The Killing of Death

Cover image: Original image by NASA/ESA and G. Bacon (STScl)

Front cover: Artist's View of a black hole in a globular cluster

Author's note: Stars that come too close to black holes of extremely dense stellar mass are doomed to be ripped apart by the tidal forces that the holes generate. In this context experts talk about 'cosmic violence' in which particles 'fight for their cosmic lives'. The gravitational field of a black hole is so intense that no particle, not even light, can escape from it. Black holes are therefore the truly dark places in the universe (www.nasa.gov; http://chandra.harvard.edu). In discussions on the phenomenon of genocide, which encompasses the annihilation of a people, it has been noted that those who deny genocide try to shove that history of victimisation down a black hole.

School of Human Rights Research Series, Volume 73

The titles published in this series are listed at the end of this volume.

The Killing of Death

Denying the genocide against the Tutsi

Roland Moerland

intersentia

Cambridge – Antwerp – Portland

Intersentia Ltd
Sheraton House | Castle Park
Cambridge | CB3 0AX | United Kingdom
Tel.: +44 1223 370 170 | Email: mail@intersentia.co.uk
Email: mail@intersentia.co.uk
www.intersentia.com | www.intersentia.co.uk

Distribution for the UK and Ireland:
NBN International
Airport Business Centre, 10 Thornbury Road
Plymouth, PL6 7PP
United Kingdom
Tel.: +44 1752 202 301 | Fax: +44 1752 202 331
Email: orders@nbminternational.com

Distribution for Europe and all other countries:
Intersentia Publishing nv
Groenstraat 31
2640 Mortsel
Belgium
Tel.: +32 3 680 15 50 | Fax: +32 3 658 71 21
Email: mail@intersentia.be

Distribution for the USA and Canada:
International Specialized Book Services
920 NE 58th Ave. Suite 300
Portland, OR 97213
USA
Tel.: +1 800 944 6190 (toll free) | Fax: +1 503 280 8832
Email: info@isbs.com

The Killing of Death. Denying the genocide against the Tutsi

ISBN 978-1-78068-351-5
D/2016/7849/30
NUR 828

British Library Cataloguing in Publication Data. A catalogue record for this book is available from the British Library.

Avant le génocide, sa préparation est dissimulée,
pendant le génocide, sa réalité est démentie,
après le génocide, sa nature même est niée.
Jean-François Dupaquier
Rwanda: Le révisionnisme,
poursuite du génocide par d'autres moyens

The essence of genocide is denegation.
Marc Nichanian
The historiographic perversion

Preface

Normally, in the tradition of PhD manuscripts, the acknowledgments would feature here. I admit that it is somewhat ironic to have a manuscript about denial that does not have acknowledgments. This does not mean that I do not appreciate the help I received. I am grateful to those who participated in my research and I am indebted to those who were always willing to hear me out. I am, however, also thankful to those who did not inquire about my research and temporarily relieved me from this subject which has been dominating my life for several years now. The last remark already reveals how topical the subject of this study is. People need denial in order to lead healthy lives; it is often a normal and human reaction that is necessary to cope with the burdens of existence. However, as this study will show, denial cannot only be constructive, it can also be destructive. This is the case when denial operates in the context of genocide and serves the perpetration of that crime. My research addresses the problem of such genocide denialism and it more particularly focuses on the denial of one specific genocide, namely the genocide against the Tutsi in Rwanda. *The broader aim of this study is to come to a more profound understanding of genocide denialism and how it operates in the specific case of the genocide against the Tutsi.* The inquiry into these issues has resulted in an elaborate study that can be found in the 7 Chapters that follow. Although I introduce the abovementioned research topic and the approach taken in this study in Chapter 1, I think it is nonetheless important to briefly address the following aspects at the outset of this study.

It is first of all important to notice that my study does not aim to deal with the conflict in Rwanda and the Great Lakes Region in an exhaustive manner. In this study I have focussed on those elements of the conflict history that are helpful (functional) in understanding the denial of the genocide against the Tutsi. I am aware of the fact that the reality of the conflict is more complex and multifaceted than presented in this manuscript. The same can be said for how I have approached the conceptualisation of genocide. In my analysis of the phenomenon I have highlighted those aspects that were most helpful in understanding the role denial plays in the process of genocide.

Due to the multidisciplinary nature of the study, a wide variety of theoretically and methodologically relevant concepts are discussed. I have, however, tried to strike a fair balance between "information" and "communication" in order not to overwhelm the reader. That is also why certain theories, concepts and methods are not elaborated in a single chapter at the beginning of the manuscript as is generally the case. Instead, they are dealt with at that point in the manuscript where they are most relevant for the analysis.

As to the style of writing, it must be noted that the manuscript is written for a mixed audience. I have a background in law and criminology and I branched out into the field of genocide studies. My audience is thus a mixed bag of people including, jurists, sociologists, psychologists, political scientists, etc. I therefore tried to write in a manner that makes the subject matter accessible to such a broad audience.

Research on the genocide against the Tutsi, almost always leads to a dichotomy between the Tutsi as victims and the Hutu as perpetrators. It cannot be denied that the genocide was staged by a group of Hutu extremists and that many Hutu participated in the genocide against the Tutsi. One should, however, also be careful about the creation of such categorical differences, because it could result in a situation in which the entire Hutu population becomes collectively labelled and demonised as the perpetrators of genocide. This is however not my intention. In 2014 I visited a conference in Rwanda, where Holocaust survivor Simon Winston spoke to a group of Rwandan youth about the persecution of his people and his remarkable story of survival. When asked by some participants whether he hated the Germans, Simon had a crucial message. He said: "I do not hate all Germans. That would be wrong, because some of them were good people." He added, "So, when you discuss the genocide against the Tutsi, don't make the mistake to blame all Hutus." If we categorically lump every individual into a group, we are actually following the absolute logic on which genocide thrives.

Lastly, genocide denialism is a delicate topic and the analysis of the cases in this book can be misinterpreted as an accusatory (*ad hominem*) exercise. Although I do refer to actors by name, it is not my intention to attack them personally or to discredit them. It is not about the particular individual actor but about the actions performed and *my analysis of these actions serves to illustrate the complex and problematic nature of genocide denialism and its far reaching implications.* It is important to read the entire study, because otherwise things can easily be misunderstood or be taken out of context.

Roland Moerland

Contents

List of abbreviations

AI	Amnesty International
ASF	Avocats Sans Frontières
AVEGA	Association des Veuves du Génocide Agahozo
CDR	Coalition pour la Défense de la République
CNLG	National Commission for the Fights against Genocide
DRC	Democratic Republic of Congo
EU	European Union
FDLR	Forces Démocratiques de Libération du Rwanda
HRW	Human Rights Watch
ICCPR	International Covenant on Civil and Political Rights
ICTR	International Criminal Tribunal for Rwanda
ICTY	International Criminal Court for the former Yugoslavia
IRDP	Institute of Research and Dialogue for Peace
LM	Living Marxism
MDR	Mouvement Démocratique Républicain
MRND	Mouvement Républicain National pour la Démocratie et le Développement
NGO	Non-Governmental Organisation
RAF	Rwandan Armed Forces
RDR	Rassemblement pour le Retour des Réfugiés et la Démocratie au Rwanda
RGE	Rwandan Government in Exile
RIG	Rwandan Interim Government
RPA	Rwandan Patriotic Army
RPF	Rwandan Patriotic Front
RTLM	Radio Télévision Libre des Milles Collines
UDF	United Democratic Forces
UN	United Nations
UNAMIR	United Nations Assistance Mission for Rwanda
UNCHR	United Nations Commission on Human Rights
US	United States
VOR	Voices of Rwanda

Table of figures

Introduction

CHAPTER 1
SETTING THE SCENE

1.1. INTRODUCTION

This study deals with the phenomenon of genocide denialism and it more particularly addresses how genocide denialism operates in the context of the genocide against the Tutsi. Genocide denialism denotes that we are not dealing with a single act or type of denial but with a more elaborate process of denial that involves a variety of denialist and denial-like acts which all play a role throughout the process of genocide.[1] The topic of this study was mainly inspired by two lacunae. The first is a substantial lacuna which entails the general lack of research on the aftermath of the genocide against the Tutsi and more particularly the neglect of the denial of the genocide. The second is a disciplinary lacuna which includes the failure of criminology to study genocide and its denial. These two lacunae have greatly determined the flow and content of this study, shaping the research questions and the approach taken to answer them. The second part of this Chapter will address the abovementioned lacunae and

1 Note that I use the term *genocide denialism* instead of *genocide denial*. The suffix "ism" might create some confusion due to the different connotations that it has. The Oxford English Dictionary clarifies that it can suggest a philosophical system or a social, political or religious belief, a teaching, a class of doctrines and principles. It can denote an affinity and "ism" could also imply a clear ideology. It can furthermore point out the name of a practice founded on the name of its object/subject or founder. So, why did I add this suffix? Why denial*ism*? According to the Oxford English Dictionary, one of the uses of the suffix "ism" is naming an act, practice, process or the result thereof. In this context, the last two elements are most significant. The term was chosen because, as will be explained in Chapter 3, in this study the term "genocide denial" refers to only one particular type of denial. The term genocide denialism is broader in scope and encompasses various denialist behaviours that operate throughout the *process* of genocide. *The "ism" thus denotes that we are not dealing with a single act or type of denial, but with a more elaborate multifaceted process of denial that involves a variety of denialist and other denial-like behaviours relevant in this context, which all play a role throughout the perpetration of genocide. All these different actions together result in genocide denialism.* Furthermore, "ism" also often has a negative connotation. Genocide denialism also hints at this, as genocide *denialism* furthers the genocidal dynamic. While, as will become clear in Chapter 2 (Sections 2.5.–2.7.), *denial* can also have a positive connotation. Tatz (2003) in his book *With intent to destroy: Reflections on genocide* also uses the term denialism to denote a range of denialist and denial-like behaviours. Tatz, however, does not develop a typology as to which denialist and denial-like behaviours would fall within the scope of the term genocide denialism. This study develops such a typology in order to create a better understanding of how denial operates throughout the process of genocide (Chapter 3, Section 3.3.). Interestingly, scholars in other fields also prefer to use the term denialism when studying the lack of acceptance of a certain reality. For instance, Diethelm & McKee (2009) and Hoofnagle & Hoofnagle (2008) also refer to denialism in the context of their research that addresses the lack of acceptance that our climate is changing, because what is generally referred to as "climate change denial" is actually also a process that encompasses many types of different denialist actions. At certain points throughout this study, I also refer to genocide denialism as a framework or perspective, because it is linked to a coherent set of ideas and it provides for a(nother) way of looking at how denial operates throughout the process of genocide and the implications that it might have.

discuss the ramifications of these two "voids", thereby illustrating the theoretical and social relevance of this study. The third part of this Chapter will continue to present a detailed outline of this study which will also introduce the research questions posed. The discussion of the research questions will be followed by a brief elaboration on how the fieldwork and data collection for this study were conducted. Lastly, some issues concerning the scope of this study are addressed. This Chapter will, however, start by introducing the topic of the denial of the genocide against the Tutsi, which is the focus of this study.

1.2. 'I AM NOT ONE OF THOSE WHO DENY THE GENOCIDE OF THE TUTSIS.'

On the 1st of May 1998, Jean Kambanda became the first head of state in history to plead guilty to the international crime of genocide.[2] Kambanda had been the Prime Minister of Rwanda at the height of the genocide against the Tutsi and he pleaded guilty to multiple charges including genocide, conspiracy to commit genocide, incitement to genocide, and complicity in genocide.[3] At a specially convened session of the International Criminal Tribunal for Rwanda (ICTR) in Arusha (Tanzania), Kambanda made clear that he had understood the charges being brought against him and that he had entered his plea knowingly and voluntarily. After having confirmed that no one forced him and that his plea was unequivocal, judge Laity Kama declared Kambanda guilty (1998).[4] It was the first verdict of the ICTR, which was set up four years earlier in 1994.

Kambanda's guilty plea was presented as being of great significance. An ICTR press release stated that:

> In a historic event that accentuated not only the role of the International Criminal Tribunal for Rwanda as a court of justice but also as an instrument to facilitate national reconciliation in Rwanda, Jean Kambanda, former Prime Minister of Rwanda, today pleaded guilty to the crime of genocide and other charges at his initial appearance before the Tribunal's Trial Chamber 1 [...]. Kambanda's *confession* of guilt before the Rwanda Tribunal in Arusha is the first time in history that an accused person has acknowledged and affirmed his or her guilt for the crime of genocide before an international criminal tribunal. (International Criminal Tribunal for Rwanda, 1998, emphasis added).

2 According to his trial records, Jean Kambanda was born on the 10th of October 1955 at Mubumbano (Butare prefecture). He is married and is the father of two children. He holds a *Diploma d'Ingenieur Commercial* and, until April 1994, he was employed by the *Union des Banques Populaires du Rwanda* where he became the director of the network of those banks. Kambanda was politically active as the Vice President of the Butare Section of the *Mouvement Démocratique Republicain* (MDR) and he was also a member of its Political Bureau. Kambanda became Prime Minister of the Interim Government on the 9th of April 1994, after his predecessor Prime Minister Agathe Uwilingiyimana was assassinated. Prior to his guilty plea, Kambanda had never been convicted for a criminal offence (The Prosecutor vs. Jean Kambanda, ICTR 97-23-S, Judgment and Sentence, 4th of September 1998, par. 45).

3 Kambanda was indicted with these charges by the ICTR on the 16th of October 1997 (The Prosecutor vs. Jean Kambanda, ICTR 97-23-S, Indictment, 16th of October 1997).

4 See also The Prosecutor vs. Jean Kambanda, ICTR 97-23-S, Judgment and Sentence, 4th of September 1998.

Louise Arbour, the Chief Prosecutor of the ICTR expressed the "hope that this admission of guilt will bring some solace to the survivors" (Office of the Prosecutor International Criminal Tribunal for Rwanda, 1998). The guilty plea was furthermore hailed as a big step for the prosecution, because the court had been criticised for its slow progress. A *New York Times* article referred to Deputy Prosecutor Bernard Muna, who noticed that Kambanda's plea could be of importance to the prosecution strategy as Kambanda was expected to testify against other defendants. The article furthermore pointed out that Kambanda's conviction "marked the first time prosecutors have cracked the wall of silence and denial among Hutu officials like Kambanda who are accused of orchestrating the slaughter of both Tutsi and moderate Hutu" (McKinley, 1998). This was indeed remarkable because *génocidaires* do not tend to acknowledge the crime they have been involved in. Therefore, Kambanda's case was hailed as "a monumental step towards truth" and it was noted that his "confession [...] destroy[ed] the creditability, if it existed, of revisionist historians, who claim a genocide never took place" (Magnarella, 1998). Hopes were high and people were anxiously awaiting Kambanda's full confession that they expected him to provide during the sentencing hearing that was scheduled in September 1998.

On the 4th of September 1998, roughly four months after his guilty plea, Jean Kambanda was sentenced by judges Laity Kama, Lennart Aspegern, and Navanethem Pillay. Both the prosecution and defence urged the Chamber to interpret Jean Kambanda's guilty pleas as "a signal of his remorse, repentance and acceptance of responsibility for his actions" (The Prosecutor vs. Jean Kambanda, ICTR 97-23-S, Judgment and Sentence, 4th of September 1998, par. 52). The prosecution furthermore explained that Jean Kambanda's prime motivation for pleading guilty was "the profound desire to tell the truth, as the truth was the only way to restoring national unity and reconciliation in Rwanda" (The Prosecutor vs. Jean Kambanda, ICTR 97-23-S, Judgment and Sentence, 4th of September 1998, par. 50). According to the prosecution Jean Kambanda had condemned the *massacres* that occurred in Rwanda and he considered his confession as a contribution to the restoration of peace in Rwanda (The Prosecutor vs. Jean Kambanda, ICTR 97-23-S, Judgment and Sentence, 4th of September 1998, par. 50). Despite the calls from the defence and the prosecution to take the guilty pleas into account as a mitigating circumstance, Kambanda was sentenced to life imprisonment. The Chamber concluded that:

> Jean Kambanda [had] offered no explanation for his voluntary participation in the genocide; nor [had] he expressed contrition, regret or sympathy for the victims in Rwanda, even when [he was] given the opportunity to do so by the Chamber, during the hearing of 3 September 1998. (The Prosecutor vs. Jean Kambanda, ICTR 97-23-S, Judgment and Sentence, 4th of September 1998, par. 51)

Everybody had been waiting for Kambanda to publicly confess to his crimes thereby shedding light on what had been done to the Tutsi people, how and why. However, as the Chamber noted, the confession everybody had been waiting for remained absent. Kambanda eventually heard his life-sentence, remained silent and was taken to prison.[5]

Although Kambanda remained silent and did not publically confess, he had prepared a speech titled *Le Manifeste de la vérité sur "l'apocalypse" au Rwanda en 1994*, but it was not presented to the public (Cruvellier, 2010, p. 44).[6] In this speech Kambanda talks about the genocide against the Tutsi, but the language he uses is telling:

> I confirm that the objective was to exterminate them, insofar as they were killing men, women, and children indiscriminately. If the international community feels that, legally speaking, the acts I just described constitute genocide, then there was a genocide of the Tutsis during the period from April to July 1994, when I was Prime Minister. (Kambanda quoted in Cruvellier, 2010, p. 44)

In addition, Kambanda points out that the Tutsi-led Rwandan Patriotic Front (RPF), which invaded the country in October 1990, had also "massacred hundreds of thousands of Hutu civilians". He adds that if according to the international community, legally speaking, these acts amounted to genocide, then a genocide against the Hutu had also been perpetrated (Cruvellier, 2010, p. 44). Furthermore, from Kambanda's account of the events, the idea emerges that both parties involved were guilty, as it was a matter of "the eternal struggle for power between Hutus and Tutsi in Rwanda" (Kambanda quoted in Cruvellier, 2010, p. 45). As Cruvellier (2010, p. 44) notes, what becomes clear from Kambanda's speech is that he did not intend to assume personal criminal responsibility for the genocide. In contrast, Kambanda only assumed political responsibility:

> Solely for the political responsibility of the interim government I headed and [I] loudly and clearly proclaim my innocence as an individual who, on the contrary, did everything possible, despite being powerless, as everyone knew, to spare his people from the worst. (Kambanda quoted in Cruvellier, 2010, p. 46)

A couple of days after the judges had passed his sentence, Kambanda appealed the judgment. He argued that he had been denied the right of counsel, and motioned to set aside the guilty plea and requested a new trial. He felt betrayed because, despite his cooperation, Kambanda was still given a life sentence (Hirondelle News Agency, 2013). After pleading guilty on all counts, Kambanda now tried to get his trial before the lower court invalidated. At this point Kambanda continued to present himself as a "scapegoat for a tragic situation over which [he had] absolutely no control"

---

5 Jean Kambanda is currently being detained in Koulikoro Prison in Mali. There have been reports by the Rwandan newspaper *The New Times* that Kambanda and other prisoners live lavish lives, run businesses in Mali and can leave the prison to visit their families (Musoni, 2012). For a short impression of life in Koulikoro prison see: Jeune Afrique (2014).

6 Although Deputy Prosecutor Bernard Muna had initially advised Kambanda to prepare the speech in order to publically address his role in the genocide, because of its questionable content the speech was deemed unacceptable to Muna and it was not to be read out in public (Cruvellier, 2010, p. 44).

(Kambanda quoted in Cruvellier, 2010, p. 46 and 47).[7] Years later, Kambanda was called as a witness for the defence in the trial against Colonel Théoneste Bagosora, who was also being prosecuted for his role in the genocide against the Tutsi. During Bagosora's trial, Kambanda made the following interesting statement:

> The events that took place in my country were so serious and so difficult to understand that as a former prime minister, I had the duty to explain them and politically assume that responsibility. That is what I recognise. I did not perpetrate any crimes. I did not send anybody to kill anybody. [...] People talk about the genocide of the Tutsis. There are some people who deny that. *I am not one of those who deny the genocide of the Tutsis.* Obviously, I am not a legal expert to give you a definition of what is meant by genocide. But during the period between April and July 1994, I saw that people of [Tutsi] (*sic*) ethnic groups were hunted down and killed for what they were, specifically, because they were Tutsis. There were men, women, children, young people, and old people who were killed. I am not a legal expert, but I believe that that is genocide. Unfortunately, Mr. President, during the same period and under the same circumstances, I saw that people from the Hutu ethnic group were massacred because they were Hutus. Men, women, elderly people, young people and children were killed. They were hunted down and killed. If what I have described as -- first was genocide, then the second aspect was also a genocide. So I believe there was a double genocide in Rwanda: Genocide of the Hutus, and genocide of the Tutsis. Now, the question that arises is who perpetrated these genocides, and I have answers for that. Regarding the genocide of the Hutus, this is easy to demonstrate. It's much easier because one does not need a lot of information to know that the genocide of the Hutus was committed by the current president of Rwanda, his regime, his army, his militia. I have evidence which has been forwarded to you, Mr. President. (The Prosecutor vs. Théoneste Bagosora, Gratien Kabiligi, Aloys Ntabakuze, Anatole Nsengiyumva ICTR 98-41-T, Transcript continued trial hearing, 11th of July 2006, emphasis added)

7 Kambanda based his appeal on the following grounds: "(1) failure to consider the denial of the right to be defended by a counsel of one's own choice; (2) failure to consider the Appellant's unlawful detention outside the Detention Unit of the Tribunal; (3) acceptance of the validity of the plea-agreement without a thorough investigation of whether the plea was voluntary and/or informed and/or unequivocal; and failure to satisfy itself that the guilty plea was based on sufficient facts for the crime and the accused's participation in it, either on the basis of independent indicia or of lack of any material disagreement between the parties about the facts of the case; (4) failure to apply the general principle of law that a plea of guilty as a mitigating factor carries with it a discount in sentence (5) failure to consider [...] mitigating circumstances, personal circumstances of the convict, the substantial co-operation of the convict with the Prosecutor and the general practice regarding prison sentence in the courts of Rwanda be taken into account in the determination of the sentence; (6) failure to pronounce and impose a separate sentence for each count in the indictment, each count being a separate charge of an offence; (7) the sentence is excessive; (8) considering the non-explanation of the convict when asked whether he had anything to say before sentence as militating against any discount" (Jean Kambanda vs. The Prosecutor, ICTR 97-23-A, Judgment, 19th of October 2000, par. 10). The Appeals Chamber upheld the guilty verdict and the life sentence against Kambanda arguing that: In this case, the Trial Chamber balanced the mitigating factors against the aggravating factors and concluded that "the aggravating circumstances surrounding the crimes negate the mitigating circumstances. The Appeals Chamber considers that this sentence falls within the discretionary framework provided by the Statute and the Rules, and so sees no reason to disturb the decision of the Trial Chamber" (Jean Kambanda vs. The Prosecutor, ICTR 97-23-A, Judgment, 19th of October 2000).

Colonel Théoneste Bagosora himself had always vigorously denied that a genocide against the Tutsi had taken place: *"Génocide? Mon œil! Des Tutsi, Il y en a encore plein à Kigali!"* (Bagosora quoted in Ntakirutimana, 2013, p. 49).[8] Kambanda's testimony at the Bagosora's trial makes clear that Kambanda was now denying the genocide he initially pleaded guilty to.[9] It is therefore questionable whether Kambanda's guilty plea is really the unprecedented historical event people often claim it to be. In the end Kambanda does what *génocidaires* generally do; they deny the genocide they are involved in.

1.3. Beyond the stereotypical ...

The phenomenon that genocide perpetrators do not acknowledge what they have done is not unique to those who perpetrated the genocide against the Tutsi. Many Nazi perpetrators who appeared in court also refused to acknowledge the genocide they had committed. The *Nürnberger Tagebuch* of Gustave Gilbert (2004), a psychologist working at the Nuremberg trials, details the many conversations he had with Nazi officials. Gilbert's *Tagebuch* tellingly reveals how the indicted Nazis structurally denied the genocidal crimes they had perpetrated. It is however important to realise, as Finkielkraut (1998, p. 3) points out, that those who perpetrated the genocidal extermination and those who would expunge the record are not always interchangeable. Often, those who perpetrate genocide and those who deny that it ever happened are not the same people.

Finkielkraut (1998, p. 4) concludes that:

> Negation cannot be put down to the evil that it strives to excuse or, even better, to abolish: its discourse exceeds the bounds of ideology to which it is ascribed, and its followers do not fit the image that the general public has of them.

---

8 For other examples of Bagosora's denialist narrative see: Bagosora (1995), Aboganana (1996) and Essoungou (2005). McGreal (2008) quotes Bagosora saying: "People say Bagosora did this or that, that I have the blood of the Tutsis on my hands. But where are all these people who were killed? If they died it is because they are rebels, or because the people were angry with them" Bagosora adds: "But it's true the Tutsis are trouble. They have taken over a Hutu country. We will fight them again until all the Tutsis are gone." Interestingly, Hirondelle News Agency (2011) published an article titled *Bagosora recognizes Rwandan genocide at last.* During his appeal Bagosora "admitted" to the "Rwandan genocide" stating that: "I kneel down before all the victims of Rwandan genocide. I still claim that I am a victim of strong RPF (Rwandese Patriotic Front Rebels) propaganda which started the massacres and hence triggered genocide of which the prosecution failed to prove the planning". It is questionable whether this is truly an acknowledgment of the genocide. Bagosora still does not accept his responsibility for what happened; instead he holds Paul Kagame and the RPF ultimately responsible for the genocide against the Tutsi. Paul Kagame used to be RPF's military leader and is now President of the Republic of Rwanda.

9 For other examples of Kambanda's denialist discourse see also: Kambanda (2011, 2013). The case of Kambanda already makes clear that genocide denial often involves more than complete or factual denial. Kambanda attempts to deny the genocide by making comparative trivialisations and by shifting the responsibility for the events. This is generally referred to as implicatory denial. The various forms of denial will be elaborated in Chapter 2, Section 7.

Finkielkraut's observations are important as they force us to challenge our stereotypical image of those who deny genocide. Genocide denial does not always happen by genocide perpetrators and bigots out of belief in a Hutu Power or Nazi ideology. Not only Kambanda spoke of two genocides, also French Premier Mitterrand talked about "*les génocides*" when questioned about what was happening in Rwanda (Dupaquier, 1995, p. 130).[10] Journalists who wrote about Rwanda in 1994, when the extermination of the Tutsi was being implemented, have often misrepresented what was truly happening. The first reports on the genocide portrayed the genocidal violence as savagery that was caused by ancient tribal hatreds or it was simply represented as a brutal civil war (Pottier, 2002, pp. 64–67; Power, 2002, p. 355).[11] Straus (2004, p. 86) notes that the problem with these "analyses" is that they dealt with the genocidal violence as spontaneous and unorganised without a specific and complex history. Scholars have been very critical about such qualifications and descriptions because they do not address the true nature of what happened. On the contrary, such qualifications obscure the genocide (Chrétien, 1995b).[12] Especially in terms of genocide denialism, this is a questionable tendency. For example, the December 1995 issue of Living Marxism's *LM* magazine ran an article by journalist Fiona Foster (1995) titled *Massacring the truth in Rwanda* in which she stated that "we must reject the term 'genocide' in Rwanda." In her article, Foster argued that the situation is more complex than generally portrayed, but nonetheless what happened in Rwanda was simply a war. According to Foster (1995), the term genocide has been politically used inside and outside Rwanda "to criminalise the majority of ordinary Rwandan people, to justify outside interference in the country's affairs, and to lend legitimacy to a minority military government imposed on Rwanda by Western powers."[13] Throughout the article, the term genocide is persistently put between inverted commas. Forster's article caused a storm and received many critical comments.[14]

One of the remarks came from the director of the Simon Wiesenthal Centre, Efraim Zuroff (1996), who argued that:

> Invariably, one of the most horrifying and painful phenomenon associated with genocide is the attempt of the perpetrators and their supporters to deny that the atrocities took place. This has been well-documented in the case of the Holocaust and is also true regarding the mass murders of the Armenians by the Turks. Now Living Marxism has joined the ranks of the deniers vis-a-vis the mass annihilation of civilians which took place in Rwanda in 1994. To question the validity of the use of the term genocide to describe the mass murders in Rwanda is to lend credence to the lies being disseminated by the perpetrators

10 For a discussion of how French state officials engage in denialist discourse concerning the role of France in the genocide against the Tutsi see: Survie France (1996).

11 For a concrete example of such reporting see: Schmidt (1994).

12 For a discussion of how simplistic depictions lead to a de-contextualisation which might perpetuate negative stereotypes concerning explanations of why the violence took place see: Adhikari (2008).

13 As will become clear throughout Chapters 4 and 5, this is the general gist of a powerful denial discourse spawned by a variety of actors, ranging from officials who were actually involved in the genocide, to lawyers, scholars and journalists who somehow end up recycling this narrative.

14 For a critical discussion of Foster's work on Rwanda see: McGreal (2000).

> and to pave the way for their exculpation. And to virtually mock the justified call for the prosecution of the murderers is to help pave the way for a recurrence of those terrible events.

Mick Hume (1996), the editor of *LM* reacted by arguing that Zuroff had missed the point about their approach to what happened in Rwanda. According to the Hume (1996), nobody denied that government militias killed many civilians, the problem was however that:

> [U]sing emotive and exceptional terms like "genocide" and "Holocaust" to describe a civil war of a kind that is all too prevalent in Africa only serves to mystify the real causes of the Rwandan conflict (particularly the role of outside powers), and to distract from the crimes committed by the new Rwandan government.

Instead of clarifying the genocidal nature of the situation in Rwanda, Hume's rhetoric further obfuscates the events. To make things worse, in a subsequent article published in *LM* in March 1996 titled *Rwanda: The great genocide debate*, journalists Helen Simons & Barry Crawford (1996) "spell[ed] out the case against those who claim that the Rwandan killings were 'the third genocide of the century'."[15] Although Living Marxism and its *LM* magazine seized to exist in 2000,[16] the denial of the genocide against the Tutsi did not and the last decade has witnessed a worrying proliferation of the denial of the genocide against the Tutsi.

1.4. A PROBLEMATIC ISSUE?

When I raised the issue of the denial of the genocide against the Tutsi in conversations, people often wondered whether it is actually a serious problem.[17] They asked whether there really are people who doubt that the genocide against the Tutsi took place. Or they wondered whether it is only a fringe phenomenon that one should simply ignore. Often they argued that, in the face of the facts, such denial is too idiotic to do any serious damage; nobody would believe these stories. Ultimately such remarks raise

15 Hintjens (1999, pp. 283–284) also makes some interesting observations concerning the issue of denial and Living Marxism. Hintjens' observations indicate that denial is not simply an individual action but often a collective exercise which requires that others collude in the denial. This interpersonal aspect of denial will be specifically addressed in Chapter 2, Section 2.6.4. and more generally throughout Chapters 4, 5, and 6.

16 Living Marxism had to close due to losing a libel suit brought against them by ITN for misrepresenting certain events that had happened during the conflict in the former Yugoslavia (Wells, 2000).

17 I noticed this regularly when conversing with people about the topic of my research, but one can also discern this trend in reactions to articles and blogs on the internet that address the issue of the denial of the genocide against the Tutsi. For instance, in a reaction to an article by George Monbiot (2011a) on the issue of genocide denial in the "comment is free" section of *The Guardian*, one of the comments reads: "This is one of George's "odd" articles. He sets up a target of whom most are unaware and whose influence is minimal and then proceeds to attack them. I cannot help but think the victims of these crimes are belittled by the process." The gist of the remark is clear: why pay attention to this. It is even presented as being disrespectful to the survivors. Interestingly, a substantial number of comments that follow continue the denial that Monbiot had initially pointed out in his article.

the question why it is important to pay attention to the denial of the genocide against the Tutsi. It is, of course, perfectly legitimate to raise these questions, but there are nonetheless several pressing reasons why the phenomenon of genocide denial, and more particularly its manifestation in the context of the genocide against the Tutsi, is problematic and therefore warrants serious scholarly attention.

1.4.1. Understudied

No crime on the African continent has been the subject of such extensive inquiry as the genocide against the Tutsi in Rwanda. Over the past two decades, a massive amount of scholarship has been published on this hitherto virtually unknown country (Cruvellier, 2007, p. 271; Totten, 2007, p. 205). The contributions are eclectic and range from books by journalists (Gourevitch, 1998; Keane, 1996; Temple-Raston, 2005), to books by those who directly experienced what happened (Immaculée, 2006; Salem, 2000; Totten & Ubaldo, 2011), and from books by United Nations (UN) and other personnel (Dallaire, 2003; Khan, 2000; Wilkens, 2011) to reports published by governmental and non-governmental organisations (Carlsson, Han, & Rufus, 1999; De Waal & Omaar, 1995; Des Forges, 1999). States, such as France and Belgium, have also published lengthy reports on the issue (Assemblée Nationale du France, 1998; Sénat du Belgique, 1997).[18] In addition to this already impressive volume of accounts, books and reports, an enormous amount of scholarly work has been published by academics from various backgrounds. The work ranges from concise articles (Chrétien, 1995b; Kimonyo, 2000; Verwimp, 2006) to elaborate and insightful books (Prunier, 1995; Straus, 2007; C. C. Taylor, 2001). Journals, such as the *Journal of Genocide Research* (2004) and *the International Journal of Genocide Studies and Prevention* (2008), have published issues specifically dealing with the genocide against the Tutsi. In addition to these contributions, the genocide has also been the inspiration for various literary projects (Courtmanche, 2003; Pierce, 2000; Stassen, 2006). Especially the *Rwanda: écrire par devoir de mémoire* (1998) project which resulted in various novels on the topic is worth noting, because it was organised as a reaction to the Western "colonisation" of the genocide (Hitchcott, 2009, p. 152). Most of the works cited above, except for survivor accounts, were written by Western authors.[19]

When considering the volume of work on the genocide, of which the contributions mentioned above only represent a small fraction, it is important to notice that authors have taken different approaches, focussing on different aspects of the genocide. First of all, some of the work is purely descriptive, while the work of others is theoretically informed. Secondly, in their approaches, some authors have taken a more structural or macro, top-down approach, while others have focused on local dynamics, thereby taking a micro, bottom-up approach. Thirdly, authors have approached the study

18 As noted before, also French officials are still denying the role played by France in the genocide against the Tutsi.

19 For a more in-depth discussion on many of the works mentioned above, I suggest one turns to Uvin's (2001), Longman's (2004) or Lemarchand's (2013) comparative reviews.

of the genocide using different time-frames. Some have focused on what was happening before the genocide, while others focused on what happened during or after the genocide. If one categorises the available material on the genocide according to its level of analysis, its time-frame and whether it is descriptive or theoretically informed, one can gain quite an accurate impression of which areas of research received scholarly attention and which did not and which areas have therefore remained understudied. When categorising the contributions, it turns out that most work is situated on the macro level and focuses on the period before and during the genocide. In comparison, the aftermath has received relatively little attention. Scholars interested in the aftermath seem predominantly legal scholars that study the International Criminal Tribunal for Rwanda (ICTR) and the local Rwandese (grass roots) *Gacaca* courts (P. Clark, 2007; Oomen, 2006; Schabas, 2005) and, although scholarly interest in the aftermath is increasing (Cook, 2004; Ingelaere, 2009; Straus & Waldorf, 2011), it still remains one of the most understudied areas of the genocide against the Tutsi.[20] In addition to these scholarly contributions, the work available on the aftermath consists mainly of reports by human rights organisations (African Rights & Redress, 2008; Amnesty International, 2004; Penal Reform International, 2010). This material is mainly descriptive and not theoretically informed. Taking into account the little research that has been done on the aftermath of the genocide, Uvin (2001, p. 99) notes that "the scholarly world appears to be interested in Rwanda only as a case study of genocide but not as a place whose ongoing political, social, and economic dynamics merit in-depth research." Authors have mainly tried to understand and explain why and how the genocide could have happened and, in doing so, they have failed to look at the stunning challenges Rwanda and its people are currently facing (Uvin, 2001; Van Hoyweghen, 2000).[21]

It is interesting to notice that most scholars in their research do generally acknowledge that the genocide had (and still has) enormous consequences for Rwanda and its people. They are aware of the extreme human, material and immaterial damage and destruction it caused. They know that the genocide killed, wounded and traumatised people and that it destroyed virtually every sector in society (Kumar et al., 1996). It is therefore rather peculiar that, despite the awareness of the consequences of the genocide, the aftermath remains largely neglected in scholarly research. Despite this neglect, Longman (2004) points out that the aftermath of the genocide is however of considerable academic interest due to the fact that "[t]he genocide was not a finite

20 Most scholarly work is situated at the macro or structural level and clear lacunas exist when it comes to theoretically informed micro work on the specifics and local dynamics of the genocide. Uvin (2001, p. 98) even argues that there are virtually two parallel volumes when it comes to work on the Rwandan genocide; on the one hand, there is a volume of descriptive micro level data devoid of scientific theorising and, on the other hand, there is a volume of theory-informed macro level analysis. On this issue also see some remarks made by Rose (2007, p. 50). Since the start of this research, more micro orientated research has been published. See for instance the contributions of de Brouwer (2009), Fuji, (2009) and Smeulers & Hoex (2010).

21 Notable exceptions are the edited volumes by Straus & Waldorf (2011) and Clark & Kaufman (2008). In their research of the aftermath of the conflict in Rwanda, scholars such as Prunier (2009) have also focussed on how the post-genocide Government of Rwanda has been involved in military actions in neighbouring countries such as Congo.

event whose total impact came to a close with the arrival of the RPF into power in July 1994. Instead, the social, economic, political, and even spiritual effects continue to be profoundly felt within Rwanda and throughout the region." The denial of the genocide against the Tutsi also vividly illustrates that the genocide is definitely not a finite event. However, due to the fact that scholars have largely neglected the aftermath of the genocide, the denial of the genocide against the Tutsi has not received much attention. Notable exceptions are the book by Fierens (2009) and the edited volume by Semujanga and Galabert (2013).[22] Also Jones (2013), Caplan (2009a) and Chrétien (2012) have paid attention to the denial of the genocide against the Tutsi in their work.

That the denial of the genocide against the Tutsi remains largely understudied is problematic, because, in contrast to what people generally tend to assume, it is not an occasional fringe phenomenon and a worrying proliferation of genocide denial can be discerned (Caplan, 2009a; E. Clark & Z. D. Kaufman, 2008, p. 4 and 6; Evans, 2005; Kayigamba, 2008, p. 42; Martin, 2009; Ndahinda, 2011). Research on the phenomenon of genocide denial tends to primarily focus on denial of the Holocaust and the Armenian genocide.[23] Holocaust denial and denial of the Armenian genocide have been systematically countered by academic and journalistic work and political actions. In contrast, the "spectre of continued denial of the Tutsi genocide" has received only little attention (Rusagara, 2009). The lack of research causes a lack of understanding of the denial of the genocide against the Tutsi that facilitates the deniers in their denialist enterprise, which has detrimental consequences due to the harm that such denial does.

1.4.2. Harmful

Scholars generally agree that genocide denialism, and therefore also the denial of the genocide against the Tutsi, is harmful due to the fact that denial is an intrinsic part of the genocidal process (Charny, 1991; Hovannisian, 1999a; Stanton, 1998b, 2004).[24] The harm that denial in the context of genocide does was also highlighted by the Director of the Simon Wiesenthal Center in his reaction to the abovementioned Living Marxism publications. According to Zuroff (1996), the denial empowers the lies being spread by those involved in the genocide and it helps the perpetrators

22 Note that both contributions are in French, which means that to date no comprehensive study and analysis of the denial of the genocide against the Tutsi is available in English. Another notable contribution is the book by Coquio (2003b). Although Coquio's book is an edited volume that takes a comparative approach, it still pays considerable attention to the denial of the genocide against the Tutsi. Furthermore, Chretièn's book *Le défi de l'ethnisme: Rwanda et Burundi* (2012) is worth mentioning, because it also addresses the denial of the genocide against the Tutsi (See also: Chrétien, 2010).

23 Note that Nichanian (2003, p. 127) actually problematises the use of the word genocide to denote what happened to the Armenian population, not because he denies the genocide but because that generic word genocide, "does not respect the identity of the Event that has shaped [the Armenians] for the last eighty years." – "they use a common name as a proper name." He therefore prefers to refer to it as the Catastrophe, or Aghed in Armenian.

24 This will be explained in more detail in Chapter 2 and 3.

to avoid their responsibility, thereby risking (re)new(ed) genocides. Stanton (2014) notices that denial harms the victims and the survivors:

> Around the world, victims of genocide ask first for recognition of the crime committed against them. It is as essential to healing as closing an open wound. Without such healing, scars harden into hatred that cripples the victim and cries out for revenge.

The denial of the genocide against the Tutsi is thus problematic for various reasons. It is an intrinsic part of the genocidal victimisation; it rehabilitates the perpetrators and undermines international justice. Furthermore, by continuing the racism and hatred against the victimised people, it prevents their recovery while inciting new genocidal violence. The harm that the denial does is extensive and it should therefore be taken seriously.

1.4.3. Linguistic community

The earlier discussed case of Living Marxism's publications on Rwanda confronts us with another problem. In the article *Massacring the truth in Rwanda*, Foster (1995) namely presents the genocide as a propaganda ploy, a political tool used by the Rwandan Patriotic Front (RPF) to consolidate its power in Rwanda as it "lend[s] legitimacy to a minority military government imposed on Rwanda by Western powers." Such uncritical and decontextualised statements are problematic because they reiterate elements from the denial discourse of the former genocidal regime that is responsible for the planning organisation and implementation of the genocide against the Tutsi. The denial of the genocide was part and parcel of the ideological propaganda of the former regime and denialist accounts, such as those of Foster, empower and lend credibility to the denialist propaganda of the *génocidaires*. The case of Foster is not an isolated incident and, over the years, there has been a proliferation of such denialist accounts by journalists, lawyers, scholars, human rights activists, etc., which make direct linguistic community with the denial discourse propagated by the former genocidal regime.[25] It seems that the denial is becoming more mainstream and more acceptable, which is a worrying development. Among other things, this development seems to be related to the complex nature of the conflict in the African Great Lakes region, as a result of which questionable accounts concerning what happened are not readily met with suspicion. Those who deny the genocide against the Tutsi claim to present the other side of a misunderstood story. Also, in recent years the current government of Rwanda has been heavily criticised by human rights activists. Those who deny the genocide against the Tutsi (ab)use this critical climate and they present their denialist accounts under the cover of legitimate critiques.

25 As will become clear later on in this Chapter in Section 1.6., this issue is actually one of the central problems addressed in this study.

1.4.4. Global impact

The sphere of influence of those who deny the genocide against the Tutsi has grown because of certain modern technological developments. For instance, the internet is an ideal tool for those spreading xenophobic and racist speech. Gerald Caplan (2009b, p. 283) notes that:

> [T]he deniers' reach and influence has been spreading, metastasising like a malignant cancer, thanks to the anarchy of the blogosphere and to the embrace of the deniers' arguments by a small but influential number of left-wing, anti-American journals and websites.

The problem is that the internet allows people, such as genocide deniers, to post their denial accounts without censorship and for basically everyone in the world to read.[26] In order to get a message across, one no longer requires sophisticated and expensive means. Some of the most influential and most visited sites are low tech and low budget. This is what Roversi (2008, pp. 23–27) calls the dark side of internet. Tatz remarks that, although deniers are isolated in their communities, they do tend to collectivise and, although they are geographically dispersed, they do turn themselves into a coterie (Tatz, 2003, p. 128). The internet allows them to get connected and organise themselves more efficiently and it seems that a "global racist subculture" has come into existence in contrast to the more isolated groups that existed previously (Banks, 2011, p. 3). The size of the group of deniers does not necessary determine their impact, because with use of the internet and other social media a small persistent clique can have a global impact (Bastian, 1997, p. 75; Ternon, 1999a, p. 14). These modern technological developments have been facilitating the denial of the genocide against the Tutsi to a great extent.

1.4.5. Underestimated

Not only does their sphere of influence grow, genocide deniers also learn, refine and become more sophisticated in their denial. According to Tatz (2003, p. 128), they have become "more credible as alternative explainers or revealers of 'truth', more subtle and less 'kooky'." Some have argued that genocide denialism is based on stupidity, bigotry and the main intention is to rehabilitate the perpetrators (Janssens, 1999; Korteweg, 2010). However, such a stereotypical image is far removed from the truth. It misjudges the nature of the phenomenon and as a result underestimates its consequences. As pointed out earlier by Finkielkraut (1998, p. 4), not only stereotypical bigots or hardliners engage in denial. What is particularly troublesome is that the group of those who deny the genocide against the Tutsi also consists of Western intelligentsia, including academics, researchers, journalists, lawyers, etc. Many of these professionals, such as academics and journalists, actually have a

26 For an analysis of how the internet is used in the denial of the genocide against the Tutsi see: Rinn (2013).

professional responsibility to uphold the truth but, instead of acknowledging the truth, they use their intellectual authority to spread the denialist message. Israel Charny's work on the denial of the Armenian Genocide reveals that the joint dynamic between scholars and perpetrators creates a powerful genocide denial, because the scholars provide the perpetrators' claims with credibility (Charny, 2000).[27] Fierens (2009), in her research on the denial of the genocide against the Tutsi, also indicates that not only those who perpetrate the genocide deny that it happened. The denial is perpetuated by other actors such as the Church and various media outlets. Not only is the group of deniers more complex, their denials can also be complex and it entails much more than the simple claim that genocide did not happen. Genocide deniers are often astonishingly knowledgeable about specific aspects of a genocide making it difficult for those who are not versed in these specifics to question and counter their claims (Abicht, 1997, p. 51; Shermer & Grobman, 2000, p. 2). What complicates the matter even further is that, because of people's poor understanding of what genocide entails and how it operates, they themselves can end up engaging in certain behaviour that unintentionally fosters and empowers the denial.

1.4.6. Implausibility of genocide

Earlier it was pointed out that people often wonder whether there really are those who still doubt that the genocide against the Tutsi happened. Nowadays, everybody knows that the Holocaust happened. Is it not the same with regard to the genocide against the Tutsi? Is that not also common knowledge? The issue is however that denial stories are generally much more believable than stories about the reality of genocide. To illustrate this, Tatz (2003, p. 123) refers to des Pres' book *The Survivor* which features the testimony of a Dachau survivor explaining that when they would have gotten the chance to come out alive, "the rest of the world would not believe what happened" (Des Pres, 1976, p. 35). During the Holocaust, the Jewish population living in the United States (US) did not put much pressure on the US government because they simply could not believe what was happening; what was being suggested was unimaginable (Horowitz, 1989, p. 26). To further illustrate this issue, Tatz (2003, p. 123) asks us to imagine a class of students in the past, the present and the future who are trying to decide which story is more credible. He provides us with the following contrasting scenarios concerning the Holocaust and the Armenian genocide:

Scenario I: Refugee Jews were treated for louse in showers before they went to work in labour camps where sadly many of them perished.

Scenario II: A handful of Nazi's were intentionally killing 12,000 Jews per day in specially designed and built death factories disguised as showers.

[27] See also the work by Charny & Fromer (1998).

Scenario I: More Turks died in the civil war than Armenians and the Turks had to fight the Armenians in order to control their rebellious elements which threatened the security of the state.

Scenario II: The Turks organised a death march in which the Armenian population was forced to walk through the desert until no Armenian was left alive.

The following scenario concerning the genocide against the Tutsi could be added:

Scenario I: A large number of Hutu died in a terrible civil war that was started by the Tutsi rebels invading the country, who subsequently also killed the President. As a result, the Hutu population, out of fear and self-defence, killed many of their Tutsi neighbours.

Scenario II: A handful of masterminds who saw the Hutu people and their power threatened thought up a genocidal Hutu Power ideology that was subsequently implemented reaching its peak in 1994. During a three-month period, almost a million Tutsi and moderate Hutu were slaughtered by their neighbours, who used mainly gardening tools as their weapons, making it the most efficient genocide to date.

Which of these contrasting scenarios are more likely to be judged as credible? What sounds more reasonable? It appears that denial thrives on the logic of Occam's razor, which entails that the most straightforward or simplest explanation is often the most plausible. Which scenario is the audience most likely to choose, that of an uncontrollable devastating civil war or that of genocide, that of a resettlement gone wrong or that of genocide? Thus, the unimaginability of the genocidal scenario facilities the denial dynamic. Finkielkraut (1998, p. 71 and 72) therefore points out that genocide denial "has the future on its side" and he wonders whether with the passage of time the gas chambers will return to the 'realm of the unreal' because they seem the least plausible. It is not only that the genocidal scenario's seem the least plausible, also the direct witnesses – the survivors – have died and therefore our direct human connection to what has happened is lost.[28] Thus, as time passes we become more and more vulnerable to genocide denial. That denial has the future on its side is also illustrated by the figure presented below, which shows the trend in internet searches for the terms "Rwandan genocide".[29]

---

28 Furthermore it is significant that survivors are dying off and all we have in the end are 'inert documents' which, according to Varon (1997, p. 84), "can be too easily ignored or distorted in potentially dangerous revisions." Varon (1997, p. 84) adds that the "fading into remote history" of the genocides against native populations "attests to the destructive effects of time when combined with a resistance to accountability."

29 The term 'Rwandan genocide' is most often used to designate the genocide against the Tutsi but, as will become clear throughout this study, the term raises some serious questions in terms of denial (see for instance Chapter 4, Section 4.4.).

Figure 1. Results Google internet search for the "Rwandan genocide"

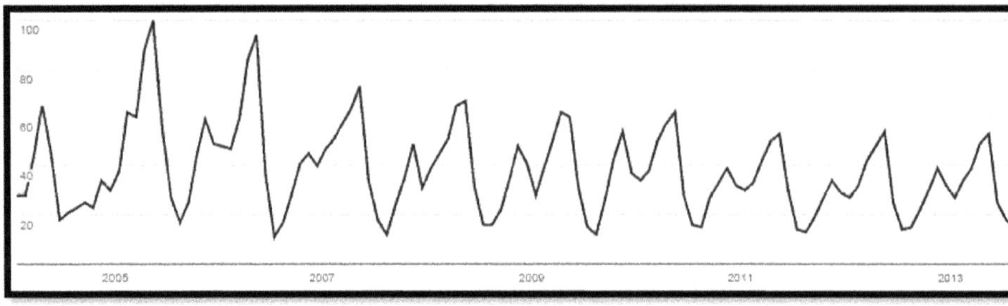

The graph shows how every year the interest in the genocide peaks around the period of April, the month in 1994 in which the extermination phase was implemented. It however also shows how attention immediately wanes and, by July, the month in which the extermination phase was halted by the RPF, interest in the genocide against the Tutsi has become marginal. The trend that we can glean from the graph is that over time the general interest in the genocide seems to become less and less.

1.4.7. Theoretical grounding

Genocide denialism remains a relatively understudied phenomenon. Spencer (2012) notes that when the field of genocide studies developed, genocide scholars were not at the forefront of efforts to study and deal with the phenomenon. He explains that:

> Perhaps some of the reason for this reluctance to engage was an assumption that denial would be too easy to disprove. What deniers claim is so obviously untrue, so demonstrably false and unsubstantiated that it is not worth wasting time on or that, if scholars had drearily to be called upon to confront denial directly, their expertise would easily expose its inherent weaknesses and absurdity. (Spencer, 2012)[30]

Over time the phenomenon has attracted more academic interest and especially the denial of the Armenian genocide and the Holocaust has received serious scholarly attention. Despite the rise in consideration, in books on genocide, discussions on denial are often excluded or only receive limited or marginal attention. For instance, in *The genocide studies reader* (Totten & Bartrop, 2009) only one text deals with genocide denialism and in the *Oxford handbook of genocide studies* (Bloxham & Moses, 2010) there is not a single article that focuses on the issue of denial.[31] Charny (2009a, p. 518), who is one of the few scholars who has systematically conducted research on genocide denialism, argues that "[t]here is an urgent need for a concerted

30 Spencer (2012) furthermore notes that the "confidence in the power of truth, evidence and reason may, however, be slightly misplaced, not least in our postmodern times." Spencer points out an important issue that will also receive considerable attention towards the end of this study, namely that the post-modern academic stance can actually facilitate denial (see Chapter 7, Section 7.4.).

31 Individual texts do refer to it in their analysis, but it is not their prime focus.

battle against deniers which will penetrate the inner-mind structures and propaganda techniques of the deniers so as to combat their explicit and implicit strategies more effectively."[32] This, according to Charny (2009a, p. 518), means that "[t]he battle against denials can no longer be limited to reproving again and again the evidential proofs of a genocide, although one also must not cease from continuing to marshal historical data." To this end, scholars such as Shermer & Grobman (2000), Hovannisian (1999a) or Lipstadt (1993) have attempted to discern strategies, templates and forms of denial in their studies. Although these scholars do provide many essential insights, a more fundamental theoretical grounding of genocide denialism remains predominantly lacking in their analyses. As a result, they do not provide for the necessary deeper theoretical understanding of the phenomenon which sheds light on issues such as how genocide and denial are related, how denial operates in the context of genocide, how it can do violence and what is the nature of that violence. The problem seems to be that, in scholarly work on the topic of genocide denialism, one discerns the tendency to use the term genocide denial in a self-explanatory fashion without really going into detail concerning the conceptualisation and theoretical foundation of the phenomenon and as a result our understanding of phenomenon remains limited.

Tatz (2003, p. 125) furthermore notices that the reasons and especially the political motives of denial are rarely discussed in these scholarly works. He, for instance, refers to the work of Manne (2001), who wrote on the Stolen Generations and the work of Cohen (2001), who wrote on denial more in general. Although Tatz praises the books for their dissection, explanation and demolishment of what deniers do, he is also critical of their analysis because it does not dismantle political motivation. They discuss what deniers do in great detail, but "[n]either work comes to grips with what Noam Chomsky would call, and what I call, political denial" (Tatz, 2003, p. 125). It is striking and tragically ironic that Tatz refers to Chomsky who, despite much insightful and valuable work, at moments has also empowered very questionable denialist narratives (Moerland, 2011; Vidal-Naquet, 1992).[33] What is

32 Charny is of course not the only scholar studying denial. However, where the work of other scholars is more case driven and descriptive, Charny tries to come to more theoretical and comparative insights concerning how denial operates. In his work he furthermore attempts to develop a general typology of genocide denials.

33 Chomsky is an influential scholar and intellectual, but his otherwise excellent work has been questioned on several occasions, because he engaged in or facilitated a denialist discourse. Most known is his involvement in the so-called Faurisson affair. Chomsky was criticised for contributing an introductory Chapter to the book *Mémoire en défense* (1980) published by the notorious Holocaust denier Robert Faurisson who claimed that the gas chambers had not existed. Chomsky's Chapter was titled *Some elementary comments on the rights of freedom of expression* and, according to him, freedom of speech also protected speech that was unpopular, such as genocide denial. Chomsky later claimed that he did not approve of nor had knowledge of the use of his work (Fresco, 1981). Chomsky's views concerning what happened in Srebrenica were also criticised. In an interview with *The Guardian*, Chomsky had said that the Srebrenica massacre of 1995 was "probably overstated" and was not an actual massacre (Hoare, 2005). Chomsky also wrote the preface to the book *The politics of genocide* written by Edward S. Herman and David Peterson (2010, 2011). The book contains an analysis of the events in Rwanda amounting to a brazen denial of the genocide against the Tutsi. Herman & Peterson's book will be central to the analysis of denial in this study and Chomsky's contribution to the book will also be addressed (see: Chapter 6, Section 6.2.1.) For Chomsky's replies to the criticism see: www.chomsky.info.

required is a more elaborate theoretical grounding of genocide denialism as it can contribute to a better understanding of the phenomenon. Such an understanding is important, because of the issue addressed in the Section above, but also because it can better inform us on how to deal with this phenomenon.

The above described issues reveal why it is theoretically and socially relevant to pay serious attention to genocide denialism and how it operates in the context of the genocide against the Tutsi. There is however an additional reason why particularly research of the denial of the genocide against the Tutsi is theoretically relevant. The following Section will reflect on this matter.

1.5. Criminology's neglect of genocide and its denial

When looking at the impressive amount of work published on the genocide against the Tutsi, it does not only become clear that a lacuna exists regarding research on the aftermath and more particularly on the issue of denial of that genocide. In addition to this substantial lacuna, a disciplinary lacuna exists as well. Scholars and authors from all kinds of disciplines have contributed to the study of the genocide against the Tutsi except for criminologists. This is quite peculiar because one would expect criminologists to have studied the crime of genocide quite extensively. Criminology, as an academic discipline, is specifically occupied with the scientific study of crime, and genocide is after all often denoted as "the crime of all crimes". The absence of criminological scholarship relating to the study of genocide is unfortunately not limited to the case of Rwanda. Chris Cunneen (1999) has for instance criticised the neglect in criminology of the forced removal of indigenous children from their families in Australia, which according to the so-called Stolen Generations Inquiry and the *Bringing them home* report could be defined as genocide (National Inquiry into the Separation of Aboriginal and Torres Strait Islander Children From Their Families, 1997).[34] Already in 1970, Schwendinger & Schwendinger (1970) had put forward the argument that the legalistic definition of crime as acts defined and punished by criminal law restricts the scope of criminological inquiry. They suggested a redefinition of crime to include all acts that violate human rights and in their text they specifically refer to international crimes including the crime of genocide. Although Schwendinger & Schwendinger strongly urged criminologists to study human rights violations, such as genocide, not much has happened in the field. Georges Yacoubain Jr. (2000) tested the proposition that criminology has largely ignored the crime of genocide. Yacoubain searched through and examined presentations at two annual criminal justice conferences and papers published in 13 prestigious periodicals that are devoted to the discipline of criminology between 1990 and 1998. The outcome was astonishing. Of the almost 20,000 presentations given

[34] On the issue of genocide in Australia, either with regard to the stolen generations or cultural and colonial genocide more in general see the contributions by Crewcock (2008), O'Malley (1994), and Van Krieken (1999). On how the genocide is being denied see: Kiernan (2002), Manne (2001) and Barta (2008b). Barta furthermore makes the insightful remark that we should see the stolen generations not in a vacuum, instead it is the outcome of a larger genocidal process that already started in the 19th century.

at annual criminological conferences, only 18 presentations dealt with the crime of genocide. The result of the content analysis for international periodicals was similar. It turned out that of the almost 3,200 articles published, only 1 article specifically dealt with the crime of genocide.[35] A relevant example of this neglect comes from a Dutch criminologist Willem Nagel. Nagel explains that he began his academic career before World War II and during this time he visited many conferences. He points out that at these conferences criminologists were mainly preoccupied with stereotypical mundane offences. After the war, the conferences resumed and Nagel started to visit them again. However, to his great surprise and major disappointment these post-war conferences were again about the same "trivial" offences, while a genocide had been perpetrated that killed more than five million people (Bovenkerk, 2000, p. 246).

1.5.1. Supranational criminology

Recent developments in criminology, however, seem to indicate that the abovementioned critique has been taken seriously. Several scholars (Haveman, 2005; Haveman & Smeulers, 2008; Haveman, Smeulers, Parmentier, & de Poot, 2011; Pruitt, 2014; Smeulers, 2006) have proposed that the study of international crimes and other gross human rights violations should be included in criminological research.[36] They argue that it should be a "separate and fully fledged specialisation" within the field of criminology: a supranational criminology (Haveman & Smeulers, 2008, p. 4).[37] Since the first calls for a supranational criminology, some significant developments have been made and in recent years we have witnessed a growing interest in the criminological study of gross human rights violations, including genocide. There have been several attempts to develop a general criminology of crimes against humanity and genocide (Anderson, 2011; Hagan & Rymond-Richmond, 2008, 2009b; Hagan, Rymond-Richmond, & Parker, 2005; Maier-Kaitkin, Mears, & Bernard, 2009; Rothe & Mullins, 2009) and there is even a growing body of work that specifically focuses on the genocide against the Tutsi in Rwanda (Ducey, 2008; Mullins, 2009; Smeulers & Hoex, 2010; Thiry & Verwimp, 2008; Winton, 2008). Furthermore, new criminological bachelor and master programs in this particular field have been introduced and the first professorships in the criminology of international crimes have been established. At conferences, more papers on the topic are presented and more special panels are convened. Criminological journals now also publish articles on international crime and the *Dutch Journal for Criminology* (*Tijdschrift voor Criminologie*) published an edition organised around the topic of international crimes. An important step for the recognition of supranational criminology came

---

35 See also Yacoubain (1997). Similar research conducted by Laufer (1999) revealed basically the same results.

36 See also www.supranationalcriminology.org.

37 They give a provisional demarcation of the field of study, which can be summarised as comprising the following issues (Haveman & Smeulers, 2008, p. 18): Defining and conceptualising the respective international crimes; Quantifying and mapping these forms of crime; Developing theories and ideas that may explain and model these forms of crime; Analysing and making an inventory of the ways to conduct post-conflict justice; Developing preventive and repressive strategies to fight these forms of crime.

in 2009, when Hagan and Zaffaroni were awarded the prestigious Stockholm Prize in Criminology for their research on genocide.[38] Although the criminological study of gross human rights violations remains relatively new, it must be noticed that the criminological study of white collar, organisational and state crime has also (to a certain extent) addressed crimes perpetrated by governments and their representatives.[39]

1.5.2. Challenges

The criminological study of genocide and other gross human rights violations, however, raises some significant challenges. For instance, criminologists have primarily focused on deviant or abnormal behaviour in their studies. In a number of criminological theories, this deviation from the norm is also explained with reference to the pathology of the deviant person. Also, the question is whether those who participated, for instance, in the genocide against the Tutsi committed acts of deviance in the first place. Given the unique circumstances, is it correct to define their behaviour as deviant? In their book *Crimes of obedience*, Kelman & Hamilton (1989) show that those who participated in atrocities, such as the My Lai massacre, did so because they followed the norm created by the authorities. In the situations that Kelman and Hamilton describe, the use of extreme violence was not a deviation from the norm, because the use of violence was the norm.[40] Not participating would have been deviant. Cunneen (1999, p. 137) also points out that core categories of criminology, such as normality and deviance, order and disorder collapse in the context of genocide: "It was the order and normalcy of a colonial regime which facilitated the attempt to eliminate Indigenous people in Australia". So in the case of Rwanda maybe those who participated were not deviant, but obedient and followed the rules. Another question is whether those who participated in the genocide against the Tutsi were abnormal people. In her work on the banality of evil, Hannah Arendt (2005) makes clear that many of those who participated in the Holocaust were actually normal people.[41] Studies of the psychological make-up of SS-personnel

---

38 For an overview of how criminology has engaged with the topic of international crime see: Haveman et al. (2011).

39 There is a large volume of work that focuses on the concept of state crime. The concept was introduced by William Chambliss in 1988 in his presidential address to the American Society of Criminology. Chambliss (1989, p. 184) defined state crime as "acts defined by law as criminal and committed by state officials in the pursuit of their job as representatives of the state". This concept was further conceptualised by authors such as Barak (1991), Ross (2000), Kauzlarich & Kramer (1988), and Green & Ward (2004).

40 See also Kelman (1993).

41 In this context it is also interesting to mention Browning's (1992b) study on the members of a German police battalion that killed many Jews during the Holocaust. Browning's study also confirms that the members of the battalion were ordinary people with no particular history of violence. Others have been more critical concerning this issue and question the ordinariness of the perpetrators. For a discussion on this issue see: Goldhagen (1997) and Matthäus (1996). De Swaan (2014), in his book *Compartimenten van vernietiging* (*Compartments of destruction*), is also critical of the insights gained by Arendt (banality of evil) and Milgram (shock experiments) in their studies which are often used to argue that normal people in abnormal circumstances would engage in violence against their fellow human beings.

done by Douglas Kelly, George Kren and Leon Rapoport revealed that the majority of the people under study would have passed psychological tests because they were perfectly normal human beings. An expert that extensively studied Adolf Eichmann concluded that Eichmann was extremely normal; "even more normal than I am after having investigated him" the expert added (quoted in Welzer, 2005, p. 11).[42] The idea that those who participate in genocide are abnormal people is therefore disputable; most of them were ordinary people. This also became clear from the interviews that I conducted with imprisoned *génocidaires* in Rwanda. They were normal people: youth, fathers, and mothers, farmers, taxi drivers, teachers, etc. Basically, they were individuals without a prior history of violence. The awareness that normal people in abnormal circumstances are capable of the most horrible things is confronting because it reveals to us that the perpetrator is not always "the other". It makes clear that, under the "right" circumstances, it could also have been you or me. The public, however, rarely tends to acknowledge this unpleasant reality, which in terms of denial is an interesting reaction. Apparently we somehow want to defend ourselves against this unpleasant reality.

The abovementioned issues indicate some of the fundamental challenges the criminological study of genocide is facing. Instead of dealing with crimes of deviance committed by abnormal people, criminologists are now confronted with crimes of obedience perpetrated by normal persons. It seems that concepts and assumptions taken for granted in criminology differ significantly from the reality of genocide and this raises the critical question whether mainstream criminological frameworks have limitations when it comes to their use for understanding genocide. If this is the case, it leaves criminologists with a serious handicap because they cannot simply fall back on existing criminological theorising. Trying to understand international crimes thus poses significant challenges for criminologists. Some criminologists hold the view that it is up to criminology to make sense of this seemingly incomprehensible complexity; the multi-disciplinary character of the discipline renders it suitable for this job. Although I support this idea, I also want to add that criminologists should be careful because criminologists are not familiar with the study of *international crimes,* such as genocide. The existing criminological framework has been developed with regard to *national crimes*, which are of a very different nature. Simply applying this framework to phenomena such as genocide, for which it was not specifically developed, raises serious concerns. Are criminologists running the risk of (over) simplifying things? And knowing that criminology has Western roots, would these concepts be able to grasp the complexity of phenomena that happen in non-Western countries, such as Rwanda? In their edited volume on Supranational Criminology, Smeulers & Haveman (2008, p. 491) also notice the abovementioned issues and furthermore point out that when studying international crimes, criminologists should rely on methodological sound empirical research in which specific methodological issues that arise when studying international criminality are taken into account. But despite their recommendation, the discussion on how to approach the study of

According to de Swaan, a normal human being would, under the circumstances described by Milgram, refuse to inflict suffering on others.

42 See also Gilbert (2004).

international crimes remains limited methodologically. The problem is, however, that carrying out sound research remains challenging as the chaos and destruction in conflict areas makes gathering reliable evidence and drawing conclusions problematic (Haveman et al., 2011, p. 300). Some scholars, like Woolford, however reveal a more fundamental scepticism concerning the abovementioned supranational endeavour. Woolford (2011, p. 137 and 138) is afraid that criminology might actually provide "little purchase" in such complex situations and he wonders how to "transport conventional criminological theories designed to understand street crime into such inter-regional, deeply historical, and dangerously political situations without engaging in gross simplification?" According to Woolford (2006, p. 97), if the baseline assumptions of the discipline remain unchanged it is questionable whether criminological theorising can grasp complex phenomena such as genocide. What Woolford (2006, p. 97) thus primarily argues is that the criminological study of genocide should be more than "add criminology and stir." It should genuinely help to advance the field of genocide studies and therefore it should encompass more than the "mundane task of testing and extending criminological discourses" (Woolford, 2006, p. 97). The discussion in supranational criminology should thus shift from what criminologists can contribute to how this can be done. The focus should shift from the question of legitimising this new criminological enterprise to the question of how to conduct sound criminological research on such a complex phenomenon such as, for instance, the genocide against the Tutsi and its denial. The following Sections will therefore explain the approach followed in this study. To this end, the content of each Chapter will be briefly discussed and the main research questions will be defined. Note that, for the purpose of clarity, the research questions are printed in *italics*.

1.6. Outline of study, research questions and sensitising frameworks

The research conducted for this study was organised in a particular order. This research flow has subsequently shaped the order of this book, which is structured in three parts: Exploration (Part I), Inspection (Part II), and Reflection (Part III). The following Sections will elaborate the outline of the study, including the leading research problems and the research questions that follow from these problems. Lastly, the main sensitising theoretical frameworks used to address the research questions will be very briefly introduced. As noted in the Preface, they are dealt with in more detail at the point in the manuscript where they are most relevant for the analysis.

Part I. Exploration

The first part of this study aimed at expanding and deepening the perception of the field of research and it entailed digging deeply into the area under study (Blumer, 1969, p. 39). Exploration is a flexible process in which the goal is to move towards a clearer understanding of the social phenomenon being studied by getting a comprehensive picture of the area of study (Blumer, 1969, p. 40 and 41). The first phase of the research was thus about exploring the field and getting an idea of the phenomenon of genocide denialism and its significance in the particular context of the genocide against the Tutsi. How was it a meaningful object for stakeholders involved, such as, victims, perpetrators and bystanders? What did it mean to them? From this exploration several pressing issues arose. Thus, in a more grounded theory fashion, instead of defining specific research problems upfront, after having been immersed in the field, the specific research problems emerged from the field through the initial exploratory data collection (Glaser, 1992, p. 4). One of the most pressing issues turned out to be the lack of clarity among stakeholders concerning what genocide denialism exactly entailed. There was considerable confusion amongst interviewees. Also in academic literature a deep theoretical grounding and conceptualisation of the phenomenon was lacking. From the interviews and the subsequent study of relevant scholarly literature on the topic, it became clear that the term genocide denial is often used in a self-explanatory way. As a result, it is rarely thoroughly (theoretically) defined. In order to be able to study and analyse the denial of the genocide against the Tutsi, it was imperative that I gained a more profound understanding of what the phenomenon entails. This required that the self-explanatory use of the term genocide denial and its lack of theoretical grounding were addressed. *Therefore, the first part of this study, which encompasses Chapter 2 and 3, explores what the phenomenon of genocide denialism entails.*

Chapter 2. Genocide and denial

In order to gain a better understanding of what genocide denialism exactly entails, *it is first of all necessary to explain what the two main conceptual building blocks of "genocide" and "denial" entail and it furthermore requires an explanation of how these two concepts are related.* The 2nd Chapter addresses these questions by firstly discussing the relevant conceptual dimensions of the concepts of genocide and denial. The analysis of the main conceptual dimensions of genocide will rely heavily on the ground-breaking work of Raphael Lemkin (1944), who was the first person to coin the term genocide and to conceptualise it. The analysis will furthermore elaborate how the two concepts are interrelated by focussing on genocide not as a specific act, but as a complex process in which denial plays several significant roles. Denial is often designated as the last stage in the process of genocide. However, the presence of denial cannot be limited to the last stage and instead denial seems to operate throughout the entire genocidal process. The situationally dependent and dynamic nature of denial indicates that it assumes different functions and meanings depending on the specific situation and broader context in which it operates. This also applies to how denial operates throughout the genocidal process. The designation "genocide denial" therefore tends to obscure the various ways in which denial operates throughout the process of genocide.

Chapter 3. Genocide denialism

The 3rd Chapter continues the analysis of how denial is related to genocide by looking more closely into how denial operates throughout the process of genocide. *The aim is to clarify which function denial performs at which stage in the genocidal process.* The analysis of the various functions performed by denial throughout the process of genocide will result in a typology of genocide denialism that identifies various types of denial and other practices that facilitate the denial dynamic on which genocide thrives. I will suggest that the term "genocide denial" should be reserved only for specific instances of denialist practices.

Due to the lack of theoretical grounding and the self-explanatory use of genocide denialism, it remains largely unclear how genocide denialism exactly functions. Scholars have revealed in their research the main linguistic or verbal strategies and mechanisms used in genocide denial, but a deeper analysis of how these mechanisms operate is rarely provided for. *The second part of the 3rd Chapter will therefore elaborate how verbal or discursive genocide denial operates.* The analysis will be grounded in some key cultural criminological notions and it will subsequently be extended by conceptualising genocide denialism in terms of speech act theory. Ferrell et al.'s (2008) invitation to cultural criminology sets out the main elements of the cultural criminological framework, including the notion that crime is a meaningful construct. Through social interaction, people create the reality of crime and language plays a central role in this. Language is thus performative and this notion of performativity is also central to speech act theory, which holds that when words are uttered something is done in the moment of their utterance; action is performed. In order to explain this, the analysis will furthermore draw on the theoretical framework of Austin (1962) and Searle's (1969) speech act theory.

Part II. Inspection

Inspection is important because examination of the empirical world is not limited to gaining a comprehensive and accurate account of what is taking place. It also includes (theoretical) analysis: an "intensive focussed examination of the empirical content" (Blumer, 1969, p. 43). Thus after deepening the perception of the field and having become familiar with some of the most pressing issues shaping it, the stage of inspection begins in which these issues are thoroughly studied, analysed and theorised. The research during the inspection phase was influenced by two other pressing issues that were revealed when exploring the field. In addition to the abovementioned problem concerning the lack of understanding of what genocide denialism entails, it became clear that the denial by the former Rwandan authorities who were responsible for the genocide against the Tutsi had not been systematically analysed. Also, it became clear that the network of genocide deniers was expanding, increasingly involving actors who were initially not implicated in the genocide. The denial of the genocide against the Tutsi was thus not only promoted by those intimately involved in the planning, organisation and execution of the genocide; it appeared that this official denial was also being recycled by agents who were not implicated in the genocide. This group often entailed Western academics, journalists, lawyers, etc. Thus, after having clarified which function denial performs at which stage in the process of genocide and having more specifically explained how linguistic genocide denial functions, the second part of this study will utilise these insights in order to study denial "at work" in several concrete instances of denial of the genocide against the Tutsi. *The aim of the second part of this study, which encompasses Chapters 4 and 5, is thus to inspect how genocide denial operates in the particular case of the genocide against the Tutsi.*

Chapter 4. Official denial of the genocide against the Tutsi

In order to come to a better understanding of the denial of the genocide, *the analysis in Chapter 4 will focus on addressing the official denial of the genocide against the Tutsi.* The term *official denial* denotes the denial by certain governmental, military and political organisations that were officially aligned with the former regime and were somehow involved in the planning organisation and/or implementation of the genocide. The focus on official denial is pertinent, because it has not been extensively and systematically analysed. Furthermore, official genocide denial, due to the power of the institutions disseminating it, and because of its highly ideological content, has had (and still has) an impact on people. *The analysis of official genocide denial in this Chapter focuses on the following organisations: the Rwandan Interim Government (RIG), the Rwandan Armed Forces (RAF) and the Rassemblement pour le Retour des Réfugiés et la Démocratie au Rwanda (RDR).* The first Sections of Chapter 4 introduce the aforementioned organisations and discuss the documents authored by these organisations on which the analysis throughout the rest of the Chapter relies.

To address the official denial of the genocide against the Tutsi, it is pertinent to analyse how the official genocide denial discourse of the abovementioned organisations is constructed. In order to study such genocide denial "at work", the analysis will draw on insights from Laclau & Mouffe's (2001) discourse theory. The introduction to the official agents of denial is therefore followed by a discussion of the relevant dimensions of Laclau & Mouffe's discourse theory. Having clarified Laclau & Mouffe's discourse theoretical approach, *the 4th Chapter discusses how the official denial discourse of the aforementioned organisations is constructed by presenting a synthesis of their discourse and highlighting the major discursive elements used to construct the official denial.*

Chapter 5. Recycling official denial

Chapter 4 focuses on the official denial of the genocide against the Tutsi, but the group of genocide deniers has expanded increasingly involving actors who were initially not officially implicated in the genocide. The denial of these actors will be under study in Chapter 5. This group entails Western academics and journalists who, for some reason, have been presenting alternative discursive constructions about what happened in Rwanda. These alternative theories are dangerous, because they empower and lend credibility to the official denial discourse of the genocide against the Tutsi. In constructing and transmitting their version of history, these actors draw on crucial elements contained in the official denial discourse analysed in the previous Chapter and they thereby recycle the denial of the genocide against the Tutsi. Therefore, *the 5th Chapter of this study will look more closely at how the official genocide denial discourse is being recycled.* The analysis has been limited to certain specific illustrative actors and documents. It will focus on journalists and academics, because they have a professional responsibility to enlighten the public about what is happening in the world, instead of clouding their minds. At the centre of the attention will be the work of Edward S. Herman, David Peterson and Keith Harmon Snow. Harmon Snow is an independent journalist, war correspondent and investigator. Edward S. Herman is professor emeritus of finance at the Wharton School of the University of Pennsylvania. David Peterson is an independent journalist and researcher. The work of these authors on Rwanda entails some of the most elaborate and brazen denials of the genocide against the Tutsi and their work is illustrative of how elements of the official denial discourse are being recycled. Note that the work of these authors has been discussed and criticised before, and the value of the analysis therefore (also) lies in the insight that their discourse recycles the official denial, which makes it very problematic. This aspect has been neglected in earlier analysis of their work. By focussing on genocide denial by academics and journalists, *the analysis thus also serves to debunk the stereotypical image of the agents of genocide denial.* In addressing these issues, I hope that the reader comes to understand that not only are there different types of denial, but there are also different types of deniers.

The first part of Chapter 5 will introduce the aforementioned agents and their work on Rwanda on which the analysis throughout the following Sections will predominantly rely. *In order to address the question how the official genocide denial discourse is being recycled, it is pertinent to analyse how the discourse of Herman & Peterson and Harmon Snow concerning the events in Rwanda is constructed* and *how it merges with the official denial discourse of the Rwandan Interim Government (RIG), the Rwandan Armed Forces (RAF) and the Rassemblement pour le Retour des Réfugiés et la Démocratie au Rwanda (RDR).* In answering these questions, the analysis will again draw on insights from Laclau & Mouffe's discourse theory to show how the discursive constructions of these actors in many ways resemble the discursive construction of those who promote the official denial discourse. Although Herman & Peterson and Harmon Snow recycle much of the official denial discourse, the discourses are not entirely identical in their discursive constructions. *Therefore, the analyses will not only address how their discourse merges with the official denial discourse of the earlier mentioned authorities, but it will also examine at which points it diverges from the official denial discourse.*

In scholarly work on the topic of genocide denialism, it is often argued that genocide denial incites (re)new(ed) genocide(s) and, as such, it is seen as a cause of genocidal violence. This also appears to be the main reason why in certain countries the denial is criminalised. Genocide denial in this approach facilitates genocide. The question is, however, *whether denial is only facilitative to the violence of genocide or whether it can also constitute violence in itself and, if so, what would the nature of such violence be.* The last part of Chapter 5 will reflect on these questions. In order to address them, I rely on insights from the framework developed by Butler (1997) which addresses the problem of injurious speech.

Part III. Reflection

The analysis of the role that denial plays in the process of genocide and the insights gained from the analysis of official genocide denial and how it is being recycled results in a particular way of looking at genocide denialism. The approach developed throughout the first two Parts of this study has broader implications that go beyond the already discussed instances of official genocide denial and the recycling of it. The perspective on genocide denialism developed throughout this study allows for a critical reflection of actions that one might not readily associate with the problem of genocide denialism. As will become clear, denial is an interpersonal phenomenon and it relies heavily on the actions of other actors. These actions do not only include the hard-core denials of fellow deniers, but there is also much behaviour that actually unintentionally facilitates the denial dynamic. The insights gained throughout this study have significant implications for a wider variety of actions that somehow engage with the flow of meaning concerning the specific events in Rwanda or genocide more in general. *The aim of the third Part of this study, which encompasses Chapters 6 and 7, is therefore to reflect critically on how the discursive actions of other actors, not readily associated with genocide denialism, can facilitate the denial dynamic.*

Chapter 6. Broader implications

To this end, *Chapter 6 will reflect on how the discursive actions of a variety of actors (described below) can possibly be problematic in terms of genocide denialism.* The aim of this reflection is to illustrate the far-reaching complexity of the phenomenon of genocide denialism and to show that genocide thrives on a broader denial dynamic that encompasses much more than official denial and its recycling. The analysis has been limited to certain actors and documents, which are an illustration of this broader denial dynamic. The first part of the Chapter problematises the endorsements of Herman & Peterson's work on Rwanda by notable intellectuals such as Noam Chomsky and Jon Pilger. Subsequently, the work of Christian Davenport & Allan Stam is discussed since it has often been referred to in discourse that denies the genocide against the Tutsi. The question is whether their findings are simply abused or whether there are more fundamental issues concerning their research that could explain why it is used in denialist articulations. Furthermore, Lemarchand's work on Rwanda is interesting in this context. Lemarchand is one of the most notable Rwanda scholars, but in some of his writings on Rwanda he appears to have developed a revisionist stance that raises some serious questions in terms of denial. The second part of Chapter 6 will address the intriguing relationship between criminal defence and genocide denial and it more particularly examines how the right of the defence to question the criminal charges and to raise alternative explanations can cause considerable problems in terms of genocide denialism. The third part of Chapter 6 focuses on one of the most intriguing implications of the genocide denialism approach, which is that even actions of the current Government of Rwanda can raise problems. Two aspects receive specific attention in this discussion. Firstly, the criminalisation of genocide denial and the problems that flow from it will be addressed. Secondly, the implications of how the current government deals with gross human rights violations perpetrated by the Rwandan Patriotic Front's (RPF) military wing the Rwandan Patriotic Army (RPA) will also be discussed. The Chapter will end with a brief reflection of the work of human rights organisations, such as Human Rights Watch, and how their advocacy on Rwanda also raises some significant questions from the perspective developed throughout this study. *The aim of addressing the abovementioned cases is not to scrutinize all the actions of the mentioned actors exhaustively. Instead, it entails a "short", but critical, analysis in order to show that the actions of these actors can also raise questions in terms of genocide denialism.* The discussion of these cases will reveal that the web of denial is much more extensive than one might have thought.

Chapter 7. A look in the mirror

Throughout the previous Chapters, the actions discussed and deemed problematic in terms of genocide denialism were situated outside the two academic fields that have informed this study, which are the fields of genocide studies and criminology. As a result, the discussion of the implications of the developed approach so far has mainly been an exercise in reflection but not self-reflection. There is, however, no reason to believe why the developed approach would not have implications for the work carried out in the abovementioned two academic fields. *Therefore, Chapter 7 addresses the question whether the developed approach also has implications for the field of genocide studies and criminology.* The discussion will first address how critical scholarly discussions on how genocide was defined by Lemkin and subsequently by the international community in the 1948 Genocide Convention can have implications in terms of genocide denialism. The field of criminology will subsequently be addressed. In contrast to the field of genocide studies, where too much critical debate seems to be the problem, in the field of criminology traditionally the absolute lack of discussion on the topic of genocide appears to be the problem; criminology is very much a discipline "in denial". The aim of addressing the fields of criminology and genocide studies is not to scrutinize the fields of study exhaustively. Instead, it entails a brief, but critical, look in the mirror in order to show that the work of genocide scholars and criminologists can also raise questions in terms of genocide denialism.

The second part of Chapter 7 will furthermore address how the revisionist scientific climate, in which knowledge and truth claims are constantly questioned, is favourable to genocide denialism and how the post-modern turn in academia has exacerbated this climate. Apparently, the problem of genocide denialism might be more closely related to legitimate scholarly revisionism than one might think.

The reflection in Chapter 7 will however not be limited to a general discussion of several implications for the two abovementioned fields. *It will furthermore address the implications of the developed approach for the study at hand.* In developing my approach, I have relied on insights from cultural criminology and speech act and discourse theory. *These sensitising frameworks have their roots in constructionism, which raises the question whether the relativist worldview underlying the approach I developed would allow for some of the most sophisticated denial.* From a cultural criminological perspective, such critical reflection is an inherent part of criminological study. Cultural criminology is a critical criminology, in the sense that it not only deconstructs how the reality of crimes is constructed by various stakeholders, but also how criminology, as one of these stakeholders, is implicated in this process. A crucial element of cultural criminological analysis is thus a critical reflection that addresses the implications of the insights yielded by the research for their own scholarly enterprise.

Figure 2. Flow of research

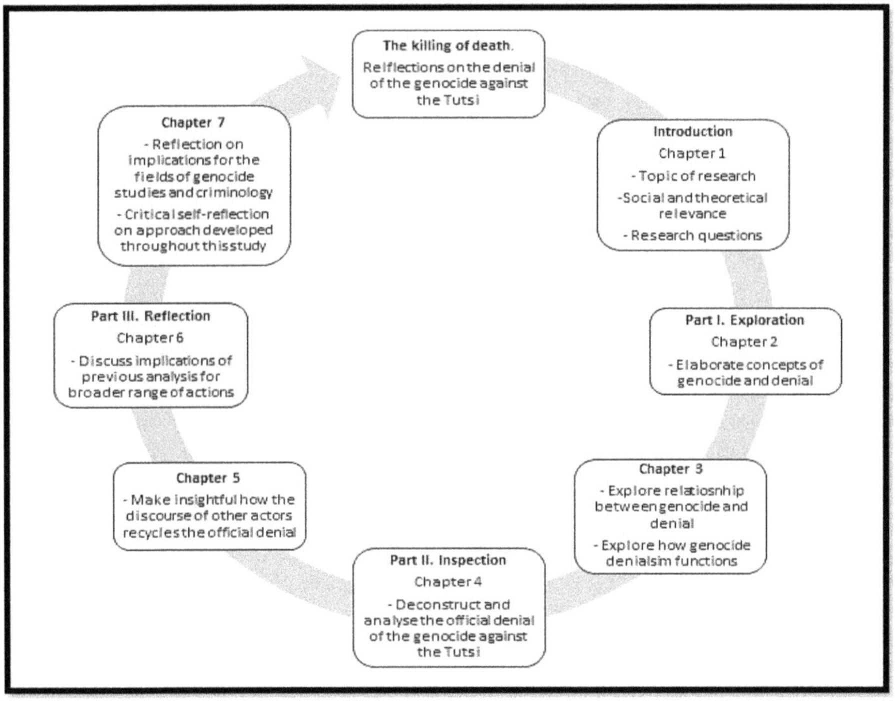

The above flow-chart gives a concise overview of the outline discussed above and it furthermore visualises the chronological order in which the research was conducted.

Sensitising frameworks

As will become clear already from the analysis of the phenomena of genocide and denial in the second Chapter, in this study I draw on insights from a wide variety of disciplines and scholarly research. For instance, the analysis of the phenomenon of denial draws on insights from fields of psychoanalysis and sociology to nursing and genocide studies. There are thus multiple concepts and frameworks that have sensitised my criminological imagination. However, as already noted during the discussion of the research outline, the frameworks of cultural criminology, speech act and discourse theory, the ground-breaking work of Lemkin on genocide and Butler's approach to injurious speech have been particularly influential. In addition, the work Cohen on the denial of human suffering has been a continuous inspiration. Especially Cohen's (2001) phenomenal work *States of denial* has been of great influence in how I have approached and made sense of the subject of denial. These perspectives have all been the main sensitising frameworks and they were utilised in a creative and functional manner in order to make sense of the phenomenon of genocide denialism and the research questions raised above. These frameworks gave "reference and guidance" and informed "directions along which to look".[43] Due to the setup of the study and how it is presented in this manuscript, the theoretical frameworks will not be elaborated at the beginning of the study and subsequently applied, as is traditionally the case. The approaches and methods that shaped this study will be elaborated in the specific parts of the study where they are applied. However, at this point, it is nevertheless insightful to introduce the frameworks briefly and address why they were so influential. Such a brief introduction might also be warranted, because it is possible that readers are familiar with some but not all of these frameworks.

Lemkin's work, especially parts of his study *Axis rule in occupied Europe*, has been particularly relevant for understanding genocide denial and genocide denialism more in general (Lemkin, 1944). This is because of his broad and inclusive conceptualisation of genocide as a complex process that involves many techniques of genocide which operate in a wide variety of domains. It is vital to understand that genocide not only involves physical violence, but it also includes all other kinds of violence. Genocide involves thus much more than mass killing. Lemkin's approach to genocide raises this awareness, which is crucial for coming to understand the significance of the role denial plays in the perpetration of genocide.

The influence of cultural criminology on my approach can be explained with regard to the neglect of criminology to study genocide discussed earlier. Due to this, a

[43] The notion of sensitising frameworks is derived from Blumer's notion of sensitising concepts. In contrast to so-called definitive concepts, which are fixed and involve specified and rigid procedures to identify and study phenomena, sensitising concepts, according to Blumer (1969, p. 148), give "a general sense of reference and guidance" when approaching empirical phenomena for study. The difference between definitive and sensitising concepts is significant, because definitive concepts give "prescriptions of what to see", while sensitising concepts "suggest directions along which to look" (Blumer, 1969, p. 148).

body of criminological theory that is tailored to the study of genocide is not readily available for research purposes. Instead of choosing a specific criminological theory and testing it, I decided to choose a more open criminological approach guided by several elements that are central to cultural criminology as set out by Ferrell et al. (2008) in their book *Cultural criminology an invitation*. Firstly, cultural criminology has an open character that invites researchers to explore criminological phenomena in new and different ways. Furthermore, its political agenda appealed to me. It recognises that research is inherently political and it does not hide behind the *façade* of a neutral, objective and positivist criminology. It holds that doing cultural criminology is doing politics, but a politics that empowers and strives for social justice. Thirdly, cultural criminology puts human agency and meaning at the centre of attempting to understand crimes, criminals and criminal justice policy. It acknowledges that people construct their reality through social interaction, through language. This last insight is valuable in coming to understand genocide denialism.

To come to a deeper understanding of the role played by language in social interaction and reality construction, the frameworks of speech act and discourse theory were explored. Austin's (1962) *How to do things with words* and Laclau & Mouffe's (2001) *Hegemony and socialist strategy* have been of major influence. These speech and discourse frameworks were particularly valuable in the context of my research for two reasons. Firstly, they provided theoretical notions that allowed me to further ground how genocide denial functions and to explain what action genocide denial speech performs. Secondly, they also provided for the necessary methodological tools to analyse concrete instances of genocide denial, which is vital if one wants to study how exactly genocide denial operates in the context of the genocide against the Tutsi.

Lastly, in addressing the question whether genocide denial can enact its own violence or whether it can only facilitate genocidal violence, I was inspired by the ideas concerning the specific nature of linguistic violence, as set out by Butler (1997) in her book *Excitable speech*. In her work, Butler analyses how, for instance, racist speech in the moment of its utterance can be violent because it marginalises and oppresses. Butler's insights helped to shed light on the specific violence that genocide denialism does and how it is different from other kinds of violence, such as physical violence.

These brief descriptions of the five leading sensitising frameworks already indicate that the study has used different lenses and has taken different angles to demystify the phenomenon of genocide denialism and how it operates in the genocide against the Tutsi. With reference to Denzin & Lincoln (2003), one could argue that my research has resulted in a *bricolage*, which is "a pieced-together set of representations that are fitted to the specifics of a complex phenomenon," instead of one final and coherent exhaustive theory of genocide denialism that has been developed by rigorously applying one specific method (Denzin & Lincoln, 2003, p. 5). This also means that this book, although it certainly follows a logical structure, is nonetheless eclectic in its approaches, levels of analysis and angles taken. This also already becomes clear from the earlier discussed outline. I realise that this also means that it is somewhat of an endeavour for the reader to go through this study. As already noted in the Preface, it is not a book from which you can easily pick and choose; one has to go through it in its entirety from beginning to end.

1.7. Data collection

Having introduced and outlined the topic of study and having presented the main sensitising frameworks used, what remains is to provide some important insights as to the type of data used to address the abovementioned research questions and how the data was collected.

1.7.1. From exploration to inspection

Data collection broadly followed the research flow of exploration and inspection described above. As noted, broader research interests (lacunae) led the study into the area of genocide denialism, but the specific research problems initially remained unclear (Glaser, 1992, p. 22; 1998, p. 118). Therefore, in the earlier exploratory stages the open "all is data" approach was followed because all kinds of data could be relevant in terms of figuring out what was going on in the field of research (Glaser & Strauss, 1967). This way, a deeper understanding of the field could be gained. "All is data" is a well-known grounded theory dictum and it means that "what is going on in the research scene is the data, whatever the source" (Glaser, 2001, p. 145). Generating good and insightful ideas requires the researcher to treat "all as data." He thus has to be open to all kinds of data whether it is hard or soft data. Cultural criminologists promote a similar stance as Presdee (2000, p. 15) reveals: "Cultural criminology uses the 'evidence' of everyday existence, wherever it is found and in whatever form it can be found; the debris of everyday life is its 'data'." One collects such "rich data" in order to achieve "thick description" (Geertz, 1973). The implication of seeking "thick" description is that, because all kinds of data must be collected, many data collection methods are applied: interviews, observation, data mining, etc.[44] The dictum of "all is data" was especially influential during the exploratory phase in which the research problems and questions were outlined.

As the research progressed, data collection started to be carried out in a more focussed manner and, instead of exploring the field inspired by general and open questions, the research became mainly driven by more clearly delineated questions that arose from exploring and engaging with the field. For instance, the first stint of fieldwork in Rwanda was guided by general questions, such as how people experience life after conflict, while the second stint of field work was driven by questions specifically

44 The process of data collection is important as the quality of the data will determine the quality of the research. One should thus avoid "smash and grab" data collection as it leads to superficial analysis (Charmaz, 2006, p. 18). Therefore a substantial part of the research consisted of exploring the field, obtaining all kinds of data that would allow for a better understanding of what is going on, that is, what the main issues are concerning the phenomenon of genocide denialism.

targeting the phenomenon of genocide denialism. Although various kinds of data were collected, when the research problem became more clearly delineated, narrative data quickly became of primary importance as it turned out to be particularly helpful in understanding the phenomenon of genocide denialism, which is often a linguistic phenomenon. Studying genocide denialism thus required the collection of narrative data of people and organisations. The term "narrative data" indicates that relevant narratives can be found in different forms of data. As a result, narratives were gathered by conducting interviews over the phone or in the field by talking to people or by observing and listening to them. Relevant narratives were also collected from written materials, such as newspapers, journals, magazines, manuscripts, reports, books, court documents, etc. A vast array of narratives was collected mining the internet. From this follows that, throughout the process of data collection, the bulk of the data was collected in mainly three ways.[45] Interviews were conducted. In addition to conducting interviews in the "real" world, much narrative data was collected in the "virtual" world by mining the internet. Lastly, observations were insightful. The following Sections will briefly address each of these methods.

1.7.2. Interviews

Much narrative data was collected by conducting interviews. I had gained experience in conducting interviews during several research projects, including an elaborate comparative legal study (Faure & Moerland, 2006). The problem was, however, that these earlier interviews were predominantly structured interviews using detailed questionnaires. In order to further my interview skills, I took an intensive course in qualitative interviewing. Furthermore, many of the people I was interested in spoke French. Therefore, I took a French language course. This also greatly facilitated the desktop research which also included the consultation of French publications. After these preparations, I conducted interviews with a wide variety of stakeholders. The interviewees ranged from Rwandese students to Rwandese Ph.D. researchers and from the Rwandan ambassador to the Netherlands to Rwandese refugees. I also conducted interviews with NGO representatives and lawyers who had been dealing with Rwanda and non-Rwandans (expats) who had lived and worked in Rwanda. Also, several months of fieldwork was conducted in Rwanda to collect data from relevant stakeholders, resulting in interviews and consultations with a variety of people and organisations, ranging from genocide victims and perpetrators to lawyers and politicians and from human rights organisations to church organisations. The fieldwork in Rwanda was divided into two stints. The first stint was in 2008 and lasted from the end of October until mid-December. The second stint of research was in 2011 and spanned the month of January. I briefly returned to Rwanda for 10 days in July 2014 to conduct some final interviews and to participate in a conference on the denial of the genocide against the Tutsi.

45 Throughout the exploratory phase, literature on the topic of genocide and denial was studied. This desktop research made use of the university library meta-search engines in order to search for relevant literature. The fact that literature is now available electronically greatly facilitated the research.

The interviews conducted in Rwanda often led to insightful additional information in the form of documentation. For instance, interviews with a judge allowed me to obtain verdicts in genocide denial cases and interviews with trauma counsellors resulted in documentation on their methods of treatment. Furthermore, consultations with the National Commission for the Fight Against Genocide (CNLG) and the Institute of Research and Dialogue for Peace (IRDP) yielded various reports and other relevant materials. At the back of this study a chronological overview of the most significant interviews, consultations and events including those mentioned above is provided. Lastly, it must be noted that, although one of the main ways to collect narrative data was by conducting interviews, much narrative data was also obtained in a less formal manner, "on the go" whenever the opportunity arose, through informal conversations and (small)talks. As noted, part of the research was conducted in Rwanda. The following Sections will briefly address some methodological aspects concerning the fieldwork.

Interpreters

My interpreter or research assistant was very important because I conducted fieldwork in a setting and a language I was not intimately familiar with. My interpreter represents me and I should be able to rely on him or her. Therefore, the person must not only know about my research, more importantly, the person should understand what it is I am trying to do. The better he or she understands my research, the better he or she is able to assist me in my research. I eventually managed to find two interpreters: a man and a woman. They were recommended to me by researchers who had worked closely with them during their fieldwork. The woman was in her thirties and had grown up in the countryside. She was an experienced interviewer having translated for numerous scholars and human rights organisations. She spoke French and Kinyarwanda and she was skilled and experienced in handling the bureaucracy that comes with applying for research permits.[46] The man was in his twenties and he had grown up in the city. He had less professional research experience but was incredibly street-smart and he spoke English, French and Kinyarwanda. He was recommended by a researcher who I had been in close contact with for quite a while and who followed a similar approach in her research. She had spent time informing him on the methods and the underlying ideas. He therefore understood how I approached doing research, which was of great help. His familiarity with my approach also allowed him to collect additional data independently when I left Rwanda.

[46] In order to conduct research in Rwanda, the permission of several governmental ministries and agencies had to be obtained. I needed permission from the Ministry of Internal Affairs, the Ministry of Internal Security, the Ministry of Justice, the National Service of Gacaca Jurisdictions and the Commission for the Fight against Genocide. In preparation for obtaining the required research permits, the interpreters reviewed the requests and provided me with feedback. After having integrated their feedback, the requests for a research permit were handed in at the respective authorities. It took a lot of effort, going back and forth between different authorities, before I had obtained all the required permits.

Interview protocol

In order to respect the privacy of the interviewees, the interviews were almost always conducted in a quiet location. For instance, the interviews in Kigali prison took place in a separate room or the interviews would take place somewhere outside on the prison compound. If people stood by or came too close, they were asked to leave and they always respected our request. The interviews were generally held in Kinyarwanda, which is the native language that most Rwandans speak. Only if people spoke English fluently, the interview was conducted in English. The interviews started off with a brief introduction by my interpreter. I subsequently continued with a more elaborate introduction of the research which my interpreter translated. In the exploratory phase of the research, the questions were broad and open. Often I asked the interviewees only one question: judging from your experiences what do you think is important for us to know? Or, when we leave after our conversation is over, what do you think we should have learned and understood? This allowed those being interviewed to discern for themselves what they thought was important to tell. Interviewees indicated that they appreciated this approach as it showed a sincere interest in their experiences. Over the course of the research, one of the issues that started to stand out was the issue of genocide denialism. This was so for various reasons: some people directly engaged in it, others raised it as a serious challenge in the aftermath, some had difficulty grasping the concept and how it related to genocide ideology, or people noticed that it was not easy to talk about the genocide because of its political sensitivity and the risk of being charged under the legislation criminalising genocide denial. Later interviews focussed more directly on the particular issue of genocide denialism.

Before asking questions, I emphasised that the interviewees were in no way obliged to participate in the interview and that they could (for whatever reason and at any time) decline the interview. It was also pointed out to them that this would have no repercussions. I nonetheless noticed that some interviewees participated because they were asked to participate and they thought it was impolite to refuse or they were afraid of repercussions. Explaining to people that they have a right to decline is one thing, but also making sure that they make use of it is another thing. I also explained that the data collected would not be provided to other agencies or authorities and that I would also, to the best of my capabilities, try to safeguard their anonymity. Anonymity however raises some issues, not only in terms of research transparency, but also because it is often virtually impossible to remain anonymous in Rwanda. People will always know that you have been talking to a *muzungu* (white person). For instance, the second time I visited Rwanda in 2011, I conducted interviews in an office in Kigali with several youth. At one point, my interpreter got a phone call from someone who knew him and who was living on the hill opposite the office that we were in. The person asked what he was doing with that *muzungu*. Lastly, I did not record the interviews and I therefore also did not ask for a signed consent. I mainly took notes, but if the matter was too sensitive I refrained from that was well. It was interesting to notice that some interviewees actually demanded to sign a consent form, because, according to the interviewees, this made everything official and it showed that they were serious about and responsible for what they were telling.

1.7.3. Observations

In addition to gathering data through interviews, conversations and talks, I also used the settings I found myself in to conduct observations. Observing what was happening during the interviews was informative. Often people's body language said more than they were actually telling during the interview.[47] Also, in order to make sense of the interview, the broader situation and context needed be taken into account. It matters, whether one conducts in an interview in an overcrowded prison or by the poolside of a four star hotel. The method of observation became particularly relevant at meetings and conferences, and it was insightful to observe how people act out or not.[48] In 2009, for instance, I visited the ICTR Defence Conference in The Hague and the conference held in memory of Alison Des Forges in London, in order to observe what was going on or to make use of the opportunity to conduct more interviews. During the period of commemoration of the genocide against the Tutsi, several commemorative meetings were held in the Netherlands, which I attended. During my fieldwork in Rwanda, I was often unexpectedly confronted with a situation and the only thing I needed to do was to watch it unfold and observe. An example of such a situation was when Rose Kabuye, former mayor of Kigali and Chief of State Protocol to Rwandan President Paul Kagame, was arrested in November 2008 in Frankfurt. She was subsequently extradited to France. Kabuye was one of several high-ranking Rwandan officials and former RPF soldiers who were indicted by French investigative judge Bruguière. According to Bruguière, these officials were responsible for downing the plane of former President Juvénal Habyarimana, which, according to Bruguière, triggered the outbreak of the genocide. The arrest and extradition of Kabuye lead to considerable unrest in Rwanda with orchestrated mass demonstrations throughout Kigali. There was also considerable animosity towards foreigners, especially Europeans. For instance, I was asked on multiple occasions what I was still doing in Rwanda – it was better if I left the country. I furthermore noticed how aid agencies, in fear of being targeted, removed logos from their cars and offices. The story of the arrest is relevant in terms of denial, because, in his arrest warrant, Bruguière tried to make the Tutsi-led RPF responsible for the genocide against the Tutsi people. Bruguière's warrants were later undermined, when a new investigation into the shooting down of the plane was started by judges Poux and Trévidic (Malagardis, 2012, 2013).[49]

---

47 Communication involves more than speech, also the way people look, facial expressions and posture can be very insightful in understanding what is being communicated.

48 See the appendix for a chronological overview of significant interviews, consultations and events.

49 In terms of genocide denial, Bruguière's indictment is significant and it will therefore receive more substantial attention throughout Chapters 5 and 6 of this study.

1.7.4. Mining the internet

I also researched the "virtual" world of the internet extensively. In terms of data collection, the internet can of course be used as a tool for straightforward desktop research, as it gives easy access to a virtually limitless e-library. For instance, much of the criminological and other journals are made available digitally through the internet. However, internet 2.0 has led to the development of a virtual life world consisting of virtual communities that one can enter for research and, as a result, the boundaries between desktop and field research have become blurred (Roversi, 2008, p. 1). Nowadays people not only live their lives in the physical world, many frequently inhabit the "virtual" world of the internet or cyberspace, as William Gibson (1984) referred to it in his phenomenal novel *Neuromancer*. This is especially the case since internet 2.0 has been developed, which uses technology that moves beyond the static non-interactive earlier versions of the internet. In contrast to its earlier versions, internet 2.0 has real-time interactive features that allow for participation to the extent that for many people cyberspace has become a digital extension of their life in the physical world. It is not simply media, but social media. For many others, however, cyberspace also seems to constitute an alternative reality that in many ways is as real as the "real" world. Also, due to the prominent place the internet has taken in people's daily lives, one could argue that it has become part and parcel of the "real" world.

When it came to collecting data that was particularly relevant in the context of genocide denialism, cyberspace turned out to be a goldmine. Websites, blogs, chats, and posts enabled people to publish their views and experiences virtually in anonymity and without censorship. Moreover, access to the internet is also almost global and so is its reach. Nowadays, it seems that the whole world can make use of and engage on the internet. When I was in Rwanda for fieldwork, construction companies were busy building a state of the art fibre optic cable network that was to connect Rwanda to the internet. In larger towns and cities, cybercafés can be found. As a result, I spent a substantial amount of time mining the internet for data, which turned out to be very fruitful when it came to narrative data. This data varied from official reactions of the Government of Rwanda posted on their website to online comments on articles published in newspapers such as *The Guardian*, and from discussions on yahoo-groups, to all kinds of documentation posted by extremist political groups and individuals on their websites and blogs.

1.7.5. Relevance of the data

Much of the materials collected, of course, also consisted of relevant scholarly and academic literature. As already became clear from the earlier discussion of the "sensitising frameworks" (Section 1.6. Part III), I drew on the work of other scholars to create an understanding, a vantage point, from which to start my exploration of the phenomenon of genocide denialism and more particularly how it operates in the context of the genocide against the Tutsi. However, in order to grasp the complexity of the phenomenon and to (come up with and) answer the research questions discussed in Section 1.6., it was imperative to move beyond a literature study. This observation already indicates the significance of the other data collected during my fieldwork. Although virtually all the collected materials were valuable to my study, not all the data that was gathered features prominently in the manuscript. As noted earlier, because denial is often a linguistic phenomenon, the data that I draw upon most directly in this study, and therefore also most prominently features as illustration in the manuscript, is narrative data from a variety of sources ranging from interviews and talks to official documents and internet blogs. This however does not mean that the other fieldwork experiences and observations are less significant. Although they do not feature prominently in the manuscript, they are nonetheless important for various reasons. Firstly, the insights gained during my fieldwork helped me to make better sense of the situations and issues I encountered. It helped to increase my understanding. Secondly, I do sometimes discuss my fieldwork experiences in this manuscript at the point where I think the information from observations or interviews, etc. is useful for the reader's comprehension of the subject matter under discussion. In such cases, I use the materials to contextualise, to add more depth, etc. Using stories of my fieldwork experiences at certain stages can also open up dense texts and such stories also have the ability to convey complex meaning to the reader in a comprehensible way.

1.8. Some last notes on the scope of the study

The general goal of this study is to obtain a better understanding of the denial of the genocide against the Tutsi and the problem of genocide denialism more in general. To this end, the study addresses many questions, but at the same time it probably raises plenty more. Although there is an end to this manuscript, this does not mean that the analysis presented is final. I hope that the analysis triggers critical thinking and generates constructive feedback. It thus remains a work in progress.

Furthermore, having a background in criminology and law, I was at times forced to work outside my criminological and legal comfort zone. This meant working with theories and approaches that I was not readily familiar with and therefore learning the tricks of these other trades became part of the research process. I, for instance, took part in an intensive course on discourse analysis in order to familiarise myself with the relevant theory and method. Although crossing disciplinary boundaries led to many valuable new insights, I nonetheless acknowledge that there is still much to learn from other fields of research. There is a vast knowledge base out there that could be tapped into in order to come to an even better understanding of genocide denialism.

In addition to disciplinary boundaries, I was also limited by language barriers. This was foremost the case in Rwanda; Kinyarwanda is a language that I am not familiar with. Due to my language skills, the materials studied were limited to English, German, Dutch, and French sources. The bulk of the materials was, however, in

English. Although I did incorporate a significant number of French sources on the topic, there is still much more ground to be covered.

As noted already in the preface, my analysis of genocide is not exhaustive and I have focussed on those aspects that were most helpful in understanding the role denial plays in the process of genocide. This has also resulted in a focus on the work of Raphael Lemkin, who conceptualised the phenomenon and coined the term genocide. I understand that readers could be critical of my focus on Raphael Lemkin's original framing of the concept of genocide. The approach could raise the question to what extent Lemkin's ground-breaking work should be guiding definitions and applications of the concept of genocide. I surely do not mean to convey that later scholarly work on the topic of genocide is less significant, because it is not. However, I do also think that later scholarly work often "neglects" important aspects that were central to Lemkin's approach to genocide. I took Lemkin's work as a vantage point, because certain aspects of his original framing of the crime of genocide are highly insightful in the context of this study.

Although I have based my analysis and conclusions of how denial operates in the context of the genocide against the Tutsi on a wide variety of concrete empirical examples, it is possible that the empirical materials are still too specific to justify the broader generalisations that I make. Furthermore, some of the implications and conclusions that I discuss do go beyond the specific case of Rwanda in relation to which the framework was "tested". The framework that I develop in Part I of this study is a general framework and therefore also more general implications and conclusions follow from it. Whether the framework can truly be applied generally still remains to be tested by applying it other cases of genocide. Therefore, although I do draw (more) general implications and conclusions, which I think are theoretically merited, one still has to be careful with how strong such claims are as long as the framework has not been applied exhaustively to other cases.

What also could be perceived as a "limitation" is that the research does not substantially address the crimes committed by the Rwandan Patriotic Army (RPA) that were, for instance, perpetrated during the war in Rwanda or in neighbouring Congo.[50] In conversations about my research, people often tried to convince me that these crimes should also be included in the study. They argued that the crimes of the RPA were also largely being denied and they deserved attention; they presented the other side of a much more complex story. It is true that the crimes perpetrated by the RPA after their invasion in 1990 or the crimes perpetrated later by the Government of Rwanda led by President Paul Kagame do receive less attention. These crimes and their implications do merit further study and should not be disregarded, but to include them in this particular research that focuses on the denial of the genocide against the Tutsi would be inappropriate. My research focuses on genocide denialism and it tries to bring insight to the relationship between denial and genocide. Formally, the war crimes and crimes against humanity perpetrated by the RPA are therefore not the

50 For an analysis of these issues consult the books by Prunier (2009), Clarck (2002) and Jones (2014).

topic of this study. Substantially, a more pressing concern is that such an approach could lead to comparative trivialisations. I think that the acknowledgement of these issues should not come at the cost of distorting the reality of the genocide and there is a real danger of conflating the genocide against the Tutsi with the war and the aftermath in Rwanda and the Democratic Republic of Congo. Those who deny the genocide against the Tutsi often focus on the crimes the military wing of the RPF has perpetrated and they use the violence inflicted by the RPA to turn around the roles of perpetrators and victims of the genocide. Also, trying to account for the suffering of all people in the conflict can cut along the same discursive lines as the rhetoric of genocide denial. In genocide denial discourse, it is often promoted that all parties have suffered and therefore it is a zero sum game. It is because of these reasons, which will become much clearer throughout the rest of this study, that I decided not to pay close attention to the abovementioned matters.

The outline presented in Section 1.6. of this Chapter furthermore makes clear that an (introductory) description of the historical events concerning the genocide against the Tutsi will not be provided. For such a historical overview, I suggest that the excellent work of scholars such as, Des Forges (1999), Melvern (2006) or Prunier (1995), can be consulted.

Lastly, this research was concluded by the end of July 2014. Developments after that date have not been included in the analysis.

Part I
Exploration

Chapter 2
Genocide and denial

2.1. Introduction

In order to address the lack of theoretical grounding discussed earlier and to address the self-explanatory use of the concept of genocide denial, the first part of this study (Chapter 2 and 3) will elaborate on how genocide denial can be more clearly conceptualised and defined so that it can be used for research purposes. *This requires first of all an explanation of what the concepts of genocide and denial, which are the main conceptual building blocks, entail and it furthermore requires an explanation of how the two concepts are related.* These questions will be the focus of this Chapter.

The complex nature of both phenomena (genocide and denial) has led to lengthy scholarly discussions concerning their delineation. However, due to the fact that the discussion of these two concepts should provide for a better understanding of the phenomenon of genocide denial, the analysis of the two concepts will be limited to a critical discussion of the conceptual dimensions that are relevant in the light of this study. The Chapter will first address the dimensions of the concept of genocide and subsequently address how this concept is related to the concept of denial. Lastly, the relevant dimensions of the concept of denial will be elaborated on.

The discussion of genocide in the next Sections goes back to the roots of the concept and focuses predominantly on how Raphael Lemkin, who developed the concept, understood genocide. Lemkin's original insights concerning genocide are valuable in understanding the role genocide denial plays in the process of genocide. What is particularly insightful about Lemkin's work is that he acknowledged the many ways (techniques) by which genocide can be perpetrated, which is an insight that was severely marginalised in subsequent scholarly conceptualisations of genocide. When discussing the concept of denial, the "opposite" approach is taken and, instead of focusing on the original conceptualisation of denial by Freud, the discussion elaborates how other scholars have contributed to the development of the concept. These critical scholarly elaborations on Freud's initial conceptualisation of denial are most insightful for understanding the phenomenon of genocide denial.

2.2. Genocide

Since its inception by the Polish-Jewish jurist Raphael Lemkin in 1944 and its subsequent criminalisation in the 1948 Genocide Convention, the concept of genocide and its definition have been heavily debated and criticised. Lemkin (1944, p. 79) defined genocide as "a coordinated plan of different actions aiming at the destruction of essential foundations of the life of national groups, with the aim of annihilating the groups themselves." Scholars have criticised Lemkin's focus on national and ethnic groups for several reasons. Lemkin saw these particular groups as the carriers or vehicles of unique and therefore indispensable cultures. The problem with such a focus on groups is that the collective is valued more than the individual creating competition amongst suffering. Lemkin's definitional focus on culture also had the unwanted effect that to kill people of a single ethnicity is somehow different and more serious than killing a group of people of mixed ethnicities (Jones, 2006, p. 11; A. D. Moses, 2010, p. 29). Lemkin's restriction to national and ethnic groups has also been criticised, because it excludes other groups that do deserve protection. Scholars argue, for instance, that the victimisation of the Kulaks in the former Soviet Union has shown that political groups can also become the targets of destructive campaigns (Alvarez, 2001, p. 37; Jones, 2006, p. 11). The 1948 Genocide Convention aims to protect more groups than only national and ethnical groups. The Convention defines genocide as "acts committed with intent to destroy, in whole or in part, a national, ethnical, racial or religious group, as such." The protected groups thus also include racial and religious groups. However, the Convention has also been severely criticised by scholars for excluding political groups and other social groups (Andreopoulos, 1994, p. 2; Semelin, 2007, p. 316).[1] It is however interesting to note that Lemkin, when he addresses the issue of the repression of the crime of genocide, seems to be more inclusive as to the groups to be protected: "An international multilateral treaty should provide for the introduction, not only in the constitution but also in the criminal code of each country, of provisions protecting *minority groups* from oppression because of their *nationhood, religion, or race*" (Lemkin, 1944, p. 93 emphasis added).[2] When the international community criminalised genocide in 1945 by adopting Resolution 96 on the crime of genocide, it also seems to have had a much broader perception of genocide and the protected groups:

> Genocide is a denial of the right of existence of entire human groups, as homicide is the denial of the right to live of individual human beings; such denial of the right of existence shocks the conscience of mankind, results in great losses to humanity in the form of cultural and other contributions represented by these human groups, and is contrary to moral law and to the spirit and aims of the United Nations. Many instances of such crimes of genocide have occurred when racial, religious, political, and other groups have been destroyed, entirely or in part. (United Nations General Assembly, Resolution 96, fifty-fifth plenary meeting, 11 December, 1946)

---

1 For an analysis of the political dimensions of the definition of genocide in the 1948 Convention see Kuper (2002).

2 In one of his first articles on the crimes of barbarity and vandalism, Lemkin (1933b) referred to "Menschheitsgruppen" (groups of people) more generally, mentioning, in addition to national and ethnic groups, also religious and social groups. In an article published years later, Lemkin (1945) refers more generally to minorities. He states that "The disease of criminality if left unchecked is contagious. Minorities of one sort or another exist in all countries, protected by the constitutional order of the state. If persecution of any minority by any country is tolerated anywhere, the very moral and legal foundations of constitutional government may be shaken."

In trying to deal with these and other discerned conceptual and definitional ills, scholars have come up with a wide variety of alternative conceptualisations and definitions of genocide.[3] One of the first alternative definitions of genocide was proposed by Peter Drost (1959, p. 125), who defined genocide as "the deliberate destruction of physical life of individual human beings by reason of their membership of any human collectivity as such." After Drost, many other scholars followed in presenting alternative conceptualisations and definitions. Fein, for instance, proposed a definition which focused on the idea that genocide involves an organised and structural effort. She defines genocide as "sustained purposeful action by a perpetrator to physically destroy a collectivity directly or indirectly, through interdiction of the biological and social reproduction of group members, sustained regardless of the surrender or lack of threat by the victim" (Fein, 2009, p. 54). Charny (2009b, p. 37), furthermore, proposed an inclusive humanistic definition of genocide in which he defined genocide as "the wanton murder of human beings on the basis of any identity whatsoever they share."[4] In contrast to Lemkin's and the Convention's limited focus on certain specific groups, these definitions focus on collectivities and groups in general.

The list of alternative definitions seems to be endless. Straus', Jones' and Alvarez's comparative analyses of genocide definitions already reveal more than 20 different definitions (Alvarez, 2001; Jones, 2006; Straus, 2001).[5] Some scholars have been critical of new conceptualisations and definitions of genocide because, in their

3 The ambiguity of the concept of genocide has also led to the introduction of a range of so called *cide*-terms, such as ethnocide, democide, gendercide, politicide, urbicide, etc. Another term that gained "popularity" during the conflict in Yugoslavia is ethnic cleansing. These terms however often describe and define aspects of the general process which is genocide as Shaw (2007, p. 64) remarks: "The many new '-cides' are, in fact, the many sides of genocide." It is confusing however that, instead of being presented as part of a general genocide framework, these new terms are often presented as substitutes for the general concept of genocide, thereby adding to the confusion (Shaw, 2007, p. 77). Shaw explains that Lemkin himself also did not include political groups as protected groups because they lacked the permanency and characteristics of the other protected groups. Shaw, however, points out that political elites are often the first targets of genocide and when totally exterminated one could wonder how such victimisation is qualitatively different from genocide. According to Shaw (2007, p. 70 and 71) it is therefore better to view politicide as a variant of genocide. Shaw (2007, p. 78) ultimately argues that "it is better to use genocide as the master-concept, accepting that its meaning has expanded from the narrow meaning of genos as nation or ethnic group, to cover the destruction of any type of people or any group."

4 Other influential alternative definitions have been the presented by Chalk & Jonassohn (1990): "Genocide is a form of one-sided mass killing in which a state or other authority intends to destroy a group, as that group and membership in it are defined by the perpetrator." Harff & Gurr (1988) discuss "the promotion and execution of policies by a state or its agents which result in the deaths of a substantial portion of a group." They however make a distinction between politicide and genocide: "The difference between genocides and politicides is in the characteristics by which members of the group are identified by the state. In genocides the victimized groups are defined primarily in terms of their communal characteristics, i.e., ethnicity, religion or nationality. In politicides the victim groups are defined primarily in terms of their hierarchical position or political opposition to the regime and dominant groups." Katz (1994) argues that "the concept of genocide applies only when there is an actualized intent, however successfully carried out, to physically destroy an entire group (as such a group is defined by the perpetrators)."

5 This also shows that genocide is a dynamic and fluid concept and can develop over time. Theriault (2010, p. 481) notes that "Genocide is not a fixed object but varies by context and evolves in methods and

attempts to (re)conceptualise and (re)define genocide, many scholars tend to reduce genocide to mass murder or they end up proposing different concepts altogether (A. D. Moses, 2010, p. 21). It seems that, in many scholarly elaborations of the concept and the definition of genocide, Lemkin's original insights have become merely an introduction to further critical discussions on genocide. They elaborate on Lemkin's biography and more particularly his lobby to get genocide criminalised, but they often refrain from substantially addressing his insights and the fundamental understanding that they provide (A. D. Moses, 2010, p. 20).[6] Sometimes scholars tend to criticise Lemkin to the extent that they seem to instruct him on how to understand a concept which he himself coined (A. D. Moses, 2010, p. 21). Shaw (2007, p. 18) argues that if one wants to understand genocide, it is essential to understand what Lemkin understood by it and as a result "[w]e should approach his contribution with more than the ritual piety."

I am aware of the fact that tensions exist between definitions of genocide. This is especially the case when it comes to definitions raised in different academic disciplines. For legal scholars or jurists, social scientific definitions of genocide might raise some eyebrows. For instance, some scholars, such as Huttenbach (1988), define genocide as any act which jeopardises the existence of a group. In terms of explaining genocide, such a definition might be helpful. However, when it comes to holding perpetrators criminally liable, such a definition raises some serious questions: what constitutes "jeopardising" and what is the exact meaning of "existence"? From a legal perspective, such a definition would have serious shortcomings, because legal definitions have to comply with other requirements than social scientific definitions. As Tatz (2003, p. 71) concludes, socio-scientifically Huttenbach might be correct, but legally he is wrong. Tatz's observation also applies to much of what is written in this book, because it addresses the dimensions of genocide predominantly not from a legal point of view.[7] When addressing a broader public, such issues are bound to arise. However, the point of the following analysis is not to come to a definite definition of genocide, nor to engage in definitional battles. Instead, in order to come to a better understanding of genocide denial, genocide as one of its conceptual elements will be addressed. To this end, drawing on Lemkin's conceptualisation, the main dimensions of genocide are elaborated and the relationship between these dimensions is discussed.

---

forms over time. In fact, as relevant laws, legal interpretations, and political commitments develop, so do would-be perpetrators modify what genocide is in order to avoid political and legal consequences."

6 This does not mean that such research on the life of Lemkin is unimportant, because it is. His life greatly shaped his academic and political work. For biographical work on Lemkin see: Freeze (2013), Jacobs (2012) and Cooper (2008). For comprehensive articles on Lemkin see the contributions by Ignatieff (2013a, 2013b).

7 For an interesting kaleidoscopic reflection on the legal reality of genocide from various perspectives, which for instance discusses the legal definition in the Convention, the application in court and the interpretation in jurisprudence see Akhavan (2012) *Reducing genocide to law: Definition, meaning, and the ultimate crime*.

2.3. Dimensions of genocide

Especially in the context of this research on genocide denialism, it is important to pay specific attention to Lemkin's conceptualisation of genocide, as it provides us with key insights for understanding the phenomenon of genocide denial and its implications. As will become clear throughout this study, those who (attempt to) deny genocide basically do this by attacking one or more of the constitutive dimensions of genocide, which allow us to determine whether an event can be defined as genocide. The following analysis will therefore mainly deal with these constitutive dimensions of Lemkin's conceptualisation of genocide, because they are functional in gaining an understanding of the phenomenon of genocide denial. More importantly, Lemkin's insights help us to understand how genocide and denial are related. This is an aspect that will also be discussed more elaborately in the following Chapter of this study.

Lemkin coined the term genocide in 1944 in his book *Axis rule in occupied Europe*. As introduced above, according to Lemkin (1944, p. 79), the term genocide signified "a coordinated plan of different actions aiming at the destruction of essential foundations of the life of national groups, with the aim of annihilating the groups themselves." It is generally argued that Lemkin's definition of genocide consists of five interrelated dimensions, which include: 1) the *aim* to be achieved by genocide, 2) the *victim* that is being targeted by genocide, 3) the *actions* involved in genocidal victimisation, 4) the *agents* that perform these actions, and 5) the *intent* with which such actions are performed (Alvarez, 2001; Jones, 2006, 2010c; Straus, 2001). The following Sections will first address the *aim* to be achieved by genocide and the *victim* that is being targeted. The specific goal of genocide and the unique nature of the victim that it targets have profound implications for the pervasiveness and the scope of the *actions* involved in genocidal victimisation, which is the third dimension that will be addressed. The last two dimensions, *agent* and *intent*, follow from the first three dimensions. Genocide requires *agents* that perform certain acts with a *genocidal intention*. Based on the presented conceptual dimensions, one could also generally define genocide as the intentional annihilation of a people. As will become clear throughout the analysis, this process involves various actors and a wide variety of genocidal techniques. The analysis of the dimensions of genocide will end with a brief discussion of the role that ideology plays in the perpetration of genocide. Although ideology is not listed as a specific dimension, it is nonetheless crucial for understanding genocide and its denial.

2.3.1. Annihilation

In understanding what genocide meant to Lemkin, we should pay attention to the specific terminology that he used to describe the phenomenon; for Lemkin words mattered. He was not only a lawyer, he had also studied linguistics. Samantha Power notes that Lemkin seemed to place an unusual trust in words, because, in contrast to many of those who deemed language inadequate to capture what happened during the Holocaust, Lemkin "reinvested in language" and coined the term genocide

(Power, 2002, p. 42). Although, in his conceptualisation of genocide, Lemkin was influenced by the Nazi Final Solution, it was not his intention to capture the Holocaust specifically (Power, 2002, p. 43). Instead, genocide was a concept which was supposed to capture a general phenomenon of which the Holocaust, but also, for instance, the Armenian genocide, were each specific and unique instances. That words mattered to Lemkin does not only become clear from the fact that he used language to describe a phenomenon that many deemed indescribable or even unintelligible, it also becomes clear from how he approached finding a word suitable for the phenomenon he was conceptualising (Power, 2002, p. 41 and 42). Power explains that, in trying to find an adequate term, Lemkin read extensively in linguistic and semantic theory and he was inspired by Eastman's arguments for choosing the term "Kodak" to name his camera (Power, 2002, p. 41 and 42). According to Eastman, who founded the corporation that produced the famous Kodak camera, the term was most suitable because it was short, could not be mispronounced, did not resemble other words and, as a result, could not be associated with anything else but Eastman's camera. Lemkin looked for a term that had these characteristics and that, at the same time, could convey a strong moral judgement (Power, 2002, p. 41 and 42). Before settling on the term genocide, Lemkin (1933b) had used the terms *vandalism* and *barbarity*, but these terms also had different connotations and failed to capture the unique character of the events Lemkin was confronted with.[8] Lemkin thus paid serious attention to the words he used to describe the phenomenon he was studying. It is therefore important to pay attention to the specific terminology he used to invest his term genocide with a unique meaning, which set it apart from other terms such as "mass murder" or "denationalisation".

[8] Although Lemkin coined the term genocide in 1944, the ideas underlying the crime of genocide were already formulated in a 1933 paper which he wanted to present at the 5th *Madrid Conference for the Unification of Penal Law*. The document in which Lemkin coined these terms was originally published by Paris law publisher A. Pedone and was titled *Les actes constituant un danger général (interétatique) considérés comme délites des droit des gens* (Lemkin, 1933a). It was later published by Lemkin in the *Austrian Law Journal* titled *Akte der Barbarei und des Vandalismus als delicta juris gentium* (Lemkin, 1933b). In that paper, he proposed a law banning what he then referred to as the international crimes of *barbarity* and *vandalism*. In the early descriptions of these crimes, one finds the central elements of what Lemkin later would term genocide. With regard to barbarity, Lemkin (1933a) argued the following: "Let us consider, first and foremost, acts of extermination directed against the ethnic, religious or social collectivities whatever the motive (political, religious, etc.); for example massacres, pogroms, actions undertaken to ruin the economic existence of the members of a collectivity, etc. Also belonging in this category are all sorts of brutalities which attack the dignity of the individual in cases where these acts of humiliation have their source in a campaign of extermination directed against the collectivity in which the victim is a member. Taken as a whole, all the acts of this character constitute an offense against the law of nations which we will call by the name 'barbarity'". With regard to vandalism, Lemkin (1933a) argued: "An attack targeting a collectivity can also take the form of systematic and organized destruction of the art and cultural heritage in which the unique genius and achievement of a collectivity are revealed in fields of science, arts and literature. The contribution of any particular collectivity to world culture as a whole, forms the wealth of all of humanity, even while exhibiting unique characteristics." Especially the idea underlying the crime of vandalism shows that genocide is not only about the physical destruction of human beings. Annihilation also requires the destruction of their ways of life, cultural heritage and collective memory. Lemkin thus conceptualised a general crime that consists of specific types of crimes, but which is more than the sum of these individual types of crime (Shaw, 2007, p. 18).

According to Lemkin's definition of genocide stated above, Lemkin saw the *annihilation* of a national or ethnic group of people as the aim of genocide. He furthermore noticed that, in order to reach this aim, the foundations of life of the group had to be *destroyed* by a coordinated effort (Lemkin, 1944, p. 79).[9] The terms destruction and annihilation are presented in Lemkin's description in a specific relation to each other; destruction is presented as a means to the end of annihilation. By destroying the foundations of life of groups, the groups themselves can be annihilated. In contrast, many scholars seem to describe the aim of genocide mainly in terms of the destruction of groups. The definitions of Drost and Fein presented above describe genocide in terms of the destruction of collectivities. Also the 1948 Genocide Convention in its definition of genocide states "acts committed with the intent to destroy."[10] The problem is however that the meaning of the term destruction differs from the meaning of the term annihilation, which Lemkin specifically used to designate the aim of genocide. By describing the aim of genocide in terms of annihilation, Lemkin conveyed the unique character of the phenomenon he was trying to conceptualise.

According to the Oxford English Dictionary, to destroy something is to demolish or ravage it, to reduce it to fragments. It also more specifically refers to the action of putting to death or the slaughter of people. What remains after destruction is the state of being destroyed: ruin. Hence, destruction leaves behind wreckage, waste or remains. The destruction of a building leaves behind bricks and the destruction of people leaves behind human remains or other artefacts signifying their victimisation. It thus leaves behind remnants reminding us of their existence. Although annihilation is sometimes also used as a synonym for destruction, the impact of annihilation is much more pervasive (all-encompassing). According to the Oxford English Dictionary, the term annihilation has its roots in the Latin word *nihil*, which means "nothing" and literally translated annihilation means "to make into nothing" or "blotting out of existence". In contrast to destruction, which always seems to leave something behind, annihilation seems to disintegrate its targets to such an extent that it leaves nothing behind. What remains when something is annihilated is "a state of nothingness resulting from blotting out of existence". In contrast to destruction, after annihilation no remnants are left behind. Lemkin's definition does mention the term destruction, but he makes clear that "destruction" is a means to the end of

9 In the Preface to his book Lemkin (1944, p. xi) talks about the "practice of extermination" and he explains that genocide is "effected through a synchronized attack on different aspects of life".

10 For a discussion of jurisprudence on the meaning of the word "destroy" as an element of the legal definition of genocide see: Van den Herik (2012). The analysis reveals that in the jurisprudence of, for instance, the International Criminal Court for the former Yugoslavia (ICTY), there is a tension between more traditional interpretations which require the material or biological, and thus physical, destruction of the protected group and interpretations which I think are more in line with Lemkin's conceptualisation that genocide can also be perpetrated by other means, such as forcibly transferring people of the targeted group or destroying their culture. Interestingly, Herik notes that the push for a broader interpretation seems to come from national cases. She points out that "In some domestic cases, perpetrators have also been charged with genocide for crimes committed in Bosnia and Herzegovina, other than the Srebrenica killings. Most notable is the German case against Jorgić. In this case, the German Court concluded that genocide also encompasses the situation where group members survive but the group ceases to exist as a social unit". (Van den Herik, 2012, p. 10).

annihilation. By destroying the foundations of life of groups, the groups themselves can be annihilated. It is significant that, in his early article on the crimes of barbarity and vandalism, Lemkin talked about the *Ausrottung* of *Menschheitsgruppen* (Lemkin, 1933b). *Ausrotten* does not simply connote destruction (*zerstören*), instead it means to eradicate or to wipe something out. It is typically used to describe the annihilation of vermin (*Ungeziefer*) or weeds. These words are meaningful in the context of the genocide, because, in genocidal propaganda, the victims of genocide are often designated as vermin. For instance, in anti-Tutsi propaganda, the Tutsi were denoted as cockroaches.[11, 12]

The idea that genocide aims for annihilation and not merely destruction is of profound importance for understanding the forms genocidal violence can take and how meaningful certain violent acts are in the context of genocide. If genocide is approached from the perspective of annihilation, certain acts committed during the Holocaust or the Armenian genocide become much more meaningful than if they are approached solely in terms of destruction. For instance, during the Armenian genocide and the Holocaust, victims' lives were not merely destroyed by putting them to death. The genocidal violence went much further, beyond the destruction of their life; what remained of those who were killed also had to disappear. During the Holocaust, bodies were burnt in crematoria, pits and trenches, thereby reducing them to ashes, to virtually nothing. During the Armenian genocide, people were forced to go on death marches leading into the desert, where, after death by starvation, their remains would wither away by the power of blasting sandstorms to the point where nothing was left behind. In both cases, human beings were reduced to a state where nothing remained of their human *being*. Such violent actions, which literally aim to evaporate people, are especially significant in the context of a crime the aim of which is to annihilate. Although these examples are meaningful, they also limit the genocidal violence to the physical destruction of human beings. As will become clear in the next Section, due to the unique character of the victim which is to be annihilated, genocidal violence involves much more than physical destruction of human beings. It, for instance, also targets their culture.

11 Dehumanisation is crucial to the perpetration of genocide. When perpetrators no longer see the victims as humans the moral responsibility towards them seizes to exist and the infliction of violence is facilitated. When people are dehumanised, they are often reduced to animals. However, humans still have empathetic feelings for certain animals. We, for instance, have close ties with cats and dogs. As a result, perpetrators tend to reduce their victims to insects, which are a threat and nuisance and can be crushed with your foot or eradicated with poison. In their reality, *génocidaires* are not annihilating a people; instead they are exterminating a pest. The true nature of the actions is obscured and harmful behaviour is presented in a more positive light, which is telling in terms of denial.

12 The focus here lies on physical or material destruction, but what will become clear throughout this study is that, in order to achieve annihilation, much of the destruction is linguistic and involves the reinterpretation of the reality of the event. How this is possible will be addressed at greater length in later Chapters. For now it is important to understand that, for instance, the victims of genocide can be destroyed, not only by physically destroying them, but also by reinterpreting the nature of their victimisation, thereby turning them into victims of war or forced labour, but not an intentional campaign to annihilate them.

2.3.2. A people

The targets of annihilation, according to Lemkin (1944, p. 79), are national or ethnic groups and he more importantly explains that "[g]enocide is directed against the national group as an entity, and the actions involved are directed against individuals, not in their individual capacity, but as members of the national group".[13] Therefore, although the measures are initially directed at individual human beings, their aim is to negatively affect the collectivity of which they are members. Lemkin (1944, p. 79), for instance, explains that:

> The confiscation of property of nationals of an occupied area on the ground that they have left the country may be considered simply as a deprivation of their individual property rights. However, if the confiscations are ordered against individuals solely because they are Poles, Jews, or Czechs, then the same confiscations tend in effect to weaken the national entities of which those persons are members.

Thus by victimising individual human beings, genocide aims to annihilate the group to which they belong. The victimisation of individuals is therefore only a means to the end of group annihilation.[14]

To describe the groups targeted for annihilation, Lemkin uses the specific term *entity*. The idea that "[g]enocide is directed against the national group as an entity" is of great importance to the meaning of genocide. When conceptualising and defining genocide, scholars often talk of groups or collectives as the victims, however, by using the specific term entity, Lemkin seemed to make clear that what genocide wants to annihilate is not simply a group of people or collection of individuals. According to the Oxford English Dictionary, the term group means an assemblage of persons forming a unity due to mutual or common relations or because they can be classed together due to a certain degree of similarity. A group is therefore an aggregation of individual persons. In contrast, entity is defined as "that which constitutes the being of a thing"; its existence. The word "entity" furthermore denotes that a group has a distinct, separate or independent existence; it can be distinguished from its attributes. An entity is thus more than the sum of its individual parts or attributes. An entity is therefore not a mere aggregate of beings; it is a conglomerate which encompasses much more than the sum of its human individuals. It includes other material and immaterial constituents, such as, artefacts, customs, beliefs, collective memories, and other elements shaping the social and collective identity of the entity. What this signifies is that, in constituting a people, culture turns out to be of great importance, as it is through their cultural norms and traditions that a people are

13 Although Lemkin specifically mentions national groups, in other work he also refers to human groups or minorities more generally. See footnote 2, Chapter 2.

14 In an article written after the United Nations General Assembly approved Resolution 96 (I) on December 11, 1946, Lemkin (1947) notes "The crime of genocide involves a wide range of actions, including not only deprivation of life but also the prevention of life (abortions, sterilizations) and also devices considerably endangering life and health (artificial death in special camps, deliberate separation of families for depopulation purposes and so forth). All these actions are subordinated to the criminal intent to destroy or to cripple permanently a human group."

able to meaningfully position and define themselves.[15] The point is that an entity encompasses more than its individual biological constituents, which has implications for the discussion of which types of violence are utilised in the process of genocidal annihilation.

In addition to the issue of which groups should be protected, another important issue is what constitutes such a group. Are there objective elements that allow us to determine whether a group of people constitutes *a* people?[16] Does such a group exist independently from the perception of those trying to annihilate them? It is important to understand that, instead of a people being a well-defined entity whose existence can be objectively determined, in constructing the victim of genocide (the other), the subjective perceptions of the perpetrators can play a significant role.[17] Irvin (2012) explains:

> In genocide, death serves as a reality effect. Genocidal ideologies obscure the possibility that cultural identity is plastic and group boundaries are fuzzy. The genocidal act thus

15 This explains why cultural genocide is possible as Lemkin concluded: "the destruction of cultural symbols is genocide," because the destruction of such elements "menaces the existence of the social group which exists by virtue of its common culture" (Lemkin quoted in A. D. Moses, 2010, p. 25). For cultural destruction to amount to genocide, it must be undertaken with a genocidal intention, thus with the aim to annihilate a people.

16 Akhavan (2005) elaborates how in the context of the genocide against the Tutsi this issue became clear as the ICTR struggled to define the Tutsi as an ethnic and therefore protected group. The differences were not ethnic because the Hutu and Tutsi social groups spoke the same Bantu language, had the same religion, occupied the same geographical space, and frequently inter-married. Originally, the distinction between the Hutu and Tutsi had socio-economic origins and it was about lineage instead of ethnicity (Akhavan, 2005, p. 1000). Early pseudo anthropological studies had racialised the socio-economic differences making them seem something immutable. The colonial powers and later the *génocidaires*, each for their own purposes, exacerbated these racialised differences. The Belgian colonisers, for instance, made a reference to "ethnic" affiliation on identity cards and this was maintained, even after Rwanda's independence. But this immutable difference was born out of a racialist mythology. The ICTR in the Akayesu case defined an "ethnic group" as "a group whose members share a common language or culture" (The Prosecutor v. Akayesu, Case No. ICTR-96-4, Judgment Sept. 2, 1998, par. 513). As Akhavan (2005, p. 1001) notes, this "definition disqualifies the Tutsi vis-a-vis the Hutu, since both shared a common language and culture." The Chamber solved this problem by arguing that "the intention of the drafters of the Genocide Convention was patently to ensure the protection of any stable and permanent group" and they subsequently concluded that "at the time of the alleged events, the Tutsi indeed constituted a stable and permanent group and were identified as such by all" (The Prosecutor v. Akayesu, Case No. ICTR-96-4, Judgment Sept. 2, 1998, par. 516 and 702). As a result, the Tutsi could be seen as a legally protected group under the Convention. Akhavan (2005, p. 1001) however concludes that such an interpretation is inconsistent with the language of the Convention and the *nullem crimen sine lege* principle. In the subsequent Kayishema case, the Chamber defined an ethnic group more broadly as one "whose members share a common language and culture; or, a group which distinguishes itself, as such (self-identification); or, a group identified as such by others, including perpetrators of the crimes (identification by others)" (Akhavan 2005, p. 1001). Akhavan (2005, p. 1002) however criticises the proposed constructivist approach to identity because it could lead to absurdity as the "perpetrator could define virtually any group as ethnic, irrespective of its objective attributes, and be held guilty of genocide." In the Rutaganda case (The Prosecutor v. Rutaganda, Case No. ICTR-96-3-T, Judgment and Sentence, Dec. 6, 1999) the Chamber developed an approach that takes into account subjective and context dependant nature of group identity but it still notes the importance of objective aspects (Akhavan 2005, p. 1002).

17 Straus (2001, p. 366) notes that the victims of genocide can be perceived as constituting an organic collectivity by the perpetrator. Genocide attempts to annihilate a present and future threat. In doing

> confers a sense of actuality upon the victim group by identifying them as a group with concrete boundaries, naming them as an "other", and then rendering them as deserving to die.

Actually, how we react to genocide often facilitates this othering-dynamic, as Irvin (2012) adds:

> Long afterwards, we keep these identities locked into place ensuring that the genocide continues to shape our world decades and centuries later. Where the victims were seen as others deserving to die during the genocide, afterwards the victims are seen as others deserving to be tolerated. The belief that they are "others" and not part of "our" society remains in place. In the entire debate on the denial ban, you don't hear many people claiming that the victims of genocide are part of our one shared human society. The good-hearted liberal thing to do now is say that the Algerians or Armenians (or any other victim minority) are "others" who have to be tolerated and protected and we can't deny what happened to them. These are noble, good, and necessary sentiments. But they threaten to preserve the us/them, victim/perpetrators binaries. What about true and radical acceptance? Not many people suggest that.

The point is that the discussion over protected groups raises the danger that, in distinguishing those groups, we rely on the same absolutist ideas as the *génocidaires* (Shaw 2004 p. 104). The real or objective approach tends to mimic the clarity on which genocide thrives.

From the above it becomes clear that the entity that genocide aims to annihilate is therefore not simply a group of people. The entity that genocide aims to annihilate is *a people*. Lemkin was a known proponent of "groupism", which saw ethnic and national groups or *Menschheitsgruppen*, as substantial entities to which agency could be attributed (A. D. Moses, 2010, p. 22). Unlike other human groups, entities have the power (agency) to produce culture and are able to endow individual human life with meaning; they are crucial to civilization (A. D. Moses, 2010, p. 23). The fact that a people includes, in addition to individual human beings, also all kinds of other material and immaterial elements, has important implications for what is targeted by the genocidal violence. In addition to violence that can be directed against the individual human beings of which the entity is comprised, genocide also targets other elements than its human constituents that are constitutive of the entity. This means that the genocidal violence involves much more than the killing of people. The violence also attacks their cultural legacy: it attacks their ideas by taking away freedom of thought and expression and the documents in which their ideas have

so, genocide attempts to destroy the reproductive capacity of its living members. According to Straus, genocide thus arises when a people are perceived by the perpetrator to have biological immutable or hereditary qualities and they are therefore capable of reproducing themselves. As noted above, in Rwanda the groups were very similar in many ways and creating the ethnic divide among the people thus required some considerable effort (Mirzoeff, 2005, p. 38).

been written are burnt and the libraries in which they are archived are demolished. Fournet (2007, p. 43) notices:

> [I]f the cultural heritage of the group targeted for destruction is eradicated, this group will disappear from collective memory, its whole existence will be eliminated, all traces of this group's life on earth will be annihilated – the genocide, the destruction will be complete.

That is why during the Holocaust and the Armenian genocide, monuments and other cultural meaningful objects were demolished. In Rwanda, artefacts that were seen as representing Tutsi culture were destroyed or not even acknowledged in the first place. When visiting the former state house of president Juvenal Habyarimana in 2008, I noticed that the woodcarvings which "decorated" the main lobby only displayed representations of what was traditionally presented as the work of the Hutu, such as, for instance, cultivating the land. The woodcarvings did not contain any references to herding cattle, which was something that was seen as typically Tutsi. Although these woodcarvings predate the genocidal violence that occurred in 1994, they already depict a society in which Tutsi were non-existent.

Lemkin understood very well that, in addition to its individual members, culture was also an important constitutive element of the group as an entity, which genocide therefore targeted. This does not mean that the targeting of cultural elements is simply being equated with the victimisation of human beings. The burning of a book is not the same as the killing of a human being. Lemkin, however, did not want to equate the genocidal techniques. What he did want to convey is that both techniques, the burning of a book and the killing of a human being, like many other genocidal techniques, are different but necessary means to the same end of genocide.

2.3.3. Action

If the national and ethnic groups that Lemkin discerns as the victims of genocide encompass more than their individual human members due to the fact that they are targeted as entities, then this has implications for the question what the annihilation of these entities requires. If the entity that is to be annihilated consists of more than its individual human members, the annihilation involves more than the physical destruction of its human counterparts. As a result, basically every element, beyond physical human beings, that acknowledges and is constitutive of the existence of a people, such as their monuments, museums, archives, and galleries of art, can be targeted (Lemkin, 1944, p. 85). That genocide, due to the fact that it aims for annihilation, involves more than, for instance, the mass murder of human beings becomes clear when Lemkin discusses the techniques of genocide. Lemkin (1944, p. 79) explains that:

> The objectives of such a plan would be the disintegration of the political and social institutions, of culture, language, national feelings, religion, and the economic existence of national groups, and the destruction of the personal security, liberty, health, dignity, and even the lives of the individuals belonging to such groups.

Thus, the techniques of genocide operate in a wide variety of fields: political, social, cultural, economic, biological, physical, religious and moral (Lemkin, 1944, pp. 82–90; 1945). Due to the fact that the techniques of genocide operate in various fields, the violence is multidimensional and involves a combination of different actions that can range from taking measures to reduce the birth-rate, and economic exploitation, to deprivation of education and destruction of cultural heritage (Power, 2002, p. 40).

In contrast to Lemkin's conceptualisation of genocide, many scholars tend to reduce genocide not only to destruction but to the physical destruction of human beings. Shaw is very critical of such narrow conceptualisations of genocide that focus on killings and massacres. He argues that those who perpetrated the Holocaust did not only aim to simply massacre the Jewish people; their violence also directed itself against their ways of life and their social institutions. What gives genocide its distinct character is that it is about much more than *biological destruction*. It is about *social destruction* – it tries to annihilate a people's real or imagined (putative) social power (Shaw, 2007, p. 22). Shaw (2007, p. 106) concludes that because the entities Lemkin described "are social constructions, they can be neither constituted nor destroyed simply through the bodies of their individual members". Card (2003) also argues that genocide is essentially about social death and that this is an aspect that sets genocide apart from mass murder. Genocide is not simply about killing but about "loss of social vitality", because this "is loss of identity and thereby of meaning for one's existence." Such an approach, according to Card (2003, p. 63), "takes our focus off body counts and loss of individual talents, directing us instead to mourn losses of relationships that create community." From such a perspective, genocide does not always require the physical destruction of people.

According to Lemkin (1944, p. 21):

> Genocide has two phases: one, destruction of the national pattern of the oppressed group; the other, the imposition of the national pattern of the oppressor. This imposition, in turn, may be made upon the oppressed population, which is allowed to remain, or upon the territory alone, after the removal of the population and the colonization of the area by the oppressor's own nationals.

Lemkin clarifies that, in the course of genocide, it is possible that the oppressed population is allowed to remain. Although theoretically genocide does not require the physical destruction of individuals, in his analysis of genocide, Lemkin did not discuss the destruction of culture separately from the physical destruction of individual human beings. According to Moses, Lemkin saw them as parts of the process of genocide in which "physical and biological destruction are always preceded by cultural genocide" (Lemkin quoted in A. D. Moses, 2010, p. 34). The forced removal of so-called "half caste" indigenous children from their families, which took place in Australia, illustrates that genocide can indeed take place without killing human beings.[18] From 1910 to 1970 Australian governments took

[18] For literature on this particular case see footnote 34, Chapter 1.

away thousands of children from their families in order to "breed out the colour". According to Queensland's Chief Protector of Native Affairs between 1913 and 1942, the aborigine population was a "degraded race" and presented a "grave social danger" to the "purity of the white race" (Quoted in National Inquiry into the Separation of Aboriginal and Torres Strait Islander Children From Their Families, 1997). The Northern Territory's Chief Protector between 1927 and 1939 promoted eugenics in order to "eradicate" all "native characteristics of the Australian aborigines". The Western Territory's Chief protector expressed his views during a conference in 1937 and argued that the "pure black" will eventually be extinct, but the problem were the "half castes", whose number was increasing. The "pure blacks" needed only to be segregated, but the "half castes" needed to be "absorbed into the white population". In order to make sure that the assimilation was effective, the "half castes" were taken from their mothers and raised in white families in accordance with "white ideas". Once the policy was successfully implemented, people would "eventually forget that there were any aborigines in Australia" (Quoted in Kiernan, 2002, p. 177). By removing children from their native setting, their cultural heritage would no longer be passed on and it would eventually vanish. The aim was to embed them in a different more "civilized" white culture that they would internalise and adhere to. Moreover, by forcing indigenous people to live and be among the "civilised" white population, the colonial power hoped to "breed out the colour", which also is essentially a perverse form of biological destruction without literally having to take the life of a single human being.[19]

Lemkin's conceptualisation of genocide makes very clear that the physical destruction of human beings, by for instance killing them, is only one genocidal technique among the many other techniques that he described. For Lemkin, strategies that do not cause mass death but marginalise a people in many other ways are as important in the process of annihilation. In contrast to conceptualisations that see marginalising processes as *facilitative* to mass death, Lemkin sees them as violent genocidal strategies *in their own right,* as they are different means to the same end of annihilation. It is tempting to argue that annihilation involves direct and indirect strategies or "pre-genocidal acts" and "actual genocide". Direct strategies would include, for instance, mass-killing of individuals and indirect strategies, for instance, would include not allowing them to celebrate their religion or burning their books. According to Huttenbach (1988, p. 292), one of Lemkin's main contributions was to distinguish between "pre-genocidal acts" and "actual genocide"; "between policies that endanger the existence of a group and naked acts of direct killing, between making the group's life increasingly difficult, thereby denying it a future, and outright mass murder." I however think that, according to Lemkin, both killing and creating economic hardship can be techniques involved in the annihilation of a people, as they can both directly target a people as an entity. To present some of these techniques as "pre-genocidal" and others as "genocidal" is misleading

---

[19] Although by removing the children from their families, genocide took place without physically destroying them, this does not mean that the victims were not to endure any physical violence. The report of the Australian Human Rights Commission (1997) notes that these children often ended up in abusive situations where they had to endure physical and psychological violence.

and it contributes to the false perception that genocide involves only the physical destruction of human beings by, for instance, killing.[20]

The fact that the general crime of genocide consists of many specific types of crimes has implications for which agents can be involved in genocide.

2.3.4. Agents

In contrast to the elements discussed above (aim, victim, action), which are explicitly mentioned in Lemkin's description of genocide, Lemkin does not specifically denote the *agents* that can engage in genocide. Lemkin's broader analysis reveals a focus on the state and authorities. He notices that "by its very nature [genocide] is committed by the state or by powerful groups which have the backing of the state" (Lemkin, 1946). As a result, "The offenders may be representatives of the state or of organized political or social groups" (Lemkin, 1945). Although genocide is predominantly described by Lemkin as a state crime, one should be aware of the fact that the agents of genocide are not only comprised of states and their main representatives.[21] As Bauman (1989) reveals in his study *Modernity and the Holocaust*, the top cadres might plan and start to organise the genocide, but, for its full organisation and execution, they are dependent on lower echelons and as a result the organisation and execution of genocide deeply penetrates the capillaries of society, thereby involving whole communities in the perpetration of genocide. Although both German and Rwandan society were organised for the genocide, there is a significant difference in how these societies were organised for this goal and the degree to which ordinary civilians were involved in the direct physical violence against their fellow human beings. According to Bauman (1989, p. 13) the Holocaust "arrived [...] in a factory produced vehicle, wielding weapons only the most advanced science could supply, and following an itinerary designed by scientifically managed organization." Those who participated in the extermination phase of the genocide against the Tutsi lacked such technical genocidal machinery, but the lack of such machinery was compensated by the sheer number of people that participated in the genocidal crimes against their fellow human beings. In Rwanda the genocidal machinery consisted of hundreds of thousands of ordinary people who, with the help of the military, attacked their fellow human beings, their neighbours, using whatever they could find, including garden tools and other ordinary household utensils, such as machetes, hammers, clubs, and

20 Ironically, the reduction of genocide to killings or massacres also seems to be facilitated by Lemkin himself. Lemkin (1944, p. 79), when introducing the term genocide, explained that "[t]his new word, coined by the author to denote an old practice in its modern development, is made from the ancient Greek word genos (race, tribe) and the Latin cide (killing)." Lemkin's term directly refers to killing, which is confusing because, from the above analysis of Lemkin's conceptualisation, it becomes clear that genocide encompasses much more than killing (Lemkin, 1946).

21 Note that genocide in theory could also be perpetrated by actors who are not related to the state. Here one could think about roving rebel groups that operate in areas where the power of state structures is declining or in situations of failed states. In this context one could think of the situation in the Central African Republic where Christian and Muslim groups are targeting each other, but also the situation in Iraq where the Islamic State (IS) is engaging in violence against minorities in northern Iraq.

screwdrivers. Mahmood Mamdani (2002, p. 5 and 6) describes this unique aspect of the genocide against the Tutsi clearly in his book *When victims become killers*:

> Unlike the Nazi Holocaust, the Rwandan genocide was not carried out from a distance, in remote concentration camps beyond national borders, in industrial killing camps operated by agents who often did no more than drop Zyklon B crystals into gas chambers from above. The Rwandan genocide was executed with the slash of machetes rather than the drop of crystals, with all the gruesome detail of a street murder rather than the bureaucratic efficiency of a mass extermination. The difference in technology is indicative for a more significant social difference. The technology of the holocaust allowed a few to kill many, but the machete had to be wielded by a single pair of hands. It required not one but many hacks of a machete to kill even one person. With a machete, killing was hard work that is why there were often several killers for every single victim. Whereas the Nazis made every attempt to separate victims from perpetrators, the Rwandan genocide was very much an intimate affair. It was carried out by hundreds of thousands, perhaps even more, and witnessed by millions.

This gruesome but unique aspect of the genocide against the Tutsi has challenging implications for the aftermath. Due to the lack of distance, perpetrators and victims are forced to live together as they inhabit the same communities.[22]

As discussed in the last Section, the genocidal techniques operate in fields ranging from the political to the economic, and from the moral to the biological. This indicates that the agents of genocide not only comprise of leading politicians that spawn a genocidal ideology or executioners who, when influenced by such ideological rhetoric, obediently followed orders and massacred people.[23] In contrast, due to the broad scope of victimisation, agents also include, for instance, local civil administrators involved in heavy taxation to create hardship, or librarians who remove banned books from the shelves in order for them to be destroyed. Most often genocidal evil has a very banal character, as Arendt (2005) made clear in her book about the Eichmann trial.[24] Those involved in the perpetration of great evils, such as genocide, do not necessarily have to be stereotypical virulent fanatics; instead such crimes are often perpetrated by ordinary people performing their ordinary (bureaucratic) jobs

22 In Germany the final extermination was carried out by certain groups mostly outside the German territory. People were taken from their local communities and exterminated elsewhere. The killers were generally not personally acquainted with their victims. In Rwanda, the way the genocide was organised involved much intimate violence, because perpetrators and victims often knew each other as they lived in the same communities.

23 Note that people are also pressured and threatened into perpetrating crimes against their fellow human beings.

24 Arendt's analysis has been criticised and it has been argued that Arendt misrepresented Eichmann, who in reality was a racist fanatic bent on exterminating as many Jews as possible (Cassese, 2009). Although Arendt's portrayal of Eichmann can be criticised, one of the central ideas presented in her book *Eichmann in Jerusalem* remains valid: you do not have to be a racist bigot to participate in the perpetration of genocide. Very often it is about ordinary people in extra-ordinary circumstances, which for various reasons can make people participate in the process of genocide. Note that, due to the division of labour, people are performing jobs not readily seen as violent and due to compartmentalisation they often do not see the end result of their actions.

with the best intentions, work that they were good at and they were often already doing before the genocidal campaign started. Due to the compartmentalisation of the process, they often do not realise the full consequences of their actions.[25]

2.3.5. Intention

Intention signifies that action is undertaken in order to achieve certain ends; that action is purposeful. What genocidal intention entails is thus closely related to the core idea that the annihilation of a people is the objective of genocide. Genocide is the actualisation of that specific intent. It is this special intent of group annihilation that defines genocide and sets it apart from other violence, such as murder (Jones, 2006, p. 22). The problem is however that there are different approaches in locating the required intention. In his book *Axis rule in occupied Europe*, Lemkin conceptualised genocide as a coordinated plan of different destructive actions with the ultimate aim of annihilating a group as an entity. The genocidal intention can be demonstrated by the fact that genocide is a planned, organised and sustained effort to annihilate a people. Chalk (1994, p. 53), for instance, explains, that:

> A genocidal society exists when a government and its citizens persistently pursue policies which they know will lead to the annihilation of the aboriginal inhabitants of their country. Intentionality is demonstrated by the persistence in such policies whether or not the intent to destroy the aboriginal groups is verbalized.

However, in later publications, instead of locating the intent in the general organisational or systematic manifestations of genocide, Lemkin described intent as a particular state of mind of individual genocide perpetrators. In an article published in 1945 and titled *Genocide – A modern crime*, Lemkin (1945) argues that "[t] he intent of the offenders is to destroy or degrade an entire national, religious or racial group by attacking the individual members of that group". Here it seems that intention is formulated not as the *element of a concept of genocide* which refers to a planned and systematic effort to annihilate (organisational policy), but as an *element of the crime of genocide* which refers to individuals having a particular state of mind (mental element) that informs their actions. Here Lemkin describes intent in the specific context of criminal legal liability, which requires that the punishable act is committed intentionally (Bergsmo, 2009, p. 22; Schabas, 2010, p. 137). In contrast to social scientists who locate intention in the systemic character of the process leading to a certain outcome, legal scholars and jurists have to demonstrate a particular state of mind involved in the performance of a certain act. From the legal approach it becomes clear that "[g]enocide is a crime with a double mental element, i.e. a general intent as to the underlying acts, and an ulterior intent with regard to the ultimate aim of the destruction of the group" (Ambos, 2009, p. 833). A special intention is thus

---

[25] This division of labour is also a mechanism used by the orchestrators of genocide to facilitate perpetration.

required. Akhavan (2005, p. 992) furthermore notes that this legal *dolus specialis* concerns the degree of intent rather than its scope:

> By way of comparison, *dolus generalis* requires that the perpetrator "means to cause" a certain consequence "or is aware that it will occur in the ordinary course of events", whereas special intent requires that the perpetrator "clearly intended the result", signifying "a psychological nexus between the physical result and the mental state of the perpetrator".

Establishing genocidal intention is a challenging task because genocidal agents are not likely to admit and openly confess the intentions underlying their actions and therefore also in legal practice the intention is often deduced from the systematic pattern of action which could only arise out of specific intent (Stanton, 1998a).[26] Moreover, they often deny the reality of genocide. For instance, in Kayishema the ICTR Trial Chamber pointed out that "the specific intent can be inferred from words and deeds and may be demonstrated by a pattern of purposeful action" (Judgment Kayishema 1999, p. 200). The Chamber furthermore stated that "The Prosecution submitted that evidence of specific intent (*dolus specialis*) arises from the repetitive character of the planned and programmed massacres and the constant focus on the Tutsi members of the population" (Judgment Kayishema 1999, p. 202).[27]

Due to the difficulties with the element of intention, some scholars, such as Thompson & Quets (1990), appear to propose such broad approaches to intention that they basically result in the elimination of special intent as an element of genocide. What is important according to these scholars is whether the existence of the collectivity is threatened by destruction. The problem is however that it is the special intent which sets genocide apart from other kinds of violence such as mass murder. It is the core of the concept of genocide. The risk involved in eliminating the element of intent is that genocide is reduced to all kinds of environmental and industrial accidents, thereby emptying the concept from its specific meaning (Fein, 2009, p. 49). The problems with the element of intention makes us aware of the fact that genocide is not determined by the gruesomeness of the genocidal acts nor the number of victims, instead it is the intention that matters (Barth, 2006, p. 19). The number of victims and

[26] With regard to genocidal intent Barta (2008a, p. 112) makes some interesting observations and relates it directly to denial: "intentions are supremely important in the world's grim record of genocide – but not because they are recorded as 'intent to destroy'." They matter least where they look like the legally decisive smoking gun. They matter most because of the way they are disguised. Intentions were disguised by the perpetrators of atrocities to make sure they were not called to account and they were disguised – also to escape responsibility – by those who should have called perpetrators to account. But that is only the beginning of the difficulties for a judicial criterion of criminal intent. Perpetrators and judicial authorities were able to disguise genocidal intentions from others most effectively where they were also disguised from themselves – by appeal to the exigencies of self-defence, by reference to the larger aims of colonisation and to explicit measures asserting benign intentions towards the indigenous peoples who nevertheless continued to "disappear."

[27] The question of intent is complex and will be dealt with in more detail in Chapter 5, Section 5.5.

the way they perished is irrelevant as the "evil" is the same as Kirakosian explains in the context of the Armenian Genocide:

> The figure of 1.5 million is regularly quoted. Some may dispute this figure, but the crime is just as dreadful whether the number of victims totalled 1 million, 1.5 million or 6 million. The method of murder is also irrelevant, whether it was by the sword, starvation, death marches, or the gas chambers. The evil was the same. It would be a terrible affront to the memory of those who perished to belittle the guilt of the crime in any way. (Asbarez Armenian News, 2011)

Those who deny genocide often dispute the number of people victimised and the methods involved in their victimisation and present such aspects as relevant for the question whether an event classifies as genocide or not. Such arguments are misleading, because it is not the number of victims, but the nature of the victim (entity) that is decisive. Furthermore, not the method of violence, but the intention informing the violence is relevant to whether an event is genocidal or not.

Intention vs. motivation

The intention underlying genocide is to annihilate a people; the reasons for genocide to occur can however vary to a great degree. The different possible motivations for genocides have informed Helen Fein's typology of genocide. Fein (Fein, 1993) distinguishes the following types of genocide. *Developmental genocide* occurs when a people are seen as an impediment to the exploitation of geographical areas. *Despotic genocide* occurs when a people are perceived to be political rivals. *Retributive genocide* involves the situation where a people are targeted in order to protect a certain societal order. Alvarez (2008, p. 215) notes that the genocide against the Tutsi is illustrative for this type of genocide. The Hutu extremist utilised genocide as a tool to preserve and consolidate their power and to prevent the Tutsi minority which had enjoyed a powerful and privileged position in the past. Lastly, Fein distinguishes *ideological genocide*, which targets a people out of certain beliefs.[28] The typologies are insightful mainly because they make us aware of the fact that genocide is a means to an end and it is therefore functional. Genocidal violence is thus never its own explanation, but it is perpetrated for certain reasons. As Alvarez (2008, p. 215) notes, although genocides can seem unjustified and irrational, Fein's typology makes clear that genocide is perpetrated for understandable reasons. This is important if we are to make sense of why genocides happen. Although Fein's typology is helpful in making genocide more understandable, it is in a sense also problematic, because in the typology, ideology is predominantly connected to one type of genocide.[29] Alvarez (2008, p. 215) points out that ideology plays a crucial role in every genocide, because it is ideology that enables and facilitates the perpetration of genocide: "Genocide,

---

[28] Fein was not the only scholar to develop such a typology. Kuper (1981), Smith (R. S. Smith, 1987), Harff & Gurr (1987), and Chalk & Jonassohn (1990) also developed typologies in an attempt to clarify the motives behind genocide.

[29] Furthermore the types might not be as easily distinguished in concrete cases as they can overlap considerably.

in other words, cannot take place without appropriate ideological support." It is therefore that in the next Section ideology will be briefly discussed.

2.3.6. Genocide ideology

An ideology is a set of beliefs which enables people to understand and define the world. Often ideologies serve as guiding thoughts or principles aimed at solving societal problems. Ideologies furthermore define ideals to aspire to and they therefore often promote a utopian version of society. In addition to these theoretical elements, ideologies involve practical elements with regard to how to overcome problems and challenges and to realise the promoted utopian ideal. Ideologies are not necessarily bad or negative, but they can also create problems between groups of people when they are sectarian (excluding other peoples), dualistic (us vs them) and antagonistic (allies vs enemies) (Nyirimanzi & Nyakinama, 2007). Ideologies greatly influence human behaviour by determining what actions are appropriate and acceptable. Actions are not by definition illegitimate or legitimate, because there is no intrinsic quality in the act that determines this. Instead, it is about how actions are defined and ideologies influence processes of interpretation and definition (Alvarez, 2008, p. 218). Ideology can thus make initially questionable behaviour acceptable. In order to engage in violence against their fellow human beings, perpetrators need to accept that the violence is necessary, just and moral, in other words legitimate. To this end, people's belief systems are manipulated through ideological propaganda. This, according to Alvarez (2008, p. 218), explains that perpetrators are often normal human beings and not psychopathic monsters:

> Instead, we must accept that those who contribute to the destructive process are generally normal individuals who have come to accept an ideological framework that demands and justifies the elimination of a population. They are ordinary people engaged in extraordinary behaviour that is made possible because they have come to believe in the rightness and necessity of the killing.

Alvarez (2008, pp. 220–229) points out that genocide ideologies have several components. They are often nationalistic, draw on past victimisations, dehumanise the other, rely on scapegoating, and are absolute in their worldviews and they seek to create a utopian future. Genocide ideologies are exclusionary and create differences between groups of people which helps to demarcate the targeted group. The process of creating in and out groups is strengthened by mythologising past victimisation, which helps the perpetrators to present themselves as the victims and the targeted groups as the perpetrator. This often results in fear of the other, in xenophobia, which is a powerful motivator for destructive action, because violence is transformed from illegitimate aggression into justifiable defence (Alvarez, 2008, p. 222). Genocide ideologies furthermore transform the targeted group into sub- or nonhumans. This strengthens the process of creating in and out groups and it places the victims outside the universe of obligation (Alvarez, 2008, p. 224). Where nationalistic tendencies made people different from you, dehumanisation makes people less than you. Towards your own group the moral relationship is tightened, towards the out-group it is severed. A crucial element of genocide ideologies is that the targeted group is presented as the cause of the crises situation and blamed for the problems (scapegoating) (Alvarez, 2008, p. 225). The polarisation and intolerance are furthered by an absolutist and totalitarian worldview which allows no room for difference and tolerance. The world is divided into good and evil, creating group righteousness (Alvarez, 2008, p. 228). The last element concerns the idea that a better world or society (utopia) is one without the targeted people. They threaten society and prevent the development towards a better one (Alvarez, 2008, p. 228). As will become clear throughout the rest of this study, the framework of beliefs that provides purpose and meaning for the destruction of a population also provides input for the denial rhetoric once the genocide is being perpetrated. As the Executive Secretary of Ibuka noted: “Ideology, it releases people from the bad thing they need to do or have done” (Ahishakiye 2014, personal communication). Genocide ideology and denial are closely related.

2.4. Explaining genocide, introducing denial

Drawing on the conceptual dimensions presented above, genocide could generally be defined as the intentional annihilation of a people. However, in their work, scholars not only have attempted to (re)conceptualise and (re)define genocide by distinguishing its constitutive dimensions, they have also tried to understand and explain how and why genocide happens. The perspectives taken by scholars in explaining genocide range from (social-) psychology, sociology and anthropology, to political science and international relations.[30] I am not going to give an elaborate overview of the different approaches taken by scholars in explaining genocide. This would be impossible due to the magnitude of scholarly work available, but it would also fall outside the scope of this study. The discussion will therefore be limited to perspectives that are particularly relevant for understanding the phenomenon of genocide denial.

2.4.1. A complex process

The above analysis has made clear that genocide cannot be reduced to a single act or event. Due to its specific aim and the specificity of its victim, genocide is a multidimensional phenomenon including a wide variety of actions and which evolves over a period of time. Genocide is thus best approached as a complex process (Alvarez, 2001, p. 88; Ternon, 1995, p. 137).[31] Several scholars, such as Horowitz (1989), Stanton (1998a, 2013), Lecomte (2001) and Hilberg (2002), have discerned different stages or sequential steps involved in this process. The infinite complexity

30 In his handbook, Jones (2006) gives a comprehensive overview of the various approaches and their main contributions.

31 This also becomes clear from the work of Staub (1989) in which he explains that genocide, but also other mass violence, develops along a continuum of destruction.

of genocide is however hard to capture in its entirety and, as a result, models of the genocidal process tend to simplify things. Scholars have, for instance, presented the development of the genocidal process in stages or steps on a continuum, but the problem of such linear conceptualisations is that it separates processes that in fact can be highly intertwined. The linear conceptualisation provides for a chronological order of events that is not always necessarily prevalent because stages may overlap or continue to operate throughout the process (Mukimbiri, 2005, p. 823).[32] Furthermore, in these models the stages are leading up to the physical destruction of human beings by killing, while the other stages appear as facilitative to that end. However, Lemkin's conceptualisation revealed that the processes involved in the other stages can be genocidal in their own right, instead of merely facilitating the stage of physical destruction. We should therefore not reduce genocide to the stage of physical destruction. The process also does not always have to culminate in large scale killing, as the earlier discussed case of the forced removal of children that happened in Australia reveals. Despite such limitations, the models these scholars developed are valuable as they do allow us to make a virtually incompressible process more intelligible.

In order to illustrate the general flow of the genocidal process, it is insightful to elaborate Stanton's model briefly. Stanton (Stanton, 1998a) initially developed a model including 8 stages. Recently he added two stages to the model, which now suggests that genocide develops in 10 stages (Stanton, 2013).[33] These stages are: 1) classification, 2) symbolisation, 3) discrimination, 4) dehumanisation, 5) organisation, 6) polarisation, 7) preparation, 8) persecution, 9) extermination, and 10) denial. During the *first stage*, people are being classified into a distinct category and the classification is subsequently symbolised during the *second stage* in order to distinguish between people more clearly. This is done, for instance, through the use of signs and/or names.[34] In the *third stage*, the rights of the victim group are limited so that they become marginalised as citizens. In the *fourth stage*, the classified, symbolised and discriminated group is dehumanised by equating them with, for instance, locusts or diseases. *Fifth*, the genocide is organised by creating special units and training them for the killing. Afterwards, extremist propaganda attempts to set the dehumanised group further apart from mainstream society.

32 Stanton notes that, in his studies of genocide, he discovered that "the process of every genocide has predictable stages. They aren't linear, because they usually operate simultaneously. But there is a logical order to them, because a 'later' stage cannot occur without a logically 'prior' stage. It is also useful to distinguish them, because they can help us see when genocide is coming and what governments can do to prevent it" (Stanton, 2014).

33 In contrast, Horowitz (1989) explains that the genocidal process of the Holocaust followed a pattern consisting of six steps. The Nazi program moved by the following stages. In the first stage, it was declared that the Jewish problem was a curse to Germany. Secondly, legislation was enacted that excluded Jewish people as citizens. Thirdly, riots and pogroms against Jewish people began and the first concentration camps were constructed. This stage was followed by sealing of the ghettos and turning them into concentration camps. Fifthly, the bulk of the Jewish population were exterminated and lastly, Horowitz explains "[e]very attempt was made to obliterate all traces of the various and sundry activities committed in the name of cleansing the Third Reich by destroying the Jewish remnants" (Horowitz, 1989, p. 26).

34 The first two stages can also be witnessed in non-genocidal societies.

They furthermore attempt to polarise society by targeting the moderates and silencing and intimidating the centre. This is the *sixth stage*. During the *seventh stage* the preparations for extermination are being taken. They stockpile weaponry and indoctrinate the population in order to create fear among them. During the *eighth stage*, the victims are persecuted. Victims are singled out, lists are drawn up, and ghettoisation and deportation take place. Subsequently, the *ninth stage* of extermination is implemented and lastly, after the group has been exterminated, during the *tenth stage* the crime of genocide is denied by those who perpetrated it. Despite the fact that the abovementioned scholars use different terminology and that the number of discerned stages varies, they all describe a similar flow in which the genocidal process develops itself. An ideology is developed that defines the target group and presents them as a threat, which at the same time is instrumental in justifying the ever-increasing marginalisation and crippling of this particular group to the extent that the victimisation concerns every aspect of their existence.[35] In terms of awareness and understanding, it is important that we start to perceive genocide in such broader terms of *a process* of annihilation that develops over time, instead of reducing genocide to *an act* of extermination.[36] The models present us with important insights and the following two aspects are particularly relevant in the context of this study.

2.4.2. 100 days?

Firstly, Lecomte's and Stanton's model have also been applied to the genocide against the Tutsi (Mukimbiri, 2005; Stanton, 2004). The analyses reveal that the genocide involves a process that started already long before the 6th of April 1994. It has even been argued that the process already started in the early 1950s (Ntakirutimana,

35 For another insightful analysis of this process see the work of Semelin (2007).

36 With regard to the origins of such genocidal processes, different schools of thought exist. This discussion mainly took place with regard to the Holocaust, but it has implications for the broader field of genocide studies. Intentionalists argue that the genocide of the Jews was intended from the outset and implemented according to a "consistent dictatorial will" of the Fuhrer as Tatz (2003, p. 22) phrases it. Intentionalism holds that a perpetrator will do A, knowing that it will lead, to B, C, D, etc. (Tatz 2011, personal communication). In contrast to such a "straight path" to the genocide, functionalists argue that the path to genocide was more "twisted". Functionalism holds that A, B, C, D, etc. are factors in a certain equation and at the start it is difficult to predict the pattern that will arise out of the interplay of factors. Instead of knowing everything beforehand, an actor would do A, which led to B, which opened the way to C. Tatz notes that, in this sense, "functionalism is opportunism" (Tatz 2011, personal communication). In this approach, the genocide has an "evolutionary and contingent character" as Jones (2006, p. 157) points out. Instead of being focussed on an individual, the focus is more on a political system that enabled such destruction because all the immaterial and material elements were available. A group of "true believers" eventually put the plan into action. So instead of every detail of the genocide being planned from the outset, it develops over time. Tatz (2003, p. 22) furthermore presents an interesting third approach, which he terms inevitabilism: "One can fit all manner of genocide cases into either of these frameworks, or simply say that they are a mix of both. But by inevitabilism, I mean simply this: every genocide has to have antecedents, constituents and body parts that lead to a political-bureaucratic engine that can make it happen. Once the engine is in place – cylinders, pistons, spark plugs, batteries, fuel – it remains to find a driver(s) willing to turn the key and get it moving. Genocide doesn't erupt, it evolves" (Tatz 2011, personal communication).

2013). In contrast, it seems that many other scholars tend to reduce the genocide against the Tutsi to the 100 days of killing that happened in 1994 in the months April, May and June. The period before April 1994 is presented as a period in which the genocide was prepared and planned and when the president was assassinated, on the 6th of April, the genocide began. The shooting down of the airplane is presented as the "trigger" of the genocide. Mann, for instance, presents the period before April 1994 as leading "into the danger zone" of genocide and that the genocide would eventually begin after the president was killed (Mann, 2005, pp. 428–473). Not only do scholars reduce the genocide to the massacres that took place after the President's plane was shot down, also the general public seems to perceive the genocide in such a way. The Wikipedia entry, for instance, states the following:

> The Rwandan Genocide was the 1994 mass murder of an estimated 800,000 people in the small East African nation of Rwanda. Over the course of approximately 100 days (from the assassination of Juvénal Habyarimana and Cyprien Ntaryamira on April 6) through mid-July, over 500,000 people were killed, according to a Human Rights Watch estimate. (Wikipedia, 2011)

Even more astounding, is that the official Genocide Archive Rwanda, which is linked to the Kigali Genocide Memorial Centre, provides for a similar description:

> The 1994 Genocide against the Tutsi in Rwanda represents one of the fastest and most atrocious cases of genocide in modern history. From early April until July of 1994, members of the Hutu ethnic group systematically slaughtered approximately 1,000,000 Tutsi, politically moderate or sympathizing Hutus, and Twa people, with whom they had previously co-existed and shared cultural practices. (Genocide Archive Rwanda, 2011).

Although, the text adds that "The history of the Genocide dates back to the 1960s, when the postcolonial government instituted anti-Tutsi discriminatory practices, resulting in a deep seated hatred of and periodic violence towards Tutsis," and that "this violence peaked in 1994," the genocide is initially reduced to the period of widespread killing that happened in 1994.

Lemkin's insights concerning the techniques involved make clear that genocide involves more than massacring people. The abovementioned models also reveal that the genocide against the Tutsi cannot be reduced to the single event of massacring. The killing is part of the broader process – it is one stage among many others. The process of genocide against the Tutsi started long before it eventually culminated in the large scale organised slaughter that took place in April 1994.[37] In a booklet

---

[37] President Kagame, in his speech during the 20th commemoration on April 7th 2014, noted that "All genocides begin with an ideology – a system of ideas that says: This group of people here, they are less than human and they deserve to be exterminated. The most devastating legacy of European control of Rwanda was the transformation of social distinctions into so-called 'races'. We were classified and dissected, and whatever differences existed were magnified according to a framework invented elsewhere. The purpose was neither scientific nor benign, but ideological: to justify colonial claims to rule over and 'civilise' supposedly 'lesser' peoples. We are not. This ideology was already in place in the 19th century, and was then entrenched by the French missionaries who settled here. Rwanda's two

published in 1964, a student named Aaron Segal, who visited Rwanda during his studies, already warns for a genocide against the Tutsi. Although substantial parts of his analysis are questionable and have extremist tendencies,[38] he nonetheless states that "measures are required to retrieve Rwanda form her present situation, avert the total annihilation of the Tutsi as a people and restore some semblance of peace, hope and sanity" (Segal, 1964, p. 20).[39] Also already in 1964, the *Ministère des Affaires Etrangers du Rwanda* (Minestère des Affaires Etrangers du Rwanda, 1964) of President Kayibanda published a document titled *Toute la vérité sur le terrorisme "Inyenzi" au Rwanda* which entails many of the negative stereotypes concerning the Tutsi that would later also feature in the hate propaganda of RTLM, Kangura and publications of extremist authorities. Furthermore, the notorious Hutu Ten Commandments did not originate in the 1990ies as often noted. The Commandments published by Kangura were originally drawn up by Hutu Power Ideologue Joseph Habyarimana Gitera in 1959. In the "Ten Commandments of the Bahutu", the Tutsi were portrayed by Gitera as a menace to society, as the enemy. The Tutsi are presented as liars and thieves by nature, cannot be trusted, and are jealous and full of hatred, thus a burden to society. These early writings exemplify Stanton's first four stages which include: classification, symbolisation, discrimination, and dehumanisation.

The process approach is enriching in terms of theory and awareness, but it does lead to practical problems. The difficulty is that one can only often retrospectively define certain techniques or steps in the process as genocidal. If the intention behind the practices is revealed or once an actual event of genocide has reached its last stages and we recognise what is happening as genocide, we can start to work back to see where the process originated and what policies and structures were genocidal. The problem is that many forms of marginalisation and human rights violations can potentially be genocidal, but we can often only distinguish this clearly in hindsight. The danger is also that we start to see every marginalisation as a step towards genocide (Huttenbach, 1988, p. 292). The early stages of genocide are furthermore difficult to distinguish, because in many "ordinary" societies these developments, such as symbolisation, categorisation, etc. are at play. At such an early point (stage 1 and 2) in the process, it is thus difficult to be sure that genocide is on its way. Dehumanisation, however, seems to be a crucial step, as denial of humanity facilitates the violence towards other people (Alvarez, 2008). As noted earlier, the process of the genocide against the Tutsi in Rwanda was already on its way before the phase of large scale extermination was implemented in April 1994. The examples given above indicate that the ideology already existed by the end of the 1950ies.[40]

---

thousand years of history were reduced to a series of caricatures based on Bible passages and on myths told to explorers. The colonial theory of Rwandan society claimed that hostility between something called 'Hutu', 'Tutsi', and 'Twa' was permanent and necessary. This was the beginning of the genocide against the Tutsi, as we saw it twenty years ago."

38 It basically blames the Tutsi for their own victimisation. This is also a tenet of the denial discourse discussed in later Chapters. He proposes to relocate all the Tutsi outside the country by force.

39 See also the work of Vuillemin (1964).

40 Whether the conspiracy to perpetrate genocide was hatched already at that point in time remains the topic of discussion, but the ideology that would provide for the required mind-set did already develop back then. We can be clear on when the main extermination phase was implemented, after

2.4.3. The last stage?

What is furthermore relevant in the context of this study is that the models presented by Horowitz, and Stanton denote denial as a specific and last stage in the genocidal process.[41] This means that genocide does not end when the stage of extermination or other stages have ended. Stanton argues that genocide is always followed by denial which encompasses a variety of actions. In trying to cover up genocide, perpetrators hide the mass graves and they destroy the historical records concerning what happened. However, if the evidence can no longer be hidden, perpetrators question the number of people that were victimised and they argue that what happened does not fit the legal definition of genocide (Stanton, 1998a, 2005). This is a significant insight. However, in contrast to the above described models, which designate denial as the *last* stage in the process of genocide, other scholars have argued that genocide *begins* with denial or that it operates *throughout* the whole process.[42] Spencer (2012) even notes that denial is "rarely absent from any part of the process." Denial of previous crimes committed against specific groups can be a prerequisite for re-victimisation and therefore one could even argue that denial is not the final, but the first stage in the genocidal process (Eltis, 2008, p. 465). Thus, by denying genocide, the seeds of future genocides are planted. This argument can be illustrated with reference to Hitler's Obersalzburg speech in which he stated that "Who after all is today speaking of the destruction of the Armenians?" (Hitler 1939 Quoted in Sarkissian, 2007) Hitler's speech reveals that denial of victimisation (Armenian Genocide) facilitates victimisation (Holocaust). Denial also comes into play during the process of genocide when the social reality of heterogeneous and coexistent communities is negated and made unimaginable. Denial of coexistence is a crucial element in the process of imagining an essentialist community. This also happened in Rwanda as Berry & Berry (1999, p. 3) explain: "Hutu extremists propagated a revisionist history of relations between Hutus and Tutsis that were not based on cohabitation and exchange but rather on segregation and violence."[43] Hilberg's analysis furthermore

---

the assassination of the president on the 6th of April, but it is hard to fix such a precise moment for the decision to plan, organise and perpetrate genocide. Experts agree that the genocide was planned and organised, but the exact point of origination remains unknown. As Caplan (2013a, p. 453) notes, when it comes to the genocide against the Tutsi, there appears not to be a single meeting or document in which all this was concocted, instead its seems to be the outcome of a cumulative set of events: the outcome of a complex process.

41 See also Smith (2012).

42 Theriault (2013, p. 54) has argued that the last stage of genocide is "consolidation". During this last stage, the perpetrators and their supporters consolidate the gains made and these can include economic, military and political power, but also demographic power in terms of social and cultural security. Theriault does however also note that denial of the questionable origins of these gains is crucial in advancing the consolidation. So maybe it is the case that denial is not the last stage, but that it is also part and parcel of the last stage and that denial indeed operated throughout the entire process of genocide. Theriault (2013, p. 54), furthermore, explains that the denial during the stage of consolidation tends to preserve the genocidal ideology and attitude that was at the root of the genocide in the first place and in doing so it sets the stage for (re)newed violence.

43 Although this observation is correct, one can also not deny the fact that there was an element of oppression during the time Tutsi elites made up the ruling power in Rwanda, during several kingdoms and during the trusteeship and colonial rule. For an analysis see Newbury (1988). This is however a delicate aspect of Rwandan history because, as will become clear throughout this study, Tutsi

reveals that denial in terms of repression and rationalisation played an important role throughout the genocide (Hilberg, 2002, p. 180). His analysis of the Holocaust reveals that it was denied by repressing information concerning the destructive process. This involved shutting off the supply of information concerning the events and omitting mentioning what was happening from conversations and correspondence. This resulted in the use of camouflaged or euphemistic vocabulary; people were being "evacuated" or "resettled", instead of being exterminated. In addition to such repression of knowledge concerning the genocide, Hilberg's analysis shows that the perpetration of the genocide itself was being rationalised by those involved. Denial facilitates violent action by dealing with the moral inhibitions that normally would prevent people from victimising their fellow human beings. People argued that they were following superior orders, that it was their fate or that the particular activity they performed was not criminal. People argued that they were only pushing paper and they were not doing the shooting and those doing the killing argued that was out of self-defence. They presented their actions as legitimate. What they did was not criminal; they were not breaking the law, they were actually following it (Hilberg, 2002, pp. 179–188). As will become clear throughout later Chapters of this study, the denial of the genocide against the Tutsi also draws on many of these elements. Especially the claim of self-defence turns out to be crucial to the denial discourse.

All these instances of denial reveal that denial manifests itself in many different ways *before*, *during* and *after* the genocide (Galabert, 2013; Ternon, 2003). Before and during the genocide, denial is a mechanism that facilitates victimisation and, after victimisation has taken place, denial covers up what really happened. Thus, denial runs like a thread through all the described stages and it continues after acts of genocide have occurred (Rusagara, 2009; Totten & Bartrop, 2009). Dupaquier (1995, p. 128) therefore concludes, *"Avant le génocide, sa préparation est dissimulée – pendant le génocide, sa réalité est démentie – après le génocide, sa nature même est niée."* Denial thus appears to operate in many different ways throughout the genocidal process. To refer to all these particular functionalities simply as "genocide denial" obscures some of the fundamental differences in how denial functions in the context of genocide. It is more insightful to distinguish specific types of denial according to their purpose in the genocidal process. Therefore, in the next Chapter, a typology of genocide denialism will be presented that distinguishes between several types of denial. For now it is important to understand that the above processual models reveal that denial is an intrinsic part of the genocidal process. Genocide and denial are thus two intertwined phenomena.

2.5. Denial

Although the abovementioned scholars presented valuable insights concerning the role denial plays in the process of genocide, the problem is that they often tend to

---

oppression is a central theme in the denialist discourse as it provides for a pretext and justification for the violence unleashed upon the Tutsi population.

use denial in a self-explanatory manner, as they do not clearly elaborate what it exactly entails. Scholars use the term denial to describe a wide range of situations, but the conceptual dimensions of denial are not delineated. This makes it hard to differentiate between which situations or events involve denial and which do not. More importantly, the self-explanatory use of denial also hinders a more thorough understanding of how it operates in the context of genocide and what its possible implications are. In order to address this self-explanatory use of denial, the next Sections will clarify the concept of denial.

The self-explanatory use of denial without further elaboration on its exact meaning could be explained with reference to the fact that denial appears to be something that people are generally familiar with. Stanley Cohen (2001, p. x), who wrote extensively on the subject of denial, argues that denial seems to be everywhere. Expressions and phrases, that we all are familiar with, such as, saving face, some things are better left unsaid, being an ostrich, turning a blind eye, don't wash your dirty linen in public, mind your own business, button your lip, burying your head in the sand, ignorance is bliss, etc., all denote denial and are quite common in our daily language. We tend to apply such phrases and expressions to a wide variety of situations, which Cohen (2001, p. 2 and 3) would refer to as *states of denial*. Such states include for example:

- The smoker, who is asked why he still smokes even though he knows it is not healthy, answers that his aunt smoked two packs a day and lived up to eighty without any trouble. He adds that life is harmful in general. Should I also stop drinking because it is unhealthy? Or driving the car because it is dangerous?
- A child has taken two cookies out of the jar, although his mother allowed him to have only one. While taking the second cookie out of the jar, the child says to itself: it shouldn't be a problem, because there are still so many left.
- After stopping the fight, the teacher says to John that he is not allowed to physically abuse somebody. John answers that the other kid had it coming. It was his own fault: he had already been bullying me for a long time.
- A seriously sick individual pretends to be healthy in order not to "harm" his children, who do not know about the terminal illness. The partner also participates in this process, pretending to the children that everything is okay.

I could extend this list with the states of denial which are present before, during and after genocidal victimisation, such as:

- In a speech, the Prime Minister warns his people against the infiltration of society by the enemy and urges them to defend themselves.
- In order not to become entangled in somebody else's conflict, the Department of Foreign Affairs briefs its staff that they are not allowed to use the word genocide to define what is happening.
- A genocide perpetrator being interviewed in prison explains that he and his people had been misled by their government into committing the crimes. They thought they had no other choice.

Although the abovementioned states probably appear familiar, our *familiarity* with certain states of denial should not be mistaken for *clarity* on what denial exactly entails. As Manousos & Williams (1998, p. 15) explain:

> It is so much part of our common explanatory fabric as to be a sort of dustbin term, being used where no other explanation offers itself. So when the behaviour of another seems inappropriate, then denial may be offered as an explanation or accusation.[44]

The problem is that such use of denial not only marginalises the phenomenon, it also turns it into "an explanatory dead-end". Instead of providing insights into what is occurring, such use of the concept closes, turning its use in "an excuse not to take matters any further" (Manousos & Williams, 1998, p. 15). Explaining what denial entails is all but easy. For instance, what do all the phrases and expressions, all these different *states of denial* that I mentioned above have in common? The examples reveal different actors (perpetrators and bystanders), different intentions (coping, lack of political will), and different issues (victim blaming, non-intervention). Denial seems to be a situation-specific phenomenon, involving many factors, and this complexity turns defining and conceptualising denial into a challenging exercise. In an early discussion on the definition of denial, Weisman (1972, p. 59) pointed out that "[t]erminology simplifies communication, but it can often defeat itself" and he remarked that the term denial was an outstanding example of such "misplaced concreteness." It seems that denial is everything except self-explanatory and Weisman's observation might explain why, in another discussion on the definition of denial, Breznitz (1983, p. 98) noted the advantage of a clear example over an exact definition. However, for research purposes, a clear example is not enough as it does not provide for the abstract theoretical tools that are needed to demystify other states of denial beyond the example at hand. In order to be able to use denial as a concept, for research purposes it should be more clearly delineated.

---

44 This is also an issue raised by Skidelsky (2010) who argues that over time denial has acquired a new polemical sense and it has become "the secular form of blasphemy; deniers are scorned, ridiculed and sometimes prosecuted." He adds that "An accusation of 'denial' is serious, suggesting either deliberate dishonesty or self-deception. The thing being denied is, by implication, so obviously true that the denier must be driven by perversity, malice or wilful blindness. Few issues warrant such confidence. The Holocaust is perhaps one, though even here there is room for debate over the manner of its execution and the number of its victims. A charge of denial short-circuits this debate by stigmatising as dishonest any deviation from a preordained conclusion. It is a form of the argument ad hominem: the aim is not so much to refute your opponent as to discredit his motives. The extension of the 'denier' tag to group after group is a development that should alarm all liberal-minded people. One of the great achievements of the Enlightenment – the liberation of historical and scientific enquiry from dogma – is quietly being reversed" (Skidelsky, 2010). Although I agree with Skidelsky that denial can be used as a way to accuse and silence those who question, one should also be careful not to reduce denial to this. Interestingly Skidelsky's remark that "Few issues warrant such confidence" and "The Holocaust is perhaps one, though even here there is room for debate over the manner of its execution and the number of its victims" was actually criticised by some of the readers of the article as denialist. It shows how complex the matter is.

2.6. Dimensions of denial

Despite its general popularity, denial remains a relatively understudied and under-theorised phenomenon, which has only received limited attention from social scientists in general and criminologists in particular. Most of the research on denial originates within the field of psychology and is done in clinical settings. It thus seems that what is denied is also often ignored or avoided by academics (Zerubavel, 2008, p. 13). What complicates the matter is that the study of denial is actually the study of that which is not acknowledged, which is challenging because, as Zerubavel (2008, p. 13) points out, "it's easier to study what people do discuss than what they do not." Denial is an intriguing state of mind, but it is hard to grasp and, as a result, scholars that have studied denial seem to have predominantly done this on a case-study basis, thereby focusing on specific cases of denial. They have, for instance, looked at how in families substance abuse of particular family members is ignored, or how people that lose sight deny that they are turning blind, or how particular persons deny the Holocaust. Not many scholars have tried to transcend the specificity of the cases they studied in order to develop a more general conceptualisation of denial that can be used to study denial as a general phenomenon.[45] Some scholars have however noticed that different cases can share very similar characteristics when it comes to denial. According to Zerubavel, such a framework could be developed because there is a striking similarity in the way that individuals, couples, families, corporations, governments, and whole nations deny the presence of unpleasant realities.[46] A general analytical framework does however require that those who study denial move beyond the specific elements of cases and focus on the general properties of denial (Zerubavel, 2008, p. 14).

Conceptualising and defining denial is a challenging exercise, however, as Galtung (1969, p. 168) makes clear in the context of his research on violence, it is not so important to arrive at *the* definition, because it is more important to demystify certain theoretically significant *dimensions* of the phenomenon studied, that allow us to think about it and help us to solve the problem. The following part of this Chapter therefore does not attempt to arrive at *the* definition of denial. Instead, like in the discussion on genocide above, it will delineate its most significant dimensions. In doing so, hopefully we get a better understanding of what denial entails. To this end, following Cohen, who traced the roots of the concept of the denial in Freudian

---

45 Within the field of sociology and criminology Stanley Cohen has tried to develop an analytical framework with regard to the phenomenon of the denial of human suffering. Cohen (1988, 1993, 1995, 1996) had been working on the issue throughout his (academic) career. His efforts culminated in his book *States of denial: Knowing about atrocities and suffering* (Cohen, 2001). Irene Bruna Seu (2013) also draws on the work of Cohen to demonstrate how audiences react to human rights violations. In her research she explores the factors and dynamics which result in people's unresponsiveness (passivity) when faced with evidence of human suffering. Eviatar Zerubavel also attempted to develop a more general conceptualisation of denial. See Zerubavel (2010), The social sound of silence: Towards a sociology of denial, Chapter 2 in Efrat Ben-Ze'ev, Ruth Ginio and Jay Winter (eds.) *Shadows of war: A social history of silence in the twentieth century*, Cambridge University Press, pp. 32–46.

46 In her book *One, by one, by one: Facing the Holocaust*, Miller (1990, p. 279) also concludes: "While the vehicles of remembrance differ from society to society, the mechanisms of suppression tend to be similar. Cultures suppress what they would like to forget in remarkably similar ways even when the events are strikingly different."

psychoanalysis, the Chapter continues with a brief discussion of the origin of the concept of denial. However, in order to come to a better understanding of the concept of denial, it is important to gain an insight into how Freud's original concept was further developed. The discussion will show how the conceptualisation of denial has changed over time from being a specific static abnormal or immature intra-personal act to a general dynamic normal interpersonal process.

2.6.1. Defence

The concept of denial has its roots in psychoanalytic literature where it was introduced by Freud more than 100 years ago. Freud originally conceptualised denial as *Verleugnung* (disavowal), which is an unconscious defence mechanism against the traumatic perception of an external reality and its replacement with a more acceptable reality (Livneh, 2009, p. 226; Sacerdoti & Semi, 1989, p. 62). Freud was the first to systematically write and theorise on the issue. He was however not the first one to discern what Cohen in his book would probably refer to as *states of denial* (Cohen, 2001). Scholars such as Von Monakow had already reported on medical cases of denial, such as denial of blindness as early as 1885. In these cases, people denied having lost their eyesight by claiming not to be blind or by behaving in a way that revealed a lack of recognition of their blindness. Later scholars, most notably Babinski (1914), introduced the term *anosognosia* in order to describe a state of denial in which patients appeared to be unaware of the paralysis of their limbs (Hackett & Cassem, 1974, p. 93; Livneh, 2009, p. 226; E.A. Weinstein & Kahn, 1955, p. 3). Although now most scholars use the phrase denial, in his original work Freud did not use that particular phrase. As noted above, he used the German term *Verleugnung* instead, which in English was generally translated as denial. The problem is, however, that this translation of *Verleugnung* is not entirely correct and therefore some scholars prefer to use the term *disavowal* as the correct English translation of *Verleugnung*. The reason that denial is an incorrect translation is because denial is a more general term which carries other different connotations than Freud had originally intended with his concept of *Verleugnung* (Cohen, 2001, p. 25; Nathanson, 1989, p. 52). Denial as a general phrase could, for instance, also be used in the context of withholding a person something or the act of simply saying no, for instance, by denying somebody access to a room or denying someone a visa. Here the phrase denial is used, but its meaning is different from what Freud initially meant with *Verleugnung*. Freud conceptualised *Verleugnung* or disavowal as a psychological defence mechanism. It is a defensive response rather than a confrontation response, as it rejects or refuses to accept a problematic reality, rather than acknowledging and confronting it (Watson, Greer, Blake, & Shrapnell, 1984, p. 2008). Of course, one could argue that, through disavowal, the reality is also somehow acknowledged and confronted. However, it is a false resolution: a protection against reality instead of learning to confront it (Cohen, 2001, p. 28). What is the most intriguing element of Freud's conceptualisation and also the invention that Freud became famous for is that the "rejection" of an external reality is an unconscious process (Crombag, 2009, p. 103). Unconsciously, before information reaches the consciousness and you become aware of it, a screening occurs that somehow filters out information that is too disturbing. Throughout his work, Freud conceptualised disavowal mainly as an aspect of psychosis and neurosis and denial was therefore pathological (Goldbeck, 1983, p. 576; Livneh, 2009, p. 226). Anna Freud further developed the concept, but she conceptualised disavowal primarily as a primitive mechanism used by children to deal with unpleasant external realities (Goldbeck, 1983, p. 576; Kortte & Wegener, 2004, p. 188; Livneh, 2009, p. 226). As a result, Freudian psychoanalysis conceptualised denial (disavowal) either as an immature age-related defence against external threats during childhood or as a pathological defence when used in adulthood (Hackett & Cassem, 1974, p. 94).

Throughout his career, Freud discovered and developed a whole range of defence mechanisms ranging from the already discussed disavowal, to negation, dissociation, repression, and isolation. Vaillant (1992) however notes that the problem is that defence mechanisms, such as disavowal, are elusive phenomena: "The closer you look at them, the harder they become to study and verify." This ambiguity has led to much additional research and theorising resulting in an elaboration of Freud's concepts and the development of many new defences. In the end, all defence mechanisms have in common that they are used by individuals to hide or alleviate conflicts or stressors that give rise to fear and anxiety that would result from conscious recognition of unpleasant realities (Cramer, 2006, p. 7; Vaillant, 1992, p. 237). Over time, scholars have started to use the phrase denial, which initially only referred to Freud's concept of disavowal, to denote defences in general and it has almost become synonymous for defence (Sjöbäck, 1973, p. 209; Vaillant, 1992, p. 10). Dorpat (1985, p. 2) even argues that denial is an implicit part of all defences and that therefore defences always contain an aspect of denial. Denial is the repudiation of a reality and all the so-called defences encompass this. Dorpat is not the only scholar that makes this claim, others like Fingarette (1969), Hilgard (1949), Weisman (1972), Haan (1977) and Moore and Rubifine (1969) also argue that all of the specific defences include some element of denial. Dorpat (1985, p. 2) concludes that if "[d]enial covers situations in which individuals in words, fantasies, or overt actions attempt to avoid a painful reality. Used in this way, denial refers to the reality repudiating aspect of defensive operation rather than to a discrete defence mechanism." Haan, for instance, argues that rationalisation denies the reality of a chain of causal events and isolation denies the logical relationship between things. Repression, for instance, also involves the defence against a threatening reality, but, in contrast to disavowal (*Verleugnung*), it is a defence against inner stimuli instead of stimuli originating from the external world (Goldberger, 1983, p. 85). Denial is therefore often used as a general term which includes a range of defences (denial in the broad sense – denial as a unifying concept), instead of using it as a specific term for disavowal (denial in the narrow sense – denial as a unitary concept). Whether using denial in the broad or narrow sense, scholars seem to agree that denial is a defence mechanism that helps people to protect (defend) themselves against painful and threatening internal (emotions) and/or external realities (situations). However, on most, if not all other aspects of denial, there seems to be debate, which in turn has resulted in many modifications and corrections of the concept. In subsequent research in which the concept of denial was further developed, several issues stood out (Livneh, 2009, p. 225; R. Moses, 1989, p. 287). Scholars discussed the question whether denial is always an *unconscious* process as Freud claimed or whether it could also be a defence mechanism that people invoke *consciously*. Freud furthermore presented denial as *pathological*. Scholars however started to wonder whether denial was indeed abnormal as it seemed to be the *normal* or general way people coped with threatening realities. This issue was closely related to the issue whether denial is *maladaptive*. Research revealed that denial was invoked by people in order to help them *cope* with threatening realities, thereby eventually helping them to adapt to such situations. Scholars therefore started to wonder whether denial was adaptive, instead of maladaptive. One of the main critical issues regarding Freud's conceptualisation of denial was that he portrayed it as an *intrapersonal* phenomenon. Scholars questioned this aspect of Freud's conceptualisation, because their research showed time and again that social interaction played an important role in denial. Apparently, denial was not an intrapersonal, but an *interpersonal* phenomenon. The abovementioned scholarly discussions highlight the main dimensions of the concept of denial. The following Sections will further elaborate on each of the respective dimensions.

2.6.2. Paradox of denial

One of the most challenging aspects of denial is whether it is a conscious or unconscious process. In Freudian psycho-analytic theory denial is an unconscious process. It is assumed that an unconscious screening mechanism somehow registers stimuli and prevents them from entering into conscious awareness. In order to be able to maintain this state of knowing and not knowing at the same time, Freud introduced the idea of splitting within the ego (Goldberger, 1983, p. 87; Wurmser, 1989, p. 180). The splitting of the ego results in two perceptions: one that is accurate but unconscious and one that is in denial and thereby less threatening (R. Moses, 1989, p. 288). Moses (1989, p. 289) however points out that these two levels of awareness are probably not as separate as Freud conceptualised them when he postulated the idea of the split ego:

> To my mind, the different levels of awareness are, rather, coexisting. They are often in a state of flux; this means that denial has its ups and downs; that there are changes over time both in what is denied and in the extent to which it is denied.

Moses thus sees denial not as a single stable event but as a dynamic process which changes over time. Moreover, in contrast with Freud's views, subsequent scholars, such as Goldberger (1983, p. 88) have argued that "despite absence of conscious awareness in successful denial, registration [...] nevertheless is achieved at some level." When there is denial, there is also some registration of what is being blocked otherwise denial would not be necessary (Croog, Shapiro, & Levine, 1971, p. 386; Lazarus, 1983, p. 10; Wurmser, 1989, p. 180). This intriguing state of mind, of knowing and not knowing at the same time, is what Spence (1983, p. 103) calls the *paradox of denial*:

> The paradox of denial stems from the fact that denial is never complete. For denial to function as a defensive mechanism, it can only be partially effective; only by allowing some threatening information to register can it orient the person where *not* to look.

Spence continues to explain that it is exactly this "leakage" that keeps the process operational because, if denial was complete, its operation ceases to be necessary. According to Cohen (2001, p. 6 and 44) the denial paradox, this state of self-deception, is "the heart of the concept": "In order to use the term 'denial' to describe a person's statement 'I didn't know', one has to assume that she knew or knows about what it is she claims not to know – otherwise the term 'denial' is inappropriate."[47] The denial paradox leads to a remarkable insight, namely that denial also confirms that something happened, otherwise there is no need to deny it (Ver Eecke, 2006, p. 1). Therefore, in a strange way, denial is actually also a form of acknowledgment.

Since its inception by Freud, the concept of denial has been broadened to such an extent that it also encompasses *conscious* states of denial (Croog et al., 1971, p. 386). According to Vitousek et al. (1991, p. 650), in their study of eating disorders, denial encompasses any "consciously or unconsciously motivated omission, concealment, or misrepresentation of behaviour or internal experience". This includes deliberate distortion; lying or malingering. But it also includes inadvertent distortion when an inaccurate account is provided due to unawareness. Vitousek et al. thus seem to approach the idea that denial involves a paradoxical state of knowing and not knowing at the same time in broader terms. One could know about something and at the same time consciously lie about it against oneself or others, thereby deceiving oneself and others. Some scholars are however very sceptical about such broad conceptualisations: "By definition, denial has to be an unconscious process; to be conscious of denial would be just to lie" (Manousos & Williams, 1998, p. 16). The issue whether denial is conscious or unconscious is closely related to the psychological status of denial; the intention underlying the denial. According to Cohen (2001, p. 9) every denial has its own psychological status:

> [Denial] may be a genuine and non-culpable ignorance; a deliberate aversion of your gaze from a truth too unbearable to acknowledge; a twilight state of self-deception where some truth is hidden from yourself; a cultural not noticing because the reality is part of your taken-for-granted view of the world; or one of a variety of calculated forms of lying, deception or disinformation. [Denial] ranges from the genuine inability to grasp what the facts mean to others, to deeply cynical renaming to avoid moral censure or legal accountability. [Denials] come from some rather banal folk techniques for avoiding moral or psychological demands, but are invoked with mystifying degrees of sincerity.

Denial can therefore range from unconscious sincere coping with trauma to Machiavellian conscious and intentional political manipulation.

[47] It is important to recognise that the defensive reaction not only includes a total rejection or blotting out of a reality. The defensive reaction often involves the redefinition of the reality in which facts are acknowledged but their meaning is changed and thereby undoing the reality from its threatening elements. So, often it is not about "not looking" or "no knowledge", but about looking and knowing, but investing realities with a less threatening meaning.

When the conceptualisation of denial is so broad that it includes both unconscious and conscious behaviour, the question arises where to draw the line: when is something not denial? Two elements are important when answering this question. First of all, from the last Sections follows that denial is a defence mechanism against an unpleasant reality. As Cohen (2001, p. 25) states with reference to Bollas (1993), in the end denial is about "the need to be innocent from a troubling recognition." Secondly, this defence, in order for it to be denial, always has to involve the paradoxical state of knowing and not knowing at the same time. As mentioned above, this state can be the result of a sincere coping process as the result of victimisation, but it can also be the result of the intentional attempt to obfuscate the fact that a person has victimised somebody. The nature of the intention is thus not decisive for the question whether something is denial or not. What matters is the denial paradox, namely that you somehow know and do not know. This can be explained with reference to the issue of ignorance. If you are truly ignorant, you are unaware of a reality; you do not know. If that is the case, denial is impossible, because in order to deny a certain reality, one has to have some awareness of it. If there is no awareness or knowledge of something it cannot be denied (Kortte & Wegener, 2004, p. 188).[48] Drawing on the above insights, denial could thus generally be defined as a mechanism of defence that serves to provide an actor with protection against a reality, which is for some reason perceived as too threatening to acknowledge and when engaged in results in the paradoxical self-deceptive state of knowing and not knowing at the same time.

2.6.3. Normal

As discussed before, in Freudian psychoanalysis disavowal was conceptualised as a pathological or immature unconscious defence mechanism. However, later research has revealed that denial is used by normal and stable people as part of dealing with threatening realities, such as serious illness (Hackett & Cassem, 1974, p. 94; Shockey, 2004, p. 985). Based on these subsequent findings, the strict psychoanalytic conceptualisation of denial has undergone significant modifications (Havik & Maeland, 1986, p. 327). Denial is no longer seen as a pathological or immature defence mechanism; instead it is viewed as a coping mechanism that is frequently used by normal people when confronted with distressing or traumatising events (Croog et al., 1971, p. 385; Hackett & Cassem, 1974, p. 94; Kreitler, 1999, p. 514). Goldberger even argues that "adequate or optimal reality contact requires a good deal of denial" and, without such a mechanism, normal life would be impossible. In this context one could think of Luria's *mnemonist* who had a virtually limitless memory (Luria, 1968). Being unable to forget and being unable to make discriminations turned out to be a major handicap that made normal life impossible. With reference to Watzlawick et al. (1974), Goldberger (1983, p. 87) points out that when we grow up and throughout the rest our lives, we are socialised to deny certain things: "what [we] must not see,

48 Note that the state of ignorance can sometimes also be wilfully induced and involve a (bad faith) decision to avoid becoming knowledgeable/aware of something. The scenario in which a person puts himself in a situation where he is unaware of certain facts in order to avoid certain implications is also called wilful blindness. In that case denial is involved.

not hear, not think or say." Tavris & Aronson (2007, p. 2) furthermore explain that, as fallible beings, humans have an unconscious tendency to justify themselves and avoid taking responsibility. The unpleasant feeling – dissonance as Festinger (1957) would call it – that is generated when we do something questionable is the driving force behind self-justification (Tavris & Aronson, 2007, p. 13).[49]

Due to these insights, denial lost its negative, pathological and immature character. It is now predominantly seen as a positive, normal mechanism that people use in their everyday life as a coping mechanism. By denying threatening realities, people buy time to mobilise the resources needed to cope with the situation (Shockey, 2004, p. 985). It helps them to deal with problems and enables them to survive, preserving their well-being and protecting them from disintegration (E. L. Edelstein, D. L. Nathanson, & A. M. Stone, 1989a, p. 174; Milburn & Conrad, 1996, p. 14; Stephenson, 2004, p. 985). Scholars indicate many reasons why a reality can be distressing or unpleasant. Humiliation, grief, anxiety, shame, fear, and embarrassment, etc. are all stressors that can be too overwhelming and therefore too threatening (Zerubavel, 2008, p. 6).[50] There is also a body of literature on the Holocaust that illustrates that denial is a normal reaction to abnormal traumatic circumstances. For victims denial of the outside and inside world was part of a day to day fight for survival when life was unbearable (Davidson, 1989, p. 310; Eitinger, 1983, p. 203; Klein & Kogan, 1989, p. 300; Lifton, 1967). Laqueur's book *The terrible secret* also addresses the issue how despite there being "a steady flow of information, it had quite obviously not registered" in the minds of those who were about to be exterminated and those who stood by. Laqueur's analysis shows that not only the victims engage in denial but also those who stood by did not acknowledge what was happening. Laqueur explains that "the news about the murder of many millions of Jews was not accepted for a long time and even when it had been accepted the full implications were not understood" (Laqueur, 1980, p. 204). Laqueur (1980, p. 2 and 3) argues that the question why the information concerning the final solution did not register is "directly connected with a more general issue, that of the denial of reality, the psychological rejection of information which for one reason or another is not acceptable." For many of those who survived, the process of denial continued after the Holocaust during the phase of recovery from traumatisation (Davidson, 1989, p. 312; Klein & Kogan, 1989, p. 300). Edelstein et al. (1989b, p. 273) conclude that, often for Holocaust survivors, "[k]nowing the Holocaust sometimes means not knowing the Holocaust." From interviews that I conducted with trauma counsellors from the Rwandan organisation Avega, it became clear that this was also often the case for those who survived the genocide against the Tutsi.[51] The counsellors explained that, for survivors, denial is a crucial element in the process of coming to terms with what happened to them and their families (Umurungi and Mukamusoni, 2008 and 2011 personal communication).

49 Aronson (2008) also explains these mechanisms in his book *The social animal*.

50 In addition to these stressors, denial can also be caused by a person's struggle to maintain control. When a person is for instance diagnosed with a terminal illness or is confronted with another life threatening situation, the feeling of loss of control over one's existence can, if perceived as unacceptable, evoke a denial response. By denying the events control is restored and the person's integrity is maintained (Shockey, 2004, p. 985).

51 This was also confirmed by church organisations that helped victims of the genocide.

In the abovementioned studies, denial is presented as a coping mechanism for those who suffer; the victims of violence. However, as Cohen (2001, p. 50) points out, "the state of "both knowing and not-knowing" serves not only those who suffer. It is indispensable for those who deliberately inflict terrible suffering on their fellow human beings – and for those who come to know about this." There is ample research on how soldiers in battle deny the dangerousness of the situation in order to function properly as soldiers (Alford, Mahone, & Fielstein, 1988; R. Moses, 1989, p. 290).[52] Hilberg's research on the Nazi Holocaust furthermore reveals that denial is an indispensable mechanism for those who engage in violent action against their fellow human beings, because it helps to deal with the inhibitions that would prevent people from engaging in such actions (Hilberg, 2002).[53] They, for instance, deny victimising their fellow human beings by arguing that they act out of self-defence. In order to legitimate their actions, they present the victims as the aggressors.

2.6.4. Interpersonal

One of the main critiques of Freud's conceptualisation of denial is that it focuses on the intra-psychic or intrapersonal aspects and dynamics of denial, thereby excluding the interpersonal or interactional aspects and dynamics of denial (Nathanson, 1989, p. 47). In Freud's work and in classical psychoanalytic literature in general, denial, as a defence mechanism, seems to operate as a set of "independent mental operations dissociated from the ebb and flow of interpersonal events" (Dorpat, 1989, p. 17). By conceptualising denial in such a manner, Freudian psychoanalysis has neglected the interactional dynamics involved which influence denial (Dorpat, 1989, p. 31). It is often the case that denial is a product of individual as well as collective efforts; as such, it is a socially organised phenomenon (Zerubavel, 2008, p. 3). Some even argue that, unless supported by other people, denials cannot successfully be maintained (Goldberger, 1983, p. 87). Zerubavel (2008, p. 4) refers to this as a "conspiracy of silence", a mutual denial, in which multiple actors "collaborate to jointly avoid acknowledging something." Although the phrase "conspiracy of silence" points out that denial is socially organised, the term might actually also give a wrong impression, because denial is very often not the result of simply remaining silent. The alternative reality that is less threatening is often constructed through talk and narratives. In that sense, denial is not about being silent, but about speaking out. Zerubavel (2008, p. 9) concludes that "[b]eing silent thus involves more than just absence of action, since the things about which we are silent are in fact actively avoided." We tend to believe that when people talk they reveal and acknowledge, but talk and text can conceal as much as they reveal and according to Graziano (1992,

---

52 Also, in the aftermath of violent conflict, the traumatic experiences of those who fought are often denied. In this process the experiences of families of fallen soldiers are also often not fully recognised (Scurfield, 1992).

53 For further research on how the inhibitions that normally prevent people from harming their fellow human beings are broken down or circumvented see the work of Kelman & Hamilton (1993; 1989).

p. 5 and 7), one of the major functions of language is therefore not to reveal realities, but to obscure them.[54]

Zerubavel's "conspiracies of silence" in which "people tacitly agree to outwardly ignore something of which they are all personally aware," rely on processes of collusion (Zerubavel, 2008, p. 2). Cohen (2001, p. 64) explains that in such situations there is a "commitment between people [...] to back up and collude in each other's denials." Such collusion can exist between partners in a relationship, but it can also be more elaborate involving entire organisations, up to the point that whole communities and societies are constructed around "living in the lie" (Cohen, 2001, p. 146). These collusive denials can not only be encouraged by close personal institutions such as family; they can also be sustained by powerful authorities such as the government, businesses or the church (Goldberger, 1983, p. 87).[55] Such a conspiracy of silence or collusive denial also existed with regard to the sexual abuse of children by members of the Catholic Church.[56] Such denial not only obscures past victimisation, it also creates an environment that facilitates future victimisation. Milburn & Conrad (1996, p. 3) even argue that societies and nations in general operate on a "shared reconstruction of reality", a negotiated order, which entails a good deal of denial as painful realities concerning our past are not or only partially acknowledged.[57, 58]

Edelstein et al. (1989c, p. 273) explain that:

> Often it has been said that reality is whatever belief is shared by two people. Belief formed through denial and shared by any two people becomes their reality; when denial extends

---

54 That silence often requires speech also becomes clear from Payne's research on the role language played in the Argentine "Dirty War." Payne (2008, p. 183 and 185) explains that silence does not "mean the absence of words", instead "silence and silencing involves text" as "it requires the right words to make the past disappear."

55 Collusive denial not only operates in government agencies and corporations but also in the world of sports. Van de Bunt (2007) gives the interesting example of how journalists and professional cyclists both avoid the discussion on doping.

56 When being confronted with the issue of child abuse in a talk show Pauw en Witteman, the Dutch Cardinal Simonis used the phrase *wir haben es nicht gewusst* to explain that they were not aware of what was really happening (Van der Kolk, 2011). The phrase *wir haben es nicht gewusst*, means "we did not know" and it was often used by Germans after the Second World War and the Holocaust to explain that they did not know that the Jewish population was being targeted for annihilation. An extensive English translation of the report of the Dutch Commission Deetman, which investigated the issue of child abuse in the Catholic Church, is available at the website of the Commission: www.onderzoekrk.nl. The report deals with the so-called *doofpotcultuur* (culture of silence) in the Catholic Church.

57 Carroll (2006) introduced the "Nagasaki principle" in order to explain how the US never came to terms with their nuclear bombing of Hiroshima and Nagasaki. The sheer impact of such massive bombing of innocent civilians triggered shame and fear leading to a denial of the moral implications of the events. Carroll's excellent short article is very insightful concerning how denial first enables such events and how it subsequently allows those involved to escape the implications of their actions.

58 Generally people belonging to certain groups want to think highly of the group or social system they belong to and this can motivate individuals to deny injustices caused (Boese, 2012, p. 12). Several theoretical frameworks explain this process, such as social identity theory (Tajfel & Turner, 1986) (personal self-esteem is dependent on the outcomes obtained by the group), just world theory (Lerner, 1980) (the world is a just place and people get what they deserve) and system justification theory (Jost, Banaji, & Nosek, 2004) (people see systems that control their lives as fair and legitimate). These processes can lead to the situation where groups or entire nations slip into denial.

> from the intra-psychic realm to the interpersonal and further still into the societal, shared denial becomes culture. Just as denial can protect the individual from affect immutably linked to unacceptable perception, cultural denial can protect an entire people from understanding, from knowing the unbearable.

Also in Dutch society cultural denial exists. It is, for instance, rarely openly acknowledged that in comparison with other Western countries occupied by the Nazis, it was in the Netherlands that the number of Jewish casualties was the highest. According to Bovenkerk (2000), this is the other side of the Anne Frank story and one we do not like to acknowledge. The horrors of our colonial past also remain largely denied. Here one could, for instance, think of the extreme violence used on the islands of Java and Sumatra by the Dutch army between 1947 and 1949 in order to prevent Indonesia, a former Dutch colony, from becoming independent from the Netherlands. If the issue does come up, the violence is represented as "police actions" (*politionele acties*) instead of a brutal military offensive that also cracked down on innocent civilians. One of the gravest perpetrations happened in 1947 in the village of Rawagede, where more than 400 men (almost the entire male population) were brutally murdered by Dutch soldiers.[59, 60]

---

59 For an insightful analysis of different cases (including genocide denial) of societal slippage into denial see: Taylor (2008).

60 Scagliola (2007, p. 243) concludes that: "In the Netherlands, to this day, in spite of a growing consensus on the importance of human rights ideology, public recognition of the fact that from 1945 to 1949 the Dutch military committed 'war crimes' on a considerable scale is still not forthcoming." One could argue that Scaglolia's conclusion has become somewhat obsolete since Dutch Government officials have officially apologised on three occasions. In 2005 the Dutch Minister of Foreign Affairs and later, in 2009, the Dutch Ambassador showed remorse during the official commemorations. However, the most powerful apologies happened in 2011 when the Dutch Ambassador apologised for the mass murder in the town of Rawagede (now Balongsari) (M. Willems, 2011). It is however telling that these last apologies followed, relatively soon after a Dutch court had sentenced the Dutch state to compensate several widows for the loss of their husbands (Rechtbank 'S-Gravenhage, Sector civiel recht, zaaknummer/rolnummer: 354119 / HA ZA 09-4171, Vonnis van 14 september 2011.- Hereafter Judgment). The question is whether the victims also perceive these gestures of the Dutch Ambassador as sincere apologies. During the civil lawsuit, the Dutch State argued that the statute of limitations applied and that the victim's right to a remedy had lapsed. This claim runs counter to the so-called van Boven Principles on the Right to a Remedy and Reparation for Victims of Gross Violations of International Human Rights Law and Serious Violations of International Humanitarian Law. The Court, however, noted that the State, despite the fact that it was aware of the fact that its action were illegal, had never taken affirmative action in order to settle the cases. By taking this stance with regard to crimes of such gravity, the State itself is responsible for the position it finds itself in now before the Court and therefore it cannot invoke the statute of limitations (Judgment par. 4.15). Therefore, basically because the Dutch State *denied* the case, it cannot invoke limitations. The Court furthermore notes that apparently the State has not come to terms with these crimes it perpetrated in the past, which is problematic especially because survivors of the massacres are still alive (Judgment par. 4.16). On this subject matter, see also De Haan (2013) who draws on the abovementioned case and other historical cases to discuss the issue of anachronism. De Haan (2013, p. 91) notes that although anachronism is often approached with suspicion by legal scholars because it infringes upon the legality principle, when it comes to dealing with the massive crimes, such as those perpetrated at Rawagede, legal anachronism is not always obvious and retroactive application is apparently not simply ruled out. De Haan's discussion of anachronism is interesting in the context of this study on genocide denial, because if we are not allowed to attribute meaning to events which at that time did not have that meaning it might prevent us from acknowledging historical events as genocide, which would facilitate the dynamic of denial on which genocide thrives. De Haan (2013, 92) concludes that retrospective moral judgments about historical events can be scientifically justified when there is enough factual evidence and it is done critically and cautiously and contributes to the public debate on history.

Denial can be the result of official gag-orders, but, in contrast to such formal gag orders, often the pressures that keep people in a state of denial are less formal (Zerubavel, 2008, p. 44).[61] In contrast to being the result of Orwellian forms of extreme control, collective denial can also be the consequence of unwritten agreements about what not to acknowledge about the past and present: social amnesia, collective consensual blind spots, shared illusions, no go areas with regard to discussable issues, etc. (Cohen, 2001, p. 11 and 137; Milburn & Conrad, 1996, pp. 3–11). In many cases collective denial relies on general social conventions. The issue of what we are socially supposed to notice and ignore is addressed in the famous tale of *The emperor's clothes*. That people (willingly or unwillingly) tacitly agree that certain subjects are better not spoken about is closely related to the issue of self-censorship, because such censorship eventually requires considerable self-censorship (Zerubavel, 2008, pp. 40–44). It is interesting that in the story of *The emperor's clothes* the state of denial is broken by a small child who honestly and surprisingly speaks out about the fact that the emperor is not wearing any clothes. Apparently, the child had not yet internalised the social norms about what to notice and what to ignore; self-censorship did not occur (Zerubavel, 2008, p. 75). However, to keep a safe distance, to always be on guard and to avoid the problematic can do considerable harm to social relationships, because the secrecy and tension undermines the development of open and honest relations which require open communication. This is what also became clear when I conducted my fieldwork in Rwanda. As my research progressed, I came to understand that how people speak, including the reluctance to talk openly, is often guided by concerns regarding people's safety. One could simply say that the reluctance to talk is in their culture, but that would be a simplification and misrepresentation. How Rwandans talk is greatly influenced by Rwanda's conflict history and the contemporary political situation.[62] Due to the conflict history and the current socio-political climate, almost everything has become political in Rwanda and this has resulted in the fact that Rwandans are often not very talkative; openly talking about political issues can get you into trouble. So, when you have to speak,

[61] In Turkey the denial of the Armenian Genocide seems to have become a state policy. The denial does not limit itself to knowing not to know and to remain silent. It is also more strongly enforced by official gag orders, which do not allow people to talk openly about what happened, as an article in the *New York Times* (2006) reveals: "The Turkish government considers even discussion of the issue to be a grave national insult, and reacts to it with hysteria. Five journalists who criticized a court's decision to shut down an Istanbul conference on the massacre of Armenians were arrested for insulting the courts. Charges against four were subsequently dropped, but a fifth remains on trial." Interestingly, the current Government of Rwanda is also often criticised for cracking down on critical voices and it is accused of abusing the criminalisation of the denial of the Tutsi for political purposes (Amnesty International, 2010; Human Rights Watch, 2008b). This controversial issue will be dealt with more elaborately Chapter 6, Section 6.4.

[62] During one of my Kinyarwanda lessons my teacher explained to me that the greetings that Rwandans generally use to say good morning, good evening, how are you, goodbye, etc. are originally inquiries about someone's wellbeing. For instance, *amahoro*, which is used to say goodbye actually literally means go in peace. *Waramutse*, which means good morning, actually means did you get safely through the night. And *wiriwe* which means good afternoon, actually means get safely through the day. *"The language reveals that Rwandans have always been facing threats: first from nature and then from each other,"* my teacher concluded.

"you speak in a way that is safe," my interpreter explained.[63] Rwandans are often afraid what will happen to them when they speak up and honestly say what is on their mind. It seems that due to what happened in Rwanda this fear has become pervasive. It reminded me of the situation Green (1995, p. 105) describes in her research on Guatemala: "Fear is a response to danger. But in Guatemala, rather than being solely a subjective personal experience, it has penetrated the social memory. And rather than being an acute reaction, it is a chronic condition." However as Green (1995, p. 118) explains, "Silence can operate as a survival strategy, yet silencing is a powerful mechanism of control enforced through fear." Not only Rwandans engage in self-censorship. I noticed that bystanders also "clean up" their conversations when talking about politically sensitive issues. During my fieldwork, I noticed that also especially among non-Rwandans using the phrases "Hutu" and "Tutsi" is considered a taboo. In their native language, they referred to the two groups as "the T's and H's" or they talked about "tall and short people". Also, in a conversation with someone who had worked for a German development organisation in Rwanda, I was told that when talking critically about the current president Kagame, they would switch his name for the German word *Kaugummi* (chewing gum) in order to obscure the topic of the conversation.[64]

The story of *The emperor's clothes* reveals that there is another level to the question whether denial is an interpersonal phenomenon. Not only do we need other people to engage and stay in denial, more importantly, through interaction with other people we learn how and what to deny. In order to understand denial, it is important to recognise that the skills that enable people to participate in denial have social foundations (Dorpat, 1989, p. 32; Zerubavel, 2008, p. 17 and 18). According to Zerubavel (2008, p. 20), the way we focus our attention and how we notice and ignore things is learned in social interaction when we grow up: "Noticing and ignoring are not just personal

63 Being safe could require that people engage in vague symbolic speech or that they censor themselves and do not speak out on certain issues. Too much talk and silence are forms of self-censorship, which Rwandans can use to protect themselves.

64 From the above discussion one might get the idea that Rwandans are extremely secretive and not talkative at all and when they talk they beat around the bush, but that is incorrect. Although the issues mentioned above are important when it comes to doing research in Rwanda and understanding the impact of the history and the current situation in the country on people, I do not want to present a stereotypical image of Rwandans, nor do I intend to confirm one (but maybe I unintentionally do this). Like with many other peoples, how Rwandans talk can also be influenced by other factors such as pride, politeness or misunderstanding or simply the reluctance to talk about personal issues to someone they do not know intimately (which is the most likely explanation). It takes quite something to talk about deeply personal issues to a researcher whom you have never met and therefore do not know. Moreover, during talks and interviews I noticed that people often seemed to doubt the integrity of researchers. After what happened, the country was flooded by them. They promise a lot, but often do not live up to their promises. The interviewees often conveyed to me that they had already talked to foreigners, but their situation had not changed. Also during the interviews with Rwandan authorities, I was told that researchers come to Rwanda and take what they need for their research, but they do not see them again. The reluctance to talk can also be caused by the fact that people also argue that for an outsider it is impossible to understand what has happened and how they experience life now. These are not unique problems in this context and other researchers in other contexts have experienced these problems as well and researchers deal with these issues in different ways (See for instance De Jong, 2007; Van San, 1998).

acts, since they are always performed by members of particular social communities with particular social conventions of attention and communication". Thus, when individuals grow up they not only learn *how* to deny, they are also socialised in "*what* [we] must not see, not hear, not think or say" (Goldberger, 1983, p. 86). As a result, denial is socially or culturally dynamic and it can vary according to changes in social mores (R. Moses, 1989, p. 290). Thus, you learn denial (what, how, why) during normal socialisation when you grow up and throughout the rest of your life (Milburn & Conrad, 1996).

That denial is often part of mainstream culture can be illustrated with regard to what we call taboos. A taboo is something that society expects its people to ignore and those who defy the taboo and bring it up are considered social deviants and as such they can become the targets of various social sanctions (Zerubavel p. 26). Rules concerning taboos focus on avoidance and often involve "prohibitions" against looking and listening and practically result in conversational no-go zones: "you do not wash your dirty laundry in public" (Zerubavel, 2008, p. 27). It is particularly interesting that in this taboo process language is often sanitised by, for instance, the use of euphemisms. Examples of such euphemistic language are ample; "ladies room", "F-word", "G-word", etc. Because of their sanitising functions, Zerubavel (2008, p. 28) describes euphemisms as the "deodorants of language". The use of euphemisms allows people to point out taboo subjects, yet at the same time avoid mentioning them. Euphemisms such as "ladies room" or "the f-word" are more or less harmless, but the same technique can be used to deny genocide or other gross human rights violations. In Japan, when the issue of wartime sexual slavery is raised, state officials euphemistically talk about "the comfort women issue".[65] Furthermore, by using terms such as "medical experiments", Nazi doctors were able to point out what they were doing without mentioning explicitly the barbarous acts they directly engaged in (Zerubavel, 2008, p. 28. See also Lifton 1986). In the context of the Holocaust, instead of *Todesschwadrons* (death squads), there were *Einsatzgruppen* (taskforces) and references to deportations and killings of the Jews were camouflaged by vocabulary such as: *Endlösung* (final *solution), Sonderbehandlung* (special treatment), *Evakuierung* (evacuation), *Umsiedlung* (relocation), etc. (Hilberg, 2002, p. 181; Staub, 1989, p. 29). In Rwanda when the genocide was perpetrated, those involved referred to their genocidal actions of killing and rape as "work", "bush clearing", or "pulling out the roots of the bad weeds" (Alvarez, 2001, p. 118; Li, 2004, p. 11; C. C. Taylor, 2001, p. 142).[66]

---

65 The designation "comfort women" has also penetrated non-official language and has become the general term to denote the victimised women. The euphemistic language of the perpetrators is thus taken over by actors, such as journalists, human rights organisations and scholars. This is a troublesome development and the term obscures the true nature of what happened to these women. The story of these victims is one of a structural denial of human rights. For analysis of the system of Japanese sexual slavery and how the issue was obscured (read denied) by the government and the by-standing international community see: Moerland (2009).

66 At times, however, the message was not euphemistic at all, but crystal clear to everyone as the following example of an RTLM broadcast by Kantano Habimana on June 4, 1994 illustrates: "One hundred thousand young men must be recruited rapidly. They should all stand up so that we kill the *inkotanyi* and exterminate them. . .the reason we will exterminate them is that they belong to one ethnic group.

2.6.5. Adaptive

As discussed earlier, denial is often seen as a normal coping mechanism that allows people to deal with threatening realities. From such a perspective, denial is thus adaptive. Research by Kübler-Ross (1969) confirms that denial is essential to overcoming traumatic experience as it sets the stage for later acknowledgement. It is an essential part of the grieving process. As noted before, this insight was also acknowledged during my interviews with the Rwandan trauma counsellors (Mukamusoni, 2008 and 2011 personal communication). However, the interviews also made clear that overcoming denial is not always easy and that residing in the state of denial for too long can have negative effects. Instead of being adaptive, denial becomes maladaptive. For instance, during the interviews, one of the counsellors discussed the case of a man who denied having lost his wife in the genocide. It is known that his wife was raped and subsequently murdered, but her body had never been recovered. In order to cope with the loss, the man denies that his wife was victimised. Instead, he argued that his wife fled the violence and is alive somewhere, but until now she has been unable to return home. The denial by the man has become a burden on the family. He has instructed family members that survived to continue to look for his wife. He also does not work on his land anymore and, as a result, he does not earn any money to support his family.[67]

Davidson (1989) explains that denial by survivors of conflict often manifests itself in patterns of over-activity. He explains how the conditions after conflict demand great efforts for adaptation for victims and they seem to embark on a quest to become survivors and create new lives. Davidson (1989, p. 313) concludes:

> This capacity for work, when associated with a tenacity of purpose and the determination to succeed, has resulted in considerable productivity with economic and occupational success. The tendency to be constantly active and self-driving seems to be closely linked with the mechanisms of avoidance and denial; an association that emphasizes the primarily adaptive direction of psychic functioning after massive trauma.

The interviews with the counsellors at Avega also illustrated this aspect (Umurungi and Mukamusoni, 2008 and 2011 personal communication). One of the main problems for Rwanda is the fact that most people are traumatised by what happened, making mental health one of the main challenges for the future.[68] One counsellor explained to me that, as time goes by, more and more people come to visit them asking for help. One would think that as time goes by the number of people that

---

Look at the person's height and his physical appearance. Just look at his small nose and then break it" (Quoted in Gordon, 2012, p. 120).

67 This phenomenon is not limited to the victims of the genocide in Rwanda. Klein & Kogan (1989, p. 305), for instance, reveal how in the treatment of Holocaust survivors they observed that survivors often denied the destruction of their families, which led to searching activities in which they tried to trace missing family members.

68 For a discussion on mental and physical health in Rwanda after the genocide see: Munyandamutsa et al. (2012) and Mutabaruka et al. (2012). For a contribution focussing on the perpetrators of the genocide against the Tutsi see: Schaal et al. (2012).

seek help would become less, but the problem seems to be that, due to the complete destruction of the country, people have used the reconstruction of the country not to think about what happened to them personally. They lose themselves in hard work, toiling day and night, but at one point when the work is done they sit down and start reflecting, the genocide comes back to haunt them. Rwanda has often been hailed for its miraculous quick recovery, but this quick recovery has implications.[69] Over time, the country's material infrastructure has improved considerably, but as the counsellors at Avega reveal, the mental infrastructure seems to have worsened.

The situation in which denial can be maladaptive is not limited to genocide. It was already noticed that individuals use denial in order to cope with abuse but, although denial facilitates coping, it can also have the unwanted effect that people stay in abusive relationships. For instance, on the Heart-2-Heart website, which is a support network that helps women to deal with battered women syndrome, denial is marked as one of the key issues (www.heart-2-heart.ca). It is addressed not because of the fact that it helps women to cope with the situation they are in, by contrast, it is portrayed as a risk-factor because it keeps battered women in abusive relationships. Instead of being constructive, denial turns out to be destructive. Scholarly opinions, however, differ with regard to whether denial is adaptive or maladaptive and the debate remains over what the exact implications are (Goldbeck, 1983, p. 581; Goldberger, 1983, p. 88; Lazarus, 1983, p. 15). Denial can help people to deal with the contingencies of life, but it can also serve to exacerbate these same problems, because problems remain unacknowledged and therefore unresolved, thereby also endangering important relationships (Croog et al., 1971, p. 386; Shockey, 2004, p. 385; Watson et al., 1984, p. 2008). Edelstein et al. (1989c, p. 174) argue that, in discussing whether denial is adaptive or maladaptive, one should not limit oneself to a single point of view. Instead, where denial favours dysfunction and it becomes destructive it must be addressed, but where it protects and is constructive it should be respected. But where does coping end and exacerbation of the problem begin? In a major study, Lazarus compared studies of denial that focused on damaging outcomes with studies of denial that focused on constructive outcomes. The findings suggest that there are time-related implications in the use of denial and he summarises the adaptational consequences of denial as follows:

> If direct action to change the damaging or threatening person-environment is adaptationally essential or useful, the family of processes called denial (when they undermine such action by avoiding or disavowing the threat or danger) will be destructive. On the other hand, when direct action is irrelevant to the adaptational outcome, then denial like processes

[69] Rwanda's quick recovery has often been lauded, but critical scholars also argue that the picture is more complex. Wealth remains highly concentrated in the Kigali area and is not equally distributed. Also the tight control that drives the development comes at the cost of the limitation of social and political space. For an analysis of these and other issues Rwanda is currently facing see: Straus and Waldorf (2011). Note that the current Government of Rwanda has been critical of the book and has denounced some of its authors as genocide deniers. This a troublesome development that will be addressed in more detail in Chapter 6, Section 6.4.

> have no necessarily damaging consequences, and could even be of value by reducing stress and allowing the person to get on with other matters. (Lazarus, 1983, p. 23)

Denial is a mechanism that is used to deal with the discomfort caused by an uncomfortable reality. Denial as such protects those who deny from the additional discomfort that the uncomfortable reality generates, rather than its initial cause (Breznitz, 1983, p. 265). We should thus be aware that the alternative realities denial constructs can also lead us further astray and distance us even more from what happened and what is actually happening (Milburn & Conrad, 1996, p. 3). The danger is that the problem that caused the denial in the first place is not confronted and dealt with in a constructive manner. This can eventually escalate turning a problem into a severe crisis and bringing us closer to the problem we actually wished to evade (Milburn & Conrad, 1996, p. 17; R. Moses, 1989, p. 295; Wangh, 1989, p. 14). Nancy Raine, who was a victim of rape, reflecting on the years of silence following her rape, argued that such denial was not constructive. Instead the "continued silence was a wounding disguised as a healing" (Raine 1988 quoted in Zerubavel, 2008, p. 79).[70, 71] This duality of the adaptive and maladaptive character of denial is also illustrated in Laqueur's earlier mentioned book *The terrible secret*, which reveals how the denial that helped people cope with their victimisation in the end also facilitated their victimisation (Finkielkraut, 1998, pp. 69–70; Laqueur, 1980).

What complicates the matter is that denial is a progressive phenomenon and those in denial tend to escape confrontation and acknowledgement of what is threatening them, thereby leading them further astray. Cohen and Zerubavel explain how the progressive tendency of denial causes a spiral of denial; you start with literal denial and once you can no longer escape the facts, you reinterpret what happened and when that fails too, you deny the implications of what you did. Also, the longer you are in denial, the more difficult it becomes to acknowledge – the longer things are obscured the harder it becomes to talk about it and the more necessary it becomes to remain silent and keep things in the dark (Cohen, 1993, p. 102, 1995, p. 15, and 2001, p. 103 and 112; Zerubavel, 2008, pp. 57–59).[72] Generally actors do not always immediately start with sophisticated denials, but they tend to become more sophisticated over time and they often end up using a variety of methods ranging from absolute or unequivocal denial of the facts to distortion and deception in which the truth is mixed with lies and only half truths remain. Cohen's and Zerubavel's insights are supported by Breznitz's research with regard to how people deal with

---

70 For an analysis of how processes of denial operate in the context of rape see the book *Denial: A memoir of terror* by Stern (2010). Stern, a victim of rape herself, describes and analyses her own experiences with the trauma it caused and the implications for her life and the life of others close to her.

71 A pastor that I spoke to in Rwanda told me that in his community certain critical issues concerning the genocide and its aftermath remain undiscussed, but nonetheless every time after the religious service he blessed his people when they went home. He concluded that because he knew of the problems but nothing was practically done about it, "his blessing was actually a curse in disguise." Denial here served to normalise overt social relations in the community, but covertly the problems remained and intensified.

72 The spiral of denial can take collective or collusive shape, when other parties are drawn into the process of denial and if this happens a web of denial is formed.

being seriously ill. Breznitz (1983, p. 257) notes that people do not simply use one form or technique of denial; instead they deal with the uncomfortable reality using a variety of changing forms and techniques of denial depending on the specifics of the situation. According to Breznitz (1983, p. 257), denials are "progressive attempts by the individual to protect himself from the impending danger by resorting to different strategies" and the mechanisms can range from attempts to avoid information and minimising the information by wishful thinking and downplaying its emotional implications, to the negation of the information and its threatening character. Each kind of denial-like behaviour could thus be understood "as different ways to bias his perception of the world in a manner that is more appropriate" (Breznitz, 1983, p. 258). Breznitz's research shows how people switch to a more advanced form of denial because the reality they are confronted with makes it impossible to maintain the current level of adjustment (Breznitz, 1983, p. 262). People switch stages when it becomes impossible to maintain the previous level of adjustment, because they have been confronted with new threatening information (Breznitz, 1983, p. 263 and 266). Breznitz (1983, p. 264) also makes clear that it is not necessary for a person to go through all levels of denial, nor is it necessary that a person will start at the lowest level, but once caught in the process, it goes only in one direction, namely, forward. Payne (2008, p. 162) thus seems to be correct when arguing that "denial does not disappear or erode over time; it escalates and spirals."

In case of genocide, the question whether denial is adaptive or maladaptive is intriguing. Victims that deny their victimisation try to cope with the violence that was inflicted upon them. They need the denial in order to survive and not to disintegrate. Their coping strengthens them so that in a later stage they can start to acknowledge their victimhood, constructively deal with it and become survivors. The downside of such denial is that victims, by denying their victimisation, also unwillingly facilitate the implementation of the last stage of genocide, which encompasses the denial of the crime perpetrated against them.[73] Although the problems caused by denial are often time related, in case of genocide denial, the problems are instant: while the survivor needs the denial to cope, at the same time the broader process of genocidal victimisation is continued. Survivors do recognise this dilemma they are in as the following excerpt reveals. After thirteen years of silence, Antoinette, a survivor of the genocide against the Tutsi, volunteered her testimony to be recorded with the Voices of Rwanda (VOR) project in 2007.[74] Antoinette's entire family was killed and she is the sole survivor. At the beginning of the testimony, she gives the following motivation for breaking the silence:

[73] Elie Wiesel also makes this observation in his book *Un Juif, aujourd'hui*. He argues that survivors who stay silent or forget become accomplices: "He, who forgets, becomes an accomplice to the enemy; he who contributes to oblivion puts the finishing touches to his work. Therefore testifying was necessary in order not to side with the enemy" (Wiesel quoted in Grünfeld, 2000). For another reflection on Wiesel's work (*The town beyond the wall*) and the issue of bystanders see: Grünfeld (2009).

[74] The Voices of Rwanda (VOR) archive project was founded in 2006 by Taylor Krauss to film and preserve video testimonies of survivors and other primary witnesses of the genocide of the Tutsi in Rwanda (www.voicesofrwanda.org).

> It is important not to withhold anything from what I will say because this is what happened. Because, if I say that it should be hidden, it would be like denying the genocide. And right now what I'm looking for … and I think the reason that I have strength to talk is … if I die without telling my story here, my lineage will be snuffed out. Do you understand? I'm the sole survivor. So if I die, at least the history of the surviving member of the family will be preserved. That's what I hope for. That's also why it's going to be difficult for me. But I will do it. My wish is … Like now I'm the only one left in my family. And my legacy is a rich one if you let me go back in time and start from my grandfather's history up to now. Because no one else can talk about that. The one who was telling stories was my Dad. But they killed him and my siblings. That means if I keep it to myself, it will disappear forever. And the name of our family will disappear. I'd like to ask you a favour, for me. This video you're making of my testimony. If you can please do me this favour. This is the first thing I can do to help my future child. If my child will be able to watch this, and learn about our history. I do not want it to be hidden. I want it to be seen. Because if I die, my family's name will disappear from the root. (www.voicesofrwanda.org)

Antoinette's statement is followed by seven hours of testimony. Taylor Krauss (2014) who filmed the testimony reflects on its implications in an article titled *In the ghost forest*. His observations are insightful and deserve to be quoted at length:

> When we meet Antoinette at the beginning of what is to be her seven-hour testimony, she suggests that she will bare everything: "… to withhold anything … would be like denying the genocide." In other words, silence equals denial, a denial that would effectively negate the previous existence of her family, not just the narrative of their murder. To avoid, or rather deny *that* denial, she is compelled to speak. It is the negation of a negation that drives her to give birth to words. These words seem to be her only assurance that her family name will continue to exist. Even bringing a child into the world would not fulfil this primary need, for her "future child" must hear this testimony too. This is the same imperative I have heard again and again from *rescapés*: that they not only must build new families in order to sustain their family lineage, but they also must speak of their histories to them. This is a crisis of survival. Though not a physical survival, it is an existential one in which the witnesses endlessly strive through telling to reverse the disappearance of their already disappeared family. Telling, however, is not a solitary endeavour; it requires an audience. And if we, as secondary witnesses, choose not to hear and see these tellings, we too become guilty of a kind of denial by default, or worse, as we are warned in Elie Wiesel's words, "to forget the dead would be akin to killing them a second time."

The last part is revealing as it points out that we, as bystanders, can also come to collude in the process of denial when we are not willing to listen. It is our responsibility to acknowledge what happened.

2.7. The object of denial

Often conceptualisations of denial have become so broad that they are deceptive in the sense that they seize to be functional in terms of research as they have become almost all-encompassing (Goldberger, 1983, p. 85; R. Moses, 1989, p. 287; Weisman, 1989, p. 254). Such broad conceptualisations do not set parameters or distil clear elements and criteria for the operationalisation of research. In their attempts to deal with this difficulty of conceptualisation, scholars have started to conceptualise denial in terms of what is being denied; the object of denial. As such, denial is conceptualised as being composed of related but distinguishable components which mainly focus on what aspect of the threatening reality is being denied. Many scholars from various disciplines have tried to distinguish the different components of denial in their research.[75] When examining their work, particularly with regard to how they differentiate the components of denial, it becomes clear that they all follow a particular pattern. They might use different terms, but substantially (almost) no difference exists between them; they might use different denominations, but they are all talking about the same components. From the literature on denial a pattern thus emerges concerning what one could refer to as the major forms of denial. A form is a mode in which something, in this case denial, manifests itself. Scholars have discerned several forms of denial by studying what exactly is being denied (object of denial) and their research differentiates mainly between three forms of denial. Firstly, scholars have differentiated *complete denial* (also referred to as major denial, denial of fact, primary denial or act-denial). When agents engage in complete denial, they do not acknowledge an unpleasant reality as such. Secondly, scholars have distinguished *denial of implications* (also referred to as avoidance, denial of impact or denial of effect). When agents engage in denial of implications, they do acknowledge a threatening reality, but they do not (fully) recognise its consequences or effects. Thirdly, scholars have pointed out *denial of accurate meaning* (also referred to as minimising meaning, reinterpretation/reconceptualisation or intention denial). In case of denial of accurate meaning, a problematic reality is initially being acknowledged but reinterpreted and thereby its meaning is changed. Complete denial negates or rejects a reality, while the other two forms of denial try to play down a somehow threating reality by not accepting the consequences that follow from it or by reinterpreting it, thereby changing its meaning.

The three forms of denial distinguished above were discerned mainly by scholars in the field of (social-) psychology when studying the behaviour of individuals. It is interesting to note that Cohen's analysis shows that the abovementioned forms of denial can also be discerned in the behaviour of other actors, such as governments. Cohen's research shows how governments who react to critical reports of human rights organisations, follow a similar denialist patterns. So not only human beings engage in denial, also organisations such as companies and states engage in these denials when confronted with an uncomfortable reality. In order to further explain the forms of denial discerned above, it is insightful to elaborate briefly on Cohen's analysis. In his work, Cohen (1993, 1996, 2001) identifies three major forms of denial

[75] See for instance the work of the following authors: Cohen, 1993, 1995, 1996, 2001; Couturier & Lock, 2006; Goldbeck, 1983; Goldberger, 1983; Greer, 1992; Hackett & Cassem, 1974; Havik & Maeland, 1986; Jacobson & Lowery, 1992; Kortte & Wegener, 2004; Kreitler, 1999; Lazarus, 1983; Levine et al., 1987; Lipowski, 1970; Livneh, 2009; Moyer & Levine, 1998; Van Dijk, 1992; E.A. Weinstein & Kahn, 1955; Weisman, 1972; Wool & Goldberg, 1986.

in official (political) discourse: *literal denial, interpretative denial* and *implicatory denial.*

According to Cohen, *literal denial* asserts that something did not happen or is not true. In claiming this, the facts or knowledge of the facts is denied; events or situations are simply not acknowledged (Cohen, 1996, p. 523; 2001, pp. 7, 21, 78, 104, 126–129). Cohen's literal denial is similar to the form of complete denial described above in which a reality is not acknowledged. Those who engage in such literal denial claim that nothing happened and those who are claiming that something did happen are making it up; they are lying. In the private realm, such literal denial can take the shape of the following arguments: I am not ill … the doctor must have it wrong. Or he is a great father he would never do such a thing … they're children they must be making it up. In the public realm: it is impossible that what you are talking of happened, in fact we have legislation that prevents such abuses from happening or it is questionable whether such massacres took place, the witnesses are untrustworthy because they have links with the political opposition, it serves their interest to discredit us. However, due to the fact that we live in a media and information society, there is greater transparency concerning what is going on in the world and therefore literal denial has become more difficult to sustain (Cohen, 1996, p. 525; 2001, p. 105). Instead of denying the facts or knowledge of it, agents admit the "raw" facts, but they deny the provided interpretation of the facts; an event is acknowledged, but it is not what you think it is (Cohen, 1996, p. 525; 2001, pp. 7, 22 and 105).

Interpretative denial disputes the imputed meaning of the events under discussion by reframing or renaming them. By reframing or renaming, their imputed meaning is replaced with an alternative meaning, thereby reallocating the events to a different class of events that is less negative (Cohen, 1996, p. 525 and 526; 2001, p. 7 and 106). Those who engage in interpretative denial argue that indeed something (might have) happened, but it was not what you think, it was something else. In the private realm: I am not an alcoholic … I am a social drinker or I did not steal it, I only borrowed it. In the public realm: It was not genocide, but civil war or it was a forceful interrogation, but definitely not torture. Cohen's interpretative denial is very similar to the denial of meaning discerned above.

In addition to literal and interpretative denial, Cohen defines a third form of denial: *implicatory denial.* In implicatory denial, the facts or knowledge of the facts are not denied, nor their interpretation. Instead, the political, moral, or psychological implications that conventionally follow are denied (Cohen, 1996, p. 529; 2001, pp. 8, 22 and 109). This form of denial is similar to the denial of implications discerned above. Those who engage in implicatory denial argue that what you said did indeed happen, but it is not their responsibility or they argue that no real damage was done. In the private realm: how dare you criticise me for drinking too much, you smoke two packs of cigarettes a day … we punished you, but we did this in your best interest. In the public realm: we had to use violence, they were attacking us, we are the victims here or you have no right to criticise us now because when we were in need of your help, you also did not act. Defining denial in terms of what is being denied, also makes clear that denial involves more than the claim that something did not happen or is not true.

2.8. CONCLUDING REMARKS

In order to come to a better understanding of genocide denialism, it is imperative to acknowledge the complex nature of genocide and denial. The above discussion reveals that genocide is often reduced to the mass killing of human beings, but this is only one element of a more elaborate genocidal process. The point is that the annihilation of a people requires more than the physical destruction of individual human beings. Therefore, the violence encompasses a wide range of genocidal techniques, which systematically target the foundations of a people's existence. The violence targets not only the biological constituents of the group, but also their socio-cultural elements, which help to constitute them as a distinct, meaningful and coherent entity. Moreover, annihilation requires that the reality of the genocide is destroyed. This means that the genocide, in order to complete its process, eventually also unleashes its violence upon itself in order to erase itself as a fact. This can be done by physically destroying the machinery used to perpetrate the genocide or by destroying the remnants of its victims, but in order to leave no traces, its history and memory need to be erased as well. In addition to the physical destruction of the crime's physical artefacts, history and memory are targeted by the violence. Here the weapons are words that are used to discursively destroy the genocidal reality. If one comes to understand that genocide is a multifaceted process, involving the application of a range of genocidal acts encompassing physical, psychological and discursive violence, it becomes possible to see that mechanisms other than killing, such as denial, also play a vital to role in the perpetration of the crime.

In addition to moving beyond the stereotypical image of genocide, it is also crucial that one acknowledges the complexity of denial. The forms of denial presented above do provide us with more clarity, but several remarks have to be made. Firstly, often situations are complex and the verbal actions of those involved cannot simply be reduced to one of the abovementioned forms of denial. Although in theory the distinctions are easier to draw, in practice forms of denial often cannot be separated easily and their use might coincide. Also, in extensive denial discourses, all different forms can be used. Parts of the reality can be literally denied, while other facts concerning that reality are acknowledged. These facts are subsequently reinterpreted and afterwards the implications are not accepted.

Secondly, denial is often presented as a specific act, but denial actually involves a process that encompasses various acts (of denial) and which ultimately results in a state of denial (outcome) (Weisman, 1989, p. 254). This state of denial is a paradoxical self-deceptive state, in which one knows and does not know at the same time. Weisman (1989), in his study of denial, explains the process as follows. The first step in the process involves the confrontation with an initial acceptance of the reality. Subsequently, because of its perceived threatening character, the initially acknowledged reality is fully or partially rejected by various verbal and/or non-verbal acts of denial. In the case of verbal denial, these acts of rejection take the forms of denial discussed above. The result is a revised version of the initially accepted reality, which is more favourable than the initially accepted reality as it reduces or eliminates the threatening elements. The more acceptable revision of reality replaces the rejected reality. This sanitised version of reality now informs the behaviour of the agent involved. However, the determination that the agent is in a state of denial comes from a third person who still shares the initially accepted reality and observes that the agent does not acknowledge this reality. According to Weisman, the last step is essential because people do not "accuse" themselves of being in denial. It is very likely that, once performed, the process does not stop. Faced with new information, those who engaged in denial are forced to deal with such new threats in order to maintain denial; resulting in a re-enactment of the process (Manousos & Williams, 1998, p. 17). This again illustrates that denial is progressive and not static: it is a process that can change over time. This last aspect explains why it is challenging to deal with denial in a constructive way, because once the world view of those who are in denial is challenged, in order to keep up the protective shield, they are likely to engage in further denials. Thus, instead of acknowledging, they tend to dig themselves further in. This can result in a situation where, in order to keep up their denial, people join others in an isolated coterie because it provides them with the much needed collusive and non-threatening environment. In order to successfully maintain their denial, others have to collude in their denial. Denial is thus not an isolated exercise, but an interpersonal project often involving many more actors. The social and interpersonal nature of denial also become clear when one realises that what is being denied, the substance of denial, and how it is being denied, the practice of denial, are learned through social interaction.

Thirdly, denial is a defence mechanism that is dynamic in nature and its configuration depends on the specifics of the situation. Due to its dynamic nature, denial is difficult to define precisely. It can manifest itself in many forms. Shafir (2002) notes:

> Sometimes, denial comes in explicit forms – visible and universally-aggressive. At other times, however, it is implicit rather than explicit, particularistic rather than universal, defensive rather than aggressive. And between these two poles, the spectrum is large enough to allow for a large variety of forms, some of which may escape the eye of all but the most versatile connoisseurs of country-specific history, culture, or immediate political environment.

Shafir's remark indicates that manifestations of denial seem to cover an almost infinite spectrum. Not only can denial manifest itself in many different acts, it can also manifest itself through many different actors. The discussion revealed that those who engage in denial make up an eclectic group of actors. Denial involves thus much more than the stereotypical perpetrator simply claiming that nothing happened. From the discussion it becomes clear that all actors involved in the atrocity and conflict triangles can engage in denial. Not only the perpetrators engage in denial, also bystanders and victims can engage in denial before, during and after the events. The positions within the triangles are not fixed and over time as conflict develops, actors can change positions. Bystanders can, for instance, become perpetrators or victims and victims might become perpetrators and vice versa. This means that, although the above discussion of the dimensions and forms of denial and the different actors can engage in denial is insightful, we should be aware that it is still merely an abstraction of a phenomenon that is much more complex.

One could doubt whether it is possible to simply apply the concept of denial to all these different situations and events discussed throughout the Chapter. Is denial really such a homogeneous concept? The point is that denying genocide or denying that one is seriously ill or that the climate is changing are certainly not the same phenomena, as the nature of the events is very different. What is however similar is that in these cases the threatening reality is being dealt with using the same mechanisms. The events mentioned are unique and therefore different, however if we analyse what is happening in these cases on a more abstract level we see the same defence techniques being applied. Also, in these cases, the actors try to alleviate themselves from the threatening reality. Furthermore, all cases involve the state of knowing and not knowing at the same time. The psychological state, the intention, underlying the defence can, however, be very different. For certain actors, this paradoxical state of not knowing could be described as "truly" not knowing and knowing at the same time, such as for people who were involved in seriously traumatising events. However in the case of states who perpetrate gross human rights violations, the paradoxical state is likely less "true" and more calculated and rationally constructed to wilfully avoid the negative consequences of their actions. In this context it is also important to keep in mind that, despite the earlier mentioned common denominators (defence, mechanisms, and paradox), the denial often plays out differently in various situations due to the dynamic character of denial.

A better comprehension of genocide denialism also requires an understanding of how the two abovementioned phenomena are related. In scholarly explanations of the genocidal process, denial is often designated as the last stage in that process. The discussion however also revealed that the role of denial in the context of genocide is not limited to the last stage in the process. Denial appears to operate throughout the process of genocide and, depending on the situation, denial can perform different functions. Some scholars even argue that denial is not the last stage in the process but the first one (Ndahiro 2014, personnel communication). The next Chapter will therefore look more closely into how denial operates throughout the process of genocide.

CHAPTER 3
GENOCIDE DENIALISM

3.1. INTRODUCTION

The analysis of the dimensions of genocide in the last Chapter culminated in a discussion of some of the main explanatory frameworks (Chapter 2, Section 2.4). For the purpose of this study, the most relevant insight of the processual frameworks was that the phenomena of genocide and denial are closely interrelated and that, in these explanatory frameworks, genocide denial was generally designated as the last stage in the process of genocide. However, the discussion also revealed that the presence of denial cannot be limited to the last stage and instead denial seems to operate throughout the entire genocidal process. The discussion on the situationally dependent and dynamic nature of denial indicates that it assumes different functions and meanings depending on the specific situation and broader context in which it operates. This also applies to how denial operates throughout the genocidal process. To refer to all these particular functionalities simply as "genocide denial" obscures some of the fundamental differences in how denial functions in the context of genocide. *Which function denial performs at which stage in the genocidal process therefore still requires further clarification.* It would be more insightful to distinguish between specific types of denial according to their purpose in the genocidal process. This Chapter will start by looking more closely into how denial is related to genocide and what role/function denial performs at different stages throughout the process of genocide. This analysis will result in a typology of genocide denialism identifying various types of denial and other practices that facilitate the denial dynamic on which genocide thrives. The aim of the typology is to provide more clarity concerning the question how denial operates throughout the genocidal process. It will be suggested that the term "genocide denial" be reserved only for specific instances of denialist practices. Genocide denial as a specific type of genocide denialism will also be the main focus throughout the rest of this study.

Due to the lack of theoretical grounding and the self-explanatory use of the term genocide denial, it also remains unclear how it operates. How do actors deny? On what mechanisms do they rely? Scholars have revealed in their research the main linguistic or verbal strategies and mechanisms used in genocide denial, but a deeper analysis of how and why these mechanisms function and why such speech is problematic is rarely given. *As a result, how verbal or discursive genocide denial operates requires further elaboration.* The second and last part of this Chapter focuses on addressing the abovementioned issues. The discussion is limited to genocide denial, although much of what is discussed here is also applicable to other instances of denial in the context of genocide. The analysis will be grounded in some key cultural criminological notions and subsequently extended by conceptualising genocide denial as a speech act. Central to this analysis is the notion that language can be performative. As will become clear throughout the next Sections, denialist speech is not simply an utterance of words. When these words are uttered, something is done in the moment of their utterance: action is performed. In order to explain this, the analysis will more particularly draw on the theoretical framework of Austin and Searle's speech act theory.

3.2. Denial, an act of genocide?

As explained in Section 2.4 of the previous Chapter, denial operates on many levels and at many instances throughout the genocidal process. Denial prevents people from being confronted with what they will do, allowing them to engage in violent behaviour that they would normally not engage in. Once they have acted, denial enables them to avoid the consequences of their behaviour, which often involves denying the responsibility for their violent action and its moral implications. Such denial after violent action makes it possible for people to engage in violent action again. In these cases, denial facilitates genocidal victimisation. However, denial is also explicitly recognised by scholars such as Stanton (1998b), Lecomte (2001) and Horowitz (1989) as the primary mechanism operating in the last stage of the genocide. In that case, it is possible that denial does not facilitate acts of genocide. Instead genocide denial can be an act of genocide in itself. Although scholars do recognise the destructive nature of such genocide denial, they tend to refrain from designating it as an act of genocide. That genocide denial can constitute an act of genocide will be elaborated with reference to Lemkin's conceptualisation of genocide.

The specific aim of genocide (annihilation) and the special nature of the victim (a people as an entity) turn genocide denial into an essential (last) element in the process of genocide. To annihilate a people as an entity is to reduce them to nothing, to make them non-existent. Thus, theoretically, if genocide fulfils its aim of annihilation, a people seizes to exist. Genocidal victimisation however creates a paradoxical situation because the process of genocide is somehow also an acknowledgment of the existence of the group as an entity, because what does not exists does not require annihilation. The manifestations of the genocide itself remind us of those who were victimised, thereby continuing their existence (in memory).[76] For genocidal annihilation to be complete, the manifestations of the process of genocide need to be destroyed to the extent that nothing acknowledges or reminds us of the victims and the process by which they were victimised (Ternon, 1999b, p. 149). Annihilation

[76] The existential impact of genocidal victimisation can even become a constitutive element of the group as an entity as Tatz (2003, p. 15) notes: "In most instances, the victim's memory, however grim, is a social cement that enables them to cohere as a people. [...] Memory is also their internal narrative, their chronology, of what befell them. In that important sense, memory is what they need, or want, to commemorate, revere, and pass on. Denial [...] of that memory produces an unbearable hurt." Denial of genocide thus also prevents the victims from becoming survivors (Grünfeld, 2000, p. 133; Ternon, 1999b, p. 149).

is complete only when the event of annihilation, the genocide itself, is annihilated and it is genocide denial that performs this last action.[77] It is therefore that scholars argue that genocide attacks truth, history and memory as their last victims and, as a result, genocide constitutes a double victimisation: first the pillars of a people's existence are demolished, followed by the destruction of the remembrance of that deed (Dupaquier, 1995, p. 129; Hovannisian, 1999a, p. 229; Totten & Parsons, 2004, p. 2; Van den Berghe, 1997a, p. 28). Kirakosian notes that:

> [D]enial is similar to genocide. It is not a distinct act, rather a part of it: an "assassination of the memory;" a destruction of proof and testimony. It is inherently linked to the violence of the genocide and the growing assault on the truth. It is the ultimate stage of the genocidal process which perpetuates the crime. (Asbarez Armenian News, 2011)

Huttenbach (2008) concludes that "Denial has become an integral part of genocide; not to take this aspect into consideration is to fail to comprehend a major component of the dynamics of extermination." Smith, Markusen and Lifton (1999) also argue that genocide denial ought to be seen as a "contribution to the genocidal violence in its own right".[78] From this perspective, one could thus argue that genocide deniers are *génocidaires*.

No other scholar has captured the detrimental nature of genocide denial more accurately than Nichanian (2009) in his book *The historiographic perversion*. Nichanian (1999, p. 259) argues that, because of what it is and what it wants, genocide is destined to erase itself as a fact and therefore "the essence of genocide is denegation".[79] What is fascinating about Nichanian's analysis is that he portrays genocide as a dynamic "creature" that, in order to reach its goal of annihilation of a people, in the end also has to achieve its own destruction: "[T]hat what the genocidal will wants is an event that would be its own destruction as a fact" (Nichanian, 2009, p. 73). According to Nichanian (2009, p. 55): "The planned murder did not consist in mere killing. The planned murder consisted [...] in erasing the death of the victims, in eradicating all traces of death and (accessorily) of murder. It consisted not in the killing of life, but in the killing of death."[80]

In that way, as Dupaquier (1995, p. 129) explains *"[l]a négationnisme n'est que la continuation du génocide par l'autres moyens."* Nichanian's observation that

---

77 Note that the annihilation not only operates on physical violence and destruction but also on discursive violence and destruction. Due to the massive victimisation not all traces of the victims and the process of victimisation can be demolished through physical actions. Therefore, discursive actions, such as, denial are of crucial importance to the genocide, because it allows for the reconstruction of the genocidal reality into a non-genocidal one. Through interpretative hegemonic speech acts the nature and thereby the reality of the events is altered and the reality of genocide is, for instance, changed into a reality of civil war. How this exactly works will be explained more in depth later on in this Chapter in Sections 3.4. and 3.5.

78 See also Ternon (1999b) and Hintjens (1999, p. 282).

79 Kotek (2004) also sees denial as fundamental to genocide: *"Tout génocide, par définition, implique sa propre négation, elle est parallèle et automatique, il s'agit d'une relation de cause à effet."*

80 See also Fournet (2007, p. 14 and 15).

genocide not only requires the "killing of life" but also the "killing of death" makes clear why denial is so intimately related to the process of genocide. The insight that genocidal annihilation of a people requires denial of the crime committed against them also explains why genocide denial is much more problematic than the denial of other (gross) human rights violations. This is not to say that the denial of other (gross) human rights violations is not seriously harmful, because it definitely is.[81] However, in contrast to other (gross) human rights violations where denial is certainly possible, but not essential to perpetration, denial is an essential element of the perpetration of genocide.[82] These other crimes, such as war crimes, are not about the annihilation of a people. There might, however, be one exception. Following Graziano, one could argue that denial is also an essential part of "disappearances", for instance, perpetrated during the "Dirty War" in Argentina. Graziano (1992, p. 41) explains that "[o]fficial denial of responsibility for Dirty War abductions functioned as an act that transformed arrests into "disappearances." One can only vanish without a trace if there is denial to cover up the traces. He furthermore adds that "A 'disappearance' occurs when the acts of abduction, torture, and execution are completed by [...] denial." Where genocide tries to reduce to nothingness, disappearances aim to make people disappear into nothingness leaving only uncertainty, doubt and terror.

3.2.1. Charny's classification of denials of known genocides

The insight presented above challenges the way in which genocide denial is generally understood. In this context, it is interesting to reflect on some of the work of Israel Charny, who is a leading scholar in the field of genocide denial (Charny, 1991, 2000, 2001, 2009a; Charny & Fromer, 1998). Charny (1991, p. 3 emphasis added) argues that when one becomes aware of how similar different instances of denial of known genocides actually are:

> [O]ne begins to think of the denial of genocide also as a step in the very basic process or sequential unfolding of genocide, *beyond its original "practical purposes,"* so that the denials are in continuation of the complex motivations that inspire genocides to begin with.

---

81 This observation is not in any way intended to create a competition between sufferings.

82 This observation could trigger a question that is closely related to an issue that I also address in the Conclusion of the Chapter 2 (Section 2.8.), namely whether one could discuss genocide denial in the *same* way as the denial of other human rights violations or even climate change denial, taking into account the abovementioned claim that genocide denial is fundamentally more *problematic* than denying other gross human rights violations. As noted earlier the phenomena are all unique and therefore automatically different. However, on a more abstract theoretical level, the cases have several common denominators, they all include defensive reactions, they rely on similar techniques, and all involve the paradoxical state of knowing and not knowing. Despite these common denominators the denial plays out differently in various situations due to the dynamic character of denial. The point that I try to make by comparing genocide denial and the denial of other gross human rights violations is not that the denials are different but that one denial, because of the particular context in which it is used, has more far reaching negative consequences. Where in case of war crimes denial certainly takes place, it is not required for the finalisation of the crime. In contrast, in case of genocide, in order to finalise the crime and complete the process of annihilation, denial is required.

Charny (1991, p. 18 emphasis added) adds that:

> Denials of genocide make no sense unless one sees in them *renewed opportunities* for the same passions, meanings, and pleasures that *were at work in the genocide itself*, now revived in symbolic processes of murdering the dignity of survivors, rationality, truth, and even history itself.

Charny acknowledges that denial is a step in the process of genocide, but he does not primarily relate it to the idea that denial is required to fulfil genocide's original purpose, which is annihilation and that it can therefore also be an act of genocide. He argues that denial mainly serves other purposes beyond its original "practical purpose". Denial is thus, according to Charny, a "renewed" opportunity to victimise those targeted by, for instance, disgracing their dignity. The implication of genocide denial is that those who survived and tell their story are all liars. He furthermore adds that such victimisation is driven by the same "meanings" that were "at work in the genocide itself". Charny thus presents denial not as a means to the end of annihilation. This also becomes clear from his specification of the several possible violent meta-meanings of denial. Denial, he argues, first of all benefits the perpetrators who, by denying the crime they have perpetrated, try to avoid their responsibility. This is, according to Charny (1991, p. 22), similar to the classic way of helping a criminal "to get away with the crime" by concealing the body. However, from the analysis above, it has become clear that it is important to understand that the operation of denial as the conclusion of the process of genocide cannot be reduced to instances of self-serving opportunistic responsibility avoidance by perpetrators because they do not want to be punished. Its operation is much more profound and it is not always simply about individual perpetrators trying to safeguard their own interests after genocide has taken place. Instead, genocide denial by perpetrators can also be about furthering the process of genocide, pushing it towards finalisation.[83] Charny (1991, p. 23 emphasis added) furthermore argues that denial mocks the sensibilities of the victims and memorial needs and "in a sense *once again* to victimize the victim people". Charny (1991, p. 23) adds that one of the violent meta-meanings of genocide denial is that it is a celebration of the genocide and of renewed genocide in the future:

> To deny the countless deaths of a known event of genocide is to celebrate the deaths and to intimate cynically that the doctrine of power which brought about their destruction is still in force, to be used again when opportunity permits.

Charny in his research has presented a *Continuum of Celebration of Violence* and it shows the extent to which deniers seek through their denial to celebrate the genocidal

83 It is fascinating to observe how certain former Rwandan Government officials, prosecuted by the ICTR for participating in the genocide against the Tutsi, invest great effort in a denial discourse that, instead of simply getting them off the hook, serves the greater cause. This dynamic will also become clear from the official denial discourse discussed throughout the next Chapter. The interviews Gilbert (2004) conducted with high ranking Nazi officials being prosecuted at Nuremberg also reveal this dynamic. In the end, denial in the context of genocide can thus arise from psychological needs to cope to political necessities in order to safeguard ideological goals (Huttenbach, 2008).

violence inflicted on the victims or call for favourable images of future violence against those of other victims. Charny (2009a, p. 527) explains that:

> There are revisionists who are virulent anti-Semites or anti-Armenian, or plain generic bigots and scoundrels who delight in jumping on the bandwagon of denial of the genocide of any victim group because it serves their basic authoritarian and reactionary attitudes and their wishes to vent violence on victims.

He adds that:

> There is no doubt whatsoever that the denial of past genocide is a device through which these people are not only humiliating the remnants of the victim people, in itself a form of further psychological victimization, but are exhorting people to engage in renewed massacre and genocide - of the same or of others. (Charny, 2009a, p. 527)

There is certainly much truth in Charny's observations, especially the last one. However, from the perception that genocide denial is fundamentally about the "killing of death", it is somehow problematic to frame genocide denial in terms of the celebration of genocidal violence.[84] From the aforementioned analysis follows that denial, instead of celebrating the perpetration of genocide, actually assists genocide in eliminating itself as a fact. Instead of acknowledging victimisation, which is what I understand a celebration does, denial seeks to suppress acknowledgment of the events.[85]

3.2.2. The original crime

The insight that denial is essential and inherent to genocide thus challenges many of the views people generally have of genocide denial. Tatz (2003, p. 124) for instance argues that genocide denial "certainly does not perpetrate the original crime, but its potential to sanitise, even to obliterate the deeds, and its ability to disfigure survivors' own memories of what happened to them, makes it worthy of our attention." In contrast to Tatz, I would argue that genocide denial can perpetrate the original crime and exactly for that reason it should warrant our serious attention. Genocide denial does, under certain circumstances, constitute an act of genocide and, as long as such denial takes place, the genocidal process continues and genocide is being perpetrated. However, too often scholars separate genocide denial from the "original" crime of genocide itself; genocide happens first and it is denied afterwards. As a result, scholars generally do not perceive genocide denial as an act of genocide. Instead of focussing on the primary goal of genocide denial, which is annihilation of a people, scholars tend to perceive genocide denial as serving other ends. This severely limits

[84] Smith (2014, p. 102) notices that in ancient times the destruction of a people was often publically celebrated, however in modern times genocide has been structurally denied.

[85] However, if the violence is celebrated by referring to the genocide in euphemistic terms that cover up the true nature of the violence, there celebration could also be an instance of denial. For instance, when perpetrators claim that they won the "war".

our understanding of the phenomenon and its detrimental impact. Interestingly, some of Charny's meta-meanings of denials of known genocides come very close to denial that is inherently genocidal and not about re-victimisation. For instance, he explains that "[k]illing the record of a known event of genocide is also to 'kill recorded human history.'" He adds that "[t]o 'kill' the ability of men to differentiate between what is known and unknown is to murder truth, reality, human memory and history" (Charny, 1991, p. 23 and 24). Such denial according to Charny (1991, p. 22 and 23) also prevents a victimised people to re-create their historical process, thereby undermining their cultural continuity as an entity. If such denial is primarily directed at fulfilling the primary aim of genocide, it would be more appropriate to designate it as genocidal. Such denials do not simply move beyond the original purpose of genocide or as a renewed opportunity for victimisation. Instead, such denial of a known genocide is genocidal, because it attempts to finish the process. It is key, however, not to see these various functions, meta-meanings, purposes, etc. of genocide as excluding each other. As will be explained throughout the next Section, they can actually operate at the same time and complement each other. For now, it is important that the notion of genocide denial, as an act of genocide, allows one to take a different angle, thereby shedding new light on things. For instance, some scholars, like Stone (2010, p. 103) argue that genocide is "less amenable to willed oblivion than most events because of the deep wounds it created." However, what Stone seems to neglect is that genocide aims to destroy itself as a fact. As a result, one might have to be more careful in claiming that genocide is less amenable to willed oblivion. Denial is part of the genocidal weaponry that not only inflicts "deep wounds" but also covers them up. Also, once you realise that denial can constitute an act of genocide, it also becomes more understandable why victims react so strongly to instances of denial. Van den Berghe argues that genocide has become the archetype of evil and adds that sometimes genocide denial is being confused with that evil that is genocide. According to Van den Berghe (1997a, p. 40), this could explain why people react to it strongly, to the extent that a fundamental right such as freedom of speech is limited, because such speech is criminalised. Van den Berghe's analysis neglects how closely denial and genocide are interrelated. Survivors, like Antoinette mentioned in the previous Chapter, do not confuse genocide denial with the evil that is genocide. They are very well aware of the reality that one is a means to the end of the other; it is genocide. It is therefore understandable that people, such as survivors, react very strongly to instances of genocide denial, as it constitutes a direct existential threat: they continue to be annihilated.[86] It also provides insight as to why survivors try to force the world "never to forget" what happened, because forgetting helps to complete the last stage of their genocidal victimisation.

[86] This insight could also help to explain why the current Government of Rwanda reacts so strongly to cases of denial of the genocide and anything that resembles it. One should therefore be careful to reduce actions that attempt to combat the denial of the genocide against the Tutsi, such as the criminalisation of genocide denial, as "weapons" in a political struggle to stay in power. This is an important issue that will be discussed at length in Chapter 6 of this study.

3.3. GENOCIDE DENIALISM

Due to its situationally dependent and dynamic nature, denial can manifest itself in different ways throughout the process of genocide. Depending on the circumstances, denial can facilitate the perpetration of acts of genocide or it can be an act of genocide in itself. Moreover, such denial can have a range of additional consequences and it can (re)traumatise victims, incite hatred and suggestively call for (re)new(ed) genocide(s).[87] Thus, to recognise that under certain circumstances denial in the process of genocide can constitute an act of genocide does not mean that one has to neglect the reality that denial has various other negative consequences. As mentioned earlier, the point is not to see these various functions, meta-meanings, purposes, etc. as excluding each other. In order to come to a better understanding of this complexity, I developed the typology of genocide denialism which is presented below. The typology tries to explain that genocide denialism encompasses a variety of denials but also other denialist practices that somehow facilitate the denial dynamic on which genocide thrives. The term genocide denialism thus denotes that we are not dealing with a single act or type of denial but with a more elaborate multifaceted process of denial that involves a variety of denialist and otherwise in this context relevant denial-like acts which all play a role throughout the process of genocide.

Figure 3. Typology of genocide denialism

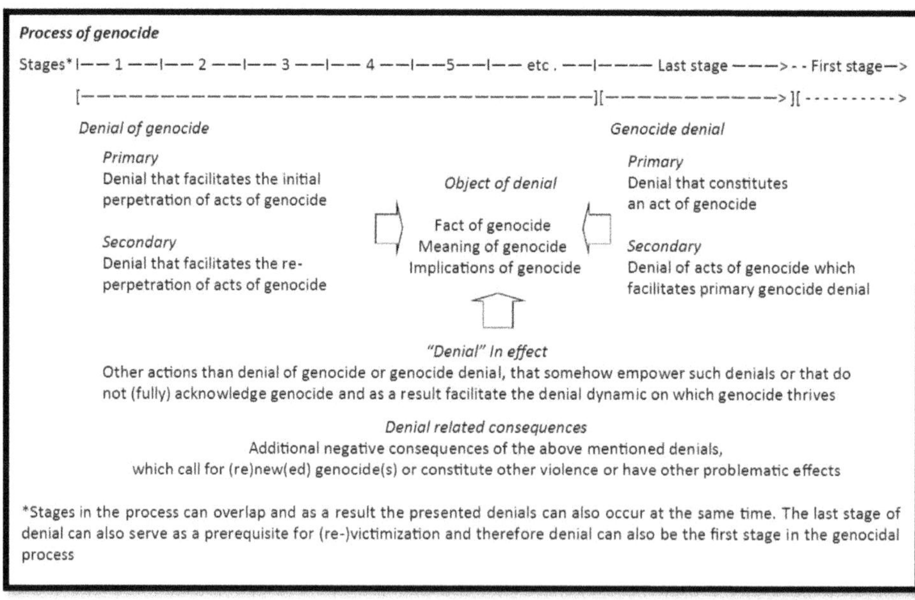

87 In her study on de the denial of the Armenian genocide, Alayarian (2008) discusses the psychological effects of genocide denial and relates them to cross generational trauma as it makes it for instance impossible for victims to make sense of their experiences. Denial turns their accounts into rumours and as a result the pain of victimisation is followed by suspicion and disbelief.

As noted in Chapter 2, denial is challenging to delineate due to its dynamic character. It is an illusion that a typology would fully capture this dynamic character. The types presented are, of course, abstractions and therefore the typology simplifies the reality concerning the operation of denial during the process of genocide. Although the reality of denial is thus more complicated than the typology presents, it nonetheless helps in clarifying the complexity, while also providing critical anchor points for further elaboration and analysis. The typology is based on the insight that denial operates throughout the process of genocide, performing different functions depending on its point in the process.[88] In order to clarify these variations, a differentiation is made between *denial of genocide* and *genocide denial.*

Following Nichanian's (2009, p. 55) observation that genocide consists not only of the "killing of life" but also of the "killing of death", it can be argued that *denial of genocide* facilitates "the killing of life" and *genocide denial* constitutes "the killing of death". Denial of genocide is denial that facilitates acts of genocide. Genocide denial involves denial that constitutes an act of genocide or facilitates this particular act of genocide. In these two cases, denial is a mechanism of defence that serves to provide an actor with protection against the reality of genocide, which for some reason is perceived as too threatening to acknowledge and when engaged in results in the paradoxical self-deceptive state of knowing and not knowing at the same time. Following from the earlier discussion in Chapter 2 on how scholars have defined denial in terms of what is being denied (the object of denial), we could add that the abovementioned denials can be factual, interpretative or implicatory. The *reality of genocide as such* can be denied, but also the *meaning of the reality of genocide* can be denied. Lastly, *the implications or consequences of the reality of genocide* can be denied. In constructing their denial, actors can engage in various forms of denial at the same time; their use might thus coincide. Parts of the reality of genocide can be literally denied (factual), while other facts concerning that reality are acknowledged. These facts are subsequently reinterpreted (interpretative) and afterwards the implications are not accepted (implicatory).

3.3.1. Denial of genocide and genocide denial

The Section above provided some general introductory comments concerning the denialism typology. The following Sections will elaborate each of the types more in depth. The main distinction made in the typology is between *denial of genocide* and *genocide denial.* Genocide denial tends to follow denial of genocide chronologically.

[88] What the process described in the figure furthermore clarifies is that denial is at the centre of genocide; it cannot take place without it. As pointed out already in Section 2.4. of Chapter 3, denial not only marks the end of the process of genocide, it also begins with denial. But also during the process, denial is essential to the perpetration of genocide; the humanity of the victims is denied and the true nature of genocidal actions is obscured. It is therefore that at the start of this manuscript I referred to Dupaquier (1995) statement that: "*Avant le génocide, sa préparation est dissimulée, pendant le génocide, sa réalité est démentie, après le génocide, sa nature même est niée.*" Thus as Nichanian (2009) concluded: "The essence of genocide is denegation." Once we come to understand that denial is essential to genocide, we come to realise the gravity of the issue.

This chronological representation, however, also simplifies the complex dynamic of denial. From the earlier discussion on the role of denial in the process of genocide follows that, as long as there is genocide denial, the process of genocide continues. As such, genocide denial does not happen after genocide, it is part of the genocide. That is why in the figure the last stage continues, which is marked by the arrows. In reality, stages might also overlap and, as a result, both types of denial might actually occur at the same time. For instance, on a micro level, an individual perpetrator might engage in denial in order to neutralise the moral inhibitions that would normally prevent him from engaging in acts of genocide. While, at the same time, on the macro level, the government engages in genocide denial by claiming that no genocide is taking place and that those who are making such claims are liars.[89, 90]

Denial of genocide

Denial of genocide facilitates the killing of life by enabling the initial perpetration of acts of genocide. Engaging in genocide against a people causes considerable psychological strain and denial helps actors to overcome these barriers, allowing them to engage in such behaviour for the first time. This is what in the model is referred to as the primary denial of genocide. Perpetrators deny the humanity of their victims as it enables them to overcome their inhibitions against violence and allows them to engage in violence against their fellow human beings (Kelman, 1993; Kelman & Hamilton, 1989). In propaganda, victims are depicted as sub-human or as vermin who pose a threat to society. This way psychological and ethical distance is created. There is less empathy as the subject is not human anymore but an object ready for destruction. By stripping the human identity, the normal ethical values that guide behaviour towards human beings no longer apply. They are placed outside the universe of moral obligations; there is no commonality, no shared humanity anymore (Alvarez, 1997, p. 167). Ideology plays a major role in this process.

---

89 The research of Kelman & Hamilton (1989) on crimes of obedience shows that such macro and micro processes are intertwined. They show how on the macro level violence is legitimised and how subsequently on the micro level perpetrators use such legitimisations to rationalise and justify their questionable behaviour.

90 Denial of genocide and genocide denial are not simply acts. Instead they involve a process that involves acts of denial and which ultimately results in a state of denial (outcome). Drawing on Weisman's study of the process of denial, one could argue that the process of denying genocide involves several stages (Weisman, 1989, p. 254). If we adopt Weisman's approach that was discussed in the last Chapter, the process could simply be presented as follows. The first step in the process involves the confrontation with and initial acceptance of the reality of genocide. Subsequently, because of its perceived threatening character, the initially acknowledged genocidal reality is fully or partially rejected by various verbal and/or non-verbal acts of genocide denial. In case of verbal genocide denial, these acts of rejection take the forms of genocide denial discussed above. The result is a revised version of the initially accepted genocidal reality, which is more favourable than the initially accepted reality as it reduces or eliminates the threatening elements. The more acceptable revision of reality replaces the rejected genocidal reality. This sanitised version of reality now informs the behaviour of the agent involved. However, the determination that the agent is in a state of genocide denial must come from a third person who still shares the initially accepted reality and observes that the agent does not acknowledge this reality. According to Weisman (1989), the last step is essential because people do not "accuse" themselves of being in denial. It is very likely that once performed, the process does not stop.

How actors deal with their first perpetration is decisive for the question whether they will engage in such behaviour again. Denial helps perpetrators to cope with what they have done; it helps them to rationalise their behaviour. If they succeed in overcoming the stress that the infliction of violence causes, it is very likely that they will be able to engage in further acts of violence. Tavris and Aronson (2007, p. 27 and 193) explain that if we self-justify the violence we inflict, a vicious circle is created: "[a]gression begets self-justification, which begets more aggression." Such denial that facilitates the re-perpetration of acts of genocide is denoted as secondary denial of genocide.[91] The barriers that perpetrators have to overcome differ greatly according to the act of genocide. Demolishing cultural heritage causes less strain than slaughtering human beings.[92] Thus, the pervasiveness of denial of genocide also depends on the type of act that it needs to facilitate. Denial of genocide defends against the uncomfortable realities of engaging in acts of genocide. It is of course possible that actors do not have problems with applying violence and in that case there might not be any inhibitions that have to be overcome. Although these actors might not engage in the denial of genocide, they could still engage in genocide denial, because they want to finish the process of genocide or they try to circumvent the negative repercussions of their acts and for instance try to avoid the responsibility for their actions.

Genocide denial

In contrast to denial of genocide, which enables the killing of life, genocide denial revolves around the killing of death. Two types of genocide denial can be distinguished: primary genocide denial and secondary genocide denial. The main difference between the two types is the intention informing the denial.[93] Primary genocide denial requires a genocidal intention and this is the case when an act of denial is undertaken with the intention to finalise the process of genocide. Denial therefore only constitutes primary genocide denial *if* such denial is a means to the end of annihilation of a people. What is happening is denied in order to be able to complete the perpetration of the crime.

In contrast, secondary genocide denial is not informed by a genocidal intention and, as a result, secondary genocide denial "merely" facilitates the process of annihilation

---

91 Primary denial of genocide *neutralises* inhibitions before the act and secondary denial of genocide *rationalises* the act afterward it has been performed. Successful rationalisations afterwards help to legitimate and justify the actions afterwards; if this is successful, the way for further action is cleared.

92 Those who plan and orchestrate genocide are aware of these difficulties and, in order to overcome them, measures are taken to mitigate the problems of those who have to carry out the gruesome task of killing innocent men, women and children. For instance, the Nazis set up an elaborate structure that helped to facilitate perpetration. This consisted of developing a "clean" industrial killing process while at the same time providing all kinds of structures and mechanisms to overcome the psychological barriers to genocide (Hilberg, 2002).

93 Intention has a different meaning in various fields of study. Sociological explanatory approaches have a broader grasp of intention and they frame intention in terms of purposeful processes, while legal approaches have a narrower understanding of intention that focuses on the mind-set of the individual perpetrator as it is a required element of criminal liability. The different approaches to intention will be addressed more in depth in Chapter 5, Section 5.5.

because it contributes to the denial dynamic on which the genocidal process thrives. By denying the genocide, one carries out acts that support the annihilation of a people and the finalisation of the process of genocide. This, for instance, involves cases of *génocidaires* who deny their actions in order to avoid responsibility. Such genocide denial serves to prevent them from being punished, but the denial also facilitates the general denial dynamic as it does not acknowledge what happened. As a result, they contribute to the last phase in the genocidal process in which the reality of the genocide is eliminated.

The above discussion of denial of genocide and genocide denial focuses on perpetrators who engage in such denials. However, denial is a general defence mechanism that is not exclusively used by perpetrators. In contrast, it can also be utilised by victims and bystanders when confronted with an uncomfortable reality. The psychological status that informs denial by victims and bystanders differs from the psychological status underlying the denial by perpetrators. Perpetrators can however also be traumatised by their crimes and as a result they deny in order to cope. Victims deny their victimisation because the reality of genocide is too confronting to be acknowledged and accepted. They would otherwise break down and denial helps them to cope and to survive. The problem is that, although it is not their intention to facilitate genocide, denial by victims and bystanders can contribute to the genocidal dynamic.[94] The example discussed earlier of the man who does not acknowledge that his wife was killed during the genocide not only allows the man to cope with his loss, it also has the unintentional but problematic effect that an instance of genocide is not acknowledged. That his wife was raped and killed did not happen; it is not a fact and that is exactly what genocide wants; its own destruction as a fact, to be a non-event. Due to the fact that the discussed denials do not primarily intent to complete the process of genocide, they can be designated as secondary genocide denials.

For bystanders, the reality of genocide can be uncomfortable because it creates obligations towards those who are victimised; they are obliged to prevent or stop their suffering.[95] Intervention, however, comes at a price, which bystanders are often not willing to pay. The psychological status of such bystander denial is, of course, questionable. It is not sincere as in the case of victims denying their suffering and it is actually *realpolitik* that often prevents states from intervening.[96] One of the most flagrant examples of this concerns the *inaction* by the US while it knew what was

94 Victims are in a dire situation, because even if they do not deny their victimisation and acknowledge what happened to them, their testimony is often presented as "proof of the fact" that genocide happened. The problem is that by presenting proof you indirectly acknowledge that what happened still needs to be proven; it is not a fact yet (Nichanian, 2009).

95 Or, as discussed earlier in relation to Antoinette's statement, they are responsible for acknowledging what happened, instead of turning away and shutting out.

96 Kiernan (2002, p. 182) notes: "Denial of genocide is often a function of simple political priorities – often ones not directly related to the genocide. In many cases the truth of the matter becomes clear and would not be denied, even if it could plausibly be. But in other cases, the stakes prove too high, or the victims too lowly."

happening In Rwanda in 1994.[97] "Inaction" might actually convey the wrong image, because it is not the case that the US did nothing. In reality it actively avoided its responsibility. On the 1st of May, a discussion paper prepared by an official in the US Office of the Secretary of Defence stated the following:

> Genocide investigation: Language that calls for an international investigation of human rights abuses and possible violations of the genocide convention. Be careful. Legal at State was worried about this yesterday – genocide finding could commit [the US government] to actually do something. (Quoted in Power, 2002, p. 359)[98]

When Christine Shelly, a spokesperson at the US State Department, was asked about how she would describe the situation in Rwanda by Journalist Alan Elsner, the following semantic limbo ensued (Quoted in Power, 2002, p. 363):

> Shelly: Based on the evidence we have seen from observations on the ground, we have every reason to believe that acts of genocide have occurred in Rwanda.
>
> Elsner: What's the difference between 'acts of genocide' and 'genocide'?
>
> Shelly: Well, I think … as you know, there's a legal definition of this … clearly not all of the killings that have taken place in Rwanda are killings to which you might apply that label … But as to the distinctions between the words, we're trying to call what we have seen so far as best as we can; and based, again, on the evidence, we have every reason to believe that acts of genocide have occurred.
>
> Elsner: How many acts of genocide does it take to make genocide?
>
> Shelly: Alan, that's just not a question that I'm in a position to answer

The denial by the US could be designated as secondary genocide denial. Although the typology attempts to clearly demarcate between denials, it is important to realise that different denials can affect and facilitate each other and genocide denial can also contribute to denial of genocide and vice versa. The secondary genocide denial of the US for instance also facilitated the perpetrators in their primary genocide denial. The role of bystanders is important because, as the analysis in Chapter 2, Section 2.6.4. revealed, in order to keep up their denial, deniers are dependent on those who stand by and are willing to collude in the denial. This indicates that

---

97 Glanville (2009), however, observes that the "ideational power" of the word genocide has waned in the sense that it has become more and more detached from legal and political demands. Where in the case of Rwanda "[o]fficials [still] believed that the use of this label would activate unwanted legal obligations and increase political expectations for an American response to the crisis. In contrast, ten years later the Bush administration willingly used the term to describe atrocities being committed in Darfur, Sudan." According to Glanville (2009), they "denied that a determination of 'genocide' activated new legal obligations, and also found that the use of the word did not lead to substantially increased political pressures to act."

98 See also Douglas (1994) for a discussion on how the Clinton Administration had instructed its spokesmen not to describe what was happening in Rwanda as genocide.

bystanders are not neutral. Whether they actively deny genocide, as the US in the example above, or genocide is simply ignored and not acted upon, such actions have far-reaching consequences. By not acknowledging genocide and condoning it, bystanders facilitate the perpetration of the crime. As Smeulers & Grünfeld (2011, p. 333) note, "Bystanders who do not interfere in effect give their tacit approval to the perpetration of the acts in question, and thus enable the perpetrator to continue committing atrocities and genocidal acts." They conclude that, by not acting, bystanders thus become collaborators. Therefore those who do not acknowledge genocide and deny it, effectively collaborate in the process of genocide. A neutral bystander to genocide therefore does not exist (Smeulers & Grünfeld, 2011, p. 334). The indifference is in the interest of the perpetrator as it allows for the perpetration of crimes. Actually, the perpetrator attempts to keep the public unaware of what is happening and by not acknowledging what is going on the "bystander" thus helps the perpetrator in keeping the public ignorant (Smeulers & Grünfeld, 2011, p. 335 en 336).[99] The secondary genocide denial of the US thus not only facilitated primary genocide denial, it also constituted denial of genocide because it facilitated the perpetration of other acts of genocide. As Des Forges pointed out, it is important to relate what happened in Rwanda to what happened in other countries and at the UN in New York because "failure to call the genocide by its rightful name, was certainly part of what made the government able to pretend that it was a legitimate exercise in self-defence" (Human Rights Watch, 2014a). The denial of the bystander can thus facilitate the denial of the perpetrator and the other way around. From the above, it furthermore becomes clear that all actors involved in the atrocity triangle can somehow become agents of denial.[100]

The above discussion of the various ways denial can manifest itself throughout the process of genocide, and how different actors rely on it, shows that it is hard to simply answer the question why actors deny the genocide they are somehow confronted with. In essence, the reality of genocide is too threatening to acknowledge, that is why they engage in denial, but the denial can be inspired by a range of motives and the psychological states therefore also vary to a great degree.

3.3.2. "Denial" in effect and denial-related consequences

The behaviour discussed above all amounted to some form of denial, either denial of genocide or genocide denial. The typology introduced in Section 3.3. also entailed actions that did not amount to denial but that are still significant because they somehow facilitate the denial dynamic. The Sections below will discuss these actions in more detail.

---

99 For an elaboration of these concepts see: Grünfeld (2000).

100 Ironically, during the 50th anniversary of World War II and the Holocaust, the international community vowed "Never Again", while at the same time genocide was happening in Rwanda. In 2004, during the 10th anniversary of the genocide against the Tutsi again the international community vowed "Never Again" while at that time genocide was underway in Darfur.

"Denial" in effect

The analysis of denial in the previous Chapter revealed that actors engage in denial for various reasons and that intentions vary from sincere and innocent coping to ill-intentioned manipulation. That the psychological status underlying genocide denial can vary also becomes clear from Charny's research. Charny (2009a, p. 527) argues that:

> [The *Continuum of Malevolence of Denial*] is defined as running from a position where the person denying the genocide really or largely does not know the facts to a position on the other side where there is full knowledge of the historical facts accompanied by brazen denial.

However, from the perspective presented throughout this study so far, the starting point of Charny's continuum raises questions. One of the elements of denial is namely the paradoxical state of knowing and not knowing at the same time (see Chapter 2, Section 2.6.2.). This paradox indicates that, if there is no awareness, denial is not possible, because one has to be aware of something in order to be able to deny it. Therefore, Charny's continuum which "is defined as running from a position where the person denying the genocide really or largely *does not know the facts*" is questionable. Charny (2000, p. 21 emphasis added) gives the example of "Israeli university students asked if they know of genocides, such as the Armenian Genocide or Cambodia or Sri Lanka, *who truly do not know of the genocide*". However, if these people are truly (and not wilfully) ignorant, it is questionable whether they are in denial. If there is no awareness, there is nothing to deny. If this is the case, it would be incorrect to define such behaviour as denial and as a result Charny's continuum should start with wilful ignorance and not ignorance. This does not mean that ignorance is not problematic. It still facilitates the denial dynamic and in the typology it would therefore fall under the scope of *"denial" in effect*, which includes other actions than denial of genocide or genocide denial that do not acknowledge genocide and, as a result, facilitate the denial dynamic on which genocide thrives. The situation changes when their ignorance is addressed and they have been confronted with the facts concerning what happened. What if after such a "reality check", there still is no acknowledgement? It might be that the reality of genocide is too threatening to acknowledge and as a result they now slip into secondary genocide denial. However, for some people, the reality of genocide might not be threatening and they just do not care. In that case "denial" in effect remains. Therefore, in addition to primary and secondary genocide denial, other behaviour than denial, such as the erosion of memory, non-recognition, indifference, ethno-centrism, lack of empathy, etc., can also facilitate the denial dynamic on which the process of genocide thrives. Moreover, the type of denial might change over time. Despite the abovementioned issues, Charny's continuum does confirm what also follows from the analysis developed so far in this study, namely that genocide denialism is dynamic (Charny, 2009a, p. 528).

The insight that acts which do not readily amount to denial can nonetheless be significant, in terms of denial, because they somehow facilitate the denial dynamic, has far reaching implications. For instance, what if genocide terminology is used in order to denote events and situations that are not genocidal in nature? Shafir (2002), for instance, gives the examples of how some people refer to the police as the *Gestapo* or call certain heads of state *Führer*. Genocide terminology is also often used in the fight against abortion. A petition against abortion titled *Abortion is genocide* explained that abortion constituted a "modern-day holocaust". Genocide terminology is used to vent disgust and moral outrage, or it is about gaining political support for a certain cause. Those who engage in such behaviour do not deliberately attempt to deny genocide. This does however not mean that such banalising and trivialising behaviour is not problematic. Fein (1994, p. 95) explains:

> [The] wave of misuse and rhetorical abuse [of genocide] parallels the alphabet: abortion, bisexuality, cocaine addiction, and dieting have also been labelled as examples of genocide – as well as suburbanization. […] Thus we study, work, and act in a public arena in which the term "genocide" has been so debased by semantic stretch that its use stirs suspicion. Virtually everything but genocide, as Raphael Lemkin first defined it […] is called genocide.

Due to its strong normative connotation, the word genocide awakens our moral conscience and it is used to vent disgust and outrage. As such, it can be used to mobilise public opinion so that action can be taken. The term can also be used in conflict situations, where parties use it to denounce each other, which can lead to stigmatisation creating a confusing picture of who the perpetrators and the victims in the conflict really are. The term has thus become a tool in accusatory propaganda (Semelin, 2007, p. 313). Persons, human rights organisations and states use the term genocide to describe events that are not genocide and, in doing so, the term genocide is "wearing out and dying". This exhaustion of meaning facilitates genocide denial (Finkielkraut, 1998, pp. 94–95). According to Kuper (1994, p. 36), the trivialising use of the concept can contribute to the resistance to charges of genocide, leading to inaction. Instead of paying serious attention when the term genocide is involved, people lose interest (Semelin, 2007, p. 312). Thus, in a tragic way, Lemkin, as a moral entrepreneur, has become maybe too successful in launching his concept of genocide. The term has become so successful that "the word might die of overuse", as Finkielkraut (1998, p. 99) concludes.

Those who have been victimised by genocide and survived place extra attention on the over-use of genocide and the use of analogies which relativise or trivialise the nature of the event that targeted them. They see great danger in satirical comments and jokes and they find it alarming when words such as "Nazi" and "Holocaust" are used recklessly to vent disgust with regard to someone's political views or to denounce the policies of certain governments. Foxman (2012), for instance, explains that:

> As Jews, we have found ourselves needing to constantly raise our voices against this kind of trivialization in an effort not only to remind others of the pain and offensiveness of these remarks, but also to protect the memory of the Holocaust […].

Lipstadt refers to such denials as "soft-core denials", and although those who engage in such behaviour do not have the same intentions as "hard-core deniers", they take events that deserve respect and abuse them for political or humorous purposes. They are thereby mangling history: "[y]ou're doing that is akin to what the deniers do" (Lipstadt quoted in Shalev, 2011). Such political abuse of genocide has denialist effects as its trivialisation and minimalisation obscures the true nature of the events. Interestingly, Lipstadt does not only refer to political abuse. She also criticises abuse of the events for humorous purposes, like using them for jokes. Lipstadt has a point there and I also think that making satirical comments or jokes about genocidal events is problematic because such actions trivialise or banalise these events. It is important to understand that the trivialisation and banalisation of genocidal events is detrimental due to the fact that, in contrast to other crimes, denial is part and parcel of the perpetration of genocide. In the typology presented above, such behaviour would not amount to denial, because the conditions for that are not met, but it would fall under the scope of what is termed "denial" in effect, which includes other behaviour than denial of genocide or genocide denial, that somehow empowers such denials or which does not (fully) acknowledge genocide and, as a result, facilitates the denial dynamic on which genocide thrives. This also means that behaviour that somehow endorses, approves of or legitimises the denial of genocide or genocide denial falls within its scope.

Denial related consequences

Above, three main forms of denial in the context of genocide (denial of genocide, genocide denial and "denial" in effect) were discussed. Although the nature of the problem was framed in terms of denial, it is important to notice that such denialist speech can at the same time also be insulting, traumatising, inciting, etc. In the typology these effects of denial in the context of genocide are referred to as *denial related consequences* and encompass additional negative implications, such as, incitement of hate and calls (re)new(ed) genocide(s) or other violent or negative effects.[101] As noted before, when discussing the work of Charny (Chapter 3, Section 3.2.), although denial speech serves its own specific purposes, this does not exclude the possibility that denial in effect can also amount to hate speech.[102] Also, sometimes hate speech can have denialist effects. Much hate speech concerning the victims of genocide revolves around the message that the victims cannot be trusted; they are power hungry liars. This was the message that was and still is being spread in anti-Tutsi propaganda (but also in anti-Jewish propaganda). The denial of the genocide against the Tutsi relies heavily on the idea that the genocide perpetrated by the Hutu against the Tutsi is a hoax: a deliberate lie of the Tutsi in order to regain power. What connects hate speech and genocide denial is the ideology of genocide in which the

---

101 That denialism has other troubling effects is possible because, due to its performative nature, speech can perform multiple speech acts at the same time. This means that one particular sentence can amount to genocide denial but also incite hatred. How this is possible will be addressed in Sections 3.8. to 3.11. of this Chapter.

102 Matsuda et al. (1993) define hate speech as speech that has a message of racial inferiority, is directed against a member of a historically oppressed group, and is persecutory, hateful, and degrading.

victim is represented in a particular way (Chapter 2, Section 2.3.6.). At one point in the process of genocide, such ideological representations against the victim are used as hate speech to dehumanise the victims and prime them for annihilation while the same ideological representation at other points in the process can serve the denial of that annihilation.

3.3.3. Innocent denial?

In contrast to bigots and self-serving opportunists, there are also people who engage in denial in order to maintain the idea that they are living in a just world. Such denial, according to Charny, is relatively innocent. These people deny the evil of genocide in order to avoid the reality that human beings are capable of extremely cruel behaviour against their fellow human beings. It is thus a sort of coping. The concept of innocent denial was developed by Charny in the context of an insidious form of denial of the Armenian genocide. A Turkish government sponsored organisation had tempted scholars to sign a petition that was used to prove that scholars questioned the validity of the Armenian Genocide. In their responses, scholars who had participated in the scheme emphasised their wish to be seen as good people, they did not want to do any harm. They were convinced that they were doing the right thing. Some even expressed that they wanted to contribute to reconciliation between the two parties. Charny (2009a, p. 526) concludes, that "unless one believes that all of these scholars are lying brazenly, which we believed they were not, many of their conscious intentions are indeed innocent." Charny's phrase "innocent denial" is confusing because, despite the good intentions, the consequences are not innocent but detrimental. Participating in such a petition can also have other pay-offs, such as research connections and, as a consequence, it can thus be self-serving (Charny, 2009a, p. 526). In that case, innocent denial is actually self-serving opportunism. Charny notices that it is important to scrutinise innocent denials for manipulation because innocence can be used as a camouflage for more questionable purposes. He explains that deniers can follow a strategy which involves presenting their work as "the other side of a controversial issue" and they ask schools, newspapers, etc. to allow them to present their story so that "all sides to the controversy" can have their say. These deniers make "innocent" appeals to fair play, freedom of speech and historical debate to poison their public with a manipulative narrative that mixes acknowledgment of facts with expressions of regret and lies about the events (Charny, 2009a, p. 528 and 529). We will see illustrations of such denials throughout the next Chapters when discussing the denial of the genocide against the Tutsi and it will become clear that such denials are far from innocent.

The discussion above revealed that denial is intrinsic to the genocidal process and it provided a more detailed understanding of what genocide denialism entails. The question remains how genocide denialism exactly operates or functions. How do actors deny? On what mechanisms do they rely and why is their denial accepted by others? Scholars have revealed the main linguistic or verbal strategies and mechanisms used in genocide denial in their research, but a deeper analysis of how and why these mechanisms function and why such speech is problematic is rarely given. Therefore, how verbal or linguistic genocide denial operates and functions still requires further clarification. The second part of this Chapter focuses on addressing the abovementioned issues. The discussion is limited to genocide denial, although much of what will be discussed is also applicable to denial of genocide. The analysis will be grounded in some key cultural criminological notions and it will subsequently be extended by conceptualising genocide denial as a speech act. Central to this analysis is the notion that language is *performative*. As will become clear throughout the next Sections, denialist speech is not simply an utterance of words, when these words are uttered something is done in the moment of their utterance; action is performed. In order to explain this, the analysis will more particularly draw on the theoretical framework of Austin and Searle's speech act theory.

3.4. Meaning in motion and the performativity of language

As explained in the first Chapter, Section 1.6., cultural criminology served as a sensitising framework for this study mainly because of three reasons. Firstly, cultural criminology has an open character that invites researchers to explore criminological phenomena in new and different ways. Furthermore, I find its political agenda appealing. It recognises that research is inherently political and it does not hide behind the façade of a neutral, objective and positivist criminology. It holds that doing cultural criminology is doing politics, but a politics that empowers and strives for social justice. Thirdly, cultural criminology emphasises the centrality of meaning in the construction of crime. It puts human agency and meaning at the centre of attempting to understand crimes, criminals and criminal justice policy. It acknowledges that people construct their reality through social interaction, through language (Ferrell, 2008).[103] This last aspect is particularly relevant for addressing the questions raised above. Cultural criminologists argue that crime does not simply exist out there; it does not carry its own meaning. Instead, it is invested with meaning by those involved before, during and after events have taken place. That is how its reality is constructed and also changed. This is a process in which meanings conflict, are contested and (re)negotiated (Ferrell et al., 2008, p. 4 and 5). Cultural criminology thus views crime as a contingent cultural product, as a creative meaningful construct whose meaning is not fixed but open to renegotiation and reconstruction (Hayward,

103 For further explanations of the cultural criminological approach see: Ferrell & Sander (1995), Hayward & Young (2004) and Ferrell et al. (2008). For applications of the framework see: Presdee (2000), Hayward & Presdee (2004) and Ferrell et al. (2004). Cultural criminology also moves away from the one dimensional over-rationalised conception of man that we can find, for instance, in rational choice perspectives and which has been criticised for not being able to explain relevant factors such as moral ambiguity, shame, impulsiveness, etc. (De Haan, 2003). Cultural criminology often features case studies that try to demystify the complexity of human life and action. In doing so, cultural criminologists try to understand (*verstehen*) how their subjects make sense of their world and how they act towards it. In these approaches human are autonomous subjects instead of automated and determined objects whose behaviour can be captured in equations, calculations and subsequently be computed. This last approach, which focuses predominantly on actuarial methods to explain and predict crime (*erklären*) and which has become more dominant in contemporary criminology, has been criticised for not being able to grasp the complexity of human behaviour (De Haan, 2005, 2011; Katz, 1988; J. Young, 2004).

2007). Ferrell et al. (2008, pp. 7–9) illustrate how meaning and thereby the reality of crime is in motion by reflecting on "the quick, snapping trajectory of arm, elbow and fist as a punch is thrown", striking somebody in the mouth and "the bloody knuckles that are pulled back in the next motion." What is the reality of this crime? Is it a crime? It all depends on how those involved and other stakeholders invest it with meaning. Thus as Ferrell et al. (2008, pp. 7–9) point out:

> Maybe it's not so much the bloody knuckles and the swollen lips as whose lips and knuckles they are, and who gets to decide what they mean. Even this most direct of crimes – flesh on flesh, bloody knuckles and busted lips – is not direct at all. It's a symbolic exchange as much as a physical one, an exchange encased in immediate situations and in larger circumstances, an exchange whose meaning is negotiated before and after the blood is spilt.

For cultural criminologists the most intriguing and leading questions are thus "[w]hat is the 'reality' of crime, and who determines it?" (Ferrell, 2007; Ferrell et al., 2008; J. Young, 2004) By emphasising meaning, cultural criminologists hold crime to be an expressive human activity in the sense that its reality is dependent on the meaning that people invest it with (Ferrell et al., 2008, p. 2). The insight that the reality of crime is under constant construction and it does not simply exist, is valuable for understanding the phenomenon of genocide and its denial. Genocide deniers also participate in this process of reality construction. They try to renegotiate and construct the reality of genocide in such a way that its reality is distorted, made unreal, or is turned into something else. Their construction of reality is thus actually the destruction of reality. Cultural criminologists furthermore recognise that language plays a central role in this process of reality construction, because it is through language that meaningful realities are created. This also indicates that language is not simply a conduit through which meaning flows, instead it has the power to create meaning and thereby reality. This is more generally referred to as the performative function of language.

Chilton, who studied the role of language in conflict including war and genocide, comes to similar conclusions with regard to these international crimes, as the above cultural criminologists do with regard to national crimes. Chilton argues that, from the perspective of the performative function of language, violent realities, such as war, are not objective natural phenomena that simply exist "out there". Instead, it is a social creation which is constructed and promoted through the use of language – it is constituted in language and communication (Chilton, 1997, p. 175 and 181). Here Chilton refers to Vasquez who reflects on the notion of "war" and states that:

> From the perspective of the constituting function of language, what is considered war is a product of history – a product of the beliefs, formal and informal laws, and customs of a particular period. This emphasizes the notion that war is a social invention, a fact created by an institution that takes certain actions and makes them a thing. The definition of war reflects the process by which the verbs to fight and to kill become nouns, the process by

which the actions become an institutional fact. (Vasquez, 1993, p. 18 and 19 Quoted in Chilton, 1997, p. 175)

Chilton's remarks with regard to war also apply to genocide, which, like war, is also a social institution that is constructed and sustained by language. Thus, what constitutes genocide "is a function of prevailing conceptualisations realised in discourse, that is, in forms of interactive linguistic communication" (Chilton, 1997, p. 175 and 179).

Cultural criminologists and other scholars, such as Chilton, approach language as constitutive of reality and this is quite different from how people normally perceive the function of language. Generally, language is perceived as a transparent medium used by people to *represent* a reality that exists independently "out there" beyond the realm of language. From such a perspective, language is seen as reflective; it is a "neutral information-carrying vehicle" (S. Taylor, 2001, p. 6). This is also how many social scientists approach language when they, for instance, interview people. In such an approach, language is primarily seen as a "device" or medium that is used to reflect a reality that exists outside of and independently from language (Van den Berg, 2004a, p. 30). This approach assumes that the world and language are separate entities and when people account for what happened they use language to "convey from one person to the other the nature of the world" (Wetherell, 2001, p. 15). In contrast to the general reflective view on language, the perspective of the constituting function of language on which cultural criminologists rely and which Chilton also addressed, is based on the idea that accounts of people do not neutrally reflect the world they live in. Instead, their accounts play an active role in creating and changing the world (Jørgensen & Philips, 2002, p. 1). People's accounts are seen as more than a representation or reflection; they are seen as a form of *social action* (Van den Berg, 2004b, p. 28). They are acts that construct the reality of the world they inhabit (Potter, 2001). From this perspective, language is constitutive; language no longer simply reflects an external reality, but it is through language that this reality is created. People, therefore, do not simply give an *account of* what happened (describe), instead they *account for* what happened. When people talk they do not describe events, but, as Buttney and Morris explain, they "interpret and rhetorically reconstruct events through talk" (Buttney & Morris, 2001, p. 286). People's accounts manage meanings and thereby (re)negotiate reality (Buttney, 1985). Thus, when victims, perpetrators and bystanders account for what happened, their accounts do not neutrally reflect the world and the genocidal conflict they are confronted with. Instead, it is through their accounts that the world which they inhabit and the genocidal conflict they were somehow involved in are constructed. In the context of violent conflict this process is, for instance, illustrated by Cuevas Valenzuela's work on the conflict in Chili. Valenzuela explains that the meaning of the coup that took place in Chili on the 11th of September 1973 depends on the discourse that signifies it because, as a phenomenon itself, it has no inherent or objective meaning which can simply be discovered. Valenzuela furthermore explains that, in the field, one encounters different and often contradictory meanings associated with the event and each depends on a specific discourse: "[T]he September 11, 1973 event is discursively created either as the tragic end of Chilean democracy or as the nation's liberation from Marxism" (Cuevas Valenzuela, 2008, p. 147). The meaning and thereby the reality of "Coup" is the result of specific discourses in which it is constructed (Wetherell, 2001, p. 16). This also applies to the reality of "genocide". This process of construction has several dimensions. Firstly, the discussion in the previous Chapter showed that the term has its origins in a legal and political discourse that was initiated by Raphael Lemkin who coined the term genocide for the first time and defined it in his scholarly works and subsequently lobbied for criminalisation. Secondly, not only genocide as a concept is a discursive construct, but also the reality of specific genocidal events is discursively constructed. The meaning and therefore the reality of the genocide against the Tutsi is constructed and sustained through elaborate linguistic acts that incorporate the accounts of victims, survivors, bystanders and perpetrators. As will become clear throughout the following Sections, on different levels we will find conflict or discursive struggles; some people try to attribute different meanings to the general concept of genocide, while others promote different interpretations of what happened in Rwanda, thereby challenging the meaning and the reality of the genocide against the Tutsi. Such challenges can involve legitimate scholarly engagement, but they often also involve instances of genocide denial.

The notion of performativity discussed above is central to speech act theory which focuses on unravelling how speech or talk can perform action.[104] The framework of speech act theory is crucial in explaining how language can construct reality. These insights are thus very helpful in coming to understand genocide denial, not simply as speech, but as an action that has the power to change reality and therefore can also undo the reality of genocide.

3.5. Speech Act Theory and Genocide Denial as Social Action

Although the term "speech act" was coined by Searle (1965), many of the general ideas underlying his speech act theory, such as the notion of performativity, were originally outlined by Austin in 1955 when he lectured at Harvard. The lectures were posthumously published in 1962 in the book *How to do things with words* (Austin, 1962). After Austin, Searle is probably the most influential scholar in the field of speech act theory. Searle published extensively on the topic of speech acts and developed the theory in different ways, as might have been originally intended by Austin.[105] Levinson (1983, p. 238) nevertheless notes that Searle's theory is basically Austin's theory, but more systematised and rigidified. Where Austin presented a more flexible and creative sensitising framework, Searle presents a more rigid, systematised and formal structure. The differences between Austin and Searle actually make it somehow problematic to refer to their body of work as "speech act theory", because speech act theory as a single coherent paradigm does not exist; a

[104] For an elaborate analysis of the notion of performativity and the roles it plays in several speech act theoretical approaches see: Loxly (2007).

[105] See for instance Searle (1965, 1968, 1969, 1975, 1976, 1979b). Later Searle (1985) also worked together with Vanderveken in elaborating the theory of speech acts.

full theory was never presented (Burkhardt, 1990, p. 94). The theoretical approach is nonetheless sufficiently elaborated and has fruitfully been applied in research (Doerge, 2004, p. 8). The following analysis will discuss some of the core dimensions of speech act theory by drawing predominantly on Austin's work. Where functional, some of Searle's contributions will be elaborated.

Austin (1962, p. 1) claimed that most scholars who studied language relied on the assumption that statements or utterances can only describe a fact or some state of affairs concerning the world. However, in contrast to this view, Austin (1962, p. 138) argued that "[o]nce we realize that what we have to study is not the sentence but the issuing of an utterance in a speech-situation, there can hardly be any longer a possibility of not seeing that stating is performing an act." Take, for instance, the following utterances: "I pronounce you man and wife." "I name this ship the Queen Elizabeth." "I bet you six pence it will rain tomorrow." Referring to examples like these, Austin (1962, p. 6) argued that "to utter the sentence (in, of course, the appropriate circumstances) is not to *describe* my doing [...]: it is to do it." By uttering the words in the above-mentioned examples, the actions of marrying, naming, betting, etc. are not simply described. Instead, they are performed. Austin (1962, p. 13) called such sentences or utterances performative because in saying something we are doing something: we are performing action. Thus, according to Austin (1962, p. 12) "to say something is to do something." In the moment a speech act is performed, for instance when during a marriage ceremony a couple says "I do," new social realities are created, in this example, a married couple. The same applies to many other speech act situations, such as for instance, a war declaration. Declaring war is not simply an utterance, instead it is an utterance that has profound implications for our world. Instead of describing a state of affairs, a war declaration creates a state of affairs. Parties now stand over and against each other, certain rules of engagement apply, and those involved start to perceive each other in different ways – people are at war and no longer live in peace. But how can it be that talk constitutes such action, because, as Searle pointed out, you cannot fix your roof or boil eggs simply by saying that you are fixing the roof or boiling eggs. In what way do such utterances differ from a marriage vow or a war declaration? In order to understand this, it is first of all important to explain that Austin distinguished three types of speech acts.

There are three basic ways in which to say something is also to do something and, as a result, by saying something, people can thus perform three kinds of acts simultaneously. According to Austin, when you say something, you do something because you *utter words (act of saying)*, which have a *force (act in saying)* and an *effect (act by saying)*. The act *of* uttering words – pronouncing vocabularies – should be distinguished from the act that is performed *in* saying those words and that act in turn should be distinguished from the possible effects caused *by* having said those particular words. These three acts are referred to by Austin (1962, p. 120) as the *locutionary act*, the *illocutionary act* and the *perlocutionary act*. Thus, when genocide deniers say that genocide did not happen, they can perform three speech acts at the same time. Firstly, when saying these words, they perform the locutionary speech act of uttering. Secondly, in saying these words they perform the illocutionary speech act of genocide denial. Thirdly, by denying the genocide they can also perform a perlocutionary speech act, as it has a certain effect on the audience. For the purpose of understanding how discursive genocide denial can constitute action, the illocutionary and perlocutionary speech acts are most relevant. In the next Section (3.5.1.) the perlocutionary act and its relevance for understanding genocide denialism will be discussed. Subsequently, in Section 3.5.2., the illocutionary act will be discussed. The illocutionary speech act is more complex and warrants a more elaborate discussion.

Before continuing to discuss the perlocutionary and illocutionary speech act, one brief remark concerning Austin and Searle's speech act framework is relevant for this discussion on genocide denial. The paradigm speech act cases that Austin and Searle discussed predominantly concern private one-on-one speech situations between the speaker and the hearer. According to Pratt (1986, p. 61), although such private one-to-one interaction does occur frequently, one needs to be sceptical about a framework that presents such speech situations as the norm because, in reality, speech situations often involve multiple participants with multiple intentions and people have various encounters with utterances on radio, television, etc. These are directed not at the hearer but a mass addressee. Also, often the speaker seems absent and the hearer or a mass addressee is approached by bureaucratic forms, such as job openings/postings or printed (mass) media, such as a newspaper article (Butler, 1997, p. 34). Pratt (1986, p. 61) therefore concludes that "not all communicative activity is as privatized as the speech-act model might suggest." This is important to take into account, because when it comes to genocide denial it is also often not addressed to specific individuals but to a mass addressee. This also means that its actions in perlocutionary terms can be far fetching, because it can have intended but also unintended effects on many people in various ways.

3.5.1. Denying in "effect" – Perlocutionary acts

A perlocutionary act involves the effects your speaking/saying has on others. It concerns "what we bring about by saying," because "[s]aying something will often, or even normally, produce certain consequential effects upon the feelings, thoughts, or actions of the audience, or of the speaker, or of other persons" (Austin, 1962, pp. 101, 102, and 108). When we talk of the action that a perlocutionary speech act performs, we thus mean the consequences or repercussions of speech. In contrast to illocutions which construct a conventional state of affairs (constituted by rules or conventions),[106] perlocutions cause a natural state of affairs (cause certain effects). In contrast to illocutionary acts, which require certain conventional conditions for their successful performance, perlocutions are not condition dependent. As a result, the effects a perlocutionary act may cause can be intended but also unintended and they are therefore often indeterminate (Levinson, 1983, p. 237; Searle & Vanderveken, 1985). The distinction between illocution and perlocution is important

[106] What this means will be further explained in the next Section 3.5.2. of this Chapter.

for our understanding of how people through their words can perform actions that facilitate the denial dynamic on which genocide thrives. It allows us to make sense of certain types or categories presented in the typology of denialism. Perlocution first of all explains the possibility of "denial" in effect. Utterances out of ignorance do not constitute denials, but they can have denialist effects because events remain unacknowledged. The notion of perlocution also clarifies why abuse of genocidal events for political and humorous ends can be problematic in terms of denial: it can have denialist effects. It furthermore reveals that illocutionary denials can have other violent or negative consequences, such as the incitement of hatred, the traumatisation of survivors, etc. The notion of perlocutionary effects thus also allows us to make sense of what was referred to as denial-related consequences. For instance, in Rwanda there was a case in which a radio presenter, during the commemoration, accidently mixed up certain words making it sound like he approved of the genocide and because of that he ended up being accused of genocide denial (Gasasira, 2012). According to the framework presented above this would not amount to an illocutionary speech act of genocide denial, but the speech act does have certain perlocutionary effects as the reaction of the government reveals.[107] Utterances not meant to deny genocide can still be interpreted as such by third parties. Thus, even if an utterance does not constitute a speech act of genocide denial, it can still have problematic perlocutionary consequences.

3.5.2. Doing genocide denial – Illocutionary acts

Austin's illocutionary act involves the performance of an act in saying something. But how can saying make it so? Utterances, such as "I invite you for diner" or "I urge you to close the window" are performative in the sense that by saying that sentence you are performing the act of inviting or urging. Moreover, as Austin explains, verbs, such as "inviting", "urging", "stating", "betting", and "promising" are explicit performatives because by uttering these verbs, we are performing the action that we are uttering; they constitute the action performed in the main verb. Such sentences are performative sentences and the verbs used are performative verbs (Austin, 1962, p. 32). Austin's explicitly performative illocutionary speech acts make us aware of the fact that many speech acts are directly related to words which carry the semantic meaning implied in the speech act. Ordering, commanding, etc., these verbs are performative because they "name" the action that is being performed (Ohlstain & Cohen, 1983, p. 19). The problem however is that deniers only rarely engage in denial using the performative verb "denying". If that was the case it would be relatively easy to discern instances of genocide denial, because the verb "denying" states the action that is being performed in saying that verb. Most of the time genocide denial is much more sophisticated, because deniers tend to refrain from stating what they are actually doing. They obscure the true nature of their verbal actions. This is an

107 Whether criminalisation and doling out heavy sentences will solve the problem is a different discussion, which will be addressed throughout Chapters 6 and 7.

interesting insight, because it means that those engaging in genocide denial basically deny their denial.

The abovementioned issue is not limited to the phenomenon of genocide denial. It is actually often the case that the performative verb that names the speech act performed is not used. Austin (1962, p. 32) therefore argued that illocutionary acts can also be implicitly performative and therefore can include all kinds of other utterances that do not directly rely on performative verbs. He, for instance, gives the example of someone saying "I shall be there" or "I will". Although the person does not use an explicit performative, the act of promising is implicitly performed (Austin, 1962, pp. 69–72). Searle (1979a, p. 31) was particularly fascinated by the idea of implicit performatives, because it allows one to perform one illocutionary speech act indirectly by way of performing another illocutionary speech act. Searle called such illocutionary acts indirect speech acts. In these cases, the intended meaning of the utterance and literal meaning of the sentence are different. One of the most telling examples Searle gives is the situation in which a person is saying to another man "Sir, you are standing on my foot." In that case the speaker is doing more than describing (stating) the situation; instead he is making a request to get off his foot. Another good example is "Can you reach the salt?" This is not only a question, but foremost a request. In these cases, the speakers perform the illocutionary act indirectly by way of performing another speech act (Searle, 1975; Searle & Vanderveken, 1985).

The idea that speech acts can be implicitly or indirectly performed also means that one can thus deny genocide in many other ways than by uttering "I deny that genocide happened in Rwanda." In order to deny the genocide against the Tutsi one could also utter "In contrast to what is commonly accepted, I am of the opinion that it was civil war that happened in Rwanda in 1994."; or "Those who you claim to be the victims are actually those who invaded the country and killed the president; they are the real aggressors." Here the genocide is implicitly denied by arguing that it was civil war or by insinuating that the victims are actually the perpetrators. How and why such utterances constitute genocide denial will be addressed later in this Chapter in Section 3.11. For now, it is important to understand that illocutionary acts can be implicitly performed and that this has profound implications, because it means that illocutionary acts can be performed without using the specific performative verb that carries the semantic meaning implied in the speech act: one can deny something, without using the performative verb "to deny" in the utterance. Thus, not all performatives are explicit performative and it has even been argued that the category of implicit performatives is so broad that it includes all other utterances not being explicit performatives (Doerge, 2004, p. 36; Levinson, 1983, p. 231). In order to do something by saying something you can thus employ other less explicit devices than performative verbs (Austin, 1962, pp. 73–76; Levinson, 1983, p. 233). Austin's observations make clear that the literal content of a locutionary act is not always determining for the illocutionary action being performed and what is meant is not directly determined by what is said; sometimes we mean more (and thus do more) than we literally say (Searle, 1975). This opens up an array of possible speech acts of denial and denial thus often involves doubletalk, in which something is said, but something else is meant.

Although the notion discussed above is helpful in understanding how actors can engage in sophisticated speech acts of genocide denial, it also presents us with a significant problem. When performative verbs indicating the action performed in the utterance are not used and one engages in one illocutionary act to indirectly perform another illocutionary act, how are we able to distinguish utterances as denials? How can the true meaning of what is being said be determined? In order to answer this question, we will have to elaborate our understanding of the illocutionary act a bit more. Searle provided some helpful insights to this end. Searle (1985) explains:

> In general an illocutionary act consists of an illocutionary force F and a propositional content P. For example, the two utterances "You will leave the room" and "Leave the room!" have the same propositional content, namely that you will leave the room; but characteristically the first of these has the illocutionary force of a prediction and the second has the illocutionary force of an order.

Thus, the illocutionary force determines the nature (purpose) of the propositional content. Searle's approach clarifies that utterances with the same propositional content can have different forces and that the same force can occur with different propositional contents. As a result, a certain propositional content can have the force of genocide denial, but also not. The same force of genocide denial can also occur with different propositional contents. There are thus different utterances that can perform the same act of genocide denial. Not only discussions of victimisation rates, but also discussions concerning who is responsible for what happened can therefore have the same force of genocide denial. The problem is, however, that, as the examples reveal, different illocutionary acts can have the same propositional content. How are we to distinguish the difference in illocutionary acts if the propositional acts of these illocutions are similar? The question thus arises how are we to determine the nature (purpose) of the propositional content? Searle explains that we can distinguish the two illocutions by looking at illocutionary force indicators, which indicate the force an illocution is to have – what illocutionary act is being performed in uttering the sentence. Illocutionary force indicators include: word order, stress, intonation, punctuation, mood, and performative verbs (Searle, 2001, p. 90). Also in speech situations, the specific circumstances and the context (broader speech situation) can indicate what the force of an illocution is (Searle, 1969, p. 30; Searle & Vanderveken, 1985). In order to figure out which act is being performed, it is therefore important to take the total speech act and total speech situation into account. This encompasses the specific event, its circumstances and the broader socio-cultural context (Austin, 1962, p. 147; Hatch, 1992, p. 127). Therefore, in order to figure out whether discussions of victimisation rates in the context of genocide have the force of acknowledgment or a denial, one not only has to look at the utterance itself, but one has to take the total speech situation into account. It thus matters whether the discussion of victimisation rates occurs during an academic conference on the topic of genocide or whether the discussion is posted on a website of an institute known for its revisionist views.

From the discussion of discourse theory in the next Chapter, it becomes clear that it is important to take the broader discourse structure into account when determining whether single instances amount to denial. The broader web of meaning of which they are a part is vital in understanding whether instances are denialist or not.[108] Note that even if an utterance does not constitute a direct or indirect illocutionary speech act of genocide denial, it can still have problematic perlocutionary consequences.

What the above discussion makes clear is that the force of illocutionary acts (illocution) is something different than the semantic content (locution) of an utterance or the effect that it can have (perlocution). The question arises how it is possible that illocution can have such force? Different speech acts have been discussed and their relevance was explained with regard to several types of genocide denialism. The question that remains however is what makes illocutionary speech acts performative. Thus, what is required for language to be performative? What is required for deniers to perform their genocide denial? Why can language constitute action?

3.5.3. The power of convention

Austin (1962, p. 14) explains that, in order for an illocutionary act to be performed successfully, it must meet certain conditions, which Austin referred to as felicity conditions. In order for a wedding or a war declaration to be successful, the circumstances have to be correct: people have to say the right words to the right people, at the right time, on the right occasion, the person speaking also must have the authority to speak, etc. (Austin, 1962, p. 116).[109] From Austin's analysis of the illocutionary act and its felicity conditions, we can distil the important insight that illocutionary acts are performative (have their force) because they are based on shared cultural conventions which link utterances to constitutive institutional procedures: "There must exist an accepted conventional procedure having a certain conventional effect, the procedure to include the uttering of certain words by certain persons in certain circumstances" (Austin, 1962, p. 26). In saying something, I am doing something, because through convention my saying constitutes an action. Although Austin in his argumentation relies heavily on the notion of the "conventional act", he remains rather vague on what it exactly entails. Searle paid more attention to this issue when developing his approach to speech acts. Searle (1969, p. 38) explains that illocutionary speech acts are convention governed and for their performance rely on constitutive rules. According to Searle, words constitute action because institutional conventions attribute consequences to what is said, but this is only possible in an institutional reality. Searle (1976, p. 14) explains that this is possible because many of

108 Later, in Chapter 4, Section 4.3., when discussing Laclau and Mouffe's discourse theory, it will become clear that in order to figure out the real meaning of an utterance it is important to take into account how it is embedded in discourse. Discourse theory namely holds that the meaning of a particular utterance (or any discursive element for that matter) is constructed by how it is related to other utterances or discursive elements. One therefore has to take into account the broader linguistic community in which the utterance is embedded in order to determine its exact force.

109 For a more elaborate discussion of this aspect read Doerge (2004), Levinson (1983) and Loxley (2007, p. 9).

our utterances operate on extra-linguistic institutions such as the state, church, law, etc. For instance, the institutional conventions of criminal justice result in a situation that when a judge utters that a suspect will be imprisoned for five years ("I sentence you to five years in prison."), the illocutionary act of sentencing is performed. These institutions turn words into actions. However, Searle adds that some speech acts do not require extra-linguistic institutions. In such cases, the general rules of language suffice. As Searle (1979a, p. 7) makes clear, in order to make a promise or to make an excuse, extra institutional conventions are not necessary, only the general rules of language need to be followed. Thus, according to Searle (2001, p. 100), language itself is therefore an institution that can empower a speaker to perform a speech act. To conclude, "what we find [...] are human conventions, rules, and institutions that enable certain utterances to function to create the state of affairs represented in the propositional content of the utterance" (Searle, 2001, p. 104 and 105). In fact, conventions can range from formalised institutional procedures to informal conventions that govern our everyday interaction. These conventions can be found in official institutions, such as the judiciary, or we can find them in the official rules of games, such as football or chess. Many other conventions however can be found in informal socially accepted "rituals" (Strawson, 1964, p. 443). As such, conventions do not exist *a priori*, instead they are often fairly arbitrary. Societies might develop and agree on certain rules and procedures, eventually accepting them and passing them on – they become institutionalised. This might give the impression that they exist independently from us, but that is an illusion (Loxley, 2007, p. 100; B. Smith, 1990, p. 54 and 55).[110] It is important that speech acts operate on conventions and that these conventions can be institutionalised in various ways, ranging from legal conventions to general language conventions. However, in the case of linguistic genocide denial, the requirement of a convention seems to pose a hurdle. Those who deny genocide can of course do this by simply saying that genocide did not take place; "It did not happen"; or "I deny that genocide took place." Such genocide denials rely on negation and operate on general social linguistic conventions.[111] What complicates the matter is that genocide is often denied by other linguistic means than straightforward negation. Due to the magnitude of the crime, the evidence that confirms that genocide took place is often overwhelming; trying to deny what happened by simply saying that nothing happened is untenable. Such denial has no merit. As a result, those who deny genocide engage in more sophisticated forms of genocide denial. As pointed out above, they for example discuss victimisation rates and argue that those who are accused of genocide also incurred great losses, or the victims are blamed for what happened to them, by arguing that they started the conflict. In these cases, people mean more than they actually say. But on what conventions do such more sophisticated denials rely for their performative power? When looking at how genocide is being denied, one can conclude that the bulk of denials rely on rationalising practices.[112] Therefore, the following Sections will discuss this practice and some of the main techniques used more in depth.

---

110 On the social origins and contingent nature of conventions see also Derrida (1988, 1989, 2002).

111 For an elaborate exploration of negation see the work of Horn (1978, 1985, 2001).

112 This will also become clear from the analysis in Chapters 4 and 5, when we look more closely at how the genocide against the Tutsi is being denied.

3.5.4. Rationalising genocide

Genocide deniers often try to clear themselves or others from blame by offering exculpations, or they attempt to vindicate themselves or others by pointing out the righteousness or the legitimacy of what happened. These denials do not primarily draw on invalidating or negating practices in which it is basically argued that something is not the case or simply did not happen, instead they rationalise what happened. Rationalising practices are particularly interesting because, within criminology, a substantial body of work has been developed addressing the rationalisations and neutralisations that facilitate the perpetration of criminal behaviour. A well-known study by Sykes & Matza (1957) explains how neutralising linguistic techniques allow youth delinquents to avoid a stigmatising deviant identity while at the same time enabling them to normalise their behaviour so as to make it more palatable and even acceptable to the broader public, which questions or might question their behaviour.[113] If this happens before engaging in deviant behaviour, this process is called "neutralisation"; if it is engaged in after the crime has occurred, it is referred to as "rationalization". As will become clear, both mechanisms draw on the same linguistic techniques. In their research, Sykes & Matza (1957) discerned the following discursive techniques: denial of responsibility, denial of injury, denial of the victim, condemnation of the condemners, and appeal to higher loyalties involved in how people account for their actions. Note that Sykes & Matza's actually use the phrase "denial" in their description of the techniques. Although their research does not focus on genocide denial, Sykes & Matza's work does discern many of the same rhetorical techniques on which genocide deniers rely. Through utilising these rhetorical techniques, the questionable nature of what happened is made intelligible to the actors themselves and/or to others and is explained away with the result that it is no longer perceived as problematic but accepted (Matza, 1964, p. 61).

Sykes and Matza developed their original theory to make sense of youth delinquency. According to Sykes & Matza (1957), youth delinquents engage in an interpretative and definitional process to counter the negative effects that occur when their behaviour is questioned by themselves or by others. This process leads to a renegotiation of the situation resulting in an adjusted and more favourable definition of the initially problematic reality, which allows for the opposing forces (their actions and internal and external demands for conformity) to be reconciled (Alvarez, 2001, p. 112 and 113). Another important aspect of Sykes & Matza's work is that they explain that moral rules are not categorical imperatives. Instead, they are more qualified guides for action that are limited in their application regarding time, person, space, and social circumstances (Sykes & Matza, 1957, p. 666). Think for instance of killing in peace versus killing in war time or the possibility to call upon self-defence as a neutralisation or rationalisation for your actions. Sykes & Matza (1957, p. 666) eventually argue that "much delinquency is based on what is essentially an unrecognized extension of defences of crimes." It shows that rules are not binding under all conditions; instead,

[113] Within the field of psychology Bandura (1996, 1999) came to similar insights. Instead of neutralisation Bandura talks about moral disengagement.

they are negotiable because they are flexible, conditional and relative. The meaning of the act is thus not intrinsic to the act and therefore its meaning can be renegotiated. Neutralisations and rationalisation make deviant behaviour possible because these mechanisms dismantle social controls and avoid potential damage to their (self-) image by altering the meaning of events and thereby their reality. As a result, "the delinquent both has his cake and eats it" (Sykes & Matza, 1957, p. 666 and 667).[114]

The first of the abovementioned techniques is called *denial of responsibility* and it rests on the idea that "[i]n so far as the delinquent can define himself as lacking responsibility for his deviant actions, the disapproval of self and others is sharply reduced in effectiveness as a restraining influence" (Sykes & Matza, 1957, p. 667). Denial of responsibility can take the shape of denouncing responsibility by claiming that it was an accident, to claims that what happened was due to forces from outside or beyond someone's control: "It's the way I was brought up …", "I didn't mean to do it …", "I didn't know what I was doing …".

The second technique of neutralisation described by Sykes & Matza (1957, p. 667) is *denial of injury* and it is based on the idea that wrongfulness depends on whether harm is caused. Whether this is the case is open to interpretation according to the agent of denial. Questioning whether the behaviour has caused harm aims at disconnecting the link between the individual and his act: "They can afford it …"; We were only borrowing it …"; "They are insured …"; "vandalism? It was only mischief …"; "I did not steal it, I borrowed it …". The link between the act and the consequences can be broken if there are no negative consequences. Also, by redefining deviant behaviour in terms of mischief, it becomes more acceptable. Scott & Lyman (1968, p. 51) explain that:

> The denial of injury to persons suggests that they be viewed as "deserving" in a special sense that they are oversupplied with the valued things of the world, or that they are "private" persons ("my friends," "my enemies") who have no standing to claim injury in the public, or to be noticed as injured.

Thirdly, even when responsibility is accepted and also the damage is acknowledged, it is still possible to neutralise indignation by framing the action as a rightful retaliation or punishment (Sykes & Matza, 1957, p. 668). The inflicted harm is not wrong given the circumstances: "He started it …", "He hit me first …" The victim is transformed in a person deserving the harm inflicted upon him and the perpetrator is claiming victim status. This way, the *victim is denied* because "They had it coming …" (Scott & Lyman, 1968, p. 51).

A fourth technique of neutralisation that is very closely linked to *denial of the victim* is *condemning the condemners*. By using this technique, the delinquent shifts and deflects the attention away from one's own deviant acts to the behaviour of those who

114 Matza (1964, p. 176) would eventually conclude that neutralisation or rationalisation "consists of obliterating the infractious nature of behaviour. It converts infraction to mere action."

disapprove or critique his actions: "They are hypocrites ...", "They are taking it out on us ..." (Sykes & Matza, 1957, p. 668). By criticising the character and motives of others, the focus shifts and the wrongfulness of his behaviour is lost out of view (Sykes & Matza, 1957, p. 668). This can turn into a bitter cynicism directed towards those who try to uphold the dominant values: "Isn't everybody corrupt to a certain extent?" (Sykes & Matza, 1957, p. 668).

The fifth and last technique described by Sykes & Matza is called *appeal to higher loyalties* and it rests on the idea that the delinquent neutralises internal and external social controls by arguing that certain norms are more pressing: "Always help a buddy ...", "Never squeal on a friend ..." (Sykes & Matza, 1957, p. 669). Scott & Lyman (1968, p. 51) argue that "Here the actor asserts that his action was permissible or even right since it served the interests of another to whom he owes an unbreakable allegiance of affection." This does not mean that norms are simply rejected. Instead, the delinquent presents himself as being caught up in a dilemma that he had to resolve and unfortunately he was forced to break the law (Sykes & Matza, 1957, p. 669). Cohen (2001, p. 61) argues that the moral demands of society are played down in favour of demands from intimate groups to which the person belongs and demand more immediate loyalties. Sykes & Matza (1957, p. 667) explain that through learning these techniques, the person becomes a delinquent, not by learning and adhering to alternative values that stand in contradiction to those of the dominant social order.[115] Although the techniques are discussed separately, in reality they are often combined. Narratives and discourses can draw upon several of the abovementioned techniques at the same time.

Sykes & Matza's research presents a powerful approach that has been applied to many forms of deviant behaviour. The range of applications varies from less serious forms of deviance, such as substance abuse (Peretti-Watel, 2003) to serious violent crime (Agnew, 1994), including gross human rights violations such as genocide (Hazani, 1991; Neubacher, 2006). Sykes & Matza's work has furthermore been applied in research on the genocide against the Tutsi in order to explain how (ordinary) people are able to engage in genocidal violence against their fellow human beings (Alvarez, 2001, pp. 115–128; Thiry & Verwimp, 2008). The research reveals how genocide perpetrators use the described techniques to overcome the moral constraints and dissonance that come with hurting other human beings. The techniques are used to neutralise internal and social control before a person engages in deviant behaviour. It thus facilitates denial of genocide; the killing of life. For the purpose of studying genocide denial, it is important to recall that the techniques Sykes & Matza described are also used after the behaviour has taken place, but then they are called rationalisations, instead of neutralisations. The techniques are thus also insightful in explaining genocide denial; the killing of death. As will become clear throughout the next Chapters, genocide denial often involves a denial of the victim. By blaming the victims for what happened and making them responsible for what happened, the perpetrators are able to present themselves as the real victims who do not bear the ultimate responsibility for what happened. The insight that denial draws

[115] See also the early work of Cressey (1953).

on the described mechanisms is valuable as it conceptually bounds the otherwise ambiguous concept of denial and places it within a framework that can be used to study and analyse instances of denial. Denial is often reduced to a mysterious internal state, but in this approach denial is captured in narrative accounts making it accessible for research (Cohen, 2001, p. 58).

The abovementioned applications of Sykes & Matza's research indicate that, since their inception, Sykes & Matza's insights have been applied to many different instances of deviance and due to their broad application their techniques of neutralisation have "escaped" the realm of criminology. They are now more generally used to explain how people react to inconsistencies and, as such, their insight seems to have gained an almost universal applicability (Murana & Copes, 2004, p. 3). The wide application of Sykes & Matza's insights has also led to the identification of many other additional types of neutralisations and rationalisations: metaphor of the ledger ("I have done more good than bad"), claim of normality ("Everybody is doing it"), or denial of negative intent ("It was just a joke") (Lanier & Henry, 2010, p. 180 and 181; Schönbach, 1990). One could continue to list and elaborate specific techniques, but what is important about the techniques is "not the flavours they come in", but their explanatory potential. What matters is their function/operation: how they neutralise or rationalise problematic behaviour (Lanier & Henry, 2010, p. 181; Murana & Copes, 2004, p. 64). In the context of this research, one additional neutralisation is however important to mention: *denial of humanity*. Dehumanisation plays a crucial role in the perpetration of genocide as it facilitates neutralising the inhibitions against violence. Depicting the victims as less than human creates ethical and psychological distance between the perpetrator and the victim and diminishes morality and empathy with the victim making inflicting violence easier. Denial of humanity can also be created by not only symbolically removing the victims from the universe of obligation by depicting them as vermin. Often the victims are physically treated in such a way that they start to look and smell like animals. They are undressed and put in overcrowded facilities with no sanitary means, without food and water. The lack of nutrients and hygiene almost literally turns them into sub-human (Alvarez, 2001, pp. 125–128).

Following the discussion above, I argue that instead of simply drawing on negation, deniers often rationalise what happened. This allows them to control and change the definition of the situation, rendering it less or no longer questionable. From the framework of speech act theory discussed above, the question arises on what conventions they rely. What gives them the force to deny?

3.5.5. Excuses and justifications

When explaining how these techniques work, Sykes & Matza (1957, p. 669) point out that:

> These "definitions of the situation" represent tangential or glancing blows at the dominant normative system rather than the creation of an opposing ideology; and they are extensions of patterns of thought prevalent in society rather than something created *de novo*.

Lanier & Henry (2010, p. 177) clarify the issue by explaining that mainstream culture with its conventional beliefs and values also has an "underbelly of subterranean values", which exists side by side with conventional values. Through interaction, individuals learn how society works; they learn that there is a difference between public statements and private practices, they encounter formal rules but at the same time learn how these can be bent. Lanier & Henry (2010, p. 178 emphasis added) conclude that:

> This kind of knowledge doesn't require the exclusivity of a gang of delinquents; it is there beneath the surface of every formal institution, policy, and practice. [...] [S]imply by learning and being socialized into conventional values and norms, adolescents are simultaneously socialized into *negation* of those values.

Thus, the techniques and strategies used to redefine the situation originate from society itself. These rationalisations draw on conventional practices that people use in their everyday lives and they are generally referred to as excuses and justifications. Those who engage in genocide denial invest their indirect speech acts with the illocutionary force by drawing on the socio-cultural conventions that exist in society for making justifications and excuses. The denials are thus often basically inappropriate extensions of commonly accepted rationalisations.

Excuses and justifications in turn belong to the broader category of speech acts called *motivational accounts* (Benson, 1985; Blum & McHugh, 1971; Cohen, 2001; Seu, 2010, 2011).[116] Motive talk provides the means by which the reality of questionable behaviour can be renegotiated and as a result the behaviour is perceived as less of an issue or even appropriate. Therefore, in using such verbal strategies, people do not simply state reasons for their actions, instead they try to exert influence; they negotiate reality by imposing meaning and thereby redefining the situation (Hopper, 1993, p. 801; C. W. Mills, 1940, p. 907). In later research, Stokes & Hewitt (1976, p. 838) would refer to such verbal actions that seek "to restore or assure meaningful interaction in the face of problematic situations" as aligning actions. According to Hewitt (2003, p. 161), aligning actions are "techniques people employ as they talk

116 Already in 1935, Burke argued that a motive is not simply a spring that lies behind action but that it is a linguistic device by which a person understands and explains his action to himself and others (Gusfield, 1989, p. 11). Following Burke's ideas, Mills (1940, p. 904) argued that one should approach linguistic behaviour (talk) by observing the social function of language, which is coordinating social action. Mills (1940, p. 904) conceptualised motives as typical vocabularies which have an ascertainable function in specific societal situations. According to Mills (1940, p. 905), motive talk comes into play in so-called "question situations", that is when social conduct (with reference to the actions and talk of others) raises questions. In essence, motive talk answers questions that "stand for anticipated situational consequences of questioned conduct" (C. W. Mills, 1940, p. 905). Mills (1940, p. 907) adds that different settings or situations have their own specific and appropriate vocabularies of motive. According to him, an appropriate, satisfactory or adequate motive is one that satisfies those who question an act: "As a word, a motive tends to be one which is to the actor and to other members of a situation an unquestioned answer to questions concerning social and lingual conduct." Motivational accounts have a function in social interaction as they are used to resolve conflicts and we learn the vocabularies of motive throughout our ordinary lives; we also learn which to use in what specific situation (C. W. Mills, 1940, p. 908 and 909).

about unexpected problematic behaviour, seek to protect and defend themselves from accusations, and attempt to make their conduct appear sensible and desirable in cultural terms." Young (1995, pp. 252–253) argues that although, substantially different, each of these aligning actions, just as the other ones already mentioned, are basically linguistic devices that allow people to "short-circuit conflicts" (social transgressions that threaten interpersonal relationships and create social conflict) by providing explanations that are situationally or culturally appropriate and acceptable. The concept of motivational accounts and the concept of denial are intimately related. Mills explains that motive talk comes into play when behaviour is questioned. Such talk will often take the form of a defensive (re)action, which tries to correct the problematic situation.

Where Burke, Mills and later scholars, such as Stokes & Hewitt, clarified the general function of motivational accounts, Scott & Lyman's research more particularly focuses on classifying such accounts or talk. Scott & Lyman (1968, p. 47 emphasis added) argue that accounts can be classified according to their content in excuses and justifications:

> Justifications are accounts in which one accepts responsibility for the act in question, but *denies* the pejorative quality associated with it. [...] Excuses are accounts in which one admits that the act in question is bad, wrong, or inappropriate but *denies* full responsibility.

Scott & Lyman (1968, p. 47) add that they are likely to be invoked when a person is accused of having done something that is "bad, wrong, inept, unwelcome, or in some other of the numerous possible ways, untoward". Interestingly, Scott & Lyman also use the word denial to capture the process they describe and even more interesting in the context of this research are the examples that they provide. When they discuss the justifying account, they give the example of a soldier in combat who admits to having killed other people but *denies* that he committed an immoral act because those he killed belonged to the enemy and deserved their fate (Scott & Lyman, 1968, p. 47).[117] With regard to the excusing account, they provide the example that a soldier in combat admits that it was wrong to kill other people, but he did not do this voluntarily as he was under orders, thereby *denying* the responsibility for what he has done (Scott & Lyman, 1968, p. 47). They add that "[e]xcuses are socially approved vocabularies for mitigating or relieving responsibility when conduct is questioned" (Scott & Lyman, 1968, p. 47).[118] These excuses and justifications are thus used by actors in social interactions as "social lubricants" that "enable troublesome situations to be passed over, put aside, and treated as unfortunate past history, they prevent each and every untoward act from becoming a major issue" (Hewitt, 2003, p. 166).

117 For an analysis of complete defences in international criminal law see: Krabbe (2014).

118 With regard to justifications, Scott & Lyman (1968, p. 51) furthermore explain that: "Like excuses, justifications are socially approved vocabularies that neutralize an act or its consequences when one or both are called into question. But here is the crucial difference: to justify an act is to assert its positive value in the face of a claim to the contrary. Justifications recognize a general sense in which the act in question is impermissible, but claim that the particular occasion permits or requires the very act."

Like other behaviour, actors learn which situations call for a particular account and they learn this during their daily social interaction throughout their lives from peers and institutions (Orbuch, 1997). But not only the formalities of accounting are learned from (significant) others, also what the account should entail in order for it to have merit and to be credible is learned. MacLennon (2010, p. 12) points out that:

> Actions need to be justified in legitimate ways in relation to the situation and context to be considered morally sound, which is in turn a reflection on the moral status of the individual, for the self and others. An account is accomplished during the course of interaction and rests upon the implicit indexical knowledge of social actors of the acceptable ways of accounting for actions.

Thus, both form and content of the account are socio-culturally embedded. An excusing or justifying account must have credibility in the sense that one adopts a motivational narrative because of its public acceptability (Cohen, 2001, p. 59). According to Orbuch (1997, p. 460), the current work on accounts acknowledges that accounts can actually reflect culturally embedded normative explanations. Orbuch argues that, in producing accounts, actors display "knowledge of the ideal ways of acting and ideal reasons for doing what they have done." Orbuch (1997, p. 460) also points out that "people must account for their experiences in ways that are intelligible and legitimate in their current social context." The content of the accounts thus depends on what is culturally available. Like the giving of accounts, the process of honouring of accounts is also very much socio-culturally embedded; one learns when it is appropriate to accept which accounts and when not to. Blumstein (1974, p. 558), for instance, conducted research on the honouring of accounts and his results "lend systematic support to the assertion that people do not react so much to what we do, but rather to the interpretation we provide for our acts." Thus when it comes to the honouring of accounts, what seems to matter is not what you have done, but how you talk about it – how one makes sense of it towards others (the nature of your account).

Genocide deniers often draw on the conventions on which justifications and excuses normally rely in order to engage in indirect speech acts of genocide denial. Such denials are powerful because they tap into the socially and culturally accepted vocabularies of motive to make questionable events and behaviours intelligible and acceptable.

3.6. Concluding remarks

The first part of this Chapter looked into the different functions that denial performs throughout the process of genocide and the second part addressed how genocide denial operates. In addressing these two aspects, an array of typologies and classifications was discussed ranging from a typology of genocide denialism to a classification of speech acts and from the techniques of neutralisations and rationalisations to types of motive talk. By looking into these theoretically abstract and technical aspects of genocide denialism, the analysis attempted to address the lack of theoretical grounding and the self-explanatory use of the term denial. Although one could use the typology of denialism in a practical and technical way to designate denials, I however think that there is a more important value to it. The typology namely shows that many different actions together generate the denial dynamic on which the perpetration of genocide thrives. It breaks with the stereotypical view that those who deny genocide are typically racist bigots. Apparently many more actors engage in behaviour that raises questions in terms of denial. The picture becomes even more complex, due to the fact that some actions amount to denial, while others might not, but such actions can nonetheless still facilitate the denial dynamic. Much more behaviour is thus problematic in terms of denial than one might initially think. The typology is a way to raise awareness about the complex nature of the denial of genocides. This can also be said for the other differentiations that were being addressed. Although the different speech acts, the various techniques of rationalisation and the types of motive talk discussed can be practically helpful in distinguishing instances of genocide denial, the primary aim of the analysis was to deepen our understanding of how genocide denial operates, how *speaking* denial is *doing* denial and how it can have the power to change the reality of genocide.

The theoretical and technical analysis of the role of denial, and how it operates, results in some intriguing insights. For instance, from the analysis of genocide denial as an act of genocide follows that if the *génocidaires* succeed in finalising the last stage in the genocide –the stage of denial – and thereby complete the annihilation of a people, then the event would never be known to us. The event would have been airbrushed out of history and it would never have taken place. One could of course wonder how it is possible to make such an enormous event disappear into thin air. Is it possible to destroy all the physical evidence of victimisation? What about those who witnessed the events? Exactly because much proof remains, linguistic genocide denial becomes of vital importance to the perpetrators. As briefly noted earlier in the Conclusion of Chapter 2, language and discourse are turned into weapons that are used to discursively destroy the genocidal reality. This process of destruction often involves the reinterpretation of the genocidal events, thereby turning them into something else, something non-genocidal: what happened is not what you think that happened, it was something else ... As a result, the evidence of genocide that remained becomes evidence of something else, something non-genocidal – acts of war, acts of spontaneous violence, acts of self-defence, etc. Genocide is thus a multifaceted process involving the application of a range of genocidal acts that encompass physical and psychological but also discursive violence.[119] This also makes clear that other acts of genocide also play a vital role in the perpetration of the crime. Focussing on the "*killing of life*" neglects that the violence in the process of genocide is also about the "*killing of death*". Taking this perspective on genocide and the violence involved, it also becomes clear that as long as there is denial the process of genocide continues.

119 How discourse can enact violence will be discussed in Chapter 5, Section 6.

Another interesting aspect that the analysis allows us to reflect upon is the criminalisation of genocide denial, because, instead of criminalising the illocutionary speech act of genocide denial, legislation predominantly focuses on criminalising the perlocutionary effects that denialist speech generates. In the Netherlands, for instance, the legislation does not directly criminalise genocide denial. The Dutch law criminalises genocide denial indirectly through broader anti-defamation and anti-discrimination legislation and, as a result, the legislation does not address illocutionary acts of genocide denial. Instead of seeing genocide denial as an act that is problematic in its own right, the problem of genocide denial is predominantly framed in terms of hate speech because it is offensive or threatening. Even in countries that criminalise genocide denial directly, such as in Germany, the illocutionary acts of genocide denial often remain unaddressed and the legislation focuses on the perlocutionary effects of genocide denial. Here genocide denial (Holocaust) is criminalised mainly because it reinvigorates a (Nazi) genocide ideology and incites new violence against people. Denial is thus mainly seen as facilitative to genocide and not as constitutive of genocide. To conclude, these and many other states therefore do not criminalise what is done *in* uttering genocide denial (illocution), but they criminalise what is done *by* uttering genocide denial (perlocution). In contrast, in France and Austria, where Holocaust denial is also criminalised, there is no requirement that the prohibited conduct should disturb the public peace. It thus seems that these countries do criminalise illocutionary speech acts of denial.

The following part of this study will utilise the insights gained so far in order to study several concrete instances of denial of the genocide against the Tutsi. This way we gain a better understanding of how genocide denial operates in the particular context of the genocide against the Tutsi. In addition to deepening our understanding of the denial of the genocide against the Tutsi, the discussion and analysis of this case will also further inform the elaboration of the theoretical framework of genocide denialism.

Part II
Inspection

Chapter 4
Official denial of the genocide against the Tutsi

4.1. Introduction

Ever since the genocide against the Tutsi was planned, organised and implemented, those responsible have been engaging in a virulent denial of the genocide that obscures the true nature of what they have been involved in (Ndahiro, 2008, p. 102; Totten & Bartrop, 2009, p. 518).[1] The group of responsible actors is broad and varies from governmental, military and political actors officially aligned with the former regime to civil, media and religious actors who supported their cause. *The analysis in this Chapter will primarily focus on addressing the official denial of the genocide against the Tutsi.* The term "official denial" denotes the genocide denial of governmental, military and political organisations that were officially aligned with the former regime and were somehow involved in the planning, organisation and/or implementation of the genocide. The focus on official denial is pertinent because, although this issue has been briefly addressed in several studies, it has not been extensively and systematically analysed.[2] Furthermore, official genocide denial, due to the power of the institutions disseminating it and because of its highly ideological content, has had (and still has) a substantial impact on people.[3] *The analysis of official genocide denial provided for in this Chapter is based on official documentation authored by the following organisations: the Rwandan Interim Government (RIG), the Rwandan Armed Forces (RAF) and the Rassemblement pour le Retour des Réfugiés et la Démocratie au Rwanda (RDR).*[4] In contrast to the other organisations mentioned, the RDR (Alliance for the Return of Refugees and Democracy in Rwanda) was created after the extermination phase of the genocide against the Tutsi was implemented. As will become clear throughout this Chapter, the RDR was established after the official government and military were dissolved and its members came to include many former government and military personnel. The records of the RIG, the RAF and the RDR are remarkable and powerful illustrations

1 Note that such a cover-up is not unique to the genocide against the Tutsi. The denial of other genocides, such as the Holocaust and the Armenian genocide, is very similar when it comes to the strategies, methods and techniques used (see Chapter 5, Section 5.7.). All these denials for instance dehumanise their victims and present them as the real culprits. Victim blaming and scapegoating appears to be a universal denial template. However, the specific content of each of the denial discourses is of course related to the unique situation and context of that particular genocide.

2 It has for instance been addressed by Chrétien (2012) and Fierens (2009).

3 The fact that many of the high ranking officials involved in the genocide were prosecuted does not mean that their ideology is not being spread anymore. A substantial number of these high profile actors, including Kambanda (1997, 2013) and Nahimana (2007), have written reports and published books that are freely available to the public.

4 In the context of this study, the term Rwandan Interim Government (RIG) is broadly defined and it also includes the Rwandan Government in Exile (RGE).

of official efforts to deny the genocide against the Tutsi. They are therefore also exemplary of other instances of denial by those implicated in the genocide against the Tutsi.[5] The first Sections of this Chapter introduce the aforementioned organisations and discuss the documents authored by these organisations, on which the analysis throughout the rest of the Chapter relies.

In order to be able to address the official denial of the genocide against the Tutsi, *it is pertinent to analyse how the official genocide denial discourse of the abovementioned organisations is constructed.* In order to study such genocide denial "at work", the analysis will draw on insights from Laclau & Mouffe's discourse theory. The introduction to the official agents of denial is therefore followed by a discussion of the relevant dimensions of Laclau & Mouffe's discourse theory. Laclau & Mouffe's framework is particularly valuable in the context of this research for two reasons. Firstly, it provides for the theoretical notions that allow us to further ground how genocide denial functions and explain what action genocide denial speech performs. It therefore advances the analysis developed throughout the last Chapter. Secondly, it also provides for the necessary methodological tools to analyse concrete instances of genocide denial. Such tools are vital if one wants to study how exactly genocide denial operates in the context of the genocide against the Tutsi.

After having introduced the aforementioned organisations and after having clarified Laclau & Mouffe's discourse theoretical approach, *the Chapter discusses how the official denial discourse of the organisations is constructed by presenting a synthesis of their discourse and designating the major discursive elements used to construct the official denial.* Lastly, the Chapter will end with a reflection on the official denial discourse and some relevant discursive developments, such as the so-called "double genocide thesis," which is often featured in discourses that deny the genocide against the Tutsi.

4.2. Agents of genocide denial

The analysis of official denial that follows in later Sections of this Chapter is based on documentation authored by the abovementioned actors. Before a synthesis of their narrative in the wake of the genocide against the Tutsi is presented, the following Sections (4.2.1. – 4.2.3.) will first provide background information concerning these organisations and how they are related to each other.

4.2.1. The Rwandan Interim Government – *Le peuple rwandais accuse …*

On the 7th of April, after President Juvenal Habyarimana and also Prime Minister Agathe Uwilingiyimana had been assassinated, a military crisis committee under the

[5] See for example the work of Bagosora (1995), Nahimana (1996), Barayagwiza (1995), Ruggiu (1995), Karemera (2005), and Kintu (2005).

supervision of Colonel Théoneste Bagosora and General Augustin Ndindiliyimana was established in order to coordinate the country's security and defence until a new government could be created. The crisis committee already managed to install a new Rwandan Interim Government (RIG) on the 8th of April. Theodore Sindikubwabo became the new President and Jean Kambanda was nominated as Prime Minister (President of the Republic T. Sindikubwabo, 1994a; 1994b, p. 91; Rwandan Armed Forces Command in exile, 1995). The new RIG was officially presented on the 9th of April at the *Hôtel des Diplomates* in Kigali, where it had set up its office. However, as the Rwandan Patriotic Front (RPF) moved in on Kigali, the RIG was forced to leave Kigali and it established its new office on the 12th of April at a school in Murambi, which is located in the Gitarama prefecture. The advance of the RPF continued to make the situation more desperate for the new regime and on the 2nd of June the RIG started its evacuation to Muramba, which is located in the Gisenyi prefecture. Eventually, on the 14th of July, the RIG moved into exile in neighbouring Zaire (Congo). They were followed by the Rwandan Armed Forces (RAF), the militias, and large parts of the population (Melvern, 2006). On the 21st of September 1994, Agnès Ntamabyaliro, the exiled Minister of Justice of the RIG, wrote a letter to the United Nations Commission on Human Rights (UNCHR) in Geneva from Bukavu, Zaire. In the letter, she explained that she was writing on behalf of the RIG and that she has the honour to present the UNCHR with a document titled *Le peuple rwandais accuse ...* The document was drafted in order to help the international community to better understand what happened in Rwanda. In reality, the narrative of the RIG presented in the document *Le peuple rwandais accuse ...* is one of official denial by those who were responsible for the genocide against the Tutsi and blames the Tutsi for everything that has happened. To the outside world, the RIG also included opposition parties, but in reality they were mostly represented by their Hutu power elements. Although some positions were not taken by Hutu power extremists who were directly responsible for the genocide, none of them protested against what was happening or took adequate political measures to stop the genocide (Prunier, 1995). The Prime Minister of the RIG, Jean Kambanda, would reiterate much of the discourse presented in *Le peuple rwandais accuse ...* in a political memorandum which was sent to the President of Zambia on the 3rd of January 1995 (Kambanda, 1995).[6]

[6] As noticed in Chapter 1, Kambanda, would become the first head of state to plead guilty to genocide. He was sentenced to life in prison by the ICTR. However, two years after his "confession" Jean Kambanda would deny the crimes to which he had confessed. Agnès Ntamabyaliro, who was Minister of Justice in the RIG and who was later prosecuted for genocide, never pleaded guilty. Also, when I interviewed her in Kigali Central Prison, she kept referring to the political document *Le peuple rwandais accuse ...*, which according to her presented the real truth about what had happened in Rwanda.

Figure 4. Letter of Minister of Justice Agnes Ntamabyaliro to the United Nations Commission on Human Rights

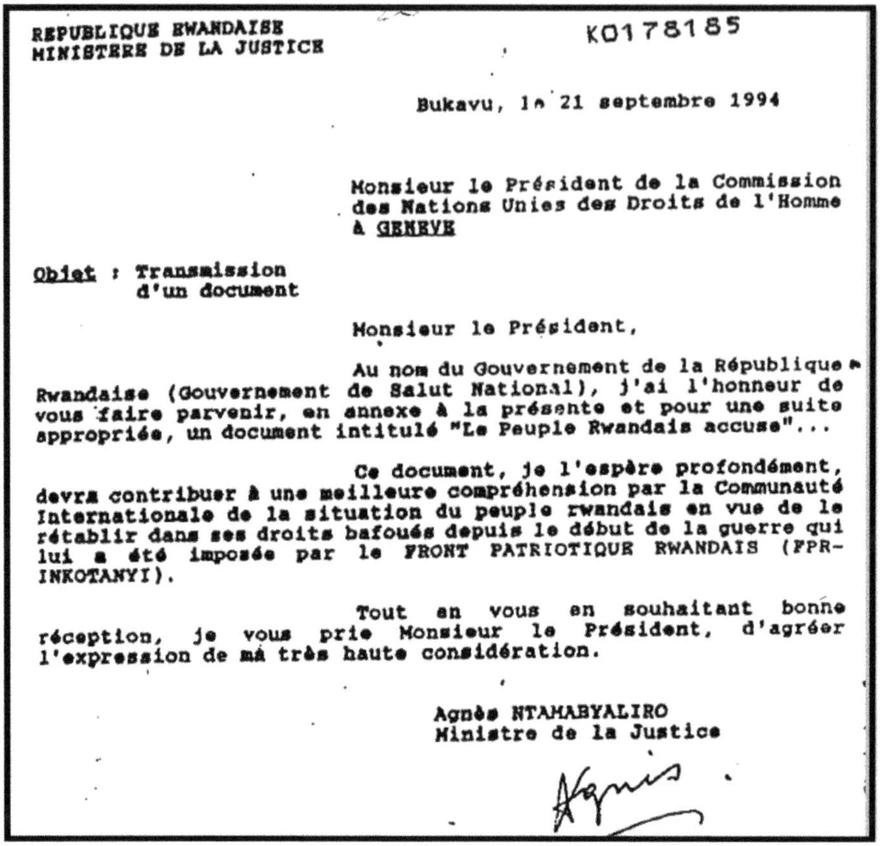

REPUBLIQUE RWANDAISE
MINISTERE DE LA JUSTICE

K0178185

Bukavu, le 21 septembre 1994

Monsieur le Président de la Commission des Nations Unies des Droits de l'Homme
à GENEVE

Objet : Transmission d'un document

Monsieur le Président,

Au nom du Gouvernement de la République Rwandaise (Gouvernement de Salut National), j'ai l'honneur de vous faire parvenir, en annexe à la présente et pour une suite appropriée, un document intitulé "Le Peuple Rwandais accuse"...

Ce document, je l'espère profondément, devra contribuer à une meilleure compréhension par la Communauté Internationale de la situation du peuple rwandais en vue de le rétablir dans ses droits bafoués depuis le début de la guerre qui lui a été imposée par le FRONT PATRIOTIQUE RWANDAIS (FPR-INKOTANYI).

Tout en vous en souhaitant bonne réception, je vous prie Monsieur le Président, d'agréer l'expression de ma très haute considération.

Agnès NTAMABYALIRO
Ministre de la Justice

From the 17th of July 1994 onwards, Jean Kambanda, Agnès Ntamabyaliro and other members of the RIG regularly met at the two major refugee camps in Goma (North Kivu) and Bukavu (South Kivu). Forced by the crisis situation, they discussed how to restructure the ministries and how to reorganise the finances of the RIG. Eventually, it was recognised that the RIG was a Government in Exile and plans were being discussed on how to best structure the organisation of such an exiled government. On the 1st of November 1994, a new Rwandan Government in Exile (RGE) was established, which in the end had only 7 of its initial 19 ministries left (Rwandan Government in Exile, 1994). The Government in Exile basically seized to exist in March 1995. At this point, a new "political" organisation, the *Rassemblement pour le Retour des Réfugiés et la Démocratie au Rwanda*, was established.

4.2.2. Rassemblement pour le Retour des Réfugiés et la Démocratie au Rwanda – *La vérité sur le drame rwandais*

Approximately one year after the assassination of President Juvenal Habyarimana, on the 3rd of April 1995, a new political organisation was created, named *Rassemblement pour le Retour des Réfugiés et la Démocratie au Rwanda* (RDR). The declaration of establishment of the RDR states that dialogue and negotiations are the best means to find a lasting solution to the Rwandan conflict. The declaration furthermore notes that the objectives of the organisation are to make possible the return of the refugees, to defend their interests, to fight for complete and impartial justice, and to contribute to making known the truth concerning the drama that happened to the Rwandan people. The RDR aspired to bring together all Rwandans who share these principles and objectives (Rassemblement pour le Retour des Réfugiés et la Démocratie au Rwanda, 1995). Although the RDR claimed to be an "autonomous and independent" organisation with apparently noble intentions, in reality, the RDR is closely related to the Rwandan Armed Forces (RAF) who were deeply involved in the genocide and, instead of noble intentions, it appears to have been driven by more questionable motives. The meeting at which the organisation was conceived was attended by officials of the RAF and also its umbrella committee lists several high ranked military personnel (Rwandan Armed Forces, 1995b). On the 4th of April 1995, the RAF issued a statement declaring their support to the RDR (Rwandan Armed Forces, 1995a). However, instead of only supporting the organisation, the RAF was actually instrumental in the establishment of the RDR as documentation of the meetings reveals. The documentation concerns a series of meetings held from the 29th of March to the 3rd of April 1995 and it provides insight as to why the RDR was created. The document states that "it was necessary to create a political organisation capable of mobilising means and ensuring unity among the population for concerted action." The organisation of such a political movement was "of the utmost concern for the RAF Commander and that is why he made contacts with refugee associations and even with the Government" (Rwandan Armed Forces, 1995b, p. 1).

The documentation elaborates on the "exchange of information" during the meeting, revealing more details as to why such a new political organisation was perceived to be necessary. It states that "interlocutors in Europe recommend a credible political organisation" and that "a solution must be found as regards the diplomatic isolation." Moreover, it was noticed that the "people have lost confidence in the Government" (Rwandan Armed Forces, 1995b, p. 1). This last issue was of great importance as the documentation continues to reveal. The document states that the decision to create a new political organisation was reached mainly because of three reasons, Firstly, "The government does not have an audience abroad, due to the embargo." Also, "[t]he government has not put in place mechanisms to liaise with the people and to safeguard unity." Thirdly, "[t]he people are worried about their confidence in the government being eroded" (Rwandan Armed Forces, 1995b, p. 2). The minutes of the meeting thus reveal that the RDR anticipated that the Rwandan Interim Government (RIG) and the national assembly would cease to operate once the Rwandan Patriotic Front (RPF) had won the war and gained support of the population and the international community. The RDR was thus created by the RAF and other extremist elements in order to bypass the embargo of the RIG, which, because of the embargo, was made politically ineffective and, as the document reveals, it would therefore probably soon seize to exist. In order to deal with this issue, a new organisation, the RDR, was created. The documentation reveals that in reality the power in the RDR lies with the so-called "umbrella committee," which is the "decision-making politico-military organ" comprised of members of the RDR executive committee, but more importantly of members of the RAF command structure.[7] However, by presenting itself as a refugee organisation, it could bypass the political embargo and engage again in political action. The organisation would fill the vacuum once the RIG would disintegrate.

That the RAF was indeed instrumental to the organisation of the RDR is revealed by the document that states that "The [Rwandan Armed Forces] lend their total support to the RDR. They are the military wing, and are represented on the umbrella committee" (Rwandan Armed Forces, 1995b, p. 8).[8] Interestingly, the document explains that, for "strategic purposes", the military has not signed the RDR declaration: "Although the RAF actively participated in the creation of the RDR, they must not sign the declaration on its establishment, for strategic reasons. However, the RAF will issue a statement of support for the RDR" (Rwandan Armed Forces, 1995b, p. 7). If the RAF had co-signed the declaration, it would have been quite obvious that the RDR was the political wing of the RAF and this would have immediately questioned the legitimacy of the RDR's objectives.

After its creation in the beginning of April 1995, the RDR suggested that units be established all over the world (Rwandan Armed Forces, 1995b, p. 5). One month after its establishment, in May 1995, the Cameroon Section published a booklet titled *La vérité sur le drame rwandais*. The booklet, like the abovementioned document presented by the RIG, claims to restore the balance of information (Rassemblement pour le Retour et la Démocratie au Rwanda Section Cameroun, 1995, p. 5). In June, 1996 the organisation published another document titled *United Nations Security Council misled about the presumed "Tutsi genocide" in Rwanda* (Rassemblement pour le Retour des Réfugiés et la Démocratie au Rwanda Cameroun Wing, 1996). This document is co-signed by Colonel Théoneste Bagosora and other officials of the RAF. This report entails the same denial narrative as also represented in earlier mentioned documents of the RIG and the RDR.

---

7 For further discussions of the RDR see: Ndahiro (2008, 2013), African Rights (2007), Terry (2002), Chrétien (2012) and Rafti (2004a, 2004b).

8 Kambanda (2013) in his book *Rwanda face à l'apocalypse de 1994. Contribution aux progrès de la justice et aux efforts de réconciliation du peuple rwandais*, also discusses the origins of the RDR and explains how the high political and military officials together cooperated in the establishment and running of the organisation as it replaced the government in exile.

Figure 5. RDR booklet published by the Section Cameroun

The RDR still exists, although it has changed its name and configuration. It changed its name to *Rassemblement Républicain pour la Démocratie au Rwanda.* On its official website www.rdrwanda.org, one used to find many of its founding documents, such as for instance the *RDR political platform* (Rassemblement pour le Retour des Réfugiés et la Démocratie au Rwanda, 1998). The headings of these documents, however, still carry the old name. On the surface, its name may have changed over time, but from the documentation presented on its website, its stance concerning what happened in Rwanda remained largely the same. Although its later publications appear to be more moderate, documents such as the *RDR political platform* that was published in 1998 and which sets out the beliefs and goals of the party still recycles much of the official denial that can be found in the abovementioned documents that were published shortly after the organisation was established. Over time, the RDR has also formed several coalitions and alliances with other political groups and parties. Most notably, in 2006 the RDR and several other parties created the United Democratic Forces (UDF) coalition and the RDR headquarters became the UDF headquarters; the address and P.O. Box remained the same. Victoire Ingabire, who was heading the organisation since 2000, was chosen as the President of the UDF political platform. Ingabire went to Rwanda in 2010 in order to participate in the elections on behalf of UDF but was arrested on several charges, including genocide denial. The outrage that her arrest caused indicates that the organisation is perceived by the public as a legitimate political opposition party.[9, 10] It therefore seems that, over time, the RDR has succeeded in its goal of being perceived as a moderate and legitimate political organisation. Note that Ingabire was nominated for the European Parliament Sakharov Prize for freedom of thought in 2012.[11]

4.2.3. The Rwandan Armed Forces – The search for the truth on the Rwandan tragedy

During meetings held in Goma from the 2nd until the 8th of September 1994, the high command of the Rwandan Armed Forces (RAF) discussed their plans for future action. Already during these meetings, they discussed the inadequacy of the Rwandan Interim Government (RIG) and the need for a more effective "politico military" organisation. The RAF was troubled by the inefficiency of the RIG (Rwandan Armed Forces High Command in exile, 1994, p. 5). It was cut off from the outside world and therefore unable to push its political agenda on its own people and the international public abroad. In order to remedy this situation, according to the RAF military high command, it was important that the population and (international) public opinion were sensitised to the cause. It was suggested that ideological documentation was drawn up and dispersed among the population by those departments who were responsible for its mobilisation (Rwandan Armed Forces High Command in exile, 1994, p. 13). RAF documentation furthermore reveals the plan that a media campaign should be organised to influence (international) public opinion in favour of the RAF by focusing on the crimes committed by the Rwandan Patriotic Front (RPF) (Rwandan Armed Forces High Command in exile, 1994, p. 32). To this end, relations with foreign news agencies were of critical importance.

---

9 Ingabire's arrest caused upheaval and she has been referred to as the "female Mandela" by, for instance, *San Francisco Bay Review* reporter Ann Garrison (2010).

10 In 1992 Jean Bosco Barayagwiza, together with other Hutu Power ideologues, cofounded a *comité d'initiative* in order to establish the *Radio Télévision Libre des Milles Collines* (RTLM), which, during the genocide, was responsible for some of the most virulent anti-Tutsi propaganda. Barayagwiza was also the co-founder of the extremist party *Coalition pour la Défence de la République* (CDR) and was one of the most outspoken Hutu Power ideologues. In 1995 during his exile in Cameroon Barayagwiza published the book Rwanda: *Le sang d'Hutu est-il rouge?* (Rwanda: Is Hutu blood red?). In his book Barayagwiza argued that the Tutsi-led RPF is responsible for what happened in Rwanda: they shot down the plane and destabilised the country in an effort to take over power. In the process they killed many Hutu in order to reduce their number for the Tutsi to become the majority people. According to Barayagwiza, the Tutsi committed genocide, not the Hutu. The first page of the book mentions several publications "*du meme auteur*" and lists among many other books also the co-authored volume *La vérité sur le drame rwandais*, which is one of the ideological RDR documents mentioned above. This example serves as an illustration of how extremist elements were linked to the RDR. During the media trial at the ICTR, Barayagwiza was prosecuted for his role in the genocide. Barayagwiza has been convicted for instigating and perpetrating genocide (Judgment and sentence of the prosecutor V. Ferdinand Nahimana; Jean-Bosco Barayagwiza; Hassan Ngeze; case No.ICTR-99-52-T, 28th November 2007).

11 See the website of the European Parliament: www.europarl.europa.eu/news/en/news-room/content/20120921FCS52015/6/html/More-about-this-year's-nominees. Furthermore in 2013 the European Parliament adopted a resolution condemning Ingabire's arrest, trial and incarceration. It criticises the political situation in Rwanda and accuses the government of using its legal framework as a political instrument to silence opposition (www.europarl.europa.eu/oeil/popups/summary.do?id=1269192&t=d&l=en).

According to RAF documentation, all possible measures were to be taken to make sure that "our journalists" were placed in these news agencies in order to establish lines of correspondence (Rwandan Armed Forces High Command in exile, 1994, p. 45). The document furthermore remarks that the press is a "double edged sword". It can help them to disperse their message and influence opinion in their favour, but it can also further stain their image. Therefore, the press is a "weapon" that should be "manipulated" with "circumspect, perceptiveness and caution" (Rwandan Armed Forces High Command in exile, 1994, p. 23).

Following their sensitisation offensive in December 1995, the command of the RAF in exile presented a report titled *Contribution of RAF to the search for the truth of the Rwandan tragedy* to the International Criminal Tribunal for Rwanda (ICTR) (Rwandan Armed Forces Command in exile, 1995). The introduction to the document states that:

> As an institution that directly confronted the RPF [Rwandan Patriotic Front] during the Rwandan conflict RAF cannot remain silent about the events that plunged Rwanda into bereavement from the outbreak to the war on 1 October 1990, and which degenerated into the disaster of April 1994.

Figure 6. Report by the RAF on the "Guerre" and the "Catastrophe"

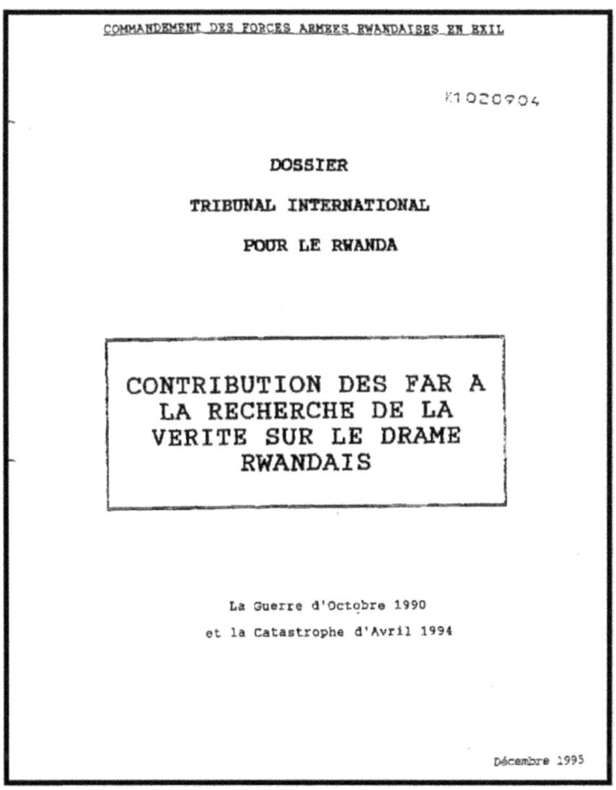

COMMANDEMENT DES FORCES ARMEES RWANDAISES EN EXIL

K1020904

DOSSIER

TRIBUNAL INTERNATIONAL

POUR LE RWANDA

CONTRIBUTION DES FAR A LA RECHERCHE DE LA VERITE SUR LE DRAME RWANDAIS

La Guerre d'Octobre 1990

et la Catastrophe d'Avril 1994

Décembre 1995

The document continues to state that the "RAF consider their opinion and contribution indispensable to the enlightenment of the International Criminal Tribunal for Rwanda" (Rwandan Armed Forces Command in exile, 1995, p. 4). To this end, the Rwandan Armed Forces accused the Rwandan Patriotic Front (RPF) of the following:

1. "Invading Rwanda from Uganda on 1 October 1990"
2. "Planning and executing the genocide of Hutu"
3. "Committing crimes against humanity, war crimes and crimes against peace"
4. "Assassinating President Juvenal Habyarimana"
5. "Causing the disaster of April 1994 by starting the war, interethnic massacres and the exodus of people and exposing them to epidemics"
6. "Destroying infrastructure, public and private property"

Taking into account the approach followed in the sensitisation campaign described above, it is not surprising that, in their report, the RAF focused on crimes allegedly perpetrated by the RPF. Although the report refers to a "contribution of the RAF to the search of truth," the document is designed to influence the situation in favour of the RAF and their cause. The RAF claimed to enlighten the ICTR concerning the truth of what had happened in Rwanda. However, as will become clear throughout the following Sections, the RAF's discourse is highly questionable in terms of denial. The document appears to do the exact opposite of what it intends to do, according to the title; instead of helping to reveal the truth about the events, it obscures what happened.

The following Sections will present a synthesis of all the above mentioned documents which represent the main sources for the official genocide denial discourse used in the analysis, resulting in what one could refer to as a blueprint or basic outline of the official genocide denial discourse. Although the synthesis is quite elaborate, it focuses on the main elements used by the aforementioned organisations in the discursive construction of their denial. As a result, the discourse of these organisations is not revealed in its entirety. Reproducing their discourse in its entirety would give it credit, while also running the risk of providing these parties with a platform. Those familiar with the abovementioned documents and the conflict they address (read "construct") could of course argue that, instead of piling lies upon lies, these documents also hold many truths. The documents, for instance, state facts concerning crimes committed by the RPF. Nobody can deny the fact that the RPF also committed gross human rights violations. However, one has to be careful here. As Krauss explains, there is a danger of conflating the genocide against the Tutsi with what happened during the war and its aftermath in Rwanda and Congo. He points out that, even when people have the best intentions, accounting for a sort of universal suffering of all these historical events can cut along the same lines as revisionism and denialism rhetoric (Krauss 2013, personal communication). The point concerning the documentation authored by the aforementioned organisations is, however, that although the documentation presents certain specific issues and elements concerning the conflict which might be correct these elements are not brought forward with the aim to reveal the reality of what happened; that is not the end of the discourse.[12] If there are facts contained in these documents, then they serve the construction of an official discourse that is bent on denying the genocide against the Tutsi. The question addressed in the following Section is how to analyse and deconstruct such a discourse.

4.3. A DISCOURSE THEORETICAL APPROACH

A powerful approach to analysing and understanding discourse has been developed by Ernesto Laclau & Chantal Mouffe (2001) in their book *Hegemony and socialist strategy: Towards a radical democratic politics*. In contrast to speech act theory, which helps us to reveal and explain some of the specific discursive practices used in order to engage in denial, discourse theory moves beyond isolated speech acts and focuses on entire discourses. Like speech act theory, discourse theory also takes as a vantage point that language is performative (or constitutive); language does not simply reflect an external reality, but it is through language that this reality is created (S. Taylor, 2001, p. 6; Wetherell, 2001, p. 15 and 16). Moreover, the conceptual elements of the discourse theoretical framework not only provide us with a better understanding of how discourses operate, they also provide useful methodological tools that are helpful in analysing how discourses are constructed. Although Laclau & Mouffe's work aimed to develop a critical democratic theory, various scholars indicate that Laclau & Mouffe's conceptual framework with regard to the analysis of discourse can be used creatively as a toolbox in other fields, such as media, cultural and political studies (Carpentier & De Cleen, 2007; Carpentier & Spinoy, 2008; Howarth & Stavrakakis, 2000; Leurs, 2009). Discourse theory is a powerful framework for analysis and it allows us to do what cultural criminologists see as a core exercise, namely to "interrogate" how crime, in this case genocide, is made into what it is by those who were implicated in it (Ferrell et al., 2008, p. 22).[13] I think that the concepts developed by Laclau & Mouffe can also serve as sensitising concepts for the study of genocide denial.[14]

---

12 The notions of reality and truth (and whether *an objective reality* or *the truth* actually exist) will be dealt with in greater detail in Chapter 7, Section 7.5., where I reflect on certain potential issues concerning the approach developed in this study. Especially, in the context of genocide denialism these are important issues that require clarification.

13 Although criminologists do not often utilise linguistic perspectives/approaches, it has been recognised that such approaches can yield valuable insights (Blommaert & Verfaillie, 2009). Content analysis has, for instance, been used in cultural criminological research. Although content analysis is useful to discern certain patterns in representation, it cannot capture the fluid dynamics of the symbolic construction of crime (Ferrell et al., 2008, p. 188). Moreover, the framework of content analysis is based on a referential or expressive function of language in which language is used to reflect on events (external realities) or feelings (internal realities) that exist outside language. It does not perceive language to be a social act and it is not based on the perspective of the constitutive function of language in which language actually constructs realities. The framework of content analysis is therefore not a very suitable approach for the purpose of this research. A more suitable linguistic approach for this study is therefore provided for by discourse theory.

14 For an explanation of the notion of sensitising concepts see Chapter 1, Section 1.6. For a more extensive elaboration see: Blumer (1969).

4.3.1. Reality?

As discussed in the previous Chapter (Section 3.4.) people's accounts determine meanings and thereby (re)negotiate reality (Buttney, 1985). The notion that language is performative, discussed earlier in the context of speech act theory, is also an important notion in discourse theoretical approaches. In speech act theory, performativity was discussed with regard to single words or sentences; in discourse theoretical approaches, performativity is connected to the idea that entire discourses perform social action. According to Jørgensen and Philips (2002, p. 9):

> Language, then, is not merely a channel through which information about underlying mental states and behaviour and facts about the world are communicated. On the contrary, language is a "machine" that generates, and as a result constitutes, the social world. [...] It means that changes in discourse are a means by which the social world is changed. Struggles at the discursive level take part in changing, as well as in reproducing, the social reality.

Language is thus functional to and constitutive of reality as it is designed to persuade and to change reality in certain ways (Wetherell, 2001, p. 17). However, the idea that all objects in the world are objects of discourse, as their meaning depends on a socially constructed system of meaning, has led to the critique that everything is reduced to language, which as a result creates scepticism about the existence of the world (Howarth & Stavrakakis, 2000, p. 4). The question is whether the idea that language is performative or constitutive indeed comes with an unbridled relativism. Is there nothing beyond spoken and written language?

Young (1988, p. 3) in his study on the issue of interpretative literary representations of the Holocaust also points to issues concerning such relativism: "[I]f Holocaust narrative is nothing but a system of signs merely referring to other signs, then where are the events themselves?" Young (1988, p. 3) points out that from such a perspective it would even be possible that "events and texts never existed outside each other and that all meanings of events created are in different representations are only relative." The point is however, as Graziano (1992, p. 1) explains, that "history consists not of events per se but rather of events under description, events that come to us in narrative form or are elaborated through narrative as a means of cognition." Laclau & Mouffe address this issue as follows in their discourse theory. They explain that, for instance, a stone indeed exists independently from discourse as a physical object and as such they do not question the existence of the world. However, they add that it is the discursive context/space in which the physical object (in our example a stone) is situated that determines its meaning and thereby its reality for us (Laclau & Mouffe, 2001, pp. X, 107 and 108). Thus, according to Laclau & Mouffe (2001, p. 108):

> An earthquake or the falling of a brick is an event that certainly exists, in the sense that it occurs here and now, independently of my will. But whether their specificity as objects

> is constructed in terms of "natural phenomena" or "expressions of the wrath of God" depends upon the structuring of a discursive field.

Following discourse theory there is nothing that intrinsically or naturally determines the reality of an object (Leurs, 2009). It is never only that material object; its reality is always discursively constructed by rendering it meaningful through interpretation (Jørgensen & Philips, 2002, p. 35; Torfing, 1999, p. 94). Therefore, Laclau & Mouffe (2001, p. 108) conclude that "[t]he fact that every object is constituted as an object of discourse has nothing to do with whether there is a world external to thought." As such, they acknowledge that "objects exist externally to thought", but they argue against the assertion that these objects "could constitute themselves as objects outside any discursive condition of emergence." As a result, "every object is constituted as an object of discourse" (Laclau & Mouffe, 2001, p. 107 and 108).

People are thus born into a world of meaningful discourses and they cannot conceive of objects outside of it (Howarth & Stavrakakis, 2000, p. 5). This also means that historical events do not naturally present themselves. They are also the result of discursive production rather than discursive representation, and such an awareness requires us to look into how such discursive construction works (Graziano, 1992, p. 2 and 3). With regard to war, Chilton (1997, p. 175) notes:

> [W]hat constitutes a legitimate concept of "war" can only be established in linguistic activity. [...] That is to say, wars would not be wars, in the sense in which late twentieth-century humans understand the term, unless certain verbal practices constituted the institution of war. From this follows an even more fundamental point concerning the relevance of language to war, or, rather, to the study of the problem of war: From the perspective of the constituting function of language, what is considered war is a product of history – a product of the beliefs, formal and informal laws, and customs of a particular period. This emphasizes the notion that war is a social invention, a fact created by an institution that takes certain actions and makes them a thing. The definition of war reflects the process by which the verbs to fight and to kill become nouns, the process by which the actions become an institutional fact.

Thus, from the perspective of the constitutive function of language, what we know as the concept of genocide, or as the genocide against the Tutsi, is constructed through discourse; it is the outcome of a process of social discursive construction. As Laclau & Mouffe explained, this does not mean that the event as such did not exist outside language, it did, but it is made intelligible to us through language. I understand that this approach to the world and its reality has serious implications as one could argue that it sets the stage for sophisticated forms of genocide denial. I will therefore address the implications of the framework at the end of this study in Chapter 7 when I reflect on various critical issues that follow from its application. For now, it is important to note that the discourse theoretical notion that discourse is constitutive of our reality provides us with an important insight concerning the action that genocide denial performs; it namely has the power to (re)construct our reality. The following Sections will continue to clarify what is meant with discourse, what the process of discursive construction entails and how denial has the power to change the reality of genocide.

4.3.2. Discourse, struggle and hegemony

Laclau & Mouffe follow the idea that through discourse people construct the world in meaning, but add the important insight that meaning can never be totally fixed. Instead, different discourses, which entail different ways of talking and of understanding the world, are in a constant struggle to try to fix meaning permanently in their particular way and thereby aim to achieve a dominant position (domination). Thus, there exists an order of discourse and this order is contested and (re)negotiated because multiple discourses strive to establish hegemony in the same domain (Jørgensen & Philips, 2002, p. 56). But why is it that meaning can never be totally fixed? Why is fixation of meaning only temporary?

Laclau & Mouffe's discourse theory is based on the notion that meaning systems are open systems that are in constant flux. This is due to the fact that there is always a surplus of meaning, which Laclau & Mouffe refer to as the field of discursivity and which provides for new and other ways of meaning creation (Laclau & Mouffe, 2001, p. 111). The field of discursivity is created when discourses try to fix a specific meaning by establishing a particular relationship among discursive elements called signifiers, while at the same time excluding other possible meanings (Jørgensen & Philips, 2002, p. 27; Torfing, 1999, p. 92). The system is thus open and in flux because the unity of meaning that a discourse has established by fixating meaning (closure) is in constant danger of being disrupted because there are also other (excluded) ways of establishing relationships between discursive elements. As such, one could argue that a discourse and the reality that it constructs are never safe against elements outside that particular discourse (Carpentier & De Cleen, 2007, p. 268). Laclau & Mouffe draw their inspiration from post-structuralist theory and the idea that meaning can never be totally fixed is more specifically based upon the deconstructionist Derridaen notion of the undecidable (Dapia, 2011; Laclau & Mouffe, 2001, p. XI). It is the dimension of structural undecidability that makes the abovementioned discursive hegemonic interventions possible (Laclau & Mouffe, 2001, p. XII). The insight that our reality is a discursive reality and that meaning can never be permanently fixed provides insight as to why even massive events such as genocide are vulnerable to language.[15] There is a constant threat that the reality of such events will be renegotiated. Genocide denial thrives on this undecidability and it allows those bent on denying the genocide against the Tutsi to engage in a discursive struggle. This struggle involves a hegemonic intervention which attempts to fix an alternative meaning concerning the events that took place in Rwanda. Thus

[15] Ndahiro had an interesting remark in this context. Concerning the methods of denial and their impact on reality, he noted that one can forge something as solid as steel, not only by heavy iron welding, but also by gently and consistently rubbing it. Although the reality of the genocide against the Tutsi seems to be solid and unbreakable as steel, it can be weakened, changed and eventually destroyed, by using less brute techniques, such as language. (Ndahiro 2014, personal communication).

they basically try to renegotiate the reality concerning the genocide against the Tutsi. But how does such (re)negotiation work? What does discursive struggle entail and what mechanisms are involved? These questions can be addressed by looking closer at Laclau & Mouffe's discourse theoretical approach to language and more particularly by looking at the mechanism of articulation, which is a central concept in their approach.

4.3.3. Articulation, elements, moments and nodal points

Laclau & Mouffe conceptualise discourse as a particular fixation of meaning that is the result of articulation, which is the practice of establishing a relationship among discursive elements or signifiers. A discourse according to Laclau & Mouffe (2001, pp. XII, 93 and 105) is thus "the structured totality resulting from an articulatory practice."[16] Signifiers include language in text and talk, but also visual communication, such as photo, fashion, architecture, etc. (Jørgensen & Philips, 2002, p. 30; Torfing, 2005, p. 14). What signifiers are therefore must thus be understood broadly and they are basically things that want to "say" or express something; things that carry meaning (Van den Berg, 2004a, p. 30). Signifiers do not have a single meaning (monosemic). In contrast, they are polysemic and their real meaning therefore remains ambiguous. Laclau & Mouffe (2001, p. 105) call these polysemic signifiers, whose meaning has not yet been fixed or articulated, elements. Polysemic signifiers or elements gain a particular meaning when they are related to other signifiers. The signifiers that are fixed in a discourse due to the established relationship between them (articulation) are called moments (Carpentier & Spee, 1999, p. 20; Jørgensen & Philips, 2002, p. 26; Laclau & Mouffe, 2001, p. 105). The following simple example will serve to clarify these abstract notions. The signifier "room" has many meanings and because of its over-determination; it is also called an empty signifier. It is empty of meaning because it overflows with meaning. The same counts for the signifier "class". These otherwise empty signifiers, which are devoid of meaning, because of the many meanings that can potentially be ascribed to them, gain a specific meaning by putting them in a relationship to each other. If one connects the signifier "class" with the signifier "room", the meaning becomes quite clear.

Laclau & Mouffe (2001, p. 112) furthermore indicate that discourses are constructed around or in relation to certain privileged signifiers which they call nodal points. The other signifiers in the discourse are ordered around these nodal points and they acquire meaning by how they are related to the nodal points (Carpentier & De Cleen, 2007, p. 268; Jørgensen & Philips, 2002, p. 26). Jørgensen and Philips, for instance, give the example of "the body" as a nodal point around which medical discourses are constructed. The concept of a nodal point draws on Lacan's idea of "point de capiton" (master signifier) and could be seen as a reference point in a discourse that

16 Discourse is an ambiguous term that has been defined in many different ways creating considerable conceptual confusion (S. Mills, 1997). Jørgensen & Philips (2002, p. 1 and 21) definition is simple but insightful. They define discourse as "a particular way of talking about and understanding the world" – "a socially constructed meaning system".

unites a particular system of meaning or constitutes the basis of discursive formation (chain of signification) (Carpentier & Spee, 1999, p. 21; Howarth & Stavrakakis, 2000, p. 8; Laclau & Mouffe, 2001, p. 112). Hoff (2000, p. 27) explains it as follows: "what discourses do is create 'islands of order' in a sea of chaos by stopping the flow of differences and constructing a centre." Nodal points, according to Hoff (2000, p. 27), serve as "knots of meaning" that tie together signifiers in a discourse. Therefore, based on the above discussion, one could argue that a discourse is a web- or netlike structure in which signifiers are related to each other (articulation) and it is their position (relation to other signifiers) that ultimately determines their meaning and the meaning of the broader discourse. What a discourse thus basically attempts to do by creating these relationships among signifiers is to transform elements into moments by reducing their polysemy to a fully fixed meaning, which is called closure (Jørgensen & Philips, 2002, p. 28). What the concept of articulation makes clear is that meaning is relational. As just explained, the meaning or identity of objects in the world can be constructed by putting them in a specific relationship.

The concept of articulation provides us with a better insight why discursive struggle exists. Articulation is possible because no discursive formation is a saturated totality and the transformation of elements into moments is never complete. The fixation of meaning (closure) is thus always threatened and always in the process of being restored. The dominant discourse on the genocide against the Tutsi has, by fixing its meaning in a particular way, excluded other ways of constructing the meaning of what happened. This dominant discourse on the genocide is however under a constant threat of being rearticulated. This "threat" is also constituted by legitimate work on the genocide. For instance, scholarly research contributes to new insights and understanding with regard to what took place and how it happened. Such insights also rearticulate the meaning of the genocide, but at the same time discursively help to construct and acknowledge its reality. However, in contrast to such scholarly endeavours, the dominant narrative is also threatened by those who are bent on denying the genocide. In order to complete the genocidal process, genocide deniers engage in a discursive struggle to redefine the reality of the events by rearticulating their meaning. They attempt to turn the genocide into a non-event. The genocidal violence thus also operates on a meta-level, resulting in a conflict about the conflict; a meta-conflict.[17]

The core notions underlying discourse theory set out above suggest that we study denials as particular expressions of articulation. By deconstructing how the official discourse of the organisation discussed earlier is articulated, we gain a better understanding of how the discourse is constructed. This requires an analysis of which signifiers they rely on and how they are related to each other.

[17] The notion that the denial involves violence that operates on a meta-level will be addressed in further detail at the end of the next Chapter in Section 5.6.

4.4. The discursive construction of official genocide denial – The Rwandan Tragedy

When analysing the documents published by the Rwandan Interim Government (RIG), the Rwandan Armed Forces (RAF) and the *Rassemblement pour le Retour des Réfugiés et la Démocratie au Rwanda* (RDR), it becomes clear that these organisations basically rely on the same set of signifiers to articulate what happened in Rwanda.[18] There might be some differences between the accounts provided for and the terminology used by these organisations, but in the end largely the same relationships are established and in doing so virtually the same meaning concerning the events that took place is being fixed. The main signifiers involved in their discursive construction of events include:

1. Lack of understanding.
2. Misleading media campaign.
3. Age-long interethnic conflict.
4. Contra-revolutionary and anti-democratic warfare.
5. Interethnic massacres.
6. Genocide against the Hutu.
7. International ramifications.
8. Equitable justice.

By relating these discursive elements to each other in the above order, a chain of signification is articulated and the meaning of these elements becomes temporarily fixed, turning them into discursive moments. As noted in the previous Sections, in the process of articulation, signifiers are organised around a master signifier, which is the nodal point in the discourse. What is furthermore important to understand is that such a nodal point or master signifier can become a floating signifier if multiple discourses struggle to fix its meaning in their own particular way (Laclau & Mouffe, 2001, p. 113). An element can thus be a nodal point in a specific discourse, while at the same time being a floating signifier in a discursive struggle between discourses (Jørgensen & Philips, 2002, p. 28 and 29). In discourses that struggle to fix the meaning of what happened in Rwanda, such as academic or public discourse, the denial discourse, or the official discourse of the current Government of Rwanda, the term "genocide" is the nodal point. It plays a central role in the structuring each of these discourses. However, because all of these discourses attempt to fix the meaning of the term "genocide" in their own particular way, "genocide" is also a floating signifier in the discursive struggle between these discourses. What can be observed furthermore is that in academic or public discourse that acknowledges the

18 The research of Fierens (2009), Mukimbiri (2013) and Chrétien (2012) also points out that denial discourses draw on a specific set of arguments. The authors list many of the arguments used, but they do not extensively analyse how the entire discourse is constructed. Nor is their analysis theoretically grounded. The elements are discussed separately, but what the analysis in this Chapter makes clear is that all these discursive elements are integrated into one coherent denial discourse. However, what makes Chrétien's and Fieren's analyses particularly interesting is that the official denial has been continuously facilitated by western actors, such as church institutions, refugee organisations, media outlets, who sympathised with the Hutu refugees or who provided a platform for the voice of extremism.

Tutsi genocide, phrases such as "Rwandan genocide" or "1994 Rwanda genocide" are often used as central and more specified signifiers around which the discourse is organised. However, although their discourse is constructed in relation to the controversial term "genocide", the RIG, the RAF and the RDR that deny that genocide took place in Rwanda tend to shy away from using the abovementioned phrases, which, because of their dominant meaning, can have self-incriminating implications. In order to break with the reality presented in these other dominant discourses, the aforementioned organisations rely on different terminology. In structuring their discourse, they prefer to use the euphemistic phrase "the Rwandan tragedy" because it does not have the dominant connotation as for instance terms such as "1994 Rwandan genocide" and, more importantly, because the term "tragedy" obscures the true nature of events. In the official documents of the aforementioned organisations, the genocide against the Tutsi is often also referred to as "the events," "the disaster," "a catastrophe," "apocalypse," "massacres," "crisis," in order to obscure the true nature of the violence unleashed upon the Tutsi population. The authors of these official denial narratives, thus, generally refrain from using the phrase "genocide". However, as will become clear in a later paragraph, when the phrase "genocide" is used, it tends to be placed between inverted commas or it is utilised to present the argument that instead of a genocide against the Tutsi a genocide against the Hutu has taken place. In these instances, the signifier "genocide" is related to the signifier "Hutu" to construct the meaning that the Hutu were the "real" victims of genocide and the Tutsi the "real" perpetrators.

Not only are the events articulated in academic, public discourse and denial discourse, also the official discourse of the current Government of Rwanda tries to fix the meaning of what happened in Rwanda in a particular way. Interestingly, one can observe that over time they also shied away from using phrases such as "Rwandan genocide" or "1994 Rwanda genocide" and instead they started to use the official phrase "the 1994 genocide against the Tutsi" (*jenoside yakorewe Abatutsi*), which since 2008 is also adopted in the constitution (Semujanga, 2013, p. 10). Phrases such as "Rwandan genocide" or "1994 Rwanda genocide" do not designate the victim group, making them prone to genocide denial as it could also be used in discourses that attempt to articulate that a genocide against the Hutu has taken place.[19] In Rwanda, they are very sensitive to vague terminology that could facilitate

19 The phrase "Rwandan genocide" is a confusing description of the events that took place because it does not clearly denote the victim group. The terminology namely implies that "Rwandans killed Rwandans." Hutu killed Tutsi and Tutsi killed Hutu; a "Rwandan genocide". The vagueness of the phrase makes it prone to genocide denial and the phrase frequently features in denialist discourses that attempt to articulate that two genocides took place. This is also more commonly referred to as the double genocide theory (Institute of Research and Dialogue for Peace, 2008, p. 89). The issue of vague and confusing terminology used to designate what happened also exist in Kinyarwanda. In Rwanda, there are several terms used to denote the genocide against the Tutsi. One is *itsembatsemba* and it means "massacres". This phrase, like the phrase "the Rwandan genocide", does not denote the victim of the genocide. Moreover, by referring to what happened as massacres, the true genocidal nature of what happened is obscured. Therefore, Rwandans also use terms, such as *itsembabwoko ry'Abatututsi, jenoside y'Abatutsi,* or *jenoside yakorewe Abatutsi*, which more specifically means genocide against the Tutsi (Fierens, 2009, p. 145). One could argue that the phrase "genocide against the Tutsi" is problematic because it obscures that during the genocide against the Tutsi, also Hutu were killed because they were

denial. This sensitivity became clear when I wrote to the Executive Secretary of the National Commission for the Fight Against Genocide (CNLG) in 2010 to "request [his] authorization to conduct research on the phenomenon of denial of the Rwandan Genocide." The Executive Secretary of the CNLG replied: "It is very important to analyse the phenomenon of denial of the "Rwandan Genocide" but I think the title has a problem: "Rwandan Genocide" or "Genocide against the Tutsi"?"

The following analysis addresses how the RIG, the RAF and the RDR articulate what exactly happened in Rwanda. The aim of the following analysis is to find out *what* meaning the aforementioned organisations try to fix with regard to what happened in Rwanda and *how* they do this. We will therefore look at the abovementioned set of signifiers more closely and analyse how they are articulated and related to each other.[20] Where appropriate, the analysis will be deepened by using insights gained in Chapter 3 concerning the rationalising techniques on which genocide denial often relies. What will become clear is that many of the discursive constructions actually involve rationalising practices, such as denial of the victim, appeal to higher loyalties and condemnation of the condemners.

4.4.1. Lack of understanding

On the 21st of September 1994, roughly two months after the Rwandan Patriotic Front (RPF) declared a unilateral ceasefire, the President of the United Nations Commission on Human Rights (UNCHR) in Geneva received a letter from Agnès Ntamabyaliro, the Minister of Justice of the Rwandan Interim Government (RIG). As pointed out above, the RIG governed Rwanda in the wake of the death of President Juvenal Habyarimana and during the genocide. She explains that she is writing on behalf of the RIG and that she has the honour to present a document titled *Le peuple rwandais accuse* ... She hopes that the document will contribute to a better understanding by

---

opposed to what was happening. The point is however that, as adviser to the Senate, Sosthène Cyitatire, explains: "*Il y a eu des Hutu qui sont morts, mais ces Hutu ne sont pas morts parce qu'ils étaient Hutu, ils sont morts parce qu'ils n'acceptaient pas d'agir contre les Tutsi. Il n'étaient pas d'accord que les Tutsi meurent*" (Quoted in Fierens, 2009, p. 146). The Tutsi perished in the genocide for who they were, while the Hutu were massacred because they were opposing it. This however does not diminish the individual suffering of these victims and their families. The acknowledgment of the genocide against the Tutsi should not lead to a denial of the suffering of Hutu who were killed because they opposed the regime. For a further discussion on the abovementioned terminology see: Moerland (2014a).

20 During the analysis of the official denial discourse, and although I do paraphrase, I often tend to stay close to the narrative of the aforementioned organisations resulting in the extensive use of excerpts of their narratives. I apply the same approach throughout the following Chapters. I understand that from a stylistic point of view this may not be considered less than ideal. One could argue that it is an intrinsic part of discourse analysis, but there are more pressing reasons for this approach. Firstly, the label genocide denial is serious and should not be applied lightly. Therefore, it is not enough to paraphrase narratives and indicate their denialist meaning. On the contrary, it is important to stay close to the speech, deconstruct it and show how it is problematic in terms of genocide denial. Secondly, only by staying close to the narrative and grounding the analysis in concrete excerpts it becomes clear to the reader what denial actually "looks like"; what words, sentence constructions, and discursive structures it entails. Otherwise it would remain too abstract. I think that staying close to the narrative of the aforementioned organisations enhances the reader's understanding of the phenomenon under study.

the international community of the situation of the Rwandan people in light of the restoration of their rights, which have been grossly disrespected since the beginning of the "war" that was "forced upon" them by the RPF (Ntamabyaliro, 1994a, p. 1). However, before analysing the document *Le peuple rwandais accuse ...* that the letter introduces, it is important to take a closer look at the cover letter itself because the denial already starts with how the letter frames the content of the attached document and how it presents those who it represents.

The letter presented the attached document as contributing to a better understanding by the international community of the situation of the Rwandan people. Thus, according to the RIG, the international community does not fully understand what happened in Rwanda. By making this claim, the cover letter creates legitimate space for the argument that the document presents in greater detail. This narrative construction allows those who were responsible for the genocide against the Tutsi to present themselves as victims of a conflict they did not choose. Moreover, the phrase "forced upon" has the connotation that they actually tried to avoid such a situation, instead of having instigated it. By implying that the international community misunderstands the current situation and by presenting themselves as victims and the RPF as aggressors, the cover letter attempts to control (or define) the situation; the letter confronts the addressee with an apparent lack of understanding concerning what happened in Rwanda and it is suggested that the report will provide a better understanding by presenting the voice of the supposed victims of the war. By pointing out the value of the document and by presenting the sender and those who the RIG is representing in a more favourable light, it is more likely that the document will be read and its content appreciated. The interim Minister obviously anticipated that her writings would arouse suspicion and, in this light, also the title of the document is remarkable. It draws on Emile Zola's open letter *J'Accuse*, that was printed in the newspaper *L'Aurore* in 1898 and which he had written to address the unlawful arrest of a French army officer named Alfred Dreyfus. According to Zola, the arrest was based on false accusations and represented a miscarriage of justice. If the investigation had been done properly, the evidence would have shown that Dreyfus was not the culprit. This is exactly the sentiment that the document being introduced by the interim Minister in her cover letter tries to evoke.

The documents produced by the RDR follow a similar tactic. The "Cameroon Section" or "wing" of the *Rassemblement pour le Retour des Réfugiés et la Démocratie au Rwanda* (RDR) started to disperse its documentation shortly after its establishment. In May 1995 it published a booklet titled *La vérité sur le drame rwandais* (Rassemblement pour le Retour et la Démocratie au Rwanda Section Cameroun, 1995). In its introduction, the booklet states that the Rwandan drama has received much attention, but it additionally presents the problem that the majority of the news coverage and testimony seems to have emanated from only one source. They originate from one party involved in the conflict; the RPF and its sympathisers or allies. It is furthermore explained that, in these representations, one party in the conflict is portrayed as the victim (the RPF and the Tutsi), while the other party (the RIG and the Hutu) has been manipulatively designated as the perpetrator. Therefore, the booklet proclaims the ambition to "restore the balance of information" that is provided to the public. The booklet claims to place the drama in its socio-historical context and it claims to address the profound causes of the conflict (Rassemblement pour le Retour et la Démocratie au Rwanda Section Cameroun, 1995, p. 5 and 6). In another document titled *United Nations Security Council misled about the presumed "Tutsi genocide" in Rwanda*, published in June 1996, the RDR questions the "lack of objectivity" of the report of UN Special Rapporteur on Rwanda, R. Degni Segui, of 28th of June 1994 in which it was concluded that, following the assassination of President Habyarimana, a genocide against the Tutsi had occurred (Rassemblement pour le Retour des Réfugiés et la Démocratie au Rwanda Cameroun Wing, 1996, p. 6). By arguing that the report was biased and not objective, the RDR has attempted to create legitimate space for the argument that it presents through the rest of its report. The appeals to objectivity are a common denial strategy and they thrive upon the idea that issues need to be approached objectively and that there is always another side to the story that also needs to be told. We also find this appeal to objectivity in the introduction to the Rwandan Armed Forces (RAF) report titled *Contribution of RAF to the search for the truth of the Rwandan tragedy* (Rwandan Armed Forces Command in exile, 1995). The introduction to the report states:

> The Rwandan tragedy has been the subject of books by many authors, who have adopted various viewpoints depending on their objectives and based on reports from human rights organizations, non-governmental organizations and the threadbare testimonies of people who were not directly involved in the Rwandan conflict. Thus, the international community was forced to swallow a version of events concocted and served up by RPF following the media embargo that was imposed on those persons that RPF had named "*génocidaires*". The absence of a juxtaposition of views did not allow the international community to consider the Rwandan tragedy in a calm and objective manner. (Rwandan Armed Forces Command in exile, 1995, p. 4)

The RAF report adds that "the ethnic massacres were deliberately termed genocide of the Tutsi at the hands of the Hutu in order to mislead public opinion and cover up the Hutu genocide" (Rwandan Armed Forces Command in Exile, 1995, p. 5). The above appeals to objectivity pervert the rationale underlying the notion why there can also be another side to the story. The rationale underlying this notion is that it facilitates getting to the truth, but the other side of the story is abused here to present a denial account that obscures the truth about the genocide.

In order to fix the meaning of what happened in Rwanda, these documents draw on signifiers, such as "a better understanding," "restore balance of information," "lack of objectivity," "absence of juxtaposing views," etc. which are related to the nodal point "Rwanda tragedy". The meaning that is created by such articulation is that what is known about the events in Rwanda follows the "RPF version of the events", which only represents the view of one party in the conflict. Following this discursive construction, a serious lack of understanding concerning what happened in Rwanda exists. What is furthermore significant is that the above articulation constructs a particular rhetorical vantage point which sets the stage from which the core of the denial discourse is subsequently presented. The discursive construction presented above is not so much about substantially redefining the reality of the event; instead the articulation involves what Goffman (1959) would refer to as impression management. It involves remedial work or face-saving techniques in order to avoid scepticism and critique from the people they are confronting with their denial. The aim is to create legitimate space for their argument, to increase its plausibility in order to have their accounts honoured. By using various defensive and protective measures, deniers thus try to control how others define them. They present themselves in a positive and empathetic light and they structure their action in such a way that it facilitates the message they are trying to convey. Hovannisian (1999a, pp. 205–228), for instance, points out that those who deny genocide often present themselves as the champions of truth, who are sincere and honest. This impression or identity management is also extended to their work, which they often try to give an objective or scientific look (Van Hennink, 1993). This strategy is combined with disclaimers that they do not want to distort history; on the contrary, they attempt "to overturn generations of faulty interpretations", which are only mystifications of what really happened (Golsan introductory notes to Finkielkraut, 1998, p. xxiii). We can see both these mechanisms "at work" in the above discursive articulations of the aforementioned organisations.

4.4.2. Misleading media campaign

The claim that what happened in Rwanda is not correctly portrayed is generally followed by the claim that this is due to propaganda of the Rwandan Patriotic Front (RPF), which supposedly has deliberately misrepresented the course of the conflict. For instance, in the introduction to the *Rassemblement pour le Retour des Réfugiés et la Démocratie au Rwanda* (RDR) document titled *United Nations Security Council misled about the presumed "Tutsi genocide" in Rwanda* it is stated that:

> [T]here is every reason to believe that the RPF first contacted the media and convinced them to provide media cover by spreading the RPF version of the events and playing down or completely ignoring the information furnished by their adversaries.

The document furthermore adds that "this explains why the international media unexpectedly took RPF propaganda for granted and dared to describe massacres that were committed in a single day, i.e. 7 April 1994, as 'genocide'." (Note the inverted commas.) The document concludes that "the use of the word 'genocide' was born of a campaign expertly orchestrated by the RPF and its allies to gain sympathy of the international community in a war they resumed and which they saw as a final solution" (Rassemblement pour le Retour des Réfugiés et la Démocratie au Rwanda Cameroun Wing, 1996, p. 4). The use of the phrase "final solution" to describe RPF action is significant. The aim of this RPF propaganda according to the document is to "forge a spirit of solidarity with the Tutsis throughout the world, while whipping up a sentiment of reprobation towards the Hutus" (Rassemblement pour le Retour des Réfugiés et la Démocratie au Rwanda Cameroun Wing, 1996, p. 5).

In the Rwandan Armed Forces (RAF) report written to "enlighten" the International Criminal Tribunal for Rwanda (ICTR), the RPF is also accused of a "misleading media campaign". According to the report, the "RPF inundated the world media with misleading information in a bid to legitimize its aggression" (Rwandan Armed Forces Command in exile, 1995, p. 9). The RAF (1995, p. 17 and 18) claims that from the outset, the strategy of the RPF consisted of stirring up ethnic unrest because they knew that the Tutsi group would eventually be the victims thereof:

> Its aim was to claim that it was a "genocide," that way it could set the international community against the Hutu and thus justify its attacks. [...] The RPF used genocide as a trump card in order to win support from the international community.

The RAF (1995, p. 24) furthermore states that:

> Public opinion was blinded, brainwashed and misled thanks to the sensational media campaign on the massacres of the Tutsis. It was claimed that all the dead bodies exposed by RPF were those of Tutsis killed by Hutu militia, whereas the civil war touched all the ethnic groups.

The notion that the civil war "touched" all the groups involved is interesting. In terms of denial, several important discursive acts are performed. Genocide is firstly reduced to a civil war, subsequently a notion of equal suffering is presented and thirdly, by making the civil war "touching" all groups, the responsible actor and the specificity of the victim group is obscured.

Thus, from the above discussion, it becomes clear that the general claim is that international opinion has deliberately covered up the truth of the situation (Ntamabyaliro, 1994b, p. 2). The discourse alleges that the lack of understanding concerning what happened in Rwanda is caused by the RPF and their allies who have disseminated the "RPF version" of "the Rwanda tragedy" which deliberately misled the public concerning "the truth" of the events. Its misleading information focussed on the "genocide" supposedly committed by the Hutu against the Tutsi. This way, according to the aforementioned organisations, the RPF was not only able to obscure its own crimes it also enabled the RPF to legitimise its own violence and to gain the sympathy of the international community. By relating the signifiers "sensational media campaign," "massive propaganda machine," "media trap," or "misleading information" to the signifier "lack of understanding" discussed above, the particular meaning of the nodal point "the Rwandan tragedy" becomes further delineated. The dominant or "official" version of what happened in Rwanda is being fixed as a misrepresentation due to propaganda and the suppression of other important information. It is essential to this discursive construction that the genocide against the Tutsi is not a reality but merely a propaganda ploy in a campaign expertly orchestrated by the RPF and its allies. By articulating the "genocide against the Tutsi" as a propaganda ploy, the Tutsi-led RPF is accused of lies and manipulation. These insinuations that the Tutsi misrepresent what happened to them, that they are liars, recycles some of the core ideas that are essential to the genocidal Hutu power ideology in which the Tutsi were portrayed as devious liars who could not be trusted. As noted before in Chapter 2, Section 2.4., the notion that the Tutsi are liars goes as far as back as 1959, when Joseph Gitera Habyarimana published the original Hutu Ten Commandments. In these Commandments, the Tutsi are presented as deceitful. The third commandment states "Never exchange ideas with a Tutsi; he is simply a liar by nature." The seventh states "Never tell lies like a Tutsi; denounce publicly his little schemes" (Quoted in Ndahiro, 2012). These original commandments were rewritten and revived by the extremist propaganda magazine *Kangura*. Rule number four of the Hutu Ten Commandments revived in *Kangura*, for instance, stated: "Every Muhutu should know that every Mututsi is dishonest in business. His only aim is the supremacy of his ethnic group." The above denial construction thus taps directly into certain notions that are central to the ideology underlying the genocide. What the aforementioned organisations engage in is basically the rationalising practice of condemning the condemners. By drawing on this practice, the deniers shift and deflect the attention away from their own criminal acts to the crimes the Tutsi-led RPF has supposedly perpetrated. Although condemnation of the condemners at this point serves to create a favourable rhetorical vantage point, as discussed earlier, it will become clear that this practice of accusing those who accuse you is part and parcel of the official denial discourse and ultimately results in a denial of the victim.

The first step in the discursive construction was to create a favourable rhetorical vantage point entailing that people have greatly misunderstood the events, which therefore require a better understanding. This raises the question what "really" happened in Rwanda. The second step in the construction of the denial discourse addresses this question. The RIG, the RAF and the RDR extend the chain of signification and continue to articulate what according to them happened in Rwanda. To deny that the genocide against the Tutsi took place, the discourse of these organisations first addresses the supposed "root causes" underlying the conflict.

4.4.3. Age-long interethnic conflict

In the document *Le peuple rwandais accuse ...*, published by the Rwandan Interim Government (RIG), it is stated that the "interethnic conflict" underlying the "current tragic situation" can be found in Rwanda's remote history (Ntamabyaliro, 1994b, p. 1). The document briefly elaborates on Rwanda's conflict history stating that the country was first inhabited by the "Twa pygmoides", followed by the "Hutu bantous" and only "much later" by the "Tutsi hamites" (Ntamabyaliro, 1994b, p. 1). The document attributes the origins of the interethnic conflict to the time when the Hutu ruled the country, they were "conquered by the Tutsi" who invaded the country much later and who gradually took over the country's institutions turning the Hutu into serfs (Ntamabyaliro, 1994b, p. 1). The booklet *La vérité sur le drame rwandais* published by the *Rassemblement pour le Retour des Réfugiés et la Démocratie au Rwanda* (RDR) also follows the argument that an age long interethnic conflict is the profound cause underlying what happened in Rwanda (Rassemblement pour le Retour et la Démocratie au Rwanda Section Cameroun, 1995, p. 7). In their reaction to the report of the Special Rapporteur Degni Segui, the RDR (1996, p. 7) furthermore argues that the Rapporteur is not familiar with "the social, political and historic realities of Rwanda," because "[o]therwise, he would have noted that those massacres had always stemmed from extremism, arrogance and murderous provocation by certain members of the Tutsi population." The meaning of the nodal point "Rwandan tragedy" is thus further elaborated by relating it to the element of "age long interethnic conflict". The exact meaning of the signifier "age long interethnic conflict" is subsequently delineated by presenting the Tutsi as the root cause of this conflict. What becomes clear from the articulation by the aforementioned organisations discussed above is that it again involves the practice of condemning the condemners, as the Tutsi are accused of being the "root cause" of the "age long interethnic conflict."

The construction of the Tutsi as the root cause relies on the following two discursive elements: "alien invaders" and "oppressors". Firstly, it is argued that the Tutsi came from abroad and conquered power; they are presented as alien invaders. They supposedly invaded Rwanda at a time when the Hutu ruled Rwanda and they had settled there long before the Tutsi arrived. Secondly, it is claimed that the Tutsi, who constitute the minority, oppressed the majority of the population, which were Hutu. The Tutsi are thus also presented as oppressors. This construction of the Tutsi as the "root cause" underlying the conflict is an essential part of the discursive process by which the Tutsi are constructed as the "real perpetrators," and the Hutu as the "real victims." The two discursive elements ("alien invaders" and "oppressors") are central to the denial narrative because the discussed documents frame "the *current* tragic situation" in more or less these same terms. With the start of the civil war in 1990, the Tutsi, who attacked Rwanda from Uganda, are again presented as invading the country to take over power; they are thus engaging in the same action that caused the conflict in the first place. Furthermore, the notion that the "majority people" were oppressed is related to the idea that the attack of the Tutsi in 1990 was a counter-revolutionary and anti-democratic attack which aimed to destroy everything the Hutu had realised after they emancipated themselves from Tutsi rule. "Invasion" and "oppression" serve as key signifiers in constructing both the meaning of the "root cause" underlying the "age long interethnic conflict" and the "Rwandan tragedy". With the articulation of the Hutu as the "real" victims and the Tutsi as the "real" perpetrators, the practice of condemning the condemners conflates with the practice of denial of the victim. By putting the Tutsi at the root of all the terrible events that happened, they become the origin of the conflict to follow for which the aforementioned organisations and the Hutu population are thus not responsible (denial of responsibility); they did not start it; on the contrary, it was "forced upon them."

4.4.4. Contra-revolutionary and anti-democratic warfare

Following the documentation discussed above, the conflict between Hutu and Tutsi thus already started long ago and, according to the document of the Rwandan Interim Government (RIG) titled *Le peuple rwandais accuse ...*, it was in that particular situation of interethnic conflict that the coloniser and missionaries arrived (Ntamabyaliro, 1994b, p. 1). The "coloniser helped the Tutsi to complete the conquest of the whole country", while the "missionaries trained the children of the Tutsi masters for their succession." The document explains that at the same time some of the Hutu also benefited from the level of education that the Tutsi received. Later these "Hutu intellectuals reclaimed the rights" of the Rwandan people which had been "confiscated by the feudal masters." In this context the document refers to the Bahutu Manifesto, which was published in 1957 by Gitera and eight other Hutu intellectuals, or *évolués* as they were called by the Belgians. One of the intellectuals included Kayibanda, who would become the president of the first Republic of Rwanda. The manifesto highlighted the "social aspect of the racial problem" and it demanded that the reforms which would liberate the "Muhutu population" which had been subjected to the "Hamite monopoly on other races which had inhabited the country earlier and in greater numbers." Although in the document *Le peuple rwandais accuse ...* the conflict is framed as inter-ethnic conflict, the ideological documents, such as the manifesto, however reveal that it is not about ethnicity but race. This manifesto was of major importance to the Hutu emancipation movement and it assisted in creating the political foundation of the genocide. Here again the relationship between ideology and denial is clear; in its narrative construction of the interethnic conflict it draws on the genocidal racial ideology. The denial that is found in these documents is thus also an elaboration of their ideological narrative.

Le peuple rwandais accuse ... continues to argue that the reclamation of the rights of the Rwandan people eventually led to a revolution and the constitution of a democratic republic. According to the document, the flow of events was caused by the Tutsi who opposed Hutu claims for emancipation and democracy. It states that the monarch of that period and his entourage reacted brutally to the demands of the Hutu who had nothing to claim from the Tutsi. This tense situation inevitably led to the revolution of 1959, which according to the document "restored the freedom and equality amongst Rwandan citizens" and introduced "democracy as the basis of the Republic", which was proclaimed on 28th of January 1961 (Ntamabyaliro, 1994b, p. 1). A similar narrative can be found in the *Rassemblement pour le Retour des Réfugiés et la Démocratie au Rwanda* (RDR) booklet *La vérité sur le drame rwandais*, which also states that Tutsi hegemony ended in 1959, when they were driven out of power by a social revolution. Since then, the Tutsi monarchy has been replaced by a republic (Rassemblement pour le Retour et la Démocratie au Rwanda Section Cameroun, 1995, p. 7).

What happened in 1959 is presented in the narrative of the RIG, the RDR and RAF as a true social revolution that emancipated and empowered the "Rwandan people". However, what actually happened was not truly revolutionary, as it only empowered the Hutu and drastically marginalised the Tutsi. The phrases "Democracy" and "Rwandan people" have obtained a particular connotation. Democracy is namely interpreted as meaning that the majority rules, thereby consolidating the power of the Hutu. When the documents refer to the "Rwandan people," they mean the majority people, the Hutu population. The democratic revolution was not about the rule of law and safeguarding the rights of others, such as the Tutsi or Twa minorities. The Hutu intellectuals who led the "revolution" (ab)used democracy to install and legitimise their dominance. In contrast, the discursive relationships that are created in the documents present the Hutu as an oppressed majority people who fought for freedom and democracy, while presenting the Tutsi as the oppressor, who were (and still are) against emancipation and democracy. This antagonistic relationship serves to further fix the meaning of the Tutsi as the "root cause" underlying the conflict. Interestingly, on several occasions the documents accuse the Tutsi and the RPF of eliminating the Hutu in order to create a numerical Tutsi majority so that they could rule the country.

The documentation of the RIG explains that, after the Tutsi were driven out of power by the revolution, "the enemies of democracy" went into exile and organised attacks against the young Rwandan Republic in order to regain power by force. The last of these "invasions" took place in 1967. From that moment onwards, the "enemies of the democracy" decided to lay low in order to better organise and equip themselves with the aim of re-conquering power by force in Rwanda. This has been "attempted since the 1st of October 1990" by the "sons of those refugees known under the name RPF-Inkotanyi" (Ntamabyaliro, 1994b, p. 1). The RDR booklet *La vérité sur le drame rwandais* adds that the Tutsi did not succeed because at that time they were not able to find "foreign powers" who were determined to reinstate them in power (Rassemblement pour le Retour et la Démocratie au Rwanda Section Cameroun, 1995, p. 7 and 8). According to the RDR (1995, p. 7 and 8), the conflict between the Hutu and Tutsi flared up again with the start of the war in October 1990 by the "sons of the feudal Tutsi".

In the above Sections, the meaning of the signifier Tutsi, who were initially signified as "invaders" and "oppressors", is further articulated as a people who do not accept the social revolution and who are "enemies of democracy." The invasions of the Tutsi refugees are articulated as part of a contra-revolutionary and anti-democratic campaign that has never stopped. The war that started with the invasion on the 1st of October 1990 by the offspring of the initial refugees is presented as a continuation of this contra-revolutionary and anti-democratic campaign. The RDR (1995, p. 11) concludes that "there is no doubt that they want the power, all the power for them alone." The RAF presents a similar picture. It argues that the RPF invoked two reasons for their invasion: "the return of the refugees and the democratisation of Rwanda". However, according to the RAF (1995, p. 9), "In reality, what the RPF [...] wanted was absolute power. The return of the refugees and democratisation were simply a ploy aimed at misleading public opinion". Again, the RAF (1995, p. 6) concludes that the Tutsi and the RPF are the root cause of the Rwandan tragedy.

The above articulation strengthens the condemnation of the Tutsi and continues to present them as perpetrators (denial of the victim). What is furthermore significant is that the violence against the Tutsi is presented as an act of defence against the invading former "feudal masters" in order to protect their "newly obtained social rights and privileges". The Tutsi are being fought in order to defend the social revolution and democracy. In doing so, the violence is being rationalised by appealing to higher loyalties. As will become clear throughout the following Sections, the element of "self-defence" that is introduced here will play an important role in articulating the violence that the Hutu perpetrated against the Tutsi.

The attacks by the Tutsi-led RPF are thus presented as part of a contra-revolutionary and anti-democratic war that has never stopped and continued with the invasion of the 1st of October 1990 by the offspring of the initial refugees. According to the RAF and the RIG, the aim of the invasions was to undo the social revolution, to overthrow democracy and to reinstall Tutsi power. The Tutsi are thus presented as aggressors who constitute a continuous threat to democracy and the Hutu people. The idea that the 1990 attacks were organised and led by the "sons" of the first Tutsi refugees is telling as it indicates that innocent children can grow up and become serious threats to Rwandan society. This narrative reveals much about the underlying intention of the violence, which also targeted pregnant Tutsi women and their children. In how Hutu ideologues had presented the conflict, these innocent women, babies and children posed an imminent threat – that is "what history had shown". To deal with such a threat once and for all, genocide was required.

4.4.5. Interethnic massacres

The Rwandan Interim Government (RIG), the *Rassemblement pour le Retour des Réfugiés et la Démocratie au Rwanda* (RDR) and the Rwandan Armed Forces (RAF) "acknowledge" that massacres happened since the war started in 1990 and that the massacres drastically increased after the assassination of the president in 1994. It is thus "recognized" that Tutsi and Hutu were victimised. The problem is however that the abovementioned organisations question the nature of the "inter-ethnic violence" that the Tutsi befell. The official discourse of the abovementioned organisations namely refutes that the violence amounted to a genocide against the Tutsi. The RDR (1996, p. 37) states that the "interethnic massacres" that followed the assassination of the president were "not planned" but "[t]hey ensued from the ethnic cleavages generated by the murderous attacks launched by the RPF over a period of 4 years against a civil population in disarray." According to the RDR (1995, p. 21), the assassination of the President of the Republic which came on top of the massive offensive of the RPF, ignites the whole country culminating in inter-ethnic massacres at an unprecedented scale. With regard to the causes of "the Rwandan tragedy" in 1994, the RAF (1995, p. 14) states that it "was caused by the war that RPF imposed on the people of Rwanda". The RAF (1995, p. 5) argues that "[t]he massacres of April to July were simply the end-result or culmination of the war" and they add that "the Tutsi were killed as a consequence of the civil war started by those who attacked Rwanda and assassinated President Habyarimana, and not an intent or general plan of the Hutu to decimate the Tutsi." The RAF continues to explain that "[f]or the RPF, the ethnic massacres were deliberately termed genocide of the Tutsi at the hands of the Hutu in order to mislead public opinion and cover up the Hutu genocide" (Rwandan Armed Forces Command in exile, 1995, p. 5). The war and assassination of the president "led to a popular uprising and a wave of massacres throughout the country" (Rwandan Armed Forces Command in exile, 1995, p. 105). The start of the war, the violation of the ceasefire and peace agreement, the massacres of Hutu, the assassination of Hutu politicians including the president, "those were all factors that caused a great deal of suffering amongst the people and forced them to defend themselves out of despair" (Rwandan Armed Forces Command in exile, 1995, p. 17). According to this discursive construction, the massacres that happened in Rwanda after the assassination of the president were not a genocide against the Tutsi; instead the violence against the Tutsi is articulated as self-defence of a Hutu population which saw itself confronted with a treacherous enemy that they had to counter. By articulating that the war was "imposed" on the "people of Rwanda" it becomes clear they were provoked and the action undertaken was a necessity.[21]

In addition to the causes listed above, the RDR lists several additional "causes" of the violence perpetrated against the Tutsi (Rassemblement pour le Retour et la Démocratie au Rwanda Section Cameroun, 1995, p. 25). They mention the unconditional Tutsi support of the RPF. It is reiterated that the massacres are the consequence of the conflict between the two ethnic groups that already exists for centuries and which resurfaced with the start of the war in October 1990 by the RPF (Rassemblement pour le Retour et la Démocratie au Rwanda Section Cameroun, 1995, p. 23). The "demons of hate between Hutu and Tutsi" are stirred up as the Tutsi became more sympathetic to the RPF, while they engaged in selective massacres during their offensives. The RDR also notes that the Tutsi were proud to have their children in the ranks of the RPF rebels (Rassemblement pour le Retour et la Démocratie au Rwanda Section Cameroun, 1995, p. 24). The RDR furthermore points out the arrogant and triumphal attitude of the Tutsi as a cause of the massacres. The booklet states that when the RPF battalion was stationed in Kigali, Tutsi from all over the country came to salute what they called their heroes and liberators (Rassemblement pour le Retour et la Démocratie au Rwanda Section Cameroun, 1995, p. 24). The Tutsi cheered at every RPF achievement and they provoked the Hutu (Rwandan Armed Forces Command in exile, 1995, p. 17). Thus, due to their "arrogance," their "triumphal attitude," and their "unconditional support" to the RPF, the Tutsi provoked the Hutu; they were responsible for their own victimisation.[22] The denial of the victim is thereby elaborated. The aforementioned organisations often refer to the violence perpetrated by the Tutsi-led RPF and not the Tutsi as a people, as such; however, the above paragraph makes clear that the RPF as a politico militant refugee organisation are equated with the Tutsi people. Not only is the Tutsi-led RPF presented as a threat

21 It is crucial to understand that the genocide did not happen spontaneously. The state did not simply disintegrate after the President's plane was shot down. Instead, as Clark (2006, p. 93) states, "the genocide resulted from the active planning of high state officials and not from the 'failure' of the Rwandan state." It was orchestrated. This however does not mean that the actions of the RPF did not have any negative impact on the situation. The hardship that the RPF invasion and the civil war created was cleverly used by the Hutu extremists to demonise the Tutsi population. It made it much easier for the extremists to instil fear of the RPF and the Tutsi in general, who were presented as the RPF's fifth column.

22 This part of the booklet really ties in with the earlier discussed Hutu Ten Commandments and the racist stereotypes concerning the Tutsi.

to the entire Hutu population, but because the Tutsi population supported the cause of the RPF they are depicted as collaborates; they present a fifth column that is bent on undermining the majority Hutu group. Moreover, the articulations discussed earlier present the Tutsi as the root cause of the conflict.

The documents further fix the meaning or nature of the contra-revolutionary and anti-democratic warfare of the RPF by stipulating that they were anything but spontaneous actions. In the document *La peuple rwandais accuse* ..., the RIG indicates that the attacks by the RPF were organised; they followed a certain plan. The document states that the "catastrophic situation" in which the Rwandan people find themselves since the start of the war to re-conquer power in Rwanda of the 1st of October in general, and more particularly since the vile assassination of President Habyarimana on the 6th of April 1994, is the "diabolical work of the RPF-Inkotanyi" (Ntamabyaliro, 1994b, p. 2). One can find a similar discursive representation of events in documentation of the RAF. The RAF argues that the "President's assassination was carefully planned by RPF" and the "RPF killed the president in order to clear the way to seizing power" (Rwandan Armed Forces Command in exile, 1995, p. 8 and 10). The discourse thus claims that the actions of the RPF followed a plan and the assassination of the president is presented as a central element of the RPF's plan to take over power. The argument that the RPF attacks followed a plan is contrasted with the argument that for those who are accused of the genocide against the Tutsi, "it was impossible to plan the 'Tutsi genocide'" (Rassemblement pour le Retour des Réfugiés et la Démocratie au Rwanda Cameroun Wing, 1996, p. 6). The "clues" which indicate that the genocide was planned, according to the RDR, do "not indicate any seriousness". The RDR generally claims that these issues were nothing exceptional or extraordinary, taking into account that the country was in a "state of war," for which the RPF was to blame in the first place (Rassemblement pour le Retour des Réfugiés et la Démocratie au Rwanda Cameroun Wing, 1996, pp. 12–14). In a subsequent paragraph titled "the inexistence of 'Tutsi genocide' in Rwanda", the RDR argues that there is no doubt that "massacres were perpetrated in Rwanda," but in contrast to what most people think, "those massacres had not been programmed" and also in these massacres "the Tutsi ethnic group was not targeted as such." Thus the RDR (1996, p. 16) concludes that "[c]riminal acts were committed in Rwanda without any intent to destroy, in whole or in part, the Tutsi group. What happened in Rwanda cannot be qualified as 'Tutsi genocide', but rather as 'interethnic massacres'." Thus, according to the RDR (1996, p. 6), "the 'Tutsi genocide' in Rwanda was an alibi or a trump card used to gain power finally, with the approval of the International Community."

In contrast to the generally accepted idea that Hutu extremists planned and executed a genocide against the Tutsi, the passages above allege that what happened was not a planned genocide against the Tutsi but a spontaneous interethnic massacre caused by the RPF's planned war effort. According to this ideology, the crimes committed by the Hutu against the Tutsi were therefore not planned; they happened spontaneously. It is acknowledged that the Tutsi were victimised in "interethnic" violence, but they were not victimised in a genocide; their genocidal victimhood is denied. In doing so, the aforementioned organisations acknowledge that they are perpetrators of justifiable "interethnic" violence (they were forced to act as they did) and they thereby automatically deny that they are *génocidaires*. As the next Section will clarify, in an ultimate denial of the victim, the Tutsi are subsequently presented as the "real" perpetrators of a genocide perpetrated against the Hutu.

4.4.6. Genocide against the Hutu

The idea that the "alien invaders" were highly organised is elaborated by the Rwandan Interim Government (RIG), the Rwandan Armed Forces (RAF) and the *Rassemblement pour le Retour des Réfugiés et la Démocratie au Rwanda* (RDR) to the extent that the only ones who were organised and worked according to a diabolical plan were the Tutsi who attacked the country. This argument culminates in the claim that, instead of a genocide against the Tutsi, it was the RPF who planned, organised and executed a genocide against the Hutu. The RAF (1995, p. 104), for instance, states that:

> Some people confuse the organization of popular self-defence in Rwanda with the organization of massacres or genocide. It is time to clear the air. [...] From the outbreak of war, RPF attacked defenceless Hutu civilians, apparently for the simple reason that they were hostile to it, but in fact to implement its plan for the genocide of the Hutus.

The RAF (1995, p. 16) furthermore adds that the "RPF steadfastly carried out its plan consisting in the genocide of the Hutus, with the view to establish a numerical Hutu-to-Tutsi balance and end the 'myth of the majority Hutu ethnic group'." In a letter to the Zairean Ministry of Defence, Commander Gratien Kabiligi stated that therefore it is also unacceptable to argue that the killings by the RPF were done in revenge. Instead, they planned the "methodological elimination of Hutu populations" (Letter from Gratien Kabiligi to the Defense Minister fo Zaire, "*Memorandum relatif au drame rwandais*", Goma, 25th of June, 1995 quoted in Terry, 2002, p. 167). The RIG (1994b, p. 2) also argues that "in their determination to re-conquer power by force in Rwanda, the RPF has made itself guilty of reprehensible crimes". These crimes committed by the RPF more particularly involve violations of international law which have been defined by the Nuremberg Tribunal and confirmed by the United Nations in 1945 (Ntamabyaliro, 1994b, p. 2 and 3). The RIG document subsequently addresses the particular criminal acts the RPF has committed, which include crimes against peace, war crimes, crimes against humanity, but also genocide. According to the RIG, with its "act of genocide", the RPF targeted "Hutu in general" and "the members of the MRND and CDR [political] parties."[23] It also targeted "those who qualified as Hutu Power or Hutu extremists" and "those who resisted the RPF." It is eventually concluded that "everywhere it passed, the RPF systematically decimated the entire population which presumed to answer to these criteria" (Ntamabyaliro,

[23] The MRND was the political party headed by Habyarimana and is an abbreviation for *Mouvement Républicain National pour la Démocratie et le Développement.*

1994b, p. 7). Following the signification of the violence against the Tutsi as spontaneous self-defence and not a planned genocide, it is articulated that the actions of the Tutsi-led RPF were meticulously planned. Moreover, their plan is signified as genocidal and the Tutsi-led RPF is thus articulated as the *génocidaires*.

According to the RIG, the RPF was "created in order to kill" and since its inception it has done nothing else but that, also today (Ntamabyaliro, 1994b, p. 10). The RAF (1995, p. 7 emphasis added) point out that that "RPF's practice has always been to hide the bodies of the people it kills in order to cover up the crime, and whenever exposed, it justifies itself cunningly misleading the public and masking *its true genocidal nature*." According to the RAF (1995, p. 6 and 47), the RPF is a criminal organisation:

> For RPF, the objective is to conquer the country, kill as many Rwandans as possible and subjugate the remaining few, and destroy all development works that bring honour to the Habyarimana regime. All this means that RPF has never been an army for the liberation of the people, but a tool to conquer a country and surreptitiously annex it to Uganda. RAF, on the contrary, facing many attacks from RPF, have always acted as a real army of the Rwandan people who, today, trust and esteem their army.

In contrast to the RPF, the RAF are presented as an organisation which did everything to prevent and stop the suffering; the "RAF were seeking peace and were not on the warpath" (Rwandan Armed Forces Command in exile, 1995, p. 6). This discursive construction strengthens the idea that the Tutsi-led RPF are the "real" perpetrators not "simply" by signifying that they perpetrated a genocide against the Hutu, but by signifying that the *raison d'être* of the organisation is to annihilate the Hutu people.

The idea of genocide against the Hutu can already be found in propaganda that was dissimulated shortly after the RPF invaded the country in October 1990. In a remarkable document titled *Toute la vérité sur la guerre d'octobre 1990 au Rwanda*, which was published by *l'Association des Femmes Parlementaires pour la Défense de Droit de la Mère et d'Enfant*, much of the discursive construction discussed can be discerned. Throughout the leaflet, the general Tutsi population and the Tutsi-led RPF are systematically conflated. The war is presented as a quest by the Tutsi and the RPF to overthrow the democratic government, install a Tutsi monarchy and to perpetrate a genocide against the Hutu (Association des Femmes Parlementaires pour la Défense de Droit de la Mère et d'Enfant, 1991).

Figure 7. AFEPADEM propaganda in collaboration with Léon Mugesera on "Toute la vérité sur la guerre"

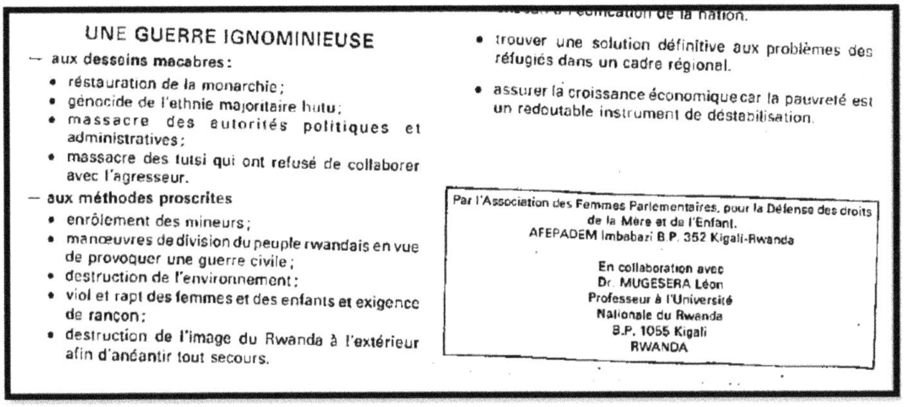

UNE GUERRE IGNOMINIEUSE

— aux desseins macabres:
- réstauration de la monarchie;
- génocide de l'ethnie majoritaire hutu;
- massacre des autorités politiques et administratives;
- massacre des tutsi qui ont refusé de collaborer avec l'agresseur.

— aux méthodes proscrites
- enrôlement des mineurs;
- manœuvres de division du peuple rwandais en vue de provoquer une guerre civile;
- destruction de l'environnement;
- viol et rapt des femmes et des enfants et exigence de rançon;
- destruction de l'image du Rwanda à l'extérieur afin d'anéantir tout secours.

... de la nation.
- trouver une solution définitive aux problèmes des réfugiés dans un cadre régional.
- assurer la croissance économique car la pauvreté est un redoutable instrument de déstabilisation.

Par l'Association des Femmes Parlementaires, pour la Défense des droits de la Mère et de l'Enfant.
AFEPADEM Imbabazi B.P. 352 Kigali-Rwanda

En collaboration avec
Dr. MUGESERA Léon
Professeur à l'Université
Nationale du Rwanda
B.P. 1055 Kigali
RWANDA

A salient detail is that the document was created in collaboration with Professor Leon Mugesera, who would later become infamous for an inflammatory speech given in 1992 at Kabaya in which he incited violence against the Tutsi population by stating the following:

> Recently, I told someone who came to brag to me that he belonged to the P.L. – I told him "The mistake we made in 1959, when I was still a child, is to let you leave". I asked him if he had not heard of the story of the Falashas, who returned home to Israel from Ethiopia? He replied that he knew nothing about it! I told him "So don't you know how to listen or read? I am telling you that your home is in Ethiopia, that we will send you by the Nyabarongo so you can get there quickly. (Supreme Court of Canada, 2005)

The Nyabarongo River is not navigable, so Mugesera did not mean that the Tutsi would leave by boat. In earlier pogroms, Tutsi victims had also been thrown into the river. During the extermination phase of the genocide, countless Tutsi bodies were dumped in the Nyabarongo River in order for them to go "home." Mugesera ended his speech by "reminding" his audience of "all the important things" he just spoke about:

> The most essential is that we should not allow ourselves to be invaded, lest the very persons who are collapsing take away some of you. Do not be afraid, know that anyone whose neck you do not cut is the one who will cut your neck. Let me tell you, these people should begin leaving while there is still time and go and live with their people, or even go to the "Inyenzis", instead of living among us and keeping their guns, so that when we are asleep they can shoot us. (Supreme Court of Canada, 2005)

Numbers game

The articulation discussed above in which the victim is being denied is elaborated with the rationalising practice of denial of injury, by playing down the numbers of Tutsi perished. In their attempt to fix the meaning of what happened, the RDR and RAF thus enter a numbers game. In order to further articulate "the Rwandan tragedy" with the meaning that a genocide against the Hutu took place, it is furthermore argued that more Hutu than Tutsi were victimised in the violence. The RDR (1996, p. 8), for instance, criticises the Special Rapporteur for the victimisation rates used in his report to the United Nations (UN): "Before advancing imaginary figures and imposing the lax theory of 'Tutsi genocide', the Security Council ought to have effectively ascertained the exact number of victims from each ethnic group." This critique of victimisation rates is further developed into the argument that the correct figures show that "many more Hutu than Tutsi were massacred" (Rwandan Armed Forces Command in exile, 1995, p. 5). It is argued that in the end approximately 2,000,000 people were killed during the inter-ethnic violence and sources indicate that between 200,000 and 500,000 Tutsi and moderate Hutu were killed by Hutu extremists. The rest of the victims thus supposedly consists of Hutu who were killed and tortured by the RPF since the start of the war and during its last general offensive after the assassination of the President (Rassemblement pour le Retour et la Démocratie au Rwanda Section Cameroun, 1995, p. 21). Although those who deny the genocide engage in a numbers game in order to inverse the role of the victim and the perpetrator, it is important to notice that the number of people killed is actually not a constitutive element of genocide. The number of people killed is basically irrelevant in order to determine whether genocide is happening or not. Instead, what matters is the intention underlying the victimisation and not how many people were victimised. As discussed earlier, genocidal techniques involve much more than killing. By fiddling with numbers, deniers try to show that there are (as many or even) more Hutu victims of the RPF than Tutsi victims of the genocidal government. According to André Sibomana:

> They are trying to outbid each other; they want the number of people killed by the RPF to be on a level with the people killed during the genocide, to restore a kind of equality. [...] It's totally absurd. Deaths don't compensate each other; they don't cancel each other out; they simply add up. (Sibomana quoted in Waldorf, 2009, p. 106)

The documentation subsequently insinuates that the violent advance of the RPF left the remaining population no other choice but to flee their country and go into exile. The RDR explains that, in contrast to the allegations of certain Western sources susceptible to RPF propaganda, the exodus was thus not orchestrated by the Hutu who had called upon the people to leave the country, instead it was the RPF who forced them to leave and who kept them deliberately in exile (Rassemblement pour le Retour et la Démocratie au Rwanda Section Cameroun, 1995, p. 40). According to the RAF (1995, p. 11), the genocide continued once the people fled went into exile: "As RPF was sure of victory, its strategy being to drive the Hutus out of the country and exterminate them." Particularly, the massacres committed by the RPF in camp Kibeho are presented as evidence that the RPF perpetrated a genocide against the Hutu. This discursive construction is significant, because it does not limit the genocide against the Hutu to the period of 1990 to 1994. On the contrary, the organisations articulate that the genocide against the Hutu continued when the population went into exile; it is an ongoing phenomenon. Furthermore, if one takes the earlier signification of the Tutsi-led RPF as a genocidal organisation into account, then it becomes clear that all the earlier actions from the 1960ies onwards are also perceived as acts of genocide perpetrated against the Hutu.

4.4.7. International ramifications

According to the abovementioned authorities, the Tutsi-led Rwandan Patriotic Front (RPF) is thus considered to be responsible for a war and a genocide waged against the Hutu and, although in the inter-ethnic violence also Tutsi perished, the RPF's violence resulted in far more Hutu casualties. However, in addition the Rwandan Interim Government (RIG) (1994b, p. 2) indicates that the RPF received substantial assistance from several African and Western powers: it was a "diabolical plan of the RPF with the massive support of certain interested super powers." The RPF might be principally responsible for what happened, however it is not the only one responsible for "the Rwandan tragedy."

According to the Rwandan Armed Forces (RAF) (1995, p. 11), the people of Rwanda were the victims of "the superpowers fight for domination":

> Although the RPF wanted to seize power, in a sense, it helped further the plan of certain superpowers for a presence in the heart of Africa to enable them to not only have easy control over the rest of the continent but also to spread their culture and influence. The RPF readily conspired with them, because they had a common goal. The uncalled-for defence of RPF's interests by the United States and Anglo–Saxon presence in Rwanda speak for themselves.

The RAF (1995, p. 7) furthermore states that:

> In view of the strong support that RPF enjoys in certain countries, RAF and Rwandan exiles suspect a conspiracy by these states to obliterate the greatness of Rwanda, which was hitherto a haven of peace and a beacon of national unity.

"The Rwandan tragedy" thus has "international ramifications" as "[c]ertain countries did not hesitate to participate in the war on RPF's side (training, logistical support, recruitment, financial support, rear bases, media support, reinforcements). By their reactions and decisions, others were overtly pro-RPF. They sinned by omission" (Rwandan Armed Forces Command in exile, 1995, p. 53). The signifier "perpetrator" is thus further articulated in the official denial discourse to include states such as Uganda, the United States, the United Kingdom and Belgium, and international organisations, such as the United Nations and its UNAMIR. The following paragraphs will reveal how the criminal role of these "perpetrators" is articulated by the aforementioned organisations.

Uganda

According to the RAF, RDR and the RIG, these countries helped to prepare and wage the war, conspired with the RPF to assassinate President Habyarimana and helped to perpetrate the genocide of the Hutu. They facilitated the cause of the RPF to take over power, because it allowed the Western powers to expand their sphere of influence. With regard to Uganda, it is argued that President Museveni participated because he saw it as an opportunity to consolidate the power of the Tutsi. The RAF (1995, p. 60) elaborates that:

> Ugandan President, Yoweri Museveni, bears a great deal of responsibility for the Rwandan tragedy. In a bid to realise his hegemonic plan of creating a Hima-Tutsi empire in the Great Lakes region, he prepared and oversaw the execution of the attack on Rwanda and all the ensuing crimes.

Therefore, the Western imperial quest is not the only conspiracy; there was apparently also a plan among the Tutsi to create a vast Tutsi empire.

Belgium

The RAF (1995, pp. 54–65), the RIG (1994b, pp. 14–16) and the RDR (1995, p. 19) furthermore accuse the Belgian United Nations Assistance Mission for Rwanda (UNAMIR) contingent's participation in the attack on President Habyarimana, which took place on 6 April 1994, the planning and execution of the genocide and the war. Moreover, the RIG (1994b, p. 16) points out that Belgian UNAMIR soldiers "did not help those who were in danger". It is suggested that at the moment that Rwanda plunged into an unjust war started by an overwhelming enemy that demolished everything in its path, the hard pressed Rwandan people were obliged to have recourse to a legitimate defence by all possible means. Instead of mediating the situation in order to avoid the worst, the Belgians recalled their UNAMIR contingent and evacuated their nationals. Although this last passage discusses the role of Belgium, the discursive construction also serves to convey the notion that what the Hutu did was justified and therefore legitimate. According to the official denial discourse, the Hutu had their backs against the wall and, having exhausted every other option to prevent the situation, they were forced to engage in spontaneous defensive action using all available means. The Hutu were forced to defend themselves but not only because the war was unjust or the enemy was superiorly equipped destroying everything it encountered; the Hutu were also forced to defend themselves because other powers, such as the Belgians, did not take appropriate action. The "inaction" of the Belgians is thus used to support the argument of a justified and legitimate defence.

United States

In addition to accusing the United States (US) of not helping those in need, The RIG (1994b, p. 16) accuses the US government of "complicity with the RPF", because at the moment the RPF resumed its hostilities against Rwanda, the US administration developed the idea, which was presented at the Security Council, to stop the resistance efforts undertaken by the Rwandan people by "imposing a military embargo" in order to "facilitate the victory of the RPF" (See also RDR 1995, p. 19). The RIG accuses the US of being part of "the conspiracy of operation *soutenir l'espoir"*. This operation reduced the direct aid to the refugees in exile, by focussing on providing aid to the national territory of Rwanda, which had been abandoned by its population as the RPF rapidly conquered Rwanda. According to the RIG (1994b, p. 17), the US devised this "strategy" which would help to "put the Rwandan people under the yoke of the RPF". The documents thus extend the conspiracy by uncovering a US imperial plan which facilitated the RPF plan to commit genocide against the Hutu. The RIG (1994b, p. 16) furthermore claims that RPF cadres were trained at US institutions and, according to the RAF (1995, p. 67), the US provided the RPF with technical, media and political support.

United Nations Assistance Mission to Rwanda

The RAF, the RDR and the RIG also hold the United Nations (UN) and its Assistance Mission to Rwanda (UNAMIR) responsible for what happened. The RAF (1995, p. 53) conclude that:

> The international community has a huge burden of responsibility for the events which plunged Rwanda into mourning. [...] During the ensuing tragedy, UNAMIR pulled out of the country as soon as the situation became more involved. The international community therefore failed to face up to its responsibilities. While the war was raging and preventing the security forces from re-establishing peace, it was unwilling to accept a ceasefire that would have enabled [RAF] to free up forces for the restoration and maintenance of law and order. On the contrary, it was quick to impose a unilateral embargo on the new Government, while it was defending itself, whereas RPF, the aggressor, continued to acquire arms at will through Uganda; it thus helped RFT to easy military victory.

The RIG (1994b, p. 2) argues that after the effort put into "the struggle to defend their sovereignty," the Rwandan people were driven from their national territory into exile, partly because "the international community decided to break their resistance efforts by ordering a military embargo against them" while on the other hand "the RPF intensified its massacres against the Rwandan people day by day". According to the RIG, the UN has become a "system of influence" of the West and more particularly the Unites States and, as a result, it adopted all projects proposed by these super powers. The UN and its UNAMIR allegedly had become imperial tools and the US and other Western powers used these organisations to actively support the RPF in order to extend their sphere of influence in francophone countries (Ntamabyaliro, 1994b, p. 16). According to the RIG (1994b, p. 18), the UN is also complicit in the crimes the RPF committed. It did not take all the necessary measures to realise the implementation of the Arusha Peace Agreements, which was the only pillar of peace for the Rwandan people. The RIG (1994b, p. 18) furthermore claims that its assistance mission, UNAMIR, has furthermore denied justice to the Rwandan people by not inquiring into the assassinations of people that occurred in the demilitarised zone and Kigali city for which it was responsible. It also did not start an inquiry into the assassination of the president which was perpetrated at the airport in Kanombe for which they were responsible. The claim that the UN and UNAMIR did not attempt to clear up the crimes committed is an interesting discursive element because it implies that such an investigation would reveal that the RPF and its Western allies were involved in the perpetration of these crimes. According to this narrative, the investigations were not undertaken by these actors because they would have turned out to be self-incriminating. The RAF (1995, p. 53) suggests that with the attack of the 6th of April 1994, the international community became an accomplice in the assassination of the Hutu presidents of Rwanda and Burundi and, even today, it appears disinterested in identifying those responsible for the said assassinations. The point is, according to the RIG (1994b, p. 2), that the truth concerning the events in Rwanda has been deliberately covered up to serve the aforementioned imperial interests.

What is significant in the above articulations is that, in contrast to the generally accepted view that the genocide against the Tutsi could occur because Western states and the international community stood by and did not undertake action,[24] the discourse of the RIG, the RDR and the RAF presents Western states and the international community as engaging in action supporting the RPF's war and its genocide against the Hutu because a RPF victory would allow these powers to expand their spheres of influence. In this context, it is furthermore interesting to notice that, although the "West" is being accused of being intimately involved in the genocidal conflict, the official denial discourse does not refer to the role played by France. France supported the Habyarimana regime politically and militarily. Its role in the war and the genocide against the Tutsi remains controversial (De Saint-Exupéry, 2009; Kroslak, 2007; Republic of Rwanda, 2007; Wallis, 2007).[25]

---

24 As noted earlier in Chapter 3, Section 3.3.1, the notion of "bystanding" is problematic in this context because it is not the case that the US and other states did nothing. In reality they actively avoided their responsibility. In this context Mwenda (2014) makes some interesting observations: "Yet the 'world' actually intervened in Rwanda in 1994; the UN having deployed a multinational peacekeeping force called the United Nations Assistance Mission to Rwanda (UNAMIR) drawn from 21 countries. If you visited Rwanda in the first months of 1994, there was not a single piece of ground in that country not occupied by UN peacekeepers. People used to joke that you cannot spit without spitting at a UN soldier or their APC. The UN Peace Keeping Operations intervened in January to stop a planned attack on ammunition stores for genocide. The Security Council intervened again in April 1994 to withdraw its troops. The story of genocide in Rwanda is not one of failure to intervene, but the failure of the intervention. Indeed, this massive presence of UN troops explains to a considerable degree why the genocide enjoyed such stunning success. Endangered Tutsi civilians, seeing UN troops everywhere and trusting in the promises of the international community stayed put thinking they were secure. When the genocide started and the UN forces pulled out, it was too late for them to escape."

25 For an extensive analysis of France's involvement see the work of Morel (2014). His book counts over 1,500 pages and is made freely available online at: www.francerwandagenocide.org.

4.4.8. Equitable justice

The last step in the discursive construction of the official denial discourse entails a call to help and reveal the truth about these events and to prosecute and punish the "real" perpetrators. To this end, the Rwandan Interim Government (RIG) (1994b, p. 19) asks the international community and all benevolent people to do everything in their power to "re-establish the truth" by all available means. The RIG (1994b, p. 19), furthermore, notes that sociological and historical research should take place before legal investigations take place. The phrase to "re-establish the truth" is telling, as it implies that the truth as we know it has been tampered with; it has been obscured and covered up by propaganda according to the articulation discussed above. The claim that sociological and historical inquiry should precede any legal inquiry is even more intriguing as the historical and sociological explanation of the conflict provided for in the document of the Interim Government attributes the conflict to the Tutsi and the RPF. Sociological and historical inquiry provides for opportunities to reconstruct the history of the conflict in their favour. It creates legitimate space and it allows those who attempt to deny the genocide to present the event as a misunderstood conflict for which the RPF and the Tutsi are primarily responsible and of which they are the "real victims." If they manage to establish *their truth* of the events as the truth, then this has, of course, far-reaching implications for any subsequent legal inquiry. Interestingly, former Chief Prosecutor at the International Criminal Tribunal for Rwanda (ICTR), Richard Goldstone (2005), noted that at the beginning he was "visited by serious historians and professors from universities, particularly from Belgium and France, who told [him] that the stories of genocide were untrue."

The RIG (1994b, p. 19) furthermore urges that the Rwandan people are being rehabilitated in their rights and it more particularly states that all the possibilities should be considered for rendering equitable justice by punishing the "real culprits" and rehabilitating those who are "innocent" (See also RDR 1995, pp. 56, 57 and 59). The fixation of the "real culprits" and the "innocent" warrants a sophisticated discursive construction, because it cannot be denied that the RAF, the presidential guard, the Interahamwe and ordinary Hutu peasants did victimise Tutsi. Literal or factual denial of the violence against the Tutsi is untenable taking into account the evidence concerning their victimisation. As a result, the denial discourse is more sophisticated. As explained above, the official denial discourse holds that the massacres that occurred have an "interethnic character" and therefore both parties in the conflict are implicated. Both parties have perpetrated crimes, while at the same time also being victimised. The discourse therefore does not try to fix the meaning of the "perpetrator" or the "culprit", but of the "genuine" or "real perpetrator." For instance, with regard to who are "really responsible" for "the Rwandan tragedy", the RDR (1996, p. 34 Emphasis added) states that:

> The massacres in Rwanda are a result of ethnic divisions [...] so the *real culprits* are individuals or bodies corporate who were responsible for the policy that led to the ethnic cleavage. [...] It emerges from this analysis that contrary to widespread belief, the inter-ethnic massacres, intentionally confounded with the "Tutsi genocide", were not conducted

> by the MRND *Interahamwe*. They were rather sparked off by the political and ethnic cleavages caused by the war waged and sustained by the [Rwandan Patriotic Front (RPF)] since 1 October 1990.

The combination of the two abovementioned discursive elements constructs the RPF and the Tutsi as the "real culprits" or "real perpetrators" and the Hutu as the "real victims" or the "innocent". Both groups have been implicated in the conflict, which means that both have perpetrated crimes and both have been victimised, but, looking at the root cause of the conflict, the "real perpetrators" are the RPF and the Tutsi, while the "real victims" are the Hutu. The notion that the Hutu are the "real victims" is, of course, even further strengthened, by the earlier discussed claim that the RPF committed a genocide against the Hutu. Interestingly, the RAF (1995, p. 107) argues that:

> The international community should consider this matter without preconceived notions, neutrally and objectively, and take a final decision to provide a peace and sustainable solution to the Rwandan question. [...] The RAF support a fair and impartial investigation to establish the truth and identify those responsible.

However, for the RAF (1995, p. 6), like for the RDR and the Interim Government, it is quite clear who is responsible for what happened:

> Indeed, as the invading force, RPF is the root cause of the Rwandan tragedy. RAF are of the view that RPF must be prosecuted for the Hutu genocide and for the other war crimes and crimes against humanity it committed in Rwanda during the war and the ones it continues to commit up to the present day.

The above calls for truth and equitable justice also involve criticism towards the ICTR, drawing on the rationalisation of condemning the condemners. The RAF (1995, p. 7), for instance, states that (See also RDR 1996, p. 12):

> The truth on the Rwandan tragedy must be established without melodrama and emotiveness. Those who are responsible for the Hutu genocide must be prosecuted without leniency, or fear of ruffling RPF's allies or the manifestly biased UN Security Council. The diktat of certain super-powers, of which the Rwandan people were victims, should not weigh on the International Tribunal for Rwanda. The Forces Armées rwandaises support an independent, fair and impartial International Tribunal for Rwanda. They believe that no one should be made a scapegoat simply because the real culprits have not been identified, as it is up to every individual to answer for his criminal acts.

The ICTR is presented as a tribunal which, because of the political influence of certain superpowers, judges only one party in the conflict, which has been made a scapegoat. The tribunal is thus not impartial. Furthermore, the victorious party in the conflict, the Tutsi-led RPF, is not being prosecuted for the crimes they have committed. Justice at the ICTR therefore not only lacks impartiality, it is victor's justice. Moreover, the RDR (1995, p. 67) criticised the ICTR for violating fundamental fair trial rights in its prosecution of cases, such as the presumption of innocence; people are arrested without a legitimate warrant. Therefore, according these parties, it is not only victor's justice, its victor's injustice. The Prime Minister of the RIG, Jean Kambanda (1995), wrote in a political memorandum that:

> [The ICTR] would only be a parody of justice, a platform for revenge, which would leave numerous crimes in impunity and condemn only the innocent ones for political and/or ethnic reasons. The arbitrary arrests and the summary executions that the RPF has perpetrated can obviously testify to this.

In addition to calls for "equitable justice", the RDR and the RAF also call for dialogue and reconciliation. According to the RAF (1995, p. 107), the solution to the problems lies in "dialogue", because dispute is "a historical problem between two ethnic groups that are one people, and who must live together." The RDR (1995, p. 71 and 72) points out that the RPF must accept dialogue and negotiations and the RPF must stop denouncing a whole people as murderers. It should abandon its theory of the "good" and the "bad" and it should engage in a sincere process of national reconciliation between all Rwandans who, despite everything, have to live together on the same territory. The war and the "interethnic massacres" have left every Rwandan citizen in sorrow. Or, as the RAF (1995, p. 24) argued, "the civil war touched all the ethnic groups". These calls for dialogue and reconciliation, which are necessary to address the problems underlying the conflict, focus on the future; both groups have suffered, but they live together again. The idea that all Rwandans have suffered, however, obscures the specific nature of the crimes perpetrated against them. Fierens (2009, p. 66) points out that such dialogue and reconciliation, in order to unify a people, can take dangerous forms in terms of denial: "*Au regard des événements des 1994, parler de 'commune culpabilité' peut paraître à tout le moins déplacé et ouvrir la porte aux arguments négationnistes.*" For instance in a report that, according to its authors Gasana and Nsegimana (1997), "aims at submitting analyses for a vision of Rwanda's society, making proposals for national reconstruction, monitoring the state of human rights and civil liberties, and creating a forum for debate and civic action." It is stated that "More than three years after the April-July 94 government that led Hutu extremists in the awful sin of genocide against Tutsis, their Tutsi successors committed an equally awful sin of genocide against the Hutus." Ntakirutimana (2013, p. 53) refers to this as *accusations symétriques* and he refers to an issue of a journal in which an author argued that:

> *La réconciliation est l'affaire de nous tous: Je ne suis pas d'accord avec ceux qui dissent que les Hutu ont tué les Tutsi vu qu'il y a des Tutsi qui ont tué les Hutu; cela veut dire que les rwandais se sont entretués.*[26]

[26] In this example, killing is used; it covers up the true nature of the violence that occurred. Sometimes equality is reached by advocating that all parties suffered genocide. See for instance Le Rwanda ou l'urgence politique, rapport de Mission by Francois Nzabahimana (1994), who reports on the situation in Rwanda in August 1994 and writes in a section titled *La confirmation des génocides*: "A Goma et à Bukavu, la plupart des personnes rencontrées sont formelles: il y a eu des massacres, du jamais vu : - Un génocide sur les Batwa dont personne ne parle. - Un génocide sur les Hutu, à l'exemple des

Denial can thus also seriously problematise and jeopardise the process of reconciliation as it could foster impunity.[27] Furthermore, if genocide is denied, forgiveness or a pardon for what happened becomes impossible because there is no genocide to forgive or pardon. According to the quote above, both sides simply killed. As will become clear throughout the next Section, the notion that both people have suffered is strengthened by the notion of a double genocide, which is often put forward in later denialist discourses.

The ultimate Orwellian Inversion

The discourse of the (RIG), the (RAF) and the (RDR) discussed above attempts to fix the meaning of the nodal point "the Rwandan tragedy." To this end, the Tutsi and the RPF are articulated as the "root cause" of the "current tragic situation." Although the Tutsi and the RPF are presented as being primarily responsible for "the Rwandan tragedy," they are not solely responsible. The articulation of the abovementioned organisations makes clear that the quest was facilitated and covered up by certain Anglophonic "super powers" who wanted to expand their sphere of influence. Moreover, the violence inflicted upon the Tutsi during the period in question was not a planned genocide but a justified and legitimate spontaneous self-defence against an overwhelming and military superior enemy. Here we thus witness a total inversion of roles (Institute of Research and Dialogue for Peace, 2008, p. 80). Cotler (1995) argues that those who participate in the Holocaust denial movement use historiography in its "ultimate Orwellian inversion":

> For we move from the genocide of the Jewish people to a denial that the genocide ever took place: then, in a classic Orwellian cover-up of an international conspiracy, the Holocaust denial movement whitewashes the crimes of the Nazis, as it excoriates the crimes of the Jews. It not only holds that the Holocaust was a hoax, but maligns the Jews for fabricating the hoax.[28]

Those who engage in genocide denial draw on historiographic practices to create a history that mystifies and erases history. Their history is an inversion of history; a contra or anti history (Van den Berghe, 1997a, p. 28). Such denial is about control. It is a means to the end of controlling the conflict. Like Orwell wrote, "who controls the past controls the future. Who controls the present controls the past." Control can not only be gained by opening up and revealing the truth, it can also be gained by closing up, and obscuring or even obliterating the past (Cohen, 1995, pp. 47–48). Cotler's Orwellian inversion template seems to be directly applicable to the official denial discourse of the RIG, RAF and RDR discussed above. Their "explanation" of what

ressortissants de la préfecture de Byumba, des personnes ont 'été tuées parce qu'elles étaient Hutu. - Un génocide sur les Tutsi, des personnes ont été tuées parce qu'elles étaient Tutsi."

27 For a discussion of these issues concerning justice and reconciliation see also Chrétien (2012, pp. 118–131). Terry (2002, p. 168) furthermore argues that the denial strategy served to justify a return to the negotiating table in order to arrange power sharing.

28 See also Ternon (1999a, p. 23) who distinguished a similar strategy with regard to how the Armenian genocide is denied.

happened effectively results in the conclusion that there was no genocide perpetrated against the Tutsi population. Their version of the events excoriates the crimes of the Tutsi-led RPF, thereby minimising and trivialising the crimes committed by the Hutu extremists. They hold that the genocide against the Tutsi is a myth and maligns the Tutsi and the RPF (and their allies) for fabricating it in order to cover up the genocide they perpetrated against the Hutu and to attain and consolidate power in Rwanda. As a result, victims become perpetrators and perpetrators become victims. Chrétien (2007, p. 55) referred to such discourse in which the *génocidaires* ascribe their agenda and actions to the victim as *accusations à mirroir*.

Although much of the official rhetoric attempts to cover up the true nature of the events, sometimes the virulent genocidal racism shows its true face. In 1995, while residing in exile, the former Prefect of the Kigali-Rural prefecture, François Karera, when asked about what happened, explained that:

> The Tutsi are originally bad. They are murderers. The Tutsi have given the white people their daughters. Physically they are weak -- look at their arms and their legs. No Tutsi can build; they are too weak. They just command. The others work. (Karera quoted in Perlez, 1995)

According to Karera, the Hutu were determined not to allow the Tutsi to repeat history. "If the reasons are just, the massacres are justified," Mr. Karera explained while adding that "In war you don't consider the consequences, you consider the causes." Karera finally concluded that "We cannot use that word genocide, because there are numerous surviving" (Karera quoted in Perlez, 1995).[29] His last remark resembles Bagosora's earlier discussed in rhetoric in Chapter 1, Section 1.2. when he questioned that a genocide had taken place because there were still so many Tutsi walking around in Kigali.

4.5. Discursive developments

On the 16th of May 1994, the French newspaper *Le Figaro* headed "*Rwanda: le double genocide*" and French President Mitterrand referred to "genocides" during the Franco-African Summit, which was held in Biarritz in November 1994. Two years later the French Minister of Foreign Affairs, Villepain, in a RFI radio show also talked about "*les génocides rwandais*" (Fierens, 2009, p. 139 and 140). When asked about his use of words by a journalist, Mitterrand replied *"Voulez-vous dire que le génocide s'est arrêté après la victoire des Tutsi?"* (Ntakirutimana, 2013, p. 52). This argument also featured in certain reports of organisations that represent the refugees, such as the *Justice et Paix pour la Réconciliation au Rwanda* (AJPR) (J.-P. Chrétien, 2012, pp. 95–101; Lanotte, 2007, pp. 308–311). Those promoting the idea of a double genocide often refer to the crimes perpetrated by the RPF during its

29 At the ICTR Karera pleaded not guilty to genocide (The Prosecutor v. François Karera, Case No. ICTR-01-74-T. Judgment and Sentence. 7 December 2007).

military advance or they draw upon the terrible situation in the refugee camps and the RPF attacks on those camps in its attempt to dismantle them. In 1995, an agent of Caritas located in Goma explained:

> *Nous sommes témoins d'un double génocide: Les uns on tué en plein jour, alignant les cadavres sur la route; les autres on fait exactement la même chose, pendant la nuit, en cachette; c'est ainsi que ses derniers sont parvenus à tromper la communauté internationale.* (Quoted in Fierens, 2009, p. 140)

The double genocide thesis conveys the idea that because both parties have committed genocide, a balance in suffering is achieved. The examples reveal that the double genocide thesis was already presented in early 1994, but it seems that it gained momentum once the evidence concerning the genocide against the Tutsi reached such an indisputable magnitude and as a result could simply no longer be literally or interpretatively be denied.[30] To rely solely on the claim that nothing happened or that what happened was a civil war or self-defence became untenable.

The official denial discourse discussed in the Sections above originated in the period 1994–1996 and it thus directly followed the genocide against the Tutsi. Discourses, however, do not always remain the same and they continue to develop over time. This is especially the case with denial discourses as they continuously need to address and deal with new threatening aspects of the reality they try to obscure. It seems that the *Rassemblement pour le Retour des Réfugiés et la Démocratie au Rwanda* (RDR), which outlived the Rwandan Interim Government (RIG) and the Rwandan Armed Forces (RAF), has altered its discourse concerning "the Rwandan tragedy" over time. Although the RDR's initial discourse sporadically referred directly to a genocide perpetrated against the Hutu,[31] like the other organisations, it vigorously denied that a genocide against the Tutsi was perpetrated. For instance, in one of their reports there is a Section that carries the title "Inexistence of "Tutsi genocide" in Rwanda", but the general argument is one of interethnic massacres (Rassemblement pour le Retour des Réfugiés et la Démocratie au Rwanda Cameroun Wing, 1996). In contrast to this earlier discourse, the *RDR political platform*, which was published in 1998, states that two genocides took place. In addition to a genocide against the Hutu, also a genocide against the Tutsi took place. According to the *RDR political platform*, "The RDR has clearly and unequivocally condemned genocide, all crimes and other violations of human rights committed against the Tutsi; it has also

---

30 Naphtal Ahishakiye, the Executive Secretary of Ibuka, noted that "The genocide can be denied in different ways that change over time. In 1994, they claimed that there was no genocide, only war. By 2000, they 'accepted' that genocide took place, but argued that it was unplanned. Today, they argue that both sides killed and ask why the genocide against the Hutu is not recognized" (Ahishakiye 2014, personal communication).

31 Their references were less direct as those of the Interim Government or the Rwandan Armed Forces. The RDR sometimes talked about *"L'autre génocide"* (Rassemblement pour le Retour et la Démocratie au Rwanda Section Cameroun, 1995). Despite the fact that the RDR seems less outspoken on the notion of a genocide against the Hutu, according to Ndahiro (2008), the RDR ideology was nonetheless influenced by the Rwandan Armed Forces, who had been instrumental in the creation of the organisation.

condemned genocide, all crimes and other violations of human rights committed against the Hutu" (Rassemblement pour le Retour des Réfugiés et la Démocratie au Rwanda, 1998). The statement continues to explain that:

> Between April and July 1994, hundreds of thousands of innocent Tutsi were massacred on the account that they belonged to the ethnic group from which most Rwandans believed came the fighters who assassinated President Juvenal Habyarimana. Automatic solidarity to the crime was attributed to the Tutsi and the whole group was held responsible for the harsh conditions in which lived millions of Rwandans displaced by the war launched by the RPF on October 1, 1990 from Uganda. Likewise, until today, many members of the Hutu community have not recognised and duly condemned the genocide committed against the Tutsi and other horrors and atrocities inflicted upon them by fellow Hutu in 1994. When they analyse current events in Rwanda where the RPF military junta rules through the oppression of one Section of the Rwandan population, they tend to minimise or to forget this horrible past so that no useful lesson can be drawn from it. (Rassemblement pour le Retour des Réfugiés et la Démocratie au Rwanda, 1998)

The RDR basically condemns those who have not yet recognised the genocide against the Tutsi, while at the same time referring to the elements that have in the broader discourse been used to justify the violence against the Tutsi population as unorganised self-defence against the RPF war effort. Moreover, the current Government of Rwanda is made responsible for the denial by members of the Hutu population.[32] Also throughout the document, the Tutsi and the RPF are still constructed as the root causes of the problems. Finally the Tutsi-led RPF is accused of perpetrating genocide against the Hutu population in the refugee camps in Congo. The gist of the discursive construction is that, in terms of the number of genocides perpetrated, the Hutu people had to endure more than the Tutsi.[33] Does the RDR now promote a double genocide thesis?

The argument that there were two genocides is referred to as the double genocide thesis, and it is often connected to the idea that because both parties have committed violence it thus becomes a zero-sum game, as both parties were basically involved in the same genocidal acts; "we are all perpetrators and we are all victims" (Dumas, 2010, p. 96; Institute of Research and Dialogue for Peace, 2008, p. 90).[34] As a result, the genocide against the Tutsi is presented at less than its true value and its significance is downplayed. Shafir in his research on Holocaust denial also refers

---

32 How the policies of the current Rwandan Government may have an impact on the denial of the genocide against the Tutsi is a complex issue and will be dealt with more in depth in Chapter 6.4. The way it is presented by the RDR does not serve to address this is issue sincerely; it is merely turned into a means to the end of an even more complex denial narrative.

33 Although the Rwandan Interim Government seized to exist, certain former government officials, such as Jean Kambanda (2011, 2013), have published documentation in which they also promote this discourse.

34 Verwimp (2003) tested the double genocide thesis for central and southern Rwanda and disproved it.

to such trivialisations which draw on relativisation as comparative trivialisations. Shafir (2002) defines comparative trivialisation as:

> [D]istortion of the record and of the significance of the Holocaust, either through the "humanisation" of its local record in comparison with atrocities committed by the Nazis, or through comparing the record of the Holocaust itself with experiences of massive suffering endured by local populations or by mankind at large at one point or another in recorded history.

Shafir draws on the work of historian Peter Gay (1978) who used the idea of comparative trivialisation to denote the argument put forward by Ernst Nolte (1974) in his book *Germany and the Cold War* (*Deutschland und der kalte Krieg*). According to Gay, Nolte developed a sophisticated apologetic denial by pointing out crimes committed by others (Stalin's Gulag) which were presumed to be as vicious as those committed by the Nazis. According to Gay, the function of Nolte's narrative was "to cover up the special horror of German barbarity between 1933 and 1945, and to divert attention from studying that barbarity in its own – that is to say its German – context" (Gay 1978, xi–xii quoted in Shafir 2002). The Holocaust has also been trivialised by arguing that the Allies have committed terrible acts, such as, the bombing of Dresden. Shafir (2002) extends Gay's framework of comparative trivialisation and it not only refers to instances in which the Holocaust is compared to other atrocities, but it also includes trivialisation by comparing it to regularly occurring events involving violence or by obliterating the difference between the victims of the Holocaust and victims of those regularly-occurring violent events. According to Shafir, comparative trivialisation draws on mainly two techniques. The first technique is to place genocide and other events on equal footing. The second technique is to put genocide in the shadow of other events. The crimes committed by the other side involved in the conflict were as bad, if not worse. Shafir notes that double genocide or symmetry theories draw on the technique of equal footing, while competitive martyrdom theories draw on the technique of overshadowing (Shafir, 2002).

The articulation of the events by the RDR discussed at the beginning of this Section moves beyond the "zero sum" argument and it thus involves competitive martyrdom. It does not involve a double genocide theory because it does not draw on the idea that there is a symmetry or equal footing of suffering. On the contrary, the suffering of the Tutsi is overshadowed by the suffering of the Hutu. This becomes most clear in the articulation that the Tutsi are the "root cause" of the conflict, the war and the genocide, but it also becomes clear from the numbers game they play in which Hutu victims greatly outnumber the Tutsi victims. The official denial discourse is thus not simply about minimisation or creating an equilibrium of suffering – a double genocide – instead, it is about overshadowing.

In the abovementioned cases, advantageous comparisons are being made by contrasting the criminal behaviour of one party with morally abhorrent behaviour of the other party in the conflict. You compare your own record with that of those who are questioning you and their record is much worse (Cohen, 1996, p. 533; 2001, p. 111). Strictly speaking one could argue that a comparative trivialisation does *acknowledge* the genocide against the Tutsi, but such an acknowledgment becomes meaningless if it is structurally followed by insinuations that the Tutsi were to blame themselves for the genocidal violence that was inflicted upon them and that they also have perpetrated a genocide against the Hutu. It therefore does not truly acknowledge the genocide. On the contrary, its "acknowledgment" served the purpose of the denial of that exact genocide, not by literally denying it but by trivialising it. It again reveals that genocide denial involves much more than simply stating that genocide did not happen. In terms of the concept of implicit or indirect speech acts discussed earlier in Chapter 3 (Section 3.9.), this is an interesting manoeuvre: deniers do more than they are literally saying.

4.6. Concluding remarks

From the analysis above, it becomes clear that the official denial discourse of the Rwandan Interim Government (RIG), the Rwandan Armed Forces (RAF) and the *Rassemblement pour le Retour des Réfugiés et la Démocratie au Rwanda* (RDR) generally does not primarily entail literal denial. Instead, it focuses predominantly on interpretative and implicatory denial. The violence perpetrated against the Tutsi is articulated as unplanned and spontaneous "inter-ethnic massacres" which excludes that an organised genocide against the Tutsi perpetrated by the Hutu ever took place. It is furthermore significant that the violence perpetrated by the RPF against the Hutu is articulated as genocidal. The redefinition of the nature of the victimisation and the victim automatically also results in a redefinition of the nature of the perpetration and the perpetrator. When Tutsi are not the victims, they are the "real perpetrators". As a result, the Hutu are not the perpetrators, but the "real victims". In the articulation of the official denial discourse, the roles of perpetrator and victims of genocide are mutually exclusive and therefore the discourse results in a reversal of roles. In contrast, double genocide discourses do enable that parties embody both roles. In that case a party can be both a perpetrator and a victim of genocide at the same time. Ultimately, in double genocide discourse the focus of denial is to create a symmetry in suffering. Although subsequent denial discourses are nowadays often designated as double genocide discourses, the analysis showed that the articulation of, for instance, the RDR does not aim to create symmetry in terms of suffering. Instead it attempts to overshadow the suffering of the Tutsi. It would thus be incorrect to refer to such discourses as adhering to the double genocide thesis.

In contrast to the first layer of interpretative denial which focuses on (re-)articulating the nature of the events and thereby of the reality of the violence perpetrated, the second layer of implicatory denial focuses on rejecting the consequences that follow from the perpetration of these "inter-ethnic massacres" by articulating the meaning of the actions as spontaneous self-defence. We could frame the first layer of denial in terms of the rationalising technique of denial of the victim, but how could this second layer of denial be framed? Is it about denial of responsibility? Denial of responsibility includes denials based on the argument that things were beyond your agency or control. Perpetrators, for instance, often claim that they were forced to act under superior orders and that they would have been severely sanctioned for disobeying. In such instances, perpetrators argue that what they did was wrong, but they had no other choice. Such denial of responsibility is thus an excuse as it acknowledges that certain acts were wrong, but no blame should be attached; it is not their fault as something or someone else is responsible for what happened (Hewitt, 2003, p. 166). In contrast, the articulation of the nature of the violence as self-defence relies on the convention of justification. In the case of justification, the responsibility for the acts is accepted, but the act is not deemed wrongful (Hewitt, 2003, p. 166). In this case, it would thus be more appropriate to speak of "denial of wrongfulness" instead of "denial of responsibility". To designate the articulation under the broader term "denial of responsibility" actually obscures the nature of the signification. In justifying their actions, the aforementioned organisations communicate that they accept the responsibility for what they did, but that the actions they engaged in were not wrong; they were justified. Moreover, it signifies that the action against which they defended themselves constituted an unlawful attack. They claim that by invading the country the RPF perpetrated crimes against peace and by slaughtering the Hutu population, they subsequently engaged in genocide.[35] The invocation of a justification thus has profound implications, because what they did was not wrong but legitimate.[36] The result of the official denial discourse is thus that there is no responsibility for a genocide perpetrated against the Tutsi, because no such violence took place. Instead there is a responsibility for the "inter-ethnic massacres", but that violence against the Tutsi was legitimate self-defence and therefore justified. The second layer of implicatory denial thus continues the denial of the victim.

It was noted that the first step in the discursive construction of the official denial discourse was to create a favourable rhetorical vantage point entailing that people have greatly misunderstood the events, which therefore requires a better understanding. This rhetorical vantage point created a legitimate space from which the denial discourse was further developed. Shermer & Grobman (2000, p. 103) explain that, in addition to creating a favourable rhetorical vantage point, genocide deniers also often follow certain rhetorical fallacies. Deniers in their approach do not critically reflect upon their own position (the position they defend) and instead focus predominantly, if not exclusively, on undermining the reality of the genocide in order to create doubt and confusion. They focus on what is not known and do not acknowledge what is known about the genocide. If genocide deniers would really critically reflect upon their own position, they would have to conclude that it was untenable. The official denial discourse discussed above also presents a biased or skewed version of what

35 They try to convey that taking into account the extreme threat and dire circumstances, they were allowed to act as they did. In contrast, if the actions had been disproportionate and excessive they would have required the invocation of an excuse, in which wrongfulness is accepted, but not the responsibility. Such an excuse would have been a "denial of responsibility". That is however not the case, the official denial discourse attempts to convey that the actions were appropriate and proportional given the circumstances.

36 To accept and acknowledge genocide, would automatically imply a wrong.

happened. It is selective in the presentation of the events as it focuses on incriminating the RPF and the Tutsi, while obscuring the planning, organisation and execution of the genocide against the Tutsi. There is no reference to the stockpiling of weapons, the training of militias, the divisive extremist politics that divided the country along Ethnic lines, or the virulent propaganda. Finkielkraut (1998, p. 35) makes clear, "they eliminate from the real any and all elements that contest the truth of the story." Shermer & Grobman (2000, p. 103) add that in constructing their argument they decontextualise, by only selecting the data that fits their denialist arguments and ignore the data that does not fit their views. This explains why, for instance, the role of France remains completely unaddressed in their discursive construction of events. The discursive construction of the discourse also shows that they tend to reduce a complex process to certain (set of) specific events. They do not elaborate on the whole process of genocide; they primarily focus on certain stages or specific elements. They for instance focus on whitewashing the physical violence against the Tutsi, but they neglect the massive anti-Tutsi propaganda they engaged in. As such, they often portray a false or skewed image of what constitutes genocide.

The denial of the genocide against the Tutsi has not only been promoted by the three organisations discussed in this Chapter; the denial of the genocide against the Tutsi has moved beyond the realm of official denial and surprisingly those who engage in the denial of the genocide also include Western academics and journalists. These actors, for some reason, have been presenting alternative discursive constructions concerning what happened in Rwanda that counter what they call "the official story" but which recycle much of the discursive elements of the official genocide denial discussed in this Chapter. In order to make this development clear, the following Chapter will address the work of Edward S. Herman & David Peterson and Keith Harmon Snow. The work of these authors namely entails some of the most brazen genocide denial and it serves as a powerful illustration of this questionable development.

CHAPTER 5
RECYCLING OFFICIAL DENIAL

5.1. INTRODUCTION

In his book *Genocide and the politics of memory*, Hirsch (1995, p. 24) points out that memory and history are not exclusively the domain of the historian. In contrast, many other actors, such as scholars from other academic disciplines, political activists, journalists, filmmakers, lawyers, etc. engage in the construction of memory and history: "It is from them more than from historians that the public mainly receives whatever conceptions, impressions, fantasies and delusions it may entertain about the past" (Vann Woodward 1989 Quoted in Hirsch, 1995, p. 24). Hirsch more particularly refers to Robertson's study on memory and history titled *American myth, American reality* (Robertson, 1980). Following Robertson, Hirsch (1995, p. 25) explains that history can be described as the memory of the lives and actions of people. Their memory is contained or embodied in a wide variety of objects, such as personal narratives, speeches, films, books, rituals, complex political institutions, etc. Whether they are true or not, these are the conduits of memory and the building blocks of history, which have been remembered and transmitted. The impact of other actors on the history of the genocide against the Tutsi should therefore not be underestimated as their ideas and representations of what happened have an impact on the construction of its history and thereby on its reality. The previous Chapter discussed how those who were implicated in the genocide against the Tutsi discursively constructed their history of the events and transmitted it to the public. The denial of the genocide against the Tutsi has however moved beyond the realm of official denial and the group of genocide deniers has expanded involving actors who were initially not implicated in the genocide. Surprisingly, this group also includes Western academics and journalists. The alternative theories these actors present are dangerous because they willingly or unwillingly "lend weight to the Hutu Power's mantra" (Odom, 2008). They empower the official denial of the genocide against the Tutsi because, in constructing and transmitting their version of history, these actors draw upon crucial elements contained in the official denial discourse analysed in the last Chapter and they thereby recycle the denial of the genocide against the Tutsi. As a result, these actors, instead of creating history, (willingly or unwillingly) obscure and destroy it. Therefore, *this Chapter will more closely look at how the official genocide denial discourse is being recycled.*[1] Like with the discussion of the official

[1] The term "recycling" is chosen to convey the idea that the discursive materials for the construction of new discourses are obtained from already existing discourses. In terms of discourse analysis this could also be seen as a form of "intertextuality" or "inter-discursivity". This means that texts draw on earlier meaning formations thereby mixing and reproducing discourses (Jørgensen & Philips, 2002, p. 72 and 73).

denial narrative presented in the last Chapter, the analysis has been limited to certain specific illustrative actors and documents. The analysis will focus on journalists and academics, because they have a professional responsibility to enlighten the public about what is happening in the world, instead of clouding their minds. As already introduced in the Conclusion to the last Chapter, at the centre of the attention will be the work of Edward S. Herman, David Peterson and Keith Harmon Snow. The work of these authors on Rwanda entails some of the most elaborate and brazen denial of the genocide against the Tutsi and their work is illustrative of how elements of the official denial discourse are being recycled. By focussing on genocide denial by academics and journalists, *the analysis thus also serves to debunk the stereotypical image of genocide deniers.*

Like in the previous Chapter, the first part of the Chapter will introduce the aforementioned agents and their work on Rwanda on which the analysis throughout the following Sections will predominantly rely. In order to address the question how the official genocide denial discourse is being recycled, *it is pertinent to analyse how the discourse of these agents concerning the events in Rwanda is constructed* and *how it merges with the official denial discourse of the Rwandan Interim Government (RIG), the Rwandan Armed Forces (RAF) and the Rassemblement pour le Retour des Réfugiés et la Démocratie au Rwanda (RDR).* In answering these questions, the analysis will again draw on insights from Laclau & Mouffe's discourse theory to show how the discursive constructions of these actors in many ways resemble the discursive construction of those who promote the official denial discourse. The analysis will show that Herman & Peterson and Harmon Snow, in fixing the meaning of the events in Rwanda, draw on many of the same signifiers and articulate very similar discursive relations as the official denial discourse. Although Herman & Peterson and Harmon Snow recycle much of the official denial discourse, the discourses are not entirely identical in their discursive constructions. Therefore, *the analyses will not only show how their discourse merges with the official denial discourse, but also at which points it diverges from the official denial discourse.*

In the previous Chapters considerable attention was paid to speech act and discourse theory. By drawing on these insights from these theoretical approaches we got a better understanding of how genocide denial operates and what it does. It became clear that utterances and discourses of genocide denial are performative and have the power to construct our reality. Those bent on denying the genocide against the Tutsi abuse this discursive power to renegotiate reality, thereby turning the genocide in a non-event. Like the official denial discourse, the discourse of Herman & Peterson and Harmon Snow discussed above draws on this performative power. In scholarly work it is, however, also often argued that genocide denial incites (re)new(ed) genocide(s) and as such it is seen as a cause of genocidal violence. This appears to be one of the main reasons why in certain countries genocide denial is criminalised. Genocide denial in this approach facilitates genocide. However, from the analysis developed throughout the current and previous Chapters of this study (Chapter 2 and 3), it becomes clear that genocide denial can also be an act of genocide in itself. This raises the question *whether denial is only facilitative to the violence of genocide, or can it also constitute violence in itself and, if so, what would the nature of such violence be.* The last part of this Chapter will reflect on these questions.

The following discussion focuses on the core of Herman & Peterson's and Harmon Snow's discourse concerning the events in Rwanda and it therefore does not deal with their discourse in its entirety. This also means that I will not engage in a substantial discussion concerning the events that took place in Rwanda in order to address what is factually right or wrong. As I already explained in the last Chapter (Section 4.2.3.), those familiar with the work of the abovementioned authors and the conflict they address could argue that, instead of piling lies upon lies, the work also holds many truths. For instance, in their work, the mentioned authors also state facts concerning crimes committed by the RPF. It cannot be denied that the RPF committed gross human rights violations and is responsible for causing mass suffering in Rwanda and in neighbouring Congo. It is legitimate to study these issues. One should, however, not (risk to) conflate the crimes of the RPF during this period with genocide. An attempt to analyse these issues critically should not distort the reality of the 1994 genocide against the Tutsi. The point is that in the discourse promoted by the abovementioned authors, these elements are not brought forward with the aim of revealing the truth about what happened in Rwanda. Instead, it will become clear that they are made to serve the distinct political ends these agents strive for.

5.2. Agents of recycling

Before discussing how Herman & Peterson and Harmon Snow articulate their discourse and how it merges and diverges with the official denial discourse, the following Section will first briefly introduce the actors and their work.

5.2.1. Edward S. Herman and David Peterson: The politics of genocide

Edward S. Herman is a Professor Emeritus at the Wharton School of the University of Pennsylvania. He has written extensively on economics, political economy, foreign policy, and media analysis. Herman published many books including *Corporate control, corporate power* (Herman, 1981); *The "terrorism" industry* (Herman & O'Sullivan, 1990). Together with Noam Chomsky, he also published the two volume work *The political economy of human rights* (Chomsky & Herman, 1979a, 1979b) and the influential *Manufacturing consent* (Chomsky & Herman, 1988). David Peterson is a writer, independent journalist and researcher based in Chicago.[2] Herman & Peterson teamed up and co-authored a book published in 2010 titled *The politics of genocide*. In the introduction to their book, Herman & Peterson (2010e, p. 13) explain that after the Second World War, the United States (US), in order to maintain its "uniquely dominant economic, political and military position in world

2 For further information on the research and publications of both authors see www.zcommunications.org and www.monthlyreview.org.

affairs", has been "aggressively pursuing US advantages by all available means," including armed interventions causing great human suffering. This "regressive, no-holds-barred foreign policy" has resulted in a vast US "empire of bases" that "encircles much of the globe" at the cost of massive gross human rights violations for which the US is ultimately responsible (Herman & Peterson, 2010e, p. 14). Regardless its "brutality and criminality", the intellectual elite and the general public have swallowed "US-directed or supported terrorism, aggression, crimes against humanity, and even genocide straight to the present day" (Herman & Peterson, 2010e, p. 15). According to Herman & Peterson (2010e, p. 16) "how bloodbaths are evaluated" apparently depends on "who is responsible for carrying them out." Their argument is captured by Chomsky whom they quote on the matter: "If it's a crime of somebody else, particularly an enemy, then we're utterly outraged. If it's our own crime, either comparable or worse, either it's suppressed or denied" (Herman & Peterson, 2010e, p. 27). Herman & Peterson conclude that, when it comes to dealing with mass atrocities, it has thus nothing to do with whether "certain thresholds of scale" are reached or whether what happened is "inherently conscience shocking". What seems to really matter, according to Herman & Peterson, (2010e, p. 27) is "*who* does *what* to *whom* – and *where does power lie.*"

According to Herman & Peterson (2010e, p. 20), through their propaganda schemes, Western imperial powers keep their citizens "properly misinformed and supportive" of their actions. As a result, the crimes for which the US and its Western allies are primarily responsible "remain out of the ambit of Western humanitarian concern and the reach of Western-enforced 'international justice'" (Herman & Peterson, 2010e, p. 20). They conclude that:

> Just as the guardians of "international justice" have yet to find a single crime committed by a Great White-Northern Power against people of colour that crosses the *threshold of gravity*, so too all of the fine talk about the "responsibility to protect" and the "end of impunity" has never once been extended to the victims of the same powers, no matter how egregious the crimes. The Western establishment rushed to proclaim "genocide" in Bosnia-Herzegovina, Rwanda, Kosovo, and Darfur, and also agitated for tribunals to hold the alleged perpetrators accountable. In contrast, its silence over the crimes committed by its own regimes against the peoples of Southeast Asia, Central America, the Middle East, and Sub Saharan Africa is deafening. *This* is the politics of genocide. (Herman & Peterson, 2010e, p. 112)

Herman & Peterson (2010e, p. 111) furthermore point out that the politics of genocide have resulted in a culture of impunity, which the US and its Western allies have enjoyed because of their "vastly superior economic and political power and nothing more":

> [The] culture of impunity which the Great Unequals have always enjoyed, an impunity that is rooted neither in their goodness nor their justice but in their vastly superior economic and political power and nothing more. The inability of any sector of the US establishment to recognize fully that the human and material destruction [...] are the consequence, not of

> accident, much less error, but of deliberate policies that produced this result, ranks among the greatest intellectual and moral failures in US history. If the phrase *genocide denial* has any validity, we find it here, in the standard practice of the richest and most well-educated classes in the world. (Herman & Peterson, 2010e, p. 111)

The politics of genocide is an important issue, which is especially interesting in the context of this study on genocide denial, because the politics of genocide effectively result in a denial of human suffering.[3] Herman & Peterson discuss many examples, such as for instance, the suffering of Iraqis under US-led sanctions in the 1990s and the US support for Israel's repression in Gaza and destruction in Lebanon, the role of the US in the massacres of Guatemalans and Salvadorans in the 1980s, and the US role in Indonesia's blood bath in East Timor.[4] This is however not where the problem lies, as also Caplan (2010a) points out: "To this stage, this little volume might on balance just be considered recommended reading. Despite its strange biases and excesses in belabouring its thesis, it's a useful reminder of American double standards that should not be forgotten." Herman & Peterson's work does raise questions when they start to examine the politics of genocide in more detail (and the same applies to Harmon Snow's work, which will be discussed later on). In Chapter 2 Section 4, which is the longest Section in their book (17 pages), Herman & Peterson address the case of "Rwanda and the Democratic Republic of Congo" as a prime example of the politics of genocide.[5] The problem is, however, as will become clear throughout this Chapter, that their work on Rwanda presents an alternative reading (articulation) of events that in its discursive construction recycles many of the core discursive elements that are central to the official denial discourse, thereby ultimately resulting in a brazen denial of the genocide against the Tutsi.

5.2.2. Keith Harmon Snow: The political economy of genocide

Keith Harmon Snow is an independent journalist, war correspondent and photographer. He has worked for more than a decade to "contest official narratives" on international crimes such as war crimes, crimes against humanity and genocide. Harmon Snow worked as a genocide investigator and consultant to the United Nations and other international bodies and he furthermore received three Project Censored awards for his Central Africa reportage (www.artsandlectures.ucsb.edu).[6] Like Herman & Peterson, Harmon Snow takes a particular interest in what he refers

---

3 The West has been complicit in war crimes, crimes against humanity and genocide but this is often not (fully) acknowledged. In that sense Herman and Peterson's notion of "the politics of genocide" is relevant. See for an overview and analysis of cases concerning Western involvement in such international crimes: Jones (2004).

4 It is however questionable whether all these events can be defined as genocide. Despite this issue, the notion that genocides have not been acknowledged is nonetheless important. For a further discussion on "forgotten" genocides see the work of Carmichael (2009), Lemarchand (2011) and Steinberg (1999).

5 This Chapter was also made available online by *Monthly Review Press* under the title *Rwanda and the Democratic Republic of Congo in the propaganda system* (Herman & Peterson, 2010f).

6 For further information on the research and publications of Keith Harmon Snow see his websites www.allthingspass.com and www.consciousbeingalliance.com.

to as "the political economy of genocide," which was also the theme of his lecture at the University of California where he was the 2009 Regent's Lecturer in Law & Society. According to Harmon Snow, "the political economy of genocide" is an issue that he became familiar with during his fieldwork and which according to him explains much of the conflict in the Great Lakes Region. In the introduction to an article he published in 2010 titled *The Rwanda hit list: Revisionism, denial and the genocide conspiracy* Harmon Snow (2010b) explains that his experience with the Great Lakes region of Africa began in 1991:

> While travelling in southern Uganda I was witness to the shooting of an unarmed man by unknown assailants believed to be rebels of the Rwandan Patriotic Army/Front. Since then I have worked tirelessly to uncover the truth about the war in the Dem. Republic of Congo (DRC).

Harmon Snow (2010b) elaborates that "[f]or the last 15 years [he has] been investigating militias and criminal rackets and propaganda about Central Africa". He adds that his early work did however not accurately capture what was happening in the Great Lakes region of Africa:

> My early reportage on Rwanda (1995–1997) unknowingly advanced false narratives about victims v. killers, and the nature of and culpability for atrocities, including "genocide" in Rwanda. The established narrative remains overly simplified and the truth has been hijacked and suppressed by the mass media. (Harmon Snow, 2010b)

It becomes clear that Harmon Snow tends to present himself as a champion of truth (Hovannisian, 1999a, pp. 205–228). In a critical article on the movie *Hotel Rwanda* he, for instance, states that:

> [A]ny hesitation in challenging the "right and proper tale" is overwhelmed by the obscenity of the obvious injustice and the machinations of empire behind it. If truth is the first casualty in war, then those of us who are lucky observers must endlessly work to resurrect it. (Harmon Snow, 2005).

As noted in the last Chapter, the champion of truth strategy is a form of impression management and draws on the idea that one judges the sincerity and reliability of somebody's work by the honest intentions of the author of the work. His dedication to the truth also implies that he has no other agenda than getting to the truth and therefore his work should not be questioned. The analysis of the denial discourse, however, seems to indicate that if people (continuously) claim to be revealing the real truth or the real facts then it is very likely that they are doing the exact opposite.

In a *Your World News* interview on the topics of "the plunder and depopulation of Central Africa", "the politics of genocide" and "white supremacy ideology and corporate control", Harmon Snow gives us an additional insight into the motivations underlying his work. He explains how Western powers have been engaging in the politics of genocide granting them impunity for crimes they themselves have committed. This political process and the propaganda scheme involved is what Harmon Snow attempts to address in his work. According to Harmon Snow, the politics of genocide have been employed by the Western super powers since the concept of genocide was introduced by Lemkin who formulated "some concept of genocide" in the 1940ies in response to the Nazi Holocaust. Harmon Snow claims that:

> Lemkin himself was a tool by the imperialist system used to produce this formulation of genocide. Which then was, of course, after its formulation was created and after Lemkin got involved with it, it was gutted by the UN, because if it had upheld the actual formulation that Lemkin had come up with, itself was compromised ... it would have implicated western powers or forced the world to try western powers as well as the Japanese and Nazi, war crimes, crime against humanity and genocide. That is the beginning of the politics of genocide on a political legalistic scale. (Your World News, 2011)

According to Harmon Snow, the politics of genocide thus also existed in 1945 with the prosecution of the Nazi war criminals:

> There is no discussion of the deeper issues, no discussion of how we supported Nazi war criminals, no discussion about how the Nuremberg trials were victor's justice, and one sided politics. Extend all of that into the present time and we have since 1945 numerous cases of mass atrocities that qualify as genocide committed by the very same powers that tried the Nazi war criminal that would be the US in particular, Britain, France, [etc.] and of course Israel. (Your World News, 2011).

Harmon Snow, like Herman & Peterson, thus argues that since the Second World War, in order to maintain their power, Western states have perpetrated imperialist crimes (including genocide) that have remained unaddressed by international criminal justice. Both actors basically set the same rhetorical vantage point from which they develop their substantial discourse on Rwanda. Their introductions reveal a sincere concern for the problem of the politics of genocide and the suffering it causes and therefore readers are not likely to approach the analysis that follows with much scepticism.

Although, Herman & Peterson and Harmon Snow make clear that their work aims to address the politics of genocide, stylistically their work is very different. Harmon Snow's work is often presented in lengthy sensational exposés.[7] In contrast to Harmon Snow, Herman & Peterson present a less emotion laden and more sophisticated account. Herman & Peterson's work is more academic and includes tables, statistics and theories. It is more compact and sober in its word use, which gives Herman & Peterson's work a much more credible appearance. In contrast to Harmon Snow's

---

7 In an introduction to one of his articles which was published in *The Black Star News*, the editor noted: "Snow writes long; he cannot help it because he feels the pain of the Congolese and the Ugandans and he wants someone somewhere –here in the United States and Britain-- to pay a price. He might be accused of being overly passionate; one has to be, when one feels the kind of indignation that Snow feels. When it is a matter of genocide no article can be too long" (Harmon Snow, 2009c).

work on Rwanda, which has basically remained "untouched," Herman & Peterson's work on Rwanda has received considerable critique. The critique of Herman & Peterson's work deals with many critical issues concerning their work, but it does not systematically analyse and deconstruct Herman & Peterson's (and Harmon Snow's) discourse using a discourse theoretical approach, which concerns how their analysis is constructed. Moreover, these critiques do not pay attention to how the discourse of these actors is related to the official denial discourse. As will become clear, it is the recycling, the fact that they make linguistic community with the official denial discourse, that makes the discourse of Herman & Peterson and Harmon Snow so problematic. Therefore, the following Section will look more closely at how they articulate the events and how they recycle crucial discursive elements of the official denial.

The following analysis is based on Herman & Peterson's work that they published on the topic of Rwanda. In addition to their book *The politics of genocide*, the analysis also draws on materials which featured on websites, such as www.zcommunications.org, www.globalresearch.ca, www.mondialisation.ca and the websites of *The Monthly Review* and *The Guardian.* As to Harmon Snow, his work on Rwanda can be found on his websites www.allthingspass.com and www.consciencebeingalliance.com. His work has also featured on websites such as www.globalresearch.ca, www.taylor-report.com, www.sfbayview.com, www.zcommunications.org, and www.blackagendareport.com.

5.3. The discursive construction of recycling

When analysing the documents published by Herman & Peterson and Harmon Snow, it becomes clear that these actors basically rely on many of the same signifiers to articulate what happened in Rwanda as the Rwandan Interim Government (RIG), the Rwandan Armed Forces (RAF) and the *Rassemblement pour le Retour des Réfugiés et la Démocratie au Rwanda* (RDR). There are of course also some differences between the accounts and at points the discourses diverge. Despite such divergences, one cannot overlook that many of the relationships established among signifiers are remarkably similar and, in doing so, virtually the same meaning concerning the events that took place is being fixed. The main signifiers involved in their discursive construction of events include:

1. Misunderstanding.
2. Propaganda.
3. Apologists and purveyors of the inversion of truth.
4. Bursts of violence.
5. Genocide against the Hutu.
6. Serving Western and US interests.
7. Victor's justice.

As with the official denial discourse, by relating these discursive elements to each other in the above order, a chain of signification is articulated and the meaning of these elements becomes temporarily fixed turning them into discursive moments. As noted earlier, in the process of articulation signifiers are organised around a master signifier, which is the nodal point in the discourse. Such a nodal point can become a floating signifier if multiple discourses struggle to fix its meaning in their own particular way (Laclau & Mouffe, 2001, p. 113). The discourse theoretical analysis of the official denial discourse revealed that it was predominantly organised around the signifier "the Rwandan tragedy" (*"le drame rwandais").* In contrast, Herman & Peterson and Harmon Snow organise their discursive construction around the general signifier "genocide" or the more specific signifier "the Rwandan genocide". It was explained that the official denial discourse was organised around the signifier "the Rwandan tragedy" because RIG, the RAF and the RDR probably wanted to avoid use of terminology that could refer to the genocide against the Tutsi. However, from the perspective of discourse theory, it is plausible that at the time the official denial discourse was developed, an absolute hegemonic intervention had not yet taken place. At the time of their discursive construction, the evidence of the genocide, which is by now overwhelming, remained largely unexcavated. There was thus more discursive space to articulate alternative discourses. However, over time the massive amount of scholarly work on the genocide has resulted in a hegemonic intervention powerfully fixing the meaning of the events. As a result, the term "Rwandan genocide" (or "1994 Rwanda genocide") has become the general and dominant term applied to describe what happened in Rwanda and the struggle now seems to revolve around this floating signifier. As will become clear throughout the analysis, an essential part of Herman & Peterson's and Harmon Snow's discursive efforts focus on instilling the signifier with the meaning of a genocide against the Hutu perpetrated by the Tutsi-led RPF. As noted in the last Chapter, this discursive construction is made possible because the terms "genocide" and "Rwandan genocide" do not specify the victim group and as such are facilitative to denial.

The following Sections will firstly reveal how Herman & Peterson and Harmon Snow articulate what exactly happened in Rwanda. The aim of the following analysis is to find out *what* meaning the aforementioned actors try to fix with regard to what happened in Rwanda and *how* they do this. We will therefore look at the main signifiers more closely and analyse how they are instilled with meaning and how they are related to each other. Due to the fact that Herman & Peterson's and Harmon Snow's discourses recycle much of the official discourse, I decided to represent their discourses not as elaborately as the official denial discourse discussed in the last Chapter. This would namely lead to extensive repetitions.

5.3.1. Misunderstandings and propaganda

In their book *The politics of genocide*, Herman & Peterson (2010e, p. 51) start their Section on "Rwanda and the Democratic Republic of Congo" stating that "the breakup of Yugoslavia" "may have been the most misrepresented series of major events over the past twenty years." But they add that "the far bloodier and destructive invasions, insurgencies, and civil wars that have ravaged several countries in the Great Lakes region of Central Africa over the same years may have been subjected to even greater misrepresentation" (Herman & Peterson, 2010e, p. 51).[8] According to Herman & Peterson (2010e, p. 62), "[v]ery big lies about Rwanda are now institutionalized and are part of the common (mis)understandings in the West." They explain that these misunderstandings exist because "[t]o a remarkable degree, all major sectors of the Western establishment swallowed a propaganda line on Rwanda that turned perpetrator and victim upside-down" (Herman & Peterson, 2010e, p. 51). Herman & Peterson (2010, p. 59) eventually conclude that:

> The established narrative's 800,000 or more largely Tutsi deaths resulting from a "pre-programmed genocide" committed by "Hutu Power" appears to have no basis in any facts, beyond the early claims by Kagame's RPF and its politically motivated Western sponsors and propagandists.[9]

Thus, according to Herman & Peterson, the events in Rwanda have been "misrepresented" due to "propaganda" resulting in grave "(mis)understandings." This involves an articulation that is very similar to the earlier discussed official denial discourse, which constructed a favourable rhetorical vantage point around "a lack of understanding" and "a misleading media campaign". The point is that both discourses, in order to create a legitimate space for their argument, articulate that people have greatly misunderstood the events, which therefore requires a better understanding that the authors subsequently will provide.

Harmon Snow follows an approach that is very similar. In the article *The US sponsored "Rwanda genocide" and its aftermath*, Harmon Snow (2008b) states:

> After more than 14 years of systematic disinformation about Rwanda there exists a collective ignorance about what really happened in Rwanda and who is responsible. The so-called "Rwanda Genocide" is one of the most widely misunderstood events in contemporary history.[10]

In an article titled *Merchants of death: Exposing corporate financed holocaust in Africa*, Harmon Snow (2008a) elaborates on how such misunderstanding supposedly has come about: "The criminality of the Kagame regime is whitewashed by the massive public relations campaigns involving Kagame's special advisor/sponsors: former Ambassador Andrew Young and former British Prime Minister Tony Blair." Also, "The New Yorker and CNN have consistently manufactured the pro-RPF/A propaganda, reported by Christiane Amanpour and Philip Gourevitch" (Harmon Snow, 2008a). In a subsequent article titled *The Rwanda genocide fabrications*

8 Peterson, in a reaction to Monbiot's critique of their work, concludes that: "The truth is that Bosnia and Rwanda rank among the most systematically misrepresented major stories of the past two decades" (Peterson, 2011a).

9 Note the inverted commas.

10 Again, note the inverted commas.

Harmon Snow (2009d) adds that "Such is the disinformation that indoctrinated the English-speaking media consumers and created a mass psychological hysteria about Rwanda that persists to this day".[11] The titles of Harmon Snow's articles are telling with regard to what the articles try to convey, namely that the misunderstanding concerning what happened in Rwanda is caused by propagandistic and flawed media coverage, which produced "the monolithic disinformation" about what happened in Rwanda. According to Harmon Snow (2011) "The propaganda system has created this story about genocide." This last excerpt makes clear that the genocide against the Tutsi is reduced to a propaganda tool.

In its articulation of the events, the official denial discourse also discursively constructs the genocide against the Tutsi as an event that is greatly misunderstood because of a misleading media campaign. At this point, Harmon Snow's and Herman & Peterson's articulation of events is very similar to how the official denial discourse is articulated. The discourses thus merge.

5.3.2. Apologists and purveyors of the inversion of truth

In contrast to the Rwandan Interim Government (RIG), the Rwandan Armed Forces (RAF) and the *Rassemblement pour le Retour des Réfugiés et la Démocratie au Rwanda* (RDR), Herman & Peterson and Harmon Snow pay significant attention to authors who in their writings have acknowledged the genocide against the Tutsi. According to Herman & Peterson (2010e, pp. 62–66), "humanitarian intellectuals", such as Philip Gourevitch, Stephen Kinzer, Samantha Power are "prime apologists" who play an important role in the misrepresentation and the institutionalisation of lies about Rwanda. One of the most prominent attacks is geared towards Alison Des Forges, who, according to them, in her expert testimony during the Military I trial at the ICTR "tried to salvage the Hutu conspiracy model, alleging plans by individual Hutu members of the coalition government to use their 'official powers' to carry out a pre-planned genocide" (Herman & Peterson, 2010e, p. 52). In a footnote to their "analysis" of Des Forges' role, Herman & Peterson (2010e, p. 129 and 130) add:

> [W]e can easily see how Des Forges work from 1991 on helped provide cover for the US takeover of as many as four countries via its proxies in Uganda and the RPF in Rwanda. In short, Alison Des Forges' career is best understood in terms of the services she performed on behalf of US power projection in Central Africa, with this policy-orientated work couched in the rhetoric of "human rights." In the process, Des Forges badly misinformed a whole generation of scholars, activists, and the cause of peace and justice as well.

Those who have acknowledged the genocide in their work are thus articulated as being part of the problem; their work facilitates the misrepresentation of reality. But, Herman & Peterson (2010e, p. 64), seem to go even further by stating that by

11 The abovementioned article was also published in the *Black Star News* under the title *False narrative: Whitewashing Rwanda genocide* (Harmon Snow, 2009c). For a similar argument see also Harmon Snow (2014).

misrepresenting what happened the human rights community has played an "active role in supporting the real aggressors and killers":

> We believe that their biases played an important role in supporting the RPF's aggression, its penetration of the country, and the execution of its final assault on power. Above all, we believe that their biases and propaganda contributed substantially to the mass killings that followed – all in accord with the needs of actual US policy.

In contrast, the discourse of the RIG, the RAF and the RDR mainly contributed the misunderstanding to a propaganda scheme set up by the RPF and its Western state supporters and it did not intensively implicate scholars, journalists and activists in this scheme. Accusing those whose work acknowledges the genocide against the Tutsi, however, seems to be an essential part of Herman & Peterson's but also of Harmon Snow's work, as will become clear. The accusations basically draw upon the rationalising practice of condemning the condemners.

Caplan (2010a) also points out that, in their analysis, Herman & Peterson ignore the work of those who have published on what happened in Rwanda and he adds that:

> Before we dismiss all these authors as tools of Yankee imperialism, it needs to be added that several of the most prominent – Des Forges, Uvin, Prunier, Lemarchand, Kuperman – are (or were) fierce critics of the post-genocide Kagame government in Rwanda. Yet none has thought to retract their original views on the reality of the genocide.

Like the official denial discourse, the discourse of Herman & Peterson thus also involves some significant rhetorical fallacies. Instead of critically reflecting upon their own position (the position they defend), they "reflect" on the "official story" of events in order to create doubt and confusion. They tend to focus on what is "not known" and do not acknowledge what is known about the genocide. Shermer & Grobman (2000, p. 103) add that, in constructing their argument, those who deny genocide decontextualise by only selecting the data that fits their denialist arguments, ignoring and in this case attacking the data that does not fit their views. It is striking to see how, for instance, Herman & Peterson (2010e, pp. 53–62) argue that, in order to accept the official, dominant or standard version of events, one has to "ignore" or "suppress" certain crucial facts, researches, reports and verdicts.[12] Their articulation of the events is predominantly based on these "obscured" sources. The point is that if genocide deniers would really critically reflect upon their own position, they would have to conclude that it is untenable. Lack of critical self-reflection is thus part and parcel of denial.

In its articulation, Harmon Snow's discourse is not very different. He also criticises people, such as Timothy Longman, Mahmood Mamdani, and Samantha Power,

---

12 Like the official denial discourse discussed in the previous Chapter, Herman & Peterson do not mention the role of France in the events, which is telling. They cannot reflect on the role of France, because this would disrupt their articulation of the events, as it would reveal that some Western powers were actually in cahoots with the Hutu Power regime.

and organisations, such as Africa Watch and Human Rights Watch, whose work acknowledges the genocide against the Tutsi, but according to Harmon Snow "endlessly perpetuate the disinformation" (Harmon Snow, 2009d). In a reaction to their critical reflection of Herman & Peterson's *The politics of genocide*, Harmon Snow (Harmon Snow, 2013b) denounces "so-called 'genocide scholars'", Caplan and "his cohort" Jones as "a necessary part of the vast money making machine that benefits from ideological bullying, using 'genocide in Rwanda' and 'genocide denialism' as weapons to silence critics, punish victims and further reward killers." Also in Harmon Snow's discourse, Des Forges appears to be a prime target. He elaborates his accusations in an article titled the *Rwanda genocide fabrications: Human Rights Watch, Alison des Forges and disinformation on Central Africa* published in *Dissident Voice* (Harmon Snow, 2009d). The title is illustrative of Harmon Snow's discursive construction of Des Forges as an agent of disinformation. He remarks that "billed as a 'tireless champion'" and "leading light in African human rights," there is much more to this story than the Western propaganda system has revealed (Harmon Snow, 2009d). According to Harmon Snow (2009d):

> [Des Forges] is the primary purveyor of the inversion of truth that covered up the deeper US role in the Rwanda "genocide" and she spent the past 10 years of her life explaining away the inconsistencies, covering up the facts, revising her own story when necessary, and manipulating public opinion about war crimes in the Great Lakes of Africa.

Harmon Snow (2009d) concludes that Des Forges' findings that the genocide resulted from the deliberate choice of a modern elite to foster hatred and fear to keep itself in power "collapse under scrutiny." He adds that "Like other researchers who have endlessly perpetuated the disinformation, Des Forges made no attempts to correct the record" (Harmon Snow, 2009d). To discredit Des Forges' acknowledgments of the genocide against the Tutsi, Harmon Snow also presents her as a US stooge. The accusations are so virulent that they basically amount to a character assassination, which attempts to cause confusion and raise doubts concerning the validity of her work.

This is thus where Herman & Peterson's and Harmon Snow's discourse diverges from the official denial discourse. Probably, the reason for this is that at the time the official denial discourse was being developed, the work of these authors was still non-existent. For instance, Des Forges' study *Leave none to tell the story* was published in 1999, while the analysed official documentation stems predominantly from the period 1994–1996. The attempts of Herman & Peterson and Harmon Snow to increase their own credibility by presenting themselves as champions of truth are thus paralleled by attempts to decrease the legitimacy of those who pose a threat to their endeavour, either because these people acknowledge what happened or because these people try to reveal their denialist enterprise.[13] This process is called altercasting and it involves placing people in a certain preferred role in order to

[13] It is insightful to look at how Herman & Peterson and Harmon Snow have reacted to critique on their work. For examples of reactions see: Herman (2011) and Herman & Peterson (2010a, 2010b, 2011b). See also Harmon Snow (2013a).

control/constrain interaction (Sandstrom, Martin, & Fine, 2003; E. A. Weinstein & Deutschberger, 1963). Such control over what others can do enables them to preserve their own world- and self-conceptions (Hewitt, 2003). By placing those who criticise you in a negative role as, for instance, being dishonest, you can also influence how others evaluate that person's behaviour and whether, for instance, their critique is credible or not. It is very similar to what Garfinkel (1956) addresses in his discussion on status degradation ceremonies by which the identity of a person is degraded by a denouncer. Garfinkel (1956, p. 424) notices that generally status degradation ceremonies occur in accordance with a set of publicly described and validated measures, but it can also occur in less formal quarrels in which one person seeks to humiliate another person.

According to Herman & Peterson and Harmon Snow, a massive propaganda scheme exists causing a misrepresentation of reality and the human rights community is deeply involved in this. But what are these facts that according to Herman & Peterson and Harmon Snow have been obscured?

5.3.3. Bursts of violence against the Tutsi and genocide against the Hutu

Herman & Peterson articulate that a planned genocide against the Tutsi did not take place; instead the Tutsi were victimised in unplanned "bursts" of violence. In *The politics of genocide*, they state that:

> [T]he Hutu members of Rwanda's power-sharing government couldn't possibly have planned a genocide against the Tutsi, the Tutsi-led RPF was well positioned to paralyze any government response to plans it had developed – and that were implemented – to avoid the threat of free election the RPF was destined to lose, to assassinate the Hutu president, and to take over the country by military force. (Herman & Peterson, 2010e, p. 52)

In an article *Kagame, our kind of guy* they furthermore explain that the Tutsi that were killed in infrequent acts of vengeance, instead of a planned genocide:

> As regards evidence on the killings, there is no doubt that many Tutsi were killed, although mostly in sporadic bursts and localized vengeance killings, not as the result of a systematically planned operation of Hutu commanders. Only the Kagame forces seem to have killed on a systematic and planned basis. (Herman & Peterson, 2010c)

Herman & Peterson furthermore insinuate that instead of a genocide against the Tutsi, a genocide against the Hutu was perpetrated by the Tutsi-led RPF. Herman & Peterson (2010e, p. 58) argue that in contrast with the Hutu power regime:

> [T]he RPF was the only well-organized killing force within Rwanda in 1994, and the only one that planned a major military offensive. Clearly, the chief responsibility for Rwandan political violence belonged to the RPF, and not to the ousted coalition government, the RAF, or any Hutu-related group.

Thus, according to Herman & Peterson (2010e, p. 63) "what Kagame turned Rwanda and the whole of Central Africa into was a rolling genocide that is ongoing". That the "rolling genocide" is "ongoing" means that it continued with the RPF "invasion" of the DRC (Herman & Peterson, 2010e, p. 66). Not only did the RPF perpetrate a genocide against the Hutu in Rwanda, they continued the genocide once the Hutu population fled to Congo. Kagame, according to Herman & Peterson (2010c), is therefore a "double-genocidist". They give the "double genocide theory" a new meaning, while distancing themselves from the classic interpretation.[14] Interestingly, in the official denial discourse, Tutsi killings were articulated as self-defence. This aspect appears to be largely neglected in Herman & Peterson's discourse.[15] The discussion below will show that this element of justifiable self-defence is articulated more clearly in Harmon Snow's discourse. Nonetheless, the discourse of Herman & Peterson and Harmon Snow is of a much less direct justificatory nature than the official denial discourse.

In contrast to Herman & Peterson, Harmon Snow (2008b) is very outspoken concerning the idea that the Tutsi-led RPF perpetrated genocide:

> [I]f anyone planned genocide in Rwanda, it was the RPF, and only the RPF. If I must accept that a pre-planned genocide was committed by the *Interahamwe* and "extremist Hutus" as defined by the official Rwanda genocide narrative that is now deeply instilled in the public mind in what can only be considered a collective insanity, then I must insist that the same people who make this claim acknowledge the genocide planned and committed by the RPF.

In an article titled *Merchants of death: Exposing corporate financed holocaust in Africa*, Harmon Snow (2008a) furthermore states:

> The "Rwanda genocide" began with the 1990 invasion of northern Rwanda by Ugandan forces that brutally targeted everyone in their path. By the time the RPF/A forces – comprised mostly of seasoned Ugandan troops – reached Kigali, more than 800,000 IDPs (internally displaced persons) were hovering around the capital city: they were terrified, they were homeless, they were hungry, they were angry and – justifiably – they took up arms.

According to Harmon Snow (2012), the violence was justified because they were "[f]orced into a life-and-death refugee existence inside Rwanda between October 1990 and April 1994" and, in this situation, "the displaced Hutu people fought back after the plane carrying the Hutu presidents of both Rwanda and Burundi, and other Rwandan high officials, was shot down over Kigali airport on April 6, 1994". Also

---

14 Herman & Peterson (2010c) criticise mainstream reports because in these reports "there was, first, the primary genocide of the Tutsi by the Hutu, which it now appears may have been followed by a secondary genocide in response by the Tutsi against the Hutu." The problem according to Herman & Peterson is that "this context is based on a monumental establishment lie about the first genocide."

15 Although one could infer it from Herman & Peterson's references to the work of Christian Davenport & Allan Stam. They refer to their work on pp. 55, 58 and 59 of their book *The politics of genocide*. The work of Davenport & Stam will be addressed in Chapter 6.

Harmon Snow presents the violence perpetrated against the Tutsi as justified self-defence and not an organised and planned genocide. This discursive construction of what happened is remarkably similar to how the official denial discourse portrayed what happened. According to Harmon Snow (2009a), the genocide against the Hutu continued once they fled into exile in neighbouring Congo: "The Kagame government, with its foreign backers, has pursued an identical strategy in Congo as they did in Rwanda". Thus, according to Harmon Snow (2008a), "If we apply the genocide label to conflicts where it surely fits, then genocide is ongoing in Congo's Orientale and Kivus provinces".

It is furthermore noteworthy that, in articulating their discourse, Herman & Peterson and Harmon Snow predominantly relate the events to Paul Kagame, who at the time was the General of the RPF and currently is the President of the Republic of Rwanda. This focus on Kagame was less strong in the official denial discourse, which focused more on the RPF in general while conflating the Tutsi with this rebel force. However, proponents of the official denial discourse at a later time also started to focus on the role of Kagame, who is presented as a genocidal master mind. For instance, Kambanda (2011) now also accuses Kagame of planning a genocide against the Hutu *and* the Tutsi. Also, Harmon Snow and Herman & Peterson do not generally articulate the Tutsi people as the root cause of the "interethnic conflict" and they also do not systematically conflate the whole Tutsi population with the RPF as the enemy. These were however central features of the official denial discourse.[16] This does not mitigate the problem that their discourse lends credibility to the official denial discourse, which does systematically conflate the Tutsi population with the RPF as the enemy. That Herman & Peterson and Harmon Snow do not articulate the Tutsi as the root of the conflict can be explained by the fact that they use the case of Rwanda as a means to an end in order to address the politics of genocide engaged in by the Western states. They articulate the US and its allies as the root of this problem. This could also explain why the discourse is much less justificatory than the official denial discourse.

5.3.4. Serving Western and US interests

According to Herman & Peterson (2010e, p. 53), the aggression of the Rwandan Patriotic Front (RPF) "led to no reprimand or cessation of support by the United States or Britain." This was because "the RPF [was] perceived as serving US

16 Such conflation does nonetheless occasionally happen. For instance, on page 56 and 57 of their book *The Politics of Genocide* Herman & Peterson state "But there is also the fact that the alleged Hutu perpetrators of "The Genocide" were the ones *driven from power* [...]. [...] If the established narrative about "who used the assassination as a pretext" were true, then Rwanda would be the first case in history in which a minority population, suffering destruction at the hands of its tormentors, drove its tormentors from power and assumed control of a country, all in the span of less than one hundred days. We find this incredible in the extreme." Jones (2010a) notes that this does conflate the Tutsi civilians with Kagame's Tutsi-led RPF and as a result "Herman & Peterson none-too-subtly adopt Hutu Power's justification for slaughtering Tutsi civilians: that they constituted a 'fifth column,' indistinguishable from the invading RPF."

interests" (Herman & Peterson, 2010e, p. 53). It "[was] doing what the United States wanted done in Rwanda" (Herman & Peterson, 2010e, p. 54). Also the "UN Security Council inaction flowed from this political bias", according to Herman & Peterson (Herman & Peterson, 2010e, p. 53). They furthermore explain that "the RPF was able to achieve a legal military presence inside Rwanda thanks to a series of ceasefires and other agreements that led to the Arusha Peace Accords of August 1993" (Herman & Peterson, 2010e, p. 54). However, these peace negotiations were "pressed upon the Rwandan government by the United States and its allies" who "called for the 'integration' of the armed forces of Rwanda and the RPF and for a 'transitional,' power-sharing government until national elections could be held in 1995" (Herman & Peterson, 2010e, p. 54). Herman & Peterson (2010e, p. 54) conclude that "These accords positioned the RPF for its bloody overthrow of a relative democratic coalition government and the takeover of the Rwandan state by a minority dictatorship." In contrast to the dominant narrative in which foreign actors are said to have been inactive in the face of the genocide against the Tutsi, Herman & Peterson argue that many foreign actors were actively involved in what happened in Rwanda. To argue like Samantha Power that the US was a bystander to the genocide is according to them thus "doubly false":

> What the United States and its Western allies (Britain, Canada, and Belgium) really did was to sponsor the US - trained Kagame; support his invasion of Rwanda from Uganda and the massive ethnic cleansing prior to April 1994; weaken the Rwandan state by forcing an economic recession and the RPF's penetration of the government and throughout the country; and then press for the complete removal of UN troops. They did this because they didn't want UN troops to stand in the way of Kagame's conquest of the country. (Herman & Peterson, 2010e, p. 63)

According to Herman & Peterson, the imperial proxy war of the US did not stop there and the US subsequently supported the invasion of the Democratic Republic of Congo (DRC).[17] Herman & Peterson (2010e, p. 66 and 67) argue that "[t]he Pentagon has very actively supported these invasions of the DRC even more heavily than it supported the RPF's drive to take Kigali." Herman & Peterson note that the successful framing of the "Hutus as villains executing a pre-planned 'genocide' against the Tutsis" and the framing of "Kagame's RPF as the defender-saviour of the Tutsis and of Rwanda and Central Africa as a whole" cleared the ground for Kagame and Museveni, "the two staunchest US clients in the region," to invade the Congo and beyond without opposition from the international community (Herman & Peterson, 2010e, p. 66). There is thus a "different set of conspirators" than the Hutu extremists and France who supported them (Herman & Peterson, 2010e, p. 56). The

[17] In an article titled *France fears U.S. advance in Africa* Howard French (1997), refers to Herman Cohen, who was Assistant Secretary of State for African affairs during the Bush Administration, who argued that: "I wish I could give credit to the U.S. Government for the broad vision and policy of doing something like this, but I can't. It's day-to-day policy. One problem at a time builds up, and the French, with their paranoia, see a grand design." This analysis stands in stark contrast with Herman and Peterson's conclusions. Following Cohen's arguments one could conclude that Herman and Peterson like the French "see a grand design" that is not there.

other "set of conspirators" consists of Washington and the RPF. Herman & Peterson (2010e, p. 55), however, see the US as having the main responsibility, because in the end "Paul Kagame and the RPF were creatures of US power."

Harmon Snow (2011) in his analysis of "the political economy of genocide" notes that "it is really about conquest, it is about empire and the United States is trying to further conquer these parts of Africa". "[W]hat I am talking about is access. That's all." He states that the reluctance of the US to use the word genocide to designate the events in Rwanda in 1994 was "not because of the so-called 'Somalia syndrome,'" but "because it likely would have forced unwanted meddling and probable intervention into a US covert operation" (Harmon Snow, 2004).[18] What is happening in Rwanda and Congo takes place off the radar screen "because the media has covered for the powerful interests and US agenda of consolidating power in the region by any means necessary" (Harmon Snow, 2001).

It thus appears that Harmon Snow and Herman & Peterson articulate the US as the root cause of the problems in Rwanda and not the Tutsi and the RPF as in the official denial discourse. It is interesting to note that despite Harmon Snow's and Herman & Peterson's discourse diverges from the official denial discourse with regard to the root cause of the conflict, both discourses signify that it is about *empire*. In the official denial discourse the notion was presented of a vast Hima Tutsi Empire, while the discourse of Herman & Peterson and Harmon Snow presents the idea of a US Empire. What is furthermore noteworthy is that although Herman & Peterson (2010e, p. 63) articulate that what the US, with the help of the RPF, overthrew was a "multi ethnic, power sharing, coalition government", they do not present the armed invasion of the RPF as a contra-revolutionary and anti-democratic war, which was what the official denial discourse articulated. Instead, the armed invasion of the RPF is presented as a "Western syndicated proxy war." A salient detail is that the forum organised by US Senator Cynthia McKinney, at which Harmon Snow (2010b) presented his "Western syndicated proxy war" reading of what happened in Rwanda, was held on the 6th of April, the day President Habyarimana was assassinated and the large scale extermination phase of the genocide was implemented. To deny the genocide against the Tutsi on the day it is collectively remembered is not a coincidence. It often happens that those who deny the genocide against the Tutsi organise parallel "commemorations", which commemorate "all victims" of the "civil war" (News of Rwanda, 2012). In Rwanda some of the most virulent denials of the genocide occur during the period of commemoration.

5.3.5. Victor's justice

Herman & Peterson (2011c) state that "in standard accounts," the International Criminal Tribunal for Rwanda (ICTR) is presented as a "genuine judicial enterprise" and not as a tool of "victor's justice and guarantor of RPF immunity," because that

18 See also: McKinney (2001).

is what it is according to them. They furthermore point out that "The ICTR's huge bias has been displayed, [...], in the fact that no Tutsi has ever been indicted by it, although vast crimes have been committed by the RPF from 1990 onward" (Herman & Peterson, 2011c). In their book they also criticise the ICTR for meeting out victor's justice:

> [All the verdicts were brought against] Hutu members of the former government and ethnic Hutus more generally, and none against members of the RPF, despite the ICTR's statute making no distinction on the basis of ethnicity or political allegiance. Neither the RPF's violent takeover of Rwanda, its massacres of "10 000 or more Hutu civilians" per month in 1994, nor any of its numerous post-war slaughters, have ever once been distributed by criminal charges at the ICTR. (Herman & Peterson, 2010e, p. 62)

They explain that "Although it has failed to convict a single Hutu of the conspiracy to commit genocide charge, the ICTR has never entertained the question of an RPF *conspiracy*" (Herman & Peterson, 2010e, p. 55).

According to Harmon Snow (2005), the ICTR perpetuates the propaganda and it "consolidates the popular mythology on genocide in Rwanda". Harmon Snow (2005) continues to explain that the ICTR does this, first of all, by "demonizing the Hutu leadership and justifying the RPF dictatorship now in control of Rwanda." Secondly, the ICTR also "serves as a means of presenting a completely false history of the events in Rwanda, and covering up the murder of the two Hutu heads of state and the massacres of hundreds of thousands of innocent people by the RPF and its allies" (Harmon Snow, 2005). Like Herman & Peterson, Harmon Snow (2009d) furthermore points out that "[s]ince the inception of the ICTR its decisions have been decisively biased – victor's justice – in favour of protecting the Kagame regime and its backers." Harmon Snow and Herman & Peterson, thus also heavily criticise the ICTR. In contrast to the official denial discourse, they do not ask for the rehabilitation of the "real victims" who have been misrepresented as the "perpetrators". Nor do they address the element of dialogue and reconciliation. Instead Harmon Snow and Herman & Peterson tend to primarily focus on the "culture of impunity" the superpowers have always enjoyed.

5.4. Recycling official genocide denial ...

Despite some significant divergences, the discourse of Harmon Snow and Herman & Peterson merges in many ways with the official denial discourse. Both discourses articulate that the events in Rwanda are greatly misunderstood due to a misleading propaganda campaign by the Rwandan Patriotic Front (RPF) and its Western allies. This campaign has obscured the true nature of events, which according to both discourses involves unplanned violence against the Tutsi that was triggered by the RPF effort to take over power by any means. The violence was justified self-defence, thereby making the victims responsible for their victimisation. Moreover, both discourses articulate that the RPF effort to take over power involved a planned and organised genocide against the Hutu that is ongoing. Western states, mainly the US, are not presented as bystanders to genocide, but they were implicated in this. Lastly, the justice meted out at the International Criminal Tribunal for Rwanda (ICTR) is biased and serves the interests of the Tutsi-led RPF and its Western backers. They thus also present the ICTR as victor's justice. This designation in both discourses is contentious in two ways. It delegitimises the important effort to prosecute the perpetrators, while at the same time it obscures the fact that there are no real victors in this conflict and only losers.[19] Those who are presented as the victors have lost many of their people. Therefore, like Cruvellier notes, it is a case of "losers justice" (Cruvellier, 2010, pp. 164–167).

Figure 8. Merging and diverging discourses

RIG, RAF, RDR	Herman, Peterson, Harmon Snow	Recycling...?
Lack of understanding	Misunderstanding	Similar discursive construction
Misleading media campaign	Propaganda	Similar discursive construction
X	Apologists and purveyors of the inversion of truth	Discursive construction added
Age long interethnic conflict	X	No such discursive construction Root cause of conflict is not addressed
Contra-revolutionary and anti-democratic warfare	X	No such discursive construction Nature of conflict is discursively constructed primarily as Western proxy war and genocide
Interethnic massacres	Bursts of violence	Similar discursive construction
Genocide against the Hutu	Genocide against the Hutu	Similar discursive construction
International ramifications	Serving Western and US interests	Similar discursive construction and elaborated
Equitable justice	Victor's justice	Similar discursive construction

Harmon Snow and Herman & Peterson thus recycle much of the official genocide denial. They draw on many of the same (key) signifiers, while also constructing similar relationships among these signifiers. Both discourses "*reallocate*", to use Herman & Peterson's phrase, the responsibility of what happened to the Tutsi-led

19 The ICTR is a troubled court as Del Ponte's book also reveals (Del Ponte, 2008). That is not a secret. However, the many issues that trouble the meeting out of fair justice at the ICTR do not justify the de-legitimisation of the attempt to prosecute the perpetrators of the genocide against the Tutsi.

RPF, who are the "prime génocidaires".[20] Despite the overlap in articulations, a significant difference can also be discerned. Earlier it was already noted that Harmon Snow and Herman & Peterson articulate the US as the root cause of the problems in Rwanda and not the Tutsi and the RPF as in the official denial discourse. For Herman & Peterson and Harmon Snow, the root cause of the problem is not an age long conflict between ethnic groups but a conflict between spheres of influence. Their neglect of the root cause of the conflict and their elaborated discourse on the nature of the conflict as a Western syndicated proxy war reveals a significant divergence from the official denial discourse. The official denial discourse is driven by a racist and genocidal anti-Tutsi ideology, while for the abovementioned authors the case of Rwanda turns out to be a means to an end to criticise the foreign policy of the US and its allies. They draw on the earlier discussed framework of the politics of genocide to develop their criticism. How the analytical concept of the politics of genocide that they present in their work is applied reveals a particular way of looking at and making sense of massive conflicts in the world, including the conflicts in the Great Lakes Region. The politics of genocide encompasses the denial of human suffering by those responsible for that suffering in order to safeguard their positions and/or to consolidate their power with the result that these powerful actors enjoy impunity for what they have done. Herman & Peterson and Harmon Snow, however, apply this framework with a singular focus on the US and its allies, which, according to these authors, are the root of all evil. Therefore, their discourse does not seem to be influenced by a genocidal ideology; instead, their denial discourse appears to follow from a radical anti-imperialist ideology.[21, 22] This indicates that Herman & Peterson and Harmon Snow initially did not intentionally recycle the official denial discourse. Although their discourse was not inspired by a genocidal ideology, it nonetheless remains problematic. It results in a denial of the genocide against the Tutsi, while at the same time enhancing the credibility of the official denial discourse.

5.5. Secondary or primary genocide denial?

Herman & Peterson's and Harmon Snow's denial is thus motivated by an anti-imperialist political ideology and, although it recycles much of the official genocide

20 This phrase was used by Herman & Peterson in an email addressed to me, in which they reacted to my open letter to Noam Chomsky. The letter will be discussed in more detail in the next Chapter, Section 6.2.

21 See also Chrétien (2012).

22 Although, the far-right and ultra-left have different political ideologies shaping their discourses and their worlds are generally far apart, it is possible as Monbiot (2011a) points out that the left and right "cohabit in the weird world of the genocide belittlers." Thus in addition to the right-wing denial of extremist political groups, the work of these actors appears to indicate a new malign intellectual subculture of left wing denial (Monbiot, 2011c). See also Monbiot (2011b, 2012b) and Jones (2011b). This is a worrying development, as the left has traditionally been critical of issues, such as abuse of power that causes human suffering, especially when it comes to the negative impact of western foreign policies. However, as Monbiot (2011c) notes, in their criticism they have taken "the unwarranted step of belittling the acts of genocide committed by opponents of the western powers." This is a dynamic that according to Coquio is often present in cases of genocide denial. Although the ideologies and the end underlying the denial discourses differ, the mechanisms used are similar (Coquio, 2003a, pp. 63–65).

denial, a clear genocidal intention seems to be lacking. By denying the genocide against the Tutsi they do not mean to annihilate the Tutsi people. Following the typology presented in Chapter 3, Section 3.3. of this study, one could therefore argue that their denial involves a case of secondary genocide denial and not primary genocide denial. Although, the required genocidal intention for primary genocide denial appears to be lacking, their discourse nonetheless has dire consequences as it empowers primary genocide denial and thereby helps to complete the genocidal process.

However, like denial in general, genocide denial is a dynamic phenomenon and it develops over time. As explained in Chapter 2 of this study, Breznitz's research shows how people switch to a more advanced stage of denial because the reality they are confronted with makes it impossible to maintain the current level of adjustment (Breznitz, 1983, p. 262). People switch stages when it becomes impossible to maintain the previous level of adjustment because they have been confronted with new threatening information (Breznitz, 1983, p. 263 and 266). Once caught in the process, it goes only in one direction, namely forward (Breznitz, 1983, p. 264).[23] Herman & Peterson and Harmon Snow have been confronted with the troublesome nature of their work on Rwanda on multiple occasions.[24] For instance, the two open letters I sent to Noam Chomsky in which he was asked to clarify why he endorsed the book *The politics of genocide* as a "powerful inquiry" were also read by Herman & Peterson. Herman & Peterson subsequently replied to me and "explained" that "In the United States, the name for the technique that [I was] employing against Noam Chomsky and [them] is called *McCarthyism*." According to Herman & Peterson (2011, Correspondence on file with author), in my letter I "never once mention, let alone attempt to analyse or dispute, facts" concerning these and other issues presented in their work. They add:

> The question therefore arises: Did you actually read Chapter 2, Section 4 of our book, or are you basing your attack on something you read or heard elsewhere? We challenge you to look at our analysis again, and to refute it by addressing the substantive issues we discuss rather than taking cheap-shots at us (e.g., "gross denial of human suffering") and at Noam Chomsky for contributing the Foreword to our book.

According to Herman & Peterson, the analysis in the letters to Chomsky had "badly mischaracterized the analysis that [they] develop and support in detail in Chapter 2, Section 4 of [their] book." They added:

> Thus in respect to the nature of the political violence that swept Rwanda, *ca.* 1990–1994, we are clearly not genocide *deniers* – we are genocide *re-allocators*. That is, we re-allocate the primary responsibility for the estimated 800,000 or 1 million or more deaths of the 100-day Rwanda *genocide* (or Genocide No. One) from the established narrative's notion of a pre-planned "conspiracy to commit genocide" by the "Hutu Power" figures who are

23 See also Payne (2008, p. 162).

24 For Herman & Peterson's and Harmon Snow's reactions to critique see: Herman (2011), Herman & Peterson (2010a, 2010b, 2011b) and Harmon Snow (2009b, 2009d, 2013a).

alleged to have assassinated Hutu President Juvenal Habyarimana so they could carry out a genocide against the Tutsi minority, to the Tutsi commander Paul Kagame and his vastly superior invading army, the Rwandan Patriotic Front, who assassinated Habyarimana and launched their final drive to seize state-power in Rwanda because they knew that under the national elections scheduled by the Arusha Accords for 1995, the Kagame-led RPF stood no chance of prevailing. (For Genocide No. Two, again with major Kagame-RPF responsibility, see the report, Mapping human rights violations in the DRC 1993–2003, UN Office of the High Commissioner for Human Rights, October 1, 2010.)

The term "genocide *re-allocators*" is a clever euphemism that mystifies the true nature of their discursive construction. The question who massively victimised the Tutsi and why remains unanswered.[25] Moreover, the explanatory gap they leave with their answer can only be filled by reiterating a discourse that recycles essential elements of the earlier discussed official denial discourse. Herman & Peterson's reactions illustrate the point made by Breznitz mentioned above concerning the progressive nature of denial. Instead of acknowledging the problems with their discourse, they further rearticulate their denialist reality. Their reaction reveals many of the mechanisms discussed before; they turn the tables and, instead of addressing the issues raised in the letter, they challenge me to look into their "facts". They downplay the analysis and the insights provided for in the letter as "cheap-shots" and they furthermore frame the approach to ask straightforward and open questions as "McCarthyism". What becomes clear from Herman & Peterson's response is that their denial has strengthened and they have gone further down the spiral. This development could have implications for the question whether their genocide denial is secondary or primary.

Despite the many critical signals concerning their discourse and the detrimental role it plays in the genocidal victimisation of the Tutsi, Herman & Peterson and Harmon Snow tend to stick to their denialist plot and they continue to sophisticate and spread it.[26] In the 2011 edition of their book, Herman & Peterson added some "reflections on *The politics of genocide*". They, for instance, discuss the regime change in Libya and they contrast this case with the situation in Sri Lanka, which did not receive the attention it should have taking into account the massive violence that occurred. Interestingly their "reflection" does not address the massive critique that their book received, which in terms of denial is a relevant reaction. Instead, they argue that "writing some two-and-one-half years later, we can state without exaggeration that [their] critique was robust" (Herman & Peterson, 2011a). Also Harmon Snow does not seriously address the critique his work has triggered. Instead, he denounces

---

25 But from the above analysis of their discourse, it nonetheless becomes clear that these deaths were probably the result of "sporadic bursts and localized vengeance killings" by the Hutu population (Herman & Peterson, 2010c). They furthermore follow the argument that the "mass killings were not directed against the Tutsi population" (Herman & Peterson, 2010e, p. 58). With regard to the calculation of victim rates Herman and Peterson rely on the work of two US academics Christian Davenport and Allan Stam. Their questionable analysis of the war and the genocide will be discussed in the next Chapter in Sections. 6.2.2. to 6.2.4.

26 See for instance the critical reviews of Herman & Peterson's work by Caplan (2010a, 2010b, 2013b) Monbiot (2011a, 2011b, 2012a), Jones (2010a, 2010d, 2011b, 2013), Shaw (2011a) and Wizeye (2011).

the critique as an "attack" that "is nothing more than a defence of the mainstream establishment narrative about 'genocide in Rwanda'" (Harmon Snow, 2013b). What do these reactions say about their intentions?

As noted earlier in Chapter 2, Section 2.3.4., the question of special intention is difficult to answer and is prone to serious discussions and conflicting views; scholars do agree that the special intention defines genocide, but there is no agreement on what defines intention (Jones, 2006, p. 21). Depending on the view on what special intention entails, different conclusions can be reached as to whether the required element of special intent is present in the cases of Herman & Peterson and Harmon Snow. When it comes to the question of intention, two aspects concerning their behaviour are important. The first aspect is their *persistence*. After being confronted with their denial, these actors can no longer legitimately claim that they were not aware of what they were doing or that they therefore did not have the intention to deny the genocide. Such arguments have become untenable and this has serious implications. If an analysis involves a denial of the genocide against the Tutsi and it recycles many crucial elements of the official denial discourse and authors insist on these views, while it has been made clear to them how dangerous their discourse is, the question arises whether their denial can still be characterised as secondary genocide denial. Are they still unwillingly facilitating the denial dynamic on which genocide thrives? The second aspect concerns the *systematic* nature of their denial. In the earlier discussion on intention in Chapter 2, Section 2.3.4., it was noted that explanatory approaches define intention as an element of a concept of genocide and it refers to a planned, persistent and systematic effort to annihilate. The idea is that the intention can be gleaned from the persistent and systematic effort of actors to implement policies of which these actors know will lead to the annihilation of a people. Herman & Peterson and Harmon Snow also systematically persist in their denial. Their denial was not a singular event, but they engage in it on a systematic basis by publishing new books and more articles. They also spread their denial through their lectures and talks. The point is that Herman & Peterson and Harmon Snow are aware of the detrimental consequences of their actions but they nonetheless systematically persist in their actions and they refrain from taking the required action to stop the harm they cause. The required intention could exist if one argues that, by acting in the above described persistent and systematic manner, they have accepted the consequences of their behaviour and, in that case, it is hard to imagine that the harm caused is accidental or undesired. What is furthermore important to note is the role in which the actors spread their views. These actors are promoting these views as professionals, as journalists or academics. This professional quality increases the level of responsibility they have for their actions (*Garantstellung*). As pointed out above, Herman & Peterson and Harmon Snow have not lived up to the standards of their profession.

Genocidal intent ...

The above discussion on intention is aimed at showing that denial is dynamic in nature and that, depending on the situation, actors can move from one type of denial to another type of denial. It is about explaining how genocide denial operates and how actors can possibly become entangled in the process of genocide to which denial is essential. The discussion is not intended to construct a criminal liability for genocide, because in that case the question whether there is intent might be answered differently. In order to be held criminally liable for genocide, regular intention does not suffice; a so-called special intention is required. Special intention requires that an act of victimisation is undertaken intentionally, but secondly that, through this particular act, one intends to annihilate a certain people. Moreover, for criminal liability, the intention, as the required state of mind, is limited to certain degrees of fault. In legal approaches, intention is generally defined as an element of the crime of genocide which refers to individuals having a particular state of mind (mental element) that informs their actions. In such approaches, it is not about explaining genocide but about holding individuals criminally responsible.[27] Thus, in contrast to social scientists who tend to locate intention in *the systemic character of the process* leading to a certain outcome, which is how the question of intention was approached above, legal scholars have to demonstrate a particular *state of mind of an individual* involved in the performance of a certain act. Among legal scholars, there is however much discussion on what this state of mind entails when it comes to the perpetration of genocide. The approaches move from strict volitional to broader knowledge-based interpretations of intention (Ambos, 2009; Goldsmith, 2010). Intention (*dolus*) spans a continuum involving different degrees. In case of *dolus directus*, the harmful effect of the behaviour was foreseen and desired by the actor (Blomsma, 2012, p. 65). *Dolus indirectus* involves the scenario in which undesired (additional) harmful effects are caused by the behaviour and these unwanted effects can be foreseen with virtual certainty by the actor. The actor has to be aware that the effects will occur in the ordinary course of events. In contrast to *dolus directus*, the actor thus acts despite the consequences and not because of that consequence (Blomsma, 2012, p. 69). Lastly, the situation can arise that the perpetrator foresees that his actions can possibly also have undesired consequences but nonetheless goes ahead with the act. This is called *dolus eventualis* (Blomsma, 2012, p. 99). Genocide is a crime with a double intentional element. There is the general intent as to the underlying acts of genocide. In addition, there is what one could refer to as the ulterior intent concerning the overarching aim of the annihilation of a people. This last mental element is also referred to as special intent (*dolus specialis*). Traditionally, interpretations of special intent have followed a strict reading of intention stressing its volitional character and the degree of intention required is *dolus directus*. In this approach, one must not only have the intention to perpetrate a specific act of genocide, one should also have the desire to bring about a

[27] Establishing such as genocidal intention is a challenging task because genocidal agents are not likely to admit and openly confess the intentions underlying their actions and therefore also in legal practice the intention is lastly often deduced from the systematic pattern of action which could only arise out of specific intent (Stanton, 1998a). For instance, in Kayishema the ICTR Trial Chamber pointed out that "the specific intent can be inferred from words and deeds and may be demonstrated by a pattern of purposeful action" (The Prosecutor v. Kayishema, Case No. ICTR-95-1, Judgment May 21, 1999, par. 527). The Chamber furthermore stated that "The Prosecution submitted that evidence of specific intent (*dolus specialis*) arises from the repetitive character of the planned and programmed massacres and the constant focus on the Tutsi members of the population" (The Prosecutor v. Kayishema, Case No. ICTR-95-1, Judgment May 21, 1999, par. 534).

certain result, in this case annihilation, by perpetrating that act. It is thus not enough that you only know this will be the result of your actions, there also has to be a desire to bring about that result. Intention here thus entails knowledge and wilfulness. This is also the approach generally followed by international criminal tribunals such as the ICTR (Van der Vyver, 2004). According to this strict interpretation of intent, the required genocidal intention would not be present in the cases of Herman & Peterson and Harmon Snow. The strict interpretation of intention has, however, been repeatedly criticised and put into question and new approaches to intention have been presented. These new approaches move into the direction of a knowledge-based approach as the most appropriate way to delineate genocidal intention. Depending on the interpretation, these approaches could move from *dolus directus* to *dolus indirectus*. Greenawalt (1999) has, for instance, argued that, "in defined situations, principal culpability for genocide should extend to those who may personally lack a specific genocidal purpose, but who commit genocidal acts while understanding the destructive consequences of their actions". Greenawalt's approach appears to come very close to how intent was approached in the above discussion.[28]

A further nuance is in order if one was to conclude that Herman & Peterson's and Harmon Snow's denial of the genocide against the Tutsi over time has moved from secondary to primary genocide denial. The world of primary denial is also inhabited by extremist racist ideologues who attempt to obscure the nature of the violence inflicted in order to complete the genocidal process. They attempt to realise a racist genocidal ideology and the denial is a means to this end. As noted before, the authors discussed above are, however, not motivated by such racism. Interestingly, in case of Herman & Peterson and Harmon Snow, the denial of their denial of the genocide against the Tutsi has elevated them to primary genocide deniers. As a result, one should not equate all agents of denial simply because they engage in the same type of denial.

5.6. Genocide denial: Violence?

It has been observed that, apart from the actual slaughtering of people, which concerns the extermination stage of the genocide, all of the stages of the genocidal process involve words which are fatal (Tatz, 2003, p. 25). Genocide denial often concerns non-verbal activities, such as the murder and intimidation of genocide survivors and other witnesses who embody the living evidence of the genocide that took place. In addition, the corpses of those who were victimised are hidden and the documentation that (somehow) revealed the genocidal process is destroyed.[29]

28 For now it is important to realise that, although from a social scientific perspective, things can become clearer and more insightful, legally the opposite can be true and more questions are raised than answered. Although it would be interesting and insightful to translate the denialism "model," including the notions of secondary and primary denial, into a model of criminal liability for genocide denial and to address the implications that arise, this is not feasible within the scope of this research which takes a social scientific approach to genocide denialism.

29 For examples of such genocide denial activities in the context of the genocide against the Tutsi see the reporting by African Rights (1996).

However, as this study has shown so far, much genocide denial does not involve physical acts of violence, but speech acts instead. In the abovementioned letter to Chomsky, who endorsed Herman and Peterson's book, I noted that "[a]s one of the most renowned linguistic experts of our time, [he] of all people should know the power of words and the role they play in the initiation and conduct of conflict." I furthermore added that "Herman & Peterson's brazen genocide denial facilitates a genocidal dynamic, and thus their words have grave, possibly mortal implications." Smith, Markusen and Lifton even conclude that genocide denial ought to be seen as a "contribution to the genocidal violence in its own right" (R. W. Smith et al., 1999). But why are the implications of denial so "grave" or "possibly mortal"? And how can denial contribute to the genocidal violence in its own right? I understand that by addressing this question, after the discussion of Herman and Peterson and Harmon Snows "recycling", I am asking much from the reader. I, however, think it is appropriate to address this question at this point in the study because, once one understands the violence involved in such speech, it becomes clear why the official denial discourse is problematic and why the recycling of such speech by the abovementioned authors is so detrimental.

5.6.1. Facilitating violence ...

In addition to physical acts, language plays an important role in the violent genocidal process, but what exactly is the relationship between language and violence? In much of the scholarly work that addresses the relationship between violence and language the role of language seems to be mainly described as facilitative to physical violence. The general argument is that through blaming, scapegoating, classifying, vilifying, devaluating, dehumanising, stigmatising, denying, etc., social relations are altered/reconstructed to such a negative extent that it makes physical violence possible. In explaining massacres and genocide, Semelin, for instance, reveals how language is being used to construct a threatening and frightening enemy of diabolical proportions which has to be destroyed. This, according to Semelin (2007, p. 22 emphasis added), is an "*imaginaire* of death" and it involves a "discourse that is perceived as coherent and credible, and able to allay individuals' anxiety. [...] Through it imaginary and real interrelate. [...] These discourses, in which myths and realities are intertwined, can serve as *a springboard towards massacre*." Here Semelin represents the role of language as facilitative to physical violence. Eltringham (2003) furthermore notes that "while conflict may have indisputable, physical manifestations in violence and coercion, these are peaks in a process that is most of the time enacted in discourse and competing verbal representations." Although Eltringham acknowledges the important role of language in the process of conflict, he nonetheless points out that the manifestations in violence are physical. The relationship between violence and language is also central to studies on the impact of media. Generally the analysis focuses on the question whether, for instance, explicit word use contributes to violence. The idea is that "violent speech begets violent behaviour" (Garlield, 2005, p. 609). These examples are not unique. In many approaches language is presented as facilitative to physical violence, while the idea that language is violent in itself is largely neglected.[30, 31] It seems that words cannot do harm, that violence is only physical and that words can facilitate such physical violence but cannot be violent in themselves. Like in the saying "sticks and stones may break my bones, but words will never hurt me." But, what if Žižek (2009, p. 51 and 52) is right and "humans exceed animals in their capacity for violence precisely because they speak."

In her study on workplace violence, Catley (2003, p. 5 and 6) makes an important observation concerning this issue:

> [T]he "obviousness" of violence as physical [...] serves to erase or marginalize other conceptions of violence. The sorts of violence, for example, that does not necessarily leave its mark on the body. The focus on discrete or sensational incidents of physical violence seals off the repeated and systematic forms of violence, for example the on-going instances of harassment, bullying and mobbing. While privileging physical representations of violence as the "real" instances of violence denies the performative aspects of language. Instances of verbal abuse are considered secondary or in support of the "real" episodes of physical violence.

In contrast to those who approach the relationship between language and violence as facilitative, Catley acknowledges that language can be violent in itself and, in her attempt to grasp such acts of non-physical violence, Catley draws on the earlier discussed speech act theory of Austin and Searle to put forward the argument that in the act of saying certain words of violence we do, we enact violence. According to Catley (2003, p. 8), "[l]anguage is not a 'do nothing' domain that reinforces or reflects 'real' violence. Language is not a promise of things to come. It is the words themselves that attack, wound and injure." Because, in this approach, language is not seen as external to violence, communication is not simply the solution to violent conflict situations. Speech is not the "antithesis of violence" (Catley, 2003, p. 8).[32] In grounding her arguments, Catley draws more specifically on the work of Judith Butler (1997) who in her book *Excitable speech* made use of speech act theory to discuss and theorise the relationship between language and violence. Butlers'

---

30 For examples of a similar approach to the role of language in genocide see for instance a document prepared by the United States Holocaust Memorial Museum (2009) and the contribution by Volhardt et al. (2007).

31 The approach that these scholars take is somehow understandable, because if language can facilitate conflict, it can also help to solve and prevent it, as Chilton (1997, p. 188) points out: "Verbal communication is essential to the initiation and conduct of conflict, so it is essential to its prevention, resolution and conclusion."

32 By arguing that "language is not a 'do nothing' domain" Catley (2003) makes an insightful point that is crucial to understanding why denialist speech is problematic as will be further elaborated throughout the following Section of this Chapter. Catley's remark is valuable because not many scholars raise awareness about this particular issue concerning the relationship between language and violence. One could of course raise the critique, also towards the approach developed in my study on genocide denialism that by bringing *linguistic violence* within the scope of "real violence" inflation of the meaning of violence occurs. I, however, think that this is not the case. Both forms of violence are "real violence" and, by bringing linguistic violence within that scope, we do justice to the nature of the phenomenon. However, it is important to note that I do not simply equate physical violence with linguistic violence, because, as will be explained later, the nature of the violence is different. To brutally beat somebody to death is something different than verbally abusing somebody.

ideas are insightful in the context of this research and they therefore warrant more attention. However, before Butler's ideas will be elaborated, it is important to briefly address how I define violence.

Defining violence

Imbusch's research addresses the origins of the concept of violence and how its meaning has changed over time. He concludes that violence is a diffuse concept and therefore hard to define (Imbusch, 2003). However, as Galtung (1969, p. 168) makes clear, it is not so important to arrive at *the* definition of violence. Instead, it is more important to demystify certain theoretically significant dimensions of violence that allow us to think about it and help us to solve the problem of violence. Galtung (1969, p. 168) argues that "violence is present when human beings are being influenced so that their actual somatic and mental realizations are below their potential realizations." Violence is thus "that which increases the distance between the potential and the actual and that which impedes the decrease of this distance" (Galtung, 1969, p. 168). This means that when the hindrance to potential realisation is avoidable, then violence is present (Galtung, 1969, p. 169).[33] Galtung thus conceives violence in terms of influence and he furthermore argues that violent action has two dimensions or modes of influence: physical and psychological. Physical violence affects human beings somatically; it works on and through the body. It varies from biological violence, which reduces the somatic capability of the human body, to violence that reduces free movement, because, for instance, a person is imprisoned. Psychological violence serves to decrease a person's mental potentials. It works on and through the soul and it can range from threats and swearing, to lies and indoctrination (Galtung, 1969, p. 169). Following Galtung, I acknowledge that physical and psychological violence can thus take many forms, as there are many possible ways in which human beings can be negatively influenced so that they are unable to reach their full potential. The idea that modes of influence are not only physical, but also psychological, makes it possible for violence to be linguistic; instead of knuckles hitting the face of a victim, people can be victimised by being negatively labelled with words.

The understanding that speech assaults victims is also a central element underlying the broader concept of "hate speech" (Armstrong, 2001; Delgado & Stefancic, 2004). Here, violence is linguistically conveyed through the written or spoken word and includes speech acts such as slandering and humiliating. Hate speech causes mental and psychological harm, such as nightmares, fear, withdrawal from society, depression, damaged self-image, and lower aspiration levels (Delgado & Stefancic, 2004, p. 14 and 15). Delgado's and Stefancic's observations make clear that, although the fact that the mode of influence of violence that hate speech causes, to use Galtung's terminology, is psychological, the effects can be both psychological and physical. It results in increased heart rates, headaches, etc. Some scholars, like Corsevski (2007, p. 513 and 514), therefore argue that linguistic violence is closely

33 Thus when the actual is unavoidable, then violence is not present.

related to physical violence, because abusive words do impact human beings in a very palpable and physical way: "The linguistic violence creates a measurable, physical result. [...] Taking a verbal beating means taking a kind of corporal beating as well." The abovementioned scholars indicate that language can be violent, but if that is the case, the question arises how this is possible? How can words actually wound?[34] It is significant in the context of this research that Galtung and the other scholars mentioned frame violence in terms of its physical or psychological impact (influence). It is however important to understand that the violence that denial does is not necessarily physical or psychological. It can have such perlocutionary effects, but, as will become clear throughout the next Sections, the violence that linguistic denial enacts in the moment it is uttered is of a more specific nature and should not be reduced to physical or psychological violence.

5.6.2. Constituting violence ...

In her book *Excitable speech*, Judith Butler (1997) addresses several relevant questions. She more particularly wonders that "when [people] claim to have been injured by language, what kind of claim do [they] make?" According to Butler (1997, p. 1), we seem to "ascribe an agency to language, a power to injure, and position ourselves as the object of its injurious trajectory." But how does language have the power to be violent and what violence does it do and how? Butler points out that the usage of terms like "wound" or "verbal beating" is actually quite problematic as it suggests that language can act and hurt people in the same way as physical or psychological violence does.[35] We see this also in the context of research on denial of known genocides when scholars describe denial as the "killing of history". Butler's critique thus is also to a certain extent applicable to the title of this study ("The killing of death"). After all, by using such terminology, the linguistic injury is described in the same way as a physical or psychological injury. Butler however argues that these are actually different phenomena that cannot be grasped in the same terms. More importantly, the use of the jargon of physical or psychological violence to describe linguistic violence obscures its unique features (Butler, 1997, p. 4). The analogue application of the framework of physical and psychological violence to linguistic violence thus hinders a better understanding of the particular violence that language does. If we want to understand the nature of the violence that language can do, we will have to look into how language can perform violence or, in Galtung's words,

[34] It is important to note that I do not claim that language can never be facilitative to violence. On the contrary, often language facilitates violence as the case of *Radio et Télévision Libre des Milles Collines* (RTLM) illustrates. This radio station was set up in 1993 and its virulent hate radio played a crucial role in the genocide. It incited hatred and urged people to kill the Tutsi (Chrétien, 1995a). However, it is pertinent to acknowledge that language in addition to being facilitative to violence can also be constitutive of violence.

[35] Such analogies are often presented. See for instance also Riley (2001, p. 41) who states that: "Verbal attacks, in the moment they happen, resemble stoning. Isn't it making heavy weather, then, to ask how they do damage: isn't the answer plain that they hurt just as stones hurt? At the instant of their impact, so they do."

how uttering words can hinder and obstruct human beings, or in this particular case a people, in reaching their full potential.

Butler (1997, p. 3) explains that, in order for an utterance like racial discriminatory hate speech, to be injurious action, it should not only communicate an offensive set of ideas which claims the inferiority of a particular people. More importantly, it should enact that very set of ideas in the moment of its utterance. Such speech effectuates the subordination of that race while making those claims (Butler, 1997, p. 3). Like Austin and Searle's illocutionary speech act, it enacts the message it communicates in the moment of communication. Key in understanding why, for instance, racial discriminatory hate speech can directly harm human beings is the insight that humans are not only biological or physical objects but also social and symbolic subjects (*Doppelkörperlichkeit*). It is because humans are also constituted in social and symbolic terms that we are vulnerable to violence that harms us on that level of being (Lemke, 2011). Humans are also linguistic beings who need language in order to be, because only through language humans can come into being (Butler, 1997, p. 1 and 2). For instance, at birth not only a physical body is brought into this world. The human body receives a name and it becomes a human individual, a subject, a social body (Krämer, 2005, p. 5). Here we see, as discourse theory explained, how objects become real and intelligible by being constructed through particular discourses. Butler furthermore explains how language is vital in constituting human beings as social and symbolic subjects by drawing on Althusser's concept of interpellation.[36] Butler (1997, p. 5 ad 6) argues that, "[l]anguage sustains the body not by bringing it into being or feeding it in a literal way; rather it is by being interpellated within terms of language that a certain social existence of the body first becomes possible" and she adds that "[i]f language can sustain the body it can also threaten its existence." Therefore, according to Butler (1997, p. 5 ad 6), "the question of the specific ways that language threatens violence seems bound up with the primary dependence that any speaking being has by virtue of the interpellative or constitutive address of the Other." Thus, our vulnerability to language is a consequence of the fact that we are constituted within its terms: "Hate speech exposes a prior vulnerability to language, one that we have by virtue of being interpellated kinds of beings, dependent on the address of the Other in order to be" (Butler, 1997, p. 26).

It is however important to notice that interpellative power is not necessarily violent, because interpellation can also construct people in a positive way; it is through processes of interpellation that they are given a social existence. This double character of naming has been explored by, for instance Dawes (1999), who explains that, on the one hand, naming is violence, because you forcibly enforce a sign upon a human subject thereby creating the other. Naming creates hierarchies, enables surveillance and control. However, on the other hand, human rights declarations, such as the International Covenant on Civil and Political Rights (ICCPR), clarify

36 According to Althusser (1971, p. 174), "ideology hails or interpellates concrete individuals as concrete subjects." Thus, ideology has the function to transform individuals into subjects. Althusser (1971, p. 174), for instance, gives the example of how an individual is transformed in a subject of state subjugation, when a police man hails a person: "Hey, you there!"

that every human being has the right to recognition and therefore article 24 Section 2 states that every child shall have a name. Thus, according to Dawes (1999, p. 215 and 216), naming has a dual character: "To be named is to suffer violence; to be named is the foundation of human dignity." However, in contrast to constructive interpellation, there are also interpellations that do the opposite when they name; they derogate, demean and oppress. Instead of creating social existence, they make it impossible, break it down and destroy it. Butler (1997, p. 2) therefore concludes that language not only constructs our subjectivity, it can also dismantle it by positioning subjects as inferior beings. Here violence is predominantly discussed in terms of racist language which in the moment of its utterance oppresses.[37] Žižek (2009, p. 51 and 52) thus appears to be right when he argued that "humans exceed animals in their capacity for violence precisely because they speak."

Human beings are thus vulnerable to language because they are constituted within its terms, but when can language be violent? How do words injure the addressee at the moment of speech? For Butler, speech can be violent in itself in the moment of utterance because it takes away the social recognition required for human *being* and it therefore threatens and destroys our position in society.[38] Butler clarifies this notion by exploring Matsuda's work on hate speech. Matsuda's argument is that hate speech not only affects its addressee in certain ways (perlocution), more importantly according to Matsuda, such speech socially constitutes the one addressed at the moment it is uttered (illocution).[39] At its moment of utterance, hate speech places a person in a position within a broader social structure and the injury lies in the fact that this is a marginalised position. In terms of Galtung's approach to violence discussed earlier, such a position would hinder the full development of a human being (and the group he or she belongs to). Such speech interpellates the addressed in a way that (re)constitutes domination and it subordinates at the moment it is uttered. Butler (1997, p. 18 and 19) concludes that:

> In Mari Matsuda's formulation [...] speech does not merely reflect a relation of social domination; speech enacts domination, becoming the vehicle through which that social structure is reinstated. According to this illocutionary model, hate speech constitutes its addressee at the moment of its utterance; it does not describe an injury or produce one as a consequence; it is, in the very speaking of such speech, the performance of the injury itself, where the injury is understood as social subordination. What hate speech does [...] is to constitute the subject in a subordinate position. [It] reinvokes the position of dominance, and reconsolidates it at the moment of utterance.

Hate speech can thus be injurious due to the fact that it names a social subject and it constructs the subject in the moment of naming, but the construction is a violent

37 The violence could, of course, also involve other kinds of speech acts. Instead of racist language, one could for instance also think of legal judgments, as Cover (1986, p. 1601) explains: "Legal interpretative acts signal and occasion the imposition of violence upon others: A judge articulates her understanding of a text, and as a result, somebody loses his freedom, his property, his children, even his life."

38 See also Krämer (2005, p. 14).

39 See Chapter 3, Section 3.8. for an explanation of these concepts.

interpellation because in the moment of uttering, it oppresses and prevents human beings from freely developing themselves (Butler, 1997, p. 49). The idea that speech can subordinate at the moment of its utterance has also been used by Langton to explain the violence involved in apartheid language. According to Langton (1993, p. 302), illocutionary speech acts of apartheid subordinated, because they ranked blacks as having inferior worth and they deprived them of their power.[40]

It is important to notice that the abovementioned scholars extend the sphere of application of speech act theory as originally developed by Austin and Searle in an important way bringing it more in line with social reality. In doing so they address some serious criticism raised by scholars, such as Pratt (1986, p. 63), who noticed that in the work of Austin and Searle the focus on those who engage in speech acts are free essential subjects and this somehow obscures the fact that when people speak they do this in a socially constituted position and these roles can differ significantly depending on the situation. What further complicates the matter is that, in Austin and Searle's speech act theory, those involved in the speech act predominantly engage in cooperative and/or collaborative behaviour as Pratt (1986, p. 64) points out: "Speech-act theory stresses language as essentially a cooperative form of behaviour, in which participants work together rationally to achieve shared or common goals." Although Austin mentions in his description of speech acts that they involve the execution of power, his analysis of speech acts does not take into account how power might impact on the speech dynamic. The scenario underlying speech act theory is that of a free essential speaker and hearer coming together in cooperative speech acts, trying to achieve common goals. The problem is, as the abovementioned examples and the specific case of linguistic genocide denial shows, that the subjects are not essential and free. In contrast, they are embedded in power structures which influence and sometimes even determine their identity and their behaviour. Also, as the phenomenon of genocide denial reveals, their speech acts are not necessarily always cooperative and constructive. Instead, they can be sabotaging, alienating and destructive.[41]

People thus manage to do all kinds of things with words and, in addition to making promises and marrying one another, people also manage to oppress one another. This critical issue has been acknowledged by Butler and the other scholars mentioned

40 Langton (1998) develops a similar argument with regard to pornography. For other illustrations that speech is violent because it reproduces social domination, it is insightful to read MacKinnon's work on the oppressive power of pornography (MacKinnon, 1987, 1993). Another insightful illustration comes from Kaplan (2009) who studied the linguistic violence of the Nazi regime focussing on how words required ever more exclusive meanings eventually leading to the exclusion of the Jewish community.

41 The idea of an open and free "talk exchange" that is underlying speech act theory suggests an interaction in which parties play an equal part. Pratt (1986, p. 68) however explains that "it is equally common for one person or group to be calling the shots for others, for one person or group to be defining the purpose of an encounter, determining what quantity is enough, what topics are relevant, what counts as truth and adequate evidence, who gets to speak at all. Think of your last interaction with a police officer, or your employer. It would be incorrect to think of speech roles as always or even normally a matter of choice, of cooperation as always or normally voluntary, of non-cooperation as always or normally irrational. For hierarchical speech situations, to do so is often to define things only from the viewpoint of the most powerful party."

above in their discussion of oppressive and subordinating speech acts. Their work shows that oppressive or subordinating language is thus violent in itself and it is not only instrumental to it. But what gives words such violent power?

5.6.3. The power to enact linguistic violence

The force to injure someone physically resides in the biological or mechanical power a human body has and can exert on another body, but where does the violent power of words originate from? In the context of his research on apartheid speech, Langton (1993, p. 304) explains that a government's action of ranking a people as inferior draws on the authority of the speaker, in this case a state institution, which imbues the utterance with its force. This oppressive force would be absent if the speaker did not occupy such an authority role. Langton thus sees authority as an essential condition for the successful performance of speech acts of subordination.[42] Subordinating or oppressive speech acts are thus authoritative speech acts and those who utter such speech must have authority. But what does such authority involve? From Langton's discussion it becomes clear that the effective or *de facto* authority that such illocutions require does not only reside in formal institutions. Less formal and even informal societal structures can also provide for the required authority. Authority can thus operate in many different domains that vary from large state bureaucracies to small family structures and, as a result, such authority can be general and formal but also local and informal (Langton, 1998, pp. 270–273). Langton thus argues that whether there is the required authority is quite dynamic and depends greatly on the specific speech situation and its context. Despite Langton's open approach to what constitutes authority, she tends to situate the authority required for illocutionary acts to be performed mainly in the institutional structures outside language.

Butler (1997, p. 32) also points out in her analysis that the power to perform illocutionary acts can rely on structures that have been vested with authority, such as the church, the police, the immigration department, the judiciary, etc. In these cases, the authority is always directly connected to an institutional speaker: a state, a police officer, an immigration department officer, a clergyman, etc. However, Butler also situates the authority to perform oppressive and illocutionary speech in the institution of language itself and its meaningful relation to history and society. According to Butler (1997, p. 51), a performative succeeds because "that action echoes prior actions, and accumulates the force of authority through the repetition or citation of a prior and authoritative set of practices." Butler argues that, in order to injure, hate speech invokes the power of community, of history, of ideology: "The subject who utters the socially injurious words is mobilized by that long string of injurious interpellations: the subject achieves a temporary status in the citing of that utterance, in performing itself the origin of that utterance" (Butler, 1997, p. 49 and 50). Thus words can be injurious because they echo prior actions and they accumulate an injurious force due to repetition or citation of a prior authoritative set of practices:

42 See also (Langton, 1998, p. 263). In terms of Austin one could refer to this as a felicity condition.

"What this means then, is that a performative 'works' to the extent that *it draws on and covers over* the constitutive conventions by which it is mobilized" (Butler, 1997, p. 51). Discursive practices to a great extent draw on earlier meaning constructions (Jørgensen & Philips, 2002, p. 139). In earlier work on gender, Butler (1993, p. 2) already noted that "performativity must be understood not as a singular or deliberate 'act', but rather as the reiterative and citational practice by which discourses produces the effects that it names." Thus, for instance, the authority of anti-Semitic hate speech thrives on a long history of anti-Semitism and persecution of the Jewish people. To give such speech its force it is not required for a speaker to have authority bestowed upon him by an institutional structure such as a state or a political party, etc. Anti-Semitic language derives its force because it echoes previous anti-Semitic (speech) acts. When such racist language is spoken, everybody exactly knows what is meant and, more importantly, what it does.[43] That is namely the reason that it is uttered in the first place. The same applies to the virulent hate speech that was part and parcel of the genocide against the Tutsi. Thus, someone who utters racist language is "citing that slur, making linguistic community with a history of speakers" (Butler, 1997, p. 52). In terms of discourse analysis we can frame the point Butler is making with reference to the notion of "inter-textuality" or "inter-discursivity" which refers to the insight that texts draw on earlier meaning formations and thereby discourses are being reproduced (Jørgensen & Philips, 2002, p. 72 and 73).

Butler thus situates the authority, the power of words to injure not necessarily in a speaker, but in the institution of language itself, its conventionality, its historicity, its *reiterability*. As a result, authority is situated in a discursive terrain of power. The author of a speech act can therefore have the required authority even if it is not officially bestowed upon him or her as a speaker. In that case a person invokes the authority that certain speech historically entails; it makes linguistic community with that history of speech. According to Butler, this insight has important implications as it means that discriminatory hate speech does not simply originate with the subject who speaks it. It derives its violent power from the fact that it is *a citation of itself*; we know its violent power because it was uttered before and that is why it is used (Butler, 1997, p. 80). It is precisely the notion of "reiterability" that it is "a citation of itself", which informs why Herman & Peterson's and Harmon Snow's recycling of the official denial discourse is so problematic. Their denialist speech has the violent power to injure, because it makes linguistic community with an extensive history of persecution; it reiterates the ideological discourse of genocide. By recycling the

43 Davis (2014), in an article on Australia's Stolen Generations, touches upon the issue how certain actors are keen to forget the historical contexts that gave birth to hate speech. Davis (2014) also notices that hate speech derives its power from the events in which it arose: "The thing that proponents of this marketplace of ideas ignore, but which minorities should never forget, is that speech has a context. Take for example a mate of mine, who was recently on the train with his primary school aged kids. A drunk on the train starts having a go for no reason; he probably would have had a problem whether they were black, white, Asian, or Muslim. But on this occasion, they were Jewish. So the guy starts on about 'rich Jews', and uses this trope to yell offensive nonsense at a seven-year-old boy. It's ghoulish, but it's also especially offensive because these insults have a history which cannot be simply brushed aside. When someone makes monkey noises directed at a football player, we all know what it means." He adds: "That context can mean that a seemingly inoffensive phrase is, in fact, offensive."

official genocide denial, they make linguistic community with a history of ideological Hutu Power speech that is racist and denialist. What is particularly notorious is that the ideology informing the anti-Tutsi propaganda was influenced by early pseudo-scientific anthropological studies undertaken by Western scholars in the Great Lakes Region. The Hamitic hypothesis that was developed in this body of work has been incorporated in the genocide ideology in order to "scientifically" strengthen the articulation that the Twa and Hutu were the original inhabitants of Rwanda and that the Tutsi were an alien race that descended from the north of Africa and invaded Rwanda.[44] The genocide ideology cites early Western scholarly "scientific" interpretations that were themselves highly ideological to begin with, thereby making linguistic community with that history of speakers. Bagilishya explains that discursive constructions on which the official discourse discussed earlier relied, existed long before the mentioned official documents were published. Bagilishya, in his analysis of the development of historical narrative presented in official documentation of the former regime and the roles it played in the genocide, makes clear that the genocidal project began with the denial of the other, with the denial of their citizenship – he points out that a continuity exists between the publication of the Bahutu Manifesto in 1957 and its republication in 1990 (Bagilishya, 2003). Due to its historical development, the discourse is meaningful to many and generations have been indoctrinated by the extremist exclusionary narrative that denies the humanity of the Tutsi. The denialist discourse discussed here thrives on and makes linguistic community with that narrative history.

5.6.4. The violence of genocide denial

The understanding gained from the above discussion allows us to clarify how genocide denial can constitute violence in itself, instead of only being facilitative to violence. To be clear, the argument is not that denial cannot facilitate violence, because it can. The typology presented earlier in Chapter 3, Section 3.3. clearly indicates that denial can facilitate acts of genocide. This was termed denial of genocide. Such denial speech can, for instance, involve the negative interpellation of the victimised group by reiterating elements of the genocidal ideology. In addition to articulating the Tutsi as being alien to Rwanda, it also presents Tutsi as power-hungry untrustworthy cockroaches, a threat against which society should be protected. This is Semelin's *imaginaire*. Denial of genocide speech that facilitates the perpetration of acts of genocide draws on this ideological interpellation of the victim as deceitful vermin that constitutes an enemy of the state and its designated people. The ideological interpellation also functions to hide the true nature of events. What is taking place is not the annihilation of an innocent people; instead a menace that is threatening society is being taken care of. Denial of genocide facilitates the perpetration of acts of genocide, by presenting the victim as being the perpetrator (and as a result the real

---

44 For an analysis of the Hamitic hypothesis and its relation to the genocide against the Tutsi see: Kayishema (2013) and Eltringham (2012).

perpetrators become victims). *Genocide ideology* and *denial of genocide* are thus closely interlinked in the process of the *killing of life*.

Genocide denial and *genocide ideology* are also intimately related and closely intertwined with the process of the *killing of death*. The analysis of the official genocide denial discourse reveals that its articulation of the "Rwandan tragedy" also relies on elements that are central to the genocidal ideology. Like in the above example, it draws on ideological misrepresentations of the Tutsi people as alien, devious and power hungry in order to renegotiate the dominant image of who are the "real" génocidaires and the "real" victims. Such genocide denial thus does not only *reflect* a genocide ideology; it *enacts* it at the moment of utterance. In this case, like the hate speech that Matsuda and Butler analysed, utterances of genocide denial also re-invoke a position of dominance and oppression and (re)consolidate this position at the moment of utterance (Butler, 1997, p. 13). The denial echoes such prior meaningful action. Although this element is central to the official denial discourse, it is much less developed in the discourse of Herman & Peterson and Harmon Snow. As discussed above, their discourse does not pay specific attention to articulating the Tutsi as the root of the conflict. They focus on the United States (US) and its imperial plot instead.

In the examples discussed above, the practice of victim blaming stands out. In that case the denial operates through the victims – the subjects – targeted in the conflict. Victim blaming is an important technique of genocide denial which in its quest for annihilation aims to obscure that the genocidal victimisation of a people took place.[45] The point is, however, that the broader event of genocide itself is also targeted by genocide denial, because, for its successful perpetration, genocide requires that the event of genocide itself is obscured and erased from history. As Nichanian (2009) pointed out, an essential part of the process of genocidal annihilation is that the perpetration of the genocide itself is no longer a historical reality. However, as the earlier discussion on the speech act of genocide denial revealed, there are many ways in which genocide can be denied and victim blaming is one of these many techniques. Genocide denial can entail discursive constructions in which the victim is blamed but also constructions in which the event is portrayed as being non-genocidal.

What seems to complicate the matter is that Althusser's concept of interpellation, on which Butler draws, focuses on the "hailing" or "naming" of human subjects, while genocide denial targets the broader historical event of genocide itself: denial of the victim is a means to this end. In Althusser's work, interpellation was presented as a way that subjects are brought into being. In these cases, people are placed in certain positions by particular ways of talking about them. Victim blaming relies on this process. From the perspective of discourse theory, one could argue that the subjects are positions in discourses and it is this idea that underlies Laclau &

45 It can also be a technique utilised in primary and secondary denial of genocide. Denial of genocide and genocide denial can rely on the same discursive elements, but according to the model the ends achieved with the denials are different. Nonetheless each of the denials can facilitate the other through its perlocutionary effects.

Mouffe's understanding of the subject. Laclau & Mouffe's and Althusser's ideas both appear to maintain that people are interpellated by discourses and subjects are subject positions in discursive structures (Jørgensen & Philips, 2002, p. 40 and 41). For instance, who we are is determined by the discourses that determine specific positions. In medical discourse, a person can be constructed as a patient, in social scientific discourses a person can be a deviant and in legal discourse a person can be a subject of law. Discourses can interpellate subjects through a process of articulation and the identity of the subject is established relationally. In ideological genocide discourses, the victim people are often meaningfully constructed by relating them to what that group equals and what it differs from (antagonistic relations). As illustrated above, in this process of interpellation, the group is often articulated as being less than human (alien) and lacking sympathetic human characteristics (untrustworthy): they are equalled with vermin and at the same time they are contrasted with what they are not, namely human beings. Denial of a victim's humanity is crucial to both denial of genocide and genocide denial.

It is, however, crucial to understand that not only subjects, the victims of genocide, are created in discourse by ways of talking about them, but also the event of victimisation, the genocide itself, is constructed in and through discourse. As Chilton pointed out, war and genocide as events are also social phenomena, which are equally dependent on language for their constitution, because through language these events are made intelligible.[46] Following Butler and Chilton, one could argue that language does not sustain the event of genocide in a literal way; instead it is because of the interpellation of these events that the social existence of the genocide becomes intelligible: it becomes a reality. It is thus by being articulated within terms of discourse that the social existence of an event of genocide becomes possible, as discourse creates the meaning and thereby the reality of genocide. However, if discourse can sustain genocide, it can also threaten its meaningful reality. The violent force of denial is thus intimately related to the dependence upon a constitutive discourse that acknowledges the genocide. The violence that genocide denial thus inflicts is that it articulates the event of genocide in a way that it is not (fully) acknowledged but (partly) excluded and thereby made unintelligible to us. If the genocide against the Tutsi is not "hailed" (recognised) or interpellated, it is not or no longer brought into being and its existence is destroyed. This denial is violent because it is an intrinsic element of the process of annihilation, which, if completed, results in the inexistence of a people. Genocide denial thus prevents a victimised people from re-creating their historical process, thereby undermining their cultural continuity as an entity (Charny, 1991, p. 22 and 23). The official genocide denial discourse is violent because it makes the genocide against the Tutsi unintelligible. The leftist anti-imperialist discourse discussed at the beginning of this Chapter is troublesome because it is a denial discourse that in

[46] Although the above example draws on the idea of interpellation to explain how human subjects or groups are interpellated by discourse, Laclau & Mouffe's discourse theoretical framework is more broadly applicable and in principle it can be used to analyse how social phenomena are discursively constructed (Jørgensen & Philips, 2002, p. 25). As explained earlier, for Laclau & Mouffe everything is discursive and objects gain meaning and become intelligible only through discursive practices of articulation.

its articulation recycles much of the official genocide denial. Following Butler, its violent power flows from the fact that it makes linguistic community with the official denial of the genocide against the Tutsi and the ideology of genocide underlying it. This official denial discourse had the power to do violence because it was spawned by powerful authorities who, in their quest to stay in power, implemented the most extreme form of oppression: the annihilation of a people. The denial of the genocide is violent because through speech it continues this most extreme form of oppression; by denying the genocide, it continues the genocide against the Tutsi.[47] Actors can intentionally make such linguistic community with histories of genocidal violence, but even the unintended discursive recycling of such histories of violence empowers the oppressive ideological structures.[48]

5.7. Concluding remarks

The problem of the politics of genocide is especially relevant in the context of genocide denial, because the politics of genocide effectively result in a denial of human suffering. Herman & Peterson and Harmon Snow raise concern in their work about many instances of gross human rights violations which were (co)perpetrated by Western powers with impunity. These cases in which justice is denied do indeed require our serious attention. However, their operationalisation of the analytical framework turns out to be problematic for several reasons. They for instance lump together crimes of a different nature without any further conceptual clarification. Moreover their application of the framework reveals a particular focus on the politics of genocide of the United States (US), a process which they claim is facilitated by many

47 Theriault (2009, p. 93) in his analysis of the denial of the Armenian genocide notes that denial is "a symptom or form of expression of [a] domination relation produced through genocide."

48 From the last Sections of this Chapter it became clear that genocide denial can also be constitutive to violence. However, as noted earlier, genocide denial is mostly presented as being facilitative to violence and only rarely do scholars attempt to capture genocide denial's unique violent nature. Nash-Marshall and Mahdessian's research is a notable exception and worth looking into, because they think out of the box when it comes to making sense of genocide denial and the violence that it does. In unravelling the violence of genocide denial, Nash-Marshall and Mahdessian (2013) focus on situations that include deliberate lying. Interestingly, they also make use of the framework of speech act theory. Nash-Marshall and Mahdessian (2013, p. 140) basically argue that the lie that genocide did not occur inflicts severe mental damage on a particular group of people. In their understanding, the violence of genocide denial lies thus primarily in the impact it has on the mental health of the targeted group; the lies impede proper functioning of the mind (Nash-Marshall & Mahdessian, 2013). The lie is thus a means to an end to cause the mental health of a people to disintegrate thereby facilitating the process of annihilation. Although Nash-Marshall and Mahdessian argue that genocide denial can be violent in its own right, they do still fail to capture the unique nature of the violence that denial does. In their approach, the violence that genocide denial does is basically psychological violence that also has severe physical effects. However, according to the analysis presented above, the nature of the violence is characterised quite differently and the violence that genocide denial does is neither physical nor psychological in nature. Instead the nature of the violence is discursive in nature. Through speech historical events of genocide are obscured and made unintelligible, thereby completing the last stage of the genocide. Nash-Marshall and Mahdessian frame the nature of the violence of genocide denial in terms of the "killing of life", while the approach set out above frames the nature of the violence in terms of the "killing of death". In the last approach, the mental disintegration could nonetheless still be a perlocutionary effect.

other actors ranging from national and international institutions and organisations to journalists, intellectuals, and the general public. In their analysis Herman & Peterson and Harmon Snow neglect a wealth of relevant data concerning other actors. When it comes to, for instance, the conflict in Rwanda they overlook influential actors, such as France and the Catholic Church, which have also played a crucial role in the events. The most significant problem is, however, that their analysis turns out to encompass an alternative reading (articulation) of events that amounts to a brazen denial of the genocide against the Tutsi and which, in its discursive construction, recycles many of the elements that are central to the official denial discourse discussed in the Chapter 4. Their articulation of events turns the history of the 1994 genocide of Rwanda's Tutsi on its head and it runs counter to the overwhelming majority of data, which consists of innumerable pieces of evidence, including eyewitness accounts, criminal investigations, academic studies, etc. (Caplan, 2010a, 2010b). In articulating the events, Herman & Peterson and Harmon Snow thus "ignore" the vast majority of research that acknowledges the genocide against the Tutsi, while at the same time they make selective use of "suppressed" evidence to articulate an alternative version of events.[49] Kearns (2010) furthermore notes that they "seem to assume that acknowledging the role of the Rwandan Patriotic Front and the Western governments that either passively or actively supported its actions requires that one deny that a genocide occurred – either you open your eyes to 'what really happened' or you're an unwitting defender of the United States' imperial designs for the Great Lakes region." The point is that, the gross human rights violations perpetrated by the RPF and whatever role various foreign actors played in what happened in Rwanda does not, in any way, make the attempted annihilation of the entire Tutsi people less of a fact. The theoretical framework that Herman & Peterson and Harmon Snow present in its application seems to be primarily a means to the end of criticising US imperialism and not the politics of genocide as such. Ultimately Herman & Peterson and Harmon Snow are not engaging in critical research on the politics of genocide. Instead, they are engaging in political activism by propagating an anti-imperialist ideology. It does not study *the* politics of genocide, but it is *a* politics of genocide that divides the world into worthy and unworthy victims (Shaw, 2011b). Thus, in the end, also for them, to use Herman & Peterson's own words, it has nothing to do with whether "certain thresholds of scale" are reached or whether what happened is "inherently conscience shocking". Again what seems to really matter is "*who* does *what* to *whom* – and *where does power lie*" and "[i]f it's a crime of somebody else,

[49] Kearns (2010) notes that there is however no thorough engagement with the existing wealth of information on the genocide against the Tutsi and where they do take such information into account, the engagement is limited to dismissing it as part of the "cover-up". Herman & Peterson and Harmon Snow do not provide strong evidence for these claims and they do not show where all other scholarship which acknowledges the genocide has it wrong. Shaw (2011) heavily criticises Herman & Peterson's methodology, which according to him can be summarised as follows: "sweeping assertions about historical events, political attitudes and intellectual positions, buttressed by selective quotation and ignoring most contending sources and arguments, with cavalier use of statistics, all calibrated via a one-dimensional media survey and offered without any attempt to define key concepts." (See also Shaw in Monbiot, 2012a; Shaw, 2011a) Although Shaw's remarks concerned the work of Herman & Peterson, it also readily applies to Harmon Snow's work on Rwanda. In contrast to Herman & Peterson's book, Harmon Snow's work has however received little critique. For critique on Harmon Snow's work see the online reactions to the following articles (Harmon Snow, 2009b, 2009d).

particularly an enemy, then we're utterly outraged" (Herman & Peterson, 2010e, p. 16 and 27).

One could wonder whether the denial of the abovementioned actors is really such an issue, because their denial is dwarfed by scholarly work that does acknowledge the genocide against the Tutsi. Despite the fact that there is an abundance of work that does indeed acknowledge the genocide, the work of these authors remains problematic for the following reasons. It should be noted that the denial of the genocide against the Tutsi is not limited to these two authors. It involves a broader phenomenon and the work of these authors is thus only an illustrative tip of the iceberg. Although Herman & Peterson's and Harmon Snow's work on Rwanda certainly does not have the power by itself to erase the history of the genocide against the Tutsi, their work does contribute to a bigger genocidal project. Denial is an intrinsic part of this bigger project, which in 1994 almost managed to annihilate the Tutsi people. That attempt was also the result not of the acts of one or two persons but of the acts of many significant and insignificant actors that all intentionally or unintentionally contributed to the realisation of a genocidal anti-Tutsi ideology. Freeman's words are relevant in this context:

> Genocide is a social process, initiated and implemented by various social agents in structured social positions. It consists of many different actions by many different agents located in different positions in the social structure. (Freeman, 1991, p. 188)

The actions of the abovementioned authors should not be overestimated, but their actions should also not be underestimated. Furthermore, following Butler's insights one could argue that, by recycling the official denial, the abovementioned authors help to maintain a system of violent repression while providing it with journalistic and scholarly legitimacy.

The recycling of the official denial discourse by others appears to create particular challenges for survivors, as became clear during a conversation with a man who had survived the genocide while the rest of his family was murdered. He had great difficulty making sense of why those who had not participated in the genocide would deny the genocide and basically cast doubt on what really happened to his family. Why would people that he did not know, had not known his family, were actually from another country, etc. question what happened to him and his loved ones. What made matters even more incomprehensible was that, during the Gacaca hearings, the killers of his family had revealed in gruesome detail what they had done to his relatives. Instead of denying their acts, the perpetrators, to his surprise, acknowledged what happened. So those who had reasons to deny did not and those who had no reason to deny the genocide did. The man explained that, even though it is difficult and painful, he could somehow understand why *génocidaires* would deny what happened; the reality is too confronting for them, they try to avoid punishment, etc. But why would these others who were not directly implicated deny the fate of his family? The fact that the man could not make reasonable sense of this (visibly) caused him much distress; it haunted and confused him. (Anonymous 2014, personal communication)

When glancing over the various denials of the genocide against the Tutsi discussed, one can conclude that they all operate on a mixture of historical (ancient hatred), defensive/reactive (self-protection), Machiavellian (power mongers), vindictive (planned and provoked), deflective (environmental factors), selective (focussing on certain actors) argumentation (Karrorero 2014, personal communication). It moves the attention away from the acts of the genocidal regime itself and presents the idea that the people quickly and easily turned on each other. It neglects the acts of planning and organisation of the former genocidal regime, such as the marginalisation of moderate political elements, stockpiling of weapons, massive propaganda, training of militia, etc.

Although the denial of the genocide against the Tutsi involves a specific discursive construction, it is interesting to observe that the official, academic and journalistic discourses discussed above also merge with other genocide denial discourses which deny the Holocaust or the Armenian genocide. Apparently genocide denials draw on similar strategies (Dumas, 2010, p. 99). In his research on denial of the Armenian genocide, Hovannisian (Hovannisian, 1987; 1999a, pp. 205–228; 1999b) explains that deniers follow a strategy that encompasses the following elements. Those who engage in genocide denial argue that stories about the alleged genocide are founded on wartime *propaganda* and they argue that the alleged *victims were not free of guilt*; they provoked the conflict and therefore action was necessary as national security was threatened. The denial often *refutes the genocidal intent* and it is argued that those who claim that genocide has happened have themselves killed many innocent people. They add that the *genocide is a myth* created by the victims and their supporters for political purposes. In addition, deniers engage in a *numbers game* aimed at minimising the impact of their crimes. The tribunals in which alleged genocides are prosecuted are, according to them, power tools of *victor's justice.* Those who did not directly participate but rally for the deniers *call on their right of freedom of speech and intellectual freedom* to dissimulate their arguments; they are *champions of truth* who are not corrupted by the established power structure. They rationalise, banalise and relativise genocide in very similar ways as is done with the genocide against the Tutsi discussed above. The strategies discerned by Hovannisian in the context of denial of the Armenian Genocide have also been distinguished in the context of denial of the Holocaust, by Vidal-Naquet (1992), Van Hennink (1993), Ternon (1989, 1999b, 2003), Stanton (2005) and Smith (2014). In addition to the abovementioned rhetorical devices, Charny (1991, pp. 13–15) mentions the following basic vocabularies of denial of known genocides. These include, for instance, the point that *more research and data is needed* to put forward the claim that genocide happened, while at the same time *attacking claims of genocide.* We can also distinguish these elements in the official denial discourse and the discourse that recycles it. Thus, although cases of genocide differ substantially, there are striking similarities between the ways genocides are being denied.

As explained in Chapter 2, denial is an interpersonal phenomenon and this means that those bent on denying the genocide are reliant on the actions of others to be able to keep up the denial successfully. Others might knowingly participate or support the denial or they can end up facilitating the denial unintentionally. These actors can end up providing a platform for denial or their speech can lend weight to the denialist mantra and provide it with credibility. Their work might contribute to confusion and uncertainty concerning the events or because they somehow unintentionally provide those bent on denying genocide with more discursive ammunition. The next Chapter reflects on these issues by looking into the actions of certain actors that are not readily associated with genocide denial but nonetheless raise serious question in terms of the approach to genocide denialism developed throughout this study.

Part III
Reflection

Chapter 6
Broader implications

6.1. Introduction

The insights gained throughout this study concerning how denial operates in the context of the process of genocide have implications for a wider variety of actors who somehow engage with the flow of meaning concerning the events in Rwanda. To this end, this Chapter will continue to reflect on *how the discursive actions of other actors not readily associated with genocide denial can be problematic in terms of genocide denialism because they somehow facilitate the denial dynamic.* The analysis does not aim to be an *ad hominem* attack, although perlocutionary, it might be perceived as such by those whose work is addressed below. Nonetheless, it is not about the specific actors, it is about their speech and discourse and the aim of the analysis is to raise awareness of how speech that is otherwise not directly deemed questionable, through the prism of genocide denialism presented in this research, can become problematic. Denial is an interpersonal phenomenon and in order to be able to deny the genocide against the Tutsi successfully, deniers rely on others who knowingly collude or unintentionally support their alternative construction of reality. One can thus get caught in the web of denial more easily than one might initially think. *By addressing the discursive actions of several actors, this Chapter aims to highlight the broader dynamics of denial on which genocide thrives.*[1] To this end, the first part of the Chapter problematises the endorsements of Herman & Peterson's book *The politics of genocide* made by notable intellectuals such as Noam Chomsky and Jon Pilger. Subsequently, the work of Professors Christian Davenport & Allan Stam is discussed. Their work in Rwanda will receive elaborate attention because it has been systematically used in discourse that denies the genocide against the Tutsi. The question is whether their findings are simply abused or whether there are more fundamental issues concerning their research that could explain why it is used in denialist articulations. Furthermore, Lemarchand's work on the genocide is interesting in this context. Lemarchand, one of the most notable Rwanda scholars, appears to have developed a more extreme revisionist stance concerning what happened in Rwanda. The development of his narrative, especially on the downing of President's Habyarimana's airplane, raises questions from the perspective developed throughout this study. It will therefore receive considerable attention. The second part of this Chapter deals with the intriguing relationship between criminal defence and genocide denial and it more particularly examines how the right of the defence

1 Throughout this Chapter I focus on several examples in order to show the various fields/areas in which such unintentional support or intentional collusion occurs. The examples discussed are however only a small fraction of the number of actors involved: in reality the web of denial is much more extensive than pictured in this Chapter.

to question the charges and to raise alternative explanations can cause considerable problems in terms of genocide denialism. Thirdly, one of the most intriguing implications of the genocide denialism approach is that certain actions of the current Government of Rwanda also raise issues. Therefore, the criminalisation of genocide denial and the problems that flow from it will be addressed. Furthermore, in terms of genocide denialism, some critical elements of the history promoted by the current Government of Rwanda will be discussed. The Chapter will end with a brief reflection on the work of human rights organisations, such as Human Rights Watch, and how their advocacy on Rwanda can also raise questions in terms of genocide denialism. The discussion of these cases will reveal that the framework developed throughout this study has broader implications and that the web of denial is much more extensive as one might initially think.

6.2. Academic engagement

6.2.1. Endorsing genocide denial

Chomsky's endorsement of Herman & Peterson's book *The politics of genocide* mentioned earlier raises questions. Although Chomsky's foreword does not address the case of Rwanda, he nonetheless endorses the book as a "powerful inquiry" (Herman & Peterson, 2010e, p. 7). As noted in Chapter 5, I wrote two open letters to Chomsky to inquire about why he endorsed the book and to raise the possible consequences of his endorsement.[2] In the letter I noted:

> In the foreword to Herman & Peterson's book, you make it clear that you are critical of the "vulgar politicization of the concept of genocide," exactly because biased usage leads to denial of human suffering, to denial of genocide. I am afraid that by endorsing Herman & Peterson's book as a "powerful inquiry", you are actually facilitating a process that directly opposes and undermines what you stand for.

I furthermore added:

> In this context, I also want to refer to the article that I mentioned at the beginning of this letter. I think that Herman & Peterson in their analysis of what happened in Rwanda have grossly neglected their intellectual responsibility. As you pointed out, intellectuals

[2] Herman and Peterson and those who endorsed their book were already being questioned about their conduct. I, however, found it rather questionable that, although Chomsky wrote the foreword to *The politics of genocide*, he was not being asked about his endorsement. Taking into account that Chomsky is a *renowned scholar in linguistics* and an *influential public intellectual*, I thought it was most pertinent to ask him about his endorsement. After writing and publishing the letters, some asked me whether I was trying to put myself in the spotlight. The point is that it is not about Chomsky or me as individuals but about the positions we hold and these professional roles come with certain responsibilities. That is also the main issue that I try to raise in my letters. Chomsky's case, furthermore, illustrates how complex the dynamic of genocide denialism can be. Chomsky does not deny the genocide against the Tutsi as such in his foreword, but by endorsing an account that does deny the genocide he is empowering and facilitating the denial dynamic.

> have a responsibility to seek the truth instead of hiding it behind a veil of distortion and misrepresentation. The fact that you wrote the foreword to their book also urges me to question your own intellectual responsibility. If you truly believe that intellectuals have a deep responsibility "to speak the truth and to expose lies", you should distance yourself from Herman & Peterson's genocide denial account at once. I think your responsibility as an intellectual requires you to critically examine their work, instead of uncritically endorsing it.

Chomsky's answer to the letter was cursory and did not in any way engage with the issues raised. The problem is that Chomsky's endorsement enhances the creditability of Herman & Peterson's work. This problem is not limited to Chomsky; it can also be extended to other actors who enhanced the credibility of Herman & Peterson's book by recommending it.

The book is namely also commended by notable intellectuals such as John Pilger, whose endorsement is on the cover of the book. Pilger states that Herman & Peterson's book is a "brilliant expose of great power's lethal industry of lies" and he adds that Herman & Peterson "defend the right of us all to a truthful historical memory." Adam Jones asked John Pilger in an open letter for an explanation about his endorsement (Jones, 2010b). Jones' letter was posted on *Pambazuka News*, but Pilger did not react. One reaction, of a reader, however aptly captures the issue at hand. He states that "there is a danger that the admirers of John Pilger may unquestioningly accept every opinion that he may put forward as correct." Being a notable and powerful intellectual, the same applies to Chomsky. By enhancing the credibility of denialist discourses, these actors do not engage in genocide denial, but their behaviour facilitates the denial dynamic on which the process of genocide thrives. This problem does not only affect scholars or intellectuals who endorse denialist accounts, in terms of facilitation, the actions of other actors can become equally problematic. In this context one could also think of the publisher of the book *Monthly Review Press* (2010), which stated the following:

> With its careful and voluminous documentation, close reading of the US media and political and scholarly writing on the subject, and clear and incisive charts, *The Politics of Genocide* is both a damning condemnation and stunning exposé of a deeply rooted and effective system of propaganda aimed at deceiving the population while promoting the expansion of a cruel and heartless imperial system.

I asked the publisher of the book to publish the letter to Chomsky, whose foreword to the book was also published on their website under the title *Genocide denial with a vengeance: Old and new Imperial norms* (Chomsky, 2010).[3] They replied stating that "[t]he editorial committee appreciated the letter but, unfortunately, the committee did not feel that it fit in MR's publishing plans" (Monthly Review 2011, Correspondence on file with author). Taking into account the typology discussed in Chapter 3, one could argue that the abovementioned behaviour is problematic not

[3] The title is remarkable when taking into account what Chomsky is actually endorsing.

because they constitute genocide denial, as such, but because they in effect facilitate the denial dynamic.

6.2.2. Selective and mendacious use?

Authors like Chomsky and Pilger facilitate the denial dynamic by endorsing a denialist discourse, but what if one's scholarly work becomes part of the articulation of a discourse that denies the genocide against the Tutsi? This seems to be the case with Christian Davenport and Allan Stam's work on Rwanda. Christian Davenport is Professor at the Department of Political Science of the University of Michigan Institute for Social Research. He is also a Research Professor at the Peace Research Institute, Oslo (PRIO). Allan C. Stam was Professor at the Gerald R. Ford School of Public Policy of the University of Michigan. Now he is Dean of the Frank Batten School of Leadership and Public Policy and Professor of Public Policy at the University of Virginia. Both Herman & Peterson and Harmon Snow have used their work to articulate their denialist discourse (Harmon Snow, 2010a; Herman & Peterson, 2010e). The way Davenport & Stam's work is used to articulate a reversal of the victim and perpetrator roles becomes most clear from Herman & Peterson's discursive construction. Their articulation of the events draws on mainly two elements from Davenport & Stam's research. Firstly, according to Herman & Peterson (2010e, p. 58), Davenport & Stam concluded that the "majority of victims were likely Hutu and not Tutsi". Herman & Peterson make it seem that Davenport & Stam made a straightforward conclusion. The quotation of Davenport & Stam's work is however selective, because if one reads the entire section from which the quotation is taken, it becomes clear that Davenport & Stam never concluded anything. Herman & Peterson refer to an article published in the *Miller-McCune Magazine*, in which Davenport & Stam (2009 emphasis added) state that:

> In the end, our *best estimate* of who died during the 1994 massacre was, really, an *educated guess based on an estimate* of the number of Tutsi in the country at the outset of the war and the number who survived the war.

Their "conclusion" is thus at best an "educated guess". Secondly, according to Herman & Peterson (2010e, p. 58), "Davenport & Stam's work shows convincingly that the theatres where the killing was greatest correlates with spikes in RPF activity [...], as a series of RPF advances, particularly in the month of April 1994, created roving patterns of killing." They furthermore quote Davenport & Stam's finding, which was also published in the *Miller-McCune Magazine*, that: "The killings in the zone controlled by the RAF seemed to escalate as the RPF moved into the country and acquired more territory. When the RPF advanced, large-scale killings escalated. When the RPF stopped, large-scale killings largely decreased" (Davenport & Stam, 2009). Herman & Peterson (2010e, p. 58) argue that "[w]ith these facts, Davenport & Stam appear to link the mass killings of 1994 to RPF actions; this work also suggests that the mass killings were not directed against the Tutsi population."

However, according to Herman & Peterson (2010e, p. 58):

> Davenport & Stam [still] shy away from asserting the most important lesson of their work – not only that the majority of killings took place in those theatres where the RPF "surged," but also that the RPF was the only well-organized killing force within Rwanda in 1994, and the only one that planned a major military offensive. Clearly, the chief responsibility for Rwandan political violence belonged to the RPF, and not to the ousted coalition government, the RAF, or any Hutu-related group.

Herman & Peterson (2010e, p. 59) thus criticise Davenport & Stam for not breaking away from "the mainstream camp". The selective use of Davenport & Stam's work becomes clear from the fact that Herman & Peterson do not mention Davenport & Stam's finding that their "research showed [that] the vast majority of the 1994 killing had been conducted by the RAF, the Interahamwe and their associates" (Davenport & Stam, 2009). This finding is the opposite of what Herman & Peterson actually claim in their discourse on Rwanda (Jones, 2010d).[4] Shaw (2011b) points out that:

> It does not seem to have occurred to [Herman & Peterson] that if "theatres where the killing was greatest correlated with spikes in RPF activity" (p 58), killing could just as easily have been committed by the threatened Rwandan regime (as Scott Straus argues in *The order of genocide*) as by the RPF themselves. But Herman & Peterson do not engage with Straus, or with much at all of the now very considerable literature on Rwanda.[5]

The question that the above discussion raises is what does Herman & Peterson's use of Davenport & Stam's work on Rwanda signify? Is it the case that Herman & Peterson simply made "selective and mendacious" use of Davenport & Stam's research as Jones indicates in his critique of their work. Or is there something else at play (or maybe both)? Interestingly, in his discussion of Herman & Peterson's abuse of Davenport & Stam's research, Jones (2010a) notes that "[t]here is almost nothing else in the scholarly literature that can be squeezed into their framework, even in denatured form." It is remarkable that Herman & Peterson "need" Davenport & Stam's research. This raises the question, what is it about Davenport & Stam's research that it lends itself for such denialist constructions?

6.2.3. Academic rigor

The fact that Davenport & Stam's work seems to have become part and parcel of a discourse that denies the genocide against the Tutsi raises some serious questions

4 If the FAR did most of the killing, how can their claim that most people killed were Hutu be explained? Did they accidently massively slaughter their own people?

5 Shaw (2011) furthermore notes that: "Herman & Peterson are only interested in the numbers of people killed, not in the rationales behind the killings. From their point of view, the difference between Auschwitz and Hiroshima would be only the larger number of people killed in the former. But should we not take into account the different, even if both deeply immoral, aims and motives of the perpetrators in these two events?"

about their work. The controversy surrounding Davenport & Stam's work on Rwanda did not start with the abovementioned article that was published in the *Miller McCune magazine* in 2009. It started already in November 2003 when they presented some of their conclusions at a genocide conference in Kigali. When they presented their conclusions, they were immediately criticised for denying the genocide against the Tutsi and their research has generated much controversy ever since (M. Green, 2003). The controversy was intensified by a 2004 press-release titled *Rwanda 1994: More than genocide*, which was published on the website of The University of Maryland and which included several sweeping statements. According to Davenport & Stam (2004a), "[a]s the world marks the tenth anniversary of one of the worst mass murders in recent history – the killing of perhaps 800,000 Rwandans – we have a chance to honour the victims by correcting the historic record." They add that "[t]he conventional wisdom has likely given us a deeply flawed picture of what really happened, overlooked some of the victims and clouded our judgments of how Rwanda and the international community responded" (Davenport & Stam, 2004a). They explain that: "The 100 days of killing and torture occurred on an epic scale. Of that much we are certain" (Davenport & Stam, 2004a). They add that:

> The generally accepted story says that the majority Hutu in Rwanda engaged in a systematic effort to eliminate the Tutsi minority – as well as a small number of politically moderate Hutu. Fanatical followers of a parasitic regime, we are told, carried out the violence with wide popular support and assistance. (Davenport & Stam, 2004a)

Davenport & Stam (2004a) however conclude that "this grossly oversimplifies what took place" and that, from their analysis, "a sharply different picture emerges." Their "correction" of the "deeply flawed picture of what really happened" involves several elements that are summarised on their GenoDynamics project website as follows:

> While there are many issues we seek to understand, thus far we have concluded several things about the violence that took place in Rwanda during 1994: 1) most research on Rwandan political violence is misleading, 2) there were several forms of political violence being enacted at once (genocide, politicide, civil war, random violence, and vendetta killings), 3) the extremist Hutu government as well as the Rwandan Patriotic Front engaged in violent activity against Rwandan citizens, and 4) the majority of victims were likely Hutu and not Tutsi. These findings have implications for public policy, advocacy, humanitarian intervention as well as post-conflict reconstruction.[6]

In the 2004 "press-release" they furthermore explain that "Our point is not to deny the scale of murder and violence as Rwandan society unravelled or to deny that ethnic motivations existed" (Davenport & Stam, 2004a). They claim that they want to do "just the opposite – we want to confront it, acknowledge that other motivations

6 Confusingly multiple versions of their website were available. The above excerpt was retrieved from: http://web.mac.com/christiandavenport/iWeb/Site%207/GenoDynamics.html. Meanwhile the site has been updated and the above statement has been edited. However under the tab "Three things to know about Rwanda" similar claims are being made.

as well as other victims existed, and that the conventional account denies the full extent of the horror" (Davenport & Stam, 2004a).

In 2009 Davenport & Stam published the already mentioned article in the *Miller-McCune Magazine* titled *What really happened in Rwanda?* in which they (attempt to) address the controversy surrounding their research. However, instead of addressing some of the issues raised concerning their research, they reiterated their claims and stated that "In the context of post-genocide Rwandan politics, however, the divergence from common wisdom was considered political heresy" (Davenport & Stam, 2009). Is it really simply the case that their "results" conflict with "common wisdom" with regard to what happened in Rwanda and because of the alleged political implications their "results" are denied?

Based on their research, Davenport & Stam draw several sweeping conclusions which they presented to the public on their websites, in several articles and during their lectures and presentations. The problem is however that Davenport & Stam have not published peer reviewed publications on this particular research that transparently ground their conclusions, elaborate their methodology and explain how exactly they got to their findings. Instead, the most elaborate explanations include two (unpublished) papers titled *Rwandan political violence in space and time* (Davenport & Stam, 2004b) and *Rashomon goes to Rwanda: Alternative accounts of political violence and their implications for policy and analysis* (Davenport & Stam, undated). Davenport & Stam do provide partial information concerning their method on their GenoDynamics website. Furthermore, Davenport & Stam make use of a 1991 census that was done under the Habyarimana regime. They explain that:

> The second finding came out of a comparison of official census data from 1991 to the violence data we had collected. According to the census, there were approximately 600,000 Tutsi in the country in 1991; according to the survival organization Ibuka, about 300,000 survived the 1994 slaughter. This suggested that out of the 800,000 to 1 million believed to have been killed then, more than half were Hutu. The finding was significant; it suggested that the majority of the victims of 1994 were of the same ethnicity as the government in power. It also suggested that genocide – that is, a government's attempts to exterminate an ethnic group – was hardly the only motive for some, and perhaps most, of the killing that occurred in the 100 days of 1994. (Davenport & Stam, 2009)

Herman & Peterson (2010e; 2011b) also use this 1991 census as their trump card. Herman & Peterson, like Davenport & Stam, however seem to take the accuracy of the census for granted. They do not raise or discuss possible validity issues. The problem is that it is very likely that the Tutsi population was seriously underreported. Under the oppressive regime, Tutsi were less likely to report themselves, but also the Habyarimana government benefited from underreporting the Tutsi population because due to the quota system it would allow for much fewer Tutsi to be empowered. So both parties basically had incentives to underreport. Note that those involved in the genocide, such as former minister Casimir Bizimungu, also claimed that more

Hutu were killed by the Tutsi. As Prunier (2009, p. 371) notes, the work of Davenport & Stam runs the risk of giving respectability to such denialist claims.

Davenport & Stam's conclusion concerning the death rates creates considerable confusion, because they do not explain where the very high number of Hutu victims actually originated from. Hutu have been killed by the RPF, but Davenport & Stam's estimate is many times higher than the highest estimate on RPF reprisal killings against Hutu. This is problematic, as Jones explains, because "unless we adopt the Herman/Peterson view that in fact the RPF *did* butcher hundreds of thousands of Hutus without anyone noticing at the time, we can only explain that holocaust of Hutus as *inflicted by Hutus themselves*" (Jones, 2011a). Davenport & Stam (2004a) do indeed seem to argue the high number of Hutu victims has been caused by mistaken identity or the settling of personal scores:

> [T]he ethnic identity of individuals within Rwanda was far from clear in the midst of the raging civil war, state-sponsored mass killing and forced migration. Some Hutus were probably accidental victims of rampages where the killers didn't try to figure out who everybody was. Other Hutus were probably deliberate targets, as individuals, Hutu and Tutsi alike, used the mass mobilization as an opportunity to settle national and more localized grievances.[7]

The problem is that this explanation is not well grounded in their research and no other credible research supports such findings.

Davenport & Stam's conclusions discussed above challenge most of the scholarly work on the genocide in Rwanda and they raise the question whether such dramatic conclusions should be drawn when thorough explanations are lacking and if the result is "somewhat ambiguous" and basically "a best guess." Jones (2011a) captures the issue as follows:

> [S]ince this runs so counter to virtually everything that is known and reported on Rwanda, perhaps the number-crunching is to blame? The methodology is in any case so random and speculative – basically guesswork, as Davenport & Stam recognize – that it should not, in my view, have been presented as a cornerstone of their research.

Despite the pitfalls, they do present their findings, with the disastrous consequence that they are used by others to deny the genocide against the Tutsi. Genocide scholarship, due to the sensitivity of the topic, requires a rigor that is lacking in the work of Davenport & Stam. It is irresponsible to draw such dramatic conclusions because of the negative and confusing impact that they can have. Their research should have been presented in the appropriate academic format, so that it can be critically engaged with by other experts in the field, instead of obscuring it in draft reports, press statements, websites and magazine articles.[8] As stated in the Section

---

7 They come up with the same argument in their Miller McCune article (Davenport & Stam, 2009).

8 In 2010 Davenport gave a lecture on his "ground-breaking study of the 1994 Rwandan Genocide" at the Kroc Institute - University of Notre Dame (https://www.youtube.com/watch?v=THyzuIPD1qc). Here

above, Herman & Peterson make "selective and mendacious" use of Davenport & Stam's work, but it seems to be the case that their lack of academic rigor has facilitated this process.

6.2.4. Problematic language

There is however more to Davenport & Stam's research that makes it controversial than the issue of academic rigor discussed above. Davenport & Stam's presentation of their research also raises some issues because of the language used. The title of their *Miller-McCune Magazine* article is illustrative for this: *What really happened in Rwanda?* What could such a title signify to others, especially if one argues that "most research on Rwandan political violence is misleading"? (Davenport & Stam, 2009). From the analysis in Chapters 4 and 5 it has become clear that this is also a claim made by those who deny the genocide. Notice also how the title carries the term "real." The use of the phrase "real" is also a pervasive feature of the genocide denial discourses. Their "press-statement" *Rwanda 1994: More than genocide* suffers from similar language issues. They state that "conventional wisdom has likely given us a deeply flawed picture of what really happened." They add that "[t]he generally accepted story" "grossly oversimplifies what took place" (Davenport & Stam, 2004a). This could have been an excerpt from the denial discourses discussed in earlier Chapters. At times, not only the language is very similar to that of the denial discourse, also the discursive construction in terms of the rhetorical vantage point they attempt to create in this way is very similar to that of the official denial discourse and those who recycle it. The danger is that by using such discursive constructions, they make linguistic community with these denialist discourses. The violent implications of such reiterations were discussed in the last part of the previous Chapter. The problem is furthermore that the discursive construction of events that follows conflates all kinds of violent events, such as war crimes, massacres, genocide, etc. Davenport & Stam do not clearly articulate (define) these concepts but lump them together under the heading of "political violence". The result is that the nature of certain events, such as genocide, becomes obscured. They furthermore state that the "political violence" "did seem to begin with Hutu extremists" (Davenport & Stam, 2009). The use of the term "seem" is confusing. It implies that it is not really clear how the violence started. Could it have been otherwise? And which violence are they referring to? Davenport & Stam (2009) note that "from there violence spread quickly, with Hutu and Tutsi playing the roles of both attackers and victims." Genocidal violence does not simply "spread". It is planned, organised and implemented. They eventually conclude that "Against conventional wisdom, we believe that the victims of this violence were fairly evenly distributed between Tutsi and Hutu" (Davenport & Stam, 2009). Here it seems that Hutu and Tutsi are victims of the same kind of violence (genocide?) and that there is some equivalence in the suffering. Due to their vague language use, the genocidal nature and the direction of the violence is continuously obscured. Also due

Davenport does much more explaining and addresses some of the questions that the abovementioned publications raise. See also Allan Stam's 2011 lecture at Ford School (https://www.youtube.com/watch?v=qi0h-EASsSU).

to the general use of the terms "Hutu" and "Tutsi," civilians are conflated with the military and rebel units that were fighting each other. By focussing predominantly on "death rates", Davenport & Stam's research tends to reduce genocide to the physical destruction of people by killing. They reduce it to mortality rates, battle map simulations, etc. The problem is however that genocide, as explained in Chapter 2, entails much more and it cannot be reduced to the physical killing of people. Instead, it is a process that involves multiple stages of violent marginalisation. Therefore when Davenport & Stam highlight who did what to whom, by solely focusing on killing, they are missing the bigger genocidal picture.

What is furthermore significant is that some of their results were published during the official period of commemoration. For, instance in 2004, an article titled *Rwandan genocide 10th anniversary: correcting the record* was published which stated that:

> Ten years after the Rwandan genocide, the worst mass killings of recent times, the historical record and basic facts need major correction, according to new research from the University of Maryland. The study, which international prosecutors are using, concludes that most of those killed may not have been minority Tutsis, as commonly believed, but majority Hutus. "We consider this more of a totalitarian purge, a politicide, rather than ethnic cleansing or genocide," says University of Maryland political scientist Christian Davenport, who has compiled and analysed evidence from independent investigations into the killings. April 6 marks the 10th anniversary of the outbreak of the slaughter. (Ascribe Newswire, 2004)

When making such critical claims concerning what happened, one should be careful because, during the period of commemoration, people, such as survivors, are extremely sensitive. Furthermore, during this period, those who deny the genocide against the Tutsi often present their alternative readings to the public and one should take care that one's claims do not mimic denialist statements.

The above discussion indicates that there is more to Davenport & Stam's work than its abuse by Herman & Peterson. There are many aspects concerning their work on Rwanda that facilitated Herman & Peterson's abuse of their work. Even though Davenport & Stam claim not to have the intention to deny the genocide, these issues result in their work facilitating the denial dynamic. Their research is taken by those who deny the genocide as "fact".[9] Lastly, on their Genodynamics website, Davenport & Stam present "reflections of others about the Hornet's nest that [they] stepped into." One of these "reflections" include Herman's article *Genocide inflation is the real human rights threat* (Herman, 2007). The other "reflection" includes Harmon Snow's article *Hotel Rwanda: Hollywood and the holocaust in Central Africa* (Harmon Snow, 2005). Davenport & Stam's references are problematic because if one's work raises the question whether it constitutes a denial of the genocide against the Tutsi and one puts other work that actually denies that genocide on one's website

9 See for instance Peterson (2011b).

as "reflections" that also engaged with subject matter concerning what happened in Rwanda, what does this mean? I asked Davenport about this in a letter:

> The fact that you present the accounts of Keith Harmon Snow and Edward Herman as "reflections" raises significant questions about how to interpret your own research and findings. Although you point out that your research does not seek to deny the genocide against the Tutsi, the articles you cite as "reflections" *do* involve a blatant denial of that genocide. Given that Harmon Snow and Herman have cited your work in their own publications, I must ask: do you agree with the accounts they present? Or, do you consider that their analysis misrepresents your research and its findings? If so, why do you lend these figures credibility by posting their "reflections" and why do you not decisively distance yourself from their denialist conclusions? (Moerland 11-06-2012 Letter on file with author)

Shortly after, I received the following reply from Davenport:

> I am in the process (with Prof. Stam) of clarifying our position relative to the others you have mentioned in your email. In brief, the webpage that you reference (which is currently being revised) listed articles largely in simplistic categories: those that outright attacked us without considering anything that was compiled/analysed and those that appeared to "reflect" on what we said at least to some extent. As much of this discussion has not been scholarly (i.e., based on the rigorous compilation and evaluation of evidence) we have tended to avoid most of it and proceeded to finish the book which should be done next year. As we complete the manuscript, then we will turn to addressing the issues you raise. (Davenport 11-6-2012 Correspondence on file with author)[10]

In his short reply, Davenport does not say a word about the serious issues that were raised concerning their research. Instead, he briefly "explains" their reference to these authors and why they tended to avoid any discussion. Davenport's reaction is telling especially when one takes into account that they never seriously addressed the critique that their work triggered. Their work on Rwanda has done its damage and is still doing it as it turns up as "credible evidence" in denialist accounts of the genocide against the Tutsi. How will their upcoming book remedy this? They will be too late.[11]

---

10 I wrote a reply to his cursory email urging him to address the issues, but he never responded. I later found out that Davenport did pay attention to my letter much later on his blog (http://christiandavenportphd.weebly.com/analog-the-anti-blog/category/rwanda). The blog was posted roughly two years after I emailed him my letter, on the 9th of March 2014. He addressed the format of the letter and how it was addressed, but he did not substantially engage with the questions that I had asked him.

11 Meanwhile Davenport and Stam have featured in a documentary that was broadcasted on BBC 2 at prime-time on the 1st of October 2014. The documentary is titled *Rwanda's untold story* and the information on BBC's *This World* website explains that: "Twenty years on from the Rwandan genocide, This World reveals evidence that challenges the accepted story of one of the most horrifying events of the late 20th century" (www.bbc.co.uk/programmes/b04kk03t). In the documentary, Davenport and Stam rehash their questionable interpretations of victim rates and eventually conclude that "What the world believes, and what actually happened, are quite different." For a critical note on the documentary and BBC's role in it see: Wallis (2014) and the letter to the Director-General of the BBC on October 12, 2014, by Linda Melvern and a list of co-signators which is available at www.lindamelvern.com.

6.2.5. The other side of the story

If one looks into the CVs of Davenport & Stam, it turns out that their case study of Rwanda is only one aspect of a much broader research interest. Most of their research does not deal with the case of Rwanda. In contrast, there are also scholars who have become notable experts on Rwanda, because they have been studying the Great Lakes Region and the history of Rwanda continuously throughout their professional careers. One of the most esteemed Rwanda scholars is Professor René Lemarchand, who has published extensively on Rwanda and on its neighbouring country Burundi. Lemarchand's work on Rwanda is interesting in the context of the discussion because, over time, his view of the events that took place in Rwanda has changed and his legitimate academic revisionism seems to have developed to such an extent that it runs the danger of facilitating the denial dynamic. In case of Davenport & Stam, one could still argue that they have underestimated the sensitive nature of the events they got themselves involved in and they therefore did not see why their well-intended words could in the end be problematic. However, one would not expect this from a notable Rwanda scholar like Lemarchand, who has decennia of experience. As will become clear, over time, Lemarchand has come to take questionable materials that portray a completely different image of the events in Rwanda too easily for granted.

In a paper titled *The politics of memory in post-genocide Rwanda*, Lemarchand (2007a) discusses the meta-conflict concerning the history of the events that took place in Rwanda, including the genocide against the Tutsi. He notes that "[t]here are the ideologues who manipulate the historical record for political purposes. They are found on both sides of the ethnic divide, and beyond" (Lemarchand, 2007a). Interestingly Lemarchand (2007a) adds that:

> Even in the absence of ulterior political motives, the deliberate travesty of the facts is not uncommon among foreign observers. [...] Christian Davenport, Professor of Political Science at the University of Maryland, also contests the appropriateness of the term "genocide", arguing that what occurred was a "totalitarian purge, a politicide rather than ethnic cleansing or genocide". Moreover, the majority of the victims, according to Davenport, were Hutu, not Tutsi. [...] Such assertions are enthusiastically received by some Hutu deniers, all too eager to bolster their claims by quoting from European "authorities".[12]

In his paper Lemarchand (2007a) furthermore refers to the so called Bruguière report:

> Recent leaks to the press of the report by the French investigating magistrate, Jean-Louis Bruguière – in which strong circumstantial evidence points to the implication of Kagame in the shooting down of Habyarimana's plane, on 6 April, 1994 – have given a new slant to the argument advanced by Hutu deniers: the mass murder of Tutsi was the direct outcome

[12] See also Lemarchand (2007c).

> of the dastardly plot concocted by the RPF, and thus has nothing to do with the planning imputed to extremist Hutu elements. If one can speak of a genocide, the argument goes, the responsibility lies squarely with Kagame. A closer look at the evidence reveals a more complex reality. Nonetheless, critical questions remain about the role of Kagame in paving the ground for the carnage, including those raised by Bruguière in his as yet unpublished report.

Lemarchand is careful with how hard Bruguière's claims are, more importantly, Lemarchand notices that Bruguière's indictment has empowered those bent on denying the genocide against the Tutsi.

The most widely believed hypothesis concerning the downing of President Habyarimana's Falcon Mystère seems to be that Hutu extremists downed the presidential plane in order to prevent the Arusha Peace Accords from being implemented and to use the assassination as a pretext for the planned extermination phase of the genocide (Grünfeld & Huijboom, 2007, p. 154). Closely related to this scenario is the idea that what happened was actually a coup d'état.[13] The problem is that who downed President Habyarimana's airplane on the 6th of April 1994 remains an enigma; none of the scenarios has been proven by hard non-circumstantial evidence. Nonetheless, in November 2006, French investigative judge Bruguière (2006) released a document accusing the RPF of having shot down the plane. Bruguière's indictment is, however, controversial for several reasons. It basically amounts to a conspiracy theory that is based primarily on witness accounts, such as those of RPF deflector Ruzibiza and extremists from the former regime, such as Bagosora. In addition to such circumstantial proof, no other solid evidence is offered. More importantly, technical questions concerning ballistics etc. are not addressed. It turns out to be a political interpretation (J.-P. Chrétien, 2012, p. 223). As Corduwener writes:

> Bruguière has presented some important material in his research. But he does not have evidence. His report is based mainly on witness statements. These are the same stories from Rwandans in the diaspora who have told these stories before. From that point of view, the materials presented in the report were not new. These Rwandan sources had reasons to take revenge, because otherwise they would not have fled the country. Revenge can sometimes alter reality. (Corduwener, 2004 translated from Dutch)[14]

In 2008 Ruzibiza, whose statements were key to Bruguière's charges, retracted his testimony in the case against Rosa Kabuye, who was one of the accused. In an interview on the matter, Ruzibiza noted that the case brought against Kabuye and

[13] For a discussion of the various scenarios see Prunier (1995).

[14] Original text in Dutch: "Bruguière heeft in zijn onderzoek belangrijk materiaal aangedragen. Maar bewijzen heeft hij niet. Zijn rapport is gebaseerd op verslagen van getuigen. Het zijn dezelfde Rwandezen uit de diaspora die deze verhalen de afgelopen jaren eerder hebben uitgedragen. Wat dat betreft was de inhoud van het onderzoek niet nieuw. De Rwandese bronnen hadden reden om revanche te nemen. Anders waren ze niet gevlucht. Wraak kan de werkelijkheid soms verkleuren" (Corduwener, 2004).

eight others by Bruguière was faulty saying that "If he is basing his investigation on me, then I have the right to say that he is a big manipulator ... he is saying what I have not said." Ruzibiza furthermore stated that "I let him manipulate me. He was desperate he had conducted an enquiry for five years and didn't get any tangible information about the downing of that plane or that accident." (Radio France Internationale, 2008). Moreover, in 2012 another French investigation into the assassination of Habyarimana led by investigating magistrate Trévidic revealed that Bruguière's thesis, which was the basis for the indictment, did not stand up to scrutiny (Wallis, 2012). According to Trévidic's investigation, the missiles were shot from the area of Kanombe, which is close to the airport and also holds the military camp of the RAF. In contrast, Bruguière had always claimed that the missiles were fired from a farm located on Masaka hill, which is also nearby the airport (Melvern, 2012b). Bruguière also claimed that it could not have been the RAF because they did not have the required surface to air missiles. Recently, however, official documents were discovered that reveal that the Rwandan army did possess such weapons and was thus equipped to down the plane (Le Point, 2012). It is not surprising that Trévidic's findings have triggered a critical response from those who adhered to Bruguière's take on what happened, because Bruguière's indictment has been extremely instrumental to those who attempt to deny the genocide against the Tutsi (Malagardis, 2012). Note that to this day the assassins have not yet been identified. Even the Trévidic report, which indicates that the missiles were launched from the Kanombe area in which Habyarimana's own army resided, does not specifically indicate who brought down the plane.

In the same year in which Lemarchand published the article in which he made the above critical remarks concerning Davenport & Stam's work and the Bruguière report, Lemarchand (2007b) published a review essay titled *Controversy within the cataclysm*. In the article, Lemarchand reviews the books of Abdul Ruzibiza (2005) and Pierre Péan (2005). Both authors have been criticised for their denialist narrative concerning the genocide against the Tutsi.[15] Lemarchand also notices that both books "clearly belong to the revisionist section" and challenge the "conventional pieties" and point to the responsibility of Kagame in creating the conditions for what happened. According to Lemarchand (2007b, p. 141), Ruzibiza's detailed description of events "produces a crushing body of evidence in support of his central argument:

[15] Both authors allege that the Kagame-led RPF is responsible for downing Habyarimana's airplane and that the assassination of the president triggered the genocide. For an elaborate critique of Ruzibiza's book see Morel (2011). Péan's book caused more critique (Basabose, 2013; Coquio, 2013; Nshimiyiman, 2013). After his book *Noires fureurs, blancs menteurs: Rwanda 1990–1994*, which was published in 2005, Péan was accused of inciting racial discrimination and hatred by *SOS Racisme* that filed a lawsuit against him. Péan was however acquitted in 2008. The issue revolved around four pages of his book in which Péan argued that the Tutsi's had a culture of lies and deceit (BBC, 2008). Péan had obtained the information on the *"culture des mensonges"* from royal descendant and historian Antoine-Théophile Nyetera. Nyetera (2009) argues that the Tutsi developed a culture of lies and deceit and he applies this idea to the Tutsi-led RPF, which are subsequently portrayed as liars and deceivers. The argument that the Tutsi have a *"culture des mensonges"* reiterates an idea central to anti-Tutsi genocidal propaganda which portrayed them as manipulative people who could never be trusted (see the Hutu Ten Commandments discussed earlier). Abtan (2010) argues that such alternative narratives reinforce the denial of the genocide against the Tutsi.

that the crimes committed by the FPR are no less horrendous than those attributed to the Hutu génocidaires." Lemarchand (2007b, p. 142) points out that Ruzibiza's contention "is that we are dealing here with a double genocide" and adds that "this is precisely where legitimate questions are bound to arise." He explains that "[d]espite persisting disagreements among scholars about what constitutes genocide, placing the carnage of Tutsi on an equal footing with the FPR-sponsored massacres of Hutu is highly debatable" (Lemarchand, 2007b, p. 142). Here Lemarchand appears to be sensitive to the issue of genocide denialism and his line of argument seems to follow his critique in the article mentioned earlier.[16] However, the remainder of the review addressing Lemarchand's analysis of the books of Ruzibiza and Péan raises several issues.

Although Lemarchand points out that the double genocide thesis raises serious questions and it is debatable to equate the RPF massacres with the genocide perpetrated against the Tutsi, he does continue to argue that the responsibility of the RPF, and specifically of Kagame himself, in creating the conditions that made mass murder possible is no longer debatable (Lemarchand, 2007b, p. 142). According to Lemarchand (2007b, p. 142):

> None of this implies that the génocidaires played a secondary role, or for that matter that Kagame knew all along that in shooting down the plane it would trigger a genocide. But neither is there any doubt about the tens of thousands of Tutsi lives that could have been saved had the FPR shown greater concern for such stakes instead of concentrating first and foremost on capturing power. Here again Ruzibiza's commentary (347–60) is entirely convincing. As is now patently clear, though seldom acknowledged, there would have been no genocide without the 1990 invasion, and if a Hutu-sponsored genocide was indeed "in the works" before the crash of Habyalimana's plane, there are reasons to believe that it would never have reached the dimension of a total extermination in the absence of such a cataclysmic event.

How can one argue that "[n]one of this implies that the génocidaires played a secondary role," while at the same time claiming that there would have been no genocide without the 1990 invasion or the shooting down of the plane by the Tutsi-led RPF? Does this not imply that they do play a secondary role with regard to the

16 In the *Online encyclopaedia on mass violence* Lemarchand (2013) also notes: "Revisionism covers a wide gamut, from the outrageous to the plausible. To this day some Hutu extremists stubbornly insist that no genocide ever occurred, only a spontaneous outburst of violence in reaction to the threats posed by the FPR." (Braeckman 1994; Lanotte 2006, 300–301). Untypical though it is, the case of Antoine Nyetera, a Tutsi claiming royal origins, is worth mentioning: on the occasion of a colloquium held in the French Senate on the 4th of April, 2002, Nyetera flatly stated that, although massacres happened, there was no genocide, a statement echoed on the same occasion by none other than the former UN Representative in Rwanda, Roger Booboh, who volunteered the opinion that to claim that a genocide occurred is closer to the politics of surrealism than to the truth (quoted in Gauthier 2002, and Lemarchand 2002, 561). "If anything can be termed surreal it is the calculated denial of the massive evidence supplied through countless testimonies and eyewitness accounts."

origins of the genocide? In his book *The dynamics of violence in Central Africa* he also points out that:

> Only recently has the responsibility of the RPF in triggering the carnage been reasonably well established thanks to the remarkably detailed accounts authored by dissident elements of the RPF, notably Lt. Abdul Joshua Ruzibiza. From the crushing body of evidence gathered in his narrative, Ruzibiza conclusively demonstrates the participation of RPF units in the killing of hundreds of thousands of Hutu civilians in Rwanda and eastern Congo, as well as Kagame's personal responsibility in the shooting down of Habyarimana's plane. (Lemarchand, 2009, p. 133).

Lemarchand's reasoning is remarkable given his earlier sensitivity to the problem of genocide denialism and the fact that, also in his abovementioned book, he notes that "[m]uch the same tendency to shift responsibility away from themselves can be seen among Hutu extremists in Rwanda when they refer to Kagame as a génocidaire, or when they claim that a double genocide was committed, one against the Hutu another against the Tutsi" (Lemarchand, 2009, p. 132 and 133). In his review of Ruzibiza's book, Lemarchand (2007b, p. 142) comes to conclude that:

> Thanks to Ruzibiza's meticulous reconstruction of the events leading to "the apocalypse" (217–52), the responsibility of Kagame in the shooting down of the aircraft is by now well established. It convincingly refutes the still widely accredited notion of a plot by Hutu extremists aimed at eliminating an all-too-liberal Habyalimana. His account fully corroborates the findings of the French investigating magistrate Jean-Louis Bruguière, and it is consistent with the previously stated position of several other defectors from the RPF; one example is found in the testimony of Jean-Pierre Mugabe at the Web site of the International Strategic Studies Association.

Lemarchand thus goes even further in his assertions and now also seems to embrace Bruguière's conspiracy theory, which initially according to Lemarchand needed to be approached more carefully.[17] Scholars who take their academic rigor seriously have to conclude that the solid evidence for Bruguière's conspiracy is lacking and that we are still in the dark as to who actually shot down the plane and why. Also the notion that it was most likely Hutu extremists who attempted a coup d'état is still only a plausible explanation and one which, in addition to Trévidic's findings, still requires more solid proof. As a scholar, to claim certainty concerning Bruguière's conspiracy and to take the "evidence" he presented for granted amounts to a dangerous speculation concerning what happened. Such scholarly accounts are problematic as they lend credit to a crucial discursive element in the official denial discourse, namely that the RPF is primarily responsible for the violence. It is fascinating and at the same time disturbing to see that the Bruguière report, which was leaked to *Le Monde* and subsequently published by Stephen W. Smith, has gained such an influence among scholars. A salient detail is that the report was leaked in March

---

17 In the *Online encyclopaedia on mass violence* Lemarchand states: "All the more so given that it substantiates the findings of the French investigating magistrate Jean-Louis Bruguière, as disclosed by Stephen Smith (Smith 1994) and corroborates the views of several other defectors from the RPA."

2004 and it dominated the news coverage during the commemorative period, which was the 10th anniversary. One wonders whether this is really a coincidence. In court, génocidaires present the report as evidence that the RPF is responsible for everything that they are accused of (Melvern, 2012a).

All of this becomes even more pressing if one realises that the question of who downed the plane is actually not decisive for the question whether the genocide against the Tutsi took place and who is responsible for it. It is however turned into a constitutive element by those who attempt to deny the genocide, because it allows them to present want happened as a spontaneous unplanned explosion of violence for which the RPF is responsible. Due to the fact that the downing of the plane is still an enigma and no hegemony has been reached by a particular discourse, there is still room for deniers to manipulate history and present their alternative discourse. Genocide denial does not get more sophisticated than this, because such a discursive construction means that there was no genocide and that, although violence against the Tutsi took place, the RPF is ultimately responsible for it. Grünfeld & Huijboom (2007, p. 155 and 156) argue that the outcome of Bruguière's investigation "means that the RPF may be considered to be instigators of the genocide, whereas the perpetrators of the genocide remain the Hutu extremists." They furthermore note that "[s]ome will make use of this report to attempt to confuse and reverse the roles of the perpetrators and the victims" (Grünfeld & Huijboom, 2007, p. 155 and 156). They conclude "Even when this last opinion turns out to be the truth these Tutsi cannot be made into accomplices in a genocide aimed at the Tutsi population in Rwanda. The trigger in this case is not the same as the cause" (Grünfeld & Huijboom, 2007, p. 155 and 156). In the *Online encyclopaedia on mass violence*, Lemarchand (2013) states that

> While it is fair to say that there would have been no genocide without an infrastructure of murder, i.e. the police and the army, the paramilitaries and the Interahamwe, and the likes of Colonel Bagosora the chief organizer of the killings; it is doubtful that any of the above would have had recourse to mass murder without the climate of ethnic hatreds and intense fears generated by the FPR invasion. The retributive element, to borrow Helen Fein's terminology, (Fein 1990, 86–91) is clearly central to an understanding of the roots of the carnage.

This last element reveals a more complex nature of the events according to Lemarchand which have so far been presented as a biased and one sided account of "good versus bad". Such argumentation tends to conflate the war triggered by the invasion of the RPF and the genocide. A single invasion and civil war does not simply lead to the targeted mass extermination of non-combatant civilians such as unborn and born babies, children, women, elderly, etc. In that sense, war is not the cause of genocide.[18] Without the mass ideological manipulation by the orchestrators of the genocide through which the Hutu masses started to see their fellow Tutsi

18 Otherwise each war would lead to genocide. In order for genocide to occur, other factors need to be fulfilled as well. This is not to say that war and genocide are not related. The work of Shaw (2007) shows this quite clearly. However genocide has also been perpetrated even if there was no direct armed conflict; take for instance the case of the forced removal of children in Australia mentioned earlier.

neighbours as existential threats, the violence would never have taken such shape. This aspect tends to be neglected by those who insinuate that the RPF is responsible for the genocide against the Tutsi.

Lemarchand's discussion of the books of Ruzibiza and Péan also raises a more significant question that is important in this context; does Lemarchand review the books or does he empower their narrative? Lemarchand (2007b, p. 143) notes that Péan's book is "equally persuasive in pinpointing responsibility for the genocide on Kagame," but he also notices that the book has some serious flaws. It has an accusatory tone, evidence is fragmentary and the conclusions lack nuance.[19] Nonetheless, Lemarchand (2007b, p. 143) concludes that the two books have something in common; they both insist on challenging the official history of the genocide. According to Lemarchand (2007b, p. 143 emphasis added), "[w]hatever reservations one may have about either one, the time has come to give serious thought to a revisionist history of the carnage, one that gives sustained attention to *the other side of the story*".[20] By arguing that the accounts presented by Ruzibiza and Péan present "another side of the story", Lemarchand did not simply review their work. Instead he helped to create a legitimate space for accounts that are questionable in terms of genocide denialism. It is disturbing to read that Lemarchand argues that it is time to give "serious thought" to such revisionist histories "whatever reservations one might have about either one." What makes matters worse is that Lemarchand (2007b, p. 143), in his final conclusion, further legitimates such revisionism by insinuating that the historical record concerning the genocide against the Tutsi is somehow crooked or manipulated: "These two testimonies – each in its own way – point to important new directions in any attempt to set the historical record straight." A formal statement by Lemarchand that his analysis does not attempt to excuse or justify what happened is not enough. Critical reflection should entail more than a formal *disclaimer*, because even reports of denialist organisations such as the RDR (1996) disclaim that "[their] analysis should [...] not be misunderstood as an attempt to minimize or justify the killings, but simply as a scientific analysis underlying political and psychological causes of the Rwandan conflict". Due to a lack of critical reflection scholars, like Lemarchand, run the risk of becoming a

19 In the *Online encyclopaedia of mass violence* he is more critical of Péan and writes: "Much the same argument is endorsed by the investigative reporter Pierre Péan, who writes that in the ultimate phase of his conquest strategy Kagame planned the downing of the plane, and therefore also planned its direct consequence: the genocide of the Tutsi perpetrated as reprisal (Péan 2005, 19). By drastically downsizing of the number of Tutsi victims, he suggests that, if anything, Kagame is guilty of an even worse genocide. Although the book leans heavily on Ruzibiza's testimony, it is radically different in tone and substance. Where Ruzibiza is coldly descriptive and factual, Péan's style is that of a pamphleteer, in turn accusatory and sarcastic; where the first attempts to reconstruct a series of events to which he was witness, the other uses the Rwanda tragedy as a pretext to settle personal scores. Woe unto those observers, journalists, scholars (e.g. Marie-France Cros, Colette Braeckman, Jean-Pierre Chrétien) and NGOs (e.g. Action Survie) whose views and actions are at odds with his own version of the truth. The polemical tone of his strictures is sometimes akin to the worst kind of yellow journalism. His characterization of Kagame is not untypical: A Fuhrer who ended up being director of Yad Vashem, the Shoah museum. From the top of his mountain of bones, here he is dispensing verdicts and morality lessons to the entire planet" (Lemarchand, 2013).

20 See also Lemarchand (2009, p. 69).

platform for groups of people with questionable political agendas. There is another downside to this as well. During my research I spoke to people in Kigali who put Lemarchand, and other scholars who take a similar stance, squarely into the camp of the hard-core deniers discussed in earlier Chapters. I, however, think that goes too far. Scholars like Lemarchand are not bent on denying the genocide and he has actually acknowledged the genocide against the Tutsi on multiple occasions. He has furthermore done excellent work, which now runs the risk of being discredited. As noticed with regard to Herman & Peterson and Harmon Snow, but this also applies to Davenport & Stam, one should be careful in lumping them together with those who promote the official denial discourse and are bent on finishing the genocide. This does, however, not diminish that the uncritical acceptation and representation of certain narratives, as discussed above, can facilitate the denial dynamic.[21]

The cases discussed above reveal that in the context of genocide, scholars should critically reflect on how their work could facilitate the killing of death. Scholars are however not the only actors which can contribute to the denial dynamic as the following Sections will reveal.

6.3. Criminal defence

6.3.1. Defending the Hutu cause

Denial is a defensive reaction to a threat, so it is not surprising that when confronted with criminal prosecution, defendants will defend themselves by denying the genocide. In that sense criminal prosecution tends to "produce" denial. When charged and prosecuted, perpetrators rarely admit to what really happened, instead they engage in denial and claim that they did not know, were not aware or never heard or saw anything (Payne, 2008, pp. 164–165). Courts, instead of being venues of justice, can thus turn into platforms for genocide denial. Such denial comes in various forms. Payne (2008, p. 158) points out that, instead of engaging in the abovementioned literal

21 Note that in June 1994, Lemarchand (1994) still wrote: "Whether Habyalimana's plane was shot down by elements of the Presidential Guard or by the Tutsi-dominated FPR has yet to be established. But when one reflects on the strong opposition of certain key members of the presidential entourage to the Arusha accords – seen as the thin edge of the wedge by which the FPR would penetrate and subvert the Republic – and on the fact that the killings began almost immediately after the crash, as if carefully planned well ahead of time, suspicions that it could have been the work of the Presidential Guard tend to harden into certainty." In 1995 Lemarchand (1995, p. 10) concluded: "This is where the shooting down of Habyarimana's plane, on April 6, seems entirely consistent with the overall strategy of MNRD extremists. Despite the absence of solid evidence in support of an akazu-sponsored plot, it is easy to see the logic that might have prompted such a move. Not only did Habyarimana's death remove once and for all the spectre of Arusha (even at the cost of losing in the process a key member of the 'akazu,' Elie Sagatwa), but by making it unmistakably clear that 'it was the RPF that did it' the same extremists could now point to their 'dastardly crime' as a moral justification for genocide. Who actually fired the missile that brought down Habyarimana's plane may never be known, any more than who ordered the missile to be fired. But if the circumstantial evidence is any index, there is every reason to view the shooting of the plane as an eminently rational act from the standpoint of the immediate goals of Hutu extremists." What happened to Lemarchand over these years?

denial, perpetrators can also engage in confessional denial. In that case perpetrators somehow admit their role in the past but attempt to justify or excuse their behaviour. However, at the International Criminal Tribunal for Rwanda (ICTR) one can witness instances of genocide denial that seem to go beyond the self-serving genocide denial of individual perpetrators described by Payne. After the ICTR indicted the first suspects, a meeting was convened in Nairobi by Belgian commercial Lawyer Luc de Temmerman, who had been taking care of the affairs of Habyarimana's family since the beginning of the 1990ies. After the President had been assassinated and the Rwandan Interim Government went into exile, de Temmerman managed to obtain powers of attorney from many of the former dignitaries.[22] This placed him in charge of their defence once they were being prosecuted. In 1996, de Temmerman managed to bring together a group of defence lawyers in Nairobi in an attempt to establish a collective defence strategy (Cruvellier 2011, personal communication). Interestingly, the meeting at which this political defence strategy was discussed was sponsored by the earlier discussed RDR (Cruvellier, 2010, p. 33). The defence strategy, as it turned out, did not focus on the cases and interests of the individual suspects, which have the right to assigned legal assistance, but de Temmerman made clear that it was about defending the Hutu cause. The aim of the joint defence strategy was to deny the genocide against the Tutsi (Cruvellier, 2010, p. 32 and 33). Cruvellier explains: "To [de Temmerman], the courtroom was just another forum to advance the 'Hutu cause' and ensure that Rwandan history was written according to this view" (Cruvellier, 2010, p. 33). Defending the cause in this case thus meant denying the cause.[23] Defence counsel Michael Karnavas, who briefly represented Akayesu, has been critical of the many problems the defence counsel faces at the ICTR. According to him, these issues have made effective criminal defence almost an impossible task, but, Karnavas (1997) adds:

> If this were not enough, one must also contend with Luc de Temmerman, a Flemish commercial lawyer with very close ties to Hutu extremist organizations. Mr. de Temmerman represented the former Rwandan President and his family clan, the "akazu," which some credit as the organizers of the genocide. Upon my formal appointment in the Akayesu case, de Temmerman cautioned me that I was not representing Akayesu, but "the Hutu nation" and "the cause." I was instructed that a genocide had not occurred, that it was simply Tutsi propaganda; but if a genocide had taken place, the Tutsis were responsible for exterminating the Hutu -- something that could be proved by exhuming the mass graves.

22 De Temmerman actually had written a standard "*mandat*" for this that could be used to obtain powers of attorney and which enable de Temmerman to represent them at the ICTR and it also gave him the power to secure the "*mobiliers et immobiliers*" of his Rwandan clients. (Document retrieved from the archive of Linda Melvern and on file with author).

23 In the *South African Mail & Guardian* of Saturday, the 4th of October 1997, de Temmerman is quoted as saying: "We are convinced that there was no genocide. It was a situation of mass killings in a state of war where everyone was killing their enemies." Interestingly he adds that "Everyone was killing but the real victims are the Hutus" (Hintjens, 1999, p. 284). De Temmerman's support also becomes clear from his correspondence to the ministers of the Rwandan Interim Government ("*Lettre ouverte*" to "*messieurs les ministres*" of the 2nd of December 1994) and from his letter to Chief Prosecutor Richard Goldstone (Letter concerning "Habyarimana – Rwanda" of the 12th of October 1995). (Documents on file with author).

> According to de Temmerman, all I needed to do was compare the body size and facial characteristics of the dead. When I refused to cooperate, he openly accused me of being an agent of the Government of Rwanda, a Tutsi spy who was sabotaging Akayesu's case, and of course "the cause." It came as no surprise that two weeks later I would be accused by my own client of having "brainwashed," "intimidated," and "manipulated" him into selecting me as his primary trial attorney.

De Temmerman also met with the refugee community in Congo to discuss and organise the defence of those implicated in the genocide. In 1996, he visited Bukavu in order to present the defence teams of Bagosora, Akayesu and others. A note to the *"Chef d'état - Major RAF"*, which was written after De Temmerman's visit, states that:

> Maître Luc De Temmerman regrette beaucoup de ce que parmi nos *leaders* il y a encore ceux qui affirment qu'il y a eu génocide de Tutsi par les Hutu. [...] Il recommande à tout Hutu de comprendre que si génocide était confirmé, c'est la fin de tout un peuple. (Harelimana, 1996)[24]

It is a fascinating statement, because it actually acknowledges that the genocide against the Tutsi took place.

6.3.2. Defending the anti-imperialist cause

Despite de Temmerman's calls to stay true to the cause, his collective defence effort was difficult to materialise. His approach did not fare well with many of his colleagues, as it prevented them from working independently and it hampered them in preparing an effective defence, which was in the interests of their clients (Cruvellier and Karnavas 2011, personal communication). Also the clients started to worry about de Temmerman's approach, which put their individual interests second (Cruvellier, 2010, p. 34). The frictions eventually caused de Temmerman to step back and, as a result, the joint defence of "the Hutu cause" as de Temmerman once had envisioned never fully materialised. Cruvellier, however, notes that with the departure of de Temmerman his line of defence did not fully disappear. Akayesu called upon Canadian lawyer John Philpot to represent him in court. While de Temmerman defended the Hutu cause, John Philpot and some of his fellow criminal defence lawyers, such as Peter Erlinder and Christopher Black, adopted a denialist line of defence as a means to an end to a different cause, namely: the fight against United States (US) imperialism. In Philpot's analysis:

> The plane was brought down. Within two hours the RPF had been activated. People defended themselves. The population resisted. There was a total societal breakdown. It was a war for political power. Excesses were committed on all sides. The government did not know what to do. It tried to maintain some semblance of power. The theory that

[24] Document retrieved from the archive of Linda Melvern and on file with author.

> the government planned the genocide is illogical. The government was weak. It had no interest in shooting down the plane. There is no proof of a plan. The so-called genocide is an excuse to keep the RPF in power. There were mass killings on both sides. I do not think that the government committed crimes against humanity. But the RPF did. It is too easy to accept the genocide theory. Why did the United Nations and the United States withdraw? Because they wanted the RPF to take power. (Philpot Quoted in Cruvellier, 2010, p. 35)

According to Philpot, the ICTR was part of a US imperialist conspiracy to cover up the crimes for which the US and its allies were primarily responsible (Cruvellier, 2010, p. 35). According to Philpot (www.johnphilpot.com) "[g]enocide is not the proper expression to describe the Rwandan conflict. It was an international war of invasion which degenerated into a political and ethnic conflict on a very large scale."[25] The resemblance to the earlier discussed official denial discourse of the former authorities is striking.

The line of defence taken by John Philpot is very similar to the plot presented in the book of his brother Robin Philpot (R. Philpot, 2003, 2004), a Canadian writer, journalist and former electoral candidate, who published a book titled *Ça ne s'est pas passé comme ça à Kigali* or *Rwanda 1994: Colonialism dies hard.*[26, 27] According to

25 Philpot (1997) argued that the fight against impunity was "a noble cause", but the problem was however that: "[T]he anti-impunity campaign has been diverted, stolen and transformed into its opposite in the Great Lakes crisis: in the name of the fight against the Culture of Impunity, the losing side in the war in Rwanda is being subjected to arbitrary and unjustified punishment." See also J. Philpot (2009).

26 The book has been made available through the website www.taylor-report.com The main proponent of the website also hosts a radio show at University of Toronto radio station, CIUT, which is prominent among the disseminators of denial. Caplan (2013b) notes that "[f]or many years, this show, named after its host Phil Taylor, has regularly offered time on his program [...] to known Rwanda genocide deniers. The vast majority who affirm the genocide do not appear." The book by Philpot's brother was recently updated and republished in English under the title: *Rwanda and the new scramble for Africa: From tragedy to useful imperial fiction.* In the acknowledgments, Robin Philpot (2013) states "Thanks to Ed Herman for insisting that I update the book and publish a hard copy." Note that The Taylor-Report also posted Herman & Peterson's replies to Caplan and Jones.

27 It is furthermore interesting to note that the introduction to the German translation of Robin Philpot's book, which carries the title *Ruanda 1994 - Die inszenierte Tragödie*, was written by Helmut Strizek. Strizek explains that Philpot's book has not lost its relevance since it was published in French in 2003, because the RPF regime and its helpers still propagate the version that was proclaimed "official" by the ICTR. Strizek (2007) adds that by now it has become clear that the whole theory of a long planned Tutsi genocide by Hutu extremists is untenable. An important detail is that Strizek was expert witness for the defence in several ICTR cases, including those against Anatole Nsengiyumva, Casimir Bizimungu and Ferdinand Nahimana (Strizek, 2003b, 2005, 2006). Strizek's view on what happened in Rwanda involves a unique quadruple genocide theory, which he explained in detail at a conference in Brussels in April 2008 (note the month!). Strizek explained that there were actually four genocides: "Personally, I talk of four genocides. The first one in 72 in Burundi. After that, a second one in Rwanda against the Tutsi, which I call a genocide *sui generis*, which means, *a genocide that does not adhere to the normal definition of genocide [in the 1948 Genocide Convention].* After that, a third one, the one that Kagame perpetrated at Byumba. And the fourth one against the refugees." (Emphasis added.) According to Strizek, the first, third and last genocide fall within the scope of the 1948 Genocide Convention, because they were "planned, with an army, and with state power." Strizek argues that the three Hutu genocides are the only real genocides because they fit the definition of the 1948 Genocide Convention, while the genocide against the Tutsi in 1994 does not, because it is a "genocide *sui generis.*" (Dumas, 2010, p. 100 and 101) Strizek adds that the second one against the Tutsi is "unique," "because it developed in a situation where there was no state." Strizek adds that the international community did nothing

Tellier (2003), who wrote a reaction to Philpot's book, both brothers are involved in defending those accused of genocide.[28] The text on the back cover of the book reveals much about the discourse Philpot constructs throughout his book:

> Robin Philpot's vast and methodical research, extensive interviews, and close analysis of events and popular writings on the subject shows not only that the Official Story is false, but that it was edified in an aim to cover-up the causes of the tragedy and to protect the criminals responsible for it. What's more, to make us believe that Story, the Story tellers have unfailingly reproduced those literary traditions, clichés, and metaphors that provided the underpinnings of slavery, the slave-trade, and colonialism. (R. Philpot, 2004)

Like many of those who deny the genocide against the Tutsi, Philpot also argues that he does not deny that a genocide against the Tutsi has taken place (CBC News, 2007). However, Philpot (2004) discursively constructs the meaning of the genocide as a political ploy used to silence critics and which is helpful for the regime in power and its allies:

> The term is a gag order. Obviously, that pleases Kigali. But it is also very helpful for Western powers, and particularly the United States, who brandish it like a weapon of mass destruction aimed at any African leader or regime that bucks the current.

Thus, the term genocide is primarily signified as a political manipulative tool.

As noted before, John Philpot is not the only defence lawyer working at the ICTR following the line of defence presented above. Christopher Black also follows such a political line of defence. Black was lead counsel in the so called Military II trial against former military leaders at the ICTR. According to Black (2002) "the truth is turned upside down" while adding that those who worked at the ICTR defending their clients have "accumulated massive evidence that paints an entirely different

---

to stop the conflict and thereby allowed hatred to foster among the population, while they knew that there was going to be violence against the Tutsi and while Kagame's RPF was a clear candidate for taking over power. Thus, Strizek concludes, "There was a genocide against the Tutsi, but not like the other ones. Not like the ICTR wants you to believe that it happened." According to Strizek there was no *"plannification."* There was no state, it was a genocide *"plus spontane"*. (See also Strizek, 2002; Strizek, 2003a). In a reaction to the conference Dutch Journalist Corduwener, a keen observer on Rwanda noted "It was about genocide, but in reality it was mostly, if not only, about the denial of that genocide." He added, that Strizek "[t]he white historian held an interesting but disgraceful presentation about the genocide of 1994. Which according to him had not been a genocide" (Corduwener, 2008). Lemarchand, who is a staunch critic of the current Rwandan Government, concludes that, by denying that the killings were planned, Strizek implicitly denies the existence of the genocide (Lemarchand, 2009, p. 101). Strizek furthermore appeared as expert witness for the defence when Nahimana's case was tried before the ICTR. In 1992 Nahimana, together with other Hutu Power ideologues, cofounded the *comité d'initiative* in order to establish the *Radio Télevision de Libre des Milles Collines* (RTLM), which during the genocide was responsible for some of the most virulent anti-Tutsi propaganda. Helmut Strizek also wrote the preface to Nahima's book *Rwanda: Les virages ratés.* (Nahimana, 2007). The examples illustrate how experts at the ICTR can facilitate the denial of the genocide against the Tutsi. In this context see also Cruvellier (2002).

28 For a critical review of Philpot's book see: Basabose (2013).

picture".[29] Interestingly, with regard to their claim that the majority of victims were Hutu, Herman & Peterson explain that they "base this on personal communications with the international criminal lawyer Christopher Black of Toronto, who, since 2000, has served as defence counsel before the ICTR on behalf of the Hutu General Austin Ndindiliyimana, a former Chief of Staff of the Rwanda Gendarmerie" (Herman & Peterson, 2010e, p. 132). The denial narratives are thus often interrelated as the actors rely on each other as sources. As noted earlier, genocide denial is an interpersonal phenomenon: they need others to collude in the denial in order to keep it up. Here the linguistic community comes into play again. It thus indeed appears to be like Caplan (2010a), in his review of Herman & Peterson's book, who argued that those who deny the genocide against the Tutsi "gleefully drink each other's putrid bathwater."

The defence counsel at the ICTR is, of course, a mixed group of people and it must be noted that it is not the defence counsel in general that follows the line of defence described above. Karnavas made crystal clear that many defence lawyers have huge difficulties with such lines of defence, because they can seriously hamper effective defences and are therefore not always in the best interest of the client (Karnavas 2011, personal communication). The above cases do, nonetheless, reveal an intriguing relationship between criminal defence and genocide denial. From a fair trial perspective, lawyers should be able to raise issues and question evidence brought forward by the defence. It is their job to take sides. However, from the perspective on genocide denialism developed throughout this study, this right of the defendant and the defence causes considerable problems. There appears to be an inherent tension. It shows how the right to a fair trial, on the one hand, can contribute to a fair criminal justice for crimes of genocide, while, on the other hand, this right creates the opportunity to follow political lines of defence that further the denial dynamic on which the genocidal process thrives. Trying to safeguard justice for genocide can thus in certain instances also facilitate further genocidal injustice. However, the denial dynamic is not only fostered by such political lines of defence or the legitimate space given to such defences because of fair trial standards, often the outcomes of judicial processes are also misrepresented by the abovementioned lawyers to serve their greater cause. It is however questionable whether such actions can still be justified by invoking the client's right to a fair trial, especially when this happens outside the courtroom.

---

[29] See also Black (2004, 2005, 2009a, 2009b, 2010). Black also collaborated with Edward Herman on an article concerning the role of Chief Prosecutor Louise Arbour (C. Black & Herman, 2000).

6.3.3. Military I

On 16 June 2006, in the case of the Prosecutor v. Karemera et al.,[30] the Appeals Chamber of the United Nations International Criminal Tribunal for Rwanda (ICTR) took judicial notice of the following facts:

1. The existence of Twa, Tutsi and Hutu as protected groups falling under the Genocide Convention;
2. The following state of affairs existed in Rwanda between the 6th of April 1994 to the 17th of July 1994: there were throughout Rwanda widespread or systematic attacks against a civilian population based on Tutsi ethnic identification. During the attacks, some Rwandan citizens killed or caused serious bodily or mental harm to person[s] perceived to be Tutsi. As a result of the attacks, there were a large number of deaths of persons of Tutsi ethnic identity;
3. Between the 6th of April 1994 and the 17th of July 1994 there was genocide in Rwanda against Tutsi ethnic group.

The Chamber furthermore made clear that the "Judicial notice of the above matters means that they are to be taken as established beyond any dispute and not requiring any proof."[31] In a subsequent press release of the ICTR is stated that:

> This is one of the most significant rulings of the Tribunal, given the consequences in terms of putting the occurrence of the genocide beyond legal dispute. It can be recalled that until now the OTP has had to in each case lead evidence and prove the occurrence of the genocide. This will no longer be necessary. In the view of the OTP the ruling should now silence the "rejectionist" camp which has been disputing the occurrence of genocide. By relieving the OTP of a substantial burden of proof the ruling has the potential to shorten the cases as each will essentially focus on the personal involvement of the accused person in genocide. (International Criminal Tribunal for Rwanda, 2006)

Approximately two years later on the 18th of December 2008, in the so-called ICTR Military I trial, which adjudicated the cases against senior military officers primarily suspected of having played a vital role in the planning, organisation and perpetration of the genocide, the Chamber found defendant Major Aloys Ntabakuze not guilty on the conspiracy to commit genocide charge (The Prosecutor v. Théoneste Bagosora et al., Case No. ICTR-98-41-T. Judgment and Sentence. 18 December 2008). In an article published a few days later on the 24th of December 2008, Ntabakuze's lead

30 Prosecutor v. Édouard Karemera. Mathieu Ngirumpatse & Joseph Nzirorera, ICTR-98-44-AR73(C), Decision on Prosecutor's Interlocutory Appeal of Decision on Judicial Notice (16 June 2006) (International Criminal Tribunal for Rwanda, Appeals Chamber).

31 For a critical analysis of the judicial notice of the genocide against the Tutsi see Jorgensen (2007) and Shannon (2006). It is noted that it infringes upon the fair trial rights of the accused as certain aspects of the case can no longer be challenged. However, in other countries such as France and Germany, courts have taken judicial notice of the Holocaust. Time and again those accused of denying the Holocaust requested proof that the Holocaust really happened and, as a result, the event of genocide was put on trial instead of the accused and his denial.

defence counsel, Peter Erlinder, published an article titled *Rwanda: No conspiracy, no genocide planning ... no genocide?*[32] In the article Erlinder (2008b), argues that:

> [I]f there was no conspiracy and no planning to kill ethnic civilians, can the tragedy that engulfed Rwanda properly be called "a genocide" at all? Or, was it closer to a case of civilians being caught up in war-time violence, like the Eastern Front in WWII, rather than the planned behind-the-lines killings in Nazi death camps?

According to Erlinder (2008b):

> [The Trial Chamber] found that the actions of Rwandan military leaders, both before and after the April 6, 1994 assassination of former Rwandan President Juvenal Habyarimana [...] were consistent with war-time conditions and the massive chaos brought about by the four year war of invasion from Uganda by Gen. Paul Kagame's RPF/Ugandan army, which seized power in July 1994.[33]

In a letter published on the World Socialist Website, Erlinder (2009a) furthermore stated, "it is true that the Rwandan Tragedy ... some call genocide ... was a product of Imperialism." However, according to Erlinder (2009a) "the anti-imperialist lawyers of the ICTR defence [...] have established that it was US/UK neo-colonialism that was behind events in Rwanda in 1994".[34] Note how Erlinder also contrasts the signifiers "the Rwandan tragedy" and "genocide", which is typical for the official denial discourse discussed earlier. The excerpt also makes the underlying anti-imperialist

---

32 The Military I case also features in the articulations of Herman & Peterson and Harmon Snow. As discussed in Chapter 5, Herman & Peterson's articulation of events involves the claim that the official version of events requires the suppression of important information. They state that: "Acceptance of this line also requires the suppression of a key verdict in a December 2008 Judgment by the ICTR. This seven-and-a-half year trial of four former high-ranking Hutu members of the Rwanda military produced an acquittal of all four defendants on the Tribunal's most serious charge: That they participated in an alleged conspiracy to commit genocide against the country's Tutsi minority" (Herman & Peterson, 2010d, p. 54 and 55). Harmon Snow (2009d), in his article The Rwanda Genocide Fabrications, also refers to the abovementioned judgment stating that: "On December 18, 2008, after the protracted 'Military I' trial, the judges at the International Criminal Tribunal on Rwanda ruled that there was no conspiracy to commit genocide by former Rwandan military leaders affiliated with the former Habyarimana government. It was war, and the actions – far from a calculated genocide – were found by ICTR judges to be "war-time conditions". According to Harmon Snow (2009d), due to the judgment, "after more than fifteen years of massive western propaganda proclaiming an organized, systematic elimination of the Tutsi people by the Hutu leaders of the former Rwandan government, the official Rwanda genocide story has finally collapsed." As will become clear, Erlinder, Herman & Peterson, and Harmon Snow, however misrepresent the judgment of the ICTR in the Military I case.

33 See also Erlinder (2009b).

34 On the Monthly Review Press website that promotes Herman & Peterson's second edition of *The politics of genocide* we can also find an endorsement by Erlinder stating that "Herman & Peterson convincingly demonstrate the U.S./NATO imperial designs lurking behind claims of 'humanitarian intervention;' the selective prosecutions carried out by all international criminal tribunals to date; and the calculated use of emotionally-laden accusations of 'genocide.' At a deeper level, this book presents a challenge to Western media and human rights activists to recognise the 'impunity for the powerful' regime that they have assisted in creating, through uncritical acceptance of the 'human rights' narrative promulgated by U.S. foreign policy elites. It is an enormous contribution to the ongoing foreign policy/ human rights discussion." (http://monthlyreview.org/books/pb2129/).

motivation very clear. They are not criminal defence lawyers but "anti-imperialist lawyers". The case of Rwanda and the ICTR are a means to an end to their quest to dismantle US imperial oppression. The problem with Erlinder's articulation of the events is however that the genocidal victimisation of Tutsi is being presented as an unplanned and uncoordinated spontaneous popular self-defence in response to the RPF war effort, while at the same time presenting the RPF crimes as planned and coordinated and comparable in scale if not much worse (Jones, 2011a).[35, 36] Erlinder thus recycles much of the official denial discourse. According to Erlinder (2008a), the truth is being kept from the public by a "US-sponsored 'cover-up' of Pentagon complicity" in the events. The documents that according to Erlinder prove "The Great Rwanda 'Genocide Cover-up'" are made available through his website www.rwandadocumentsproject.org. Erlinder currently no longer serves as ICTR defence counsel, nor does he teach at William Mitchell College of Law. He is however still the director of the International Humanitarian Law Institute.[37]

It is interesting to notice that the Chamber actually pays considerable attention to Erlinder's "alternative explanations" in relation to its judgment in the Military I case concerning the conspiracy charge. The Chamber apparently very well understood the possible implications of its judgment and it therefore attempted to fix its meaning. The Chamber explained that the prosecution had indeed not proven beyond a reasonable doubt that the four accused conspired together to plan and commit the genocide, but the Chamber added that:

> To the extent that the Defence's alternative explanations aim to raise doubt about whether a genocide occurred in Rwanda, the submissions are without merit. A review of the evidence related to the crimes underpinning the charges amply demonstrates that the

35 Erlinder is also involved in a lawsuit against President Paul Kagame, which was initiated by the widow of Habyarimana. The lawsuit accuses the Tutsi-led RPF under Kagame to provoke the genocide and it furthermore notes that those who are now accused of planning the genocide had no plans in advance to commit the killings (Ingold, 2011).

36 In 2013 Erlinder (2013) published a massive research volume in which he sets out his alternative account of what happened in Rwanda. (See also Erlinder, 2010b). The book brings together the work that he had done so far on the topic and it further substantiates his views that are also addressed in the above section. The title of the book is remarkable: *The accidental genocide*. However, when it comes to genocide this title appears to be a contradiction in terms. Genocides are never accidental.

37 The website of the institute (www.ihli.org) features much of Erlinder's work on Rwanda. Interestingly one IHLI statement concerning the evidence for Erlinder's articulation of events reads: "IHLI notes this evidence in the public record: Former prosecution expert witness, Professor Allan Stam of the University of Michigan and Professor Christian Davenport of Notre Dame, analysed all reports from the Government of Rwanda, NGO's and the UN and found twice as many Hutus were killed as Tutsis between April and July 1994, www.genodynamics.com." But Davenport & Stam did not only work for the prosecution, in their Miller McCune Magazine article they explain that they also worked for Erlinder. They even note that they "had misgivings about cooperating or working with the defence, the gravest being that such work might be seen as supporting the claim we were genocide deniers" (Davenport & Stam, 2009). Despite such doubts, they met with Peter Erlinder who "was, of course, interested in establishing his client's innocence, but he felt it would help the defence to establish a baseline history of what had taken place in the war in 1994" (Davenport & Stam, 2009). According to Davenport & Stam, "[w]hat he asked was reasonable. In fact, he made the same essential offer the prosecution had: In exchange for our efforts at contextualizing the events of 1994, Erlinder would do the best he could to assist us in getting data on what took place" (Davenport & Stam, 2009).

> perpetrators acted with genocidal intent (IV.2.2). Leaving aside the particular facts in this case, it is clear that a genocide occurred. (The Prosecutor v. Théoneste Bagosora et al., Case No. ICTR-98-41-T. Judgment and Sentence. 18 December 2008, par. 1998)

The Chamber furthermore emphasised that:

> [T]he question under consideration is not whether there was a plan or conspiracy to commit genocide in Rwanda. Rather, it is whether the Prosecution has proven beyond reasonable doubt based on the evidence in this case that the four Accused committed the crime of conspiracy. (The Prosecutor v. Théoneste Bagosora et al., Case No. ICTR-98-41-T. Judgment and Sentence. 18 December 2008, par. 2092)[38]

According to the Chamber, the problem was, however, that the evidence was not sufficient to establish that the only reasonable inference was that the four accused conspired to commit genocide. The Chamber stated that it is understandable that the evidence presented "shows a prior conspiracy to commit genocide. Indeed, these preparations are completely consistent with a plan to commit genocide. However, they are also consistent with preparations for a political or military power struggle" (The Prosecutor v. Théoneste Bagosora et al., Case No. ICTR-98-41-T. Judgment and Sentence. 18 December 2008, par. 2110). They lastly note that "Other or newly discovered information, subsequent trials or history may demonstrate a conspiracy involving the Accused prior to 6 April to commit genocide" (The Prosecutor v. Théoneste Bagosora et al., Case No. ICTR-98-41-T. Judgement and Sentence. 18 December 2008, par. 2112).[39, 40] The statements show that the Chamber made quite

---

38 The Chamber also notes that they "cannot exclude that there were in fact plans prior to 6 April to commit genocide in Rwanda. As the Prosecution argues, there are certain indications in the evidence of a prior plan or conspiracy to perpetrate a genocide as well as other politically motivated killings in Rwanda, which could have been triggered upon the resumption of hostilities between the government and the RPF or following some other significant event" (The Prosecutor v. Théoneste Bagosora et al., Case No. ICTR-98-41-T. Judgment and Sentence. 18 December 2008, par. 2107).

39 See also Jalloh (2010).

40 Although the Chamber in the Military I trial tried to give a clear signal on how the judgment should be interpreted in order to prevent abuse of the judgment, one cannot reduce the problem of denial to the misrepresentation of the verdict by authors such as Erlinder, Herman & Peterson, and Harmon Snow. There are some remarkable and, in terms of denial, questionable elements in the judgment of the Chamber that add substantial "noise" to the clear "signal" they initially tried to convey. For instance, in the verdict the Chamber makes the following statement: "The attack on President Habyarimana's plane is not charged as a crime in any of the Indictments. There are multiple theories concerning who is responsible. The Chamber has permitted the Defence to adduce some evidence related to this event as background. It remains, however, a collateral issue in the case. The Defence has presented a body of evidence suggesting that the RPF was responsible for the attack. In view of the Prosecution's position with respect to the attack and its limited significance, this evidence has not been adequately tested through cross-examination by an interested party or through rebuttal evidence, and the Chamber therefore has no view on who the perpetrators may have been" (The Prosecutor v. Théoneste Bagosora et al., Case No. ICTR-98-41-T. Judgment and Sentence. 18 December 2008, par. 1997). In addition to the fact that it was a big mistake of the prosecution to leave the downing of the plane un-investigated, the question here is why the court would allow the defence to present their alternative conspiracy theory that the RPF downed the airplane if nobody was charged with this. In fact, nobody knows who shot down the plane and it remains one of the most debated aspects of the genocide. The Chamber namely continues to state that "In sum, the alternative explanations for the events have added relevant

some effort in making clear that their judgment should not be misinterpreted and misrepresented. Despite such "warnings," Erlinder, in articulating his discourse, has misrepresented the judgment in the Military I case.[41] Also, note that, although Ntabakuze was not convicted for conspiracy to commit genocide, he was convicted by the Chamber in the same verdict for committing genocide. That is, however, something that is rarely mentioned.

6.3.4. Proving survival ...

According to Fournet (2007, pp. 127–135), when genocide is being prosecuted it can positively contribute to a collective memory of the genocide. By gathering documents, survivor testimony, etc. a lasting historical and impartial record can be created and as such trials can be a tool against genocide denial. Fournet (2007, p. 135) argues that:

> By "symbolically putting an end to the course of evil", trials not only bring a sense of closure to victims but they also constitute the ultimate rampart against denial claims and therefore against the revival of the victims' pain and suffering. And indeed, such claims will be facilitated by the lack of justice and the absence of trials which would have impeded the crimes and the victims from penetrating into collective memory.

Actually, on the website of the International Criminal Tribunal for the former Yugoslavia (www.icty.org), it is for instance stated that:

> The Tribunal has contributed to an indisputable historical record, combating denial and helping communities come to terms with their recent history. Crimes across the region

context to a few allegations against the Accused. For the most part, however, they are irrelevant to the core issues in this case, namely whether the Accused are responsible for the specific criminal allegations charged against them" (The Prosecutor v. Théoneste Bagosora et al., Case No. ICTR-98-41-T. Judgment and Sentence. 18 December 2008, par. 2001). What is the Chamber insinuating here, that some of the denial story is actually true? Does the Chamber argue that the alternative explanations presented by the defence, which basically entail a denial of the genocide, have made what happened more understandable?

41 The point is that I do not argue that it is impossible to have a discussion on the conspiracy or planning and how this was done. There are different approaches to this issue, as pointed out earlier (intentionalism, functionalism, inevitabilism). However, these discussions do always, in varying degrees, acknowledge planning and organisation, whereas Erlinder's aim of discussion seems to be to undermine this element completely and thereby the genocide: "no conspiracy, no planning, no genocide". The issues concerning the ICTR, such as how difficult it is as a lawyer to fully support your client and to guarantee a fair trial, etc., should be raised and critically discussed, but *the attack on the ICTR that adjudicates cases of genocide, often turns into an attack on the genocide itself.* Lawyers, such as Biju Duval or experts such as Des Forges have warned that the denial of the genocide might also be facilitated by the problems that haunt the court, fair trial issues, lack of rigor, problematic judgments, bias in prosecution, etc. Des Forges noted: "The question of credibility is of enormous importance. Not just in the short term [...] but in the future. We know that there are people who deny the Holocaust and there are people who deny the Rwandan genocide. If the evidence has not been solid, if the trial has not seemed to be fair, a certain number of people will reject that conviction and will use it to prove that these trials represent victor's justice or even worse are part of a larger plot" (Des Forges quoted in Cruvellier, 2010, pp. 36–37).

> can no longer be denied. For example, it has been proven beyond reasonable doubt that the mass murder at Srebrenica was genocide.

Fournet (2007, p. 136) notes that "This obviously does not presuppose that legal decisions will always succeed over denial claims, but it is argued [...] that trials and judicial recognition of the crime will participate in the fighting against such claims". Tatz (2003, p. 155) also argues that, despite some poor outcomes of trials, they still confirm that certain acts were committed and they clarify who the victims and the perpetrators are. In his opinion, trial records are "infinitively more powerful educative tools about contemporary social and political history than passive voice and the indirect speech of history texts, or of books" (Tatz, 2003, p. 156). To support his conclusion Tatz refers to ICTY/ICTR Judge Kirk McDonald who explains that the judgments are indelible records of what happened and will remain the best record of that history and therefore pose a challenge for those who are bent on denying what happened (Tatz, 2003, p. 156). The discussion above, however, revealed that, instead of being a tool in the fight against denial, those bent on denying genocide can use the court as a tool to engage in denial. Thus, it is not as simple as Stanton (1998b) portrays it when he argues that "[t]he best response to denial is punishment by an international tribunal or national courts. There the evidence can be heard, and the perpetrators punished." In reality, it provides for a levelled playing field in which those on the stand are allowed to legitimately challenge the facts, the evidence and present alternative readings of events. That is exactly what happened in the Military I trial. In paragraph 2110 of the Military I verdict, the Chamber finally reveals what "proof beyond reasonable doubt" really means in this case:

> After the death of President Habyarimana, these tools were clearly put to use to facilitate killings. When viewed against the backdrop of the targeted killings and massive slaughter perpetrated by civilian and military assailants between April and July 1994 as well as earlier cycles of violence, it is understandable why for many this evidence takes on new meaning and shows a prior conspiracy to commit genocide. Indeed, these preparations are completely consistent with a plan to commit genocide. However, they are also consistent with preparations for a political or military power struggle. The Chamber recalls that, when confronted with circumstantial evidence, it may only convict where it is the only reasonable inference. It cannot be excluded that the extended campaign of violence directed against Tutsis, as such, became an added or an altered component of these preparations. (The Prosecutor v. Théoneste Bagosora et al., Case No. ICTR-98-41-T. Judgment and Sentence. 18 December 2008, par. 2110)

Apparently, the official denial discourse presented in court by defendants and their counsel is thus seen as an "alternative explanation" that is as credible as the conspiracy to commit genocide. Denial is an intrinsic element of the genocide, and it was allowed on the stand; it was not judged, but allowed to gain a credibility that matches the conspiracy to genocide, which is reduced to a competing alternative explanation. By allowing the denial to be brought forward as proof, the process of genocide actually continued in court.[42, 43]

One could argue that the court not only provides the alleged perpetrators with a platform that allows them to obscure what happened, also the victims can speak up when they testify for the defence. This allows them to publically acknowledge what happened to them and their relatives. For victims, there seems to be a need to testify; they want to tell their stories. There are multiple reasons: it turns them into survivors, it honours the memories of those who have perished, it exorcises their pain and their stories create a memory which prevents genocide from happening again; the hope that knowing about what happened prevents such events in the future (Fournet, 2007, p. 27). Cohen (2001, p. 225) notes that for survivors the truth is known; they experienced what happened, but they want to render this knowledge explicit. They want acknowledgement, which is according to Cohen (2001, p. 225) "what happens to knowledge when it becomes officially sanctioned and enters public discourse." The information needs to move from private memory to collective memory. The urge to testify in the face of genocide denial and to tell what happened is also triggered by the specificity of the crime of genocide, which constitutes an existential threat and, through their testimony, survivors fight against the continued victimisation caused by genocide denial. As Antoinette explained earlier (Chapter 2, Section 2.6.5.): "It is important not to withhold anything from what I will say because this is what happened. Because, if I say that it should be hidden, it would be like denying the genocide." However, for various reasons, testifying in court is a perilous exercise. Testifying about the crime of all crimes somehow banalises it: "Precisely because the survivor had survived, the crimes could not have been so terrible as they were claiming – and, if they were, this necessarily implied that those who survived had had illegitimate privileges" (Fournet, 2007, p. 30). Genocide thus creates an inherent problem for survivors: simply being alive after what happened arouses suspicion; survivors might not be telling the straight story, they might be lying and they might have profited or colluded with the perpetrators. This puts them

42 In this context the remark by the trial chamber in Karemera and Ngirumpatse (also known as Government I) is also significant: "The date by which the first three Civil Defence Documents were issued, 25 May 1994, marks the point where the only reasonable inference based on the credible evidence is that Karemera and Ngirumpatse conspired with the Interim Government to adopt a policy of genocide, which they executed primarily through their Civil Defence Plan – a thinly-veiled strategy for exterminating Tutsis." But they add: "The Prosecution has not proved beyond a reasonable doubt that Karemera and Ngirumpatse, or other leaders, planned the massacre of Tutsis in advance of the assassination of President Habyarimana. The Chamber acknowledges that the genocide may have started as a spontaneous reaction to the assassination of President Habyarimana, which was fuelled by the belief that the Tutsi-led RPF was responsible, and prior anti-Tutsi propaganda" (Oral summary -The Prosecutor v. Édouard Karemera et al., Case No. ICTR-98-44-T). To state that the genocide might have started as "a spontaneous reaction to the assassination" is directly in line with the denial discourse that also Erlinder promotes. As noted earlier, genocide by nature and definition can never be spontaneous. Ordinary people do not spontaneously start to slaughter their fellow men, women and children. They need the motives, means and opportunities to do this. The required ideological mind-set, the weapons and the impunity are orchestrated and do not spontaneously fall from mid-air. For a critical reflection of the Karemera judgment see: Cruvellier (2012).

43 For a general discussion of the role of justice mechanisms such as courts, tribunal or truth commissions in fighting or facilitating denial see: Imbleau (2004).

into the situation where they have to prove their own survival (Fournet, 2007, p. 31). For victims, these trials, instead of bringing closure, can thus also be confronting, because their testimony is "made to serve as probative value regarding the fact" (Nichanian, 2009, p. 120). The testimony of their genocidal victimisation is reduced to a proof of that fact, of that reality – it could be fact, but it could also be fiction: "They [have] to prove their own death" (Nichanian, 2009, p. 28).[44] The genocide thus creates an unimaginable catastrophe for the survivor, as Nichanian (2009, p. 123 emphasis added) reveals:

> In the very moment when the first survivor has uttered a word of testimony, at the very instant the first sound came out of his mouth to tell his cavalry of his observations, the archive has already seized his speech. That is the catastrophe for the survivor. From the beginning, before the beginning even, the murderer is here, facing me, and he tells me: Prove it! Prove it then if you can! And I, for ninety years, I have stood up and proven it. [...] I answer to the injunction of the executioner. For ninety years, by proving, by making testimony function as proof, I answer to the call and injunction of the executioner. *For that is what he wanted from the beginning is it not? To kill, to eliminate, to exterminate? Of course, he wanted that too, but, above all, he wanted me to prove – and prove again.*

The last sentences powerfully capture the notion discussed earlier that genocide is not only about the "killing of life" but also about the "killing of death". By determining "the truth of the facts", by proving that genocide happened, you automatically acknowledge that it is not a fact, thereby creating room for other proofs, for historiographic perversion as Nichanian refers to it. By bringing proof, you automatically end up playing the game of those bent on denying genocide, which is to "assert that the factuality of an event has not been established and that the historical record, here too, is open to revision" (Nichanian, 2009, p. 141). The insight that the *génocidaires* not only want to kill, but that part of the violent genocidal process and therefore of the denial is that they want others, especially the victims to prove that this actually happened, sheds a critical light on ICTR proceedings in which the bringing of proof is required.

It remains a question to what extent the ICTR judgments contribute to a collective memory. Of course the genocide against the Tutsi is collectively remembered but not as extensively as the Holocaust. Although the genocide against the Tutsi happened quite recently, for Westerners, it occurred far away; there are no memorials and museums in the West that focus on the genocide. So really how collective is that memory that is being created at the ICTR? Who knows who Habyarimana, Kambanda, Bagosora, and Ntabakuze were and what they did? If people know about what happened in Rwanda it is because they read about Dallaire's perils in his book *Shake hands with devil* or they have seen the movie *Hotel Rwanda*. The discussion reveals that one cannot straightforwardly conclude that the ICTR trials are "cornerstones of social and collective memory of the crime of genocide" (Fournet, 2007, p. 128). Moreover, for many, the legacy of the ICTR is tarnished. It was criticised for its slow start,

---

44 See also Fierens (2009, p. 161).

that it is not making headway, that because of its bureaucracy and politics it is dysfunctional, too expensive and biased.[45] Especially the lack of attention for RPF crimes is deemed an issue. Despite such criticism, it also has to be noticed that the ICTR was set up from scratch under very difficult conditions and these efforts have gone largely unappreciated. The reality is also that the court and its staff cannot perform miracles (Peter, 1997). This, however, does not right the wrongs committed.

One cannot reduce the problem of denial to questionable scholarship, denialist lines of defence, ambiguous verdicts and their subsequent misrepresentations. When reflecting on actions that contribute to the denial, one also has to face the reality of how the current Government of Rwanda is dealing with the problem of denial and that this can have certain negative consequences. The implication appears to be that their fight against denial could also facilitate the denial of the genocide against the Tutsi. This is, however, a tricky subject, because one should be careful that such a critical analysis does not reiterate the criticism of the current Government of Rwanda that has also become a cornerstone of discourses that deny the genocide. Denial is namely often presented as critique and there is the risk that one makes linguistic community with such denialist rhetoric.

6.4. Governmentality

6.4.1. Genocide deniers must be countered at every turn

The current Government of Rwanda has put the problem of genocide denialism firmly on the political agenda and it addresses the issue through a variety of means. President of the Republic of Rwanda, Paul Kagame (2008, p. xxi) has, for instance, on various occasions warned that "[a] new phenomenon has emerged in the form of individuals and groups who seek to revise history for their own gain, including those who deny outright that genocide took place in Rwanda in 1994." The current Government of Rwanda also tries to address the problem of genocide denialism by giving it special attention during the commemorations of the genocide against the Tutsi. Denial of the genocide against the Tutsi, for instance, received special attention during the official 15th commemoration of the Rwandan genocide which took place in the month of April 2009 (www.rwanda15.org, www.cnlg.gov.rw). The theme of the commemoration was "Let us keep alive the memory of Genocide against Tutsi by fighting its revisionism as we build our country" (Musoni, 2009; National

[45] For a critical reflection on the workings of the ICTR see Des Forges and Longman (2004). Many of these questions also apply to international criminal courts and tribunals in general. For a discussion of the challenges these international justice mechanisms are facing see: Drumbl (2009). For a further reflection on this particular subject matter see also Mols (2009). Mols (together van der Spoel) represented Kambanda as defence counsel in his appeal process. Mols interestingly notes how the defendant, defence counsel, trial chamber judges, the prosecution, etc. all moved from The Hague to Arusha in the same plane in order to adjudicate the appeal at the ICTR (See also Heanen, 2000). Mols notes that, despite the financial costs involved, it was justified to hold the appeal trial in Arusha instead of The Hague; when cases are adjudicated on or near the *locus delicti* it helps to make locally visible that justice is being done.

Commission for the Fight Against Genocide, 2009). President Kagame (2009) spoke during the commemoration at the Nyanza Memorial Site in Kucikuro in 2009 stating that:

> There have been lots of debates and discussions on our history and what really happened in an attempt to get to the truth. Even when the truth does not come out immediately, it will do so at some point, because as we say in Kinyarwanda, "the truth passes through fire but it never burns". It looks like there are some people who are still trying to "burn the truth" but that can never happen.

In the wake of the 15th commemoration, Rwanda also hosted the international conference of genocide scholars. According to Jean de Dieu Mucyo, director of the National Commission for the Fight Against Genocide (CNLG), the conference served to establish and perpetuate the memory of the genocide and combat its ideology, negationism and revisionism (Musoni, 2009). Rwandans living abroad were also asked to commemorate the Genocide and "to fight genocide deniers and revisionists" (www.rwandan.no, www.rwanda15.org). More notably, the Rwandan ambassador and permanent representative of the Republic of Rwanda to the United Nations, during his commemorative speech at the UN General Assembly, specifically mentioned that, 15 years after the genocide, the world continues to witness the negation and denial of the genocide against the Tutsi in Rwanda (Nsengimana, 2009).[46] President Kagame (2008, p. xxi and xxiv) concludes that "[t]he genocide deniers must be countered at every turn."

In addition to, for instance, raising awareness during the commemorations, the Government of Rwanda also tries to control the problem of genocide denial by criminalising it. Like for many European countries, for the current government, the repression of genocide denial through criminalisation is seen as a valuable instrument in the fight against genocide. However, in comparison to other countries who have witnessed genocide, such as Germany or France, Rwanda is quite unique with regard to the extent in which it has tried to combat genocide through legislation; no other country seems to have passed as many hate speech and genocide denial laws as Rwanda. That the Rwandan authorities take the issue of genocide denial serious became clear when Erlinder was arrested in Rwanda on the 28th of May 2010 when visiting his client Victoire Ingabire and was detained for approximately three weeks on charges of genocide denial. Erlinder was eventually released on the 17th of June 2010 for medical reasons and was not prosecuted further. In a reaction to the criticism on the arrest, Minister of Justice Tharcisse Karugarama (2010) stated:

> Let me explain as clearly as I can: Without genocide ideology, there can be no genocide. Human beings will not engage in systematic slaughter spontaneously. It begins with

[46] The 20th commemoration of the genocide had the theme "remember-unite-renew" (www.kwibuka.org) and, although the commemoration did not specifically focus on the issue of genocide denial, during the commemorative period, certain events were organised that addressed the issue. I, for instance, participated in an international youth conference held at Gabiro (Akagera Park) that specially addressed the issue of the denial of the genocide against the Tutsi.

> hate translated into words and ideas from rational-seeming men – political and religious leaders, intellectuals and journalists – before a single gun is fired or machete raised. And what binds these belief systems – from the ancient pogroms to the Holocaust to Cambodia and Rwanda – is the pivotal role of historical revisionism. Every genocide has depended on lies about the past. This is why Rwanda treats genocide ideology as a deadly serious matter. Without it, the events of 1994 could not have happened. And this is why we see Twin Cities attorney Peter Erlinder's pattern of genocide denial as a deadly serious crime. This is not a matter of intellectual curiosity. Erlinder's actions as a high-profile genocide denier and radical ideologue are precisely why these laws were brought into being. Left unpunished, these actions give comfort to terrorists who regard him as an intellectual hero. Left unchecked, the promulgation of the Erlinder worldview – that the genocide is a figment of Rwanda's imagination and that the victims were responsible for their fate – will cause unrest and disunity. Make no mistake: The Erlinder worldview will cost lives. How do we know? Because it has happened before – on a scale that scars our soul and shames the world.

Denial is indeed "a deadly serious matter" and for the reasons mentioned by Karugarama it is understandable that it is addressed, but the fight against genocide denial by means of criminalisation also appears to cause considerable problems.

6.4.2. Criminalising denial

The criminalisation of genocide denial is for many a major concern because the possibility to express oneself freely is thereby limited. A significant political and ethical issue thus underlies the question concerning the criminalisation of genocide denial, namely whether such a limitation of the fundamental right of freedom of speech by the state is actually legitimate (Raes, 1995, p. 31 and 32). The Republic of Rwanda, like many other members of the international community, has international obligations to safeguard fundamental human rights, such as, for instance, freedom of expression as it ratified the International Covenant on Civil and Political Rights (ICCPR). Article 19 of the ICCPR deals with the right to free speech and it states that everyone shall have the right to hold opinions without interference. By ratifying the ICCPR, Rwanda is not only bound by the provisions of the ICCPR, it is also obliged to give effect to the ICCPR through national legislation. The Rwandan Constitution safeguards freedom of expression in article 33 and 34. Article 33 states that "[f]reedom of thought, opinion, conscience, religion, worship and the public manifestation thereof is guaranteed by the State in accordance with conditions determined by law." Article 34 adds that "[f]reedom of the press and freedom of information are recognized and guaranteed by the State." The preamble to the Constitution also reaffirms that the Republic of Rwanda adheres to the principles of human rights enshrined in, for instance, the Universal Declaration of Human Rights and the International Covenant on Civil and Political Rights. However, Rwanda has also ratified the Convention on the Prevention and Punishment of the Crime of Genocide of 9 December 1948. Thus, in addition to safeguarding freedom of expression, Rwanda also has the obligation to prevent and stop genocide and this includes curbing genocide denial.[47] This, of course, becomes even more pertinent due to the fact that Rwanda has witnessed genocide. Rwanda is a party to the 1948 Genocide Convention, which in article 1 states that "[t]he Contracting Parties confirm that genocide, whether committed in time of peace or in time of war, is a crime under international law which they undertake to prevent and to punish." The preamble of Rwanda's Constitution also makes crystal clear that fighting genocide is one of the main responsibilities of the state and its people. There is thus a tension between the duty of guaranteeing the fundamental human right of freedom of speech described above on the one hand and the duty to prevent and stop genocide on the other hand, which might require that freedom of speech is limited.[48]

The preamble of the Constitution of the Republic of Rwanda that was adopted in 2003 states that "[i]n the wake of the genocide that was organised and supervised by unworthy leaders and other perpetrators and that decimated more than a million sons and daughters of Rwanda" the people of Rwanda are "[r]esolved to fight the ideology of genocide and all its manifestations and to eradicate ethnic, regional and any other

47 Article 1 of the 1948 Genocide Convention states: "The Contracting Parties confirm that genocide, whether committed in time of peace or in time of war, is a crime under international law which they undertake to prevent and to punish."

48 Restrictions to the freedom of expression are admissible under Article 19(3) of the ICCPR only when they are necessary, respectful of the principle of proportionality, and established by the law for pursuing specific aims, namely for respect of the rights or reputations of others or the protection of national security or of public order, or of public health or morals. Furthermore, article 20 of the ICCPR also prohibits "any propaganda for war" as well as "any advocacy of national, racial or religious hatred that constitutes incitement to discrimination, hostility or violence". The acts listed in article 20 are all subject to restriction pursuant to article 19(3). The aims provided by the Rwandan legislator, namely "to prevent and punish genocide ideology in order not for genocide to be committed again in the country" appear to fall within the scope provided by Article 19(3). Note that the Human Rights Committee in de case of Faurisson, who had denied the existence of the gas chambers during the Holocaust and was prosecuted on the basis of the French Gayssot Act, decided that the restrictions on Faurisson's freedom of speech were legitimate, since "the statements made by the author, read in their full context, were of a nature as to raise or strengthen anti-Semitic feelings, the restriction served the respect of the Jewish community to live free from fear of an atmosphere of anti-Semitism" (Faurisson v. France, No 550/1993: France. 16/12/96. CCPR/C/58/D/550/ 1993, par. 9.6). Also in the jurisprudence of the European Court on Human Rights we find cases from which it becomes clear that genocide denial speech is not protected under the Convention. In restricting freedom of speech the commission has mainly followed the requirements set out in the second part of article 10 which states that: "The exercise of these freedoms, since it carries with it duties and responsibilities, may be subject to such formalities, conditions, restrictions or penalties as are prescribed by law and are necessary in a democratic society, in the interests of national security, territorial integrity or public safety, for the prevention of disorder or crime, for the protection of health or morals, for the protection of the reputation or rights of others, for preventing the disclosure of information received in confidence, or for maintaining the authority and impartiality of the judiciary." The main reasons given for restricting freedom of speech in case of for instance Holocaust denial were that public order was at stake, that it could incite hatred or could lead to the reoccurrence of the events and that the dignity of the victims required protection. (See for instance: H., W., P. and K. v Austria, European Court of Human Rights, Decision as to the admissibility of 12 October 1989 and European Commission on Human Rights, Nationaldemokratische Partei Deutschlands, Bezirksverband München-Oberbayern v Germany, 29 November 1989, Application No. 25992/94). For a critical analysis of the subject matter discussed above see: Kučs (2014).

form of divisions.'[49] Article 13 of the Section on fundamental human rights adds that "[r]evisionism, negationism and trivialisation of genocide are punishable by the law." The prosecutor-general Martin Ngoga was thus correct when he stated in an interview that "the fight against genocide and Rwanda's unwavering commitment to this fight through its contributions to fend off efforts by other people propagating genocide elsewhere is fundamentally entrenched in the constitution" (The New Times, 2010). Constitutionally, Rwanda is governed by the legacy of the genocide. Its Constitution is a fundamental rejection of the genocide and its underlying ideology and it provides the basis for far-reaching legislative efforts repressing genocide in general and more particularly its ideology and its denial. Buckley-Zistel (2006, p. 136) thus notes that:

> More than a decade after the event, the horror of the 1994 genocide is omnipresent in Rwanda. It serves as a foundation for private arguments and public policies; the individual and the collective *raison d'être* of the nation and its people is built around the genocide.

The Government of Rwanda has enacted various laws to implement the abovementioned constitutional obligations. Genocide denial was first criminalised in Law N° 33*bis*/2003 of 06/09/2003 Repressing the Crime of Genocide, Crimes Against Humanity and War Crimes. Chapter 2, Article 4 of the law criminalised:

> Any person who will have publicly shown, by his or her words, writings, images, or by any other means, that he or she has negated the genocide committed, rudely minimized it or attempted to justify or approve its grounds, or any person who will have hidden or destroyed its evidence.

By initially dealing with genocide denial under the Chapter of "The Crime of Genocide and its Sanctions", it becomes clear that the Rwandan legislator recognises genocide denial as being an intrinsic part of the genocidal process and thereby an intrinsic part of the crime of genocide. It is interesting to note that no references are being made to the fact that the denial should incite hatred, discrimination, disturb public peace, etc., which is often the case in, for instance, European legislation criminalising Holocaust denial.[50] As such, the legislation focussed on the illocutionary speech act

49 See also basic principles mentioned in Article 9 of the Constitution.

50 In contrast to the Netherlands, which criminalised the perlocutionary effects of denial speech, the abovementioned legislation focusses on illocutionary acts. France appears to take a similar approach. In France, denial is criminalised under the so-called Loi Gayssot which states that "anyone who disputes the existence of one or more crimes against humanity as defined in Article 639 of the Statute of the International Military Tribunal annexed to the London agreement of 8 August 1945 which have been committed either by the members of an organisation declared criminal under Article 9 of the Statute or by a person found guilty of such crimes by a French or international court shall be liable". The French legislation is limited to Holocaust denial and, in contrast to the legislation in other countries, it does not punish the trivialisation (downplaying) of the Holocaust. It furthermore does not require the prohibited conduct to disturb the public peace (Sullo, 2014). The same applies to the criminalisation of denial in the Austrian *Verbotsgesetz*, which in article 3h states that those who publically deny the Holocaust (*leugnet, gröblich verharmlost, gutheisst or zu rechtfertigen sucht*) are criminally liable. In Germany Holocaust denial is criminalised in article 130 (*Volksverhetzung*) of the German Criminal Code, which states that: "Whoever publicly or in a meeting approves of, denies or belittles an act committed under the rule of National Socialism of the type indicated in Section 6 subsection (1) of the

of denial and not necessarily its perlocutionary consequences. The harm of genocide denial is not reduced to the danger that it can lead to (re)new(ed) genocide(s), instead the denial is harmful because it is intrinsic to an ongoing genocidal process. The law concerning the repression of genocide of 2003 was, however, not the only law that addressed and criminalised genocide denial. Genocide denial also falls within the scope of genocide ideology, which has been criminalised in Rwanda since 2008.

In a 2006 report entitled *Genocide ideology and strategies for its eradication*, the government generally defined genocide ideology as "a set of ideas or representations whose major role is to stir up hatred and create a pernicious atmosphere favouring the implementation and legitimization of the persecution and elimination of a category of the population" (Republic of Rwanda, 2006, p. 16).[51] According to the report:

> [T]he ethnicist, anti-Tutsi, genocidal or pan-Hutu ideology takes the form of revisionism by *denying* genocide and its consequences, or by minimizing it. It takes a revisionist form by vaguely acknowledging genocide but, in the same breath, trying to justify it through counter accusations in order to cleanse the real culprits of any responsibility. Moreover, genocide ideology takes its traditional form consisting in demonizing the Tutsis through psychological, social or political clichés. In particular, the genocide ideology takes on the subtle form of a merciless war against any effort to rebuild consciousness of national citizenship and strives to encapsulate the Rwandan society for ever in the ethnicist deadlock. (Republic of Rwanda, 2006, p. 18 Emphasis added)

To address the problems discerned in the report, Law N° 18/2008 of 23/07/08 relating to the Prevention and Punishment of the Crime of Genocide Ideology was adopted. Article 2 of this law defined genocide ideology as follows:

> The genocide ideology is an aggregate of thoughts characterized by conduct, speeches, documents and other acts aiming at exterminating or inciting others to exterminate people based on ethnic group, origin, nationality, region, colour, physical appearance, sex, language, religion or political opinion, committed in normal periods or during war.

Article 3 furthermore dealt with the characteristics of the crime of genocide ideology and stated that the crime of genocide ideology is:

> [C]haracterized in any behaviour manifested by facts aimed at dehumanizing a person or a group of persons with the same characteristics in the following manner: 1) Threatening, intimidating, degrading through defamatory speeches, documents or actions which aim at propounding wickedness or inciting hatred; 2) Marginalizing, laughing at one's misfortune, defaming, mocking, boasting, despising, degrading, creating confusion

Code of Crimes against International Law, in a manner capable of disturbing the public peace shall be punished [...]." Here the public peace thus needs to be disturbed. Interestingly, the French, Austrian and German legislation also criminalises the denial of other crimes against humanity perpetrated by the Nazi regime. In France and Germany the sanction is up to five years imprisonment. In Austria one could however be sentenced to ten years imprisonment.

51 See also *République Rwandaise Parlement Commission Extraordinaire* (2004).

aiming at negating the genocide which occurred, stirring up ill feelings, taking revenge, altering testimony or evidence for the genocide which occurred; 3) Killing, planning to kill or attempting to kill someone for purposes of furthering genocide ideology.

From the above it becomes clear that the ideology legislation criminalised a very broad range of actions including genocide denial.[52]

6.4.3. Critique and reform …

Various human rights organisations have raised considerable critique concerning the legislation described above. Organisations, such as Human Rights Watch (2008b), Amnesty International (2010, 2011), and Article 19 (2009) do generally acknowledge that the criminalisation of genocide denial is legitimate in cases where it incites hatred, violence and discrimination. They furthermore point out that taking into account the role speech has played in the genocide against the Tutsi, it is understandable that the Government of Rwanda has resorted to criminalisation. The critique therefore does not focus on the question as to whether criminalisation is legitimate *per se*. Instead, some serious questions were raised concerning how the criminalisation precisely took place and how the abovementioned legislation was utilised in practice.[53]

---

52 But there are more laws that are possibly relevant in this context. In certain cases denial speech could also be seen as divisionary, which would bring it within the scope of the legislation criminalising sectarianism and discrimination (Law NO 47/2001 on Prevention, Suppression and Punishment of the Crime of Discrimination and, Sectarianism). According to Article 1 of this law sectarianism (or divisionism) "means the use of any speech, written statement or action that divides people, that is likely to spark conflicts among people, or that causes an uprising which might degenerate into strife among people based on discrimination." This law was reviewed with the introduction of the 2012 Rwandan Penal Code, which changed the sentences for the crime of sectarianism. Article 136 of the Rwandan penal code now states that: "Any person who commits the crime of discrimination and sectarian practices shall be liable to a term of imprisonment of more than five (5) years to seven (7) years and a fine of one hundred thousand (100,000) to one million (1,000, 000) Rwandan francs." But also in other legislation, such as for instance the so called "media law," we find references to the crime of genocide denial. For instance, in the section on "penalties for particular crimes committed through press," it is mentioned that the "apology for the crime of genocide" is punishable with penalties (Law N°22/2009 OF 12/08/2009 On Media).

53 This was also noted by the Government of Rwanda and its development partners in an assessment (Republic of Rwanda, 2008). With regard to the ideology legislation it was noted that there are several problems: "It is doubtful whether they fulfil the requirements of legal certainty meaning that the offence is sufficiently clearly drafted to allow a person to know whether or not their conduct would amount to a breach of the law. The absence of a requirement of intentionality (i.e. that the offender intended to cause harm) in the provisions adds to the problem of vagueness and leaves the provisions open to abuse and less effective in tackling the problem that they are designed for. In particular Article 3 of the proposed new law risks confusing the definition of genocide ideology to the extent that the law could be used where sanctions are not warranted or might fail to convict real acts of incitement. Other problems with the proposed legislation are the rigid specification of penalties that do not leave any judicial discretion in sentencing to reflect the facts of each case, and provisions on the sentencing of children. Given the gravity of the issue it is essential that laws against genocide ideology are as clearly formulated in order to ensure that the justice system can be brought to bear most effectively and to guard against the possibility of misuse" (Republic of Rwanda, 2008, p. 33).

The legislation was, for instance, criticised for its heavy penalties. Violation of the abovementioned legal provisions could lead to punishments ranging from a fine of 50,000 RWF and three years of imprisonment to a fine of 10,000,000 RWF and 25 years to life imprisonment, depending on the specifics of the legal provision violated, the specifics of the case and the type of actor involved. The critique was voiced that the severe penalties were not in line with what was proportionally required. Such severe criticism forced the Government of Rwanda to reform its legislation. First of all, with the introduction of the new Rwandan penal code in 2012, the abovementioned law of 2003 repressing the crime of genocide was repealed (Article 765 of Law N° 01/2012/OL of 02/05/2012 instituting the penal code). The content of the 2003 legislation is now integrated in the Rwandan penal code (Part II, Title 1, Chapter 1) and article 116 criminalises "the crime of negationism and minimization of the genocide against the Tutsi":

> Any person who publicly shows, by his/her words, writings, images, or by any other means, that he/she negates the genocide against the Tutsi, rudely minimizes it or attempts to justify or approve its grounds, or any person who hides or destroys its evidence shall be liable to a term of imprisonment of more than five (5) years to nine (9) years.[54]

Initially the definition appears to be clear and very similar as to how genocide denial is legislated in other countries. The question however remains what exactly would make a minimisation "rude"? What is noteworthy is that the sentences have been significantly reduced. Those who break the law are now liable to a term of imprisonment of more than five years to nine years.

The crime of genocide ideology is addressed in the subsequent Chapter of the penal code (Part II, Title 1, Chapter 2). Article 135 concerns "the crime of genocide ideology and other related offences" and states that:

> Any person who commits the crime of genocide ideology and other related offences shall be liable to a term of imprisonment of more than five (5) years to nine (9) years and a fine of one hundred thousand (100,000) to one million (1,000, 000) Rwandan francs.

The article furthermore notes that "[a] law shall provide for the details related to genocide ideology and other related offences." The sentences are also significantly lower compared to the legislation from 2008 discussed above. The legislation from 2008 was revised and a new law was eventually adopted in 2013 (Law N° 84/2013 of 11/09/2013 on the crime of genocide ideology and other related offences) repealing the old legislation (Article 14). It is interesting that the preamble to the new legislation states that the legislation is "[p]ursuant to the United Nations Convention on the

54 Article 96 of the penal code clarifies the required subjective element: "Criminal liability is personal. Unless otherwise provided by the law, only a person who intentionally commits an offence shall be liable to a penalty. A person who commits an offence intentionally is one who commits it consciously and willingly."

Prevention and Punishment of the Crime of Genocide of 09/12/1948." Article 3 of the law gives a "definition and acts constituting the crime of genocide ideology":

> Genocide ideology shall be any deliberate act, committed in public whether orally, written or video means or by any other means which may show that a person is characterized by ethnic, religious, nationality or racial-based with the aim to: 1° advocate for the commission of genocide; 2° support the genocide.

The new legislation rephrases article 2 of the old legislation from 2008 mentioned above in a more comprehensive manner, but the underlying idea remains the same. Article 3 of the old legislation dealt with the characteristics of the crime of genocide ideology, the new legislation refrains from giving such concrete examples. These examples gave rise to much criticism due to their vague description and therefore could cover a wide range of different behaviours. What furthermore complicated the matter was that in the old legislation the required intention was not clearly specified. Normal unintended behaviour could thus amount to the crime of genocide ideology. The new legislation therefore states that the actions have to be deliberate, that is "willingly and with an intent to promote genocide ideology" (Article 2.5). The downside of the new legislation is that descriptions of what could be concrete acts of genocide ideology are missing and this could again create uncertainty as to what behaviour amounts to genocide ideology and is therefore prohibited.[55] Ironically, the old legislation with its illustrations might have been more insightful in that respect. On the other hand, the new legislation makes a clearer difference between genocide ideology and other related offences. Now genocide denial is treated as a separate, but related, offence of which the elements are relatively well defined, while under the old legislation denial ended up being conflated with ideology. In a way this is understandable because genocide denial often draws on elements of the genocide ideology.

In addition to defining the crime of genocide ideology, the new legislation also criminalises so-called "genocide ideology related offences" and these also include among others negation, minimisation and justification of genocide.[56] The negation of genocide according to article 5 concerns a "deliberate act, committed in public" which aims at:

> 1° stating or explaining that genocide is not genocide; 2° deliberately misconstruing the facts about genocide for the purpose of misleading the public; 3° supporting a double genocide theory for Rwanda; 4° stating or explaining that genocide committed against the Tutsi was not planned.

55 For a critical analysis of the legislative developments concerning the laws discussed above see: Jansen (2014).

56 The other genocide related crimes listed in the penal code include incitement to genocide (article 4), concealment or destruction of evidence of genocide (article 8), theft or destruction of remains of victims of genocide (article 9), demolishing a memorial site or cemetery for the victims of genocide (article 10), and violence against a genocide survivor (article 11).

Minimisation of genocide is defined in article 6 as:

> Any deliberate act, committed in public, aiming at: 1° downplaying the gravity or consequences of genocide; 2° downplaying the methods through which genocide was committed.

According to article 7 justifying genocide includes:

> Any deliberate act, committed in public, aiming at: 1° glorifying genocide; 2° supporting genocide; 3° legitimizing genocide.

When the legislation mentions genocide, it means "genocide committed against the Tutsi or any other genocide recognized by the United Nations" (Article 2.2). Therefore, apparently the criminalisation does not limit itself to the denial of the genocide against the Tutsi. The sentence is also significantly reduced. Article 12 of the law refers back to article 116 of the Rwandan penal code which provides for prison sentences of more than five years to nine years. Instead of the earlier sanction of imprisonment of ten years to twenty five years or life imprisonment when found guilty of the ideology of genocide and one was convicted of the crime of genocide.

When one analyses the internal structures of the abovementioned legislative frameworks addressing genocide denial and ideology, it is not always clear how all the offences mentioned in each of the frameworks relate to each other. For instance, in the penal code denial is criminalised in article 116, which, among negation, minimisation, justification and approval also criminalises hiding or destroying the evidence. One could wonder how "approval of the genocide" falls within the scope of denial, but moreover in subsequent articles (117 and 118) theft and destruction of remains of the victims is also heavily criminalised. It seems that the same behaviour could thus fall under different articles. Also, how the two legislative frameworks are related to each other is not always clear. For instance, both criminalise genocide denial. Article 116 of the penal code mentions different denials, such as negation, justification, etc. but does not define them. The legislation on genocide ideology does define each of these denials in greater detail. It is however unclear whether that clarification also applies to the penal code. Also, while article 116 in the penal code mentions "approval" as a form of denial, this form is not listed in the definition of denial in the legislation on genocide ideology, although the definition of justification is broad enough for "approval" to fall within its scope. But if that was the case, why mention it as a separate form in the first place? However, when reading how the legislation defines genocide ideology, one also could argue that this entails "approval" of the genocide. Thus despite the improvements with regard to, for instance, the harshness of the sentences and the clarity of the legislation, the internal consistency of the two legislative frameworks and how they are related is not always clear and it could lead to confusion.

6.4.4. The perils of criminalisation

Several issues appear to haunt the criminalisation of genocide denial. These issues are however not always unique to Rwanda and many of these issues can also be observed in other countries that have criminalised genocide denial.

Proportional?

Above it was mentioned that human rights organisations found the severe penalties not in line with what is proportionally required in cases of genocide denial. However, whether a penalty is proportional is closely related to how one perceives the violent nature of the phenomenon of genocide denial and the perceptions concerning this differ greatly.[57] For instance, the rationale underlying European legislation that criminalises Holocaust denial is that it discriminates and incites new violence.[58] Here, genocide denial is something that comes after the crime; first the crime of genocide, afterwards the denial. It is seen as something separate and denial of the genocide is thus not perceived as being essential to its perpetration. Genocide denial is predominately approached as hate speech that facilitates genocidal violence and as a result, the harsh penalties are not proportional to the harm inflicted. However, as Fournet (2007, p. 95) explains: "Genocide denial is not simply the denial of a crime; it is a particular conduct which fits into the broader genocidal pattern of occurrence." It is the continuation of the genocide but now through a different strategy and it is thus part of the crime itself. As noted before, this last insight could also explain why survivors react so intensely when it comes to genocide denial; it constitutes a direct existential threat due to the fact that it is part of the genocidal process. They do not perceive it as something that might lead to a reoccurrence of what happened to them; it is a continuation of their victimisation. Thus, when it comes to dealing with genocide, it is not only about preventing genocide in the future. It is about stopping ongoing genocide in its tracks – about controlling and stopping a genocidal process that continues as long as there is denial. The Government of Rwanda apparently sees genocide denial as an intrinsic part of the crime of genocide (Republic of Rwanda, 2006, p. 15 and 17).[59] It was initially criminalised within the framework of the crime of genocide (Law N° 33*bis*/2003 of 06/09/2003 Repressing the Crime of Genocide, Crimes against Humanity and War Crimes) and, with the introduction of the new Rwandan penal code in 2012, it was again dealt with under the Chapter of crimes of genocide. It is furthermore interesting that the crimes of genocide including its denial are the first crimes addressed in the general part of the penal code describing the different offences. When one sees denial as intrinsic to genocide, the harm that denial does is much graver and as a result harsh punishments are not seen as disproportional but as appropriate and proportional.

57 See also Chapter 5, Section 5.6.

58 For a comparison between Rwanda's and Germany's legislation see: Pall (2010).

59 I also hold this view, although I am not convinced that criminalisation is the most suitable strategy to deal with the problem of genocide denial.

Does it work?

The human rights organisation Article 19, which has severely criticised Rwanda's old genocide ideology legislation, wonders whether it can be substantiated that criminalisation ensures that genocide will not happen again. According to Article 19, "there is no legislation that absolutely guarantees the prevention of genocide" (Article 19, 2009, p. 6).[60] The question thus remains whether criminalisation works.[61] Do such penalties help to prevent genocide or are they "merely" symbolic gestures that such behaviour is wrong and not tolerated. Scholars also question whether criminalisation of genocide denial really prevents genocide.[62] Janssens, in addition to noting that criminalisation does not show faith in the corrective capacities of scientific and political debate, questions whether the lies and faulty visions of history will disappear due to criminalisation. Will criminalisation really cause deniers to think differently? According to Janssens (1999), it could have the opposite and perverse effect that deniers might become hardened in their views and their prosecution would also enable them to portray themselves as victims, turn themselves in to martyrs and thereby gain attention that they otherwise would not have had. The problem is that the population that is likely to engage in denial does this for mostly ideological reasons and they are therefore often (highly) motivated fanatics (Van den Berghe, 1997b, p. 179). Criminalisation and prosecution could stimulate their denial because they see this "crack down" on their freedom of speech as part of the bigger scheme that they aim to uncover. Lasson (2007, p. 33) explains: "The deniers view themselves as messengers sounding an alarm; their self-perceived intellectual insights have enabled them to see through the conspiracy; their refusal to be victimized is testimony to the strength of their character." They see in the criminalisation a confirmation of their conspiracy and it makes them believe more firmly in the task they have assigned to themselves. Thus, instead of censoring them, criminalisation might have the effect that they speak out even more. The fact that genocide denial tends to be progressive complicates the matter. These issues were also at stake when Erlinder was arrested in Rwanda on suspicion of genocide denial. In the press, Erlinder was being represented as an inspiring human rights lawyer who took on unpopular causes and who was arrested simply for being critical of the country's President Paul Kagame and for having won the acquittal of his ICTR client on genocide conspiracy charges. Erlinder was seen as the victim of an oppressive and totalitarian regime and the National Lawyers Guild, the American Bar Association,

---

60 Note the focus on facilitation as it is framed in terms of prevention.

61 Whether criminalisation works of course depends on the goals one tries to achieve. As noted, the goal could also be to make clear to everybody that such behaviour is not tolerated in society. Or maybe the legislation tries to serve both aims: prevention and norm confirmation. Moreover, maybe the legislation does not prevent all instances of denial, but does have a certain effect and the problem of denial might be much worse without such legislation. As the discussion will reveal, if the goal is prevention, I have serious doubts whether it will prevent genocide denial. I think it can mainly be of value as a symbolic gesture which signals that this is not tolerated and confirms the norms in society. Whether we should use criminal law for that is however a different discussion.

62 On the website of Genocide Prevention Now (www.genocidepreventionnow.org), a substantial volume of articles can be found that address the issue of criminalisation of genocide denial in more detail. One particularly insightful article posted on that website is written by Spencer (2012) and titled *Genocide scholars and legislating to outlaw the denial of genocide*.

and an international grassroots campaign called for his release (W. Jacobs, 2011; Kagire & Condon, 2010; Karnowski, 2010). After his release, Erlinder embarked on a speaking tour through the US and he also published his "analysis" of the situation in an article in the *De Paul Journal for Social Justice* (Erlinder, 2010b). Erlinder made clear that he "is *not* a 'genocide denier'" and added that he is however also "not willing to accept the 'victor's version' of any war wholesale." He argues that he is simply doing everything in his power to serve the interests of his clients who have the right to a fair trial which includes the right to an attorney and the right to call things in question and offer alternative explanations (Erlinder, 2010a). Erlinder (2010a) furthermore remarks that "In Rwanda, 'genocide denial,' like an ink-blot test, can be whatever the RPF government perceives it to be." It is true that criminalisation of speech could hinder the work of criminal defence lawyers and undermine fair trial standards. The question is, however, whether Erlinder's case is a good example of this. He distributed his discourse also outside the courtroom in situations where it is questionable whether he was really acting on behalf of his client. On the other hand, even if this would not have been the case, in terms of genocide denialism the violent power of Erlinder's discourse is not simply reduced by the fact that he utters those words in or outside the court room in the service of his client.

Legality?

Another significant issue that troubles the abovementioned human rights organisations is the vagueness of the legislation. The legal principle of *lex certa* (legality) requires that the behaviour that is being criminalised is precisely defined. A clear definition of what behaviour is not allowed limits the possibility of extended and arbitrary use of the legislation. Furthermore, as long as people do not exactly know which behaviour is not allowed, it is difficult for them to adapt their behaviour to the norm prescribed. The general implication of violations of the *lex certa* principle is that they cause a situation of legal uncertainty. The problem with the above legislation is that the definition of genocide denial is vague and it furthermore remains unclear how it is related to the crime of genocide ideology. For instance, during interviews it became clear that it was extremely difficult for ordinary Rwandans and various (criminal justice) officials to define denial and ideology clearly and to explain how the two relate to each other.[63] The vagueness of the legislation leads to considerable problems when applied in practice, especially when professionals and officials lack the required experience as the abovementioned study of *Avocats Sans Frontières* reveals (Sculier, 2011). A fundamental issue concerned the imprecision of the facts of the cases that were being prosecuted and judged. Often the relevant facts and circumstances were not described clearly. In several cases it even happened that the exact date, time, and location were not mentioned. The elements of the crime were not described and also the relevant circumstances that help to constitute the nature of the defendants' behaviour were not mentioned (Sculier, 2011, p. 26). Various laws criminalise genocide denial and it often remained unclear which law applied. In addition, there was confusion concerning the legal basis due to confusing use of terminology. People were, for instance, prosecuted for violating the 2008 genocide

63 Amnesty International (2010, p. 18) also encountered these issues in their research.

ideology law, but their behaviour was framed as the minimisation of genocide, which is a term used in the 2003 law specifically criminalising genocide denial (Sculier, 2011, p. 30 and 31). The new legislation should however remedy this. Although it remains difficult to always clearly distinguish between ideology and denial. It furthermore turned out that in many cases it was not examined whether the defendant had actually fulfilled the elements of the crime. The report notes that the imprecision and indistinctness concerning the facts of the case led to situations where the judge more or less automatically deduced the guilt from the "evidence" without going into detail concerning the specific constitutive elements of the infraction (Sculier, 2011, p. 33). When asked about such issues in an interview, the Minister of Foreign Affairs, Louise Mushikiwabo, reacted by arguing that:

> There is no precision in "ideology" whether you are in France, the United States, Poland, Holland or South Africa. I have looked at 15 other countries with these laws and they are as vague as they can be. I have seen similar laws about the Holocaust and I have seen people from these countries saying we have vague laws. They have things as vague as, "insulting the memory of the dead," or "offending a group of people because of their sexual preference." What precision is there in that law? How do you interpret it? How do you think a Rwandan judge will interpret it in a way that will stop people from expressing themselves? (Kezio-Musoke, 2010)

Mushikiwabo's argument concerning the vagueness of genocide denial laws in other countries appears to be correct: many of these laws are indeed vague and use virtually the same terminology as the Rwandan legislation. But that does not mean that they are not problematic and it does not mean that how Rwanda deals with genocide ideology, including genocide denial, does not raise any problems. Despite these issues, Rwanda's Prosecutor General Martin Ngoga says the law is an important bulwark to protect against ethnic divisions. "There are people who, given the opportunity, would do it again," he says. "There are politicians who would like it to happen. There are armed groups that want it to happen. There is a population that we continue to educate but is not educated enough to the extent that they will not be manipulated again" (Wadhams, 2010).[64] One also cannot not deny that there is truth in what Ngoga states.

Genocide?

What is particularly interesting about the criminalisation of genocide denial in Rwanda is that it is not limited to the denial of the genocide against the Tutsi. The question is, however, who determines that an event constitutes genocide and thus falls within the scope of the legislation. Smith (2010) points out that:

> One of the problems with such legislation is that it is not clear what a genocide is and what it is not. Was Bosnia genocide? Is Darfur an ongoing genocide, or once a genocide, but no longer? Was Bangladesh a civil war or a genocide? And, is it the case, as some

[64] For remarks concerning the question why in Rwanda they attempted to prosecute Erlinder see: Ngoga (2010).

> international lawyers have concluded, that Cambodia was not genocide? As long as one punishes only denial of the Holocaust, privileging it above all other genocides, then at best the reference is known, but once one moves beyond that, the issue of characterization is crucial.

He adds:

> In 2009, the EU attempted to address this problem by saying that for something to be a "genocide" it must be so labelled by an international court or in the charter of the Nuremberg court. Unfortunately, there are at least four problems with this solution. First, why should such determinations be restricted to an international court, as opposed to other courts? Second, the Nuremberg court did not make a determination of Nazi genocide, but of crimes against humanity. Third, the formula currently used will make it impossible for the Armenian Genocide to be recognized as genocide since it occurred before the UN Genocide Convention went into effect. And lastly, historians have their own role in assessing what is and is not genocide; we should not conclude that genocide is a legal concept only. (R. W. Smith, 2010)

In contrast to Rwanda's general criminalisation of genocide denial, states, such as Germany, Austria, and Belgium limited the scope of criminalisation to Holocaust denial. Other genocides, such as the Armenian Genocide and the Genocide against the Tutsi are excluded and this is a questionable situation. Of course, as to the question why and which genocide denial is being criminalised also has a situational/ contextual dimension. As Lipstadt (2007) points out: "The swastika or denial of the Holocaust has a different resonance in Atlanta than it does in Berlin or Vienna." How serious genocide denial is taken thus greatly depends on the role genocide has played and still plays in national life (Kahn, 2004, p. 3; Verbeeck, 1997b, p. 11). Many states have specifically criminalised Holocaust denial but not, for instance, the denial of the genocide against the Tutsi. This issue has become even more pertinent now many of the deniers actually reside outside Rwanda. This limited scope of cases covered by criminalisation itself raises the question of genocide denial. Why are instances of genocide excluded and why have states not criminalised genocide denial in general? This is a serious issue in Rwanda because people and authorities feel that states are using double standards. During interviews in Rwanda, it became clear that this focus on denial of the Holocaust is perceived as a double standard: "you cannot deny the Holocaust, but you are allowed to deny the Genocide against the Tutsi." Janssens (1999) also points out that the criminalisation of Holocaust denial is, in itself, discriminatory towards other genocides whose denial is not being criminalised. This causes the situation in which the suffering of one people is for some reason more serious or important than the suffering of others. In terms of genocide denial, it is questionable to focus on the denial of one single genocide, as such exclusionary practices facilitate the denial dynamic, which is an integral part of the genocidal process.[65]

[65] Many of the abovementioned issues are also discussed in the context of European countries that have criminalised Holocaust denial. The discussion is thus not unique to Rwanda. For an insightful discussion on issues related to, for instance, the French Loi Gayssot see: Garibian (2003).

The above discussion reveals that there are problems concerning the genocide denial legislation and one of the main issues concerns its vagueness. The critique of especially the legislation on genocide ideology has resulted in new legislation. Whether the new legislation solves the problems remains to be seen, because many of the problems do not seem to result from how it is legislated, but from how the legislation is implemented in practice (Pall, 2010, p. 54). In addition to the abovementioned issues concerning the implementation of the legislation, human rights organisations have also raised another pertinent issue concerning the implementation. In their reports they have pointed out that the current Government of Rwanda is using the legislation for political purposes.

6.4.5. Political use

The abovementioned issues seriously jeopardise the fair and equal administration of justice. However, much of the critique of the legislation that criminalises genocide denial focuses on the problem that the current government apparently uses such legislation to silence its (potential) critics. Human Rights Watch (2008b, p. 37), for instance, notices that the prevention of genocide is a legitimate cause, but they add that "it is not the authorities' only impetus for seeking to eliminate certain views they deem inappropriate." Human Rights Watch explains that the legislation is also about ideological conformity and political control (Human Rights Watch, 2008b, p. 37).[66] No other report addresses the abovementioned issues more elaborately than Amnesty International's report titled *Safer to stay silent* (Amnesty International, 2010). Amnesty International (2010, p. 7) states that:

> Prohibiting hate speech is a legitimate aim, but the Rwandan government's approach violates international human rights law. Rwanda's vague and sweeping laws against "genocide ideology" and "divisionism" under "sectarianism" laws criminalize speech protected by international conventions and contravene Rwanda's regional and international human rights obligations and commitments to freedom of expression.

The report adds: "These broad and ill-defined laws have created a vague legal framework which is misused to criminalize criticism of the government and legitimate dissent" (Amnesty International, 2010, p. 7). According to Amnesty International (2010, p. 8):

> The cumulative result of these laws is to deter people from exercising their right to freedom of expression. This chilling effect means that people who have yet to have any action taken against them nonetheless fear being targeted and refrain from expressing opinions which may be legal. In some cases, this has discouraged people from testifying for the defence in criminal trials. The laws have had a corrosive effect on mutual trust in a society already fragile after the 1994 genocide and run counter to the government's stated commitment to national unity.

[66] See also the report of Article 19 (2009) in which they comment on the law relating to the punishment of the crime of genocide ideology of Rwanda.

Denunciations based on these laws are powerful weapons and Amnesty International (2010, p. 8 and 24) also notes that the legislation has also been abused for personal gain:

> The vague definition of "genocide ideology" has left it open to abuse at a local level where individuals appear to have used it to settle personal disagreements, including to discredit teachers, for local political capital, to acquire land and in the context of personal disputes.

The vagueness of the legislation is indeed an issue because of the abovementioned reasons, but to claim that the legislation focuses on the criminalisation of speech that is protected by international conventions and which contravene Rwanda's regional and international human rights obligations and commitments to freedom of expression is questionable. As noted in the previous Section, Rwanda, like other states, has the obligation to prevent human rights violations. However, the human rights framework that Rwanda is obliged to adhere to does not protect speech that is racist or incites genocide as it gravely infringes upon the rights of others. As already explained in the previous Section of this Chapter, such speech is not protected. However, the alleged misuse to silence dissent and the apparent danger that the legislation, due to is vagueness, could have a chilling effect are important issues that require further attention.

The criminalisation of genocide denial has triggered considerable debate not only in Rwanda but also in Europe, where genocide denial has been criminalised by various countries such as Austria, Germany, France, and Belgium. The risk of silencing is also one of the main issues raised in these discussions. Those who oppose criminalisation warn that the criminalisation of genocide denial can have perverse effects. Such a restriction of the freedom of speech can possibly deter potential critics from addressing controversial issues out of fear of being criminally charged. Not knowing when exactly they are crossing the line, they will shy away from addressing critical issues. Such a "chilling effect" could have disastrous consequences for democracy which is based on free speech and dialogue to define itself. Censorship is the opposite of toleration and censorship is also a key ingredient of totalitarian regimes. It can even limit critical discussion up to the point that it might undermine scientific freedom and, as a consequence, hamper free academic research (Raes, 1995, p. 62).[67] However, according to those in favour of criminalisation, those who fear that the criminalisation of genocide denial prevents the public and academics from having an open debate have an exaggerated "Big Brother" view. The law is not developed to look over the public's or academic's shoulder when they are conversing or doing their research (Verbeeck, 1997a, p. 177). The abovementioned concerns are unfounded because criminalisation focuses on pseudoscience and not science. Nonetheless, critics fear that in the end history will be written by lawyers and judges who they deem ill equipped to do so.

While in the above discussions, self-censorship is seen as a perverse and unintended side-effect of the criminalisation of genocide denial, in critical discussions of the

---

67 For further comments on this issue see also Raes (1997), O'neill (2007), and Lipstadt (1993, 2007).

Rwandan legislation to combat denial one almost gets the idea that in Rwanda self-censorship is not simply an unintended negative side effect of the legislation. Instead the criticism gives you the feeling that this censorship actually is what the legislation also aims at. (Especially because the criticism almost never seriously and elaborately addresses the problem of genocide denial.) That Rwandans censor themselves cannot be denied. I noticed this during my fieldwork in Rwanda. However, that people censor themselves is not a development that was triggered solely by the abovementioned legislation. Throughout the decades of conflict, remaining silent became a survival strategy. Self-censorship therefore seems to have more complex social foundations and, because of various reasons throughout their lives, Rwandans have learned what to notice and what to publically ignore. This is not to say that the problem which the human rights organisations raise is non-existent. In interviews, local human rights activists indicated that the legislative efforts of the government had increased the extent to which people engaged in self-censorship. It appears that in Rwanda a *culture of denial* has originated from the interplay of the abovementioned elements. But even non-Rwandans, who do not share Rwanda's culture and have not lived through decades of conflict, censor themselves. In conversations with Dutch expats, I noticed how they, even while speaking in their native language, spoke of "long people and short people." Paul Kagame was often referred to as "PK". They explained that they used these euphemisms because it was better that other people would not notice that they were talking about Hutu's and Tutsi's or Paul Kagame. This self-censorship not only affects talk but also what people do in general. It limits expression and society cleanses itself from critical issues; they are not mentioned – they exist, but at the same time they do not exist. Fear seems to be a common denominator in cases where both Rwandans and non-Rwandans engage in self-censorship.

The use of legislation for political ends is problematic as it infringes upon basic democratic civil and political rights and freedoms, such freedom of expression, the right to liberty and freedom of association. However, what furthermore seriously problematises the situation is that such political use lends credibility to denialist discourses, in which the legislation is presented as a Machiavellian tool to silence the truth concerning the events from being revealed. That is also the gist of Erlinder's argument, when he made the comment that "In Rwanda, 'genocide denial,' like an ink-blot test, can be whatever the RPF government perceives it to be." Such criticism can also be found in the articulations of the other actors discussed, such as Harmon Snow (2010a) who claims that "Today, anyone who steps out of line inside Rwanda will immediately be targeted, accused of genocide revisionism or participation in 'the genocide' itself." Following Erlinder's arrest, ICTR defence counsel Christopher Black also stated that "The alleged law under which he is charged is designed to suppress the truth about the war in Rwanda in order for a brutal regime to maintain its totalitarian control of a tragic country" (Bhagwat, 2010). Herman & Peterson (2010d) conclude that the "allegation of 'genocide denial' has been an important instrument of Kagame's rule, with potentially rival politicians, or in fact any Kagame target, so accused and pushed out of the way."

6.4.6. History

The fight against genocide does not only involve the abovementioned legislative measures, it also involves a complex program of civic education including initiatives, such as, *Ingando.* The first beneficiaries of *Ingando* were ex-combatants. The programme later expanded to include school-going youth and students at secondary and tertiary levels. By 2002, the training was even further extended to other social groups including survivors, prisoners, community leaders, women, and youth (www.nurc.gov.rw). During Ingando, topics are covered under five central themes: analysis of Rwanda's problems; history of Rwanda; political and socioeconomic issues in Rwanda and Africa, rights, obligations and duties and leadership. At *Ingando* Rwandans are thus educated on the conflict history of Rwanda.[68] One element or tenet of that history is particularly relevant for the current discussion. A 2006 *Ingando* manual reveals the promotion of a history which entails that, although some RPF soldiers may have victimised civilians, these crimes were the unfortunate result of wartime or were occasional acts of revenge and have been punished (Human Rights Watch, 2008b). These crimes are however well known and have been documented and several cases have actually been adjudicated by Rwandese courts.[69] Brandstetter (2012, p. 15) however indicates, that despite the evidence, the crimes committed by the RPF remain a contested issue. First of all, Brandstetter notes that official Rwandan post-genocide literature questions the extent of these killings as they have been documented by the abovementioned organizations. Secondly, according to Brandstetter, the government maintains that most of those killed were killed in combat and were not civilian casualties. Brandstetter (2012, p. 15) furthermore points out that those who challenge this run the risk of being labelled as genocide deniers or ideologues. The 2006 Government report on genocide ideology, mentioned earlier, when discussing the specific forms genocide ideology can take, gives the following examples of "revisionism" that amount to denying the genocide:

> [A]nger, hatred and violence from Hutus and native Congolese towards the Tutsis; RPF war, as the cause of genocide; RPF responsible for the killing of Habyarimana, therefore responsible for genocide; RPF military and political leaders involved in genocide, RPF secret squads that carried out genocide; Tutsi extremists in government in Kigali; Hutu genocide by RPF; genocide of Hutu intellectuals; both Inkotanyi and deposed government as criminals; *unpunished RPF crimes* ..." (Republic of Rwanda, 2006, p. 17 emphasis added)

68 Although the term "official history" has a negative feeling to it, especially because it is a common term used in denialist accounts, it is important to notice that the approach tries to overcome division and promote a unified Rwanda, but this is challenging. McLean Hilker (2011, p. 276), for instance, explains that the Rwandan government's goal to promote a unified Rwandan identity meant that it insisted on a singular 'official' narrative. This, however, conflicts with the Governments' broader aspirations to foster open, free and critical thinking. It is however important, as McLean Hilker (2011, p. 277) explains, that "[t]hese challenges need to be understood in terms of a wider political context in which the Rwandan government has argued that promoting 'unity and reconciliation' depends on ridding Rwanda of the 'divisive' identities Hutu, Tutsi, and Twa [...] and combating the persistence of genocide denial."

69 RPF crimes have, for instance, been addressed in reports by Amnesty International (1994), Human Rights Watch (1999), International Panel of Eminent Personalities (2000), and Des Forges (1999).

The report thus specifically mentions "unpunished RPF crimes" as "a revisionist form [of denial] by vaguely acknowledging genocide but, in the same breath, trying to justify it through counter accusations in order to cleanse the real culprits of any responsibility" (Republic of Rwanda, 2006, p. 17). Deviation from the Government narrative can thus have negative repercussions. Brandstetter (2012, p. 15) warns that "making these killings a taboo issue does risk the emergence of rumour and resentment, and can play into the hands of those who actually deny the genocide and downplay the extent of the violence."[70] It facilitates talk of double genocide and victor's justice (Waldorf, 2009, p. 106 and 107). The denial discourses analysed in previous Chapters indeed show that the RPF crimes are abused in discursive constructions to "present" the RPF's actions as genocidal. As long as the nature and extent of the crimes committed by the RPF remains unclear and officially unacknowledged, it will facilitate those bent on denying the genocide. The ambiguity concerning the crimes allows deniers to tweak their meaning easily in a way that empowers their denialist enterprise. The resentment can also fuel speculation concerning the real aims of the legislation discussed above. Deniers argue that the legislation puts a moratorium on the past and people are not allowed to discuss RPF crimes. The legislation is presented as a tool to control history and thereby consolidate power, because if those crimes were to be prosecuted, many of those currently in power would have to stand trial, so they argue. It is understandable that the current government has distanced itself from reprisal killings that took place, but the current president of the Republic of Rwanda, Paul Kagame, was also the highest military leader. The allegations of massacres committed by the RPF are however not limited to reprisal killings. This situation is quickly used to argue that the military that is now in government uses its power to whitewash its own crimes as Kohen et al. (2011, p. 103 and 104) reveal in the following statement:

> While not all Hutu murdered Tutsi – and while many have suffered as refugees, in Rwandan prisons, or due to the stigma of presumed guilt – the persistence of the myth of an RPF-led genocide is likely to have disastrous consequences. Indeed, one of the principal strategies employed by the architects of the genocide, in early 1994, was to claim that the invading RPF intended to take over Rwanda and either enslave or murder its rightful Hutu inhabitants for the benefit of the Tutsi. These claims rang true to many Hutu due to the memory of collective victimization suffered at the hands of Tutsi during the colonial period. The continued emphasis on Hutu victimization encourages offenders to view their participation in the genocide as legitimate action in the face of their own potential victimization while clearly discouraging an apology to those Tutsi whose families were murdered or who were themselves in grave danger. This feeling of victimization is furthered by the perception amongst Hutu that members of the RPF are not held accountable for crimes they committed, as neither the ICTR nor the Gacaca courts have jurisdiction to try these crimes.

Although the current Government of Rwanda is hesitant to fully acknowledge the crimes committed by the RPF's RPA, it is very important to note that not all denial

[70] See also International Crisis Group (2002, p. 17).

of RPF crimes can simply be reduced to grand macro political ploys to consolidate power. Buckley-Zistel's research which takes a micro approach to narrating the past reveals how at the grass roots level people also eclipsed past tensions and conflicts between Hutu and Tutsi from their narratives. Buckley-Zistel (2006, pp. 131–132) concludes that people ignore the past tensions, not out of a grand political ploy, but because it is a conscious strategy to cope with living in proximity with those who were somehow involved in the conflict, such as perpetrators, victims, etc. She notes that:

> In Rwanda the inability to remember seemed deliberate; my interviewees did not want to recall particular aspects of their past. Most strikingly, for instance, they frequently replied that they could not recollect what caused the genocide. This suggests an immediate benefit of not remembering: to choose amnesia serves a particular function deriving from particular needs in the present. [...] [Rwandans] depend on each other in their day-to-day life and hence require some form of cohesion. As a consequence, the past is distorted to establish group coherence. (Buckley-Zistel, 2006, p. 134)

This eclipsing at grassroots levels is thus not necessarily the result of an implemented official history. It is not only government coercion, she notes, but also fear of the other group. "Pretending peace" is pragmatic, because it allows people to live together (Buckley-Zistel, 2006, pp. 142–146). People can thus also omit parts from history because they need to cope, but such non-official omitting also empowers the official history promoted by the Rwandan authorities. Earlier I noted that in Rwanda a *culture of denial* seems to have developed. This culture appears to be not necessarily *official* or *private*. As the above discussion reveals, the denial seems to be the result of a dynamic between both the top-down official denial and a bottom-up private denial. Buckley-Zistel (2006, pp. 140–141) furthermore notes that in the narratives of ordinary Rwandans about the genocide, references to guilt and responsibility are often omitted:

> External parties – the pre-genocide government and elites – are blamed for causing divisions and unleashing violence. This strategy of scapegoating works to render ordinary Rwandans collectively innocent. Consequently, for many of my local Hutu interviewees, all Rwandans were victims. [...] This explanation is in line with the current government discourse, which locates the cause of the genocide in bad governance and top-down manipulation.

I also noticed that when interviewing *génocidaires* they explained that they were betrayed by a corrupt government that had lured them into attacking their Tutsi neighbours.[71] The issue illustrates how complex dealing with genocide denial can be. Instead of fighting genocide denial, one might be facilitating its dynamic.

---

71 See also Zorbas (2009), who notes that two significant factors raised during interviews were that the former government and intellectual elite exploited their ignorance and manipulated them into attacking their Tutsi neighbours and secondly they give as the reason the invasion of the RPF and subsequent civil war.

Accusing human rights defenders

Human rights organisations have brought up the issue of RPF crimes on multiple occasions. For instance, in 2008 and 2009, Human Rights Watch (2008a, 2009) sent letters to the ICTR's chief prosecutor urging for the prosecution of RPF crimes. The 2009 letter states that:

> Seeking justice for the victims of these RPF crimes neither denies the genocide nor equates these crimes with genocide. It simply asserts that all victims, regardless of the identity of the alleged perpetrator, have the right to seek redress for the wrongs done to them. (Human Rights Watch, 2009)

This was also what Des Forges argued: there is no equivalence between the crimes of the RPF and the genocide committed against the Tutsi, but there is an equivalence when it comes to the rights of the victims, who all have the right to justice. Furthermore, if impunity is to end, all crimes should be appropriately addressed.[72] Upon publication of the letter to the prosecutor, the newspaper *The New Times* subsequently published an article stating that "The New York-based organisation risks being classified among the group of those cold-blooded characters who have been amplifying the negationists/revisionists theory at the misery of the survival of the 1994 Tutsi genocide" (Kamana, 2009). The article furthermore commented on how Human Rights Watch described certain crimes perpetrated by the RPA noting that "Isn't this a clear indication that HRW watch is an apologist of the genocide?" (Kamana, 2009).[73] Although *The New Times* is officially an independent newspaper, they do very much reflect the government's opinion. Rieder (2011, p. 2) in his research analysed more than 200 *New Times* articles and concluded that he could not find a single statement that fundamentally criticised the Government of Rwanda and its policies. Although critics of the current government are not featured in the newspaper, they are actively addressed in the articles published (Rieder, 2011, p. 6). Rieder (2011, p. 9) notes that the aggressive way in which critics are addressed strongly suggests that political interests are indeed involved and not "only" historical truth.[74] Rieder (2011, p. 10) concludes that the unjustified denouncements have the potential of delegitimising the valid points of the government to combat genocide denial. To denounce Human Rights Watch's critical efforts to safeguard fair justice as negationist is problematic as it obscures the difference between legitimate critique and genocide denial. Denouncing human rights scholars and organisations however seems to have become a strategy of the government to counter criticism.[75] This is a

---

72 This is crucial, as impunity seems to be an important factor in keeping cycles of violence alive.

73 Human Rights Watch and Amnesty International have also been heavily criticised in several New Times' editorials (The New Times (Editorial), 2009a, 2009b) the question is raised whether their actions are not "just another 'whitewash' of the revisionist/negationist agenda?" In another editorial, various researchers and academics also vented their concern with regard to the ICTR, they were labelled as "professors of hate" (The New Times (Editorial), 2009c).

74 Newbury (2002, p. 70) also points out that the official representations of the current reflects political positions more than valid historical reconstruction.

75 See for example Rwanda News Agency (RNA) (2011a, 2011b), The New Times (2011) and Kagire (2012).

dangerous development. In a reaction to Amnesty's critique concerning the ideology legislation, the organisation was accused of being implicated in the genocide against the Tutsi. *The New Times* article stated that:

> The move by Amnesty International has not come as a surprise but follows a series of other events where it has been in support of the génocidaires and their sympathizers. This time it is supporting them in the process of the eighth stage of genocide and probably will give them a cover up in the preparation of another genocide. (Kagabo, 2010)

Kagame has also denounced organisations such as Amnesty International and Human Rights Watch for their critical reporting, stating that their work was "trash" and "pathetic" (Rwanda News Agency, 2011a).

The virulent attacks in the government newspaper *The New Times* do not limit themselves to human rights organisations. Also scholars who are critical of the current socio-political situation in Rwanda are being denounced. During a conference in 2008 in Kigali, Des Forges was publically accused by the Rwandan Minister of Justice of becoming a "spokesperson for genocide ideology". In an article published in 2011 titled *Remaking Rwanda: Kicking but dying all the same,* contributors to the book *Remaking Rwanda: State building and human rights after mass violence* (Straus & Waldorf, 2011) were condemned as "experts at self-destruction" (Kayinamura, 2011). In another article, it is argued that the book "should be seen as the latest project of an association of what may be appropriately called 'Genocide Deniers Inc.' and 'Hate Rwanda Ltd'. The editors have brought together the works of a wide array of members of these two groups" (Rwagatare, 2011). The attacks against the book also involved a website dedicated to smearing its authors (www.theremakingrwanda.blogspot.com). What is most worrying about such a critique is that those who have contributed to the book are lumped together with genocide deniers who do promote a virulent denial narrative.

Acknowledgment?

Crucial in fighting genocide denial is acknowledging the problems that currently exist in Rwanda, because denying such critical issues will only fuel the denialist enterprise of those bent on denying the genocide against the Tutsi. Although acknowledgment is often presented as a solution to the abovementioned issues, the reality of genocide denial is more complex, because official acknowledgment of RPF crimes can also be abused to fuel the denialist enterprise, as Amnesty International (1994, p. 2) noted in one of its reports on RPF killings:

> Reports of abuses by the RPA have already been exploited as political propaganda by supporters of the former government. This report may also be exploited for partisan propaganda by some of the very people who were responsible for genocide between April and July 1994.

Despite such dangers, the report was published because Amnesty International (1994, p. 2) considered it "unacceptable to allow killings and other human rights violations by the RPA to pass in silence". They added that:

> Given the horrendous scale of massacres committed by forces loyal to the former government, there could never be any comparison between those massacres and other human rights abuses committed by the RPA. Nevertheless, this fact should not be allowed to prevent the truth about alleged RPA abuses from being uncovered and, where appropriate, action being immediately taken to bring those responsible to justice and to prevent such abuses from recurring. (Amnesty International, 1994, p. 2)

A *catch-22* situation thus ensues, as both strategies – investigating the crimes or leaving the allegations of RPF crimes unresolved – can empower those bent on denying the genocide against the Tutsi. Leaving the crimes unaddressed is, however, most problematic, as it allows deniers the freedom to inflate the nature and scope of the crimes committed by the RPF. It enables them to create a parity between these crimes and the genocide or even to portray the RPF crimes as worse than the genocide against the Tutsi, namely as a genocide against the Hutu (Eltringham, 2004, p. 110). There is, however, also a real danger that investigations into these crimes would present those who perpetrated the genocide against the Tutsi with a platform and the RPF crimes become a means to an end of their genocidal agenda. The current Government finds itself thus in a predicament. One should therefore be careful in drawing conclusions that reduce the stance of the Government of Rwanda as driven by realist power politics only. My experience with Rwanda is that actions are very often shaped by multiple motivations which operate at the same time.

What further complicates this situation is that even sincere and legitimate calls for justice of RPF crimes can have unintended perlocutionary effects and can be misinterpreted by others as genocide denial. When it comes to the difficult task of distinguishing genocide denial from sincere calls for the acknowledgement of human suffering, the Prosecutor General Martin Ngoga made a remark that, in the light of the perspective developed throughout this study, is interesting. With regard to statements such as, for instance, "Yes, there was a genocide, but there were some other people also killed" Ngoga remarked that it is about "the philosophy behind it". He adds that "The insistence is not based on the concern that this is a group that will be forgotten. No, it is based on an attempt to play down the bigger project of the genocide" (Wadhams, 2010). Ngoga's remarks are interesting, because according to him calls for acknowledgement for the crimes committed against the Hutu are part of a broader strategy that attempts to minimise the genocide against the Tutsi and they are therefore problematic. From the discourse theoretical approach developed throughout this study, it becomes clear that such calls can indeed obtain a meaning as genocide denial, because they are embedded in a broader discursive denial construction. The problem is, however, that once you isolate them and loosen them from the broader discursive structure that gives them meaning, figuring out what they exactly mean becomes challenging. The discursive web which provides the phrase with its particular denialist meaning is now absent. As explained earlier, in Chapter 4, Section 4.3., meaning is relational and here the relation with other signifiers that gives it meaning is absent. Calls for justice for RPF crimes do not automatically amount to genocide denial. In order for them to have such a meaning, they have to be part of a broader denial discourse and in order to figure out whether an utterance constitutes denial one has to locate it in the broader discursive construction or web of meaning of which it is a part. The facts of the case and the broader context in which the utterance took place are thus crucial in figuring out its meaning. As noted in Chapter 3, Section 3.5., one should take the total speech situation in account. This is why the lack of facts and contextual description in genocide denial cases in Rwanda is so detrimental. One needs the details of the case and the broader contextual information to figure out what the real meaning of an utterance is. To denounce people or hold them criminally liable for using phrases solely because these phrases are also often used in the context of a broader denial discourse would virtually amount to "guilt by association". The problem remains, however, that by (unintentionally) citing elements of the genocide denial discourse, linguistic community is still being made with that history of speech. As explained in the previous Chapter, the power of inflicting linguistic violence is not invested in the authority of a certain individual or organisation, but it can reside in the structure of a certain language itself. As a result, words can do harm more quickly than one might initially have thought. The issue is that many of these discursive elements, such as the call for justice of RPF crimes, have become very meaningful in terms of genocide denial because they are often an intrinsic part of the denial discourse. Consequently, for many, these discursive elements have become emblematic of the discourse that denies the genocide against the Tutsi. Even when they are uttered by an actor without the intention to deny, perlocutionary, they can be taken by others to signify a denial of the genocide against the Tutsi and subsequently cracked down upon.

6.5. Defending human rights

6.5.1. The power of horror

But one can also not simply reduce the problem to how the Rwandan authorities deal with cases of genocide denial and how they have reacted to the critique concerning the political abuse of the legislation. There are also certain issues concerning human rights reporting in Rwanda that are problematic or sensitive in terms of genocide denialism. For instance, in April 2009, Kenneth Roth (2009) of Human Rights Watch published an article in the *Los Angeles Times* titled *The power of horror in Rwanda,* in which he heavily criticises the oppressive politics of the current Government of Rwanda. He notes that despite the progress made, Rwanda still has a long way to go. He furthermore states that:

> Despite the facade of occasional elections, the government essentially runs a one-party state. And ironically, it is the genocide that has provided the government with a cover for

> repression. Under the guise of preventing another genocide, the government displays a marked intolerance of the most basic forms of dissent. (Roth, 2009)

Roth (2009) also criticises other states for facilitating such politics "by closing their eyes to this repressive sleight of hand." *The New Times* subsequently published an article by one of its editors accusing Human Rights Watch of sanitising those who try to deny the genocide against the Tutsi and this "at the height of the 15th Genocide Commemorations" (Kwinjeh, 2009a).[76] In another article published in 2010, the question is openly raised whether "Kenneth Roth is in love with *génocidaires*?" (Oluoch-Ojiwah, 2010). It is disturbing that those who attack organisations such as Human Rights Watch for the harm that their reporting allegedly does, do so by using some of the most virulent language themselves. That such authors can vent their hate speech in *The New Times* undisturbed reveals a double standard when it comes to the government's commitment to fighting violent language.[77] Although the general gist of the article is to denounce Roth virulently, the remark that the letter was published "at the height of the 15th Genocide Commemorations" raises an important issue. During the time of commemoration, there is considerably more tension in Rwandan society as people are confronted again with what happened. The timing of Roth's article is thus questionable and, for some, as the reactions in *The New Times* reveals, casts doubt on the real intentions behind its publication. The period of commemoration is often used by those who attempt to deny the genocide against the Tutsi to launch a denial offensive. The denial is furthermore often shrouded under a veil of critique. Critical elements raised by Roth also feature in the discursive construction of these denial discourses. For instance Roth (2009) argues that "it is the genocide that has provided the government with a cover for repression." In the official denial discourse and the discourse that recycles much of that denial, the genocide against the Tutsi is also presented as a tool to cover up and to engage in violence against the population. From such a perspective, Roth's remark is sensitive. The question remains however why Human Rights Watch did not use the period of commemoration to seriously address the problem of the denial of the genocide against the Tutsi, which is also a very serious human rights issue.

Although Roth notices that things have improved in Rwanda these acknowledgments are basically a formality and the main focus tends to be "on the long way that Rwanda still has to go". This is a structure that one often encounters in reports on Rwanda. The acknowledgements are brief and general, while the critique that follows is detailed

---

76 See also Kwinjeh (2009b).

77 For the reaction of Human Rights Watch to the article published by Kwinjeh, see Gagnon (2009), she writes: "Human Rights Watch has never espoused the notion of a double genocide or claimed that the genocide did not happen. To the contrary. So Ms Kwinjeh's attempt to paint HRW as genocide "revisionist/negationists" is just plain wrong. Being a critic of Rwandan government policies when those policies violate basic rights does not make one a proponent of so-called genocide ideology. It just makes one a proponent of human rights." Also in 2014 Human Rights Watch was accused in *The New Times* on the 2nd of June, 2014, of collaborating with the Democratic Forces for the Liberation of Rwanda (Forces Démocratiques de Libération du Rwanda, FDLR) or of political bias. Human Rights Watch (2014b) replied that it has never attempted to "sanitise and/or legitimize" the FDLR, nor have we ever been their "campaign mouthpiece."

and elaborate. In doing so, one runs the risk of minimising the immense challenges the current government is facing and the great strides it has already made. Some of the author's interviewees referred to such critique as "Rwanda bashing".[78] In the end Roth and other critics hope that the government will take their critique seriously and that it mends its ways. However, the manner in which the critique is presented does not make the government receptive to the message that the authors attempt to convey. Speaking "truth to power" is surely important, but it should preferably be done in a way that it leads to positive change. In that case, not only is the information important, but also how it is communicated is important. The point is that, taking into account the specifics of the situation, it would have been better if Roth would have conveyed his criticism using a different rhetoric and if he made it public at a different moment than during the commemorative period, when the article was published. Critique should not only be legitimate. In order for it to contribute to positive changes it should also be perceived as legitimate by the party to whom the critique is addressed. One should take care that the message is not misinterpreted.

6.5.2. Slander ...

The implications of human rights reporting by organisations such as for instance Human Rights Watch remain largely undiscussed. It is simply not done to criticise organisations who strive to achieve noble goals. It might even be interpreted as trying to silence these organisations and, as a result, critics are denounced and put in the camp of the current RPF-led Government of Rwanda. An example of this dynamic is the critical analysis published by Richard Johnson (2013) titled *The travesty of Human Rights Watch on Rwanda*. In the article, Johnson argues that what Human Rights Watch does is not human rights advocacy, but political advocacy and according to Johnson such "reckless humanitarianism" has dire consequences.[79]

---

78 The problem is that the virulent criticism of the new regime is also part and parcel of the denialist discourse. For a further observation of how critique of the new regime and the denial of the genocide are closely related see: Chrétien (2012, p. 103 and 104).

79 HRW has been criticised before concerning its activism by an organisation called NGO Monitor (Mandel & Steinberg, 2009) in a report titled "Experts or Ideologues". The report examines HRW's activities related to the Arab-Israeli conflict. Steinberg (2009) who heads the NGO notes that "Human Rights Watch was founded in 1978 in New York (as Helsinki Watch) with the mission of using public demonstrations and other forms of "naming and shaming" to free prisoners of conscience in the Soviet Union and Eastern Europe. Many Gulag denizens, including Anatoly (now Natan) Sharansky, later recognized HRW's role in gaining their freedom. Shortly thereafter HRW began advocating on behalf of political prisoners and torture victims in other totalitarian regimes, including in Chile, Argentina, and Greece." Steinberg adds, "[b]ut since then, HRW has lost its moral compass, and the organization is using its substantial budget ($42 million in 2008) to repeatedly attack Israel by exploiting the language of human rights and international law. Tendentious reports and press conferences, using distorted legal rhetoric in place of credible evidence, target Israeli responses to terror attacks from Arafat, Hamas, and Hezbollah." The Israel-based organisation has however been accused of having ties to the Israeli government and it has been argued that it might need to be monitored. It is however significant to note that Bernstein as the actual founder of Human Rights Watch and its active chairman for 20 years noted that as the "founding chairman emeritus, I must do something that I never anticipated: I must publicly join the group's critics. Human Rights Watch had as its original mission to pry open closed societies,

According to Johnson:

> This discourse – what is said and left unsaid, what is highlighted and what is downplayed, what is averred and what is implied – can best be understood as four commands addressed to the post-genocide Government of Rwanda: 1) Let the genocidal parties back in. 2) Do not outlaw their ideology. 3) Don't hold more than a few perpetrators accountable, and forget about their foreign accomplices. 4) Admit that you are no better than they.

The article was introduced on the list-serv of the International Association of Genocide Scholars by Caplan who stated that "this is a much-needed and in [his] view substantially legitimate critique of HRW's longstanding negative bias against the RPF government of Rwanda." Caplan furthermore noted that he hoped the article would receive attention and that Human Rights Watch was compelled to reply. After one scholar had replied with several insightful additional comments, the following response was posted by Alan J. Kuperman:

> I too hope that HRW will reply . . . with a slander suit against Johnson. He makes up some facts, ignores others, and denies still others. Kagame usually pays quite well for such propaganda. If Johnson didn't get compensated for this, he missed out on a real pay day. Based on my 18 years of research, I believe that Kagame is responsible for more deaths than anyone else in Africa, and that includes Idi Amin, Omar Bashir, and the leaders of Hutu Power. HRW is to be commended for condemning human-rights violations even when it is not "politically correct" or expedient to do so. As for the western scholars and western government officials who were so traumatized by the anti-Tutsi genocide that they cannot see the massive crimes committed by Tutsi before, during, and after that event, I have only sadness. But we must condemn and reject their writings, which so obviously reflect biased misperception.

It is telling to observe how Kuperman engages in basically the same behaviour that he accuses Johnson of.[80] More importantly, the remark from Kuperman silenced any discussion on the issues raised by Johnson, which should have been discussed, because his article does raise important questions. The incident is relevant for how also the scholarly community is greatly polarised, which is a troubling development as it seriously stifles and undermines academic debate. Human Rights Watch and other human rights organisations for that matter should indeed be commended for speaking up about human rights issues that have haunted Rwanda and still haunt Rwanda today. It is legitimate to critically analyse the crimes perpetrated by the RPF and their involvement in conflict abroad, such as in Congo. It is furthermore legitimate to critically reflect on the contemporary socio-economic and political situation in Rwanda. These issues have received much less attention than the genocide and they

---

advocate basic freedoms and support dissenters. But recently it has been issuing reports on the Israeli-Arab conflict that are helping those who wish to turn Israel into a pariah state" (Bernstein, 2009).

80 Another scholar immediately replied: "Shall we take Alan's word for this? Or is evidence on offer to buttress these serious accusations of 'slander' and 'mak[ing] up' facts, and the insinuation of personal corruption? Also, which payments by Kagame, how much, when, and to whom?" (Correspondence on file with author).

do also warrant our scholarly attention. This is important because very often people have a too romanticised image of contemporary Rwanda that obscures the many and challenges and problems this society is still facing.[81] It cannot be denied that it is very difficult for human rights activists to achieve their goals and to keep up their motivation. One interviewee who represented a human rights organisation in Rwanda told me during an interview that human rights were a *"bête noir"* and that he would not be in that business for long. Human rights should be taken seriously because, as a former High Commissioner for Human Rights, Mary Robinson, once stated: "today's human rights violations are the causes of tomorrow's conflicts." However, anger and frustration over RPF crimes and how the current Government of Rwanda rules the country should not make scholars blind to how the (re)actions of human rights organisations or other actors, including scholars themselves, who address the questionable conduct of the current Government, can also turn out to be problematic. Instead of engaging in a denial of these issues, such problems should be acknowledged, reflected upon and inform subsequent action in a constructive manner.[82]

6.5.3. Marginalisation

When I talked about my research on genocide denialism and how I think it operates in the context of the genocide against the Tutsi, people often tended to move the discussion into the direction of the issues also mentioned above concerning the abuse of legislation, etc. As a result, the discussion in the end revolved around the current socio-political situation in Rwanda and how the phenomenon of genocide denial is abused for the purpose of covering up RPF crimes and consolidating political power. Although I am of the opinion that much of the critique should be taken seriously, because there is certainly a political side to the use of the legislation, one should however be careful, because it could also result in a marginalisation of the problem of the denial of the genocide against the Tutsi. The danger is that, by predominantly

---

81 Rwanda is often represented as a miracle (see for instance Grill, 2009; Kinzer, 2008) which, taking into account its recent history of violence and devastation, it definitely is. However, the image of Rwanda is often gleaned from the controlled and polished city life in Kigali, but this image is far removed from the reality of the countryside which encompasses most of the country. The contrast between the wealth in the city and the sheer poverty in the countryside is alarming. The reality of this miracle is thus more complex as often portrayed. See for an analysis of these issues, Ingeleare (2009) and Ansoms (2009). Furthermore, Gacaca, which has been hailed as a unique local solution to dealing with justice in the aftermath of genocide (Khaleeli, 2010), has also been criticised for its violation of fair trial standards (Human Rights Watch, 2011). In judging the merits of Gacaca, the specific context of the genocide and the unique challenges that arise from it should not be neglected. However, one can also not deny the many problems involved in Gacaca. The research of organisations such as Avocats Sans Frontières (www.asf.be) and Penal Reform International (www.penalreform.org) which have structurally monitored Gacaca has laid bare the many challenges and problems involved in meeting out such grass-roots justice in a volatile "post"-conflict environment.

82 There seems to be a dynamic in which if one acknowledges the genocide, one is accused of denying the crimes perpetrated by the RPA and if one acknowledges these crimes one is perceived as denying the genocide. As a result, one is either an "RPF stooge" or a "genocide denier" (Kearns, 2010). The polarised climate has led so to a situation in which both sides engage in the practice of "condemning the condemners" thereby ultimately denying the real issues at play that are raised by the actors involved.

focussing on political abuse and by not reflecting on the extensive nature of the problem of genocide denial more broadly, the idea arises that the *raison d'être* of the legislation is mainly driven by questionable political purposes.[83] Instead of discussing the problematic nature of the denial of the genocide against the Tutsi, the problem is mainly reduced to Machiavellian political ramifications.[84] This distracts the attention from the serious nature of the phenomenon and marginalizes it. Outside Rwanda, as this study reveals, the genocide is being denied, but also in Rwanda there are still many people who, for various reasons, do not want to acknowledge what happened (Semujanga, 2013, p. 10). Often this does not happen by simply saying that the genocide did not take place but, when asked about it, Rwandans will for instance respond by saying "Ah, let me tell you about the war that happened here ..." or they argue that "the consequences of what happened are the same for all of us ..." and "Why is it important to have all these memorial sites everywhere? Aren't 1 or 2 enough ...? Why always mention the genocide against the Tutsis ..."

Human rights organizations and activists, but also scholars, and other actors should therefore be careful in framing their critique, because much of the critique tends to reduce the legislative efforts of the Government of Rwanda to fight genocide denial to political tools that are abused to consolidate power. In his letter, Roth (2009), for instance stated "the government has another tool of control -- the crime of 'genocide ideology'". Genocide ideology concerns the belief system that serves as the basis for the genocide against the Tutsi. As noted earlier, the official denial discourse draws on crucial elements from this ideology. By reiterating elements of this ideology,

83 For instance, in a Human Rights Watch report published in 2014 (at the beginning of the commemorative period), it is framed as follows: "For the vast majority of families of victims of RPF killings, there is therefore little hope of seeing the perpetrators prosecuted. A few have attempted to demand justice for these crimes, but it has been a difficult struggle. There are tight restrictions on free speech in Rwanda, and few people dare broach publicly the sensitive subject of RPF crimes. Talking about those crimes, and effectively departing from the official version of Rwanda's recent history, can carry serious consequences, such as charges of genocide denial, genocide ideology or divisionism (inciting ethnic divisions). Rwanda has passed a number of laws which may originally have been intended to prevent and punish hate speech of the kind which led to the 1994 genocide, but in practice, have restricted free speech and imposed strict limits on how people can talk about the genocide and other events of 1994" (Human Rights Watch, 2014c).

84 Above this issue was discussed in relation to the reporting of human rights organisations, but we see the tendency also in the work of other actors such as for instance in the article *Who really made a mess of Rwanda?* Written by senior writer Tim Black (2012). Black argues that "It is no coincidence that in 2003, the year Kagame officially became Rwanda's president, the crime of "genocide ideology" was made a central pillar of the new Rwandan constitution. Six years later, in a grisly indication of the extent to which the idea of genocide has shored up Kagame's authority, it was revealed that of the 60,000 inmates incarcerated at Rwandan's prisons, nearly two thirds were guilty of the crime of "genocide ideology". If you are not with Kagame, it seems, you are in favour of genocide." Reyntjens, (2010, p. 33) even argues that "Domestically, the RPF has decreed one single truth and devised instruments (legislation, intimidation, 're-education', silencing alternative voices) to avoid its being challenged, at least publicly." He furthermore notes that "Law, too, became a potent instrument in the RPF's hands. Laws on 'divisionism' (2001) and on 'genocide ideology' (2008) allowed the elimination of dissident voices and the imposition of the RPF's reading of history and truth" (Reyntjens, 2010, p. 16). Reyntjens' article does raise important issues concerning the current political governance in Rwanda that cannot be denied and should be addressed, but his analysis is dangerously one sided, lacks reflection and contextualization that allows readers to understand that the measures and issues he describes not only originate from power grabbing by Kagame and RPF.

the belief system of annihilation is maintained (See Chapter 2, Section 2.3.6.). It is very telling that ideology and denial prominently feature in reports and articles on Rwanda, but not because of their problematic nature.[85]

In this context it is insightful to briefly get back to the book by Straus and Waldorf (2011) mentioned earlier titled *Remaking Rwanda: State building and human rights after mass violence* and more particularly the review Uvin (2011) wrote. His review of the book contains some insightful remarks. Straus and Waldorf's book paints a less rosy picture of Rwanda than generally portrayed in the media and by the Government of Rwanda and Uvin notes that the book is therefore a "welcome corrective" to the very positive versions of contemporary Rwanda. Uvin (2011) however makes two important additional remarks. He firstly notes that "although it can be argued that in their attempt to show the darker side of the country, many Chapters neglect the brighter side of what has been done," because "this, too, is part of the legacy of Kagame and the RPF regime he controls." Uvin (2011) furthermore notes that:

> The genocide is actually oddly underplayed in this book. It is not that the authors do not refer to it and even less that they try to deny it (the standard accusation by the regime against all its critics) – every essay mentions the genocide, typically both in the introduction and in the conclusion, and with the appropriate sense of gravity and horror. But it is as if, in the analytical pages in between, the genocide has largely disappeared.

Uvin's observation that in the main analytical parts of the book, the genocide has largely disappeared is important, because one can only make sense of what is happening in contemporary Rwanda by paying significant attention to this phenomenon that radically determines virtually everything that goes on in the country. Uvin (2011) notes that "the crucial question then is not can we judge current Rwanda policies and realities to fail by human rights standards? But rather, in light

85 A similar tendency can be observed with regard to the "abolishment" of the terms Hutu, Tutsi and Twa. The picture presented is that any use of these terms is criminal or that it is used to conceal Tutsi domination. Reyntjens (2010) for instance states the following: "One particular aspect of imposing the truth served a very concrete project. The RPF vigorously denied the reality of ethnicity, a denial that was an essential element of the hegemonic strategies of a small Tutsi elite. The claim that 'there are no Hutu and Tutsi, but only Banyarwanda' allowed the concealment of domination by Tutsi. When, in the past, Hutu were a majority in public institutions, this was called 'ethnic domination'; however, now that Tutsi were a majority, this became 'meritocracy'." Reyntjens presents a Machiavellian analysis of why the use of the labels was criminalised. In reality, the reasons for limiting the use of these terms are complex and understandable in the light of what happened and, furthermore, not every use is criminal. You can make use of these labels as longs as you do not use them in a discriminatory manner that revives the marginalisation and hatred that the country has witnessed before with disastrous consequences. Everything in contemporary Rwanda is related to the genocide; it is therefore impossible to do away with these terms and respectful use of the terms is allowed. As noted before, that is not to say there is no political side to the implementation of that legislation, but it is not as one dimensional as Reyntjens presents it. Also the implementation of the label "genocide against the Tutsi" has been criticised for only acknowledging the violence perpetrated against the Tutsi thereby obscuring the suffering of the Hutu population. However as one "advocate for the 'genocide against the Tutsis' label argued that its purpose is to reflect the intention of the perpetrators, not to deny the fact that some Hutus were killed: '[the perpetrators sought] to eliminate the human beings called Tutsis and those who have the same physique, ideology or understanding'" (Ibreck, 2001, p. 339).

of the past, what are the realistic margins for manoeuvre in modern Rwanda?" This does not mean that the current regime should not be scrutinised and held up to human rights standards. Human rights are important and human rights organisations and other actors should speak up about abuses. However, the judgement concerning the state of affairs in Rwanda should also be informed by an analysis of how the past impacts the contemporary situation. Lack of an analytical engagement with the genocide and the focus on the contemporary human rights situation results in a failure to apprehend how significant the impact of this event is. The genocide (but also the positive contributions of the current government) should not be reduced to mere introductory remarks and, as Uvin (2011) notes, such attention does not whitewash the crimes committed by the current regime.

6.6. Concluding remarks

The discussion in this Chapter has shown that the insights gained throughout this study concerning how denial operates in the context of the process of genocide has significant implications for a wide variety of actors who somehow engage with the flow of meaning concerning the events in Rwanda. The aim of this Chapter was to reveal this complexity drawing on several concrete illustrations and my intention is not to demonise the organisations and persons whose speech was discussed. It is about the acts not the individual actors. Once one acknowledges that the denial on which genocide thrives involves more than stereotypical acts of primary genocide denial, and that it relies on a variety of secondary denials and a broad range of other facilitative behaviour, then many other actions not readily associated with genocide denial become problematic. The significance of the actions illustrated in this Chapter and that somehow facilitate or empower the denial dynamic can be explained with reference to the insight that denial discussed earlier, and therefore genocide denial is also an interpersonal phenomenon (Chapter 2, Section 2.6.4.). The perpetrators who deny the genocide in order to keep up their alternative reality need the support of others to keep up their denial. They receive this support by those who willingly collude in their denial, but they are also supported by those who somehow unintentionally end up facilitating their denialist enterprise. Actors might make linguistic community and reiterate some elements of the ideological discourse; they might use confusing terminology, etc. Therefore, what you end up with is a situation in which the core consisting of ideological or official genocide denial is encircled by various layers of denial which range from intentional collusion in the denial to unintentional collaboration in and recycling of the denial. These layers of denial around the central core reinforce the alternative reality and protect it from disintegrating.

Denialism in the context of genocide, like denial in general, is an interpersonal phenomenon and, in order for it to operate successfully, it relies on the actions of other actors that somehow willingly or unwillingly support and empower the denial through their speech. Taking this into account and looking at the variety of illustrations discussed above, the question arises where does this continuum of denial end? How far does it expand? Because once one starts to look at behaviour through the prism of genocide denialism, there appears to be no end to the web of denial that is being spun. The following example provides for an illustration of how far the web of denial expands.

On the 9th of January 1994, General Roméo Dallaire of the United Nations Peace Keeping Forces in Rwanda informed the UN headquarters in New York per fax that the extermination of the Tutsi is being planned. Dallaire received this information from an informant named "Jean-Pierre", who explained that "in 20 minutes his personnel could kill up to 1000 Tutsis." Exactly 20 years later, on the 9th of January 2014, an article appeared in *The New York Times* written by Michael Dobbs (2014b) titled *The shroud over Rwanda's nightmare*. Given the date of publication, one would assume that the article sets out to commemorate the abovementioned event and the genocide against the Tutsi. The article states:

> The refusal by United Nations officials to approve the general's plan for raids on suspected arms caches has been widely condemned as paving the way for one of the worst genocides since the Holocaust. But evidence submitted to the International Criminal Tribunal for Rwanda, some of it still under seal, reveals a murkier, more complicated situation than has often been portrayed. New details about the mysterious informant known to General Dallaire as "Jean-Pierre" serve as a reminder that history can take a long time to reveal its secrets. Important documents that could shed light on the unresolved mysteries and ambiguities of the Rwanda genocide remain under lock and key. (Dobbs, 2014b)

The article furthermore states that:

> Whether the genocide was planned, and was thus foreseeable, has been hotly debated by scholars, politicians and lawyers. The "genocide fax" has been a key part of this debate. Controversy has surrounded Jean-Pierre's motives for cooperating with General Dallaire, the reliability of his information, and his fate after his request for protection was rejected by the United Nations. (Dobbs, 2014b)

When reading these introductory remarks, one wonders what exactly it is that we do not know. What are these "mysteries and ambiguities" that are being kept from us in hidden archives and that are supposed to reveal a "murkier" and "more complicated" situation than has been portrayed? Which archives does Dobbs exactly mean? And what does this have to do with Dallaire's "genocide fax"? Is there something wrong with the informant "Jean-Pierre" and the information that he provided? As Smith (2014) points out, to the unsuspected reader, the introduction leaves "nagging doubts on the details, which in turn calls into question the established facts." The point is however, as Smith explains, that we do know the important facts. We do know that "Jean-Pierre" warned Dallaire about the extermination and we know that Dallaire acted upon this information. Sadly, we also know that this information was not acted upon by the international community and three months later on the 6th of April 1994 we witnessed how the extermination phase of the genocide against the Tutsi was implemented. Thus, Smith (2014) concludes that both "Jean-Pierre" and Dallaire "were proven right": "There is no shroud. The facts remain."

What is even more disturbing about the article, as Melvern and Stanton (2014) note, is that Dobbs raises doubts concerning whether the genocide was planned and was thus foreseeable. According to him, this "has been hotly debated by scholars, politicians and lawyers" (Dobbs, 2014b). Caplan (2014) captures the significance of the statement as follows:

> If it were unplanned, that meant the killings were spontaneous. If so, perhaps there was no intent to exterminate all Tutsi. If so, according to the 1948 UN Convention on the Prevention and Punishment of the Crime of Genocide, there was no genocide at all.

Dobbs, furthermore fails to mention that the *génocidaires* follow a line of defence at the ICTR in which they claim that the violence was spontaneous and unplanned and part and parcel of this defence effort has been to cast doubt on Dallaire and his informant "Jean-Pierre" (Melvern and Stanton, 2014).

One might wonder why this story about Mr. Dobbs is relevant in light of the question raised earlier about how far the continuum of denial actually expands. The story does not explain exactly how far the continuum reaches and what acts and which actors can possibly fall within its scope. Nonetheless, the story is significant, because it is an alarming illustration of how far the web of denial can reach. Michael Dobbs is namely a fellow at the United States Holocaust Memorial Museum and he directs the Rwanda documentation and oral history project launched by the National Security Archive titled "#Rwanda20yrs".[86] It is a daunting reality that apparently even institutions whose *raison d'être* it is to memorialise, commemorate and educate on genocide, thus whose task it basically is to fight denial, can end up facilitating the denial dynamic.

The continuum of denial stretches far and can penetrate areas where you least expect it. Can it also have penetrated the scientific fields underlying this study, namely genocide studies and criminology? Although the role of scholars and science is often perceived as positive, because the scientific endeavours help to improve our lives in many ways, scholars and their science have also often played a questionable role in genocidal processes. Science contributed to the genocide as its "objectivist" and scientific absolutism was used to manufacture differences and it was often science that provided the perpetrators with the ultimate vocabularies of motive (Eltringham, 2004, p. 4; See also Tatz 2003, p. 24 and 25).[87] Science has historically played a questionable role in Rwanda's conflict history. It started with the questionable

86 The article published in the *New York Times* is an outline of a more elaborate e-book which marks the first publication of this project (Dobbs, 2014a).

87 This raises the question to what extent the scientists who promoted such views were actually perpetrators themselves. Some scientists helped to construct the ideological framework that was necessary for the perpetration of genocide, while other scientists were actually involved hands on in the perpetration of the most gruesome crimes.

pseudo-scientific work of early anthropologists who helped to create false racist histories, such as the Hamitic hypothesis mentioned earlier (J.-P. Chrétien, 2012, pp. 214–220). If the web of denial is more encompassing than one might think, it is imperative to continue the reflection and to address whether the developed approach also has implications for the fields of genocide studies and criminology.

Chapter 7
A look in the mirror

7.1. Introduction

So far, the actions discussed and deemed problematic in terms of genocide denialism were situated outside the two academic fields that have informed this study, which are the fields of genocide studies and criminology. As a result, the discussion of the implications of the developed approach has so far mainly been an exercise in reflection and not self-reflection. There is, however, no reason why the developed approach would not have implications for the work done in the abovementioned academic fields. The last Chapter therefore discusses *whether the developed approach also has implications for the field of genocide studies and criminology.* The denial dynamic can namely also be facilitated by scholars in these fields.[88] The issue of scholarly reflection becomes even more pertinent if one acknowledges the fact that scholars often also play a questionable role in genocidal process. Tatz (2003, p. 24) notices that scholars, such as, biologists, anthropologists, psychiatrists, and lawyers have often provided for the building blocks of the genocidal apparatus. That criminologists are not mentioned does not mean they were not involved. On the contrary, criminologists seem to have been deeply implicated in the process of classifying people as abnormal or deviant, thereby contributing to the process by which they were singled out for destruction (Cunneen, 1999; Morrison, 2004; Wetzell, 2000).

The discussion in this Chapter will first address how critical scholarly discussions on how genocide was defined by Lemkin and subsequently by the international community in the 1948 Genocide Convention can have implications in terms of genocide denialism. The field of criminology will subsequently be addressed. In contrast to the field of genocide studies, where intense critical debate seems to be the problem, in the field of criminology traditionally the lack of discussion on the topic of genocide appears to be the problem. The aim of addressing the fields of criminology and genocide studies is not to scrutinise the fields of study exhaustively.

[88] How subtle issues can possibly be is revealed by an insightful observation made by Tatz concerning Lipstadt's book *Denying the Holocaust.* Lipstadt's study contains a powerful analysis of various instances of Holocaust denial and their implications. However, as Tatz (2003, p. 131) observes, in the same book Lipstadt relegates the Armenian genocide to a "massacre", which was the result of Turkey's ruthless policy of expulsion and forced resettlement. Tatz (2003, p. 131) furthermore notices that, in her index, the Armenian genocide is listed as "Armenian massacre". This nuance in terminology raises an issue in terms of denial. I do not mean to say that Lipstadt denies the Armenian genocide, because she does not. On the contrary she has acknowledged the event on multiple occasions (Akçam, 2014; Lipstadt & Balakian, 2007). However, one can also not deny that using the term massacre to denote the events obscures the nature of the violence perpetrated against the Armenian people. Even if this happens unintentionally, it is still problematic in terms of denial.

Instead, it entails a brief but critical look in the mirror in order to show that the work of genocide scholars and criminologists can also raise questions in terms of genocide denialism. The problem should also not be reduced to specific issues concerning the fields of genocide studies and criminology. Yet, in order to understand that denial can be fostered by scholarly work, it is important to notice the broader scientific climate in which it is legitimate to raise questions, especially since the rise of post-modern thought. The second part of this Chapter will therefore address *how the revisionist scientific climate in which knowledge and truth claims are constantly questioned is favourable to genocide denialism and how the post-modern turn in academia has exacerbated this climate.* The problem of genocide denialism might thus be more closely related to legitimate scholarly revisionism than one might think.

The analysis in this Chapter will not be limited to a general discussion of several implications for the two abovementioned fields and the post-modern academic climate. The reflection will continue throughout the third part of this Chapter, *which will address the implications of the developed approach for the study at hand.* In developing my approach, I relied on insights from cultural criminology and speech act and discourse theory. These sensitising frameworks have their roots in constructionism, which *raises the question whether the relativist worldview underlying this approach would allow for some of the most sophisticated denial.* The analysis of the implications of the developed approach for the study at hand will culminate in a discussion of several lessons that can be drawn from this study.

7.2. Genocide studies

Lemkin's work and the 1948 Genocide Convention have presented the academic community with powerful concepts that triggered and still cause vigorous scholarly debate. However, as the following discussion will reveal, from the perspective of genocide denialism, such critical debate can also have its downsides. Although scholars are critical of how Lemkin defined genocide, most of the scholarly critique seems to focus on how genocide was finally conceptualised in the 1948 Convention. Scholars from the social sciences generally argue that legal definitions, due to their political nature, are not suitable for scientific purposes (Sellin, 1938). The definitions have different objectives. Legal definitions must be appropriate with regard to criminalisation and subsequent prosecution of criminal acts of genocide, while research definitions must be appropriate for the purpose of trying to understand and explain genocide (Chalk, 1994, p. 47). The question that thus arises according to Semelin (2007, p. 321) is: "to what extent is it legitimate to adopt an international legal norm resulting from a political compromise between states as a basis for historical, sociological or anthropological inquiry?" In addition to this general issue, scholars have raised more specific questions concerning the range of protected groups, the listed genocidal acts, the required number of victims, the element of intent and the meaning of the phrases "in whole or in part" and "as such" and the lack of concrete instruments to effectively implement the 1948 Convention. These issues motivated scholars to come up with alternative definitions and since the 1950ies many alternative definitions of genocide have been proposed by scholars from different academic disciplines.[89] This has resulted in heated debates among scholars concerning what the definition of genocide exactly is or should be (Totten & Parsons, 2004, p. 3). Genocide scholars, through their efforts, try to delineate genocide and bound it conceptually for scientific research purposes (Jones, 2006, p. 15). Some of the proposed definitions are "harder" while others are "softer". According to Jones (2006, p. 19), "harder positions are guided by concerns that 'genocide' will be rendered banal or meaningless by careless use." They are against broad interpretations of genocide and call for a more narrow delineation of the phenomenon. In contrast "[s]ofter positions reflect concerns that excessively rigid framings [...] rule out too many actions that, logically and morally, demand to be included" (Jones, 2006, p. 19). They are against narrow interpretations and take a more inclusive approach to defining genocide. In terms of denial, one could argue that the first approach guards against minimisation of the concept, while the second approach guards against the exclusion of genocidal suffering. These different positions lead to different and often opposed definitions which makes the concept of genocide a deeply contested concept. To date no definition has been accepted as definitive (Alvarez, 2001, p. 33; Jones, 2006, p. 15; Straus, 2001, p. 349). From the approach developed throughout this study, both of the abovementioned approaches have implications.

7.2.1. Too narrow?

Scholars have criticised the 1948 Convention for being too narrow with regard to the included acts of genocide. Lemkin's conceptualisation envisaged a wide range of genocidal acts and, as mentioned in the last Section, killing was the last resort. Article II of the Convention seems to partly acknowledge Lemkin's original idea that genocide entails more than killings and massacres as it, for instance, also lists causing mental harm or forcibly transferring children as acts of genocide. However, although genocide is not reduced to killing, the focus still remains on physical destruction and, as Shaw (2007, p. 27) notes, "the wider issue of the destruction of social, economic, political and cultural life and institutions of groups had largely disappeared." Tatz (2003, p. 68) however remarks that the Convention equated several genocidal acts in terms of their seriousness, such as for instance physical killing and forcibly removing children. He adds that to equate killing with causing mental harm is an equivalence that is however hard to grasp. This difficulty might hamper a broadening of the definition of genocide to include the wider issue of the destruction of social, economic, political and cultural life, and institutions of peoples as entities. Causing mental harm and killing are two different actions and generally we find killing more abhorrent than causing mental harm. However, as noted before in Chapter 2, in the context of genocide, these acts are not ends in themselves. They are two different means to the single end of genocide; they are performed with the intent to annihilate a people. The conceptualisation of genocide that focuses on

89 For an overview of definitions see for instance Abed (2006) Jones (2006) and Straus (2001).

physical destruction limits our capabilities to prevent genocide from happening or to intervene at an early stage. As Lemkin argued, killing happens at a later stage when the genocidal process is already well on its way and groups as entities have already been victimised in many other ways. A broader conception of genocide which encompasses the wide variety of acts possible in the process of genocidal victimisation as discerned by Lemkin would allow us to recognise genocide earlier and no longer neglect its many other manifestations.

Those who critique the narrow approach of the 1948 Convention reveal that delineation of the concept and definition of genocide is in itself a process of inclusion and exclusion and, as such, an over-exclusive definition can result in the denial of human suffering. Charny (1994, p. 91) argues that, when discussing definitions of genocide, the danger exists that the reality of the subject under discussion is "lost". Discussions are no longer guided by a sincere concern for the faith of the victims, but instead they focus on technicalities, super-rational argumentation and intellectual competition. As a result, cases of immense human suffering are "dumped into a conceptual black hole, where they are forgotten" (Charny, 1994, p. 92). Charny (1994, p. 91) finds this problematic and he argues that "[i]t would be a moral absurdity and an insult to the value of human life to exclude from full historical recognition any instance of mass killing as if it were undeserving of inclusion in the record." He therefore suggests that genocide be treated as a generic category that includes virtually all instances of mass killings or mass death (Charny, 1994, p. 91). Charny (Charny, 1994, p. 75; 2009b, p. 37) presents what he calls a humanistic definition of genocide: "the wanton murder of human beings on the basis of any identity whatsoever that they share". Thus, according to Charny (1994, p. 74), "whenever large number of unarmed human beings are put to death at the hands of their fellow human beings, we are talking about *genocide*." Although Charny's soft or inclusive approach is laudable because it acknowledges human suffering instead of denying it, it does present us with a dilemma. Charny's definition is so inclusive that it encompasses cases ranging from the Holocaust, to the Allied bombings of Dresden and cases of uncontrolled smog and even the hole in the ozone layer. In the context of the conflict in Rwanda, according to his definition, both the victimisation of the Tutsi at the hands of Hutu extremists and the victimisation of Hutu by the RPF would be genocide. Such an approach could facilitate double genocide discourses. Charny's humanistic or generic approach to defining genocide, despite its laudable intentions, turns out to be over-inclusive and as a result it risks rendering the crime of genocide meaningless (Ternon, 1999a, p. 9). The problem with such unbridled inclusion is, according to Fein (1994, pp. 104–105), that it not only undermines the study of genocide, but it relativises its victims into obscurity. Over-inclusive definitions tend to confuse genocide with other crimes (Chalk, 1994, p. 57). If every case of war or terrorism is included in the definition of genocide, it becomes very difficult to be precise with regard to what it is that we are studying (Chalk, 1994, p. 60). Thus, in their quest to fight the denial of genocide, certain scholars tend to present over-inclusive definitions of genocide, which ironically facilitate the denial dynamic because they neglect the essential nature of genocide and render the term meaningless.

7.2.2. Too broad?

In contrast to those who argue that genocide is defined too narrowly and promote an inclusive approach or those who use it in a popular manner, there are also scholars who find that genocide is defined too broadly and argue to limit its definitional scope. Fein (1994, p. 100) for instance explains that "discrimination of crimes and events is necessary and both scientifically and morally justified." According to her, aggregating all cases of human suffering would lead to general and even banal insights and conclusions (Fein, 1994, p. 100). Thus, according to Fein we should make a distinction between cases of mass death, between war, slavery, genocide, and terrorism. Fein is correct, aggregating all those crimes, neglects the specific nature of genocide. Also, if one neglects the character of each crime, we end up with explanations concerning the most common denominators of all aggregated crimes thereby rendering our analysis superficial. There are however also scholars whose approach is much harder than the one Fein proposes. Some scholars have, for instance, argued that there was only one genuine case of genocide, which is the Holocaust; it is the unique and only true example and cannot be compared. These particularists (or exclusivists) maintain that, because of its distinct quality, the Holocaust is a singular event that is unprecedented and unrepeatable and therefore fundamentally different from other instances of mass death. Other cases of genocide, such as those which, for instance, happened in Cambodia and Rwanda are excluded (Alvarez, 2001, p. 34; Shaw, 2007, p. 42; Straus, 2001, p. 359). Steven T. Katz, for instance, argues that what happened in Rwanda was "mass murder" and not genocide like the Holocaust was: "With certain kinds of events, one needs to be able to say, this is new, or singular, or unprecedented" (Katz quoted in lovett, 2011; Rosensaft, 2011).[90] Some particularists go even further in what ultimately are basically discriminatory practices, arguing that the Holocaust was a genocide experienced solely by the Jewish people and the fate of other people such as that of the Gypsies is excluded from the genocidal suffering (Churchill, 2000). Churchill (2000) argues that genocide deniers whose denial has its roots in a genocidal ideology is only a tiny fringe group, but the group of particularists who promote the uniqueness of the Holocaust is much larger. He notes that these particularists engage in behaviour that is very similar to that of whom we typically denounce as genocide deniers, but, instead of problematising their discriminatory actions, many tend to respect and acknowledge their discriminatory claims. The consequences of such exclusive approaches to defining genocide, according to Churchill (2000), is the devictimisation of many people who suffered genocide. Instead of engaging in genocide denial, particularists argue that extending the definition of genocide to include other cases than the Holocaust, leads to denial by trivialisation; it minimises and trivialises the suffering of those who experienced the Holocaust. Thus, particularists do not perceive themselves as deniers of genocidal suffering; on the contrary they claim that their approach aims to stop such denial of suffering. The problem is that, by taking such an approach, there is a risk of constructing a hierarchy of crimes and genocides that creates competition between horrible events and which turns victims into competitors, which is intolerable for

90 See also Lovett (2011).

those who were victimised (Ternon, 1999a, p. 11). Effectively, in these debates, both parties are accusing each other of denial. Those who claim that the Holocaust is unique argue that comparison leads to trivialisation and those who claim that the Holocaust is not unique argue that the uniqueness argument leads to minimisation of other genocidal suffering.[91] Interestingly, the over-exclusive approach of the particularists is one of the reasons why Charny takes an over-inclusive approach. Charny (1994, p. 72) explains that he objects "strongly to the efforts to name the genocide of any one people as the single, ultimate event, or as the most important event against which all other tragedies of genocidal mass death are to be tested and found wanting." Charny remarks:

> There is a disquieting pattern of claims of the "incomparable uniqueness" of the Holocaust and a good deal of political power used in many places in academia, museums, and communities to back up these claims by pushing down and out nonadherents. No less disturbing, many of the counterclaims – however justified in epistemological and moral intent to place genocide of all peoples on the same level of tragedy and evil – go on to minimize the horror of the Holocaust and display a nasty lack of reverence for the victims. (Charny quoted in Shaw, 2007, p. 38).

Comparative research does not necessarily aim to diminish or relativise genocide. Instead, many scholars recognise that, although each genocide is a unique phenomenon, these instances of genocide have elements in common that can be related to each other in order to come to a better understanding of the phenomenon (Alvarez, 2001, p. 13).[92] Alvarez (2001, p. 14) points out that "[a]ll genocides are simultaneously unique and analogues" and as such "similarities and dissimilarities can be equally instructive in understanding" genocide. It must, however, also be noticed that, during the so-called *Historikerstreit*, scholars (ab)used a comparative approach to relativise the Holocaust. Ernst Nolte drew parallels between the crimes committed by Hitler's Nazi Germany and those committed by the Stalin's Communist Soviet Union; Stalin's Gulag was the original and greater crime. Jürgen Habermas reacted arguing that by drawing such comparisons these scholars risked white washing German history (Barth, 2006, p. 52; Verbij, 2006). Above, Ternon indicated that particularist approaches create competition between genocidal events, thereby turning victims into competitors, which is intolerable for those who were victimised. This situation is not limited to the situation where genocidal events compete with each other. By introducing genocide, it seems that Lemkin wanted to create "a sacrosanct category of crime"; a crime that is more nefarious than any other crime; the crime of all crimes (Power, 2002, p. 65). According to Andreopoulos, "[n]o crime matches genocide in the moral opprobrium that it generates" (Andreopoulos, 1994, p. 1). This has resulted in a situation in which genocide, being the crime of crimes, eclipses other morally abhorrent events such as war crimes and crimes against humanity. How massive the suffering generated by genocide is, it should not make

---

91 For a discussion on the debate over the uniqueness of the Holocaust see: Rosenfeld (1999).

92 See for instance Jonassohn & Björnson (1998) Jongman (1996), Kuper (1981), Shaw (2007) for comparative approaches.

us less sensitive or outraged by other kinds of human suffering (Charny, 1994, p. 72). Other crimes against humanity also warrant our utmost concern.

Lastly, to wrap up this discussion of the implications of definitionalism, it is insightful to briefly reference the work of Theriault (2010) because, instead of promoting a narrow or a broad definition, he argues the following:

> The fact that the definition of genocide could be used as an obstacle to prevention and intervention suggests deep questions about how definition of genocide is approached. We are left with three serious problems: (1) definitional denials of a past genocide can be used to forestall perpetually recognition of that genocide, (2) definitional denials of an ongoing genocide, even when ultimately overcome, will likely do their job of stymieing intervention efforts, and (3) improving the standard fixed definition will not solve these two problems, as denials are advanced despite the fact that the UN definition might – but is not allowed to – work in these situations. As I argue below, it is not that such a definition is flawed in a way that can be addressed that is the problem, it is that the usual approach to the definition of genocide opens the door to definitional denial. To begin to see this, consideration of a third type of definitionalism will be helpful. This might be termed "anticipatory denial" of a planned but not yet executed genocide. In such a case, perpetrators intentionally misrepresent and tweak planned actions themselves to maximize the possibility of definitional denial once the actions are taken. (Theriault, 2010, p. 487)

Theriault (2010, p. 518) therefore urges us to recognise genocide as:

> [A] changing social practice through a flexible definitional process that can capture mutations can advance the goals of a proper understanding of past genocides, intervention against present genocides, and prevention of future possible genocides better than the use of a fixed definition.

What is interesting about Theriault's approach is not only that he acknowledges that genocidal practices can change, and therefore the definitions need to adapt as well, but that he notices that perpetrators will take the definitions of genocide into account when planning and organising genocide in order to obscure the true nature of their endeavour. Our definitions trigger what he calls "anticipatory denial". By misrepresenting and tweaking their planned actions genocide perpetrators attempt to maximise the possibility of what Theriault referred to as definitional denial once the planned actions become implemented. When we look at the significance of Theriault's notion of anticipatory denial from the perspective of the genocide denialism typology presented earlier (Chapter 3, Section 3.3.), it becomes clear that anticipatory denial falls within the scope of primary denial of genocide, which encompasses the denial that facilitates the initial perpetration of acts of genocide.

Figure 9. Anticipatory denial

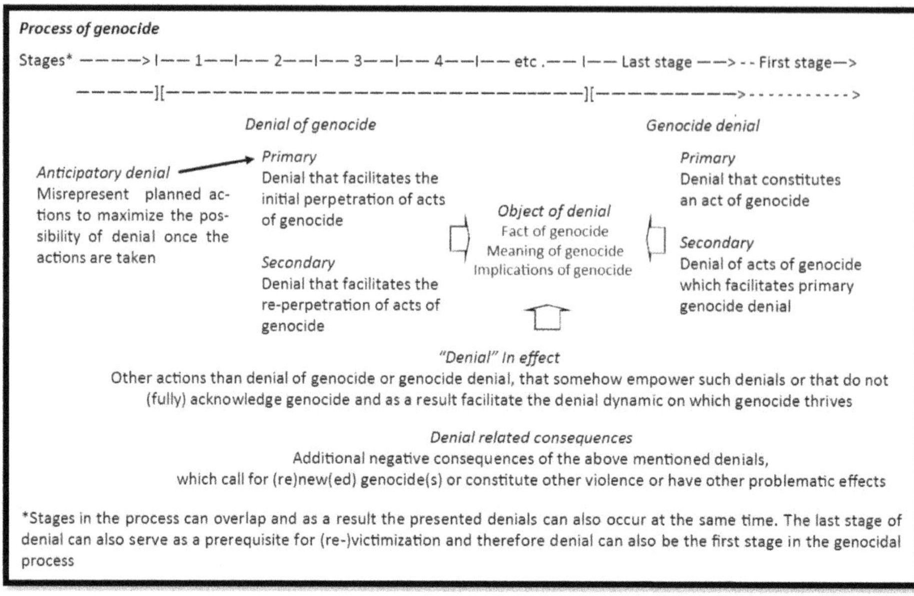

Scholarly debate and disagreement about concepts and their definition is normal and a requirement for innovation and development.[93] But as the discussion above reveals, critical debate can also result in situations that raise questions in terms of denial. In the field of criminology, the opposite situation appears to exist; there the denial dynamic is facilitated by the lack of critical debate on the crime of genocide.

[93] But such disagreement about the core attributes of genocide also has negative side effects. Strauss (2001, p. 349), for instance, points out that the existing conceptual differences are profound and limit the theoretical scope of cross/comparative study. But the effects maybe even more profound and not limit themselves to hampering the study of genocide; the disagreement might have implications for the prevention of genocide. Andreopoulos (1994, p. 4) explains that "[b]ecause genocide refers to a social process, a good definition has critical functional value: to assist in the detection of early signs of an impending crisis and, provided the appropriate mechanisms are in place, devise preventive measures. Thus a good definition can be instrumental in the creation of an early warning system for the detection of genocide-prone situations." As a result, definitional issues can thus have an impact on enforcement (Andreopoulos, 1994, p. 3 and 4). Kuper has also been critical of the definitional confusion that has been created by the overwhelming array of definitions put forward by scholars in the field. According to Kuper "it is helpful to create new definitions of genocide, when there is an internationally recognized definition and a Genocide Convention which might become the basis for some effective action, however limited the underlying concept" (Kuper 1981 Quoted in Jones 2006, p. 16). Ambiguity regarding the concept of genocide and its definition might undermine effective (preventive) action, which is a serious problem as the ultimate aim of the inception of the concept and the Convention is prevention. Ambiguity makes it difficult to clearly distinguish whether a certain case is genocide or not; it hampers the ability of recognition which is a prerequisite for action. As discussed in the last section, what constitutes genocide is often determined by political agendas of inclusion and exclusion to the extent of outright denial (Alvarez, 2001, p. 34). Genocide carries with it heavy political implications because of issues such as sovereignty, territorial integrity and non-intervention in internal affairs contribute to inaction (Kuper, 1994, p. 36).

7.3. CRIMINOLOGICAL STUDIES

In Chapter 1 it has been discussed that a disciplinary lacuna exists. It seems that scholars and authors from all kinds of disciplines have contributed significantly to the study of the genocide against the Tutsi except for criminologists. This is quite peculiar because one would expect criminologists to have studied the crime of genocide quite extensively. Criminology is after all a discipline that is concerned fundamentally with crime and, as noted before, genocide is generally perceived as being "the crime of all crimes" (Cunneen, 1999, p. 131). Cunneen (1999, p. 137) notes that this is especially tragic due to the fact that

> [T]he issue of human rights abuses goes to the heart of many questions which criminology has had so much to say about in the case of individual behaviour, but so little to say about when it comes to large scale organized and legitimized criminal behaviour by state agencies.

Cunneen's arguments are important because they force criminologists to rethink their disciplinary foundations. Cunneen was not the only one to point out criminology's neglect. Years earlier, Stanley Cohen already argued that it is incorrect to claim that the crime of genocide never appears on the radar of criminologists. According to Cohen (1993), it had been raised by, for instance Schwendinger & Schwendinger, but the implications were "conveniently" repressed by the rest of the criminological community. In the context of sociology, it was Zygmunt Bauman who, in his book *Modernity and the Holocaust*, made a similar observation. According to Bauman, sociology had ignored genocide and he described sociological research as a "collective exercise in forgetting and eye-closing" (Bauman quoted in Shaw, 2007, p. 10). The same seems to apply to criminology. Alvarez (2001, p. 2 and 3) even argues that the neglect of criminologists to study the crime of genocide when it comes to the damaging effects can be comparable to the harm done by those who deny genocide. He acknowledges that the two types of denial are, of course, not morally equivalent, but, despite such difference, they do seem to have similar results: "That is, the failure of social scientists to adequately address the study of genocide contributes to perceptions and attitudes that, through exclusion, minimize the importance and significance of genocide" (Alvarez, 2001, p. 3). According to the typology offered in Chapter 3, this behaviour, like much of the behaviour discussed above, could be qualified as "denial" in effect. But why does genocide cause such an uncomfortable reality for criminology to the extent that led it to systematically neglect the study of genocide? Is there more at play?

7.3.1. Leviathan's faithful servant

When scholars address the question why the criminological study of genocide has been neglected, they come up with various possible reasons, such as disciplinary barriers, methodological biases, lack of funding, wariness of morally charged research, etc. (Moon, 2011, p. 49; Woolford, 2011, p. 137). In these discussions on criminology's neglect, one significant issue is mostly lacking. The conclusion that criminology is in a state of denial does not mean that criminology did not engage with genocide at all. Instead, as Cunneen, in the context of the forced removal of children seems to indicate, criminology did engage with genocide; it was implicated in it. Hogg (2002, p. 194) also notices that criminology has been "a loyal servant and occasional mild critic of Leviathan," but, despite its close relationship to it, criminology has not been disturbed by the criminal violence that is related to state formation and maintenance of state power. Cunneen (1993) notes how criminological research has helped to construct the indigenous peoples as deviants, as perpetrators of crime, instead of laying bare the reality that these people have been victims of the most atrocious crimes. Criminological labelling has facilitated their genocidal victimisation by the state. According to Woolford (2011, p. 139), criminology's essentialising tendency has provided states with the legitimacy for their exclusionary practices. It helped to criminalise and stigmatise groups of people, thereby facilitating destructive projects of social engineering. History thus shows that criminology has not been a bulwark against extermination. It is however important to point out that, in these cases, criminology was not a perverted or degenerated science. Rafter (2008), in her analysis of Nazi bio-criminology, notes that "It is no longer possible to dismiss Nazi criminal-biology as a bad science concocted by mad scientists, a perversion that will not recur so long as we uphold standards for 'good' science."[94] It has become increasingly clear that the notion that there was "bad" and "good" science was promulgated after the Holocaust to exculpate the implicated scientists and their science. This is an interesting reaction in terms of denial. Morrison (2004, p. 75), who is one of the few criminologists systematically reflecting on the abovementioned issues, explains that positivist criminology, which set out to scientifically identify the determinants of criminality, has created a body of knowledge that helped to construct and legitimate the power of the state to alleviate or eliminate crime. Criminology was thus not simply a science corrupted by Nazi ideology. The evil did not only come from the outside and corrupted criminology. Instead it was also ideas central to criminology itself that made it ready to facilitate victimisation (Woolford, 2011, p. 139). The problem, as Morrison (2004, p. 76) points out, is that: "[t]he symbolic space criminology worked within was the constitution of a social order within the boundaries of the *nation-state*." As such, criminology helped to create a peaceful and ordered civilised space by identifying the "fit and unfit companions". However, reflexively it has become clear that this ordering of society was highly political.[95] Rafter's analysis reveals how criminological endeavours, for various reasons, eventually became aligned with the political program of genocide. The point that Rafter (2008, p. 288) makes is that criminology at that time was not responsible for that political programme; it did not set it up, but it nonetheless ended up providing justifications for its exclusionary policies. Rafter concludes that this could happen again. Criminological science could be enlisted again in such destructive enterprises, unless we acknowledge, as Morrison also indicated, that our criminological science is in reality socially

94 Wetzell (2000) has extensively studied how criminology was implicated in the perpetration of the Holocaust.

95 See also Morrison (2006) and Garland (2002) for an analysis of the relationship between the "Lombrosian project" and the "governmental project".

constructed and politicised and seriously address the implications that follow from it. Value free science can thus actually be dangerous, as it can be used as a tool to impose certain values violently. Morrison (2004, p. 77) concludes that we should therefore be careful about narratives of control because "[y]ou may end up defined as the problem and controlled out of existence". Criminologists thus need to reflect on their scientific endeavours in order to prevent them from facilitating violent processes, such as genocide. Otherwise we risk developing a criminology that supports such *criminological nightmares* instead of countering them (Woolford, 2011, p. 136).

7.3.2. A discipline in denial?

One could argue that the discipline of criminology is no longer in a state of denial with regard to the study of gross human rights violations as many scholars are now engaging with the topic within what seems to be a booming criminological sub-discipline: supranational criminology.[96] Those in favour of a supranational criminology argue that the deadly scope of the crime requires such attention; it is the crime of all crimes. It is furthermore argued that criminologists can positively contribute to a solution, but also criminology itself can benefit, because such study expands and enriches the discipline. This last aspect reveals that criminology, like other disciplines, is susceptible to the tendency to extend its domain and to show its applicability (Woolford, 2011, p. 136).[97] Such academic colonialism is fostered even more by the increasing competitive nature of academic markets in general (Woolford, 2011, p. 143). Cunneen's critique entailed more than criminology's neglect of the study of events that were not traditionally incorporated in its scope of research. Cunneen also pointed out that this neglect calls for a critical reflection on the criminological enterprise itself and, with regard to this aspect supranational criminology, it does still appear to be very much in a state of denial.[98] Woolford (2011, p. 142) points out that criminological research on international crimes, such as genocide, tends to be redemptive, as the core ideas and assumptions underlying the criminological enterprise are left unchallenged and the application is an illustration that criminological theory is also applicable with regard to international criminality. Woolford (2000), for example, refers to Day & Vandiver (2000) who state:

> We strongly disagree with the notion that [genocide] should be placed beyond the boundary conditions of our field. To do so results in lost opportunities to test the generalizability of our concepts and lost opportunities to integrate concepts from other disciplines.[99]

---

96 See Chapter 1, Section 1.4.

97 Carrier & Park (2013) also criticise criminologists studying mass violence for their entrepreneurial and colonizing tendencies.

98 The issue raised in the last Section how criminology itself was implicated in gross human rights violations, such as genocide, is often also neglected in supranational criminological research.

99 You encounter this argumentation also in the article by Yacoubain (1997, p. 16): "[t]o omit genocidal behaviour from scholarly exploration would not only diminish the consequences of the international community's most menacing offence, but it would deprive the discipline of criminology an untapped reservoir of criminal justice exploration."

According to Woolford (2006, p. 95), the existing literature on criminology and genocide has thus demonstrated only a limited awareness of critical issues and challenges connected to the criminological study of genocide. Reflexivity typically takes the form of a critique of absence of criminological engagement with the crime of genocide. Few go further and critically examine what it takes for criminologists to study genocide and few point out the critical issue of approach and the concerns that come with it. Applying criminology to genocidal processes that are far too complex for criminology's reductive language is problematic. In addition, providing redemptive and self-serving benefits to the discipline and ignoring its past further creates serious issues. According to Woolford (2011, p. 136), such criminology runs the risk of turning out to be a criminological nightmare. Interestingly, Woolford (2011, p. 137 and 138) takes the conflict in the Great Lakes Region as an illustration for his argument that criminology might provide "little purchase" in such complex situations and he raises the question: "How does one transport conventional criminological theories designed to understand street crime into such an inter-regional, deeply historical, and dangerously political situation without engaging in gross simplification?" Woolford (2011, p. 138) concludes that despite the many challenges that such application poses, neutralisation theory, control theory, and non-partisan conflict theory have "all been spotted in the hills of Rwanda". Supranational criminology should however be more than "add criminology and stir" (Woolford, 2006, p. 97). It should genuinely help to advance the field of genocide studies and therefore it should involve more than the "mundane task of testing and extending criminological discourses" (Woolford, 2006). The main issue is that, if the baseline assumptions of the discipline remain unchanged, it is questionable whether criminological theorising can grasp complex phenomena such as genocide (Woolford, 2006). Despite this critique, it can also not be ignored that criminological research on genocide has yielded interesting and valuable insights.[100] There is however also criminological scholarly work on genocide, and more particularly on the genocide against the Tutsi in Rwanda, that raises issues, especially in terms of the approach developed throughout this study.

7.3.3. Unintended, but problematic ...

The following Sections briefly discuss several examples of criminological encounters with the phenomenon of genocide. In these examples, the specific nature of genocide as discussed in Chapter 2 is somehow neglected resulting in analyses that raise questions in terms of the framework of genocide denialism developed so far.[101]

---

[100] See for instance Hagan et al. (2005) and Smeulers & Hoex (2010).

[101] Carrier & Park (2013, p. 305) explain that we should not categorically reject the idea that criminological insights and tools might be helpful in explaining international crimes, but they also note that: "Nonetheless, quite remarkably, the pervasive recommendations to graft criminological concepts and theories onto mass political action have almost universally evaded any meditation on whether the distinctly political quality of the actions under scrutiny makes any difference at all. The failure to account for – or even to examine seriously – the political quality of acts of mass violence results in the isolation of the criminalised act in a vacuum or the fetishization of acts, divorced from context and meaning."

Institutionalised child abuse ...

In their book *State crime: Government, violence and corruption*, Green & Ward (2004) give an overview of the nature and types of various state crimes, including genocide. They note that the concept and definition of genocide are contested and they explain that some scholars argue that only the Nazi Holocaust and the genocide against the Tutsi are deemed to qualify, while others have pointed out that genocide involves more than mass murder and therefore other cases should also be included (Green and Ward, 2004, p. 165). In this context they specifically refer to the act of "forcibly transferring children of the group to another group" which is also listed as an act of genocide in the 1948 Genocide Convention. Green & Ward point out that this gives rise to "a strong *legal* argument" that genocide was committed in Australia where indigenous children were removed from their families. Interestingly, however, Green & Ward (2004, p. 165 and 166) continue to conclude that "[f]or *criminological* purposes, it does not appear helpful to put this form of institutionalised child abuse in the same category as mass murder." The authors apparently disconnect the policy of forcibly removing children from the broader historical reality of the continuous victimisation of indigenous people. It is, however, in this broader context that the true meaning of the forced removal of children is constituted. As Crewcock (2008, p. 2) notes:

> They label forced removal as "institutionalised child abuse" [...], which apart from being an inadequate description of the assimilationist intent and devastating social impact of the policy, leaves out the whole issue of settler and frontier violence against Aboriginal people and how that might relate to the various removal practices.

To reduce the forced removal of children to a form of institutional child abuse obscures the true nature of the genocidal endeavour, which, as explained before, was to "breed out the colour". Subsequently, Green & Ward discuss many elements that are relevant for understanding the perpetration of genocide, which is insightful. They also briefly mention Bauman's work on the Holocaust. Bauman's ideas concerning the bureaucratic nature of genocide and the modernist ideas ("gardener's vision" of society) underlying processes of genocide, which are discussed in Chapter 4 of his book *Modernity and the Holocaust,* would have been very helpful in making sense of the forced removal of children from their families which occurred in Australia.

Low self-control ...

In a paper in an edited volume on control theories and delinquency, Brannigan & Hardwick (2003) discuss whether criminological theory can explain genocide and they argue that crimes such as genocide can be comprehended within the broad boundaries of the control tradition as articulated by Hirschi (1969) and Gottfredson & Hirschi (1990). Morrison is however critical of applying Gottfredson & Hirschi's theory to phenomena such as genocide. The two proponents of control theory stipulate that any general criminological theory must be faithful to the data, but Morrison wonders what exactly constituted their data. Morrison (2004, p. 72) points out that their data on which their theory was based does not include the millions destroyed by genocide or other gross human rights violations. On the contrary, they point out that "the bulk of the crimes are trivial and mundane affairs" that do not have such a significant impact. Morrison observes that this leads them to conclude that crime "has much in common with accidents, other forms of deviant behaviour and is a function of low rates of self-control." However, according to Brannigan & Hardwick, "Gottfredson & Hirschi's A General Theory seemed to [...] be a sufficiently, if not masterfully, articulated and eloquent model for the application of general criminological control theory to the phenomenon of genocide." Brannigan & Hardwick (2003) apply these insights to the case of Rwanda arguing that:

> [R]ather than pursuing complicated and time-consuming political negotiations, the political leadership in both cases sought remedies that paralleled the impulsive characteristics found in studies of garden variety crimes: the immediate gratification of desires (hatred) through righteous slaughter of enemies; easy or simple steps to achieve political ends (i.e. physical displacement and annihilation); risky, thrilling and/or exciting solutions (sadistic orgies of killing); dubious long term benefits (since the activities attract prosecutions for genocide, and result in cycles of revenge); little skill or planning in the conduct of genocide; indifference to the suffering of the victims; versatility of criminal acts (cruelty, humiliation and degradation of victims, theft of their property and desecration of their cultural symbols); and an inability to tolerate frustration in the achievement of ends (through UN negotiations, political compromise and long term investments in peace agreements).

Although some elements of Brannigan & Hardwick's analysis are definitely insightful, the main problem is that the language that is used to make sense of genocide at the same time minimises and contradicts to a great extent what genocide is about.[102] To talk about genocide in terms of "low self-control," as criminal acts that are an "easy, simple and immediate gratification of desires," as acts that are "exciting, risky, and thrilling," and which "require little skill or planning" and that the perpetrators of these crimes "often do not appear to experience any lasting trauma or shame" is problematic. Of course, on a micro or individual level, which is the focus of the control approach, this can be the case. However, genocide, as a systematic crime, is not about "loss of self-control" and "rage," instead it is about absolute control. It is not about spontaneous short-term gratification, but about planned and organised

---

102 Despite that they argue that it is applicable, Brannigan and Hardwick automatically need to rework the theory in order to make it fit: "Recall that the distal mechanism, according the Gottfredson and Hirschi's A General Theory, responsible for low self-control is ineffective or poor parenting. If we could rightly assume that all of those responsible for genocide were predisposed to criminality, then the application of this mechanism would be unproblematic. However, we have discovered that it is more likely that many if not most of the perpetrators are historically, situationally, and 'momentarily' incited to low self-control, or righteous anger. Thus, it becomes necessary to propose an alternative distal mechanism or mechanisms to the phenomenon of genocide. Here, we are searching for mechanisms or processes that can reasonably explain why individuals might be willing and ready to systematically attempt to destroy large numbers of other individuals. We suggested that it is the state or culture or a combination of both that provides the predisposition to genocide by employing propaganda, selective education, subornment of group hatred, misinformation, and the creation of special militias perhaps populated to some extent by key 'role models' (i.e. criminals)" (Brannigan & Hardwick, 2003).

annihilation of a people that has an indefinite effect. The language used to describe the phenomenon thus does not sit well with the nature of the genocidal phenomenon. The gist of the official denial discourse is that it happened because the authorities had no control and that people were out of control. The problem with Brannigan & Hardwick's application is that it tends to reduce the complexity of genocide to the common denominators found in garden variety crimes with regard to which the theory was developed, thereby moving the focus away from the elements of the crime that are crucial in understanding it.[103] Nonetheless Brannigan & Hardwick's research is referred to by others, without any critical reflection, as an illustration that criminology is taking an increased interest in international crimes such as genocide.[104]

Catalyst to genocide ...

In 2012 the *State Crime journal* featured an article by Cameron (2012) on British state complicity in genocide in Rwanda in 1994.[105] In terms of denial, Cameron's analysis of British bystander complicity in genocide for geo-political ends is important and insightful as it shows that not only the perpetrator is responsible for the genocidal process. Also those who stand by and do nothing, in this case purely out of self-interest, affect the genocidal dynamic as their (in)actions empower the perpetrator. Cameron is also a member of the International State Crime Initiative, which publishes the *State Crime Journal.* The website of the initiative featured a "critical introduction" to "state crime in Rwanda" that is written by Cameron. In the paragraph titled "the catalyst to genocide," Cameron explains that the shooting down of the presidential plane was "a critical turning point in the sequence of events that lead to genocide." In the abovementioned article in the *State Crime Journal*, she also states that the assassination triggered the genocide (Cameron, 2012, p. 77). Cameron appears to reduce the genocide to the stage of extermination, thereby obscuring that genocide encompasses a more elaborate process consisting of multiple techniques and which

103 Brannigan (2013), in a later publication, takes a more elaborate and nuanced approach with regard to control theory when explaining what happened in Rwanda and notes: "The Chapter applies the theoretical model to Rwanda. The perplexing features of the 1994 genocide include its speed, its widespread support among the Hutu majority, and the absence of widespread remorse among the perpetrators. This emotional anomaly in terms of inter-group relationships from colonial to post-colonial development and the role of massacres in political struggles from the inception of Rwanda are examined. The 1963 amnesty laws put complicity in mass violence beyond the rule of law, and created expectations that politically directed violence could be undertaken without emotional baggage. The concept of administrative closure describes a political system designed to harness the populace in a tightly managed system of control, i.e. 'over-control'. Racial closure was an ideology designed to extinguish amity along lineage lines when social control valorised Tutsi exclusion. Politically motivated inter-lineage murders had been effectively decriminalized, and were undertaken with little apprehension of guilt by their perpetrators." He appears to move away from the strict parameters by Gottfredson & Hirschi's original control theory.

104 See for instance Haveman et al. (2011, pp. 296–297).

105 Cameron's article reveals how the British state did not intervene to stop the genocide against the Tutsi, while it had substantial knowledge on what was going on. According to Cameron (2012), the British state chose to stand by and refrained from calling what was happening genocide, because it wanted to avoid the political repercussions of taking action, while inaction would help to advance political interests, such as maintaining a power status and ensuring economic interests in the region.

spans a much wider period than the 100 days in 1994. Furthermore, the genocide was not "triggered" by the assassination. The genocide was planned and organised and having moved through several stages of the genocidal process, the assassination of the president started off the large scale extermination phase. Cameron is however not alone in referring to the assassination of the president as the trigger of the genocide. It is an issue that one encounters regularly in research on the genocide against the Tutsi. To designate the killing of the president as the trigger of the genocide conveys a wrong image of what genocide entails as a complex process is reduced to the stage of physical extermination. If we want to prevent future genocides, it is imperative that we stop equalling it to physical violence, such as killing, and we need to start perceiving it as a complex process. Preventing genocide requires early intervention in this process. An issue is furthermore that, by presenting the notion that the killing of the president triggered the genocide, one risks facilitating the (official) denial discourse, which entails that the genocide was unplanned and spontaneous and triggered by the assassination of the president. Language is important because it constructs the reality of the genocide. By using confusing terminology, we can unwillingly facilitate the denial dynamic because our language helps to obscure the nature of the event. If one continues to display the plane crash as the trigger of the genocide, one can thus unwillingly empower the alternative reality that the deniers try to construct through their discourse.

What is however disquieting is that, for a long time, the website of the *State Crime Journal* (www.statecrime.org) featured an article by Cameron in which she explains that:[106]

> Despite being pivotal to the tragedy, no official investigation has been launched in relation to the attack on the plane or the death of its occupants, and as such no individual, group or organisation, has been convicted of responsibility. Alternate versions, rumours and speculation have thrived in the years since the attack on the plane. *Current international legal consensus suggests however that the RPA were responsible for the attack that set the wheels of genocide in motion.* (Emphasis added)

Cameron, without any citation or reference concludes that there is a "legal consensus" that the RPA, which is the military wing of the RPF, are responsible for the assassination of President Habyarimana, which, according to her, set the genocide in motion. No court has ever decided on the question of who is responsible for shooting down the plane. So what "legal consensus" is Cameron referring to? The problem is that in the official denial discourse the downing of the plane is presented as the trigger and the RPF are held responsible for this. Although Cameron leaves

[106] The website featured this article for a considerable period of time. I came across it for the first time in 2010 and it was featured on the website probably until the end of 2014; that is when I noticed that it was removed. It is furthermore telling that Cameron in her PhD thesis also draws on the work of scholars such as Harmon Snow, etc. without critically reflecting on the problematic nature of their broader narrative. Interestingly, later Cameron testified and spoke out against the denial of the genocide against the Tutsi during an official investigation of the Rwandan authorities into the BBC documentary *Rwanda's untold story* (Corbin and Conroy 2014), which was heavily criticised for its denialist contend.

the reader confused concerning the "legal consensus" because she does not present any substantial source for her conclusion, Cameron, at the end of her article, does provide a link to Erlinder's Rwanda documents project website. To present Erlinder's documents project as the primary source of an analysis is not only questionable in terms of academic rigor, it is also raises questions in terms of genocide denialism. Erlinder's documents project is not an objective archive, but presents the perspective of the defence. It basically grounds his defence brief in the Military-I case, which to a great extent turns the reality concerning the genocide on its head.

I have no doubt that scholars like Green & Ward, Brannigan and Cameron have sincere intentions with their research and they do not intend to deny the genocide. They should therefore not be lumped together with primary genocide deniers and those who virulently recycle their narrative as discussed in earlier Chapters. Nonetheless, their cases do reveal that their research raises problems in terms of genocide denialism and it calls for a more critically reflexive stance that allows them to approach their research in such a way that it does not facilitate a phenomenon that they actually are intending to curb.

My early "critical" analysis ...

The perspective on genocide denialism developed throughout this study has also confronted me with the problematic nature of my own actions. Especially in the early stages of my research, parts of my speech can be criticised. When reassessing some of that early work (see next paragraph), it becomes painfully clear that I was also lacking the critical awareness that allows one to discern issues that raise questions in terms of genocide denialism. When I started this study, I did not look at genocide and denial in the way it is presented throughout the previous Sections and Chapters. In the end I was simply fortunate to have ample time to conduct my research as it allowed for a prolonged engagement with the field and reflection on it. I had the luxury of time to have my ideas and insights challenged and to use the critique as new input. This allowed me, but also my work, to go through a process of maturation. Lincoln and Guba (1985, p. 301) point out that a crucial element of credibility of the research is whether he or she is able to have a prolonged engagement with the phenomenon in the broader field of inquiry. Certain aspects of the research simply cannot be forced. In the current academic climate where scholars are pressed for results this may actually become a serious problem. A saying used by one of the Rwandese interviewees is insightful in this context: "A running cow gives birth to blind calves."

When I started my research I also encountered (elements of) the earlier discussed discourse that certain scholars, defence attorneys and other actors were promoting. At that time I saw it as critical revisionism and I was actually quite receptive to it. Their questions seemed reasonable and their alternative explanations seemed plausible. I furthermore thought it was a virtue to be critical as things are often more complex than they initially seem. Only later I became aware of the questionable nature of their discourse. Especially the insight that many of these actors are basically recycling crucial elements of the official denial of the former genocidal authorities made me realise that this was not legitimate genocide revisionism, but genocide denial. Actually, in hindsight, much of *my early "critical" analysis* could have featured in one of the earlier discussions on how academics somehow facilitate the denial dynamic. In an early draft, I, for instance, wrote:

> In the approximately 100 days that the genocide raged, it killed and wounded hundreds of thousands of people and it destroyed virtually every sector in society. The violence started after the plane of Rwanda's President Habyarimana was shot down by two missiles on the 6th of April 1994. The plane crash was a coda for decades of escalating tension in Rwanda and within an hour the violence erupted. Using carefully prepared death-lists, the Presidential Garde and the Hutu-power militias, such as the *Interahamwe*, started killing the liberal and democratic opposition. They targeted ministers, members of parliament, judges, priests, journalists, activists and party leaders. Within thirty-six hours after the plane crash, the priority targets of the liberal and democratic opposition had all been killed. After the opposition had been eliminated, the killing continued, now targeting the entire Tutsi population and their (possible) supporters. From Kigali, where the plane crashed, the slaughter quickly spread outwards and systematic massacres started taking place in almost all other regions of the country. Within days the violence reached an unimaginable level of destruction with a daily killing rate of at least three times that of the Nazi death camps. The genocide came to an end on the 20th of July 1994 when the Tutsi-led rebel army, the Rwandan Patriotic Front (RPF) declared a unilateral ceasefire. General Augustin Bizimungu, a high ranking official in the Rwandan Army and one of the leading perpetrators argued that those who govern Rwanda after the genocide will rule over a desert. (Moerland draft 2007)

I reduced the genocide to 100 days of killing and only focused on the physical violence involved. I presented the shooting down of the plane as the trigger of the genocide and I furthermore argued that the genocide ended when the RPF took over power.[107] It reveals that I was doing many of the same things as those whose work I have scrutinised throughout his study. In this respect, my comments on some of the articles contained in my research archive are also revealing. The archive included the work of Reyntjens, who, in a 2004 article, wrote that "it has become increasingly clear that the RPF was responsible for shooting down the airplane of Kagame's predecessor, a crime that ignited the genocide" (Reyntjens, 2004). It is doubtful whether such "clarity" exists and to claim that it does exist is dangerous as explained earlier. I furthermore also archived several articles written by Lemarchand, some of which are discussed in the previous Chapter, but, back in 2004 or 2007, I apparently did not find them problematic. They just revealed "another side to the story" or were instances of critical academic scholarship. I had added the note "unknown story" to these articles. My early records also included the paper by Davenport &

[107] Also due to the massive trauma triggered by the events, the genocide continues to live on in the minds of the survivors. Moreover, during the genocide *génocidaires* who were HIV positive transmitted the virus to their rape victims. These women fell victim to HIV and many died in the years that followed. Also because of these reasons we have to be careful to say that the genocide ended in July 1994, because, for the people mentioned above, the realities of the genocide continued.

Stam titled *Rashomon goes to Rwanda: Alternative accounts of political violence and their implications for analysis and policy*. My first encounter with Davenport & Stam's "alternative account" however did not raise any questions. I did not see the danger involved. I saw the contrasting accounts as critique without realising the implications of such accounts in terms of denial. This also becomes clear from how I experienced some of my early interviews. One interviewee noticed that not all actors in the conflict were judged equally and I was asked how I thought the conflict had started and who exactly the victims and perpetrators were; "Who is who?" The interviewee pointed out that people were "ignorant," that they were not willing to listen: "For instance, foreigners they know little on the Rwandan issue. Most people have closed their eyes and ears." The interviewee concluded "when studying the history of the conflict the other story must also be revealed." Apparently there was a "known story" concerning what had happened and that has become widely accepted in the West: "Everyone knows the known story." However, "there are other issues involved, there is also an unknown story." My annotations to the interview did not signal issues of denial. Now, years later, when I look back at the interview, I know what such language signifies and does. The point is that my study of genocide denialism has made me much more aware of the destructive power of speech, especially in the context of genocide. It has raised my awareness about the problematic meaning that certain words or phrases can have because, by uttering such words, one makes linguistic community with the discourse of the perpetrators or, by uttering such speech, one somehow relativises or trivialises the nature of the genocide. This changed my perception concerning responsible and appropriate language use and as a result I value the words spoken in interviews, published on the internet, printed in books, or spoken in documentaries, etc. differently from how I used to. I have changed my way of talking and writing and I refrain from using certain words or phrases in order to avoid the risk of empowering the denial dynamic. I have been criticised by some of my peers for taking this all too seriously. They, for instance, claim that in the end a joke is just a joke or that certain cinematic representations of genocide should not be taken that seriously. However, once you start to see how the genocide denial of the perpetrators and their supporters also feeds on such a broader set of actions one starts to value jokes about victims of genocide very differently.

The reflection above requires some nuance, because it might seem that the awareness has somehow enlightened me and that it prevents me from engaging in questionable behaviour. This is, of course, not the case and I am sure that people who critically reflect on my work might find certain aspects of my actions problematic because they somehow contribute to the denial dynamic. I am thus certainly not infallible.

7.4. A FAVOURABLE SCIENTIFIC CLIMATE ...

The above discussion on genocide studies and criminology also reveals that critique appears to be essential to scientific progress. Scholarly definitions, concepts and theories are applied, scrutinised and revised by the academic community. The discussion, for instance, revealed how both Lemkin's concept and its subsequent definition in the 1948 Genocide Convention triggered a critical scholarly debate in which the concept and the 1948 definition were further (re)defined. Also, the critical discussion of certain criminological approaches and studies of the genocide against the Tutsi illustrates the critical nature of the scientific endeavour. Revisionism appears to be part and parcel of science, which, in light of the approach developed throughout this study, is a significant insight. The following Sections will address why.

7.4.1. Scientific revisionism

Revisionism is a normal and necessary part of scientific research, because the perception of researchers and historical witnesses is fallible.[108] Human perception is bound by situation, place, time, culture, etc. and because they are subject bound they are always partial, improvable and revisable (Van den Berghe, 1997a, p. 21). Established theories and knowledge can be revised because new facts, insights or methods have become available. Often researchers rely on the personal accounts of human beings that experienced the conflict as victims, perpetrators or bystanders. Such lived experience is unique and people can experience and interpret real life events quite differently. To distil one history from such accounts is difficult (Hirsch, 1995, p. 16). History might therefore be more fluid and disorderly as we might think. Of course historians also draw on written evidence and other materials, but in essence history is partially reconstructive:

> [P]ersonal memory is not an orderly phenomenon, and, since history is often based on personal memory, history is not as clear cut and orderly as some interpreters would like us to believe. History is, [...], a form of reconstructed memory, but it is memory reconstructed after historians have attempted to corroborate the memories and recollections by using documents and gathering other testimony. (Hirsch, 1995, p. 15)

Not only historians engage in revisionism. On the contrary, revisionism can be found in every academic discipline, because in science it is a general practice to examine critically, reinterpret and revise established theories and knowledge. It is this critical attitude that moves science forward (Van den Berghe, 1997a, p. 25 and 26; Verbeeck, 1997b, p. 8). Revisionism is thus a legitimate academic activity and necessary research tool (Lipstadt, 1993, p. 20 and 21; Shermer & Grobman, 2000, p. 238). Because revisionism is essential to scientific research, scholars should be able to discuss historical issues freely, without the fear of being accused of denial (Verbeeck, 1997a, p. 176). It can nonetheless be the case that academic revisionism when critically analysing genocide is perceived as an endeavour that is damaging the history of genocide. Survivors who fear denial of what happened can be sceptical about such critical academic reflection. Academic revisionists who engage in critical analysis often have to clearly explain and justify their work, because they run the

108 For a detailed discussion and development of the concept of revisionism see: Gkotzaridis (2008).

risk being seen as genocide deniers (Van den Berghe, 1997a, pp. 39–41).[109] Critical revisionism can not only be problematic because of the fear of the victims, but it is also often hampered by the political-ideological weight of genocide (Van den Berghe, 1997a, p. 41).[110] I also encountered scepticism towards my research on the genocide when undertaking my fieldwork in Rwanda. The fear of historical perversion triggers a tight control over the research that takes place on the genocide against the Tutsi. It is however important to understand that academic revision of certain aspects is necessary in order to deal with the deniers' arguments more effectively. Stereotypical images and simplistic perceptions concerning genocide should be addressed because genocide deniers will exploit such simplistic notions to claim that what happened was exaggerated or a lie (Van den Berghe, 1997a, p. 40).[111] The more the complex reality of the genocide is refined and acknowledged, the harder it becomes to deny it.

The problem is, however, that genocide denial and revisionism are not always easy to distinguish and scholars might begin with revisionism and end up denying (Shermer & Grobman, 2000, p. 243). Moreover, those bent on denying genocide can present themselves as legitimate revisionists. It is therefore not an accident that one of the documents of the Rwandan Interim Government discussed earlier is titled *Le peuple rwandais accuse*. As noted before in Chapter 4, Section 4.2.1., the title refers to Zola's now famous open letter that was published in the French paper *L'Aurore* and which carried the title *J'Accuse*. The movement that called for the opening of the Dreyfus case, which was addressed in Zola's letter, was referred to as *les révisionnistes*. The fact that deniers started to portray themselves as belonging to the legitimate historiographic academic tradition of re-evaluating the past has caused a development in which the term revisionism started to be used to denote genocide denial (Abicht, 1997, p. 54; Lipstadt, 1993, p. 20; Vidal-Naquet, 1992, pp. 79–98). This is a questionable development because genocide denial and revisionism are two different acts. In contrast to scholarly revisionism, deniers rewrite the past for personal or political purposes; they engage in pseudo-history, not history (Shermer & Grobman, 2000, p. 2). The problem is however that they tend to portray themselves as committed to revealing the truth and they often pretend to pursue this aim in an academic fashion (Verbeeck, 1997a, p. 165). By using the mantle of historical revisionism and claiming that they have no other objective than getting to the facts, deniers have acquired an intellectual credibility that cloaks their real intentions (Lipstadt, 1993, p. 20). They mimic scientific inquiry – they have extensive bibliographies, numerous references, they follow methods, etc. – and actively invoke academic and liberal arguments (Finkielkraut, 1998, p. 66 and 67). In contrast to genocide deniers, revisionists are critical about the interpretation of a phenomenon, but they do not question the phenomenon itself. Reality is explained

109 Eltringham (2004) makes this danger very explicit in his work on the conflict in Rwanda and how different actors narrate what happened and why.

110 Doing historical research on genocide is a delicate undertaking; for a discussion on issues involved see: De Graaf (2006).

111 For instance, the emblematic image of the holocaust focusses on the gas chambers and this allows Holocaust deniers to confuse people by only attacking this element, but the Holocaust as a genocidal process entailed much more.

in a more sophisticated way revealing (acknowledging) its complexities, but it is not denied (Van den Berghe, 1997a, p. 27). In that sense, revisionists work in an inclusive manner, providing new insights that reveal the complexity of the phenomenon under study. Deniers however do not refine history, they defraud and falsify it; they *un*write history. According to Ternon (1999a, p. 13), "*[c]e sont des menteurs et des imposteurs.*"[112] Therefore the term revisionism should be used to denote a legitimate academic activity and it should not be used to denote genocide denial (Shermer & Grobman, 2000, p. xv and xvi).

The problem is however more complex and it is more fundamental in nature than deniers presenting themselves as legitimate revisionists. Genocide denialism namely appears to thrive on the revisionist scientific climate in which research findings are always under scrutiny. Post-modern thinking has made the scientific climate even more favourable to denial. This indicates that the problem of genocide denialism might be more closely related to legitimate scholarly revisionism than one might think.

7.4.2. Modernism and post-modernism

The revisionist notion underlying modern scientific research creates a climate that is favourable to those who attempt to deny the genocide, because challenging the facts is a legitimate endeavour and is not necessarily met with scepticism. Post-modern thinking has furthered this tendency to the extent that there is always another side to the story.[113] Those who deny genocide often claim to present another more complex side of a simplified and misunderstood story. In doing so, they draw on the general notions of objectivity and fair play (Najarian, 1997). The willingness to hear critical

[112] Because of this, certain scholars prefer to use the term negationism instead of denial because it more clearly expresses what genocide deniers really do (Van den Berghe, 1997a). Especially, in French literature on genocide denial, scholars tend to use to term *négationnisme*, which was first coined by Jean-Pierre Rioux in an article in *Le Monde* on the 22nd of September 1987 and subsequently that year by Henry Rousso in his book *Syndrome du Vichy* (Ternon, 1999a, p. 41). Ternon (2003, p. 207) points out that "*négationnisme*" and "*révisionnisme*" are "deux mots miroir". For a discussion of the term revisionism and negation and its usages see: Fresco (2003) and Traverso (2003).

[113] Deborah Lipstadt (1993, p. 15), who wrote extensively on the phenomenon of Holocaust denial, notes that denial is empowered by the post-modern intellectual developments that have made their mark in the scholarly world throughout the past two decades. According to Lipstadt (1993, p. 18), this post-modern thinking has created an atmosphere of permissiveness toward questioning the meaning of historical events. One could indeed be critical of post-modern perversions, however post-modern thinking is not always automatically problematic. See for a good example Eaglestone's book *The Holocaust and the post-modern* (Eaglestone, 2004). Pendas (2007) reviewed Eaglestone's book and concluded: "This claim that postmodernism is ethically incapacitated by its epistemological relativism has been particularly potent among historians, some of whom (e.g., Richard Evans and Deborah Lipstadt) have alleged that questioning of the positive truth of history is a slippery slope to Holocaust denial. In light of [...] the use by some deniers of postmodern seeming arguments, these are hardly unwarranted concerns (although most Holocaust deniers actually claim to be empiricists). Yet anyone tempted to dismiss postmodernism on these grounds, as either well-intentioned but misguided relativism or as obscurantist posturing, would do well to read Robert Eaglestone's thoughtful, provocative, and cogent defense."

arguments is part of our democratic society in which free speech and reasonable enquiry are important elements. Free speech and reasonable critical enquiry are however not only important elements of democracy, they are also the cornerstones of academic methodology (Najarian, 1997). The idea that there are more sides to the story became highly valued during the Enlightenment as it helped to nourish critical reflection that limited established powers and helped to create important liberties, such as liberty of thought (Des Pres, 1986). Des Pres (1986, p. 2) argues that it is exactly this argument that the deniers use to dehistorise genocide: "the method of hearing both sides [has] become a gimmick for turning history on its head." Well documented genocides, such as the Armenian and the genocide against the Tutsi, are challenged by other views with regard to what happened; "Two sides – the [denial] begins". Des Pres (1986, p. 2) concludes and adds, "then we are told no genocide took place but only a vague unfortunate mishap determined by imponderables like time and change, the hazards of war, uncertain demographics." In this culture, where there are always two sides to every story which require rightful hearing, denial has automatically become a plausible argument, while in fact it is a deterioration of the true purpose of the two-sided scheme which was about acknowledgment of truth and not about denial of truth (Des Pres, 1986, p. 2).[114] The purpose of science is to know, but as Charny & Fromer (1998, p. 46) point out, in case of denial, science is used in a manner that it creates a situation of "know-nothingness". Des Pres (1986, p. 3) explains that "[w]hat has happened is that the two-sided argument has degenerated into mere relativism on the one hand, and on the other into the mechanical belief that there must always be 'another' point of view." Denial thrives on the perverted version of the two-sided arrangement. It claims legitimacy simply because it provides for an alternative take on what happened (Najarian, 1997). Najarian (1997) argues that deniers use the two-sided arrangement to reduce an indisputable historical event to a conflict between two opposing sides with regard to what happened and in doing so "deniers have constructed a linguistic ground where none existed before." Najarian (1997) therefore concludes that:

> [To break genocidal events such as] the Holocaust down into opposing camps is already to deny its reality, even before one starts making excuses for the gas chambers. [...] To begin to argue numbers and sides is already to give in to denial. It is our own decorum, our fascination with the paraphernalia of objectivity that makes denial possible.[115]

Those who deny genocide use "modernity's ordinary behaviours: the scrambling of information through interpretation, the denial of fact turned into the exegesis of discourse, the refusal to know what is said sublimated in the will to know more about the person speaking" (Finkielkraut, 1998, p. 36). Moreover, Finkielkraut (1998,

114 For a discussion on this issue see also Coquio (2003a, pp. 65–75).

115 The following reaction that was posted on a web log illustrates the abovementioned issue: "Dear Charles, Every sentence you write is based on a false notion. If the Holocaust narrative is so accurate, why do 17 nations have Holocaust Denial Laws? Pushed by the Jewish Lobby worldwide - Israel was the first nation to pass such laws in 1986. Can I send you a copy of a book in exchange for yours? *Debating the Holocaust: A New Look At Both Sides* by Thomas Dalton. Which I can't even advertise virtually in any mainstream publication, with tens of thousands of dollars in my advertising budget, because of the power of the Jewish Lobby" (http://michaelsantomauro.blogspot.com / www.reportersnotebook.com).

p. 57) points out that genocide deniers often claim that what they are doing falls with the tradition of enlightenment and democracy. Think of Chomsky who defended Faurisson's brazen Holocaust denial with reference to Voltaire's ideas on democracy and free speech. It is also relevant that Nahimana's denialist book *Rwanda: Les virages ratés*, to which historian Strizek wrote the preface, is published by *Editions Source du Nil* in their series "*le droit á la parole*".

Moreover, Cohen (2001, p. 282) notes that Western post-modern intelligentsia have been marketing a scientific framework that provides "just the right theory for boosting even the most untenable forms of denial." In this influential constructionist post-modern theoretical framework, a unitary objective truth and reality no longer exists; instead truth has become subjective and realities are multiple (Cohen, 2001, p. 280). This relativism has reduced truth and reality into social constructs and as a result "[n]arratives compete equally and openly in indeterminate truth-games" (Cohen, 2001, p. 283). As a result, there is no way of determining which truth or reality is more valid – they are all equally valid (Cohen, 2001, p. 281).

Nichanian (1999, p. 258) argues that it is exactly this post-modern relativist mind-set that has become the "message of the modern discourse of denial" and, according to him, this method of denial is the "worst of all kinds":

> It does not attack the facts, which cannot be revised any more [...]. It attacks the significance of the facts, [...] [and], in doing so it is undermining the reality of the event. *The reason for this is simple, albeit infinitely profound: there is reality only where there is meaning.* (Nichanian, 1999, p. 262 emphasis added).

But "meaning", according to Nichanian (1999, p. 262), "does not wait in the heart of events in the moment when they take place." Instead, "It can occur only as the result of an interpretation, that is, of a labour directed against other interpretations or the lack of interpretations" (Nichanian, 1999, p. 262). Thus, facts do not just exist with the objective existence of the events. Instead, facts are constructed after the events, when they are infused with meaning and become meaningful objects to people. Nichanian (1999, p. 262) therefore observes that "a raw fact and a real fact are two different things". Or, as Finkielkraut (1998, p. xxxiii) explained, "in the world in which live, facts are not stubborn; facts are precarious, docile, malleable." This constructionist framework has resulted in a relativism that provides deniers with a scientific foundational base for their denial and as a result "disingenuous denials now look respectable, even intellectually dignified" (Cohen, 2001, p. 285). The pervasive idea that there is another side to the story has resulted in a situation whereby added latitude is given to ideas that once would be dismissed as mere fabrications (Lipstadt, 1993, pp. 208–209). Cohen (1993, p. 112; 2001, p. 286) concluded that "these confusing times" force us to think about "the role of the intellectual" in all of this because post-modern theory is potentially destructive due to the fact that it basically "denies any way of knowing what has really happened." The question is however, as Housepain Dobkin (1987) wonders, whether there are really two sides to everything – including genocide?

The above remarks, especially those concerning the constructivist approach in which there is only reality where there is meaning, also raise serious questions concerning the study at hand, because with its constructivist cultural criminological and discourse theoretical underpinnings, it might actually provide for some of the most sophisticated denial. Does it turn out to be a criminological nightmare?

7.5. A CRIMINOLOGICAL NIGHTMARE?

7.5.1. Destruction or deconstruction?

The issues discussed above raise questions concerning the cultural criminological and discourse theoretical approaches underlying this research, which are also based on the constructionist framework. Cultural criminology has its roots in the broader symbolic interactionist perspective, which holds that truth and reality are under continuous construction through a process of symbolic negotiation (Ferrell et al., 2008, p. 5). Discourse theory, like most post-structuralist discourse and language theories, holds that knowledge is contingent and that the world is discursively constructed and therefore its character is not pre-given (Jørgensen & Philips, 2002, p. 5). For cultural criminologists, to engage with this framework is a means to "offer a radical critique of authorities' truth claims" about criminal justice and it enables them to address the "reifications through which progressive alternatives are made unimaginable" (Ferrell et al., 2008, p. 20). Moreover, they hope that cultural criminology can operate as "counter-discourse" on criminal justice that shorts out the "circuitry of official meaning" (Ferrell et al., 2008, p. 20). Discourse theorists question the "taken for granted" in order to reveal that truth and reality are the outcome of political discursive struggles and therefore there is no objective truth (Jørgensen & Philips, 2002, p. 5). For discourse theorists, the main aim of their analysis is not to figure out whether discursive constructions are true or false or which representation most accurately represents reality. Instead, the "regimes of truth" that determine whether something is true or false are the focus of study (Jørgensen & Philips, 2002, p. 14 and 21). In the context of what has been discussed before, phrases, such as "radical critique of truth claims" and "counter-discourse", "questioning the taken for granted" raise suspicion. Do cultural criminology and discourse theory maybe provide for another framework of sophisticated denial because there is the risk of slipping into unbridled relativism?

As pointed out earlier in Chapter 3, Section 3.4., cultural criminologists critically engage with the flow of meaning in order to come to a better understanding of what the reality of crime is and by whom it is determined (Ferrell et al., 2008, p. 21). But this question also forces criminologists to look at their own criminological endeavours and how they shape the reality of crime: "If [they] claim the right to critically examine the cultural worlds of those [they] study, shouldn't [they] be willing to examine [their] own cultural world as well?" (Ferrell et al., 2008, p. 168) Cultural criminology thus demands critical reflection from the researcher that addresses the implications of the insights yielded by the research for their own scholarly enterprise. They are also stakeholders in the process of reality construction. Thus, critical self-reflection is essential to cultural criminological research. It furthermore has to be noted that cultural criminology is not an objective criminology; instead it is morally and politically engaging. It aims to contribute to a more just world and, as a result, it is critical of injustice (Ferrell et al., 2008, p. 13). This insight has implications for how to engage in criminological research. For instance, in their criminological struggle against injustice, cultural criminologists have often embraced those marginalised groups who have been the victims of abuses of power. Cultural criminology's self-reflexive character and critical political agenda, which focuses on furthering social justice and helping to create a better and more just world, prevents it from slipping into unbridled nihilism. With regard to discourse theory, the discussion in Chapter 4, Section 4.3.1. is relevant, in which it is explained that discourse theory does not dispute the existence of an objective reality or world. Instead, discourse theory holds that it is only accessible through language. Thus, discourse theory also does not promote an unbridled relativism. It is important to notice that, in this particular research, discourse theoretical analysis is combined with a cultural criminological approach, which is not simply guided by the rules of science, which preach neutrality and objectivity. The dangers discussed in Section 7.3.1. are acknowledged and cultural criminology refuses to be Leviathan's faithful servant. It acknowledges that criminological endeavours are inherently political and the politics of cultural criminology involve critical engagement with the flow of meaning that constructs the reality of crime "in the hope of turning this fluidity towards social justice" (Ferrell et al., 2008, p. 13 and 14). To give in to a relativism and nihilism that allows for genocide denial to flourish would be contradictory to that which cultural criminology according to its political agenda attempts to achieve. Moreover, because of its agenda, cultural criminology is the opposite of nihilistic. It is hopeful as it does not take crime as a given; people are not absolutely predetermined criminal objects, they are subjects, who create and recreate the world they live in and in that world things can change ... for the better. Ironically, the non-relativist positivist criminological approaches often present a grim nihilistic reality of human beings and the world they live in. It is exactly this criminology that is based on positivism and absolutism that turns human subjects into controllable objects.

The discussion in the previous Section, focused on the downsides of constructionist approaches and such critique should be taken seriously. However, the authors who criticised constructionism fail to mention that this same approach also allows for a deconstruction of reality that enables scholars to reveal how, for instance, the less powerful in society have been ignored or oppressed. This ability to deconstruct has also driven the analysis of genocide denialism in this study and it allowed me to demystify how denial discourses are constructed and to clarify the role they play in the process of genocide. The combination of cultural criminology and discourse theory thus results in a framework that allows one to deconstruct, not to destruct.[116]

116 Smith (2014, p. 102) raises the questions whether research that analysis and demystifies the strategies, methods and techniques of denial actually could also inform perpetrators and their collaborators on how to deny the crimes they are involved in or are somehow supportive of.

7.5.2. Resistance: counter discourse and taking sides

Earlier it was mentioned that traditional criminology has neglected the study of gross human rights violations. Despite the fact that cultural criminology is often sensitive to phenomena that are neglected in traditional criminology, the same can be said for cultural criminology. If cultural criminologists want to contribute to the supranational criminological enterprise, critical reflection is important, because such engagement can also have implications. (See Chapter 7, Section 3.2. and Chapter 1, Section 5.) The case of Herman & Peterson that was discussed in Chapter 5 is insightful in this regard. Although Herman & Peterson are certainly not cultural criminologists, their work is interesting in this particular context, because certain aspects of their resistance against the politics of genocide show similarities with how cultural criminologists often attempt to resist injustice as they often position themselves strongly and thereby end up taking sides.

Cultural criminologists have an ambivalent relationship to resistance. On the one hand, they are critical of resistance, because in contemporary society resistance is turned into a popular commodity. They however also acknowledge that reality is a meaningful construction that can never be fully fixed and therefore resistance will always be possible: "the exhaustion of meaning is never complete, the illicit subversion never quite conquered" (Ferrell et al., 2008, p. 19 and 20). Cultural criminologists hope that their "counter-discourse" can serve as a "radical critique" of the "truth claims" that authorities make and that it breaks down structures that obscure alternatives for achieving social justice (Ferrell et al., 2008: 20). The struggle for progressive transformation and social injustice that cultural criminologists engage in can result in taking sides in an attempt to empower those who are marginalised and oppressed.[117, 118] Cultural criminology has been criticised for this partisan stance and

---

117 In his article *Whose side are we on?* Becker (1967, p. 239) addresses the question whether we should be neutral and engage in "technically correct and value free" research or whether research should "express a deep commitment to a value position". According to Becker (1967, p. 239), this dilemma actually does not exist because it is impossible to conduct research that is not influenced by personal and political sympathies. Becker (1967, p. 239) concludes "that the question is not whether we should take sides, since we inevitably will, but rather whose side are we on." Becker (1967, p. 244) furthermore argues that, especially in political situations, "[w]e usually take the side of the underdog". Taking sides is however generally seen as a serious flaw, as the research provides a one-sided account in which our sympathy has distorted the research rendering it invalid and scientifically useless (Becker, 1967, p. 239). Becker argues that the problem with taking sides is not so much the danger that people will hide certain damaging findings out of sympathy for those they have sided with. Or they might only publish the findings that support their beliefs and sympathies. But there is a more likely meaning of the bias charge according to Becker (1967, p. 240); due to our sympathy for certain marginalised or deviant groups, we run the risk of whitewashing their behaviour, while at the same time condemning those others who denounce the groups for whom we have sympathy. Becker does note that, although we cannot avoid taking sides, this however does not mean that we should indulge in bias – that we should take sides. Instead we should make sure that our research meets the standards of good scientific work so that our sympathies do not make our work invalid (Becker, 1967, p. 246 and 247). Moreover, Becker (1967, p. 247) notes that we should make clear what the limitations of our research are and mark the boundaries beyond which our findings cannot safely be applied. This should however not include the conventional disclaimer. It should convey the vantage point taken and its implications.

118 See for a similar argument in the context of the criminological study of genocide Hagan & Rymond-Richmond (2009a, p. 509) who argue: "Howard Becker (1967) long ago asked us to consider seriously

it has been argued that it romanticises crime and criminals; it paints portraits that are too sympathetic, glorifies their behaviour, praises their resistance and minimises the harm done to society (Ferrell et al., 2008, p. 21). Interestingly, this critique also raises the questions that are crucial for cultural criminology, what the reality of crime is and by whom it is determined. On what reality do those who vent this criticism rely? What is their baseline? Official statistics and media representations also turn criminality into fiction. These representations are also romanticised (Ferrell et al., 2008, p. 21). Cultural criminologists therefore conclude that:

> When critics chide cultural criminologists for romanticizing crime and resistance, then, they risk reproducing by default the manufactured misunderstandings that should in fact be the object of criminology's gaze. [...] [C]riminal acts are never quite so obviously little or large, never inherently consequential or important; they're made to be what they are, invested with meaning and consequence, by perpetrators, victims, lawyers, news reporters, and judges, all operating amidst existing arrangements of power. [...] The key isn't to accept criminal acts for what they are, but to interrogate them what they become. (Ferrell et al., 2008, p. 22)

Resistance and partisanship appear to be part and parcel of cultural criminology and, although this approach is inspired by noble causes, the case of Herman & Peterson's work on Rwanda illustrates that one has to be careful when taking such a stance, especially when it comes to genocide.

In the context of genocide, one needs to be cautious in propagating a counter discourse, because such counter discourses can empower discourses that deny the genocide. To demystify the politics of genocide, Herman & Peterson have propagated a counter discourse that attempts to short circuit the official meaning of the genocide against the Tutsi. That way they create space for an alternative reality construction, which aims to signify the politics of genocide in the case of Rwanda. Despite the noble cause, their counter discourse recycles many elements of the official denial discourse. Denial is an intrinsic part of the genocidal process and therefore the fight against genocide would require that the dominant discourse concerning the genocide against the Tutsi is supported. In that case, resistance against genocide does not require a counter discourse.[119]

Herman & Peterson's noble aim to address and confront the politics of genocide takes the shape of a critical mission against the US and its allies. In the case of Rwanda, the role of the US and its allies was certainly questionable, because they

the question of 'Whose Side Are We On?' He recognized that we have an obligation as social scientists to maintain our efforts at objectivity, but he encouraged acknowledging our own political positions as a means of doing so while also fulfilling our responsibilities as citizens. There is a place for an activist criminology alongside similar disciplinary commitments to action anthropology and public sociology. This includes the use of terms such as 'genocide' that are intended to highlight elemental processes of a deeply political as well as destructive nature."

119 This does not mean that critical discussion would no longer be possible. It is vital that critical elements of genocide, such as the genocide against the Tutsi, are discussed and explained. This acknowledges the complexity of genocidal events which makes them harder to deny.

failed to intervene in a constructive way, although they were aware of the genocide against the Tutsi. However, by critiquing the abovementioned parties, Herman & Peterson neglect the problematic roles played by other parties in the conflict. They, for instance, do not talk about the questionable role of France. Instead of critiquing the US and its Allies, Herman & Peterson should have critically analysed how the politics of genocide operated in the context of the genocide against the Tutsi in Rwanda and such an approach requires an analysis of how all parties involved contributed to the problem. By focussing on the US and its allies, Herman & Peterson have thus effectively taken sides, which turns their work into *a* politics of genocide instead of an analysis of *the* politics of genocide.

In the case of genocide, it is tempting to take sides, because the absolute character of the crime has created a clearly demarcated victim and perpetrator. Furthermore, the extreme level of violence inflicted upon the victim and the immensely deep suffering caused can trigger a strong concern for the interests of the victims. However, in the context of this study it is clear that all parties involved – perpetrators, victims and bystanders – each in their own specific way could contribute to the denial dynamic on which genocide thrives. Critically addressing genocide is not "simply" about choosing the side of the oppressed (victim) and resisting the oppressor (perpetrator), because this would, for instance, overlook the role of an important party: the bystander. The problem is that in the discussion on "taking sides," the bystanders are often left out of the equation. Research on conflict and atrocity has, however, shown that bystanders play a crucial role (Grünfeld, 2000, 2008; Grünfeld & Huijboom, 2007; Grünfeld & Vermeulen, 2014). Due to the imbalance in power, the dynamic between victim and perpetrator is not likely to change and only the intervention of the bystanders will change or stop the conflict dynamic. Bystanders can aid the victim and become rescuers, but by doing nothing they facilitate the perpetrator and thereby become collaborators. Denial is an interpersonal phenomenon that relies on the action of others, not only perpetrators and their sympathisers, but also the bystanders and even the victims. Due to the interpersonal character of denial, bystanders come to play an important role, because deniers can only successfully keep up their denial if third parties collude in the process. Thus, it does not suffice to take a side in the conflict. Instead, one needs to adopt a critical stance against genocide and that requires that the behaviour of all parties involved is scrutinised.

The brief discussion aims to illustrate that certain phenomena, such as genocide, possibly require a form of resistance that does not directly correspond with how resistance within cultural criminology is often shaped. An approach that attempts to function as a counter-discourse can have negative effects and strong positioning can obscure the role of other parties in the conflict, including the role of the party that you are siding with. It is important to reflect on one's resistance and one's positioning because, if such critical reflection is lacking, opposition out of a noble cause can end in collaboration in the same genocidal processes that one actually attempts to curb.

7.5.3. A fundamental paradox?

Although above I argued that the cultural criminological and discourse theoretical approaches underlying this study do not lead to an unbridled relativism, the constructionist view of the world underlying these frameworks does present this study with a fundamental paradox given its specific focus on genocide denialism. As Cohen (2001, p. 278) points out, denial comes with an ontological prerequisite, namely a modernist assumption of truth and unity. It only makes sense to talk about denial if there is truth which is unified and single: the truth – instead of a fragmented truth (Cohen, 2001, p. 278). The concept of denial is thus dependent on a clear notion of the truth that one wishes to deny. In the context of genocide, this ontological prerequisite of the truth becomes even more pertinent as Friedlander (1992, p. 3) notes because denial is an intrinsic element of genocide, the obligation to bear witness and record the events is even more compelling: "Such a postulate implies, quite naturally, the imprecise but no less self-evident notion that this record should not be distorted or banalized by grossly inadequate representations." Friedlander (1992, p. 3) concludes that in the context of genocide "some claim to 'truth' appears particularly imperative." However, from the constructionist perspective, underlying cultural criminology and also discourse theory, truth would be a social construction; the outcome of a socio-political process in which multiple truths struggle for hegemony. As a result *the truth* does not exist. Instead, *the truth* is *a truth* that has won the discursive struggle and successfully conquered other truth claims. This has implications in the context of genocide.[120]

The phenomenon of genocide and its denial thus presents this study with a paradox. On the one hand, this study draws on approaches that are based on a constructionist framework that takes a relativist approach to truth and reality, but, on the other hand, this study assumes a modernist assumption to a unitary truth when it comes to the existence of the genocide against the Tutsi. The anti-essentialist underpinnings of the cultural criminological and discourse theoretical approaches are valuable as they enable the deconstruction of denialist discourses revealing the violence and harm involved. They furthermore allow us to confront what escapes or is denied in established historical representations of genocidal events (Friedlander, 1992, p. 20). However, curbing genocide and its denial also requires the acknowledgment that genocide happened. It requires acknowledgement of *this truth*. An absolute truth and reality seem to be required; contending otherwise would be to give in to denial, to the other side of the story. An earlier Section (7.4.2.) of this Chapter already briefly touched upon the danger involved in constructionist approaches, which can lead to an unbridled relativism that questions the possibility of historical objectivity, as there is

[120] In Rwanda there is a saying that "the truth will pass across the fire, but it will never burn". It conveys the idea that the truth is indestructible and will come out no matter what. This notion is however problematic in this context for two reasons. As pointed out above, truth is not simply a given; it is a discursive construction and multiple discourses struggle to define it, which makes it vulnerable. Secondly, in the context of genocide we are faced with a phenomenon that is actually also geared towards its own destruction. In that case, the discursive struggles are fought in order to obscure the true nature of the events.

no unmediated access to facts whose meaning are *a priori* given (Varon, 2005, p. 17). As a result, history is turned into a meaningful, but mythical, representation of reality (Varon, 1997, pp. 83–89). The danger with such an approach is, as Browning notes (1992a, pp. 31–32), that all accounts concerning what happened during a historical event become equally valid. Browning (1992a, pp. 31–32) notes that if this relativism is accepted and followed through, it would also be valid to write the history of a genocide based on the testimony of the perpetrators who claim that something else or nothing happened. From such a perspective, it is actually questionable whether they were the perpetrators in the first place.

Denial can thrive on these relativist assumptions and it is therefore required that the status of relativism in the approach taken in this research is clarified. In the context of historical science, the status of relativism has led to considerable debate. The discussion that is probably best known is the one between historians White and Ginzburg who both have opposing ideas on the nature of historical truth. In his work White (1989, p. 75) has propagated a far-reaching relativism claiming that scholars must "face the fact that when it comes to apprehending the historical record, there are no grounds to be found in the historical record itself for preferring one way of construing its meaning over another." White (1989, p. 75) concludes that:

> The human and social sciences, insofar as they are based on or presuppose a specific conception of historical reality, are as blind to the sublimity of the historical process and to the visionary politics it authorizes as is the disciplined historical consciousness that informs their investigative procedures.

For White, writing history is about the politics of interpretation. Interestingly, in his discussion, White does point out that the claim that "any historical object can sustain a number of equally plausible description or narratives of its processes" promotes a relativism that permits manipulation and denial. White notes that those who have such a stance are confronted with questions, whether the nature and occurrence of a genocidal event is a matter of opinion or whether any account of such an event is as valid as any other account. Instead of being sensitive to the issues at stake, White (1989, p. 76) concludes that "in such questions we come to the bottom line of the politics of interpretation." Thus, according to White, because of indeterminacy there is no objective way of establishing truth. Although over time White's relativism has become less radical, Ginzburg is nonetheless critical of White's approach.[121] He reflects on White's stance in an article titled *Just one witness* and he elaborates some of the far-reaching implications of White's approach, the most fundamental one being that a denialist narrative concerning a genocidal event could be true, according to White, if it is widely believed and politically effective. Thus Ginzburg (1992, p. 93) concludes that "if Faurisson's narrative were ever to prove *effective*, it would be regarded by White as true as well." In contrast to White, Ginzburg argues that even the voice of one single witness can give us access to historical reality.[122]

121 See for instance White (1992).

122 For an elaborate analysis of the discussion between White and Ginzburg see: Varon (1997).

Positioning – Relativism or realism?

So where do I stand in this? Somewhere between a post-modern historical relativism and modern historical realism. Somewhere between White and Ginzburg. I found Vidal Naquet and Browning's observations in this particular context insightful. Naquet, to which Ginzburg refers in his critique of White's post-modern approach to history and who reflected extensively on the Faurisson affair, acknowledges that everything has to go through an ongoing discourse, but he adds that "beyond this or before this, there was something irreducible which, for better or for worse, I would still call reality. Without this reality, how could we make a difference between fiction and history?" (Vidal Naquet quoted in Ginzburg, 1992, p. 86).[123] I do think that the notion that genocide is a real event and not a mere abstraction also makes perfect sense from the earlier discussed perspective of discourse theory. Discourse theory presents us with a complex understanding of reality. According to discourse theory an objective reality does exist. It is however socially contextualised and only accessible through language. As to genocide, the material fact of genocide existed long before it was conceptualised by Lemkin. He did not create this reality. Instead, he constructed a theoretical framework that conceptualised it, which basically is a discourse that defines the genocidal event in meaningful terms thereby making it intelligible to us. He presented us with a particular way of understanding the reality of genocide. Thus the fact that this is a discursive construction does not make genocide less real. The problem is however that we can never access the true and universal reality because we are not able to approach it from a position outside discourse and for us its reality always remains a discursive construction (Jørgensen & Philips, 2002, pp. 8–12).[124] Objective reality thus exists, but it is extremely hard to capture in full, because for us it will always be mediated. That reality is the outcome of an interpretative discursive process also explains why genocide denial is such a powerful mechanism. If the reality was objectively given and universally accessible to us, it would be hard to temper with, in fact it would be impossible and denial would be ineffective and easy to unmask as an outright lie.

123 Browning (1992a, p. 25) also notes that his narrative research on Reserve Police Battalion 101 sets the basis for a discussion on the limits and difficulties of narrative constructions of such genocidal events. According to Browning (1992a, p. 29 and 33), it is difficult to make a distinction between self-evident facts and interpretations which meaning is constructed: there are no clear-cut methods to decide this. Browning (1992a, p. 25) nonetheless concludes that the Holocaust is "not an abstraction"; it is "a real event".

124 An objective reality does thus exist, but it is only accessible to us through language and discourse and as such the reality of the event as we know it is a mediated reality: it is representation not a reflection. It is accessed and reflected upon in different ways leading to different truths depending on whether the access is individual, collective and what purpose it means to serve. These elements become clear in the context of the South African Truth and Reconciliation Commission (TRC) which took place in South Africa and which had several purposes, but also aimed at getting to the truth about what happened, which is an important basis for reconciliation. Interestingly, the TRC distinguished four different notions of truth: factual/ forensic truth, which is about factual or scientific evidence, 2 personal/narrative truth, which refers to the individual stories of those involved, 3 social/dialogue truth, which encompasses the truth that is established through discussion and debate, and lastly, healing/restorative truth, which is about what the facts and their meaning within the context of human relationships (Smeulers & Grünfeld, 2011, p. 451). This thus shows that there can be multiple truths.

If reality is mediated, the question arises how to distinguish between valid interpretations and invalid interpretations, between truths and falsehoods, between the real and the unreal. As Browning noted, there is no straightforward method that allows us to make such distinctions. Because universal truth and objective reality are beyond our reach for the reasons explained above, I think the question is not about whether one is able to capture the exact truth concerning the reality of the events. Instead, it turns into a question whether one is able to approach the reality of events as closely as possible. I think that we can only try to represent what happened as truthfully as possible. It is thus not about *the truth*, but about *truthfulness*. Certain claims about genocidal events are more truthful, are more in accord with reality, than others. It is important to understand that the truthfulness of a claim is not necessarily dependent on whether it is empirically correct or not. Some claims or statements can be deemed factually incorrect but still acknowledge and be truthful about the nature of events. Take for instance the following excerpt:

> [A] conference of historians, psychoanalysts, and artists gathered to reflect on the relation of education to the Holocaust, watched the videotaped testimony of the woman in an attempt to better understand the era. A lively debate ensued. The testimony was not accurate, historians claimed. The number of chimneys was misrepresented. Historically, only one chimney was blown up, not all four. Since the memory of the testifying woman turned out to be, in this way, fallible, one could not accept – nor give credence to – her account of the events. It was utterly important to remain accurate, [lest] the revisionists in history discredit everything. A psychoanalyst . . . profoundly disagreed. "The woman was testifying," he insisted, "not to the number of the chimneys blown up, but to something else, more radical, more crucial: the reality of an unimaginable occurrence." One chimney blown up in Auschwitz was as incredible as four. The number mattered less than the fact of the occurrence. The event itself was almost inconceivable. The woman testified to an event that broke the all compelling frame of Auschwitz, where Jewish armed revolts just did not happen, and had no place. She testified to the breakage of a framework. That was historical truth. (Laub, 1992, pp. 59–60)

The point is that in discussions on genocidal events there will always be contradictions, issues and opposing claims as to the details of what exactly happened. The fact that you are incorrect about or disagree on the number of chimneys, the number of victims, etc. does not turn an "invalid" claim into a denialist one. Here the nature of the events is not at stake. Denial is untruthful because it attacks the fundamental nature of the genocidal event, transforming its reality into something else. Denialist discourses are not truthful because, instead of bringing us closer to reality, they lead us further astray concerning what happened. In that sense they are deceptive. From a constructionist perspective, this study is thus inherently biased as certain truth claims are rejected. The term "rejecting" is used deliberately because the term "privileging" as in "privileging one truth over the other" would still give too much credibility to denialist claims.[125] It is therefore that over some questions, such as genocide, "one

[125] Scholars such as Najarian (1997) also warn for this trap: "The historical project of refuting Holocaust denial may not even be useful; one has to beware that one does not authenticate denial by treating it as if it were a serious scholarly approach." When one approaches denialist claims as lies (see for instance

must be biased to be truthful", because "[t]o consider another side is to consider a fiction" (Najarian, 1997). This does not mean that the reality concerning the genocide against the Tutsi is a more complex and sophisticated one than currently presented. Through the negotiation of truth claims concerning the reality of the genocide, we come to a fuller and more complex truth about what happened. There is however no alternative truth or perverted "other side to the story" with regard to what happened. It is possible to have competing claims concerning the number of victims based on different scientific approaches, or a discussion on the methods of victimisation. Such critical discussion is acceptable as it is part of getting closer to the reality of the events. As noted earlier, scientific revisionism is a legitimate part of scholarly work.[126] In this context one could say that certain "truths" can be "privileged" over other "truths" because some bring us closer to the reality of genocide than others. However, if the numbers are, for instance, being (ab)used to turn the tables and to turn victims into perpetrators, we tend to become further removed from reality and in that case it is not about presenting an "alternative truth" but about spreading lies and deception.

7.6. Safeguarding Reality

The question has been raised why reality should be protected, for instance, by enforcing it through the criminalisation of acts that question it; "Is she that vulnerable?" (Raes, 1997, p. 74) In case of genocide, reality is vulnerable because it concerns a phenomenon which is geared towards its own destruction. In addition to the killing of life, it needs to engage in the killing of death in order to reach its ultimate aim of annihilation. This vulnerability requires us to safeguard the reality of genocide, but how?

7.6.1. Criminalisation?

Whether criminalisation is a viable option is controversial. Criminal law is the *ultimum remedium* and it is not designed to solve such complex social problems. Criminalisation often does not address the root of the problem as it mainly focuses on managing the symptoms. Criminalisation also raises issues because it might actually contribute to a breakdown in democratic values due to its limitation of fundamental rights, such as freedom of speech.[127] It could provide deniers a platform

Ternon, 1999b; Ternon, 2013), it also stops being an issue of privileging one truth over the other. The other truth is simply a lie. According to Chretien (2012, p. 65), it is a *dialectique du mensonge* which turns the quest for truth into an intoxicating racist game.

126 As Withuis (2012) notes, academics can take different approaches in their research focusing on different aspects, but this does not mean that historical realities do not exist and that one simply can interpret the history of genocide at one's own discretion.

127 In discussions on the criminalisation of genocide denial it has been argued that it would lead to a situation where freedom of thought is under pressure and one is no longer allowed to have controversial ideas and opinions. To frame the criminalisation of genocide denial in terms of "thought crimes" and all the Orwellian implications that come with it is misleading. Thoughts, ideas, and opinions are not

and it can possibly strengthen them in their views. The question also remains whether criminalisation really prevents genocide denial. It only addresses certain instances of genocide denial, while this study has shown that the phenomenon of genocide denialism is much broader in scope and involves much more problematic behaviour. It is not desirable to criminalise all these behaviours. Taking into account such criticism, one could nonetheless argue that the main function of the criminalisation of genocide denial is that it is a symbolic measure which acknowledges genocides and makes clear that denial of such events is not accepted in society. It gives a signal of moral condemnation that is strengthened by punitive force. From a discourse theoretical perspective, criminalisation for symbolic reasons makes sense as it basically involves a hegemonic intervention which attempts to permanently fix the meaning of events. The problem is however, that such powerful fixations also cannot preclude being challenged by alternative discursive constructions. Another issue is how the legislation is drafted and enforced, because much legislation only focuses on the perlocutionary effects of genocide denial and not its illocutionary power. It is criminalised because it can facilitate new violence and genocide denial is not criminalised because it can constitute violence in itself. Furthermore, not all countries criminalize genocide denial or they do criminalise genocide denial but in different ways. As discussed, legislation tends to focus on the denial of certain genocides, such as the Holocaust, while the denial of other genocides is being denied. Moreover, genocide denial is not limited to state boundaries. On the contrary, with the rise of the internet it seems to have no boundaries. How do you curb such a globalised phenomenon? Enforcement thus appears to be problematic for various reasons.

When it comes to criminalisation, there is another issue that is worth mentioning. Criminalisation of denial can also lead to considerable net widening when denial of crimes other than genocide are being criminalised. For instance, in 2014 the Latvian parliament approved the amendments to a law that proposes criminal liability for glorifying, denying, white-washing or doubting the Soviet and Nazi occupation (Russian Legal Information Agency, 2014). People may also be prosecuted for holocaust denial and the denial of crimes against humanity. In 2008 the Council of the European Union adopted the Council Framework Decision 2008/913/JHA on combating certain forms and expressions of racism and xenophobia by means of criminal law. The Decision stipulates that each Member State shall take the measures necessary to ensure that the following intentional conduct is punishable: publicly condoning, denying or grossly trivialising crimes of genocide, crimes against humanity and war crimes as defined in the Statute of the International Criminal Court or the Charter of the International Military Tribunal appended to the London Agreement of 8 August 1945. The Decision thus not only criminalises genocide denial but also denial of crimes against humanity and war crimes. Although I am not in favour of criminalisation for the reasons discussed earlier, a valid rationale for the criminalisation of genocide denial could be the fact that such denial constitutes

criminalised here, but presenting them in public is. Thoughts are thus not criminalised but violent speech acts of genocide denial are.

an essential element of the perpetration of the crime of genocide. The problem is, however, that denial does not constitute a crucial element of the perpetration of war crimes and crimes against humanity and, because of this, a major rationale for the criminalisation of denial speech for other international crimes is lacking. This is not to say that these crimes are not denied, because they often are. The point is, however, that denial is not required to fulfil the process of perpetration of these crimes. However, like with genocide, the denial of these other international crimes is not criminalised because of the violent illocutionary nature of the denial; their denial is mainly criminalised because of its negative perlocutionary effects (inciting intolerance, hatred, violence, etc.).

7.6.2. Toleration?

If criminalisation is not a suitable strategy to safeguard the reality of genocide, what other strategies remain? Toleration is also not a viable option. By doing nothing and allowing the denial to flourish, we would aid the *génocidaires*. It would turn us into collaborators or accomplices and not simply bystanders as explained in Chapter 3, Section 3.3.1. It has been argued that the state should tolerate such speech and let the "free market place of ideas" deal with it. It is first of all questionable whether the "market place" is really that free. In the discussion on speech act theory and the violence of language in Chapter 5, Section 5.6.2., it was noticed that speech situations are often not free and open. Furthermore, if this means entering a debate, then we have a problem, as Finkielkraut (1998, p. 1) points out, because: "[t]o denounce a lie is to nourish it with the energy one devotes to it, and the slightest comment that it inspires one to make, no matter what is pertinence, is an offering for which it can be grateful." Also Lipstadt (1993, p. viii) refuses to legitimise genocide denial by entering "a debate that is not debate". The problem is that the ideas of deniers can also not simply be tolerated because, due to their sophistication and aggressive lobbying, they do have a negative impact (Abicht, 1997, p. 53). For instance, denialist publications end up in high school or university libraries and they stand next to the other books as another version concerning the truth of what happened. As a result, historical truth is put under pressure (Raes, 1997, p. 66 and 67). I experienced this myself when the high school that I attended in the Netherlands was provided with a copy of the *Rudolf Report*, a so-called "Expert report on chemical and technical aspects of the 'gas chambers' of Auschwitz." In this report, German trained chemist Rudolf tries to show "scientifically" that no Jews had been gassed in Auschwitz. Also, books that spawn or recycle the official denial narrative concerning the Genocide against the Tutsi, such as Herman & Peterson's book, are available to students in libraries. Convinced by the idea that simply ignoring them is not an option, Lipstadt (1993, p. 217) lets the deniers' factual claims go unanswered and instead aims at removing their cloak of respectability by unmasking their efforts for what they really are. She analyses how genocide deniers engage in denial, thereby making their method the subject of study while leaving out "the other side of the story" (Lipstadt, 1993, p. 2 and 28). Because you cannot discuss *with* them, the debate should be mostly *about* them and their work and how memory is pushed "down the hole" (Van Galen Last,

1998). Also Tatz (2003, p. 126) concludes that exposing who denies and how, and revealing what they really stand for is much more effective than trying to counter them in a debate or to re-educate their audiences on the historical facts.

7.6.3. Unmasking

The strategy of unmasking, which is basically about demystifying what genocide deniers do with their words, seems promising as it circumvents many of the dilemmas involved in criminalisation and toleration. One point of serious critique is however that unmasking can also turn into an *ad hominem* attack or it can be perceived as such. This is also an important issue in the context of this study. Some are critical of this approach; Kahn (2004, p. 11), for instance, argues that the attacks against the person of the denier do not address whether the debated argument is correct or not. Also *ad hominem* attacks are unfair, as fairness requires hearing from both sides. Furthermore, those who are attacked *ad hominem* are often seen as victims. To avoid these issues, the approach of unmasking should therefore focus on the acts and not the individual actors, although their professional roles can be significant as the analysis throughout previous Chapters revealed (it can namely create a *Garantstellung*). The point is that the analysis should not be a witch hunt in which individual human beings are being stigmatised; it is not the person but the act that is problematic. Research should focus on the techniques, methods and strategies used by deniers to engage in their denial. By uncovering how deniers engage in their denial, it is possible to reveal the deceitful qualities of their claims. As noted, such an approach could still be perceived as an *ad hominem* attack. These perlocutionary effects are however hard to prevent. The second issue Kahn raises concerning "fairness" is sensitive in this context. It is exactly the argument of "fairness", the idea that there is "another side to the story" that must also be heard, that deniers use to create a legitimate space for their ideas. In that sense, dealing with denial is unfair or, as was noticed in an earlier Section, in this case one has to be biased in order to be truthful. The third issue Kahn mentions is a problem that could indeed complicate the strategy of unmasking; *ad hominem* attacks allow deniers to present themselves as victims and this can create sympathy for those who, because of their questionable agenda, do not deserve it. Such an attack places the denier in a position of the underdog, which can possibly arouse sentiment among the public. This sympathy might even give them more leverage. Thus, although the strategy of unmasking deals with many of the issues that one would have when one enters the debate, criminalises or tolerate genocide denial, it is not the panacea. Also unmasking, especially when it turns into or is perceived as an *ad hominem* attack, has its drawbacks.

7.6.4. Strategic issues

There are two additional issues that further complicate the abovementioned strategies of criminalisation and unmasking. Firstly, what adds to the complexity is that, because of its interpersonal nature, denial also thrives on the actions of other actors. You can try to curb primary and secondary genocide denial by criminalising and/or unmasking it, but what about all those other actions that amount to genocide denial in effect. The approaches of unmasking and criminalisation do not take this interpersonal aspect of denial into account. Those who promote these approaches focus on hard-core genocide denial and neglect the broader web of denial on which such hard-core denial relies. Secondly, what complicates the question on how to deal with genocide denial is that denial is not abnormal and has social foundations. As discussed in Chapter 2, Section 2.6., denial is a normal coping mechanism that allows people and communities to deal with life's burdens. That we have the capacity to deal with threatening realities allows us to live healthy lives and it prevents us from psychologically and socially disintegrating. Furthermore, the way we focus our attention and how we notice and ignore things is learned through social interaction. We learn the social conventions that help us to deal with threatening realities. We, for instance, learn how to make justifications and excuses that allow us to control how situations and events are defined and subsequently played out. It is one of the first things that you learn as a child when you grow up. Moreover, when individuals grow up they not only learn how to deny, they are also socialised with regard to the substance of denial: what realities should be avoided, what we are not supposed to acknowledge. Often denial of certain realities is required in order to have efficient and fluid social interactions. Also academic scholars are professionally socialised in particular traditions of paying attention, which affect how and what they notice, as the previous Sections revealed. In many ways denial is thus socio-culturally embedded. This socio-cultural embeddedness of denial makes it difficult to actually have or create the conditions under which troubling recognitions are not denied but acknowledged. Thus, whether genocide denial is criminalized or unmasked, all these strategies of dealing with the issue seem to be problematic to a certain degree as the above analysis illustrates; apparently there is no clear cut solution to the problem.

7.7. Concluding remarks

The above insights concerning the problems related to criminalisation and unmasking lead me to conclude that a constructive approach to dealing with genocide denialism should primarily focus on education and research.[128] This is also in line with the quote by Nichanian that can be found at the beginning of this study and which states that "the essence of genocide is denegation". If the essence of genocide is denial, this means that a constructive approach to dealing with genocide should

128 I do not mean to say that dealing with denial is limited to this. As Willems (2014) explains with regard to the denial of child abuse, overcoming denial is a process involving various stages. In this process, awareness raising and building knowledge on the phenomenon of denial and what is being denied are crucial elements. This process of overcoming denial also involves: the alignment of different actors who put the problem on their agenda, followed by more activism on behalf of the cause, the raising of alternatives (solutions), the politisation as structural human rights violations (human, social and economic costs), eventually alternatives appear on political agendas and in programmes of political parties, followed by the implementation of policies and legislation. Willems basically describes a process of acknowledgement which triggers constructive action that remedies the denial.

focus on acknowledgment. I think education and research can contribute to such acknowledgment.

Education should first of all provide the public with historical information about genocides. Above, it was noted that unmasking genocide denial might be more effective than to (re)-educate audiences on the historical facts, but this does not mean that such education is not important. Unmasking cannot substitute such historical knowledge. People should be knowledgeable on historical events of genocide, because not knowing is already problematic due to the fact that genocide also thrives on ignorance. Such education should furthermore be inclusive in the sense that it not only deals with cases that have directly impacted the particular society that we reside in.[129] Genocide is a threat to humanity and therefore genocides perpetrated in other places against other peoples should be included in the education: there should be no discrimination between genocides. Such education on *histories of genocide* should also be combined with education on *theories of genocide* that allow people to make sense of such complex phenomena.

The call for education seems cliché but the reality is that, in raising awareness on genocide, the element of denialism is often neglected. I noticed that, when visiting exhibitions, much attention is paid to the process of genocide. The history of genocide is elaborated, but the last stage of denial remains virtually always unaddressed. The Kigali Memorial Centre that houses the main exhibition on the genocide against the Tutsi does not address the problem of the denial of the genocide. Only in the comparative section where it deals with the Holocaust, the Armenian genocide and genocide in former Yugoslavia it briefly mentions the denial of these genocides. To fight genocide, it is, however, not enough to acknowledge the histories of these and other genocides. It is crucial that such knowledge is complemented with an acknowledgment of the denialism on which genocides thrive. In conveying this, unmasking does play an important role. The restrictions of such an approach are however that the knowledge is often limited to specific cases and it tends to focus on hard-core denials while neglecting the broader denial dynamics illustrated in this study. Because denial is essential to the perpetration of genocide, I suggest that awareness should be raised not only about the facts and the cases but also on their denial. Raising such awareness should not only focus on genocide denial spawned by virulent ideologues. Denial is a broad multifaceted phenomenon and it is important that people start to become aware of the fact that much more behaviour is problematic because it somehow facilitates *the killing of death*. Education should thus pay attention to genocide denialism more broadly, instead of limiting the attention to genocide denial. People should not only be educated on the brazen denials of racist bigots, they should also be made aware of what joking or the use of imprecise vocabulary does.

Such education can only be provided for if it is backed up by substantial scholarly research on genocide and its denialism. I therefore also urge other scholars to take

[129] For an overview of so called "hidden" or "forgotten" genocides see the contributions by Hinton et al. (2014) and Lemarchand (2011).

up the framework developed throughout this study and apply it to other cases of genocide, to criticise it constructively and elaborate it. It remains a work in progress. It is, furthermore, important that the insights from research are carried beyond the confines of the ivory towers in which academics often reside. Knowledge should not only sit on the shelves of scholars and nor should its use be limited to the education of students at universities. The knowledge should also be made available to the broader public in various ways and the format should be tailored to the needs of the specific audience. Here one could think of panels or posters that can "travel" around and be added to exhibitions on genocide in order to raise awareness and one could combine this with lectures on the issue of genocide denialism.

Due to the problems related to criminalisation and unmasking, I came to conclude that a constructive approach to dealing with genocide denialism should primarily focus on education and research. However, what furthermore informed my conclusion was the following. Throughout this study, it became clear to me that the knowledge I had gained allowed me to break with existing paradigms on the role denial plays in the process of genocide and it enabled me to look at things differently. This not only allowed me to reflect critically upon the actions of others, more importantly, it also made me aware of the sometimes questionable nature of my own actions. Being knowledgeable on the role denial plays in the process of genocide not only makes people less vulnerable to attempts to deny genocide, in addition, such an understanding also makes people more aware of the problematic nature of their own actions. Often the denialist consequences of actions are unintended and critical knowledge on genocide denialism allows actors to address and change their behaviour once they become aware of its possible negative impact. I therefore think that a critical awareness of genocide denialism can not only make people more able bodied against genocide denialism, it can also make it less likely that they engage in actions that somehow facilitate the denial dynamic on which genocide thrives.

Chronological overview of significant interviews, consultations and events

2008

- Klaas de Jonge, Research Coordinator Penal Reform International Rwanda (PRI), Amsterdam, The Netherlands, 8-10-2008
- George Weiss, Director, La Benevolencija, Amsterdam, The Netherlands, 9-10-2008
- Marco de Swart, Consultant and Civic Education Advisor, The Netherlands (telephone), 17-10-2008
- Gisoze Genocide Memorial Centre, Kigali, Rwanda, 29-10-2008
- Ntarama Church, Genocide Memorial, Bugasera, Rwanda, 1-11-2008
- Leslie Haskell, Researcher, Africa Division, Human Rights Watch, Kigali, Rwanda, 3-11-2008
- Juvénal Sebishwi, Director, Communauté des Potiers du Rwanda (Coporwa), Kigali, Rwanda, 3-11-2008
- Anonymous, Researcher, Kigali, Rwanda, 3-11-2008
- Johan Blancquaert, Head of Finance and Administration, Radio La Benevolencija, Kigali Rwanda, 4-11-2008
- Anonymous, Teacher, Kigali, Rwanda, 4, 11, 18, 25-11-2008
- Ariane Inkesha, Communications Officer, Institute of Research and Dialogue for Peace, Kigali, Rwanda, 5-11-2008
- Andrew Karima, Programme Officer, Safer Rwanda, Kigali, Rwanda, 06-11-2008
- Christine Namuwonge Muhongerwa, Program Co-ordinator, Safer Rwanda, Kigali, Rwanda, 06-11-2008
- Gacaca monitoring Nyakabanda sector, Kigali, Rwanda, 7, 16, 23, 30-11-2008
- Anonymous, Prisoner, Kigali Central Prison, Kigali, Rwanda, 8-11-2008
- Anonymous, Prisoner, Kigali Central Prison, Kigali, Rwanda, 8-11-2008
- Attended Rwandan wedding ceremony, Kigali, Rwanda, 8-11-2008
- Anonymous, Socio-therapist, Kigali, Rwanda, 9-11-2008
- Adriaan Verwijs, Pastor, Anglican Church, Kigali, Rwanda, 10-11-2008
- Arrest Rosa Kabuye leads to orchestrated mass protests, Kigali, Rwanda, 10/19-11-2008
- Guma Alexandre, Officer, Prison Fellowship Rwanda, Kigali, Rwanda, 10 and 18-11-2008
- Assumpta Umurungi, Executive Secretary, Association des Veuves du Génocide Agahozo (Avega), Kigali Rwanda, 11-11-2008
- Jean Gakwandi, Founder and Director, Solace Ministries, Kigali, Rwanda, 11-11-2008

- Roelof Haveman, Vice Rector in charge of Academic Affairs and Research, Institute of Legal Practice and Development (ILDP), Kigali, Rwanda, 11-11-2008
- Gilbert Mwenedata, Conflict Advisor USAID/Rwanda, Kigali, Rwanda, 12-11-2008
- Francois Sobo, Coordinator of Research and Gacaca Monitoring, Penal Reform International (PRI), Kigali, Rwanda, 12-11-2008
- Stefan Gilbert, Parliamentary Development Project Coordinator, Political Governance Program, IDASA, Kigali, Rwanda, 12-11-2008
- Veronique Geoffroy, Attaché, Délégation de la Commission Européenne en République du Rwanda, Kigali, Rwanda, 13-11-2008
- Jean de Dieu Kyiranga, Communications Officer/Program Associate, United Nations Development Program Rwanda (UNDP), Kigali, Rwanda, 13-11-2008
- Julienne Uwamariya, Portfolio Coordinator, Netherlands Development Organisation SNV, Kigali, Rwanda, 13-11-2008
- Jeanne Mukamusoni, Responsible de Départment Psycho-Médical, Association des Veuves du Génocide Agahozo (Avega), Kigali Rwanda, 14-11-2008
- Agéé Shyaka Mugabe, Center of Conflict Resolution (CCM), National University of Rwanda, Kigali, Rwanda, 15-11-2008
- Moctar Al Housseinou, Program Coordinator, Reseau Citoyen Network Justice and Democracy (RCN), Kigali, Rwanda, 17-11-2008
- École Technique Officielle (ETO), Site of Memory, Kicukiro, Rwanda, 18-11-2008
- Nyamata Church, Genocide Memorial, Bugasera, Rwanda, 20-11-2008
- Edward Kalisa, Technical Services Director, World Vision Rwanda, Kigali, Rwanda, 20-11-2008
- Youth summit, Amohoro Stadium, Kigali, Rwanda, 20-11-2008
- Consolate Bigirimana, Center of Conflict Resolution (CCM), National University of Rwanda, Butare, Rwanda, 21-11-2008
- Ethnographic Museum, Butare, Rwanda, 21-11-2008
- King's Palace Museum, Nyanza, Rwanda, 21-11-2008
- Hilde Baele, author/creative writer, Kigali, Rwanda, 20-11-2008
- Anonymous, Prisoner, Kigali Central Prison, Kigali, Rwanda, 24-11-2008
- Anonymous, Prisoner, Kigali Central Prison, Kigali, Rwanda, 24-11-2008
- Anonymous, Prisoner, Kigali Central Prison, Kigali, Rwanda, 24-11-2008
- Anonymous, Prisoner, Kigali Central Prison, Kigali, Rwanda, 24-11-2008
- Epimack Kwoko, Coordinateur Régional, Ligue des Droits de la Personne dans la région des Grand Lacs (LDGL), Kigali Rwanda, 24-11-2008
- Anonymous, Prisoner, Kigali Central Prison, Kigali, Rwanda, 26-11-2008
- Anonymous, Prisoner, Kigali Central Prison, Kigali, Rwanda, 26-11-2008
- Anonymous, Prisoner, Kigali Central Prison, Kigali, Rwanda, 26-11-2008
- Rudi Drigo, Wood Energy Planning and Policy Development, Food and Agriculture Organization of the United Nations (FAO), Kigali, Rwanda, 29-11-2008
- Anonymous, Prisoner, Kigali Central Prison, Kigali, Rwanda, 01-12-2008
- Anonymous, Prisoner, Kigali Central Prison, Kigali, Rwanda, 01-12-2008
- Simon Ndimubanzi, Human rights lawyer, SYNDIC, Kigali, Rwanda, 3-1-2008

- Fatuma Ndangiza, Executive Secretary, National Unity and Reconciliation Commission (NURC), Kigali, Rwanda, 4-12-2008
- Zarir Merat, Head of Mission, Avocats Sans Frontières (ASF), Kigali, Rwanda, 8-12-2008

2009

- Anonymous, PhD researcher, Maastricht, The Netherlands, 08-01-2009
- Alison Des Forges, Antwerp, Belgium, 27-01-2009
- Conference, Reconstructing Rwanda: Fifteen Years after Genocide A Tribute to Alison Des Forges, Centre for International Human Rights (Institute of Commonwealth Studies), School of Advanced Study, University of London, London, England, 20-3-2009
- Anonymous, Ghent, Belgium, 26-3-2009
- Consultation Meeting Rwanda, Dutch Ministry of Foreign Affairs, The Hague, The Netherlands, 27-5-2009
- Conference, The ICTR, Law and International Politics: A Defence Perspective, International Institute of Social Studies, Erasmus University, The Hague, The Netherlands, 14/16-11-2009

2011

- 17th Commemoration of the Genocide Against the Tutsi, Tilburg University, Tilburg, The Netherlands, 5-4-2011
- 17th Commemoration of the Genocide Against the Tutsi, Maastricht School of Management, Maastricht, The Netherlands, 12-4-2011
- Immaculée Uwanyiligira, Ambassador of the Republic Rwanda to the Netherlands and Permanent Representative to the OPCW, Maastricht, The Netherlands, 12-4-2011
- Michael Karnavas, Defence Council ICTR and ICTY, The Hague, The Netherlands, 22-06-2011
- Inauguration ceremony primary school Nyarafunzo, Kigali, Rwanda, 07-01-2011
- Emmanuel Musaba Koloni, Archbishop Anglican Church, Kigali, Kigali, Rwanda, 8 and 18-01-2011
- Gisoze Genocide Memorial Centre, Kigali, Rwanda, 9-01-2011
- Irakoze Pierre Claver, Communications Manager, Ibuka, Kigali, Rwanda, 10-01-2011
- Tom Ndahiro, Researcher and journalist, Kigali, Rwanda, 10, 15, 21 and 25-01-2011
- Patrice Mulama, Executive Secretary, Media High Council, Kigali Rwanda, 10-01-2011
- Olivier Isatibasumba, Project Coordinator, Radio Projet Heza, Maison des Jeunes, Kigali, Rwanda, 12-01-2011

- Focus group youth A, Maison des Jeunes Kimisagara, Kigali, Rwanda, 12-01-2011
- Focus group youth B, Maison des Jeunes Kimisagara, Kigali, Rwanda, 12-01-2011
- Oswald Rutimburana, National Unity and Reconcilliation Commission (NURC), Kigali, Rwanda, 13-01-2011
- Residence Dutch Ambassador to Rwanda, 13-01-2011
- Pascal Nyilibakwe, Secretaire Exécutif, Ligue des Droits de la Personne dans la région des Grand Lacs (LDGL), Kigali Rwanda, 14-01-2014
- Valerie Bemeriki, former RTLM, Kigali Central Prison, Kigali, Rwanda, 17-01-2011
- Isaac Nkubito, former chairman of the MRND Kacyiru commune, Kigali Central Prison, Kigali, Rwanda, 17-01-2011
- Anonymous, Prisoner, Kigali Central Prison, Kigali, Rwanda, 17-01-2011
- Anonymous, Prisoner, Kigali Central Prison, Kigali, Rwanda, 17-01-2011
- Agnes Ntamabyaliro, former Minister of Justice of Interim Government and Government in Exile, Kigali Central Prison, Kigali, Rwanda, 18-01-2011
- Anonymous, Prisoner, Kigali Central Prison, Kigali, Rwanda, 18-01-2011
- Anonymous, Prisoner, Kigali Central Prison, Kigali, Rwanda, 18-01-2011
- Faustin Bismarck Murangwa, a, Member Kigali Bar Association (KBA) and Legal Officer in the Rwandan judiciary dealing with international crimes and transferred cases, Kigali, Rwanda, 19 and 24-01-2011
- Jeanne Mukamusoni, Responsible de Départment Psycho-Médical, Association des Veuves du Génocide Agahozo (Avega), Kigali Rwanda 19-01-2011
- Aloisea Inyumba, Senator National Senate of Rwanda, Kigali, Rwanda, 20-01-2011
- Presidential palace, Kigali, Rwanda, 20-1-2011
- Diogene Bideri, Principal Legal Adviser Commission for the Fight Against Genocide (CNLG) and Chairperson Regional Committee on Genocide Prevention International Conference on the Great Lakes Region (ICGLR), Kigali, Rwanda, 21-01-2011
- Evariste Kalisa, Chairperson of the Committee on National Unity, Human Rights and Fight against Genocide and Vice President of the Chamber of Deputies, Kigali, Rwanda, 24-01-2011
- Paul Rutayisire, Director Center of Conflict Resolution (CCM), National University of Rwanda, Kigali, Rwanda, 25-01-2011
- John Bosco Siboyintore, Head Genocide Fugitive Tracking Unit, Kigali, Rwanda, 25-01-2011
- National Public Prosecution Authority (NPPA), Archives, Kigali, Rwanda, 26-01-2011
- Régis François Rukundakuvuga, Inspector General of the Courts and Tribunals, Kigali, Rwanda, 26-01-2011
- Eugène Ntaganda, Research Regional Coordinator, Avocats Sans Frontières, Kigali, Rwanda, 26-01-2011
- Agéé Shyaka Mugabe, Center of Conflict Resolution (CCM), National University of Rwanda, Kigali, Rwanda, 28-01-2011
- Anonymous, Human rights lawyer, Kigali, Rwanda, 10 and 28-01-2011

- Thierry Cruvellier, Investigative journalist and author, Phnom Penh, Cambodia (skype), 11-7-2011
- Colin Tatz, ANU research scholar; senior lecturer sociology & politics, Monash; professor of politics UNE and Macquarie University, Canberra, Australia (email), 14-7-2011

2012

- Linda Melvern, Investigative journalist and author, Brussels, Belgium, 29-2-2012

2014

- Jean-Damascène Gasanabo, Director General, Commission for the Fights Against Genocide (CNLG), Kigali, Rwanda, 2-7-2014
- Youth against Genocide Conference, Gabiro, Rwanda, 2/3-7-2014
- Kwibohora 20, 20th Liberation Day Ceremony Amohoro Stadium, Kigali, Rwanda, 4-7-2014
- Joseph Karorero, Legal Officer, Commission for the Fights Against Genocide (CNLG), Kigali, Rwanda, 7-7-2014
- Tom Ndahiro, Researcher and journalist, Kigali, Rwanda, 7-7-2014
- Naphtal Ahishakiye, Executive Secretary Ibuka, Kigali, Rwanda, 8-7-2014
- Simon Winston, Holocaust survivor, Kigali, Rwanda, 9-7-2014
- Gisoze Genocide Memorial Centre, Kigali, Rwanda, 9-7-2014
- Anonymous, The Hague, The Netherlands, 9-10-2014

Selected Bibliography

Abed, M. (2006). Clarifying the concept of genocide. *Metaphilosophy, 37*(3–4), 308–330.

Abicht, L. (1997). Moet het negationisme bestreden worden? Persoonlijke en filosofische beschouwingen. In G. Verbeeck (Ed.), *De verdwenen gaskamers: De ontkenning van de Holocaust* (pp. 49–62). Leuven: Acco.

Aboganana, J. M. (1996). De sa prison de Yaoundé, Bagosora s'explique. *Africa International, 296*, 18–21.

Abtan, B. (2010). Le renforcement du négationnisme du génocide des Tutsis. *Le Monde*.

Adhikari, M. (2008). Hotel Rwanda: The challenges of historicising and commercialising genocide. In H. Melber & J. Y. Jones (Eds.), *Revisiting the heart of darkness: Explorations into genocide and other forms of mass violence* (pp. 173–195). Uppsala: Dag Hammarskjöld Foundation.

African Rights. (1996). Killing the evidence. London: African Rights.

African Rights. (2007). A welcome expression of intent: The Nairobi communique and the ex-far/interahamwe. Kigali.

African Rights, & Redress. (2008). Survivors and post-genocide justice in Rwanda. Their experiences, perspectives and hopes. Kigali/London.

Agnew, R. (1994). The techniques of neutralization and violence. *Criminology, 32*, 555–580.

Akçam, T. (2014). An open letter to: Madame la Conseillère fédérale, Simonetta Sommaruga, Cheffe du Département fédéral de justice et police (DFJP). Retrieved from The Armenian Weekly website: www.armenianweekly.com/

Akhavan, P. (2005). The crime of genocide in the ICTR jurisprudence. *Journal of International Criminal Justice, 3*, 989–1006.

Akhavan, P. (2012). *Reducing genocide to law: Definition, meaning, and the ultimate crime.* Cambridge: Cambridge University Press.

Alayarian, A. (2008). *Consequences of denial: The Armenian genocide.* London: Karnac Books.

Alford, J. D., Mahone, C., & Fielstein, E. M. (1988). Combat and behavioral sequelae of combat: Conceptualization and implication for treatment. *Journal of Traumatic Stress, 1*(4), 489–501.

Alvarez, A. (1997). Adjusting to genocide: The techniques of neutralization and the Holocaust. *Social Science History, 21*(2), 139–178.

Alvarez, A. (2001). *Governments, citizens, and genocide: A comparative and interdisciplinary approach.* Indiana: Indiana University Press.

Alvarez, A. (2008). Destructive beliefs: Genocide and the role of ideology. In A. Smeulers & R. Haveman (Eds.), *Supranational criminology: Towards a criminology of international crimes* (pp. 213–231). Antwerpen: Intersentia.

Ambos, K. (2009). What does 'intent to destroy' in genocide mean? *International Review of the Red Cross, 91*(876), 833–858.

Amnesty International. (1994). Rwanda: Reports of killings and abductions by the Rwandese Patriotic Army, April - August 1994. Retrieved from Amnesty International website: www.amnesty.org/en/library/info/AFR47/016/1994/en

Amnesty International. (2004). Rwanda: The enduring legacy of the genocide and war. London: Amnesty International.

Amnesty International. (2010). Safer to stay silent: The chilling effect of Rwanda's laws on 'genocide ideology' and 'sectarianism'. Retrieved from Amnesty International website: www.amnesty.org/en/library/info/AFR47/005/2010/en

Amnesty International. (2011). Unsafe to speak out: Restrictions on freedom of expression in Rwanda. Retrieved from Amnesty International website: www.amnesty.org/en/library/info/AFR47/002/2011

Anderson, K. (2011). *The dehumanisation dynamic: A criminology of genocide.* National University of Ireland, Galway.

Andreopoulos, G. J. (1994). Introduction: The calculus of genocide. In G. J. Andreopoulos (Ed.), *Genocide: Conceptual and historical dimensions* (pp. 1–28). Philadelphia: University of Pennsylvania Press.

Ansoms, A. (2009). *Faces of rural poverty in contemporary Rwanda: Linking livelihood profiles and institutional processes.* University of Antwerp, Antwerp.

Arendt, H. (2005). *Eichmann in Jeruzalem: De banaliteit van het kwaad.* Amsterdam: Moussault NV.

Armstrong, E. G. (2001). Gangsta misogyny: A content analysis of the portrayals of violence against women in rap music 1987–1993. *Journal of Criminal Justice and Popular Culture, 8*(2), 96–126.

Aronson, E. (2008). The social animal. New York: Worth Publishers.

Article 19. (2009). Rwanda: Comment on the law relating to the punishment of the crime of genocide ideology of Rwanda. Retrieved from Article 19 website: www.article19.org/resources.php/resource/483/en/rwanda:-comment-on-the-law-relating-to-the-punishment-of-the-crime-of-genocide-ideology

Asbarez Armenian News. (2011). Attorney Levon Kirakosian discusses criminalizing genocide denial. Retrieved from Asbarez Com website: http://asbarez.com/95937/attorney-levon-kirakosian-discusses-criminalizing-genocide-denial/

Ascribe Newswire. (2004). Rwandan genocide 10th Anniversary: Correcting the record -- University of Maryland expert, *Ascribe Newswire.*

Assemblée Nationale du France. (1998). Rapport d'information, mission d'information sur le Rwanda, No 1271.

Association des Femmes Parlementaires pour la Défense de Droit de la Mère et d'Enfant. (1991). Toute la vérite sur la guerre d'octobre 1990 au Rwanda.

Austin, J. L. (1962). *How to do things with words.* Oxford: Clarendon Press.

Ayoub, N. (2011). New book on Rwanda becomes target. Retrieved from The Chronicle of Higher Education website: http://chronicle.com/blogs/pageview/university-press-book-on-rwanda-becomes-target/28615

Bagilishya, L. (2003). Discours de la négation, dénis et politiques. In C. Coquio (Ed.), *L'histoire trouée. Négation et témoignage* (pp. 731–752). Nantes: Librairie L'Atlante.

Bagosora, T. (1995). L'assassinat du Président Habyarimana ou l'ultime opération du Tutsi pour sa reconquête du pouvoir par la force au Rwanda. Yaoundé Cameroon.

Bandura, A. (1996). Mechanisms of moral disengagement in the exercise of moral agency. *Journal of Personality and Social Psychology, 71*(2), 364–374.

Bandura, A. (1999). Moral disengagement in the perpetration of inhumanities. *Personality and Social Psychology Review, 3*(3), 193–201.

Banks, J. (2011). European regulation of cross-border hate speech in cyberspace: The limits of legislation. *European Journal of Crime, Criminal Law and Criminal Justice, 19*, 1–13.

Barak, G. (1991). *Crimes by the capitalist state: An introduction to state criminality.* Albany: State University of New York Press.

Barayagwiza, J.-B. (1995). *Rwanda: Le sang Hutu est-il rouge? Vérités cacheées sur les massacres.* Cameroun Yaoundé.

Barta, T. (2008a). Responses to Gunter Lewy's contribution: 'Can there be Genocide without the intent to commit genocide?'. *Journal of Genocide Research, 10*(1), 111–133.
Barta, T. (2008b). Sorry, and not sorry, in Australia: How the apology to the stolen generations buried a history of genocide. *Journal of Genocide Research, 10*(1), 2.
Barth, B. (2006). *Genozid: Völkermord im 20. Jahrhundert*. Muenchen: Verlag C.H. Beck.
Basabose, P. (2013). Discours du déni: De la vérisimilitude à la verisimulation. In d. J. Semujanga & J.-L. Galabert (Eds.), *Faire face au négationnisme de génocide des Tutsi* (pp. 73–89). Saint-Jean: Éditions Izuba.
Bastian, T. (1997). *Auschwitz und die "Auschwitz-Luge": Massenmord und Geschichtsfalschung*. Muenchen: Beck.
Bauman, Z. (1989). *Modernity and the Holocaust*. Cambridge: Polity Press.
BBC. (2008). French author in dock over Rwanda. Retrieved from BBC News website: http://news.bbc.co.uk/2/hi/europe/7633449.stm
Benson, M. L. (1985). Denying the guilty mind: Accounting for involvement in a white collar crime. *Criminology, 23*(4), 590–599.
Bergsmo, M. (2009). Intent. In S. Totten & P. R. Bartrop (Eds.), *The genocide studies reader* (pp. 22–30). New York: Routledge.
Bernstein, R. L. (2009). Rights watchdog, lost in the Mideast, *The New York Times*. Retrieved from www.nytimes.com/2009/10/20/opinion/20bernstein.html?_r=2&em=&pagewanted=print
Berry, J. A., & Berry, C. P. (Eds.). (1999). *Genocide in Rwanda: A collective memory*. Washington: Howard University Press.
Bhagwat, N. (2010). Lawyers who reveal the truth: The arrest and threats to the life of attorney professor Peter Erlinder. Retrieved from Global Research website: www.globalresearch.ca/lawyers-who-reveal-the-truth-the-arrest-and-threats-to-the-life-of-attorney-professor-peter-erlinder/19621
Black, C. (2002). Racism, murder and lies in Rwanda. Retrieved from Race and History website: http://raceandhistory.com/selfnews/viewnews.cgi?newsid1010700918,2310,.shtml
Black, C. (2004). Persecution not prosecution. Retrieved from Cirque Minime/Paris Blog website: http://cirqueminime.blogspot.nl/2005/04/persecution-not-prosecution-by.html
Black, C. (2005). The Dallaire genocide fax: A fabrication. Retrieved from Scoop Independent News website: www.scoop.co.nz/stories/HL0512/S00081.htm
Black, C. (2009a). The hidden story behind Rwanda's tragedy. Retrieved from Whale website: www.whale.to/c/hidden_story.html
Black, C. (2009b). The truth about Rwanda. Retrieved from Cirque Minime/Paris Blog website: http://cirqueminimeparis.blogspot.nl/2010/01/truth-about-rwanda-by-christopher-black.html
Black, C. (2010). The Rwandan Patriotic Front's bloody record and the history of U.N. cover-ups. Retrieved from Monthly Review Magazine website: http://mrzine.monthlyreview.org/2010/black120910.html
Black, C., & Herman, E. S. (2000). An unindicted war criminal: Louise Arbour and the International Crimes Tribunal. Retrieved from Whale website: http://whale.to/c/unindicted_war_criminal.html
Black, T. (2012). Who really made a mess of Rwanda? Retrieved from Spiked website: www.spiked-online.com/newsite/article/12708#.VBdJJvmSySo
Blommaert, J., & Verfaillie, K. (2009). Discoursanalyse. In T. Decorte & D. Zaitch (Eds.), *Kwalitatieve methoden en technieken in de criminologie* (pp. 312–337). Leuven: Acco.
Blomsma, J. (2012). *Mens rea and defences in European criminal law*. Cambridge: Intersentia.
Bloxham, D., & Moses, A. D. (Eds.). (2010). *The Oxford handbook of genocide studies*. New York: Oxford University Press.

Blum, A. F., & McHugh, P. (1971). The social ascription of motives. *American Sociological Review, 36*(1), 98–109.
Blumer, H. (1969). *Symbolic interactionism: Perspective and method.* Berkeley: University of California Press.
Blumstein, P. W. (1974). The honoring of accounts. *American Sociological Review, 39*, 551–566.
Boese, G. D. (2012). *The social psychology of genocide denial: Do the facts matter?*, The University of Manitoba, Winnipeg.
Bollas, C. (1993). *Bring a character: Psychoanalysis and self-experience*. London: Routledge.
Bovenkerk, F. (2000). The other side of the Anne Frank story: The Dutch role in the persecution of the Jews in World War Two. *Crime, Law & Social Change, 34*, 237–258.
Brandstetter, A. M. (2012). Contested pasts: The politics of remembrance in post-genocide Rwanda. Wassenaar: Netherlands Institute for Advanced Study in the Humanities and Social Sciences.
Brannigan, A. (2013). *Beyond the banality of evil: Criminology and genocide*. Oxford: Oxford University Press.
Brannigan, A., & Hardwick, K. H. (2003). Genocide and general theory. In C. L. Britt & M. R. Gottfredson (Eds.), *Control theories of crime and delinquency* (Vol. 109–131). New Brunswick: Transaction Publishers.
Breznitz, S. (1983). Seven kinds of denial. In S. Breznitz (Ed.), *Denial of stress* (pp. 257–280). New York: International Universities Press, INC.
Brouwer, A. de (2009). *The men who killed me: Rwandan survivors of sexual violence*. Vancouver: Douglas and McIntyre.
Browning, C. R. (1992a). German memory, judicial interrogation, and historical reconstruction: Writing perpetrator history from post-war testimony. In S. Friedlander (Ed.), *Probing the limits of representation: Nazism and the "Final Solution"* (pp. 22–36). Cambridge: Harvard University Press.
Browning, C. R. (1992b). *Ordinary men: Reserve police battalion 101 and the Final Solution in Poland* New York: Aaron Asher Books.
Bruguière, J. L. (2006). Issuance of international arrest warrants: Tribunal de Grande Instance de Paris.
Buckley-Zistel, S. (2006). Remembering to forget: Chosen amnesia as a strategy for local coexistence in post-genocide Rwanda. *Africa, 76*(2), 131–150.
Burkhardt, A. (1990). Speech act theory - The decline of a paradigm. In A. Burkhardt (Ed.), *Speech acts, meaning and intentions* (pp. 91–128). Berlin: Walter de Gruyter.
Butler, J. (1993). *Bodies that matter. On the discursive limits of sex.* New York: Routledge.
Butler, J. (1997). *Excitable speech*. New York: Routledge.
Buttney, R. (1985). Accounts as a reconstruction of an event's context. *Communication Monographs, 51*(1), 57–77.
Buttney, R., & Morris, G. H. (2001). Accounting. In W. P. Robinson & H. Giles (Eds.), *The new handbook on language and social psychology* (pp. 285–301): John Wiley and Sons td.
Cameron, H. (2012). British State Complicity in Genocide: Rwanda 1994. *State Crime, 1*(1), 70–87.
Caplan, G. (2009a). Remembering Rwanda or denying it? *Peace Review, 21*(3), 280–285.
Caplan, G. (2009b). Rwanda: Memory and denial - The genocide 15 years on. Retrieved from Pambazuka News website: www.pambazuka.net/en/category/comment/55324
Caplan, G. (2010a). The politics of denialism: The strange case of Rwanda. Retrieved from Pambazuka News website: www.pambazuka.net/en/category/features/65265
Caplan, G. (2010b). Sources and testimonies: A response to Herman and Peterson. Retrieved from Pambazuka News website: www.pambazuka.net/en/category/features/65974/print
Caplan, G. (2013a). The 1994 genocide of the Tutsi of Rwanda. In S. Totten & T. Parsons (Eds.), *Centuries of genocide: Essays and eyewitness accounts* (pp. 447–476). New York: Routledge.

Caplan, G. (2013b). Why does the University of Toronto's radio station promote genocide denial? Retrieved from Rabble Canada website: http://rabble.ca/blogs/bloggers/gerry-caplan/2013/04/why-does-university-torontos-radio-station-promote-genocide-deni

Caplan, G. (2014). Genocide against the Tutsi and inflammatory falsehoods by the Holocaust museum staff. Retrieved from Umuvugizi website: http://umuvugizi.wordpress.com/2014/02/25/rwanda-genocide-and-inflammatory-falsehoods-by-a-holocaust-museum-staff-kwibuka20/

Card, C. (2003). Genocide and social death. *Hypatia, 18*(1), 63–79.

Carlsson, I., Han, S.-J., & Rufus, M. K. (1999). Report of the independent inquiry into the actions of the United Nations during the 1994 genocide in Rwanda. New York: United Nations

Carmichael, C. (2009). *Genocide before the Holocaust.* Cornwall: Yale University Press.

Carpentier, N., & De Cleen, B. (2007). Bringing discourse theory into media studies. The applicability of discourse theoretical analysis (DTA) for the study of media practises and discourses. *Journal of Language and Politics, 6*(2), 265–293.

Carpentier, N., & Spee, S. (1999). Een mening hebben over prostitutie? Een kritische kijk op de prostitutie-uitzending van Jan Publiek aan de hand van theorieën van Foucault en Laclau & Mouffe. Retrieved from Universiteit Antwerpen website: http://uahost.uantwerpen.be/psw/pswpapers/PSWpaper%201999-02%20carpentier.pdf

Carpentier, N., & Spinoy, E. (2008). Introduction: From the political to the cultural. In N. Carpentier & E. Spinoy (Eds.), *Discourse theory and cultural analysis: Media, arts, and literature* (pp. 1–28). Cresskill: Hampton Press.

Carrier, N., & Park, A. S. J. (2013). On an entrepreneurial criminology of mass political violence. *Crime, Law and Social Change, 60*, 297–317.

Carrol, J. (2006). The Nagasaki principle. *The Boston Globe*. Retrieved from Boston.com website: www.boston.com/news/globe/editorial_opinion/oped/articles/2006/08/07/the_nagasaki_principle/

Cassese, A. (2009). Eichmann: Is evil so banal? *Journal of International Criminal Justice, 7*, 645–652.

Catley, B. (2003). Philosophy: The luxurious supplement of violence. Retrieved from Department of Management, University of Otago website: www.mngt.waikato.ac.nz/ejrot/cmsconference/2003/proceedings/philosophy/catley.pdf

CBC News. (2007). Rwandan group attacks PQ over candidate who questions genocide, *CBC News*. Retrieved from www.cbc.ca/news/canada/montreal/rwandan-group-attacks-pq-over-candidate-who-questions-genocide-1.676220

Chalk, F. (1994). Redefining genocide. In G. J. Andreopoulos (Ed.), *Genocide: Conceptual and historical dimensions* (pp. 47–63). Philadelphia: University of Pennsylvania Press.

Chalk, F., & Jonassohn, K. (1990). *The history and sociology of genocide.* New haven: Yale University Press.

Chambliss, W. (1989). State-organized Crime. *Criminology, 27*, 183–208.

Charmaz, K. (2006). *Constructing grounded theory: A practical guide through qualitative analysis.* London: SAGE Publications.

Charny, I. W. (1991). The psychology of denial of known genocides. In I. W. Charny (Ed.), *Genocide: A critical bibliographic review* (Vol. 2, pp. 3–37). London: Mansell.

Charny, I. W. (1994). Toward a generic definition of genocide. In G. J. Andreopoulos (Ed.), *Genocide: Conceptual and historical dimensions* (pp. 64–94). Philadelphia: University of Pennsylvania Press.

Charny, I. W. (2000). Innocent denials of known genocides: A further contribution to a psychology of denial of genocide. *Human Rights Review, 1*(3), 15–39.

Charny, I. W. (2001). The psychological satisfaction of denials of the Holocaust or other genocides by non-extremists or bigots, and even by known scholars. *6*(1). Retrieved from IDEA: A journal of social issues website: www.ideajournal.com/articles.php?id=27

Charny, I. W. (2009a). A classification of denials of the Holocaust and other genocides. In S. Totten & P. R. Bartrop (Eds.), *The genocide studies reader* (pp. 518–537). New York: Routledge.
Charny, I. W. (2009b). The definition of genocide. In S. Totten & P. R. Bartrop (Eds.), *The genocide studies reader* (pp. 36–39). New York: Routledge.
Charny, I. W., & Fromer, D. (1998). Denying the Armenian genocide: Patterns of thinking as defence-mechanisms. *Patterns of Prejudice, 32*(1), 39–49.
Chilton, P. A. (1997). The role of language in human conflict: Prolegomena to the investigation of language as a factor in conflict causation and resolution. *Current Issues in Language and Society, 4*(3), 174–189.
Chomsky, N. (2010). Genocide denial with a vengeance: Old and new imperial norms. Retrieved from Monthly Review website: http://monthlyreview.org/2010/09/01/genocide-denial-with-a-vengeance-old-and-new-imperial-norms/
Chomsky, N., & Herman, E. S. (1979a). *After the cataclysm: Post-war Indochina and the reconstruction of imperial ideology.* Cambridge: South End Press.
Chomsky, N., & Herman, E. S. (1979b). *The Washington connection and third world fascism.* Boston: South End Press.
Chomsky, N., & Herman, E. S. (1988). *Manufacturing consent: The political economy of the mass media.* New York: Pantheon Books.
Chrétien, J.-P. (1995a). *Rwanda, les médias du génocide.* Paris: Karthala.
Chrétien, J.-P. (1995b). Un "Nazisme tropical" au Rwanda? Image ou logique d'un génocide. *Vintième Siècle. revue d'Histoire, 48*, 131–142.
Chrétien, J.-P. (2007). RTLM propaganda: The democratic alibi. In A. Thompson (Ed.), *The media and the Rwanda genocide* (pp. 55–61). London: Pluto Press.
Chrétien, J.-P. (2010). Le génocide du Rwanda: un négationnisme structurel. Retrieved from LDH Toulon website: http://ldh-toulon.net/Jean-Pierre-Chretien-Le-genocide.html
Chrétien, J.-P. (2012). *Le défi de l'ethnisme: Rwanda et Burundi.* Paris: Karthala.
Churchill, W. (2000). Forbidding the "G-word": Holocaust denial as judicial doctrine in Canada *Other Voices, 2*(1). Retrieved from Other Voices website: www.othervoices.org/2.1/churchill/denial.php
Clarck, J. F. (Ed.). (2002). *The African stakes in the Congo war.* New York: Palgrave Macmillan.
Clark, E., & Kaufman, Z. D. (2008). Introduction and background: After genocide. In E. Clark & Z. D. Kaufman (Eds.), *After genocide: Transitional justice, post-conflict reconstruction and reconciliation in Rwanda and beyond* (pp. 1–19). London: Hurst Publishers.
Clark, J. F. (2006). Rwanda. Tragic land of dual nationalisms. In L. Barrington (Ed.), *After independence: Making and protecting the nation in postcolonial and post-communist states* (pp. 71–106). Ann Arbor: University of Michigan Press.
Clark, P. (2007). Hybridity, holism and "traditional" justice: The case of the Gacaca courts in post-genocide Rwanda *George Washington International Law Review, 39*(4).
Clark, P., & Kaufman, Z. D. (2008). *After genocide: Transitional justice, post-conflict reconstruction and reconciliation in Rwanda and beyond.* London: Hurst Publishers.
Cohen, S. (1988). *Against criminology.* Oxford: Transaction Books.
Cohen, S. (1993). Human rights and crimes of the state: The culture of denial. *Australian and New Zealand Journal of Criminology, 26*(2), 97–115.
Cohen, S. (1995). State crimes of previous regimes: Knowledge, accountability, and the policing of the past. *Law and Social Inquiry, 20*(1), 7–50.
Cohen, S. (1996). Government responses to human rights reports: Claims, denials, and counterclaims. *Human Rights Quarterly, 18*, 517–543.
Cohen, S. (2001). *States of denial: Knowing about atrocities and suffering.* Cambridge: Polity Press.

Cook, S. E. (2004). The politics of preservation in Rwanda. In S. E. Cook (Ed.), Genocide in Cambodia and Rwanda. New perspectives Genocide Studies Program Monograph Series no. 1, 2004. Retrieved from www.yale.edu/gsp/publications/new_perspectives.html.

Cooper, J. (2008). *Raphael Lemkin and the struggle for the Genocide Convention*. New York: Palgrave Macmillan.

Coquio, C. (2003a). À propos d'un nihilisme contemporain. Négation, déni, témoignage. In C. Coquio (Ed.), *L'histoire trouée: Négation et témoignage* (pp. 23–89). Nantes: Librairie L'Atlante.

Coquio, C. (2003b). *L'histoire trouée. Négation et témoignage*. Nantes: Librairie L'Atlante.

Coquio, C. (2013). le génocide des Tutsi du Rwanda vu de France: De la scène politique au voile esthétique. In d. J. Semujanga & J.-L. Galabert (Eds.), *Faire face au négationnisme du génocide de Tutsi* (pp. 117–142). Saint-Jean: Éditions Izuba.

Corduwener, J. (2004). Een explosief Rwanda-rapport, *NRC*. Retrieved from http://vorige.nrc.nl/buitenland/article1597924.ece

Corduwener, J. (2008). Als de zon schijnt. Retrieved from Jeroen Corduwener Blog website: www.corduwener.nl/blog/15-Als-de-zon-schijnt#.VDKWnvmSySo

Corsevski, E. W. (2007). The physical side of linguistic violence. *Peace Review, 10*(4), 513–516.

Cotler, I. (1995). The human rights revolution and counter-revolution: Dance of the dialectic. Atlantic Human Rights Centre.

Courtmanche, G. (2003). *A Sunday at the pool in Kigali*. Edinburgh: Canongate.

Couturier, J. L., & Lock, J. (2006). Denial and Minimization in Adolescents with Anorexia Nervosa. *International Journal of Eating Disorders, 39*(3), 212–216.

Cramer, P. (2006). *Protecting the self: Defense mechanisms in action*. New York: Guilford Press.

Cressey, D. R. (1953). *Other people's money*. Illinois: The Free Press.

Crewcock, M. (2008). Colonial genocide and state crime. In C. Cunneen & M. Salter (Eds.), *Proceedings of the 2nd Australian & New Zealand critical criminology conference 19–20 June 2008 Sydney, Australia* (pp. 91–106). Sydney: Crime & Justice Research Network and the Australian and New Zealand Critical Criminology Network.

Crombag, H. (2009). *De Man uit Susquehanna. Over Psychologie, Recht en Moraal*. Amsterdam: Uitgeverij Contact.

Croog, S. H., Shapiro, D. S., & Levine, S. (1971). Denial among male heart patients. *Psychosomatic Medicine, 33*(5), 385–398.

Cruvellier, T. (2002). Le discours de la négation. *Diplomatie Judiciaire. Chroniques et reportages sur la Justice pénale internationale*.

Cruvellier, T. (2007). The contingent genocide. *Genocide Studies and Prevention, 2*(3), 271–274.

Cruvellier, T. (2010). *The Court of remorse: Inside the International Criminal Tribunal for Rwanda*. Madison: The University of Wisconsin Press.

Cruvellier, T. (2012). ICTR legacy: Fragile and confusing. Retrieved from Radio Netherlands Worldwide website: www.rnw.nl/international-justice/article/ictr-legacy-fragile-and-confusing

Cuevas Valenzuela, H. (2008). Chilean traumatized identity: Discourse theory and the analysis of visual arts. In N. Carpentier & E. Spinoy (Eds.), *Discourse theory and cultural analysis: Media, arts, and literature* (pp. 141–165). Hampton Press: Cresskill.

Cunneen, C. (1999). Criminology, genocide and the forced removal of indigenous children from their families. *The Australian and New Zealand Journal of Criminology, 32*(2), 124–138.

Dallaire, R. (2003). *Shake hands with the devil: The failure of humanity in Rwanda*. Toronto: Random House Canada.

Dapia, S. G. (2011). Logics of antagonism, of difference, and of the limit: Questions of cultural identity in Latin American cultural studies. *Dialogos Latinamericanos*.

Davenport, C., & Stam, A. C. (2004a). Rwanda 1994: More than genocide. *University of Maryland*.

Davenport, C., & Stam, A. C. (2004b). *Rwandan political violence in space and time (Unpublished manuscript).*
Davenport, C., & Stam, A. C. (2009). What really happened in Rwanda? (November - December). Retrieved from Millar McCune website: www.psmag.com/navigation/politics-and-law/what-really-happened-in-rwanda-3432/
Davenport, C., & Stam, A. C. (undated). Rashomon goes to Rwanda: Alternative accounts of political violence and their implications for policy and analysis. Retrieved from University of Maryland website: www.gvpt.umd.edu/davenport/dcawcp/paper/mar3104.pdf
Davidson, S. (1989). Avoidance and denial in the life cycle of holocaust survivors. In E. L. Edelstein, D. L. Nathanson & A. M. Stone (Eds.), *Denial: A clarification of concepts and research* (pp. 309–320). New York: Plenum Press.
Davis, F. (2014). I used to believe I had the right to be a bigot. But reason prevailed, *The Guardian.* Retrieved from www.theguardian.com/commentisfree/2014/mar/31/i-used-to-believe-i-had-the-right-to-be-a-bigot-but-reason-prevailed
Dawes, J. R. (1999). Language, violence and human rights law. *Yale Journal of Law & Humanities, 11*, 215–250.
Day, L. E., & Vandiver, M. (2000). Criminology and genocide studies: Notes on what might have been and what still could be. *Crime, Law & Social Change, 34*(1), 43–59.
De Graaff, B. (2006). *Op de klippen of door de vaargeul? De omgang van de historicus met (genocidaal) slachtofferschap.* Amsterdam: Uitgeverij SWP Amsterdam.
De Haan, W. (2003). A crying shame. The over-rationalized conception of man in the rational choice perspective. *Theoretical Criminology, 7*(1), 29–54.
De Haan, W. (2005). Een mond vol tanden. Enkele gedachten over de zin van casuïstische criminologie. *Ontmoetingen: Voordrachtenreeks van het Lutje Psychiatrisch-Juridisch Gezelschap, 11.*
De Haan, W. (2011). Making sense of 'senseless violence'. In H. Strang, S. Karstedt & I. Loader (Eds.), *Emotions, Crime and Justice* (pp. 37–54). Oxford: Hart.
De Haan, W. (2013). 'Met kennis van nu' Internationale misdrijven in historisch perspectief. In C. Kelk, F. Koenraadt & D. Siegel (Eds.), *Veelzijdige gedachten* (pp. 85–94). Den Haag: Boom Lemma Uitgevers.
De Jong, J. D. (2007). *Kapot moeilijk: Een etnografisch onderzoek naar opvallend delinquent groepsgedrag van 'Marrokaanse' jongens.* Amsterdam: Aksant.
De Saint-Exupéry, P. (2009). *Complices de l'inavouable: La France au Rwanda.* Paris: Editions Les Arènes.
De Swaan, A. (2014). *Compartimenten van vernietiging: Over genocidale regimes en hun daders.* Amsterdam: Prometheus Bert Bakker.
De Waal, A., & Omaar, R. (1995). Rwanda: Death and despair. London: African Rights.
Del Ponte, C. (2008). *Mevrouw de aanklager: Oog in oog met de grootste misdadigers van deze tijd en de cultuur van de straffeloosheid.* De Bezige Bij: Amsterdam.
Delgado, R., & Stefancic, J. (2004). *Understanding words that wound.* Boulder: Westview Press.
Denzin, N. K., & Lincoln, Y. S. (2003). Introduction: The discipline and practice of qualitative research. In N. K. Denzin & Y. S. Lincoln (Eds.), *Strategies of qualitative inquiry* (pp. 1–45). London: Sage Publications.
Derrida, J. (1988). *Limited Inc.* (S. Weber, Trans.). Evanston: Chicago University Press.
Derrida, J. (1989). *Memoires: For Paul de Man* (C. Lindsay, J. Culler, E. Cadava & P. Kamuf, Trans.). New York: Columbia University Press.
Derrida, J. (2002). *Negotiations* (E. Rottenberg, Trans.). Stanford: Stanford University Press.
Des Forges, A. (1999). *Leave none to tell the story: Genocide in Rwanda.* New York: Human Rights Watch.

Des Forges, A., & Longman, T. P. (2004). Legal responses to genocide in Rwanda. In E. Stover & H. M. Weinstein (Eds.), *My neighbour, my enemy. Justice and community in the aftermath of mass atrocity* (pp. 49–68). Cambridge: Cambridge University Press.

Des Pres, T. (1976). *The survivor: An anatomy of life in the death camps.* New York: Oxford University Press.

Des Pres, T. (1986). On governing narratives: The Turkish-Armenian case. *The Yale Review, 75*, 1–9.

Diethelm, P., & McKee, M. (2009). Denialism: What is it and how should scientists respond? *European Journal of Public Health, 19*(1), 2–4.

Dobbs, M. (2014a). *The Rwanda "genocide fax": What we know now. New documentation paints complex picture of informant and his warnings.* Washington: National Security Archive.

Dobbs, M. (2014b). The shroud over Rwanda's nightmare, *The New York Times.* Retrieved from www.nytimes.com/2014/01/10/opinion/the-shroud-over-rwandas-nightmare.html?_r=0

Doerge, F. C. (2004). *Illocutionary acts: Austin's account and what Searle made out of it.* (Doktor der Philosophie), Eberhard-Karls-Universität, Tuebingen.

Dorpat, T. L. (1985). *Denial and defense in the therapeutic situation.* New York: Jason Aronson, Inc.

Dorpat, T. L. (1989). Interactional perspectives on denial and defense. In E. L. Edelstein, D. L. Nathanson & A. M. Stone (Eds.), *Denial: A clarification of concepts and research* (pp. 17–35). London: Plenum Press.

Douglas, J. (1994). Officials told to avoid calling Rwanda killings 'genocide', *The New York Times.* Retrieved from www.nytimes.com/1994/06/10/world/officials-told-to-avoid-calling-rwanda-killings-genocide.html

Drost, P. (1959). *The crime of state: Penal protection for fundamental freedoms of persons and peoples* (Vol. 2). Leiden: Sythoff.

Drumbl, M. (2009). International criminal law: Taking stock of a busy decade. *Melbourne Journal of International Law, 10*(1).

Ducey, K. A. (2008). Using the 1994 Rwanda genocide to integrate critical criminology and liberation sociology. *Critical Criminology, 16*, 293–302.

Dumas, H. (2010). Du 'double genocide' à la négation du génocide: Evolution du discours négationniste. *Dialogue* (190), 94–102.

Dupaquier, J.-P. (1995). Rwanda: Le révisionnisme, poursuite du génocide par d'autres moyens. In R. Verdier, E. Decaux & J.-P. Chrétien (Eds.), *Rwanda: Un génocide du XXe siècle* (pp. 127–136). Paris: L'Harmattan.

Eaglestone, R. (2004). *The Holocaust and the postmodern.* Oxford: Oxford University Press.

Edelstein, E. L., Nathanson, D. L., & Stone, A. M. (1989a). Clinical implications. In E. L. Edelstein, D. L. Nathanson & A. M. Stone (Eds.), *Denial: A clarification of concepts and research* (pp. 171–174). New York: Plenum Press.

Edelstein, E. L., Nathanson, D. L., & Stone, A. M. (1989b). Social and political implications. In E. L. Edelstein, D. L. Nathanson & A. M. Stone (Eds.), *Denial: A clarification of concepts and research* (pp. 273–276). New York: Plenum Press.

Edelstein, E. L., Nathanson, D. L., & Stone, A. M. (Eds.). (1989c). *Denial: A clarification of concepts and research.* New York: Plenum Press.

Eitinger, L. (1983). Denial in concentration camps: Some personal observations on the positive and negative functions of denial in extreme life situations. In S. Breznitz (Ed.), *Denial of stress* (pp. 199–212). New York: International Universities Press, INC.

Eltis, K. (2008). A constitutional "right" to deny and promote genocide. Pre-empting the usurpation of human rights discourse towards incitement from a Canadian perspective. *Cardozo Journal of Conflict Resolution, 9*(2), 463–477.

Eltringham, N. (2003). 'The blind men and the elephant': The challenge of representing the Rwandan genocide. In P. Caplan (Ed.), *The ethics of anthropology: Debates and dilemmas* (pp. 96–112). London: Routledge.

Eltringham, N. (2004). *Accounting for horror: Post genocide debates in Rwanda*. London: Pluto Press.

Eltringham, N. (2012). 'Invaders who have stolen the country': The Hamitic hypothesis, race and the Rwandan genocide. *Social Identities, 12*(4), 425–446.

Erlinder, P. (2008a). The "Rwanda genocide" cover-up. Retrieved from Jurist website: http://jurist.org/forum/2008/02/rwanda-genocide-cover-up.php

Erlinder, P. (2008b). Rwanda: No conspiracy, no genocide planning ... no genocide? Retrieved from Jurist website: http://jurist.law.pitt.edu/forumy/2008/12/rwanda-no-conspiracy-no-genocide.php

Erlinder, P. (2009a). Letters on Rwanda: Peter Erlinder's response to the article "Rwanda: Perpetrators of genocide jailed" Retrieved from Hungry for Truth, Peace and Justice Blog website: http://hungryoftruth.blogspot.com/2009/02/letters-on-rwanda-peter-erlinders.html

Erlinder, P. (2009b). The real authors of the Congo crimes. Nkunda has been arrested but who will arrest Kagame? Retrieved from Global Research website: www.globalresearch.ca/the-real-authors-of-the-congo-crimes-nkunda-has-been-arrested-but-who-will-arrest-kagame/12139

Erlinder, P. (2010a). Rwanda: Flawed elections and the politics of 'genocide denial'. Retrieved from Jurist website: http://jurist.org/forum/2010/08/rwanda-flawed-elections-and-the-politics-of-genocide-denial.php

Erlinder, P. (2010b). The UN Security Council ad hoc Rwanda Tribunal: International justice or juridically constructed "victor's impunity". *DePaul Journal for Social Justice, 4*(1), 131–214.

Erlinder, P. (2013). *The accidental genocide. Research edition*. Saint Paul, Minnesota: International Humanitarian Law Institute.

Essoungou, E. M. (2005). Bagosora face à ses juges: Un négationniste combatif. Retrieved from Radio France Internationale website: http://www1.rfi.fr/actufr/articles/070/article_39372.asp

Evans, L. (2005). The people who cover up genocide. Retrieved from UCLA International Institute website: http://www1.international.ucla.edu/article.asp?parentid=21398

Faure, M. M. G., & Moerland, C. A. R. (2006). *Griffierechten. Een vergelijkende beschrijving van griffierechten- en vergelijkbare stelsels in een aantal landen van de Europese Unie*. Den Haag/Maastricht: Faculteit der Rechtsgeleerdheid, Universiteit Maastricht, WODC, Boom Juridische uitgevers.

Faurisson, R. (1980). Mémoire en défense. Paris: La Vieille Taupe.

Fein, H. (1993). *Genocide: A sociological perspective*. London: Sage Publications.

Fein, H. (1994). Genocide, terror, life integrity, and war crimes: The case for discrimination. In G. J. Andreopoulos (Ed.), *Genocide: Conceptual and historical dimensions* (pp. 95–107). Philadelphia: University of Pennsylvania Press.

Fein, H. (2009). Defining genocide as a sociological concept. In S. Totten & P. R. Bartrop (Eds.), *The genocide studies reader* (pp. 44–56). New York: Routledge.

Ferrell, J. (2007). Criminological *Verstehen*: Inside the immediacy of crime. *Justice Quarterly, 14*(1), 3–23.

Ferrell, J. (2008). *Cultural criminology*. Retrieved from www.culturalcriminology.org.

Ferrell, J., Hayward, K., Morrison, W., & Presdee, M. (2004). *Cultural criminology unleashed*. London: Glasshouse Press.

Ferrell, J., Hayward, K., & Young, J. (2008). *Cultural criminology: An invitation*. London: Sage Publications.

Ferrell, J., & Sander, C. R. (1995). *Cultural criminology*. Boston: Northeastern University Press.

Festinger, L. (1957). *A theory of cognitive dissonance*. Stanford: Stanford University Press.

Fierens, M. (2009). *Le négationnisme du génocide des Tutsi au Rwanda*. Villeurbanne: Golias.

Fingarette, H. (1969). *Self-deception*. New York: Routledge and Kegan Paul.
Finkielkraut, A. (1998). *The future of a negation: Reflections on the question of genocide*. Lincoln: University of Nebraska Press.
Foster, F. (1995). Massacring the truth in Rwanda. *LM*, (85). Retrieved from Web Archive website: http://web.archive.org/web/20010521175331/www.informinc.co.uk/LM/LM85/LM85_Rwanda.html/
Fournet, C. (2007). *The crime of destruction and the law of genocide: Their impact on collective memory*. Hampshire: Ashgate.
Foxman, A. H. (2012). When holocaust analogies run amok. Retrieved from Anti-Defamation League website: http://archive.adl.org/adl_opinions/holocaust/120109_jta.html#.VA71tvmSySo
Freeman, M. (1991). The theory and prevention of genocide. *Holocaust and Genocide Studies, 6*(2), 185–199.
Freeze, D.-L. (Ed.). (2013). *Totally unofficial. The autobiography of Raphael Lemkin*. New Haven: Yale University Press.
French, H. (1997). France fears U.S. advance in Africa, *The New York*. Retrieved from www.nytimes.com/1997/04/04/world/france-fears-us-advance-in-africa.html?pagewanted=print
Fresco, N. (1981). The Denial of the dead. On the Faurisson affair. Retrieved from Anti Revisionism website: www.anti-rev.org/textes/Fresco81a/
Friedlander, S. (1992). Introduction. In S. Friedlander (Ed.), *Probing the limits of representation: Nazism and the "Final Solution"* (pp. 1–21). Cambridge: Harvard University Press.
Fuji, L. A. (2009). *Killing neighbors: Webs of violence in Rwanda*. Ithaca: Cornell University Press.
Gagnon, G. (2009). Response to The New Times article on Rwandan genocide. Retrieved from Human Rights Watch website: www.hrw.org/news/2009/05/18/response-new-times-article-rwandan-genocide
Galabert, J.-L. (2013). Non reconnaissance, négation, déni du génocide. Faire la part des choses pour fair face au négationnisme. In d. J. Semujanga & J.-L. Galabert (Eds.), *Faire face au négationnisme du génocide des Tutsi* (pp. 369–392). Saint-Jean: Éditions Izuba.
Galtung, J. (1969). Violence, peace and peace research. *Journal of Peace Research, 6*(3), 167–191.
Garfinkel, H. (1956). Conditions of successful degrading ceremonies. *American Journal of Sociology, 61*, 420–424.
Garibian, S. (2003). La loi Gayssot ou le droit désaccordé. In C. Coquio (Ed.), *L'histoire trouée. Négation et témoignage* (pp. 223–246). Nantes: Librairie L'Atlante.
Garland, D. (2002). Of crimes and criminals: The development of criminology in Britain. In M. Maguire, R. Morgan & R. Reiner (Eds.), *The Oxford handbook of criminology* (pp. 7–50). Oxford: Oxford University Press.
Garlield, A. E. (2005). Protecting children from speech. *Florida Law Review, 57*, 566–651.
Garrison, A. (2010). Africa's female Mandela? Victoire Ingabiré Umuhoza on trial. Retrieved from San Francisco Bay View Newspaper website: http://sfbayview.com/2010/africa%E2%80%99s-female-mandela-victoire-ingabire-umuhoza-on-trial/
Gasana, J., & Nsengimana, N. (1997). Breaking Hutu - Tutsi enmity in Rwanda through reconciliation. Can there be hope again. Lausanne.
Gasasira, S. (2012). Reporters without borders deplores Rwandan radio presenter held pending trial after slip of the tongue. Retrieved from Umuvugizi The Voice of Rwanda website: www.umuvugizi.com/?p=5246&lang=en
Geertz, C. (1973). *The interpretation of cultures*. New York: Basic Books.
Gibson, W. (1984). *Neuromancer*. New York: Ace Books.
Gilbert, G. M. (2004). *Nürnberger Tagebuch*. Frankfurt am Main: Fisher Taschenbuch Verlag.

Ginzburg, C. (1992). Just one witness. In S. Friedlander (Ed.), *Probing the limits of representation: Nazism and the "Final Solution"* (pp. 82–96). Cambridge: Harvard University Press.
Gkotzaridis, E. (2008). Revisionism in the Twentieth Century: A Bankrupt Concept or Permanent Practice? *The European Legacy, 13*(6), 725–741.
Glanville, L. (2009). Is "genocide" still a powerful word? *Journal of Genocide Research, 11*(4), 467–486.
Glaser, B. G. (1992). *Basics of grounded theory analysis*. Mill Valley: Sociology Press.
Glaser, B. G. (1998). *Doing grounded theory: Issues and discussions*. Mill Valley: Sociology Press.
Glaser, B. G. (2001). *The grounded theory perspective: Conceptualization contrasted with description*. Mill Valley: Sociology Press.
Glaser, B. G., & Strauss, A. L. (1967). *The discovery of grounded theory: Strategies for qualitative research*. New York: Aldine de Gruyter.
Goffman, E. (1959). *The presentation of self in everyday life*. New York: Prentice Hall.
Goldbeck, R. (1983). Denial in physical illness. *Journal of Psychosomatic Research, 43*(6), 575–593.
Goldberger, L. (1983). The concept and mechanisms of denial: A selective overview. In S. Breznitz (Ed.), *The denial of stress* (pp. 83–95). New York: International Universities Press, INC.
Goldhagen, D. J. (1997). *Hitler's willing executioners: Ordinary Germans and the Holocaust*. London: Abacus.
Goldsmith, K. (2010). The issue of intent in the Genocide Convention and its effect on the prevention and punishment of the crime of genocide: Toward a knowledge-based approach. *Genocide Studies and Prevention, 5*(3), 238–257.
Goldstone, R. (2005). Justice now, and for posterity, *Herald International Tribune*.
Gordon, G. S. (2012). Incitement in Rwanda: The Path to Genocide. In A. Baker (Ed.), *The changing forms of incitement to terror and violence: The need for a new international response* (pp. 117–126). Jerusalem: Jerusalem Center for Public Affairs and the Konrad-Adenauer-Stiftung.
Gourevitch, P. (1998). *We wish to inform you that tomorrow we will be killed with our families: Stories from Rwanda*. New York: Farrar, Strauss and Giroux.
Graziano, F. (1992). *Divine violence: Spectacle, psychosexuality, and radical Christianity in the Argentine "Dirty War"*. Boulder: Westview Press.
Green, L. (1995). Living in a state of fear. In C. Nordstrom & C. G. M. Robben (Eds.), *Fieldwork under fire: Contemporary studies of violence and survival* (pp. 105–127). Berkeley: University of California Press.
Green, M. (2003). Rwanda 1994 killings weren't "genocide" - U.S. study, *Reuters*.
Green, P., & Ward, T. (2004). *State crime: Governments, violence, and corruption*. London: Pluto Press.
Greenawalt, A. K. (1999). Rethinking genocidal intent: The case for a knowledge-based interpretation. *Colombia Law Review, 99*, 2259–2294.
Greer, S. (1992). The management of denial in cancer patients. *Oncology, 6*(12), 33–40.
Grill, B. (2009). Der Antrieber, *Die Zeit*.
Grünfeld, F. (2000). The role of bystanders in human rights violations. In F. Coomans (Ed.), *Rendering justice to the vulnerable: Liber amoricum in honour of Theo van Boven*. Den Haag: Kluwer Law International.
Grünfeld, F. (2008). The role of bystanders in Rwanda and Srebrenica: Lessons learned. In A. Smeulers & R. Haveman (Eds.), Supranational criminology: Towards a criminology of international crimes (pp. 457–486).
Grünfeld, F. (2009). The role of the bystander. In A. Jones (Ed.), *Evoking genocide* (pp. 97–100).
Grünfeld, F., & Huijboom, A. (2007). *The failure to prevent genocide in Rwanda: The role of bystanders*. Leiden/Boston: Martinus Nijhoff Publishers.

Grünfeld, F., & Vermeulen, W. N. (2014). *Failure to prevent gross human rights violations in Darfur. Warnings to and responses by international decision makers.* Leiden-Boston: Brill-Nijhoff.
Haan, N. (1977). *Coping and defending: Processes of self-environment organization.* New York: Academic Press.
Hackett, T. P., & Cassem, N. H. (1974). Development of a quantitative rating scale to assess denial. *Journal of Psychosomatic Research, 18*, 93–100.
Hagan, J., & Rymond-Richmond, W. (2008). Collective dynamics of genocidal victimization in Darfur. *American Sociological Review, 73*(6), 875–902.
Hagan, J., & Rymond-Richmond, W. (2009a). Criminology confronts genocide: whose side are you on? *Theoretical Criminology, 13*(4), 503–511.
Hagan, J., & Rymond-Richmond, W. (2009b). *Darfur and the crime of genocide.* New York: Cambridge University Press.
Hagan, J., Rymond-Richmond, W., & Parker, P. (2005). The criminology of genocide: The death and rape of Darfur. *Criminology, 43*(3), 525–562.
Harelimana, C. (1996). Note au Chef D'Etat Major FAR.
Harff, B., & Gurr, T. R. (1987). Genocide and politicide since 1945: Evidence and anticipation. *Internet on the Holocaust and Genocide, 13*, 1–7.
Harmon Snow, K. (2001). Prepared statement of Keith Harmon Snow. Retrieved from All Things Pass website: www.allthingspass.com/journalism.php?catid=10
Harmon Snow, K. (2004). Mass rape and genocide in Rwanda 1994 - The untold story of how the Western press both ignored and manipulated the issue of rape of women and girls during the 1994 cataclysm in Rwanda, and why. Retrieved from Whale website: www.whale.to/c/mass_rape.html
Harmon Snow, K. (2005). Hotel Rwanda: Hollywood and the Holocaust in Central Africa. Retrieved from Global Research website: www.globalresearch.ca/hotel-rwanda-hollywood-and-the-holocaust-in-central-africa/1096
Harmon Snow, K. (2008a). Merchants of death: Exposing corporate financed holocaust in Africa. Retrieved from Global Research website: www.globalresearch.ca/merchants-of-death-exposing-corporate-financed-holocaust-in-africa/11311
Harmon Snow, K. (2008b). The US sponsored "Rwanda genocide" and its aftermath. Retrieved from Global Research website: www.globalresearch.ca/the-us-sponsored-rwanda-genocide-and-its-aftermath/8657
Harmon Snow, K. (2009a). Ben Affleck, Rwanda, and corporate sustained catastrophe. Retrieved from Dissident Voice website: http://dissidentvoice.org/2009/01/ben-affleck-rwanda-and-corporate-sustained-catastrophe/
Harmon Snow, K. (2009b). Ben Affleck, Rwanda, and Corporate Sustained Catastrophe, Part 2. Retrieved from Dissident Voice website: http://dissidentvoice.org/2009/01/ben-affleck-rwanda-and-corporate-sustained-catastrophe-part-2/
Harmon Snow, K. (2009c). False narrative: Whitewashing Rwanda genocide. Retrieved from Black Star News website: www.blackstarnews.com/others/extras/false-narrative-the-rwanda-genocide.html
Harmon Snow, K. (2009d). The Rwanda genocide fabrications: Human Right Watch, Alison Des Forges and disinformation on Central Africa. Retrieved from Dissident Voice website: http://dissidentvoice.org/2009/04/the-rwanda-genocide-fabrications/
Harmon Snow, K. (2010a). Apocalypse in Central Africa: The Pentagon, genocide and the War on Terror. Retrieved from ZMagazine website: http://zcomm.org/zmagazine/apocalypse-in-central-africa-by-keith-harmon-snow/

Harmon Snow, K. (2010b). The Rwanda hit list: Revisionism, denial, and the genocide conspiracy. Retrieved from Conscious Being Alliance website: www.consciousbeingalliance.com/2010/03/the-rwanda-hit-list
Harmon Snow, K. (Producer). (2011). The plunder and depopulation of Central Africa: The politics of genocide: White supremacy ideology and corporate control. Retrieved from https://www.youtube.com/watch?v=Yg6kPY7QC3M
Harmon Snow, K. (2012). Pentagon produces satellite photos of 1994 Rwandan genocide. Retrieved from Dissident Voice website: http://dissidentvoice.org/2012/04/pentagon-produces-satellite-photos-of-1994-rwanda-genocide/
Harmon Snow, K. (2013a). Dr. Gerald Caplan and the Rwanda genocide cranks. *Black Agenda Report.* Retrieved from Blackagendareport.com website: www.blackagendareport.com
Harmon Snow, K. (2013b). White slaughter in black Africa: Genocide and denialism - Dr. Gerald Caplan and the Rwanda genocide cranks. Retrieved from Dissident Voice website: http://dissidentvoice.org/2013/05/white-slaughter-in-black-africa-genocide-and-denialism/
Harmon Snow, K. (2014). Real Rwandan genocide and brainwashing of the Western mind. Retrieved from Dissident Voice website: http://dissidentvoice.org/2014/04/real-rwandan-genocide-and-brainwashing-of-the-western-mind/
Hatch, E. (1992). *Discourse and language education.* Cambridge: Cambridge University Press.
Haveman, R. (2005). Supranationale criminologie. In P. A. M. Mevis & J. Wöretshofer (Eds.), *Praktisch Strafrecht* (pp. 197–211). Nijmegen: Wolf Legal Publishers.
Haveman, R., & Smeulers, A. (2008). Criminology in a state of denial - Towards a criminology of international crimes: Supranational criminology. In S. Smeulers & R. Haveman (Eds.), *Supranational Criminology: Towards a Criminology of International Crimes* (pp. 3–26). Antwerp: Intersentia.
Haveman, R., Smeulers, A., Parmentier, S., & de Poot, C. (2011). De Staat van de criminologie van internationale misdrijven. *Tijdschrift voor Criminologie, 53*(4), 287–309.
Havik, O. E., & Maeland, J. G. (1986). Dimensions of verbal denial in myocardial Infarction. *Scandinavian Journal of Psychology, 27,* 326–339.
Hayward, K. (2007). Cultural criminology. In B. Golson (Ed.), *The Dictionary of youth justice.* Cullompton: Willan.
Hayward, K., & Young, J. (2004). Special issue: Cultural criminology. *Theoretical Criminology, 8*(3).
Hazani, M. (1991). The universal applicability of the theory of neutralization: German youth coming to terms with the Holocaust. *Crime, Law and Social Change, 15,* 135–149.
Heanen, M. (2000). Oorlogsmisdadiger per business class naar Afrika, *NRC Handelsblad.* Retrieved from http://retro.nrc.nl/W2/Nieuws/2000/06/28/Vp/03.html
Herman, E. S. (1981). *Corporate control, corporate power* Cambridge: Cambridge University Press.
Herman, E. S. (2007). Genocide inflation is the real human rights threat: Yugoslavia and Rwanda. Retrieved from ZMagazine website: www.zmag.org/znet/viewArticle/15696
Herman, E. S. (2011). Reply to George Monbiot on "genocide belittling". Retrieved from ZNet website: http://zcomm.org/znetarticle/reply-to-george-monbiot-on-genocide-belittling-by-edward-herman/
Herman, E. S., & O'Sullivan, G. (1990). *The "terrorism" industry.* New York: Pantheon.
Herman, E. S., & Peterson, D. (2010a). Adam Jones on Rwanda and genocide: A reply. Retrieved from Monthly Review Magazine website: http://mrzine.monthlyreview.org/2010/hp140810.html
Herman, E. S., & Peterson, D. (2010b). Genocide denial and genocide facilitation: Gerald Caplan and the politics of genocide. Retrieved from Monthly Review Magazine website: http://mrzine.monthlyreview.org/2010/hp040710.html

Herman, E. S., & Peterson, D. (2010c). Kagame, our kind of guy. Retrieved from ZCommunications website: www.zcommunications.org/paul-kagame-our-kind-of-guy-by-edward-herman-1
Herman, E. S., & Peterson, D. (2010d). Peter Erlinder jailed by one of the major génocidaires of our era - Update. Retrieved from Monthly Review Magazine website: http://mrzine.monthlyreview.org/2010/hp170610.html
Herman, E. S., & Peterson, D. (2010e). *The politics of genocide*. New York: Monthly Review Press.
Herman, E. S., & Peterson, D. (2010f). Rwanda and the Democratic Republic of Congo in the propaganda system (Excerpted from *The Politics of Genocide*, Monthly Review Press, 2009). *Monthly Review, 62*(1).
Herman, E. S., & Peterson, D. (2011a). *The politics of genocide*. New York: Monthly Review Press.
Herman, E. S., & Peterson, D. (2011b). We are not genocide deniers. We just want to uncover the truth about Rwanda and Srebrenica, *The Guardian*. Retrieved from www.theguardian.com/commentisfree/2011/jul/19/not-genocide-deniers-uncover-truth
Herman, E. S., & Peterson, D. (2011c). Yugoslavia and Rwanda: On "genocide denial" and "revisionism" media disinformation, George Monbiot and The Guardian. Retrieved from Global Research website: www.globalresearch.ca/yugoslavia-and-rwanda-on-genocide-denial-and-revisionism/26363
Hewitt, J. P. (2003). *Self and society: A symbolic interactionist social psychology*. Boston: Allyn and Bacon - Pearson Education.
Hilberg, R. (2002). The Nazi Holocaust: Using bureaucracies and overcoming psychological barriers to genocide. In M. D. Ermann & R. J. Lundman (Eds.), *Corporate and governmental deviance: Problems of organizational behavior in contemporary society* (6th ed., pp. 167–188). Oxford: Oxford University Press.
Hilgard, E. R. (1949). Human motives and the concept of the self. *American Psychologist, 4*, 374–382.
Hintjens, H. M. (1999). Explaining the 1994 genocide in Rwanda. *Journal of Modern African Studies, 37*(2), 241–286.
Hinton, A. L., La Pointe, T., & Irvin - Erickson, D. (Eds.). (2014). *Hidden genocides: Power, knowledge, memory*. New Brunswick - New Jersey: Rutgers University Press.
Hirondelle News Agency. (2011). ICTR/Military I - Bagosora recognizes Rwandan genocide at last. Retrieved from Hirondelle News Agency: International Justice Reporting website: www.hirondellenews.com/ictr-rwanda/343-trials-ended/military-i-trial/24982-en-en-010411-ictrmilitary-i-bagosora-recognizes-rwandan-genocide-at-last1403314033
Hirondelle News Agency. (2013). Convicted ex-Prime Minister Jean Kambanda publishes damning portrait of Rwanda Tribunal. Retrieved from Hirondelle News Agency: International Justice Reporting website: www.hirondellenews.com/ictr-rwanda/387-trials-ended/kambanda-jean/34309-70813-convicted-ex-prime-minister-jean-kambanda-publishes-damning-portrait-of-rwanda-tribunal
Hirsch, H. (1995). *Genocide and the politics of memory*. London: The University of North Carolina Press.
Hitchcott, N. (2009). A global African commemoration - Rwanda: Écrire par devoir de memoire. *Forum for Modern Language Studies, 45*(2), 151–161.
Hoare, M. A. (2005). Chomsky's genocidal denial. Retrieved from Bosnian Genocide website: http://bosniangenocide.wordpress.com/2012/06/17/chomskys-genocidal-denial/
Hoff, J. (2000). Technology and social change: The path between technological determinism, social constructivism, and new institutionalism. In J. Hoff, I. Horrocks & P. Tops (Eds.), *Democratic governance and new technology* (pp. 13–33). London: Routledge

Hogg, R. (2002). Criminology beyond the nation state: Global conflicts, human rights and the "new world disorder". In K. Carrington & R. Hogg (Eds.), *Critical Criminology: Issues, Debates, Challenges.* (pp. 185–217). Devon: Willan Publishing

Hoofnagle, M., & Hoofnagle, C. (2008). What is denialism? *Denialism Blog.* http://scienceblogs.com/denialism/about.php

Hopper, J. (1993). The rhetoric of motives in divorce. *Journal of Marriage and the Family, 55*(4), 801–813.

Horn, L. R. (1978). Some aspects of negation. In G. J. H., C. A. Ferguson & A. Moravcsik (Eds.), *Universal of Human Language Volume 4: Syntax* (pp. 127–210). Stanford, California: Stanford University Press.

Horn, L. R. (1985). Metalinguistic negation and pragmatic ambiguity. *Language, 61*(1), 121–174.

Horn, L. R. (2001). *A natural history of negation.* Leland Stanford Junior University: CSLI Publications.

Horowitz, I. L. (1989). *Taking lives: Genocide and state power.* New York: Transaction Publishers.

Housepain Dobkin, M. (1987). What Genocide? What Holocaust? News from Turkey, 1915–1923: A case study. In R. G. Hovannisian (Ed.), *The Armenian Genocide in Perspective* (pp. 97–110). Oxford: Transaction Books.

Hovannisian, R. G. (1987). The Armenian genocide and patterns of denial. In R. G. Hovannisian (Ed.), *The Armenian genocide in perspective* (pp. 111–133). New Brunswick: Transaction Books.

Hovannisian, R. G. (1999a). Denial of the Armenian genocide in comparison with Holocaust denial. In R. G. Hovannisian (Ed.), *Remembrance and denial: The case of the Armenian genocide* (pp. 201–236). Detroit: Wayne State University Press.

Hovannisian, R. G. (1999b). L'hydre à quatre têtes du négationnisme: Négation, rationalisation, relativisation, banalisation. In CDCA (Ed.), *Colloque CDCA (1998) / L'actualité du génocide des Arméniens.* Paris: Edipol.

Howarth, D., & Stavrakakis, Y. (2000). Introducing discourse theory and political analysis. In D. Howarth, A. J. Norval & Y. Stavrakakis (Eds.), *Discourse theory and political analysis: Identities, hegemonies and social change* (pp. 1–23). Glasgow: Bell & Bain.

Human Rights Watch. (1999). 'Leave none to tell the story': Genocide in Rwanda. New York: Human Rights Watch.

Human Rights Watch. (2008a). ICTR: Address crimes committed by the RPF. Retrieved from Human Rights Watch website: www.hrw.org/news/2008/12/12/ictr-address-crimes-committed-rpf

Human Rights Watch. (2008b). Law and reality: Progress in judicial reform in Rwanda. Retrieved from Human Rights Watch website: www.hrw.org/news/2008/07/25/rwanda-progress-judicial-reforms-falls-short

Human Rights Watch. (2009). Letter to the prosecutor of the International Criminal Tribunal for Rwanda regarding the prosecution of RPF crimes. Retrieved from Human Rights Watch website: www.hrw.org/news/2009/05/26/letter-prosecutor-international-criminal-tribunal-rwanda-regarding-prosecution-rpf-c

Human Rights Watch. (2011). Justice compromised: The legacy of Rwanda's community-based Gacaca courts. New York.

Human Rights Watch (2014a). Confronting evil: Genocide in Rwanda (Featuring Alison Des Forges). Retrieved from www.hrw.org/video/2009/02/13/confronting-evil-genocide-rwanda-featuring-alison-des-forges

Human Rights Watch. (2014b). Letter to Johnston Busingye, Minister of Justice, Ministry of Justice, Republic of Rwanda. Retrieved from Human Rights Watch website: www.hrw.org/sites/default/files/related_material/Letter%20to%20Minister%20of%20Justice%2012%20June%202014.pdf

Human Rights Watch. (2014c). Rwanda: Justice after genocide – 20 years on. Retrieved from Human Rights Watch website: www.hrw.org/news/2014/03/28/rwanda-justice-after-genocide-20-years

Hume, M. (1996). Reaction to Zuroff letter concerning article Fiona Foster. London: Living Marxism.

Huttenbach, H. R. (1988). Locating the Holocaust on the genocide spectrum: Towards a methodology of definition and categorization. *Holocaust and Genocide Studies, 3*(3), 289–303.

Huttenbach, H. R. (2008). The psychology and politics of genocide denial. In A. Jones (Ed.), *Genocide* (pp. 306–316). Los Angeles: Sage Publications.

Ibreck, R. (2001). The politics of mourning: Survivor contributions to memorials in post-genocide Rwanda. *Memory Studies, 3*(4), 330–343.

Ignatieff, M. (2013a). Raphael Lemkin and genocide. Retrieved from Notting Hill Editions website: www.nottinghilleditions.com/uploads/essaywinners/NHEessayIGNATIEFF.pdf

Ignatieff, M. (2013b). The unsung hero who coined the term "genocide". Retrieved from The New Republic website: www.newrepublic.com/article/114424/raphael-lemkin-unsung-hero-who-coined-genocide

Imbleau, M. (2004). Initial truth establishment by transitional bodies and the fight against denial. *Criminal Law Forum, 15*, 159–192.

Imbusch, P. (2003). The concept of violence. In W. Heitmeyer & J. Hagan (Eds.), *International handbook of violence* (Vol. 2, pp. 13–40). Dordrecht: Kluwer Academic Publishers.

Immaculée, I. (2006). *Left to tell: Discovering god amidst the Rwandan Holocaust.* London: Hay House.

Ingelaere, B. (2009). Do we understand life after genocide? Centre and periphery in the knowledge construction in/on Rwanda (working paper). Antwerp: Institute of Development Policy and Management.

Ingold, J. (2011). Lawsuit over Rwandan genocide appealed in federal court in Denver. Retrieved from Denver Post website: www.denverpost.com/ci_19643670

Institute of Research and Dialogue for Peace. (2008). *The fight against genocide denial.* Kigali Institute of Research and Dialogue for Peace.

International Criminal Tribunal for Rwanda. (1998). Ex-Rwandan Prime Minister Jean Kambanda pleads guilty to genocide. Retrieved from International Criminal Tribunal for Rwanda website: www.unictr.org/tabid/155/Default.aspx?ID=494

International Criminal Tribunal for Rwanda. (2006). ICTR Appeals Chamber takes judicial notice of genocide in Rwanda [Press release]. Retrieved from http://ictr-archive09.library.cornell.edu/ENGLISH/PRESSREL/2006/481.html

International Crisis Group. (2002). Rwanda at the end of the transition: A necessary political liberalisation. Retrieved from International Crisis Group website: www.crisisgroup.org/en/regions/africa/central-africa/rwanda/053-rwanda-at-the-end-of-the-transition-a-necessary-political-liberalisation.aspx

International Panel of Eminent Personalities. (2000). Rwanda: The preventable genocide. Organization of African Unity.

Irvin, D. (2012). Discussion article - Genocide denial bans: What would Raphael Lemkin do? Retrieved from The Worldbuzz Blog website: http://worldbuzz.blogs.france24.com/article/2012/02/03/genocide-denial-bans-what-would-raphael-lemkin-do-0

Jacobs, S. L. (Ed.). (2012). *Lemkin on genocide*. Plymouth: Lexington Books.

Jacobs, W. (2011). Prof. Peter Erlinder speaks on Rwanda genocide. Retrieved from Afro Beat Radio website: http://afrobeatradio.net/2011/02/09/prof-peter-erlinder-speaks-on-rwanda-genocide/

Jacobson, B. S., & Lowery, B. J. (1992). Further analysis of the psychometric properties of the Levine denial of illness scale. *Psychosomatic Medicine, 54*, 372–381.

Jalloh, C. (2010). (Re)writing history after Rwanda's genocide: A response to Peter Erlinder. Retrieved from the Jurist website: http://jurist.org/forum/2010/08/rewriting-history-after-rwandas-genocide-a-response-to-peter-erlinder.php

Jansen, Y.-O. (2014). Denying genocide or denying free speech? A case study of the application of Rwanda's genocide denial laws. *Northwestern Journal of International Human Rights, 12*(2), 191–213.

Janssens, A. L. J. (1999). De loochenaars van Auschwitz. *Ontmoetingen: Voordrachtenreeks van het Lutje Psychiatrisch-Juridisch Gezelschap, 5*, 31–42.

Jeune Afrique - AFP. (2014). Mali: La vie des génocidaires rwandais à la prison de Koulikoro. Retrieved from Jeune Afrique website: www.jeuneafrique.com/Articleimp_ARTJAWEB20140407174548_mali-la-vie-des-genocidaires-rwandais-a-la-prison-de-koulikoro.html

Johnson, R. (2013). The travesty of Human Rights Watch on Rwanda. Retrieved from The Travesty of Human Rights Watch on Rwanda Blog website: http://travesty-of-hrw-on-rwanda.blogspot.ch/

Jonassohn, K., & Björnson, K. S. (1998). *Genocide and gross human rights violations in comparative perspective*. New Brunswick: Transaction Publishers.

Jones, A. (2006). *Genocide: A comprehensive introduction*. New York: Routledge.

Jones, A. (2010a). Denying Rwanda: A response to Herman and Peterson. Retrieved from Genocide Studies Media File website: http://jonestream.blogspot.nl/2010/11/denying-rwanda-response-to-herman.html

Jones, A. (2010b, 29th December). Denying Rwanda: An open letter to John Pilger, *Pambazuka News*. Retrieved from www.pambazuka.net/en/category/letters/70038

Jones, A. (2010c). *Genocide: A comprehensive introduction* (2nd ed.). London: Routledge - Taylor & Francis Publishers.

Jones, A. (2010d). On genocide deniers: Challenging Herman and Peterson, *Pambazuka News*. Retrieved from www.pambazuka.net/en/category/features/65977

Jones, A. (2011a). *Rwanda and the politics of genocide denial*. Paper presented at the 9th Biennial Conference of the International Association of Genocide Scholars (IAGS), Buenos Aires, Argentina.

Jones, A. (2011b). Why do leading leftists deny the Rwandan Genocide of 1994? Retrieved from Genocide Studies Media File website: http://jonestream.blogspot.nl/2011/12/why-do-leading-leftists-deny-rwandan.html

Jones, A. (2013). Denying Rwanda. In A. Jones (Ed.), *The scourge of genocide. Essays and reflections* (pp. 346–359). New York: Routledge.

Jones, A. (2014). The Great Lakes genocides: Hidden histories, hidden precedents. In A. L. Hinton, T. La Pointe & D. Irvin - Erickson (Eds.), *Hidden genocides: Power, knowledge, memory*. New Brunswick: Rutgers University Press.

Jones, A. (Ed.). (2004). *Genocide, war crimes and the West: History and complicity*. London: Zed Books.

Jongman, A. J. (Ed.). (1996). *Contemporary genocides: Causes, cases, consequences*. Leiden: PIOOM.

Jørgensen, M., & Philips, L. (2002). *Discourse analysis as theory and method*. London: Sage Publications.

Jorgensen, N. H. B. (2007). Genocide as a fact of common knowledge. *International and Comparative Law Quarterly, 56*, 885–898.

Jost, J. T., Banaji, M. R., & Nosek, B. A. (2004). A decade of system justification theory: Accumulated evidence of conscious and unconscious bolstering of the status quo. *Political Psychology, 25*, 881–919.

Kagabo, E. (2010). Amnesty International is operating at stage eight of a genocide, *The New Times*. Retrieved from http://allafrica.com/stories/201009131087.html
Kagame, P. (2008). Preface. In P. Clark & Z. D. Kaufman (Eds.), *After genocide: Transitional justice, post-conflict reconstruction and reconciliation in Rwanda and beyond* (pp. xxi - xxvi). London: Hurst Publishers.
Kagame, P. (2009, 7th April). Speech by His Excellency Paul Kagame: 15th commemoration of the genocide against the Tutsi at the Nyanza memorial site in Kicukiro. Retrieved from www.paulkagame.com/speeches07-04-09.php
Kagire, E. (2012). Kigali will this time around not be bullied into a war of words, *The East African*. Retrieved from www.theeastafrican.co.ke/Rwanda/News/Rwanda+denies+Amnesty+report+on+J2+torture+and+detention+/-/1433218/1531992/-/gjk2m6/-/index.html
Kagire, E., & Condon, P. (2010). Peter Erlinder, American lawyer, arrested by Rwandan police. Retrieved from Huffington Post website: www.huffingtonpost.com/2010/05/29/peter-erlinder-american-l_n_594440.html
Kahn, R. A. (2004). *Holocaust denial and the law: A comparative study*. New York: Palgrave Macmillan.
Kamana, E. (2009). Dancing to the revisionist tune in the name of promoting "rights", *The New Times*. Retrieved from www.newtimes.co.rw/news/index.php?i=13915&a=16270&icon=Results&id=2.
Kambanda, J. (1995). Memorandum on the political situation prevailing in Rwanda submitted to the President of Zambia by Rwanda Government in Exile.
Kambanda, J. (1997). Testimony and confession.
Kambanda, J. (2011). La planification du genocide des Tutsi et des Hutu par Paul Kagame. Koulikoro.
Kambanda, J. (2013). *Rwanda face à l'apocalypse de 1994. Contribution aux progrès de la justice et aux efforts de réconciliation du peuple rwandais*. Bruxelles: E.M.E. & InterCommunications.
Kaplan, T. P. (2009). The language of the Nazi genocide: Linguistic violence and the struggle of Germans of Jewish ancestry. New York: Cambridge University Press.
Karemera, E. (2005). La vérite d'abord, la justice ensuite. Arusha.
Karnavas, M. G. (1997). Rwanda's quest for justice: National and international efforts and challenges. *The Champion Magazine*. Retrieved from National Association of Criminal Defence Lawyers website: www.nacdl.org/CHAMPION/ARTICLES/97may01.htm
Karnowski, S. (2010). US Lawyer held in Rwanda critical of its president. Retrieved from Bet website: www.bet.com/news/news/2010/06/02/uslawyerinrwanda.html
Karugarama, T. (2010). Denial is the seed of future genocide. Retrieved from Star Tribune website: www.startribune.com/opinion/97195164.html
Katz, J. (1988). *Seductions of crime: Moral and sensual attractions in doing evil*. New York: Basic Books.
Kauzlarich, D., & Kramer, R. C. (1988). *Crimes of the American nuclear state at home and abroad*. Boston: North Eastern University Press.
Kayigamba, J. B. (2008). Without justice no reconciliation: A survivor's experience of genocide. In E. Clark & Z. D. Kaufman (Eds.), *After genocide: Transitional justice, post-conflict reconstruction and reconciliation in Rwanda and beyond* (pp. 33–42). London: Hurst Publishers.
Kayinamura, N. (2011). Remaking Rwanda: Kicking but dying all the same, *The New Times*. Retrieved from www.newtimes.co.rw/news/index.php?i=14624&week=18&a=6818
Kayishema, J.-M. (2013). Du mythe Hamite au génocide des Tutsi et á sa négation. In d. J. Semujanga & J.-L. Galabert (Eds.), Faire face au négationnisme du génocide des Tutsi (pp. 91–106). Saint-Jean: Éditions Izuba.
Keane, F. (1996). *Season of blood: A Rwandan journey*. London: Penguin Books.

Kearns, O. (2010). Polarising the debate over Rwanda. Retrieved from ZNet website: http://zcomm.org/znetarticle/polarising-the-debate-over-rwanda-by-oliver-kearns/

Kelman, H. C. (1993). The social context of torture: Policy process and authority structure. In R. D. Crelinsten & A. P. Schmid (Eds.), *The politics of pain: Torturers and their masters* (pp. 21–38). Leiden: COMT.

Kelman, H. C., & Hamilton, V. L. (1989). *Crimes of obedience*. New haven: Yale University Press.

Kezio-Musoke, D. (2010, 3th May 2010). There is no political crisis in Rwanda, it's the rules, *The East African*. Retrieved from www.theeastafrican.co.ke/news/There%20is%20no%20political%20crisis%20in%20Rwanda/-/2558/910496/-/item/1/-/hu4n18/-/index.html

Khaleeli, H. (2010). Rwanda's community courts: A unique experiment in justice, *The Guardian*. Retrieved from www.theguardian.com/world/2010/jan/11/rwanda-gacaca-courts

Khan, S. M. (2000). *The shallow graves of Rwanda*. New York: I.B. Tauris Publishers.

Kiernan, B. (2002). Cover-up and denial of genocide: Australia, The USA, East Timor and the Aborigines. *Critical Asian Studies, 34*(2), 163–192.

Kimonyo, J.-P. (2000). *Revue critique des interpretations du conflict rwandais* (Vol. Cahier no. 1). Butare: Université Nationale du Rwanda.

Kintu, R. (2005). The truth behind the Rwandan tragedy. Langly Park.

Kinzer, S. (2008). *A thousand hills: Rwanda's rebirth and the man who dreamed It*. London: John Wiley & Sons.

Klein, H., & Kogan, I. (1989). Some observations on denial and avoidance in Jewish Holocaust and post-Holocaust experience. In E. L. Edelstein, D. L. Nathanson & A. M. Stone (Eds.), *Denial: A clarification of concepts and research* (pp. 299–308). New York: Plenum Press.

Kohen, A., Zanchelli, M., & Drake, L. (2011). Personal and political reconciliation in post-genocide Rwanda. *Social Justice Research, 24*, 85–106.

Korteweg, D. (2010). Strafbaarstelling negationisme: Geschiedschrijving via het recht. *Mediaforum, 3*, 79–83.

Kortte, K. B., & Wegener, S. T. (2004). Denial of illness in medical rehabilitation populations: Theory, research, and definition. *Rehabilitation Psychology, 49*(3), 187–199.

Krabbe, M. (2014). *Excusable evil: An analysis of complete defences in international crimes law*. Antwerpen: Intersentia.

Krämer, S. (2005). *Gewalt der Sprache - Sprache der Gewalt*. Berlin: AAD Trescom.

Krauss, T. (2014). In the ghost forest. In M. Cave & S. M. Sloan (Eds.), *Listening on the edge: Oral History in the aftermath of Crisis*. Oxford: Oxford University Press.

Kreitler, S. (1999). Denial in cancer patients. *Cancer Investigation, 17*(7), 514–514.

Kroslak, D. (2007). *The role of France in the Rwandan genocide*. London: C. Hurst & Co ltd.

Kübler-Ross, E. (1969). *On death and dying*. New York: Macmillan.

Kučs, A. (2014). Denial of genocide and crimes against humanity in the jurisprudence of human rights monitoring bodies. *Journal of Ethnic and Migration Studies, 40*(2), 301–319.

Kumar, K., Tardif-Douglin, D., Knapp, C., Maynard, K., Manikas, P., & Sheckler, A. (1996). Rebuilding post-war Rwanda: The role of the international community. Aid evaluation special study report No. 76. Washington DC: U.S. Agency for International Development (Center for Development and Evaluation).

Kuper, L. (1981). *Genocide*. New haven: Yale University Press.

Kuper, L. (1994). Theoretical issues relating to genocide: Uses and abuses. In G. J. Andreopoulos (Ed.), *Genocide: Conceptual and historical dimensions* (pp. 32–46). Philadelphia: University of Pennsylvania Press.

Kuper, L. (2002). Genocide: Its political use in the twentieth century. In A. L. Hinton (Ed.), *Genocide, An anthropological reader* (pp. 48–73). Oxford Blackwell Publishers.

Kwinjeh, G. (2009a). 15 years after the 1994 Genocide against the Tutsi, why we must never forget, *The New Times*. Retrieved from www.newtimes.co.rw/news/index.php?i=13889&a=15520

Kwinjeh, G. (2009b). 'Group of academics' Or have the HRW genocide negationists come out clean?, *The New Times*. Retrieved from www.newtimes.co.rw/news/views/article_print.php?i=13917&a=16353&icon=Print
Laclau, E., & Mouffe, C. (2001). *Hegemony and socialist strategy: Towards a radical democratic politics* (2 ed.). London: Verso.
Langton, R. (1993). Speech acts and unspeakable acts. *Philosophy and Public Affairs, 22*(4), 305–330.
Langton, R. (1998). Subordination, silence and pornography's authority. In R. Post (Ed.), *Censorship and silencing: Practices of cultural regulation* (pp. 261–284). J. Paul Getty Trust and Oxford University Press.
Lanier, M. M., & Henry, S. (2010). *Essential criminology*. Boulder: Westview Press.
Lanotte, O. (2007). *La France au Rwanda (1990–1994) Entre abstention impossible et engagement ambivalent*. Bruxelles: P.I.E. Peter Lang.
Laqueur, W. (1980). *The terrible secret*. London: Penguin.
Lasson, K. (2007). Defending truth: Legal and psychological aspects of Holocaust denial. *Current Psychology, 26*(3–4), 223–266.
Laub, D. (1992). Bearing witness, or the vicissitudes of listening. In S. Felman & D. Laub (Eds.), *Testimony: Crises of witnessing in literature, psychoanalysis, and history* (pp. 57–74). London: Routledge.
Laufer, W. S. (1999). The forgotten criminology of genocide. In W. S. Laufer & F. Adler (Eds.), *The Criminology of Criminal Law* (pp. 71–82). London: Transaction Publishers.
Lazarus, R. S. (1983). The costs and benefits of denial. In S. Breznitz (Ed.), *The denial of stress* (pp. 1–30). New York: International Universities Press, INC.
Le Point. (2012). D'étranges missiles français dans l'arsenal rwandais. Retrieved from Le Point.fr website: www.lepoint.fr/societe/d-etranges-missiles-francais-dans-l-arsenal-rwandais-01-06-2012-1468153_23.php
Lecomte, J.-M. (2001). *Teaching about the Holocaust in the 21st century*. Strasbourg: Council of Europe Publishing.
Lemarchand, R. (1995). Rwanda: The rationality of genocide. *Issue: A Journal of Opinion, 23*(2), 8–11.
Lemarchand, R. (2007a). The Politics of memory in post-genocide Rwanda. Minneapolis: Centre for Holocaust and Genocide Studies University of Minnesota.
Lemarchand, R. (2007b). Review essay: Controversy within the cataclysm. *African Studies Review, 50* (1), 140–144.
Lemarchand, R. (2007c). Scholarly review: Rwanda: The state of research. Retrieved from Online Encyclopedia of Mass Violence website: www.massviolence.org/RWANDA-THE-STATE-OF-RESEARCH,742
Lemarchand, R. (2009). *The dynamics of violence in Central Africa*. Philadelphia: University of Pennsylvania Press.
Lemarchand, R. (2013). Rwanda: The state of research. Retrieved from Online Encyclopedia of Mass Violence website: www.massviolence.org/IMG/article_PDF/RWANDA-THE-STATE-OF-RESEARCH,742.pdf
Lemarchand, R. (Ed.). (2011). *Forgotten genocides*. Philadelphia: University of Pennsylvania Press.
Lemke, J. L. (2011). Violence and language: The signs that hurt. Retrieved from Columbia University website: www.columbia.edu/cu/21stC/issue-1.2/Language.htm
Lemkin, R. (1933a). Acts constituting a general (transnational) danger considered as offences against the law of nations - Additional explications to the special report presented to the 5th Conference for the Unification of Penal Law in Madrid (14–20 October 1933). Retrieved from Prevent Genocide website: www.preventgenocide.org/lemkin/madrid1933-english.htm

Lemkin, R. (1933b). Akte der Barbarei und des Vandalismus als *delicta juris gentium. Internationales Anwaltsblatt (Wien), 19*(6). Retrieved from Prevent Genocide website: www.preventgenocide.org/de/lemkin/anwaltsblatt1933.htm

Lemkin, R. (1944). *Axis rule in occupied Europe: Laws of occupation - Analysis of government proposals for redress*. Washington D.C.: Carnegie Endowment for International Peace.

Lemkin, R. (1945). Genocide - A modern crime. *Free World*. Retrieved from Prevent Genocide website: www.preventgenocide.org/lemkin/freeworld1945.htm

Lemkin, R. (1946). Genocide. *American Scholar, 15*(2), 227–230. Retrieved from Prevent Genocide website: www.preventgenocide.org/lemkin/americanscholar1946.htm

Lemkin, R. (1947). Genocide as a crime under international law. *American Journal of International Law, 41*(1), 145–151. Retrieved from Prevent Genocide website: www.preventgenocide.org/lemkin/ASIL1947.htm

Lerner, M. (1980). *The belief in a just world*. New York: Plenum Press.

Leurs, R. (2009). The 'chain of equivalence'. Cultural studies and Laclau & Mouffe's discourse theory. Retrieved from Politics and Culture website: http://politicsandculture.org/2009/11/09/the-chain-of-equivalence-cultural-studies-and-laclau-mouffes-discourse-theory/

Levine, J., Warrenburg, S., Kerns, R., Schwartz, D., Delany, R., & Fontana, A. (1987). The role of denial in recovery from coronary heart disease. *Journal of Psychosomatic Medicine, 38*, 109–117.

Levinson, S. C. (1983). *Pragmatics*. Cambridge: Cambridge University Press.

Li, D. (2004). Echoes of violence: Considerations on radio and genocide in Rwanda. *Journal of Genocide Research, 6*(1), 9–27.

Lifton, R. J. (1967). *Death in life: Survivors of Hiroshima*. New York: Random House.

Lincoln, Y. S., & Guba, E. G. (1985). *Naturalistic inquiry*. London: Sage Publications.

Lipowski, Z. J. (1970). Physical illness, the individual and the coping process. *International Journal of Psychiatry in Medicine, 1*, 91–102.

Lipstadt, D. E. (1993). *Denying the Holocaust: The growing assault on truth and memory*. New York: The Free Press.

Lipstadt, D. E. (2007). Denial should be defeated by facts, not laws. Retrieved from Spiked website: www.spiked-online.com/index.php/site/article/3609/

Lipstadt, D. E., & Balakian, P. (2007). Turkey must acknowledge its past. Retrieved from Deborah Lipstadt's Blog website: http://lipstadt.blogspot.nl/2007_09_01_archive.html

Livneh, H. (2009). Denial of chronic illness and disability: Part 1. Theoretical, functional, and dynamic perspectives. *Rehabilitation Counselling Bulletin, 52*(4), 225–236.

Longman, T. P. (2004). Placing genocide in context: Research priorities for the Rwandan genocide. *Journal of Genocide Research, 6*(1), 29–45.

lovett, I. (2011). The Shoah Foundation widens scope, *The New York Times*. Retrieved from www.nytimes.com/2011/11/17/arts/shoah-foundation-institute-examines-other-genocides.html?_r=2&pagewanted=all

Loxley, J. (2007). *Performativity*. London: Routledge.

Luria, A. R. (1968). *The mind of a mnemonist: A little book about a vast memory*. Cambridge: Harvard University Press.

MacLennon, S. (2010). *Account giving as a fundamental social practice and a central sociological concept: A theoretical and methodological reconceptualisation and a practical exploration in a critical case*. (Doctor of Philosophy), University of Edinburgh, Edinburgh.

Magnarella, P. J. (1998). The U.N. Criminal Tribunal for Rwanda concludes its first case: A monumental step towards truth. *African Studies Quarterly, 2*(3), 21–26.

Maier-Kaitkin, D., Mears, D. P., & Bernard, T. J. (2009). Towards a criminology of crimes against humanity. *Theoretical Criminology, 13*(2), 227–255.

Malagardis, M. (2012). Rwanda, la preuve d'un génocide planifié, *Libération*. Retrieved from www.liberation.fr/monde/2012/01/11/rwanda-la-preuve-d-un-genocide-planifie_787468
Malagardis, M. (2013). Un dossier relancé par le juge Trévedic, *Libération*. Retrieved from www.liberation.fr/monde/2013/01/09/un-dossier-relance-par-le-juge-trevidic_872892
Mamdani, M. (2002). *When victims become killers: Colonialism, nativism, and the genocide in Rwanda*. Princeton/Oxford: Princeton University Press.
Mandel, S., & Steinberg, G. M. (2009). Experts or Ideologues? A systematic analysis of Human Rights Watch's focus on Israel. www.ngo-monitor.org/article/experts_or_ideologues_a_systematic_analysis_of_hrw_s_focus_on_israel_executive_summary_english_
Mann, M. (2005). *The dark side of democracy: Explaining ethnic cleansing*. Cambridge: Cambridge University Press.
Manne, R. (2001). *In denial: The stolen generations and the right*. Melbourne: Black Inc.
Manousos, R., & Williams, D. I. (1998). The locus of denial. *Councelling Psychology Quarterly, 11*(1), 15–22.
Martin, B. (2009). Managing outrage over genocide: Case study Rwanda. *Global Change, Peace & Security, 21*(3), 275–290.
Matsuda, M. J., Lawrence III, C. R., Delgado, R., & Williams Crenshaw, K. (1993). *Words that wound: Critical race theory, assaultive speech, and the first amendment*. Boulder: Westview Press.
Matthäus, J. (1996). What about the "ordinary men"?: The German order police and the Holocaust in the occupied Soviet Union. *Holocaust and Genocide Studies, 10*(2), 134–150.
Matza, D. (1964). *Delinquency and drift*. New York: John Wiley.
McGreal, C. (2000). Genocide? What genocide?, *The Guardian*. Retrieved from www.theguardian.com/comment/story/0,3604,181819,00.html
McGreal, C. (2008). 'If Tutsis died it was because the people were angry with them', *The Guardian*. Retrieved from www.theguardian.com/world/2008/dec/19/theoneste-bagosora-rwanda-tutsis
McKinley, J. C. (1998). Former Rwandan premier pleads guilty to genocide, *The New York Times*. Retrieved from http://partners.nytimes.com/library/world/africa/050298rwanda-genocide.html
McKinney, C. (2001). *Covert Action in Africa*.
McLean Hilker, L. (2011). The role of education in driving conflict and building peace: The case of Rwanda. *Prospects, 41*(2), 267–282.
Melvern, L. (2006). *Conspiracy to murder: The Rwandan genocide*. London/New York: Verso.
Melvern, L. (2012a). The expert investigation of the 'perfect crime' that was the trigger for the Rwandan genocide. Retrieved from Genocide Prevention Now website: www.genocidepreventionnow.org/Home/GPNISSUES/Issue9Winter2012/tabid/165/ctl/DisplayArticle/mid/1024/aid/464/Default.aspx
Melvern, L. (2012b). Rwanda: At least we know the truth, *The Guardian*. Retrieved from www.theguardian.com/commentisfree/2012/jan/10/rwanda-at-last-we-know-truth
Melvern, L., & Stanton, G. H. (2014). The Rwandan Genocide, *The New York Times*. Retrieved from www.nytimes.com
Milburn, M. A., & Conrad, S. D. (1996). *The politics of denial*. London: MIT Press.
Miller, J. (1990). *One, by one, by one: Facing the Holocaust*. New York: Simon and Schuster.
Mills, C. W. (1940). Situated actions and vocabularies of motive. *American Sociological Review, 15*, 904–913.
Mills, S. (1997). *Discourse*. London: Routledge.
Minestère des Affaires Etrangers du Rwanda. (1964). Toute la verite sur le terrorisme "Inyenzi" au Rwanda.
Mirzoeff, N. (2005). Invisible again: Rwanda and representation after genocide. *African Arts, 38*(3), 36–39, 86–91, 96.

Moerland, C. A. R. (2009). Japanese sexual slavery. In D. P. Forsythe (Ed.), *Encyclopedia of Human Rights* (pp. 279–290). Oxford: Oxford University Press.

Moerland, C. A. R. (2011). Endorsing denial of the 1994 genocide against the Tutsi: Open letters to professor Noam Chomsky. Retrieved from Urumuri Rw'izuba website: http://rolandmoerland.blogspot.nl/2011/02/endorsing-denial-of-1994-genocide.html

Moerland, C. A. R. (2014a). Unacceptable or appropriate? UN Security Council adopts new terminology to denote the genocide that was perpetrated in Rwanda in 1994 – Update. Retrieved from Maastricht University Denialism and Human Rights website: http://law.maastrichtuniversity.nl/denialismandhumanrights/?p=93

Moerland, C. A. R. (2014b). Verzet of collaboratie? Hoe de strijd tegen genocide kan bijdragen aan genocide. *Tijdschrift over Cultuur & Criminaliteit, 4*(1), 80–96.

Mols, G. (2009). Omzien in tevredenheid? Retrieved from Scherp in Strafrecht website: www.scherpinstrafrecht.nl/site/column/column2.html

Monbiot, G. (2011a, 13th of June). Left and libertarian right cohabit in the weird world of the genocide belittlers, *The Guardian*. Retrieved from www.theguardian.com/commentisfree/2011/jun/13/left-and-libertarian-right

Monbiot, G. (2011b). Media cleanse. Retrieved from George Monbiot website: www.monbiot.com/2011/08/04/media-cleanse/

Monbiot, G. (2011c). Naming the genocide deniers. Retrieved from George Monbiot website: www.monbiot.com/2011/06/13/naming-the-genocide-deniers/

Monbiot, G. (2012a). Genocide denial: Expert assessments. Retrieved from George Monbiot website: www.monbiot.com/2012/05/21/genocide-denial-expert-assessments/

Monbiot, G. (2012b, 21st of May). My fight may be hopeless, it is as necessary as ever, *The Guardian*. Retrieved from www.theguardian.com/commentisfree/2012/may/21/ratko-mladic-genocide-denial

Monthly Review Press. (2010). The politics of genocide. Retrieved from Monthly Review Press website: http://monthlyreview.org/books/pb2129/

Moon, C. (2011). The crime of crimes and the crime of criminology: Genocide, criminology and Darfur. *The British Journal of Sociology, 62*(1), 49–55.

Moore, B. E., & Rubinfine, M. D. (1969). The mechanism of denial. In B. D. Fine, E. D. Jospeh & H. F. Waldhorn (Eds.), *The Kris Study Group of the New York Psychoanalytic Institute monograph III* (pp. 1–57). New York: International Universities Press, Inc.

Morel, J. (2011). "Rwanda. L'histoire secrète" de Abdul Joshua Ruzibiza ou mensonges made in France? Retrieved from Umuvugizi website: http://umuvugizi.wordpress.com/2011/11/10/%C2%AB-rwanda-l%E2%80%99histoire-secrete-%C2%BB-de-abdul-joshua-ruzibiza-ou-mensonges-made-in-france/

Morel, J. (2014). *La France au cœur du génocide des Tutsi*. Paris: L'Esprit Frappeur/Izuba.

Morrison, W. (2004). Criminology, genocide, and modernity: Remarks on the companion that criminology ignored. In C. Summer (Ed.), *The Blackwell Companion to Criminology* (pp. 68–88). Oxford: Blackwell.

Morrison, W. (2006). *Criminology, civilisation & the new world order*. New York: Routledge-Cavendish.

Moses, A. D. (2010). Raphael Lemkin, culture, and the concept of genocide. In D. Bloxham & A. D. Moses (Eds.), *The Oxford handbook of genocide studies* (pp. 19–41). Oxford: Oxford University Press.

Moses, R. (1989). Denial in political process. In E. L. Edelstein, D. L. Nathanson & A. M. Stone (Eds.), *Denial: A clarification of concepts and research* (pp. 287–297). New York: Plenum Press.

Moyer, A. M., & Levine, E. G. (1998). Clarification of the conceptualization and measurement of denial in psychosocial oncology research. *Annals of Behavioral Medicine*, 149–160.

Mukimbiri, J. (2005). The seven stages of the Rwandan genocide. *Journal of International Criminal Justice, 3*, 823–836.
Mukimbiri, J. (2013). Pour une déconstruction du négationnisme du génocide anti-Tutsi: Arguments et contre-arguments. In d. J. Semujanga & J.-L. Galabert (Eds.), Faire face au négationnisme du génocide des Tutsi (pp. 335–354). Saint-Jean: Éditions Izuba.
Mullins, C. W. (2009). We are going to rape you and taste Tutsi women. *British Journal of Criminology, 49*(6), 719–735.
Munyandamutsa, N., Nkubamugisha, P. M., Gex-Fabry, M., & Eytan, A. (2012). Mental and physical health in Rwanda 14 years after the genocide. *Social Psychiatry and Psychiatric Epidemiology, 47*, 1753–1761.
Murana, S., & Copes, H. (2004). Excuses, excuses: What have we learned from five decades of neutralization research. *Crime and Justice, 32*.
Musoni, E. (2009). Plans for 15th genocide anniversary in top gear *The New Times*. Retrieved from www.newtimes.co.rw/news/views/article_print.php?15320&a=13568&icon=Print
Musoni, E. (2012). Rwandan genocide convicts imprisoned in Mali reportedly living "lavishly", *The New Times*. Retrieved from www.biyokulule.com/view_content.php?articleid=5489
Mutabaruka, J., Séjourné, N., Bui, E., Birmes, P., & Chabrol. H. (2012). Traumatic grief and traumatic stress in survivors 12 years after the genocide in Rwanda. *Stress and Health, 28*, 289–296.
Mwenda, A. M. (2014). Rwanda's self-emancipation, *The Independent*. Retrieved from www.independent.co.ug/the-last-word/the-last-word/8872
Nahimana, F. (1996). Rwanda. L'elite Hutu accusee. Retrieved from Ferdinand Nahimana website: www.nahimana.info/index.php?id=29
Nahimana, F. (2007). *Rwanda. Les virages ratés*. Lille: Éditions Sources du Nile.
Najarian, J. (1997). Gnawing at history: The rhetoric of Holocaust denial. *The Midwest Quarterly*(Autumn).
Nash-Marshall, S., & Mahdessian, R. (2013). Lies, damned lies, and genocide. *Metaphilosophy, 44*(1–2), 116–144.
Nathanson, D. L. (1989). Denial, projection, and the empathic wall. In E. L. Edelstein, D. L. Nathanson & A. M. Stone (Eds.), *Denial: A clarification of concepts and research* (pp. 37–60). New York: Plenum Press.
National Commission for the Fight Against Genocide. (2009). Raporo yo kwibuka ku nshuro 15 jenoside yaorewe Abatutsi. Kigali.
National Inquiry into the Separation of Aboriginal and Torres Strait Islander Children From Their Families. (1997). Bringing them home: Report of the national inquiry into the separation of Aboriginal and Torres Strait Islander children from their families. Retrieved from Australian Human Rights Commission website: https://www.humanrights.gov.au/publications/bringing-them-home-report-1997
Ndahinda, F. (2011). Rising revisionism of the Tutsi genocide in Europe, US and Canada. Retrieved from Friends of Evil website: http://friendsofevil.wordpress.com/2011/03/18/the-rising-revisionism-of-the-tutsi-genocide-in-europe-us-and-canada/
Ndahiro, T. (2008). Genocide-laundering: Historical revisionism, genocide denial and the role of the Rassemblement Republicain Pour La Democratie Au Rwanda. In P. Clark & Z. D. Kaufman (Eds.), *After genocide: Transitional justice, post-conflict reconstruction and reconciliation in Rwanda and beyond* (pp. 101–124). London: Hurst Publishers.
Ndahiro, T. (2012). Pierre Péan: Europe allows genocide denial in the age of 'never again'. Retrieved from Umuvugizi website: http://umuvugizi.wordpress.com/pierre-pean-europe-allows-genocide-denial-in-the-age-of-%E2%80%98never-again%E2%80%99/
Ndahiro, T. (2013). *Friends of Evil*. Retrieved from http://friendsofevil.wordpress.com/category/book/

Neubacher, F. (2006). How can it happen that horrendous state crimes are perpetrated? *Journal of International Criminal Justice, 4*, 787–799.
New York Times. (2006). Turkey, Armenia and denial. Retrieved from www.nytimes.com/2006/05/16/opinion/16tue3.html?_r=0
Newbury, C. (1988). *The cohesion of oppression: Clientship and ethnicity in Rwanda 1860–1960.* New York: Columbia University Press.
Newbury, C. (2002). Ethnicity and the politics of history in Rwanda. In D. E. Lorey & W. H. Beezley (Eds.), *Genocide, collective violence, and popular memory* (pp. 68–83). Wilmington: SR Books.
News of Rwanda. (2012). Rwanda: Belgian police arrests Rwandan for genocide negation. Retrieved from Rwanda News Agency website: http://rnanews.com/politics/5942-belgian-police-arrest-rwandan-politician-for-genocide-negation
Ngoga, M. (2010). Why we're prosecuting Peter Erlinder, *The Guardian*. Retrieved from www.guardian.co.uk/law/2010/jul/03/why-prosecute-peter-erlinder/print
Nichanian, M. (1999). The truth of the facts: About the new revisionism. In R. G. Hovannisian (Ed.), *Remembrance and denial: The case of the Armenian genocide* (pp. 249–270). Detroit: Wayne State University Press.
Nichanian, M. (2003). Between genocide and catastrophe. In D. L. Eng & D. Kazanjian (Eds.), *Loss. The politics of mourning.* (pp. 125–147). Berkeley: University of California Press.
Nichanian, M. (2009). *The historiographic perversion.* New York: Columbia University Press.
Nolte, E. (1974). *Deutschland und der kalte Krieg.* München: Piper.
Nsengimana, J. (2009). 15th commemoration of the Rwandan genocide. New York.
Nshimiyiman, E. (2013). Profession de haine: Du syndrome du "Hutu Power" au négationnisme du Génocide contre les Tutsis. In d. J. Semujanga & J.-L. Galabert (Eds.), *Faire face au négationnisme du génocide des Tutsis* (pp. III - XV). Saint-Jean: Éditions Izuba.
Ntakirutimana. (2013). Le négationnisme du génocide rwandais en paroles et en actions. In d. J. Semujanga & J.-L. Galabert (Eds.), *Faire face au négationnisme du génocide des Tutsi* (pp. 45–58). Saint-Jean: Éditions Izuba.
Ntamabyaliro, A. (1994a). *Cover letter document Le peuple rwandais accuse ...* Republic of Rwanda Ministry of Justice.
Ntamabyaliro, A. (1994b). Le peuple rwandais accuse ... Bukavu: Interim Government of Rwanda.
Nyetera, A. T. (2009). *Education au mensonge et la calomnie.* Paper presented at the International Criminal Tribunal for Rwanda: An independent conference on its legacy from the defence perspective, The Hague.
Nyirimanzi, G., & Nyakinama, N. (2007). *The genocide ideology (Training manual).* Kigali.
Nzabahimana, F. (1994). Le Rwanda ou l'urgence politique. Staumont: Comite rwandais d'action pour la democratique.
O'Malley, P. (1994). Gentle genocide: The government of Aboriginal peoples in Central Australia. *Social Justice, 21*(4), 46–65.
O'Neill, B. (2007). 'Genocide denial laws will shut down debate', *Spiked Online*. Retrieved from www.spiked-online.com/index.php?/site/article/2824/
Odom, T. (2008). Book review - Conspiracy to murder: The Rwandan genocide. Retrieved from Small Wars Journal website: http://smallwarsjournal.com/blog/book-review-conspiracy-to-murder-the-rwandan-genocide
Office of the Prosecutor International Criminal Tribunal for Rwanda. (1998). Statement by Prosecutor Louise Arbour regarding the International Tribunal for Rwanda. Retrieved from United Nations International Criminal Tribunal for the former Yugoslavia website: www.icty.org/sid/7674

Ohlstain, E., & Cohen, A. D. (1983). Apology: A speech act set. In N. Wolfson & E. Judd (Eds.), *Sociolinguistics and language acquisition* (pp. 18–35). MA: Newbury House.
Oluoch-Ojiwah, F. (2010). Is Kenneth Roth in love with génocidaires?, *The New Times*. Retrieved from www.newtimes.co.rw/news/index.php?i=14242&a=28453
Oomen, B. (2006). Rwanda's Gacaca: Objectives, merits and their relation to supranational criminal law. In R. Haveman (Ed.), *Sentencing in supranational criminal law* (pp. 1–20). The Hague: Intersentia.
Orbuch, T. L. (1997). People's accounts count: The sociology of accounts. *Annual Review Sociology, 23*, 455–478.
Pall, Z. (2010). Light shining darkly: Comparing post-conflict constitutional structures concerning speech and association in Germany and Rwanda. *Colombia Human Rights Law Review, 42*(5), 6–54.
Payne, L. A. (2008). *Unsettling accounts: Neither truth nor reconciliation in confessions of state violence*. Durham: Duke University Press.
Péan, P. (2005). *Noires fureurs, blancs menteurs: Rwanda 1990–1994*. Paris: Mille et une nuits.
Penal Reform International. (2010). The contribution of the Gacaca jurisdictions to resolving cases arising from the genocide. Contributions, limitations and expectations of the post-Gacaca phase. London: Penal Reform International.
Pendas, D. O. (2007). The Holocaust and the postmodern (review). *Holocaust and Genocide Studies, 21*(3), 519–521.
Peretti-Watel, P. (2003). Neutralization theory and the denial of risk: Some evidence from cannabis use among French adolescents. *British Journal of Sociology, 54*(1), 21–42.
Perlez, J. (1995). Under the Bougainvillea. A litany of past wrongs, *New York Times*. Retrieved from www.nytimes.com/1994/08/15/world/under-the-bougainvillea-a-litany-of-past-wrongs .html
Peter, C. M. (1997). The International Criminal Tribunal for Rwanda: Bringing the killers to book. *International Review of the Red Cross, 321*.
Peterson, D. (2011a). George Monbiot and the anti-"genocide deniers" brigade. Retrieved from ZNet website: http://zcomm.org/znetarticle/george-monbiot-and-the-anti-genocide-deniers-brigade-by-david-peterson/
Peterson, D. (2011b). Rwanda's 1991 census. Retrieved from ZBlogs website: http://zcomm.org/zblogs/rwandas-1991-census/
Philpot, J. (1997). The Rwandan impunity issue: The theft of truth and justice in Central Africa. *Living Marxism* (103).
Philpot, J. (2009). *Impunity at the ICTR*. Paper presented at the ICTR Defence Conference, The Hague.
Philpot, R. (2003). *Ça ne s'est pas passé comme ça à Kigali*. Paris: Les Intouchables.
Philpot, R. (2004). *Rwanda 1994: Colonialism dies hard*. Retrieved from www.taylor-report.com
Philpot, R. (2013). *Rwanda and the new scramble for Africa: From tragedy to useful imperial fiction*. Montréal: Baraka Books.
Pierce, J. R. (2000). *Speak Rwanda*. New York: Picador.
Potter, J. (2001). Wittgenstein and Austin. In M. Wetherell, S. Taylor & S. J. Yates (Eds.), *Discourse theory and practice: A reader* (pp. 39–46). London: Sage Publications.
Pottier, J. (2002). *Re-imagining Rwanda: Conflict, survival and disinformation in the late twentieth century*. Cambridge: Cambridge University Press.
Power, S. (2002). *A problem from hell: America and the age of genocide*. London: Flamingo.
Pratt, M. L. (1986). Ideology and speech act theory. *Poetics Today, 7*(1), 59–72.
Presdee, M. (2000). *Cultural criminology and the carnival of crime*. London: Routledge.
President of the Republic T. Sindikubwabo. (1994). Arrêté présidentiel du 8 avril 1994 portant désignation des membres du gouvernement.

Pruitt, W. R. (2014). How criminology can engage in the theorizing on genocide? *International Journal of Criminal Justice Sciences, 9*(1), 1–15.
Prunier, G. (1995). *The Rwanda crisis: History of a genocide*. New York: Columbia University Press.
Prunier, G. (2009). *Africa's world war: Congo, the Rwandan genocide, and the making of a continental catastrophe*. Oxford: Oxford University Press.
Radio France Internationale. (2008). Key witness in Kabuye trial retracts testimony. Retrieved from Rfi English website: http://www1.rfi.fr/actuen/articles/107/article_2190.asp
Raes, K. (1995). Vrijheid van meningsuiting en de revisionistische geschiedvervalsing. In G. A. I. Schuijt (Ed.), *Vrijheid van meningsuiting. Racisme en revisionisme* (pp. 31–77). Gent: Academia Press.
Raes, K. (1997). De wet ter bestrijding van het negationisme: Ethisch-politieke vragen bij het beteugelen van de meningsvrijheid. In G. Verbeeck (Ed.), *De verdwenen gaskamers: De ontkenning van de Holocaust.* (pp. 63–80). Leuven: Acco.
Rafter, N. (2008). Criminology's darkest hour: Biocriminology in Nazi Germany. *Australian & New Zealand Journal of Criminology, 41*(2), 287–306.
Rafti, M. (2004a). The dismantling of the Rwandan political opposition in exile. *L'Afrique des Grands Lacs. Annuaire 2003–2004*, 22–42.
Rafti, M. (2004b). The Rwandan political opposition in exile: A valid interlocutor vis-à-vis Kigali? *(IDPM-UA discussion paper, 2004:1)*: Institute of Development Policy and Management, University of Antwerp.
Rassemblement pour le Retour des Réfugiés et la Démocratie au Rwanda. (1995). Declaration de creation du RDR.
Rassemblement pour le Retour des Réfugiés et la Démocratie au Rwanda. (1996). Rwandese crisis: The other side of the story. Bruxelles.
Rassemblement pour le Retour des Réfugiés et la Démocratie au Rwanda. (1998). RDR political platform. Paris.
Rassemblement pour le Retour des Réfugiés et la Démocratie au Rwanda. Cameroun Wing. (1996). United Nations Security Council misled about the presumed "Tutsi genocide" in Rwanda.
Rassemblement pour le Retour et la Démocratie au Rwanda. Section Cameroun. (1995). *La vérité sur le drame rwandais*.
Republic of Rwanda. (2006). Genocide ideology and strategies for its eradication. Kigali.
Republic of Rwanda. (2007). Commission nationale indépendante chargée de rassembler les éléments de preuve montrant l'implication de l'État français dans la préparation et l'exécution du génocide perpétré au Rwanda en 1994. Kigali.
Republic of Rwanda. (2008). Rwanda: Joint governance assessment report. Kigali.
Republique Rwandaise Parlement Commission Extraordinaire. (2004). Rapport de la Parlement Parlementaire Extraordinaire mise en place le 20 Janvier 2004, chargé d'examiner les massacres commis a Gikongoro et analyser l'idéologie du génocide et ceux qui la propagent partout dans le pays. Kigali.
Reyntjens, F. (2004). La transition politique au Rwanda. In F. Reyntjens (Ed.), *L'Afrique des grands lacs: Annuaire 2003–2004* (Vol. 1–21). Paris: L'Harmattan.
Reyntjens, F. (2010). Constructing the truth, dealing with dissent, domesticating the world: Governance in post-genocide Rwanda. *African Affairs, 110*(438), 1–34.
Rieder, P. (2011). Commemoration, criticism and the encompassing acknowledgement of suffering in Rwanda. *Paper presented at 2011 IAGS Conference*. Retrieved from UNTREF website: www.untref.edu.ar/documentos/ceg/51%20PHILIPPE%20RIEDER.pdf
Riley, D. (2001). Bad words. *Diacritics, 31*(4), 41–53.

Rinn, M. (2013). La sophistique négationniste sur internet. Passions du déni du génocide des Tutsi rwandais. In d. J. Semujanga & J.-L. Galabert (Eds.), *Faire face au négationnisme du génocide du Tutsi* (pp. 247–258). Saint-Jean: Édtions Izuba.

Robertson, J. O. (1980). *American myth, American reality*. New York: Hill and Wang.

Rose, L. L. (2007). Land and genocide: Exploring the connections with Rwanda's prisoners and prison officials. *Journal of Genocide Research, 9*(1), 49–69.

Rosenfeld, G. D. (1999). The Politics of uniqueness: Reflections on the recent polemical turn in Holocaust and genocide scholarship. *Holocaust and Genocide Studies, 13*(1), 28–61.

Rosensaft, M. Z. (2011). Criminalizing mass-murder: 65 years after the UN's first condemnation of genocide. Retrieved from The World Post website: www.huffingtonpost.com/menachem-rosensaft/criminalizing-massmurder-_b_1150463.html

Ross, J. I. (2000). *Controlling state crime*. London: Transaction Publishers.

Roth, K. (2009). The power of horror in Rwanda, *Los Angeles Times*. Retrieved from www.latimes.com/opinion/la-oe-roth11-2009apr11-story.html

Rothe, D. L., & Mullins, C. W. (2009). Toward a criminology of international criminal law: An integrated theory of international criminal violations. *International Journal of Comparative and Applied Criminal Justice, 33*(1), 97–118.

Roversi, A. (2008). *Hate on the net: Extremist sites, neo-fascism on-line, electronic jihad*. Alderschot: Ashgate.

Ruggiu, G. (1995). *Dans la tourmente rwandaise*.

Rusagara, F. (2009, 24th November). Nation's resilience despite continuing denial of the genocide, *The New Times*. Retrieved from http://allafrica.com/stories/200911240071.html

Russian Legal Information Agency. (2014). Latvian parliament approves criminalization of Soviet occupation denial. Retrieved from RAPSI website: http://rapsinews.com/legislation/20140328/271031585.html

Ruzibiza, A. (2005). *Rwanda, L'histoire secrète*. Paris: Édition du Panama.

Rwagatare, J. (2011). Remaking Rwanda: Only Rwandans can do it, *The New Times*. Retrieved from http://josephrwagatare.wordpress.com/2011/04/19/remaking-rwanda-only-rwandans-can-do-it/

Rwanda News Agency. (2011a). President Kagame attacks critical human rights reports as "trash". Retrieved from http://rnanews.com/politics/5087-president-kagame-attacks-critical-human-rights-reports-as-trash

Rwanda News Agency. (2011b). Rwanda's Ministry of Justice calls Human Rights Watch report "distorting" and "misleading". Retrieved from www.rnanews.com/health/5023-rwandas-ministry-of-justice-calls-human-rights-watch-report-distorting-and-misleading

Rwandan Armed Forces. (1995a). Declaration de Soutien des Forces Armees rwandaises au Rassamblement pour le Retour et la Democratie au Rwanda (RDR).

Rwandan Armed Forces. (1995b). Meeting of 29 March - 3 April 1995.

Rwandan Armed Forces Command in exile. (1995). Contribution of RAF to the search for the truth on the Rwandan tragedy.

Rwandan Armed Forces High Command in exile. (1994). Report de la reunion du haut commandement des forces armees rwandaises et des membres des commission tenue.

Rwandan Government in Exile. (1994). Le Gouvernement en exil du 1er novembre 1994.

Sacerdoti, G., & Semi, A. A. (1989). Denial and Weltanschauung. In E. L. Edelstein, D. L. Nathanson & A. M. Stone (Eds.), *Denial: A clarification of concepts and research* (pp. 61–70). New York: Plenum Press.

Salem, R. A. (Ed.). (2000). *Witness to genocide: The children of Rwanda. Drawings by child survivors of the Rwandan genocide of 1994*. New York: Friendship Press National Council of Churches.

Sandstrom, K. L., Martin, D. D., & Fine, G. A. (2003). *Symbols, selves, and social reality: A symbolic interactionist approach to social psychology*. Los Angeles: Roxbury Publishing Company.
Sarkissian, R. (2007). The Armenian Genocide: A contextual view of the crime and politics of denial. In R. Henham & P. Behrens (Eds.), *The criminal law of genocide: International, comparative and contextual aspects* (pp. 3–15). Hampshire: Ashgate.
Scagliola, S. (2007). The silences and myths of a 'dirty war': Coming to terms with the Dutch–Indonesian decolonisation War (1945–1949). *European Review of History, 14*(2), 235–262.
Schaal, S., Weierstall, R., Dusingizemungu, J. P., & Elbert, T. (2012). Mental health 15 years after the killings in Rwanda: Imprisoned perpetrators of the genocide against the Tutsi versus a community sample of survivors. *Journal of Traumatic Stress, 25*, 446–453.
Schabas, W. A. (2005). Genocide trials and Gacaca courts. *Journal of International Criminal Justice*(3), 879–895.
Schabas, W. A. (2010). The law and genocide. In D. Bloxham & A. D. Moses (Eds.), *The Oxford handbook of genocide studies* (pp. 123–141). Oxford: Oxford University Press.
Schmidt, W. E. (1994, 9th of April). Terror convulses Rwandan capital as tribes battle, *The New York Times*. Retrieved from www.nytimes.com/1994/04/09/world/terror-convulses-rwandan-capital-as-tribes-battle.html
Schönbach, P. (1990). *Account episodes: The management or escalation of conflict*. Cambridge: Cambridge University Press.
Schwendinger, H., & Schwendinger, J. (1970). Defenders of order or guardians of human rights. *Issues in Criminology, 5*(2), 123–157.
Scott, M. B., & Lyman, S. M. (1968). Accounts. *American Sociological Review, 33*(1), 46–62.
Sculier, C. (2011). La pratique judiciaire du contentieux de l'ideologie du genocide et infractions connexes au Rwanda: Limites er defis d'application 2007–2010 Retrieved from Avocats Sans Frontières website: www.asf.be/blog/publications/asf_rwanda_pratiquejudiciairecontentieuxgenocide/
Scurfield, R. M. (1992). The collusion of sanitization and silence about war: An aftermath of "Operation Desert Storm" *Journal of Traumatic Stress, 5*(3), 505–512.
Searle, J. R. (1965). What is a speech act? In M. Black (Ed.), *Philosophy in America* (pp. 221–239). London: Allen & Unwin.
Searle, J. R. (1968). Austin on locutionary and illocutionary acts. *The Philosophical Review, 77*(4), 405–424.
Searle, J. R. (1969). *Speech acts*. New York: Cambridge University Press.
Searle, J. R. (1975). Indirect speech acts. *Syntax and Semantics*, 59–82.
Searle, J. R. (1976). A classification of illocutionary acts. *Language in Society, 5*(1), 1–23.
Searle, J. R. (1979a). *Expression and meaning: Studies in the theory of speech acts*. Cambridge: Cambridge University Press.
Searle, J. R. (1979b). What is an intentional state. *Mind, 88*(349), 74–92.
Searle, J. R. (2001). How performatives work. In D. Vanderveken & S. Kubo (Eds.), *Essays in speech act theory* (pp. 85–108). Amsterdam: John Benjamins Publishing Company.
Searle, J. R., & Vanderveken, D. (1985). *Foundations of illocutionary logic*. Cambridge: Cambridge University Press.
Segal, A. (1964). *Massacre in Rwanda*: Fabian Society.
Sellin, T. (1938). *Culture conflict and crime*. New York: Social Science Research Council.
Semelin, J. (2007). *Purify and destroy: The political uses of massacre and genocide*. New York: Columbia University Press.
Semujanga, d. J. (2013). Le négationnisme de l'Itsembabwoko, dénégation et manipulation politique. In d. J. Semujanga & J.-L. Galabert (Eds.), *Faire face au négationnisme du génocide des Tutsi* (pp. 9–30). Saint Jean: Éditions Izuba.

Semujanga, d. J., & Galabert, J.-L. (Eds.). (2013). *Faire face au négationnisme du génocide des Tutsi*. Saint-Jean: Éditions Izuba.
Sénat du Belgique. (1997). Commission d'enquête parlemetaire concernant les événements au Rwanda, Sénat de Belgique, session de 1997–1998, 6 décembre 1997, Rapport fait au nom de la commission d'enquête par MM Mahoux et Verhofstadt.
Seu, I. B. (2010). 'Doing denial': Audience reaction to human rights appeals. *Discourse & Society, 21*(4), 438–457.
Seu, I. B. (2011). 'Shoot the messenger': Dynamics of positioning and denial in response to human rights appeals. *Journal of Human Rights Practice, 3*(2), 139–161.
Seu, I. B. (2013). *Passivity generation: Human rights and everyday morality*. New York: Palgrave Macmillan.
Shafir, M. (2002). Between denial and "comparative trivialization": Holocaust negationism in post-Communist East Central Europe. Analysis of current trends In The Vidal Sassoon International Center for the Study of Antisemitism (Ed.), *Analysis of current trends in antisemitism, Acta no. 19*. Jerusalem: The Hebrew University of Jerusalem.
Shalev, C. (2011). Full interview with holocaust historian Deborah Lipstadt. Retrieved from Haaretz website: www.haaretz.com/jewish-world/full-interview-with-holocaust-historian-deborah-lipstadt-1.401823
Shannon, K. G. (2006). Judicial notice of genocide. *Revue Québécoise de Droit International, 19*(2), 95–122.
Shaw, M. (2007). *What is genocide?* Cambridge: Polity Press.
Shaw, M. (2011a). Book reviews. The politics of genocide. Edward S. Herman and David Peterson. New York: Monthly Review Press, 2010. *Journal of Genocide Research, 13*(3), 353–387.
Shaw, M. (2011b). Edward S. Herman and David Peterson, *The politics of genocide* Draft Review to appear in the *Journal of Genocide Research,* 13, 3, 2011.
Shermer, M., & Grobman, A. (2000). *Denying history: Who says the Holocaust never happened and why do they say it?* Berkeley: University of California Press.
Shockey, P. (2004). Understanding denial. *Oncology Nursing Forum, 31*(5), 985–988.
Simons, H., & Crawford, B. (1996). Rwanda: The great genocide debate. *LM,* (88). Retrieved from Web Archive website: http://web.archive.org/web/20000325071207/www.informinc.co.uk/LM/LM88/LM88_Rwanda.html
Sjöbäck, H. (1973). *The psychoanalytic theory of defensive processes*. New York: John Wiley & Sons.
Skidelsky, E. (2010). Words that think for us. Retrieved from Prospect Magazine website: www.prospectmagazine.co.uk/regulars/words-that-think-for-us
Smeulers, A. (2006). Criminologie in een 'state of denial'? Ook internationale misdrijven vergen criminologische benadering. *Tijdschrift voor Criminologie, 3*(48), 275–289.
Smeulers, A., & Grünfeld, F. (2011). *International crimes and other Gross human rights violations: A multi- and interdisciplinary textbook*. Leiden: Martinus Nijhoff Publishers.
Smeulers, A., & Hoex, L. (2010). Studying the microdynamics of the Rwandan genocide. *British Journal of Criminology, 50*, 435–454.
Smith, B. (1990). Towards a history of speech act theory. In A. Burkhardt (Ed.), *Speech Acts, Meaning and Intentions* (pp. 29–61). Berlin: Walter de Gruyter.
Smith, R. S. (1987). Human destructiveness and politics: The twentieth century as an age of genocide. In I. Walliman & M. Dobkowski (Eds.), *Genocide and the modern age: aetiology and case studies of mass death* (pp. 21–40). New York: Greenwoood.
Smith, R. W. (2010). Legislating against genocide denial: Criminalizing denial or preventing free speech? Retrieved from Genocide Prevention Now website: www.genocidepreventionnow.org/Home/tabid/39/ctl/DisplayArticle/mid/971/aid/209/Default.aspx

Smith, R. W. (2012). Le négationnisme, étape ultime du génocide. Retrieved from Collectif VAN (Vigilence Arménienne contre le Négationnisme) website: www.collectifvan.org/article.php?r=0&id=60908

Smith, R. W. (2014). Genocide denial and prevention. *Genocide Studies International* (8), 1.

Smith, R. W., Markusen, E., & Lifton, R. J. (1999). Professional ethics and the denial of the Armenian genocide. In R. G. Hovannisian (Ed.), *Remembrance and denial: The case of the Armenian genocide* (pp. 271–295). Detroit: Wayne State University Press.

Smith, S. D. (2014). The fine line of genocide history. *Huffington Post.* www.huffingtonpost.com/stephen-d-smith/the-fine-line-of-genocide_b_4719666.html

Spence, D. P. (1983). The paradox of denial. In S. Breznitz (Ed.), *The denial of stress* (pp. 103–123). New York: International Universities Press, INC.

Spencer, P. (2012). Genocide scholars and legislating to outlaw the denial of genocide. (12). Retrieved from Genocide Prevention Now website: www.genocidepreventionnow.org/Home/tabid/39/ctl/DisplayArticle/mid/1161/aid/664/Default.aspx

Stanton, G. H. (1998a). The 8 stages of genocide (Paper was originally written in 1996 and was presented as the first Working Paper (GS 01) of the Yale Program in Genocide Studies in 1998). Retrieved from Genocide Watch website: www.genocidewatch.org/genocide/8stagesofgenocide.html

Stanton, G. H. (1998b). Eight stages of genocide (Originally written in 1996 at the Department of State); presented at the Yale University Center for International and Area Studies in 1998.

Stanton, G. H. (2004). Could the Rwandan genocide have been prevented. *Journal of Genocide Research, 6*(2), 211–228.

Stanton, G. H. (2005). Twelve ways to deny genocide. Retrieved from Genocide Watch website: www.genocidewatch.org/aboutgenocide/12waystodenygenocide.html

Stanton, G. H. (2013). The ten stages of genocide. Retrieved from Genocide Watch website: http://genocidewatch.org/genocide/tenstagesofgenocide.html

Stanton, G. H. (2014). The cost of genocide denial. Retrieved from Genocide Watch website: www.genocidewatch.org/aboutus/thecostofdenial.html

Stassen, J. P. (2006). *Deogratias, A tale of Rwanda.* New York: First Second Books.

Staub, E. (1989). *The roots of evil: The origins of genocide and other group violence.* Cambridge: Cambridge University Press.

Steinberg, G. M. (2009). From Gulag liberators to Saudi retainers: Human Rights Watch has betrayed its original mission. Retrieved from National Review website: www.nationalreview.com/articles/227921/gulag-liberators-saudi-retainers/gerald-m-steinberg

Steinberg, M. (1999). Le génocide, l'histoire ou un imbroglio juridique. In K. Boustany & D. Dormoy (Eds.), *Génocide(s)* (pp. 161–177). Bruxelles: Etablissement Emile Bruylant.

Stephenson, P. S. (2004). Understanding denial. *Oncology Nursing Forum, 31*(5), 985–988.

Stern, J. (2010). *Denial: A memoir of terror.* New York: Harper Collins Publishers.

Stokes, R., & Hewitt, J. P. (1976). Aligning actions. *American Sociological Review, 41*(October), 838–849.

Stone, D. (2010). Genocide and memory. In D. Bloxham & A. D. Moses (Eds.), *The Oxford handbook of genocide studies* (pp. 102–119). New York: Oxford University Press.

Straus, S. (2001). Contested meanings and conflicting imperatives: A conceptual analysis of genocide. *Journal of Genocide Research, 3*(3), 349–375.

Straus, S. (2004). How many perpetrators were there in the Rwandan genocide? An estimate. *Journal of Genocide Research, 6*(1), 85–98.

Straus, S. (2007). The order of genocide: The dynamics of genocide in Rwanda. *Genocide Studies and Prevention, 2*(3), 259–269.

Straus, S., & Waldorf, L. (2011). *Remaking Rwanda: State building and human rights after mass violence.* Madison: The University of Wisconsin Press.

Strawson, P. F. (1964). Intention and convention in speech acts. *The Philosophical Review, 73*(4), 439–460.
Strizek, H. (2002). Linda Melvern is right, but ... Short analysis of 'A people betrayed. The role of the West in Rwanda's genocide' by Linda Melvern (2000). *Internationales Afrika-Forum, 38*(4), 375–390.
Strizek, H. (2003a). Human rights in Rwanda. Life after genocide. Aachen: Pontifical Mission Society Human Rights Office.
Strizek, H. (2003b). Rapport synthetique sur les aspects sociaux, politiques, economiques et militaires de la situation du Rwanda dureant les annees 1990–1994 Berlin.
Strizek, H. (2005). Rapport d'expertise dans le procès d'Anatole Nsengiyumva devant le Tribunal Pénal International pour le Rwanda. Berlin.
Strizek, H. (2006). Rapport du temoin expert Dr Helmut Strizek dans le proces contre Casimir Bizimungu et al. devant le Tribunal Penal Internatinal pour le Rwanda - Le gouvernement interimaire rwandais face a un genocide provoque. Bonn.
Strizek, H. (2007). *Ruanda 1994 - Die inszenierte Tragödie: Vorwort zur deutschen Übersetzung*, Retrieved from Philpot, R. Rwanda 1994: Colonialism dies hard, www.taylor-report.com.
Sullo, P. (2014). Lois mémorielles in post-genocide societies: The Rwandan law on genocide ideology under international human rights law scrutiny. *Leiden Journal of International Law, 27*(2), 419–445.
Supreme Court of Canada. (2005). Mugesera v. Canada (Minister of Citizenship and Immigration), [2005] 2 S.C.R. 100, 2005 SCC 40. Retrieved from Judgments of the Supreme Court of Canada website: http://scc-csc.lexum.com/scc-csc/scc-csc/en/item/2273/index.do
Survie France. (1996). La France a fait obstacle à la reconnaissance du génocide. Des dirigeants français ont tenté d'accréditer la thèse du "double génocide" Retrieved from Survie website: http://survie.org/publications/les-dossiers-noirs/dossier-noir-no1-rwanda-depuis-le/article/la-france-a-fait-obstacle-a-la
Sykes, G. M., & Matza, D. (1957). Techniques of neutralization: A theory of delinquency. *American Sociological Review, 22*(6), 664–670.
Tajfel, H., & Turner, I. C. (1986). The social identity theory of intergroup behavior. In S. Worchel & W. G. Austin (Eds.), *Psychology of intergroup relations* (pp. 7–24). Chicago: Nelson-Hall.
Tatz, C. (2003). *With intent to destroy: Reflecting on genocide*. London: Verso.
Tavris, C., & Aronson, E. (2007). *Mistakes were made (but not by me)*. Orlando: Harcourt, Inc.
Taylor, C. C. (2001). *Sacrifice as terror: The Rwandan genocide of 1994*. New York: Berg.
Taylor, S. (2001). Locating and conducting discourse analytic research. In M. Wetherell, S. Taylor & S. J. Yates (Eds.), *Discourse as data: A guide for analysis* (pp. 5–48). London: Sage Publications.
Taylor, T. (2008). *Denial: History betrayed*. Carlton: Melbourne University Press.
Tellier, L. N. (2003). Le Rwanda de Robin Philpot. Retrieved from Le Devoir website: www.ledevoir.com/non-classe/26081/libre-opinion-le-rwanda-de-robin-philpot
Temple-Raston, D. (2005). *Justice on the grass: Three Rwandan journalists, their trial for war crimes, and a nation's quest for redemption*. London: Free Press.
Ternon, Y. (1989). *Enquete sur la negation d'un genocide*. Marseille: Parentheses.
Ternon, Y. (1995). Les éléments de la preuve. In R. Verdier, E. Decaux & J.-P. Chrétien (Eds.), *Rwanda: Un génocide du XXe siècle* (pp. 136–145). Paris: L'Harmattan.
Ternon, Y. (1999a). *Du négationnisme: Mémoire et tabou*. Paris: Desclée de Brouwer.
Ternon, Y. (1999b). Négationnisme, régles générales et cas particuliers. In K. Boustany & D. Dormoy (Eds.), *Génocide(s)* (pp. 143–160). Bruxelles: Etablissement Emile Bruylant.
Ternon, Y. (2003). Le spectre du négationnisme. Analyse du processus de négation des génocides du XXe siècle. In C. Coquio (Ed.), *L'histoire trouée. Négation et témoignage* (pp. 207–221). Nantes: Librairie L'Atlante.

Ternon, Y. (2013). Approche comparée de la négation des génocides avérés du XXe siècle. In d. J. Semujanga & J.-L. Galabert (Eds.), *Faire face au négationnisme du génocide des Tutsi* (pp. 107–114). Saint-Jean: Éditions Izuba.

Terry, F. (2002). *Condemned to repeat: The paradox of humanitarian action*. New York: Cornell University Press.

The New Times. (2010). France needs to do more on génocidaires. Retrieved from Friends of Evil website: http://friendsofevil.wordpress.com/2010/09/27/france-needs-to-do-more-on-genocidaires/

The New Times (Editorial). (2009a). HRW and company, wake up, let the truth set you free, *The New Times*. Retrieved from www.newtimes.co.rw/news/index.php?i=13917&a=16352

The New Times (Editorial). (2009b). HRW when will this end?, *The New Times*. Retrieved from www.newtimes.co.rw/news/views/article_print.php?i=15449&a=16281&icon=Print

The New Times (Editorial). (2009c). Professors of Hate, *The New Times*.

The New Times (Editorial). (2011). Amnesty International dishonest. Retrieved from www.newtimes.co.rw/news/views/article_print.php?i=14370&a=33100&icon=Print

Theriault, H. (2009). Genocide, denial, and domination: Armenian - Turkish relations from conflict resolution to just transformation. *Journal of African Conflicts and Peace Studies, 1*(2), 82–96.

Theriault, H. (2010). Genocidal mutation and the challenge of definition. *Metaphilosophy, 41*(4), 481–524.

Theriault, H. (2013). Denial of ongoing atrocities for not attempting to prevent or intervene. In S. Totten (Ed.), *Impediments to the prevention and intervention of genocide* (pp. 47–76). New Jersey: Transaction Publishers.

Thiry, I., & Verwimp, P. (2008). Daders van genocide bevraagd. Een bijdrage vanuit de criminologie met veldonderzoek in Rwanda. *Panopticon, 1*, 27–49.

Thompson, J. L., & Quets, G. A. (1990). Genocide and social conflict: A partial theory and comparison. In L. Kriesberg (Ed.), *Research in social movements, conflicts and change* (Vol. 12). Greenwood: JAI Press.

Torfing, J. (1999). *New theories of discourse: Laclau, Mouffe and Zizek*. Oxford: Blackwell Publishers Ltd.

Torfing, J. (2005). Discourse theory: Achievements, arguments, and challenges. In D. Howarth & J. Torfing (Eds.), *Discourse theory in European politics: Identity, policy and governance* (pp. 1–32). New York: Palgrave Macmillan.

Totten, S. (2007). Editor's introduction. *Genocide Studies and Prevention, 2*(3), 205–208.

Totten, S., & Bartrop, P. R. (Eds.). (2009). *The genocide studies reader*. New York: Routledge.

Totten, S., & Parsons, W. S. (2004). Introduction. In S. Totten, W. S. Parsons & I. W. Charny (Eds.), *Century of genocide: Critical essays and eyewitness accounts* (2nd ed., pp. 1–13). London: Routledge.

Totten, S., & Ubaldo, R. (2011). *We cannot forget: Interviews with survivors of the 1994 genocide in Rwanda*. New Brunswick: Rutgers University Press.

Traverso, E. (2003). Révision et révisionnisme. In C. Coquio (Ed.), *L'histoire trouée. Négation et témoignage* (pp. 157–168). Nates: Librairie L'Atlante.

United States Holocaust Memorial Museum. (2009). Hate speech and group targeted violence: The role of speech in violent conflicts. Washington: United States Holocaust Memorial Museum.

Uvin, P. (2001). Reading the Rwandan genocide. *International Studies review*, 75–99.

Uvin, P. (2011). Review of Straus, Scott; Waldorf, Lars, eds., Remaking Rwanda: State building and human rights after mass violence. *H-Africa H-Net Reviews*. Retrieved from H-Net website: www.h-net.org/reviews/showrev.php?id=33141

Vaillant, G. E. (1992). *Ego mechanisms of defense: A guide for clinicians and researchers*: American Psychiatric Press.

Van de Bunt, H. (2007). Muren van stilzwijgen. In H. Van de Bunt, P. Spierenburg & R. Swaaningen (Eds.), *Drie perspectieven op sociale controle* (pp. 113–136). Den Haag: Boom Juridische Uitgevers.

Van den Berg, H. (2004a). Discoursanalyse. *KWALON, 9*(2), 29–39.

Van den Berg, H. (2004b). Discoursanalyse in de praktijk: De discursieve constructie van sociale categorieen. *KWALON, 9*(3), 27–34.

Van den Berghe, G. (1997a). Een oorlog die, omdat hij nooit meer gebeuren mocht, blijft duren. In G. Verbeeck (Ed.), *De verdwenen gaskamers: De ontkenning van de Holocaust* (pp. 15–47). Leuven: Acco.

Van den Berghe, G. (1997b). Huiswerk voor Holocaust ontkenners. In G. Verbeeck (Ed.), *De verdwenen gaskamers: De ontkenning van de Holocaust* (pp. 179–182). Leuven: Acco.

Van den Herik, L. (2012). The meaning of the word "destroy" and its implications for the wider understanding of the concept of genocide. Retrieved from SSRN website: http://ssrn.com/abstract=1989848

Van der Kolk, T. (2011). Kardinaal Simonis: Ik wilde niemand misleiden, *De Volkskrant*.

Van der Vyver, J. D. (2004). The International Criminal Court and the concept of *mens rea* in international criminal law. *University of Miami International and Comparative Law Review, 12*, 58–149.

Van Dijk, T. A. (1992). Discourse and the denial of racism. *Discourse & Society, 3*(1), 87–118.

Van Galen Last, D. (1998). Wetenschapsbeoefening en revisionisme. In J. Van Donselaar & T. Da Silva (Eds.), *Weerzinwekkende 'wetenschap': Verslag van de studiedag over holocaustontkenning en andere uitingen van historisch revisionisme op 8 december 1997 te Amsterdam* (pp. 16–33). Amsterdam: Anne Frank Stichting.

Van Hennink, M. (1993). De ontkenning van het verleden. Het revisionisme en de jodenvervolging. *Kleio: tijdschrift van de Vereniging van Geschiedenisleraren in Nederland, 34*(4).

Van Hoyweghen, S. (2000). Book review: Do I still have life? Voices from the aftermath of war in Rwanda and Burundi. John M. Janzen & Reinhild Kauenhoven Janzen. Lawrence: University of Kansas, 2000. *African Studies Quarterly, 6*(1/2).

Van Krieken, R. (1999). The barbarism of civilization: Cultural genocide and the 'stolen generations'. *British Journal of Sociology, 50*(2), 297–315.

Van San, M. (1998). *Stelen en steken: Delinquent gedrag van Curaçaose jongens in Nederland.* Amsterdam: Het Spinhuis.

Varon, J. (1997). Probing the limits of the politics of representation. *New German Critique, 72*, 83–114.

Varon, J. (2005). Probing the limits of the politics of representation. In S. C. Feinstein (Ed.), *Absence/presence: Essays and reflections on the artistic memory of the Holocaust* (pp. 12–38). New York: Syracuse University Press.

Ver Eecke, W. (2006). *Denial, negation and the forces of the negative.* Albany: State University of New York Press.

Verbeeck, G. (1997a). De erfenis van de schuld: Historisch revisionisme in Duitsland. In G. Verbeeck (Ed.), *De verdwenen gaskamers: De ontkenning van de Holocaust* (pp. 161–178). Leuven: Acco.

Verbeeck, G. (1997b). Holocaust-ontkenning: Een stormloop tegen de geschiedenis. In G. Verbeeck (Ed.), *De verdwenen gaskamers: De ontkenning van de Holocaust* (pp. 7–13). Leuven: Acco.

Verbij, A. (2006). Twintig jaar *Historikerstreit. Historisch Nieuwsblad,* (6). www.historischnieuwsblad.nl/nl/artikel/25755/twintig-jaar-historikerstreit.html

Verwimp, P. (2003). Testing the double genocide thesis for central and southern Rwanda. *Journal of Conflict Resolution, 47*(4), 423–442.

Verwimp, P. (2006). Machetes and firearms: The organization of massacres in Rwanda. *Journal of Peace Research, 43*(1), 5–22.

Vidal-Naquet, P. (1992). *Assassins of memory: Essays on the denial of the Holocaust*. New York: Columbia University Press.

Vitousek, K., Daly, J., & Heiser, C. (1991). Reconstructing the internal world of the eating-disordered individual: Overcoming denial and distortion in self-report. *International Journal of Eating Disorders, 10*(6), 647–666.

Vollhardt, J., Coutin, M., Staub, E., Weiss, G., & Deflander, J. (2007). Deconstructing hate speech in the DRC: A psychological media sensitization campaign. *Journal of Hate Studies, 5*(15), 15–35.

Vuillemin, G. (1964, 4th of February). L'extermination des Tutsis. Les massacres du Ruanda sont la manifestation d'une haine raciale serieusement entretenue, *Le Monde*.

Wadhams, N. (2010). Rwanda: Anti-genocide law clashes with free speech. Retrieved from TIME website: http://content.time.com/time/world/article/0,8599,1986699,00.html

Waldorf, L. (2009). Revisiting Hotel Rwanda: Genocide, ideology, reconciliation, and rescuers. *Journal of Genocide Research, 11*(1), 101–125.

Wallis, A. (2007). *Silent accomplice: The untold story of France's role in the Rwandan genocide*. London: I.B. Tauris & Co Ltd.

Wallis, A. (2012). Rwanda: A step towards truth. Retrieved from Open Democracy website: https://www.opendemocracy.net/andrew-wallis/rwanda-step-towards-truth

Wallis, A. (2014). "Rwanda: The untold story": Questions for the BBC. Retrieved from Open Democracy website: https://www.opendemocracy.net/andrew-wallis/rwanda-untold-story-questions-for-bbc

Wangh, M. (1989). The evolution of psychoanalytic thought on negation and denial. In E. L. Edelstein, D. L. Nathanson & A. M. Stone (Eds.), *Denial: A clarification of concepts and research* (pp. 5–15). London: Plenum Press.

Watson, M., Greer, S., Blake, S., & Shrapnell, K. (1984). Reaction to a diagnosis of breast cancer: Relationship between denial, delay and rates of psychological morbidity. *Cancer, 53*(9), 2008–2012.

Watzlawick, P., Weakland, J., & Fish, R. (1974). *Principles of problem formation and problem solution*. New York: Norton.

Weinstein, E. A., & Deutschberger, P. (1963). Some dimensions of altercasting. *Sociometry, 26*(4), 454–466.

Weinstein, E. A., & Kahn, R. L. (1955). *Denial of illness: Symbolic and physiological aspects* (Vol. 249). Springfield: Charles C Thomas Publisher.

Weisman, A. D. (1972). *On dying and denying*. New York: Behavioral Publications, INC.

Weisman, A. D. (1989). Denial, coping and cancer. In E. L. Edelstein, D. L. Nathanson & A. M. Stone (Eds.), *Denial: A clarification of concepts and research* (pp. 251–259). New York: Plenum Press.

Wells, M. (2000). LM closes after losing libel action, *The Guardian*. Retrieved from www.theguardian.com/uk/2000/mar/31/medialaw.media

Welzer, H. (2005). *Daders: Hoe heel normale mensen massamoordenaars worden* (C. v. Bree & C. Kloos, Trans.). Amsterdam: Anthos.

Wetherell, M. (2001). Themes in discourse research: The case of Diana. In M. Wetherell, S. Taylor & S. J. Yates (Eds.), *Discourse theory and practice* (pp. 14–28). London: Sage Publications.

Wetzell, R. F. (2000). *Inventing the criminal: A history of German criminology, 1980–1945*. Chapel Hill: The University of North Carolina Press.

White, H. (1989). *The content of the form: Narrative discourse and historical representation*. Baltimore: The Johns Hopkins University Press.

White, H. (1992). Historical emplotment and the problem of truth. In S. Friedlander (Ed.), *Probing the limits of representation: Nazism and the "Final Solution"* (pp. 37–53). Cambridge: Harvard University Press.

Wilkens, C. (2011). *I am not leaving*. Spokane: World outside my shoes.

Willems, J. C. M. (2014). *Lecture "My parents can't take care of me". Denialism in child rights and child maltreatment research*. Faculty of Law, Maastricht University. Maastricht.

Willems, M. (2011). Excuses Nederland aan nabestaanden Rawagede - 'unicum', *NRC*. Retrieved from www.nrc.nl/nieuws/2011/12/05/excuses-nederland-aan-nabestaanden-rawagede/

Winton, M. A. (2008). Dimensions of genocide: The circumplex model meets violentization theory. *The Qualitative Report, 13*(4), 605–629.

Withuis, J. (2012). Goed en fout bestaan weldegelijk, *De Volkskrant*. Retrieved from www.volkskrant.nl/vk/nl/2844/Archief/archief/article/detail/3323885/2012/09/29/Goed-en-fout-bestaan-wel-degelijk.dhtml

Wizeye, J. (2011). To claim Tutsis caused Rwanda's genocide is pure revisionism. All the facts point to a carefully targeted Hutu plan of extermination, *The Guardian*. Retrieved from www.theguardian.com/commentisfree/2011/jul/25/tutsi-rwanda-genocide-hutu

Wool, M. S., & Goldberg, R. J. (1986). Assessment of denial in cancer patients: Implications for intervention. *Journal of Psychosocial Oncology, 4*, 1–14.

Woolford, A. (2006). Making genocide unthinkable: Three guidelines for a critical criminology of genocide. *Critical Criminology, 14*, 87–106.

Woolford, A. (2011). Criminological nightmares: A Canadian criminology of genocide. In A. Doyle & D. Moore (Eds.), *Critical criminology in Canada: New voices, new directions* (pp. 136–161). Vancouver: UBC Press.

Wurmser, L. (1989). Blinding the eye of the mind: Denial, impulsive action, and split identity. In E. L. Edelstein, D. L. Nathanson & A. M. Stone (Eds.), *Denial: A clarification of concepts and research* (pp. 175–202). London: Plenum Press.

Yacoubain Jr, G. S. (1997). Underestimating the magnitude of international crime: Implications of genocidal behavior for the discipline of criminology. *Injustice Studies, 1*(1). www.csudh.edu/dearhabermas/yacoubiandoc.htm

Yacoubain Jr, G. S. (2000). The (in)significance of genocidal behavior to the discipline of criminology. *Crime, Law & Social Change, 34*(1), 7–19.

Young, J. (2004). Voodoo criminology and the numbers game. In F. Ferrell, K. Hayward, W. Morrison & M. Presdee (Eds.), *Cultural criminology unleashed* (pp. 13–27). London: Glasshouse Press.

Young, J. E. (1988). *Writing and rewriting the Holocaust: Narrative and the consequences of interpretation*. Bloomington: Indiana University Press.

Young, R. L. (1995). Misunderstandings as accounts. *Sociological Inquiry, 65*(3/4), 251–264.

Your World News (Producer). (2011). Interview with Keith Harmon Snow on the politics of genocide. Retrieved from https://www.youtube.com/watch?v=OlPY2fWBUeU

Zerubavel, E. (2008). *The elephant in the room: Silence and denial in everyday life*. Oxford: Oxford University Press.

Zerubavel, E. (2010). The social sound of silence: Towards a sociology of denial, Chapter 2 in Efrat Ben-Ze'ev, Ruth Ginio and Jay Winter (eds.) *Shadows of war: A social history of silence in the twentieth century*, Cambridge University Press, pp. 32-46.

Žižek, S. (2009). *Violence: Six sideways reflections*. London: Profile Books.

Zorbas, E. (2009). What does reconciliation after genocide mean? Public transcripts and hidden transcripts in post-genocide Rwanda. *Journal of Genocide Research, 11*(1), 127–147.

Zuroff, E. (1996). *Letter Living Marxism concerning article Fiona Foster*. Simon Wiesenthal Center. Jerusalem.

Curriculum Vitae

Roland Moerland (born 1976 in Roosendaal, The Netherlands) is currently Assistant Professor of Criminology at the Faculty of Law of Maastricht University in the Netherlands. He obtained his degree in Criminal Law from Maastricht University in 2002. He furthermore holds a Master's Degree in Criminology from the University of Sydney, Australia, that he received in 2004.

Roland Moerland's main interest lies in the fields of supranational and organisational criminology. Supranational criminology encompasses the criminological study of international crimes, such as genocide and other gross human rights violations. Organisational criminology entails the criminological study of white collar, corporate, state and governmental crime.

Roland Moerland has taught a variety of courses: Introduction to Law, International Development Law, European Integration, Tort Law, Substantive Criminal Law and Criminal Procedure, and Criminology. He currently coordinates and teaches research-related courses, such as Organisational Criminology, Causes of Gross Human Rights Violations, and Cultural Criminology and Transitional Justice. Roland Moerland is also a board member of the Maastricht Centre for Human Rights.

School of Human Rights Research Series

The School of Human Rights Research is a joint effort by human rights researchers in the Netherlands. Its central research theme is the nature and meaning of international standards in the field of human rights, their application and promotion in the national legal order, their interplay with national standards, and the international supervision of such application. The School of Human Rights Research Series only includes English titles that contribute to a better understanding of the different aspects of human rights.

For previous volumes in the series, please visit http://shr.intersentia.com.

Published titles within the Series:

65. Gustavo Arosemena, *Rights, Scarcity and Justice. An Analytical Inquiry into the Adjudication of the Welfare Aspects of Human Rights* ISBN 978-1-78068-275-4.
66. Etienne Ruvebana, *Prevention of Genocide under International Law. An analysis of the obligations of states and the United Nations to prevent genocide at the primary, secondary and tertiary levels* ISBN 978-1-78068-273-0.
67. Evgeni Moyakine, *The Privatized Art of War. Private Military and Security Companies and State Responsibility for Their Unlawful Conduct in Conflict Areas* ISBN 978-1-78068-281-5.
68. Esther Janssen, *Faith in Public Debate. On Freedom of Expression, Hate Speech and Religion in France and The Netherlands* ISBN 978-1-78068-309-6.
69. Stefanie Jansen-Wilhelm, *Accepting Assistance in the Aftermath of Disasters* ISBN 978-1-78068-329-4.
70. Helen Beckmann-Hamzei, *The Child in ICC Proceedings* ISBN 978-1-78068-339-3.
71. Karel De Meester, *The Investigation Phase in International Criminal Procedure: In Search of Common Rules* ISBN 978-1-78068-305-8.
72. Nelleke Koffeman, *Morally sensitive issues and cross-border movement in the EU. The cases of reproductive matters and legal recognition of same-sex relationships* ISBN 978-1-78068-349-2.

www.ingramcontent.com/pod-product-compliance
Ingram Content Group UK Ltd.
Pitfield, Milton Keynes, MK11 3LW, UK
UKHW051919100926
8556IPUK00021B/1264

9 781780 683515